CHIMNEYS IN THE DESERT

CHIMNEYS IN THE DESERT

Industrialization in Argentina During the Export Boom Years, 1870–1930

FERNANDO ROCCHI

STANFORD UNIVERSITY PRESS

Stanford, California

2006

CONTENTS

LIST OF FIGURES

LIST OF TABLES

ACKNOWLEDGMENTS

This book, like any book, has its particular story. Naturally, most of its interest lies in personal details wholly uninteresting to the reader. Let me, however, evoke its geographic evolution. The book was first imagined in Argentina; became a doctoral dissertation at the University of California, Santa Barbara; transformed into a book while I was a visiting scholar at the London School of Economics and Political Science; and took its final shape in the same place it started, my native Argentina. The book traveled with me along the various paths of my professional and personal life of the past several years.

I owe the completion of this book to a great number of people and institutions, in Argentina, the United States, and the United Kingdom. With regard to funding, I was able to begin research in 1994 thanks to a grant from the Department of History at the University of California, Santa Barbara. I continued my fieldwork in 1995 and completed the writing between 1995 and 1997 thanks to an International Doctoral fellowship from the Fundación Antorchas in Argentina. The fact that this dissertation obtained the Louis and Winifred Lancaster Award for the best dissertation in the Humanities and Social Sciences at UCSB was good news that encouraged me to continue the project. My enlightening stay as a visiting scholar at the LSE was supported by both this institution and a postdoctoral fellowship from the Argentine Scientific Agency (CONICET) during 1998 and 1999. Finally, I completed the book thanks to the support of my own university, the Universidad Torcuato Di Tella, in Argentina. I owe a lot of gratitude to this university, an institution that always encourages and helps its faculty to publish in distinguished presses and journals.

I had the opportunity to bring a fresh approach in this book thanks to the research I have done in several libraries and archives, to which I am extremely grateful. The UCSB Library helped me with all its resources as well as with the assistance in obtaining original sources from the Department of State and the Department of Commerce in Washington, D.C. The staff of the Biblioteca Tornquist, at the Argentine Central Bank, especially its director Marta Gutiérrez and Amelia del Compare, provided me with all the support necessary to consult the library's magnificent collection on Argentine economic history. The staffs at the Archivo General de la Nación, the Biblioteca Nacional, the Archivo del Banco de la Provincia de Buenos Aires, and the Archivo del Banco de la Nación Argentina, all in Buenos Aires, kindly helped me to find new archival sources. I also thank the personnel at the Foreign Office Archives at Kew Gardens and of the LSE library, both in London, and the Ministero degli Affari Esteri, in Rome.

I have a special debt to those who allowed me to consult company archives. The owners of the cookies and crackers company Bagley, the textile firm Fábrica Argentina de Alpargatas, and the metallurgical firm La Cantábrica kindly granted me unrestricted access to their archives. I was also lucky that the archives of two major companies were available at other universities. The archives of the Compañía General de Fósforos had been rescued in 2000 by the Programa de Estudios en Historia Económica y Social Americana (PEHESA) at the Facultad de Filosofía y Letras, Universidad de Buenos Aires. I am grateful to Silvia Badoza for letting me consult that material. The Archive of SIAM Di Tella S.A. is located at the Universidad Torcuato Di Tella library. I am especially indebted to Norma Palomino, Yrma Patrone, and the rest of this library's personnel for helping me find fresh sources and letting me dig into company papers. In the cases where those were lost, I had the support of owners and former managers in reconstructing the companies' evolution by means of interviews. I appreciate the help of Hugo and Jorge Fontana from the metallurgical Talleres Fontana Hermanos; of Juan María Veniard for lending me the unpublished memoirs of his grandfather Daniel Bassi (the owner of the chocolate firm that carried his last name); of Mauricio Morris, manager of the textile firm Grafa in the 1930s; and of Mario Piñeyro, manager of the soap company Alejandro Llauró e Hijos.

As this project was unfolding, I discussed it with several people whose comments enriched my learning. In Buenos Aires I benefited from my exchanges with Juan Carlos Korol, Jorge Schvarzer, and the late Leandro Gutiérrez; together we undertook an ambitious project of business history at the PEHESA, in which I was first exposed to industrial history. In Buenos Aires I also embarked upon a rewarding intellectual undertaking with Michael Johns, a geography professor at UC Berkeley, to examine the relationship between industry and the urban sphere. My endless conversations about my first drafts with María Inés Barbero, Mirta Lobato, and Juan Manuel Palacio were invaluable. I was delighted to share my research results with the late Adolfo Dorfman, whose ninety years of age (of which seventy have been dedicated to the study of Argentina's industry) and his unstinting scholarly enthusiasm inspired me to continue this project. I have a special debt to Stephanie Bower, whose careful reading and editing of my manuscript was a source of both help and friendship.

I also received along the way valuable comments on the book from Paula Alonso, Samuel Amaral, Ted Beatty, Natalio Botana, Roberto Cortés Conde, Ezequiel Gallo, Pablo Gerchunoff, Donna Guy, Stephen Haber, Tulio Halperin Donghi, Alejandra Irigoin, Alan Knight, Colin Lewis, Lucas Llach, Carlos Newland, Andrés Regalsky, Hilda Sabato, Graciela Silvestri, Juan Carlos Torre, and Eduardo Zimmermann. The intellectual atmosphere among my fellow editors at the journal *Entrepasados: Revista de Historia* in Buenos Aires—Emma Cibotti, Silvia Finocchio, Patricio Geli, Lucas Luchilo, Gustavo Paz, Leticia Prislei, and Juan Suriano, in addition to the already mentioned Mirta—provided me with the opportunity to discuss my work from a wide variety of historiographical perspectives. Finally, I deeply appreciate the referees' reports at Stanford University Press, which were extremely useful in giving the argument a better content and shape. My friends Didier Maleuvre and Emily Stern have helped me in parts where my native Spanish slipped in place of the English language. Christian Scaramella and Gastón Rossi efficiently helped with map and graphs.

Several of my friends at the University of California provided me with continuous help in the writing stage. I express gratitude to Erik Ching, Elizabeth Marchant, Viviana Marsano, Karen Mead, Mónica Orozco, and Rafael Pérez-Torres for their varied support and to Adán Griego, Sara Poot-Herrera, and Silvia Bermúdez for providing the blessing of friendship to the life of an expatriate.

I profoundly thank my adviser at UCSB, David Rock, with whom I have worked for more than six years. David, together with Sarah Cline, Carl Harris, and Fernando López-Alves, the other members of my doctoral committee, have helped substantially to broaden my approach, my methods, and my knowledge. Sarah supported me intellectually and probed my dissertation with acutely relevant comments. Carl introduced me to the new issues of American history set next to Argentinian differences and similarities. Fernando helped me with the learning of comparative politics and economics which allowed me to see Argentina's events with more informed eyes.

I am also very grateful to Stanford University Press. The referees have made useful suggestions that improved the quality of this book. I thank Norris Pope and Mariana Raykov for all the support as editors. And I am especially indebted to David Horne, the copyeditor of this book, who did a wonderful job. I really feel it makes a big difference to have a knowledgeable and smart copyeditor such as David.

Finally, I thank the tireless help and faith of my family and my friends in Argentina. No one thought I could make a living as a historian in this country. This book is a tribute to their faith.

Buenos Aires, January 2005

ABBREVIATIONS

CGF, BD	Libros de Actas del Directorio. Minutes of the Board of Directors meetings.
DOT	United Kingdom, Department of Overseas Trade. Commercial, Economic and Financial Conditions in the Argentine Republic.
DE	Desarrollo Económico, Buenos Aires
DSCD	Diario de Sesiones de la Cámara de Diputados
DSCS	Diario de Sesiones de la Cámara de Senadores
Exposición	Exposición Nacional de 1898, Buenos Aires
Finanzas	Finanzas, comercio e industria en la República Argentina, Buenos Aires
FO	United Kingdom, Public Record Office Archives, Foreign Office
MSA	Monitor de Sociedades Anónonimas, Buenos Aires
RRP	The Review of the River Plate, Buenos Aires
SAJ	South American Journal and Brazil and River Plate Mail, London
USDCBFDC	United States, Department of Commerce, Bureau of Foreign and Domestic Commerce
USDCBFDC-SAS	Special Agents Series
USDCBFDC-SCR	Special Consular Reports

CHIMNEYS IN THE DESERT

Introduction:
Industrialization in an
Agrarian Economy

This book describes how industry changed Argentina, an allegedly agrarian country, during a historical period of major transformations. The period begins in the 1870s—when an already ongoing modernization deepened—and ends with the 1930 Depression—when many dreams associated with this process died. In those sixty years, the country's economic, social, political, and cultural traits dramatically changed. Argentina became a rising star in an internationalized economy; its population grew from two to twelve million, its gross domestic product (GDP) multiplied by twenty, its exports by eighteen, and its imports by fifteen. The country, wrecked by decades of civil wars and severe instability after gaining independence from Spain in the 1810s, seemed to be experiencing a miracle, attracting immigrants and capital in a way that surprised contemporaries. During that period, Argentina enjoyed its best economic performance in its entire history.

This so-called "belle époque" has usually been considered the outcome of a successful agrarian and export experience. From this perspective, the transformation was founded on wool, grain, and beef sales abroad, to the effect that scholar research has focused, for better or for worse, on this aspect of the Argentine experience. By contrast, this book attempts to demonstrate that this traditional approach only partially accounts for a more complicated process.

Chimneys in the Desert focuses on an atypical economic sphere and moves in a direction different from traditional studies on international trade. Whereas scholarly research focused on sales abroad from agrarian activities,

1

this book investigates instead the features of a domestic market (growing in parallel with and largely thanks to exports, but achieving a dynamic of its own). Recent estimates of the GDP of that period have shown that activities oriented to internal consumption, such as industry, affected the national income. Social studies also have illustrated the significance of manufacturing mills, which prompted the rise of social unrest. However, we have a limited understanding of the evolution and performance of these activities.[1]

The origin of Argentina's industry is the target of this book. Manufacturing was then (and continues to be) oriented toward domestic consumption. Industry's share of Argentine wealth, however, was as large as that of agriculture by the 1920s. Moreover, as this study will show, industry's impact on society surpassed the significance of its output numbers. The analysis will focus on industrialization rather than on industry, a choice that reveals a spectrum of topics from factories to the symbols they engendered. To achieve its goal, the book investigates the production realm and, in parallel, how the world of manufactured goods encompassed consumers, the market rules, the minds of industrialists, the development of politics, and the formation of an Argentine nation. As a result, the hidden force of industrialization emerges as one of the keys to understanding a historical process traditionally associated just with the export sector.

Contemporaries had already noted industrial growth, some with alarm and fearing the changes it might provoke. A report produced in 1902 by a special commission appointed to study tariffs on imports captures these feelings. The commission members concluded that once protected, industrial firms had been free to erect large mills, the size of which fostered an atmosphere of social unrest, ripe for the violence advocated by Anarchists:

> Modern machines have brought serious responsibilities. They remove
> the worker from the ennobling environment full of affection and hu-
> man stimulus that home and family provide to convert him into one of
> the many wheels that the continuing movement of the workshops pro-
> duces. . . . These working masses present an enormous danger since they
> are linked to life only with the unstable and precarious bond of salary
> and animated by resentment rather than hope. All this creates germs that
> spread from person to person and explains the immolation of presidents
> and monarchs, with astonishing cynicism, in broad daylight, before the
> entire world, without taking care, as in classical times, to hide their dag-
> gers behind myrtle boughs.[2]

The commission's comments referred to the ambience of growing social discontent gripping the country as it entered the twentieth century. Strikes, bombings, and tumultuous rallies angered and frightened the elite. The new problems, by then labeled *la cuestión social* (the social question), impelled the government to institute measures in response. Inquiries into the causes for the uneasy times began, and the recent industrial growth became one of the favorite targets for blame.[3]

At that time, people accused industry of destroying the country's old pastoral society—which was fondly, though idyllically, remembered as peaceful—and dragging in the accompanying irritations of modern life. Women and children, the most vulnerable element of the Argentine social fabric, were trapped in the dreadful environment of the factories, which posed dangers for both their physical health and moral behavior, a topic skillfully portrayed in the fashionable literary style known as naturalism. The elegance of the booming capital city was dimmed by the gloomy neighborhoods surrounding the mills. Monopolistic industries were the supposed sources of ill-achieved personal wealth, squeezing consumers, while small-scale farmers and landowners described themselves as victims of an unscrupulous group of grain sack manufacturers who halted exports by charging outrageous prices. Usually, financiers were equated with opulent industrialists as the symbols of capitalist robbery.

Whereas contemporaries blamed industry for a variety of disasters, scholars by contrast have judged it insignificant. When depicting the economic features of the belle époque, they have paid—as said before—almost exclusive attention to activities related to international trade. This approach has some basis in fact, since exports were the economic engine, the most dynamic sector, and the area in which productivity gained momentum. Agriculture and cattle-ranching articles produced on Argentina's fertile prairies, the *Pampas*, lay at the root of a transformation that allowed the country to become one of the world's most notable cases of economic prosperity. Its achievements, however, went beyond international trade and included, just as an example, an impressive social mobility. This made the country different from other successful Latin American export economies during the same period, such as Cuba or Mexico. Whatever Argentina became as a result of the turn-of-the-twentieth-century expansion, an important part of the explanation should take into account the domestic economy, which contains some of the keys to understanding how Argentine society was shaped.[4]

Perhaps unsurprisingly, social historians also have delved into the impact of the rise of factories on the country. In so doing, they encountered a paradox: while most of the wealth was created in the countryside, social conflict developed primarily in the fast-growing cities, mainly Buenos Aires. A reconsideration of the domestic economy's role will transform this paradox into an understandable outcome of the transformations experienced by Argentina.[5] By the beginning of the twentieth century, Argentina was supposed to replicate in Latin America some features of recent settlement countries, such as Canada or Australia.[6] A marginal place during Spanish rule and in the first half of the nineteenth century, Argentina showed growth from the 1860s up until 1930 that was so impressive that it was expected eventually to become the United States of South America. This expansion halted with the 1930 Depression and has never really recovered. With the exception of some years, stagnation has prevailed since the Second World War. The country had a slow rate of growth in the pre-1973 period—especially in the 1950s and part of the 1960s—when most of the rest of the world enjoyed a golden era, and experienced a decline in economic performance following the oil crisis in the 1970s, through the 1980s, and in the last years of the 1990s. During the twentieth century, the country fell from having one of the world's ten highest GDP per capita to the fiftieth or sixtieth position. Argentinians began to see themselves as Francesca da Rimini in hell: "There is no greater sorrow than to recall, in wretchedness, the happy time."[7]

Argentina's peculiar economic experience from prosperity to poverty during a century of peace captivated onlookers; it is comparable only with countries that suffered the consequences of a war, such as Lebanon from the 1970s to the 1990s, which was not its case. Discussion among academics was sparked with the first signs of economic decay in the 1940s and grew in the following decades, along with the continuing economic deterioration. This academic debate centered on the reasons for Argentina's alleged failure and a search for the roots of this decay—a perspective that did not consider the possibility that forecasts of the country's grandeur might have been overly optimistic. Industry was at the center of discussion, held accountable not for its evil consequences (as with contemporaries) but for its plain absence. Historians and economists blamed not industry itself but its failure to develop during the prosperous years as the reason for the country's future underdevelopment. And they did it with the same passion with which contemporaries had complained about its presence.[8]

Research on industry for this period has been minimal. The lack of scholarly works is such that Adolfo Dorfman's book is still the finest piece, despite being published in 1942.[9] Conversely, from the 1940s to the 1970s the presumed lack of industrialization prompted an abundant debate, the roots of which can be traced back to when the limits of agro-exporting expansion became apparent. A consensus was reached in the form of a shared body of knowledge that I label the "canonical version." According to this narrative, the lack of state support was the most serious restraint to growth that

Argentine industry encountered. This perspective blamed the state for not using its banks to provide convenient long-term and low-interest loans for industrial firms and for not supporting tariff barriers against imports of manufactured goods.

Although its popularity increased notably after the 1940s, the historical construction of the canonical version had started at an earlier age. From its foundation in 1887, the Unión Industrial Argentina (UIA)—the industrialists' lobbying group—was especially active in the projection of this image.[10] It is not surprising that a corporate association would use this tactic to obtain more benefits for its constituency. More problematic is the fact that its view became so widely accepted. Indeed, the canonical version tightened its hold on politicians, scholars, and the public at large until it turned into an article of faith.

Beyond UIA's intentions, this interpretation of events was part of a movement that saw a powerful industrial sector and a state actively involved in the economy as the modernizing forces that would eventually lead the country toward development. In the formulation of this interpretation, the canonical version provided the historical background that gave legitimacy to industrialists' claims for credit and tariffs. A major thrust for this stance came in the 1920s with the support of Alejandro Bunge, the influential director of the *Revista de Economía Argentina* and a UIA consultant. Foreseeing an expansion in the population that would consume additional goods (thus decreasing commodities available for export and increasing the demand for imports), Bunge advocated industrialization as the only way to sustain economic growth and maintain a healthy balance of trade. The Great Depression gave a more defined shape to his proposals, in which he urged the state to take that task seriously, as clearly outlined in his *Una Nueva Argentina* (*A New Argentina*), published in 1939 and destined to have a resounding impact. The conclusion was simple: if industry could not progress for lack of governmental support, it was the task of the New Argentina's standard bearers to make up for lost time by pushing manufacturing with all their strength.[11]

To some, this news came not a second too soon. In 1944, Américo Guerrero published a book, with a foreword by Luis Colombo, the incumbent president of the UIA, which described the history of Argentine industry as a secular crucifixion, while announcing its final victory, the arrival of a glorious era when state help could be taken for granted. The long-awaited time finally became a reality with the creation of the state-owned Banco de Crédito Industrial (Bank for Industrial Loans) the very same year, and the launching of a preposterous import-substitution program that president Juan Domingo Perón carried out after 1946. From that time to the mid-1970s, industrial growth became a major aim for any administration, whether civilian or military.[12]

In the academic sphere, the canonical version enjoyed a success as striking as that in the political arena. In the 1940s and 1950s, professional engineers such as the previously mentioned Dorfman produced valuable studies.[13] Yet a more academic discussion began only in the 1960s and 1970s. A group of scholars, encouraged by the prospect of finding in history the origins of the country's decline, looked to the past for reasons why Argentina had not developed an industrial sector comparable to that of First World nations. The canonical version provided a perfect answer to this question for two reasons. First, fashionable theoretical assumptions led academics to believe that industry could not obtain any support (private or public) from an economy (and a state) dominated by agriculture and cattle-raising interests. Second, the essays overwhelmingly drew with little critical analysis on the biased sources published by industrialists themselves.

As a result, a group of scholars, who could be labeled Structuralists, coalesced around an argument claiming that a state held captive by a landed elite blocked industrial development until a major external shock occurred. According to these scholars, it was not until the 1930 Depression that industrialization was promoted as the direct result of forced import-substitution policies aiming to overcome the trade deficit induced by the collapse of the world economy.[14] The Rostowian approach followed by Guido Di Tella and Manuel Zymelman is an example; they supported the idea that Argentina had had an opportunity to industrialize with the First World War and the shortages it brought. The state's narrow-minded policies, however, had prevented the country from seizing this chance until the world depression forced its leaders to put the economy on the path to modernity; the period in between the possibility and the actuality came to be known as the "long delay."[15]

Suggestions that industrial growth had occurred in the period of agrarian expansion prior to 1930 came in a twofold movement. First, scholars looking with more detail at data found the existence of a certain degree of industrialization in agricultural and cattle-related activities.[16] Second, adherents of staple-theory (the idea that the export sector shapes the domestic economy) not only claimed that the country had experienced such a growth but also provided a theoretical context—based on the idea of comparative advantages—to explain its origin.[17] One of these authors, Ezequiel Gallo, called into question some of the very pillars of the canonical version, such as the alleged lack of state support, and set the agenda for further research.[18] This agenda seemed to hold great promise at the time, especially with the iconoclastic analysis of Carlos Díaz Alejandro. Drawing upon neoclassicism, he suggested that some manufacturing development during the agro-export boom was nothing but the outcome of free-trade policies, since they promoted an optimal recourse allocation.[19]

Structuralists and neoclassicists confronted each other with hostility and prepared for battle. The debate, however, was short-lived and disappointing. For one thing, theoretical challenges did not go as deep as first anticipated. Neoclassicism merged with the canonical version when Díaz Alejandro's study finished with more of the same in the sphere of industrial financing and tariffs; he concluded that the Argentine state did not consciously work in favor of industry before 1930. His emphasis on the benefits of free-trade policies, indeed, prevented him from seeing any active effort regarding the manufacturing sector.[20] In addition, the methodology and the data used in different essays were unchanged; it was only variations in the theory that promoted different interpretative frameworks. Macroanalysis monopolized the debate while the aggregate census results continued to be the main source relied upon. As a result, as some scholars have pointed out, "the discussion ceased before it had finished, probably because it could only go on producing more of the same arguments with the tools available."[21]

Chimneys in the Desert strives to break the stalemate by studying new topics, by applying a new methodology, and by using new primary sources. First, it deals with neglected subjects beyond the usual focus on production. Production is analyzed in depth here, but this study also delves into the sphere of consumption and the interaction between supply and demand. As a result, taste, fashion, and commercialization changes are investigated as closely as the evolution of productive strategies. Second, the book examines industry through a different lens: in its component production units, rather than the traditional macroeconomic approach. Therefore, this book abandons the standard idea of a homogeneous "industrial sector" acting as a block and adopts the firms' perspective. In pursuing this approach, the book draws on the methods and recent empirical achievements provided by "business history," although it just takes advantage of its methodology as a basis for the examination of the larger stage on which production units interact, thus combining micro and macro analyses.[22] Finally, this research has mined unused archival sources—such as company, financial, and bank records—while looking at the traditional ones with the detail that microanalysis permits.[23]

To capture the interaction of micro and macro perspectives, this study works in parallel with branch and firm levels of analysis, a methodological approach that requires the use of disaggregate data. The aggregate census results, indeed, present a variety of problems. Each of the censuses—undertaken in 1887, 1895, 1904, 1908, and 1913—used different criteria that inhibited reliable comparison. The Municipal Census of 1904, for example, shows a diminishing workforce in comparison with data from 1895. Since industry grew substantially during those years, a quick assessment might suggest a dramatic increase in labor productivity, a misleading conclusion since the drop in workforce was, simply, the consequence of poor data collection in 1904.[24] In addition, censuses lumped together establishments of different sizes and productive natures. These data offer a general overview of industrial growth, but their conclusions are tainted by the problems of aggregation. The industrial scene depicted by these averages is, then, a constellation of small- to middle-size workshops, a description that cannot be further from the truth since, as will be shown, it hides the important role that large factories played in the origin of Argentine industrialization.

Chapter 1 focuses on the sphere of supply, a choice that requires some explanation, since I myself consider supply and demand two sides of the same coin. This choice, then, encourages a more logical organization of the argument, rather than a historiographical stand. The book starts with the beginning of Argentine industry, which has itself been a subject of discussion. Scholars have traditionally adhered to the idea of "radical ruptures," insisting that the 1930 Depression was a dramatic watershed that changed the country's economic orientation from the external to the domestic market. In this shift, industry would have played a key role as an almost entirely new force. By contending that the Depression sparked the country's first period of industrial growth, this approach took on the appearance of a local version of Alexander Gerschenkron's paradigm of big spurts, very much in fashion in the 1960s.[25]

Glimpses of continuity regarding Argentine industrial history began to emerge with Javier Villanueva's pathbreaking study, published in 1972. Challenging what he called the "Olympian version" depicting the 1930 Depression as a sharp rupture, Villanueva opened the field for renewed discussion by providing evidence of a significant increase in manufacturing in the 1920s, led by foreign investments in response to increasing domestic market demand.[26] His assertions did not fall on deaf ears; through a series of case studies, evidence began to accumulate that factories of significant size existed in the pre-1930 period.[27] Moreover, recent research has found a surprising degree of industrial growth during that period, when imports were rising, disproving the claim that manufacturing thrusts are necessarily the outcome of trade balance problems.[28] This time frame for industrial development, showing ruptures as well as continuities, is reinforced in this book.

Chapter 2 analyzes the demand for manufactured goods from the consumption perspective, in which market formation links material and cultural lives. Consumption encompasses changes in taste, fashion, and commercialization of these goods. It also implies the parallel arrival of economic modernity to the Argentine market, demonstrated by the increasing presence of advertising, sales catalogues, and department stores in what was—as will be argued—the rise of a consumer society. The study of the formation of a consumer market in Argentina is a novelty.[29] Consumption as a field for historical research has given rise to a new perspective, so-called "consumerism," to analyze economic changes.[30] Consumerism has been subject to an array of strong criticisms, not the least of which is the overemphasis on the demand side. It provides, however, a number of analytical tools that will be widely used in this chapter. By working with demand and supply as they interact with one another, this book attempts to develop a more integrated approach than consumerist or supply-side studies.

The chapter focuses on the city of Buenos Aires, the place where changes in consumption were most evident, and deals with firms' efforts to enlarge their circle of customers and promote changes in people's habits.[31] The implications this transformation had for the country's industrialization were significant. Thanks to it, domestic factories underwent a previously unknown rate of growth and expansion, for the first time producing some goods in massive quantities. However, the process that transforms people into consumers goes beyond factory production and blends changing ideas, customs, and relationships between persons and things, as well as between people themselves. Adopting this perspective, Chapter 2 will also analyze the cultural and social shifts fostered by the rise of a consumer society and the first signs of a massive market for manufactured goods.

With the arrival of a new century, the reshaping of industrial capitalism changed the very nature of supply, as will be studied in Chapter 3. Argentine economic history during the export boom period has usually been considered a homogeneous period in terms of its main structural features—basically, an export-oriented and open economy. In the domestic market and at a microeconomic level, change rather than continuity prevailed in the turn-of-the-century period. By the first decade of the twentieth century, as this chapter will show, industrial supply moved toward "trustification" (as was the fashionable label at that time), capital concentration, and big business.[32] Transforming the nature of market relations was not unique to Argentina. Most industrialized countries, as well as the largest Latin American economies, witnessed a trend toward capital concentration at the time. By moving in that direction, through a domestic market that closely followed the world's lead, Argentina revealed how deeply it was integrated into the international market. Scholars differed in their interpretation of these changes;

some considered them a qualitative readjustment in the market, while others saw them as a major qualitative transformation of the capitalist system. Different perspectives offer useful analyses and conclusions that will be taken into account in this chapter.[33]

For Argentina, the process was partially the result of a recession in 1897, followed by a highly prosperous decade that started around 1903. Despite its importance, scholars did not make note of this recession. This is not a surprise but rather the consequence of an export-oriented bias in the analysis of Argentine economic history—the end-of-the-nineteenth-century slump, indeed, mainly affected the domestic market. After 1903 and until a new depression hit the country in 1913, Argentina experienced glory days, which would be partially renewed in the 1920s. The golden years were shorter than usually perceived, and their extension to the whole export boom period is quite arbitrary. But the origin of the major structural features of the economy lay in its transformation at that time; any further opening of the domestic market to the international economy would follow this path.

A country has a national market for goods when their prices in any of its territory are just the result of adding transport costs to production values. A national market, then, is more than a sum of regional economic spaces in which people buy and sell; it implies a convergence of goods prices. The replacement of local transactions by national ones was, in many countries, the result of a process that cracked internal barriers to trade, such as domestic tariffs on the circulation of goods. The formation of a national market for manufactured goods as a major event in the building of Argentine capitalism is the subject of Chapter 4.[34] In this transformation, nationwide manufacturers replaced regional producers operating in more restricted areas; this process has received scant scholarly attention. Such indifference, which again arises from the alleged insignificance of the domestic market during the years of the export boom, finds an exception in Roberto Cortés Conde's study of the formation of a factors-of-production market.[35] The role of goods, however, has been especially neglected; no study of the formation of a national market for products has yet been undertaken.

This chapter delves into the complexities of the evolution of the national market for products by showing that the cheaper transportation provided by railways was a necessary but insufficient condition for the formation of such a market. Some regional studies have foreshadowed this assertion by indicating how long it took for some areas to become part of an integrated national economy.[36] As in the case of consumption, this process was not linear; every product had its own story, every region its own evolution. In addition, the formation of this market was a collective effort in which the state and the private sector played a conscious and active role. Moreover, the historical construction of this market was one of the battlefields in the struggle to create an Argentine nation. Following decades of civil war, the central state defeated the last local rebellion in 1880. The next step was to create an entity that could foster a feeling of identification and common experience for the main bulk of the population. Efforts to firmly establish this nation became an obsession with the massive arrival of European immigrants in the late 1880s and grew to fanaticism in the first years of the twentieth century. Thus, the formation of a national market was not merely a field for contesting economic interests but also an arena for competing ideological positions, which interacted with market forces.[37]

As this book is a study of the world that industrialization helped to build, it includes a discussion of labor's contribution to this process. Chapter 5 studies the complex relationship that linked factory owners and workers, and especially how it transformed their collective behavior. Traditionally, the industrialists' performance has been regarded as an extension of the activity of the UIA. Moreover, information produced by this association has been considered a direct expression of industrialist views.[38] This chapter challenges this assumption, which might be true for the 1940s but is of doubtful certainty for the pre-1930-Depression years. A long-standing vision, therefore, is replaced with a description of an unfolding process of industrial-identity formation. In the view of the entrepreneurs, workers played a significant role in this evolution by withdrawing from the paternalistic industrial family and becoming antagonists in the public sphere.

The birth of the Argentine working class has been one of the most researched topics in the country's historiography. Nevertheless, labor history has barely taken into account the relationship between the workers and the industrialists. When it has, it relied largely on the sources provided by the workers themselves. This story tells us a great deal about the work routine but not very much about the features of the mentioned relationship. The exceptions to this gap reveal a highly complex story in which paternalism coexisted with modernity and even prevailed over other more "rational" organizational tools, such as Taylorism.[39] In researching labor's influence on industrial growth, historians have examined it as a factor of production. However useful this analysis is, we still lack information on its qualitative effect on the entire society, let alone on industrialists.[40] In addressing this gap, Chapter 5 will concentrate on one of the most sensitive issues raised by industrialization, the appearance of the *fabriqueras* (factory girls). They were central to the Argentine government's formulation of the "social question" and to the preoccupation of Catholic, Reformer, Socialist, and Anarchist groups.[41] Their very existence has been the subject of debate. Some feminist studies, for instance, have stated that the incorporation of women into the factory workforce was a limited phenomenon, a myth created by contemporaries, attractive only because of the very nature of work—an escape from the home and domesticity.[42] This chapter will question this "image" and look at the actual role of these women, revealing the importance of their presence in the transformations wrought by industrialization.

Chapters 6 and 7 directly challenge the widely accepted canonical version, which portrays the origins of Argentine industry as a quixotic epic undertaken by factory owners against a hostile capital market and an antagonistic state. Chapter 6 not only shows that the issue of industrial financing needs to be revisited but also suggests it was not a major bottleneck for growth, as has been traditionally thought. The pioneer studies of manufacturing financing coincided with the well-established belief in the alleged anti-industrial bias of financing institutions prior to the 1940s. Not surprisingly, these studies only touched briefly on the issue—as an unquestionable truth, it did not need further research. This lack of attention was reinforced in the 1960s and 1970s, when an overemphasis on the real sector in economic analysis promoted an even wider acceptance of the canonical version.[43] Providing some relief from this version's homogenous perspective, a few works offered important nuances that could have provided a basis for further debate, but such a debate never took place. With its variants, the canonical version held that, beyond personal ties, industry was bereft of access to credit, while the market mechanisms that could have provided loans to the industrialists did not work.[44]

This chapter draws upon aims and methods provided by perspectives, such as neo-institutionalism, that have focused on this topic.[45] In so doing, it shows that firms found a variety of alternative methods to increase their working capital and to obtain money for their investments. As will be seen, they had access to capital in a simpler and more fluid manner than has ever been supposed. Moreover, some of this money was provided by the very institutions considered to embody the anti-industrial bias of the capital market: the state banks. Not only does the microanalysis challenge the canonical version, but company data, primarily from balance sheets rather than industrialist propaganda sources, also support this conclusion. Most of this information comes from the two major state banks reputed to be most hostile to industry, the Banco de la Nación Argentina (Bank of the Argentine Nation) and the Banco de la Provincia de Buenos Aires (Bank of the Province of Buenos Aires). In addition, this chapter analyzes the role of some forgotten economic institutions, such as the Stock Exchange, which just recently has been recovered as a significant channel of finance for the export boom years.[46]

The study of industrial policy in Chapter 7 tackles this issue by analyzing the economic role of the state within a flexible framework. This chapter focuses on the political and ideological meaning of industrial policy in order to examine the place of manufacturing on the political map from 1880, when the central state consolidated, to 1930, when military intervention ended seven decades of constitutional administration. On this terrain, parties, bureaucracies, and institutions battled. Traditionally, scholars have looked for a one hundred percent protectionist policy during this period; when they did not find it, they concluded that free trade prevailed. Some historians have even argued that the different administrations engaged in a *proteccionismo al revés* (reverse protectionism) by not only failing to protect domestic industry but also placing high tariffs on the foreign inputs that local producers desperately needed.[47] This vision fails to take into account the many possible settings that lie between a coherent and well-enunciated industrial policy and its absence. It is on this middle ground that this study focuses. In so doing, it demonstrates the existence of industrial policies notwithstanding their restricted nature.[48]

For many supporters of the canonical version, a state controlled by landowners (as was supposed to be the case prior to 1930) presumably would have been anti-industrial. This perspective has theoretical and historical flaws. Studies on the nature of the state have illustrated the complexities in the interaction between interest groups and the implementation of policies. The school of thought that stresses the relative autonomy of the state, for instance, has shown that the idea of its alleged captivity and performance as the instrument of a particular group is shortsighted, as well as empirically rare.[49] Even if some degree of captivity is accepted, the canonical argument remains historically unproven. The assumption that landowners had substantial power in the government of a country experiencing an agro-export boom makes sense. But, as some scholars have shown, these landowners were a diverse group with a wider web of interests that went beyond agriculture and included commerce, industry, and any profitable activity at hand. This makes it difficult to equate social actors with economic interests taken as separate activities.[50] Actually, industrial and exporting interests were not necessarily at odds; both supported the same monetary and exchange policies, which aimed at keeping local currency cheap.[51] Beyond theory and common sense, the evidence upon which the canonical version was constructed—mainly sources from the industrialists themselves—reveals another shortcoming of an already weak argument.

Scholars generally accept that any discussion of industrial policy during an era when national states were not yet involved in the production of goods and services must target the impact of tariffs on foreign imports. Crucial to understanding the importance of Argentine tariffs during the export boom is an analysis of the parliamentary debates, especially those preceding the long-lasting customs law of 1906, a project not yet accomplished by scholarship.[52] Díaz Alejandro challenged the belief in anti-industrialism by demonstrating how beneficial open market policies could be to industrialists. Nevertheless, as already stated, he emphasized the laissez-faire nature of the Argentine economy prior to 1930 and consequently left out any discussion of the political nature of tariffs. Moreover, when evidence forced scholars to recognize the existence of some tariffs, they continued to highlight the subservience of the state to agricultural interests.[53] Some studies have questioned the laissez-faire policies of the export boom period.[54] These challenges to the canonical version stress the need to reassess the nature of the relationship between the Argentine State and economic policies. By studying the meaning of industrial policies, this chapter delves into the complexities of this relationship and depicts a state more favorable toward industry than previously thought.[55]

In sum, this book attempts to reveal the importance of the domestic economy in different spheres of Argentina's social life by studying industry during the export boom years, a neglected subject in Argentina's history. On the one hand, it focuses on production for Argentine internal consumption, since its aim is to study industry as a part of the domestic market. It excludes export manufacturing such as meatpacking houses and cereal mills, which were also (and in the first case mainly) oriented toward foreign customers; nor does it delve into regional production, such as wine and sugar, which have already been extensively studied.[56] On the other hand, this book deals especially with the industrial world of large factories, those which—by the eve of the Great Depression—were involved in substantial production (in many cases, already standardized), usually employed hundreds of workers, and almost always used steam power. This choice is not arbitrary, for these were the production units in which real industrial activity took place, while the dense universe of simultaneously operating small establishments worked a slower handicraft production. This is not an easy task. What might be considered a large factory in turn-of-the-twentieth-century Argentina is a highly complicated issue discussed extensively in the first chapter. And this is just one of the complexities that a study on industrial growth in Argentina implies.[57]

The complexities, nuances, and contradictions that characterized industrialization will dog our steps through the following pages. By focusing on this topic, this book will delve into the nature of a country carving its way to economic growth, social expansion, political consolidation, and nation building before the rift of a military coup and a world depression changed its history. In this slow-motion wave of modernization, industry played a leading role.

Chapter 1

The First Factories:
The Dawn of Argentine Industry,
1870s–1890s

The First Industrial Setting

By the 1890s, the landscape of Buenos Aires had experienced noticeable transformations, and its skyline had been transformed by the presence of a new type of building: the factory. Adrián Patroni, a labor union activist, wrote a report in 1897 depicting the grimy life of workers in an industry that "without dispute, only twenty years ago . . . was unknown in here." As a result, the city of "Buenos Aires has changed its appearance; once, it was only distinguished by the great number of belfries, but very soon, very tall chimneys dominating the landscape could be seen wherever one looked."[1] The newspaper *La Nación*, mostly unsympathetic to the bustling industrial activity, had made a similar comment three years before:

> Those who used to take a stroll along the outskirts of the capital city must have noticed what we assert; at every corner one meets the erect chimneys of masonry, tall and sharp, culminated in a tuft of smoke, the unequivocal sign of a national industry.[2]

Another publication, also noted for its lack of enthusiasm for manufacturing—*The Review of the River Plate*, a local magazine for the British community in Buenos Aires—went further in complaining about the inconveniences that the new buildings caused:

The fact of a large extension of manufactured goods in our midst is not to be gainsaid. One has to ascend to some point in the city of Buenos Aires from which he can command an extensive view . . . to become convinced of the fact that this has at least begun to be a manufacturing city. The number of new factory chimneys is astonishing, and an unwelcome evidence, if further evidence were desired, is to be found in the extension of the soot plague, especially in the southern districts, and in the center when the south wind blows.[3]

If factories were evident across the landscape, their products were not as obvious in the stores. In the 1890s, many of the items manufactured in Argentine factories copied foreign models and were sold as if they had been made abroad. As the same journal noted,

For the truth of it is that every manufactured article in this city is sold, not for what it is, but for what it imitates; and the art of imitation is carried to a very high pitch of perfection indeed.[4]

As a consequence, domestic goods turned out to be quite invisible to unquestioning eyes.

Industry either existed or did not exist, according to what the observer perceived. This simultaneous visibility and invisibility has led to different conclusions in scholarly research. For social and urban historians, industry was of paramount importance; for all other academics, especially those interested in economics, it was insignificant. This chapter will untangle this confusion by showing that these conflicting conclusions arose from the complexities and paradoxes permeating early Argentine industrialization.

Argentine factories were virtually nonexistent until the 1870s. In 1876, the scientist Ricardo Napp explained the reasons for such an absence: "No industry can prosper in a country with only one inhabitant for each 2 square kilometers, where the labor force is very expensive, and where there is no capital and technological knowledge."[5] Between the year when Napp described the manufacturing prospects of the new nation and 1900 — around the time when the first observers mentioned in this chapter spoke — industrial output had grown seven-fold and was especially perceptible in the city of Buenos Aires (see Table 1.1 and Figure 1.1).

The rise of factories in the last quarter of the nineteenth century resulted from a see-saw movement comprising two opposing forces both supportive of industry: depressions and demand growth. The deeper incorporation of Argentina into the world market in the mid-nineteenth century changed the national history. Cycles of world capitalism began to set off booms and

TABLE 1.1
Argentina: Economic Indicators, 1875–1930

(GDP per Capita and Industrial Output, base year 1900 = 100.00)

	Population	Exports (gold pesos)	Imports (gold pesos)	GDP	GDP per Capita	Industrial Output
1875	2,161,000	52,009,113	57,624,481	17.45	55.82	14.46
1880	2,492,000	58,380,787	45,535,880	21.78	53.02	14.57
1885	2,880,000	83,879,100	92,221,969	44.70	82.64	22.40
1890	3,377,000	100,818,993	142,240,812	58.59	88.25	31.62
1895	3,956,000	120,067,790	95,096,438	82.69	115.32	60.37
1900	4,607,000	154,600,412	113,485,069	100.00	100.00	100.00
1905	5,289,000	322,843,841	205,154,420	164.35	159.26	169.56
1910	6,586,000	389,071,360	379,352,515	197.43	162.95	217.85
1915	8,148,000	558,281,000	305,488,006	216.30	137.63	235.14
1920	8,968,000	1,044,085,000	963,123,000	231.73	135.50	271.50
1925	10,500,000	867,930,000	877,973,000	304.94	162.10	389.66
1930	12,046,000	614,104,000	740,088,000	326.93	149.15	417.35

SOURCES: My own elaboration based on the following:

Population: For the period 1875–1910, Vicente Vázquez Presedo. *Estadísticas históricas Argentinas: Primera parte* 1875–1914 (Buenos Aires: Macchi, 1971)15–16; for the period 1915–1930, Dirección Nacional de Estadísticas y Censos, Informe demográfico de la República Argentina, 1944, p. 14.

For exports and imports: Anuarios del comercio exterior Argentino, 1875–1930; and Ernesto Tornquist & Co., Ltd., *Buenos Aires: The Economic Development of the Argentine Republic in the Last Fifty Years*, 1919, pp. 15–18 and 139–40.

For GDP, GDP per capita, and industrial output: Roberto Cortés Conde, "Estimaciones del producto bruto interno en Argentina 1875–1935," pp. 17–20.

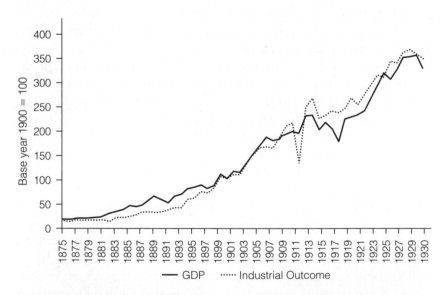

Figure 1.1. Growth of GDP and Industrial Outcome: Argentina 1875–1930

SOURCE: My own elaboration based on Roberto Cortés Conde, "Estimaciones del producto bruto interno en Argentina, 1875–1916," mimeograph, Department of Economics, Universidad de San Andrés, Buenos Aires, Victoria, 1994, 17–20.

depressions in the local economy. Argentina experienced an economic boom from the 1850s to the 1870s thanks to the export of wool.[6] This affluence spurred the arrival of immigrants to a country with a scarce population and where the promotion of European immigration became an obsession. Everybody in power shared the motto created by Juan Bautista Alberdi, the man who wrote the outline of the National Constitution of 1853, in effect until 1949—"Gobernar es poblar" (to govern is to populate). By 1869, according to the data from the first national census, foreigners already composed 11 percent of the population. But the number reached 50 percent in the city of Buenos Aires and 17 percent in the region most benefited by the export growth.[7]

A recession in 1866 that hit the wool international market, however, halted this long-lasting period of prosperity. But this recession was mild compared to the one the country experienced, as did most of the world, in 1873. The tenacity of the 1873 crisis, which lasted until 1877, halted the arrival of foreign capital, drove government incomes downward, and jeopardized the process of state formation. But it also promoted an opportunity for manufacturing. After years of confusion, during which the administration discussed whether to default or to pay the external debt with substantial changes in economic policies, President Nicolás Avellaneda chose the second alternative. In 1876, the national government decided to abandon the gold standard begun in 1867 and to impose higher duties on a variety of imported goods, including some previously untaxed, in order to reduce the trade deficit, swell the state treasury, and pay the international financial debt. The first policy led to devaluation and raised the price of imports through the exchange rate. The second policy went in the same direction.[8]

As a result, some (albeit few) industrial firms took advantage of import substitution, and their installations started to resemble real factories. Imports fell more than a third between 1875 and 1876, and the level of the first year was not recovered until 1881. In the late 1870s, the amount of industrial inputs in the entire group of imports doubled compared to the pre-crisis level—a clear demonstration of a rise in local manufacturing. The parallel maintenance of the rate of capital goods in the total number of imports, however, reveals the rather unmechanized nature of this first wave of import substitution (see Table 1.2). The first fruits of this nascent industrial sector appeared in an 1881 exposition that, according to bystander Emile Daireaux, succeeded because "domestic industrial progress was already important [enough] to justify a continental exhibition of manufactured goods." Although growing, industry still was handicraft in nature. This was apparent in the kind of artisanal artifacts displayed, as well as in the mixing of sculptors and painters with industrialists.[9]

TABLE 1.2

Imports According to Their Productive Nature, 1876–1930

Total Imports (million gold pesos)	Consumer Goods (%)	Capital Goods (%)	Industrial Inputs (%)	Consumer Goods (%)	Food	Beverage	Textiles	Durables	Tobacco
1876	36.8	93.4	2.4	5.2	46.7	18.0	26.2	6.4	2.8
1880	45.5	83.9	3.2	12.9	44.5	16.3	31.8	5.0	2.3
1881	55.7	77.6	8.6	13.8	26.4	17.9	47.9	5.0	2.9
1885	92.2	49.5	24.5	26.0	27.3	21.3	39.1	8.1	4.2
1890	142.2	42.2	36.7	21.1	18.4	14.0	58.3	5.6	3.6
1895	95.1	66.2	8.5	25.3	18.8	11.4	55.8	9.2	4.9
1900	113.5	56.4	8.6	35.0	17.8	9.4	53.3	14.6	4.8
1905	205.2	42.2	21.8	37.0	21.1	10.1	43.9	20.7	4.1
1910	379.3	38.9	16.8	44.3	18.1	2.7	68.2	8.5	2.4
1915	301.5	38.0	14.2	47.8	19.5	1.3	57.5	19.8	1.9
1920	868.4	42.2	17.4	40.4	12.8	0.8	52.6	32.6	1.2
1925	830.7	40.7	17.4	41.9	16.5	0.7	52.8	28.6	1.3
1930	636.4	35.8	21.2	43.0	46.7	18.0	26.2	6.4	2.8

NOTES: Consumer goods includes food, beverages, tobacco, and durable textiles.

Capital goods includes agriculture and industrial machinery, materials for transportation, and wire for fences.

Industrial inputs includes yarn, oil, coal, metals, iron and steel, and construction materials.

SOURCE: My own elaboration based on *Anuarios del Comercio Exterior*, 1876–1930.

Import substitution could show only minimal results in a country with around two million people, as was the case of Argentina in the 1870s. Sustained industrial growth could take place only with a rise in demand, a phenomenon that began to occur in the 1880s, after the depression was over. Between 1875 and 1890, the Argentine population increased from 2,161,000 to 3,613,000, mostly under the influx of almost one million immigrants, mainly from Northern Italy. In addition, the GDP per capita grew 60 percent, thanks to a remarkable economic performance. By then, the country had become a major destination not only of European immigrants but also of British overseas investments. By 1875, Argentina attracted 12 percent of this country's capital in Latin America and was rated fourth after Peru, Brazil, and Mexico in the British capital preferences. By 1890, the percentage reached 35 percent, and Argentina was at the forefront of British investment interest, with numbers that doubled the sums going to Brazil and Mexico.[10]

With immigration, Argentina could profit from the benefits of human capital provided by recent arrivals, an issue especially important for manufacturing—many factories, indeed, could not have opened had the skills of the immigrant population not been available. But the new settlers also provided a demand market as well as a source for workforce. By 1890, consumers, labor, capital, and technology were no longer as scarce as in 1876,

TABLE 1.3

Annual Growth Rate, GDP, GDP per Capita, and Industrial Output, 1875–1930

	GDP	GDP per capita	Industrial Output (1)	Industrial Output (2)	Food	Textile
1875–1890	8.4	3.1	5.2	—	5.6	3.9
1890–1900	5.5	1.3	11.5	—	4.2	12.7
1900–1910	7.0	5.0	7.8	6.0	6.7	7.4
1910–1920	1.6	−1.8	2.2	0.7	1.4	0.3
1920–1930	3.5	1.0	4.3	5.1	3.1	3.9

SOURCE: My own elaboration based on Cortés Conde, "Estimaciones del producto bruto interno en Argentina 1875–1935," pp. 17–20 (1); and CEPAL, *Análisis y proyecciones del desarrollo económico. Vol V: El desarrollo económico de América Latina* (Mexico City: 1959), pp. 11 and 18–19 (2).

when Napp had analyzed the reasons for the lack of industry. Nevertheless, the results were still modest: this period's estimates show an industrial annual growth of 5.2 percent, well behind that of the overall economy, which increased at an annual rate of 8.4 percent (see Table 1.3).[11]

Numbers at the turn of the twentieth century indicate the magnitude of industrial growth. Census data offer a general overview—capital, the use of steam power, and the size of the workforce all increased (see Tables 1.4 and 1.5)—but their conclusions are tainted by the already mentioned problems of aggregation and lack of potential comparison. Disaggregate data, showing the workforce evolution, reveal a much more impressive increase in the largest firms, which turned out to be the leaders in the industrial activity (see Table 1.6).[12]

The influence of large companies sparked a momentous change in the late 1880s, when a few firms located in the city of Buenos Aires started to produce on the basis of an incipient standardization by higher consumption. The booming economy changed dramatically in 1890, when Argentina suffered an economic depression that exceeded the 1873–1877 one. A monetary experiment had started in 1883 with the idea to go back to the gold standard that had ended in 1876, but it was short-lived. At the beginning of 1885 a crisis in the balance of payments forced the Argentine government to end the brief experience with gold standard. That year the price of gold went up from one to 1.36 paper pesos (the local currency—there were two currencies, the gold-backed one [peso oro] and the nonconvertible paper pesos). Economic growth regained strength in 1886 and reached momentum in 1887 and 1888. Difficulties began in the southern summer of 1888–1889, and by March of 1889 the price of gold had increased to $1.55 paper pesos. The government closed the Stock Exchange to end what was called a speculative movement, but when it reopened in September the price of gold had risen to

TABLE 1.4

Industrial Growth in the Argentine Republic, 1895–1914

	Number of Firms	Workers	Capital (1000 pesos moneda nacional)	Workers per Firm	Steam Force (horsepower)	Capital per Firm (1000 pesos moneda nacional)
1895	23,300	167,000	475,000	8	59,500	20.4
1908	32,000	329,500	727,590	12	56,000	22.7
1914	48,800	410,000	1,800,000	8	265,000	36.9

SOURCE: My own elaboration from Segundo Censo Nacional de la República Argentina, May 10, 1895 (Buenos Aires: Talleres Tipográficos de la Penitenciaría Nacional, 1898), volume III, for number of firms, capital, steamforce, and workers pp. 17–20; Censo Industrial de la República Argentina levantado por la Dirección de Comercio e Industria del Ministerio de Agricultura, 1908 in Pablo Storni, "La industria y la situación de las clases obreras en la capital de la República," Informe presentado al ex ministro del interior Dr. Joaquín V. González como antecedente para la preparación del Proyecto de Ley Nacional de Trabajo. Revista Jurídica y de Ciencias Sociales, July-September 1908, 25(3), for number of firms and capital, p. 239, for workers, p. 240, for steamforce, p. 249.; and Tercer Censo Nacional levantado el 1° de junio de 1914, (Buenos Aires: Talleres Gráficos de L. J. Rosso y Cía, 1917), Vol. VII, for number of firms and capital, pp. 187–92, for steamforce, pp. 302–309, for workers, 395–403.

TABLE 1.5

Industrial Growth in Buenos Aires City, 1887–1914

	Number of Firms	Workers	Capital (1,000,000 pesos moneda nacional)	Workers per Firm	Steam Force (horsepower)	Capital per Firm (1,000 pesos moneda nacional)
1887	6,128	42,321	n.d.	7	6,277	n.d.
1895	8,439	70,469	143	8.5	8,729	16.9
1904	8,877	68,512	99	9	10,000	11.1
1908	10,427	118,435	266	11.5	25,000	25.6
1914	10,275	149,281	548	14.5	178,493	53.3

SOURCE: My own elaboration from Censo General de Población, edificación, comercio e industrias de la ciudad de Buenos Aires levantado en los días 17 de agosto, 15 y 30 de septiembre de 1887 (Buenos Aires: Companía Sudamericana de Billetes de Banco, 1889), volume II, for number of firms, p. 370, for workers, p. 379, for steamforce, p. 389; Segundo Censo Nacional de la República Argentina, May 10, 1895 (Buenos Aires: Talleres Tipográficos de la Penitenciaría Nacional, 1898), volume III, for number of firms, capital, steamforce, and workers, pp. 272–73; Censo general de población, edificación, comercio e industrias de la ciudad de Buenos Aires, levantado en los días 11 y 18 de septiembre de 1904 (Buenos Aires: Compañía Sud-Americana de Billetes de Banco, 1906), for number of firms and capital, pp. 174–75, for steamforce and workers, 186–87; Censo Industrial de la República Argentina levantado por la Dirección de Comercio e Industria del Ministerio de Agricultura, 1908, for number of firms and capital, p. 239, for workers, p. 240, for steamforce, p. 249; and Tercer Censo Nacional levantado el 1° de junio de 1914, (Buenos Aires: Talleres Gráficos de L. J. Rosso y Cía, 1917), Vol. VII, for number of firms and capital, p. 120, for steamforce, p. 255, and for workers, p. 320.

TABLE 1.6

Evolution in the Workforce of Argentine Large Firms, 1877–1916

Firm	Branch	circa 1877	1887	circa 1893	1895	circa 1898	circa 1905	1910	circa 1916
Godet-Bassi	Chocolate	45	40	120	120	150	170	200	210
Bagley	Biscuits				161			500	
Noel	Jam		140		160			300	
Saint	Coffee		40		72	150	160	450	
Bieckert	Beer	250	230		450				
Quilmes	Beer			200		800		1000	1200
G–Lauret	Tannery			300		400			
Luppi	Tannery	80			101	120		180	
C. Gomez	Leather			120	550			800	1000
Piccardo	Cigarettes						130	426	1059
CGF	Various			600	828	1330	1500	4000	2450
F.Argentina	Alpargatas		530	600	600			1200	1600
Franchini	Hats				300	480			
Prat	Textile	40	150				400		
P. Merlini	Metallurgical				40	100		150	
Sternberg	Shirts			80	288			700	
Dell'Acqua	Textile				500	800		1300	
Vasena	Metallurgical		68	130		500	500	600	1500
S. Zamboni	Metallurgical	150				300			
F.N. Calzado	Shoes				269		300	600	
Marti	Shoes				400		1000		
Rigolleau	Glass				220			600	1500
La Argentina	Paper				700		800		
Ferrum-Schnaith	Pots and pans				160		700		
Barolo	Textile				14		500		650
Gath y Chaves	Ready-to-wear				76			6000	
La Primitiva	Burlap bags		700		250			700	1000

SOURCES: For the sources for this table, see Appendix 5.

$2.20 paper pesos. In 1890, the crisis moved to the political arena, and by July the incumbent president Miguel Juárez Celman was forced to resign in favor of his vice president, Carlos Pellegrini. Pellegrini had to face a banking crisis in March of 1891 and a further devaluation of the local currency. The gold quoted at $4 paper pesos in the worst months of that year. The new president launched a program of fiscal reforms designed to tackle the economic turmoil by reducing the trade deficit and increasing state revenues through the raising of import tariffs (see Table 1.7).[13] In an atmosphere in which both foreign investments and confidence in the country's future were scarce, the collapse of domestic currency and the rise in tariffs combined to create a favorable milieu for local industry. Not surprisingly, the *Unión Industrial Argentina* (UIA) maintained an optimistic outlook amidst the depression:

It is an ill wind that blows no good. The crisis which sweeps the nation is enormous. . . . [The] nation is in a situation that no one can envy.

TABLE 1.7

Evolution of the Argentine Tariff, 1876–1928

(% ad valorem over items)

	1876	1880	1889	1891	1905	1918	1923	1925	1928
Consumer goods									
Clothing	40	40	50	60	40	47	47	40	50
Shoes	40	60	50	60	40	47	47	40	32
Linseed fabric	20	25	15	15	20		40		
Cotton fabric	20	25	15	15	20	25	22	25	25
Wool fabric	20	25	15	15	30	37	37	30	30
Chocolate	20	25	50	60	47	E	E	E	E
Wine	30	40	E	E	92	E	E	E	E
Beer	40	40	E	E	E	E	E	E	E
Liqueurs	40	40	E	E	E	E	E	E	E
Tobacco	40	40	55	55	58.6	E	E	E	E
Matches	40	40	45	45	E	E	E	E	E
Furniture	40	40	50	60	40	47	47	E	E
Perfumes	40	40	50	50	50	57	57	50	50
Capital goods									
Industrial machinery	—	—	—	—	—	—	—	—	—
Motors	—	10	5	5	—	—	—	—	—
Inputs									
Paper	—	10	20	10	E	32	32	25	25
Iron	10	10	10	10	5	7	7	5	5
Wood pulp	20	25	—	—	5	—	—	—	—
Cotton yarn	20	25	25	—	5	7	7	5	5
Sulphuric acid	20	25	5	5	10	32	32	25	25
Cloth for bags	10	10	5	5	E	E	E	E	E
Cement	20	25	10	10	25	32	32	25	25
Coal and combustible	—	—	—	—	—	—	—	—	—

NOTE: E = specific duties according to quality and other characteristics.

SOURCE: My own elaboration based on Francisco Latzina, *Estadística retrospectiva del comercio exterior Argentino, 1875–1904* (Buenos Aires: Cía. Sudamericana de Billetes de Banco, 1905); and Vicente Vázquez-Presedo, "Sobre un período de protección industrial inevitable," Buenos Aires, 1969, mimeograph, pp. 10–11.

At the same time the wind blows ideally for national industry, and it should be seen as providing the opportunity to elevate industry by a supreme effort to the heights that we desire.[14]

In the 1890s, industrial growth surpassed that of GDP (see Table 1.3). Although the already established firms faced an initial drop in their demand due to recession, import substitution soon increased their output. During the last years of the golden 1880s, machinery had been introduced in the production of beer, cigarettes, matches, soap, candles, paper, and *alpargatas* (a cheap slipper with a rope sole and canvas body). The recessive but protective atmosphere of the 1890s solidified this trend. Firms already producing large quantities in the late 1880s increased their output after an initial fall in demand; others switched from small- to large-scale production; and new companies began operating.

By the time the nineteenth century ended, industry was a significant force in Argentina's economy. Manufacturing, however, was still very new and, not surprisingly given its recent evolution, was characterized more by its omissions than achievements. Because the Argentine case resembled the beginning of a smooth and slow process rather than a big spurt or a take-off, the nascent manufactories faced major limitations. This became apparent by 1897, when the country faced a new depression. As explained at the end of this chapter, the industrial growth that spanned the last three decades of the century was largely responsible for the crisis.

The Features of the First Factories

The early growth in manufacturing activities was very modest and limited to a restricted number of goods of simple manufacture. Textile manufacturing, the alleged mainstay of an early industrial economy, was almost nonexistent in the 1880s. Prior to 1888 only one firm—the Fábrica Nacional de Paños (National Clothing Factory)—was dedicated to producing woolen textile items. Its story is almost mythical since it symbolizes, for some scholars, the failed attempt to fully industrialize and the conspiratorial atmosphere faced by industrialists in the export boom period. In this particular case, at least, the perception is partially accurate. As I said before, in 1866 an international crisis affected wool, the main staple export of Argentina, and the very same year landowners created an association, the Sociedad Rural Argentina (Argentine Rural Society), to defend their interests. As a response, local wool producers found an alternative to diminishing external purchases in the potential domestic demand created by textiles. The Fábrica Nacional opened in 1873 with a labor force of sixty workers, most of them women and children. The depression that began this year reinforced the idea of promoted industrialization. The end of the crisis, however, killed wool producers' enthusiasm for this project. In later years, the factory struggled to survive, and in 1879 it went to bankruptcy.[15] This failed attempt to substitute imports was just one part of a larger story that involved more successful developments of manufacturing activities, such as those resulting in shoes, tobacco products, furniture, carriages, metal goods, and food processing.

Labor-intensive activities, made-to-order production, and lack of mechanization characterized most of the first mills until the late 1880s. Some of them employed hundreds of people, resembling those of other countries at the dawn of industrialization, but the Argentine pattern of early industrial growth differed from those that experienced proto-industrialization (a step before the rise of modern factories in which workers manufactured in the countryside in agreement with a city merchant who sold the output). Buenos Aires, where most of the industry grew, was a marginal city during most of the colonial times. The area in which it was settled had been inhabited by nomadic indigenous people who were killed or incorporated into the white world. Colonized by few people for two centuries after its founding in 1580, Buenos Aires grew mainly as a commercial port in the late eighteenth century. Thus, it did not possess an artisan group that would have been transformed and ultimately destroyed by the arrival of mills. Nor did the number of people involved in the activity of the mills match the numbers of the more populated areas in Latin America.[16] The first Argentine factories did initially employ handicraft methods, but this was not the result of a previous tradition in the country; it was based on the human capital provided by immigrants, some of them already artisans in their native countries. Argentine industry, then, started almost from scratch, and its factories rose like chimneys in a desert.

The use of handicraft labor on a large scale pervaded early industry in Argentina. This scenario differed from standardization, but it was suitable for a small and unstable market. Shoe production provides a good example. According to one industrialist source, shoe making employed ten thousand people in Buenos Aires in 1872, many of them recent arrivals to the city and only sporadically productive. Rising popular income during the booming economic years of the early 1870s prompted an increased domestic demand for shoes; however, imports soon filled the market. The number of workers dropped to twenty-eight hundred because

> That enormous mass of shoes in a country without enough consumers
> forced the owners to offer their merchandise to the merciless hammer
> of the auctioneer who sold it at a very low price. This meant a financial
> loss for some establishments and bankruptcy for most of them. Due to
> the lack of orders, they had to quit the shoe industry to work as car
> drivers, maids, tramway stagecoach drivers, and other professions.

Relief for the shoemakers came with the previously mentioned tariffs of 1876 that followed the 1873 depression and the subsequent fall in imports. The number of workers recovered and jumped to thirteen thousand by the end of the decade.[17] Fostered by the rise in domestic demand in the 1880s, shoe manufacturers increased the number of laborers but did not mechanize (as late as 1887, and with a single exception, the industry lacked steam-powered machines, even in establishments employing as many as three or four hundred people).[18] As a chronicler later remembered, by then "subdivision of labor and better use of raw material lacked importance"; most of the work was done under the putting-out system, a type of production in which factory owners provided (or "put out") inputs to workers who finished them at home and returned the final output to the industrialist. Soles were usually given to the official, who cut them however he wanted since he obtained materials that supplemented his meager salary.[19] Moreover, some of these factories were using noncapitalist methods to obtain their workforces, such as "contracting" abandoned children from the *Defensoría de Menores* (Defense of Minors Office).[20] By the 1880s, local shoe production was so primitive that it could not compete with higher-quality imported articles and was limited to the production of the coarsest goods sold on the market.[21] But by doing so, it was able to find a niche in the satisfaction of local demand and, thanks to its flexibility, bear with success the ups and downs of the Argentine economy.

Artisan methods also characterized the furniture, metal, and carriage industries. The owner of one of the main furniture factories, for instance, boasted of not using any machinery in the transformation of machine-cut wood into fine articles: "In finishing the products and communicating their artistic shape a man's hand could not be replaced."[22] Not surprisingly, a benevolent observer stated in 1884 that "the furniture industry is, in spite of its efforts, an industry of tomorrow."[23] Local shops did not produce the highest-quality goods (which were still imported from Europe), nor could they manufacture the poorest-quality items that were produced elsewhere at a low cost thanks to standardization; thus, cheap chairs from mechanized factories in the United States flooded the market. But the production methods allowed domestic output to produce at least one type of inexpensive item—those made of white wood made in small quantities and based upon the made-to-order system.[24]

Various metal industries were also based on made-to-order production, carried out by immigrants in small workshops.[25] Using a machine to produce nails was a pioneering move in 1880, while human skills were the main capital.[26] Carriage production followed a similar scenario. A French observer stated that "[t]here is no other industry where the division of labor has become so pervasive." By "division of labor", however, he meant a shop whose owner worked side by side with his employees, though referring to himself as the "best worker."[27]

Tobacco manufacturing inaugurated a new trend: handicraft labor used in large numbers. This was one of the few activities that can be traced back to colonial times. After independence, tobacco rollers gave their final product, mainly cigars, to the *almacenero* (storeowner) in exchange for food, drink, and a little bit of cash.[28] In the 1880s, cigarettes, a popular and cheap article, displaced other forms of smoking, such as cigars. Large-scale production made this putting-out system unsuitable for these factories. Long rows of skilled workers rolling items in an ever-expanding mill became typical of the tobacco industry. As a result, an increase in production could be achieved only by employing more people, a situation that created supervision bottlenecks in the most successful firms.[29]

At the dawn of Argentine industry, the most dramatic steps took place in food processing, a branch which had introduced some machinery at its inception. A group of skilled confectioners, all of them foreigners with some dexterity acquired in their native countries who boasted of their exquisite taste, had been producing goods on a small scale since the middle of the century.[30] A combination of factors presented them with the possibility of becoming real industrialists: import tariffs, growth of aggregate demand, and a passion for eating and drinking European products in a country eager to forget old colonial tastes and to adopt more "civilized" customs. Three chocolate factories expanded by introducing steam-powered machines in the 1880s. At the same time, wholesale operations replaced previous retail selling.[31] Mr. Noel, a Basque entrepreneur who had opened a confectionery store in 1847, made the transition from selling his locally crafted or imported delicacies directly to the public to producing in substantial large-market quantities. The key to his success was the use of machinery in large-scale production targeted on only one good: *dulce de membrillo*, a jellied quince introduced by a Catalan in 1880 and destined to become one of Argentina's favorite desserts.[32]

Biscuits, liqueurs, pasta (demanded by the large Italian community), cooking oil, and even some canned foods started to pour out of establishments more akin to real factories than workshops.[33] Domingo Faustino Sarmiento, who had been president in the period 1868–1874, noticed the fall in imports by 1878, especially in those goods that could be easily substituted.[34] The case of one particular firm illustrates the possibilities and the limits of this type of production. In 1864, the North American inventor M. S. Bagley started to produce a liqueur made from orange peels called Hesperidina. Supported by the success of his "European-style" liqueur (popular enough to be used widely in cholera epidemics and during the Paraguayan war that elapsed from 1865 to 1870), Mr. Bagley and his Argentine commercial partner moved into the production of biscuits in 1877.[35] Bagley succeeded; by the 1880s his factory had become the largest in the city of Buenos Aires and began to replace imports, most of them British, which dropped from 1,444,567 to 176,927 kilos between 1875 and 1877.[36] This production became, according to an industrial source, "the one that gained major victories" and, as a French observer commented, "it has vanquished the perfidious Albion."[37] Albion was only defeated, however, in the provision of the coarsest goods, since high-quality biscuits were still supplied by British factories.[38]

A Precocious Mechanization

Limited mechanization in a few firms—producing foodstuffs, beer, alpargatas, cigarettes, matches, soap, candles, glass, and paper—was the main industrial novelty of the late 1880s. In these activities, a small group of factories even fostered a tenuous standardization. This trend toward a more massive production continued after the 1890 depression, with the devaluation of local currency and the rise in tariffs on imports through a process of import substitution. After the worst of the recession was over, most of these firms grew during the 1890s (see Table 1.6). The extent of this evolution differed according to production type and was strongest in easy-to-manufacture (and, consequently, to substitute) consumer goods. We can divide these goods into three categories: weak, middle, and strong substitution. In all of them, numbers from 1891 show the drop in consumption and its damage to imports. But the demand recovered rapidly and, by 1895, surpassed predepression levels. This is clear in the first group, in which numbers can be seen as a sign of the revival in the consumer market, actually an underestimation because some domestic production of these goods had begun in Argentina. This was the case of bottles, writing paper, and, to a lesser extent, nails, in which the demand of imported items in 1895 doubled the predepression quantities. The second group of middle substitution includes wrapping paper and candles, whose case approximated that of nails for the same reason: local manufacturing. Imports of wrapping paper and candles reached just one half and a third, respectively, of predepression numbers in 1895 because the rest of their consumption was supplied by local production. For the articles composing the third group, import substitution was deeper and even almost complete in some instances. This was the case of wooden matches; stearine (the input for the most common wax matches that had already displaced imports after the 1876 tariff); and clothing such as shirts, shoes, ties, vests, and hats (see Table 1.8).

Besides import substitution, manufacturing grew as a result of changes in consumption patterns (which will be more deeply studied in Chapter 2) and the creation of new demand, which developed because of lower prices and changing tastes. Beer, crudely made and meagerly consumed until two large breweries opened in the late 1880s, was one of the most noticeable examples. The aim of those firms was to manufacture a cheap and decent-quality product on a massive scale. The French immigrant Emile Bieckert founded one of the breweries in 1860 and had a moderate degree of success in its first years

TABLE 1.8

Imports and Import Substitution in Argentina, 1890–1895

(Bottles, hats, shirts, shoes, and ties in dozens, candles, matches, nails, paper, stearine, and vests in kilos)

	WEAK SUBSTITUTION			MIDDLE SUBSTITUTION				STRONG SUBSTITUTION				
	Bottles	Writing Paper	Nails	Wrapping Paper	Candles	Wood Matches	Stearine	Shirts	Shoes	Ties	Vests	Hats
1890	238,624	420,953	1,105,242	931,370	678,339	103,021	448,497	16,044	40,339	26,530	265,823	86,641
1891	97,186	172,857	509,914	321,022	72,927	87,431	64,608	2,029	1,267	3,802	93,961	9,285
1892	179,330	436,155	871,449	523,624	144,944	25,502	6,273	645	119	1,157	93,961	19,500
1893	501,918	490,438	868,338	573,211	188,918	9,236	10,115	1,033	4,338	2,041	110,352	46,417
1894	580,876	815,123	564,025	517,491	141,856	1,982	3,432	720	1,721	521	44,434	14,060
1895	467,052	835,013	970,628	586,156	192,240	3,711	48,361	549	841	144	26,686	12,458

SOURCE: My own elaboration based on *Anuarios de la Dirección General de Estadística correspondiente a 1894*, *Estadística retrospectiva*, pp. 245–251; and *Anuario correspondiente a 1898*, pp. 312–320.

of existence. Nevertheless, the qualitative jump to large-scale production did not occur until 1889, when British investors mechanized the establishment and increased its production.[39] Otto Bemberg, a German entrepreneur who later became one of the wealthiest men in Argentina, opened an even larger brewery, which is still the largest in the country: Quilmes. Prompted by his success in the distilling industry, Bemberg had inaugurated a large, many-storied mill with the latest European technology and, with the support of German technicians, began production of quality beer in a Buenos Aires sub-urb in 1888.[40] Investments in breweries soon paid off as the product found a growing market among consumers, which prompted a new expansion. In addition, the nature of the market made large installations necessary. Beer consumption in Argentina was highly seasonal; it spiked in the summer months and tapered off during the rest of the year. Huge installations were required to keep the beer cold during the winter low season, in contrast to countries such as Britain and Germany, where sales were more stable and small breweries could survive by running the whole year.[41]

Alpargatas found a large market when the urban and rural working class adopted these cheap articles as their usual footwear. In 1885, an Argentine entrepreneur established a joint venture with a Scottish firm, which developed the first piece of machinery capable of assembling this kind of sandal, and created the Fábrica Argentina de Alpargatas. Later joined by the Manchester textile firm of Ashworth, it succeeded in capturing a third of the national market for alpargatas as well as manufacturing a type of canvas to protect harvests from rain and humidity on the way to the port.[42]

The tobacco industry found a solution to the overcrowding in its cigarette factories by implementing an invention imported from the United States: Bonsack, a cigarette-rolling machine invented in 1880 by James Albert Bonsack and adopted by James Buchanan Duke for his firm in 1883. In 1889, the Fábrica Nacional de Tabacos became the first South American company to use them, which reduced production costs substantively and solved the problem of labor supervision. Each Bonsack produced fifteen thousand cigarettes an hour, whereas a dexterous worker could roll only around six hundred in that time and had to stop to rest and eat. Moreover, machine-made cigarettes were of a much better quality; they were softer and more tightly packed.[43] Old scenes of expert cigarette makers rolling at high speed with sensitive fingers started giving way to those of less skilled workers packaging the output of Bonsack machines, though mechanization was not completed until the first years of the twentieth century. The resulting rise in labor productivity was important; in Britain, with wages closer to those of Argentina than to those of the expensive American workforce, estimations were made that the Bonsack reduced production costs to about seventeen percent of what they were before.[44]

The production of matches, soap, and candles also experienced similar changes. In the match industry, the 1889 merger of the three largest companies into the Compañía General de Fósforos (CGF) created conditions for growth. Output rose due to economies of scale and produced an article that could substitute for imports (see Table 1.8).[45] Mechanization was the source of this expansion; by the end of the decade workers had, according to the proindustrial newspaper *El País*, "been reduced to watching the machinery and turning some of its springs from time to time."[46] Similarly, manufacturers expanded soap supply by concentrating on large-scale production of one item that ousted imports, coarse yellow bars used for laundry purposes.[47] As an illustration, by 1893, the major soap factory had doubled the number of workers since 1890.[48]

The use of machines intensified in the food industry, which had undertaken some mechanization before the late 1880s. Biscuits produced in automatic ovens, however, could not yet substitute for the *paladares delicados* (delicate palates) supplied by English firms.[49] Food production expanded in peanut oil, canned food, starch (which overtook imports), rice processing, and, even more successfully, the increasingly popular *dulce de membrillo* jellied quince, a cheap article that fit well into depression times.[50] Similarly, domestic liqueur production became concentrated on a few products that displaced imports after a long battle.[51] Nevertheless, the most dramatic of all these changes occurred in a new product that Argentines learned to consume in a different way: "packaged coffee." Its creator, Abel Saint, based his success on new marketing strategies, transforming bulk sales into brand-name commercialization, the same strategy employed contemporaneously in the food industry in the United States and Western Europe. Mr. Saint's cans of *café torrado* (toasted coffee) flooded stores when customers realized they could keep the article at home and enjoy a cup of coffee whenever they wanted instead of depending upon store owners' schedules.[52]

The expansion of some forms of industrial production had a multiplier effect. Expansion of beer production, for instance, promoted the manufacture of bottles. Supplying multiple breweries enabled firms—such as the one founded by the French immigrant Leon Fourvel Rigolleau—to achieve economies of scale.[53] Likewise, the rate of growth in the match industry propelled the increase of cardboard production to package its products. In the 1890s, a large paper company, La Argentina, produced mostly thin cardboard. But the small size of the market forced this firm to take another strategy. Soon the largest match producer—the Compañía General de Fósforos—opened a cardboard factory of its own and stopped buying from La Argentina. As a result, La Argentina expanded its production to include the wrapping paper used in the commercialization of goods. Since the CGF and La Argentina battled for the market, paper industry fostered new production.[54] Increasing food production also fostered parallel development in the packaging industry, because most processed edibles were sold in tin boxes to protect them against humidity. Establishments called *hojalaterías mecánicas* (mechanized tin-package stores) started to produce these boxes domestically, due to the advantages of developing an intermediate industry that imported tin-plate instead of finished boxes. The story of the largest company at the time illustrates this process. Alfredo Molet—another Frenchman—opened a canned poultry factory in 1882. Due to the difficulties he faced in procuring tin packages, he started a mechanized tin-plate shop, a business that turned out to be so lucrative that Molet abandoned his first undertaking and devoted himself exclusively to the latter production.[55]

Mechanization was even more humble and unfolded over a longer period in the shoe and furniture industries; the 1890s witnessed a transition from handicraft to factory work in only the largest companies. Shoe industrialist Juan Videla implemented "modern" methods in his mill such as putting workers in circles where each one accomplished a task, a practice that foreshadowed the assembly line.[56] A few factories even incorporated machines, producing a lighter and more resistant article. Yet mechanization existed alongside manual labor. At one factory, workers in charge of machines were separated by a wire fence from those operating under the traditional system; the idea was to prevent the machine workers from passing finished shoes to the traditional workers, who were paid on a piece-work basis. In the furniture industry, domestic output replaced some cheap American chairs but thanks to tariff protection and low salaries rather than productive changes.[57]

In the 1890s, some changes took place in the textile industry, which had been largely absent from the industrial scenario up to then. This branch grew at an annual rate of 12.7 percent during the decade, exceeding the total increase in manufacturing (11.5 percent) and far surpassing that in food processing (4.2 percent).[58] Transformations occurred in three different areas: (1) woolen and worsted textiles, (2) cotton weavings, especially in the manufacture of hosiery (*artículos de punto*), and (3) ready-to-wear clothes. All were labor intensive and did not require a large amount of capital, as economies of scale were minimal and complicated technology was unnecessary.[59]

Woolen and worsted textile production developed unevenly. According to the UIA, "some [factories] had large capital resources while some had nothing but the personal work of their proprietors."[60] Entrepreneur Adrián

Prat bought the old Fábrica Nacional, which expanded as other companies entered the market.[61] Low capital requirements for opening a woolen textile mill allowed Mr. Bozzala (whose family owned a similar firm in Italy) to begin producing cashmeres and cloth in limited facilities. His factory's buildings could not have been more modest; they were made of wood and zinc without much masonry. His wool-washing sites lay in the open air, while the dying department consisted of two pots and one pool. Carding, spinning, and weaving took place on manual machinery. In an interview, Mr. Bozzalla explained his factory's humility:

> We look to produce many ponchos [a greatcoat widely used by the city and especially country people] and cashmeres, not large buildings. When the factory works, it will allow us to install stories and buildings. . . . [He did not use mechanical looms] First of all, because a mechanical loom . . . is very expensive. . . . We do not repudiate the use of mechanical looms. But for the time being, we believe that with this system we will be able to accomplish our plan, especially having a large number of experienced artisans [mainly Italians and Spaniards] in this city and the capacity to build looms at a low cost.[62]

The new firms showed signs of primitive production methods. Prat's firm began as an integrated factory; all the standard steps of woolen textile production—washing, sorting, yarn spinning, cloth weaving, finishing, and dying—were done at the same mill. A French observer expressed surprise at this situation, since "all these tasks represent different factories and personnel in Europe, whereas here [at Prat's firm] groups and directs them all at the same time, establishing a system that has no precedent in labor history."[63] This observer was unaware that integration rather than specialization was taking place simultaneously in the Yorkshire mills. In the Argentine ones, however, integration was a costly response to a meager market rather than a sign of modernization.[64] In contrast to Yorkshire, in Argentina only a few factories existed, and their output consisted of the coarsest cloths and finished goods, such as blankets and bedcovers. Moreover, domestic production grew but was still unable to meet demand; by 1900, 60 percent of these goods consumed in Argentina were imported.[65]

The cotton textile industry presented an even more backward picture. In Argentina, cotton-weaving firms started as semi-integrated factories. But instead of integrating spinning and weaving as they did in Europe and the United States, Argentine mills blended the latter with the production of hosiery goods. The reason for this was simple: there was no cotton-spinning activity at all. Hosiery, however, was a success, and its production advanced greatly when some European import firms opened mills in Buenos Aires.[66] In the 1880s, Enrico Dell'Acqua, a successful textile industrialist in Italy, found an attractive market in Argentina, to which he began to export his products. Post-1890-crisis tariffs, however, forced him to switch plans, and, in 1894, the Dell'Acqua company opened a factory in Buenos Aires that produced 1,500,000 meters of cotton cloth annually (by using imported yarn), plus socks and vests.[67] The same considerations prompted Sternberg, a German textile company that used to export to Argentina, to open a mill in the country's capital.[68] By the end of the decade, imports of vests had been reduced to less than 20 percent of predepression levels, while imported shirts, ties, hats, necks, cuffs, and blankets fell to negligible numbers. A similar scenario unfolded in ready-to-wear domestic production, partially taking place in the same hosiery factories.[69] When referring to the clothing industry, a commissioner sent to Argentina in 1897 to study the prospects for British products concluded that "[a]s a consequence of this protective policy, the national production has at last gradually dislodged all importation of common goods."[70] The case of the textile industry illustrates the kind of initial industrialization that took place in the late nineteenth century in Argentina. It started with the domestic production of finished goods and encompassed the import of inputs. The reason was simple: factories began to produce the goods that were easy to substitute in a country with no industrial or artisanal past.

Not all industries grew in the 1890s. With the crisis, construction plummeted and all related activities were hurt. Antonio Zanotti's steam-powered sawmill and mechanical carpentry, which had enlarged its labor force to 400 people during the boom of the late 1880s, was forced to cut back to 150 workers in 1891.[71] In addition, building activity had created a major part of the demand for the metalworking industry, which subsequently contracted. A few large firms, however, survived the disaster by converting to the production of simple goods in large quantities. In the late 1880s, this strategy had some success in a metallurgical factory that stood out in a universe of handicraft workshops: Casa Amarilla, founded in 1859 by the German immigrant Felipe Schwartz. His mill possessed, by 1887, the fourth largest steam-powered motor in the city. This fact enabled Schwartz to produce an increasing supply of two kinds of goods in relatively high numbers: simple farming implements for an expanding agriculture economy and the lockers and strongboxes demanded in a city whose crime rate rose along with its growth.[72]

A wider transformation in the production of metal goods, however, took place in the 1890s with the expansion of domestic output of nails, screws, nuts, and pins.[73] The manufacturing process was simple, since a worker

> puts the iron wire in its place while the machine takes charge of cutting it to the desired size, of making the head and of sharpening. A couple of peons collect the goods that the machine with mathematical precision manufactures and conduct them to the drums to receive their shine. These goods are later packed in the boxes to be wholesaled and distributed in hardware stores.[74]

In spite of its simplicity, the production of these nails, screws, nuts, and pins represented a major turning point in the Argentine metallurgical industry, as it heralded the shift from made-to-order to standardized production. Pedro Vasena, who possessed a factory that had enjoyed success in the 1880s during the construction boom of Buenos Aires, responded to the changing economic situation without abandoning his old business. The firm moved to volume nail and pin production, a strategy that allowed it to continue its growth. Similarly, José Ottonello's bolt company prospered from the manufacture of screws, nuts, and nails for railways, while El Ancla foundry progressed by producing rivets and screws. As we will see later, these establishments, which became the cornerstone of the country's metallurgical activity, faced the same major limitations as the rest of the newly risen factories.[75]

The Shortcomings of a Nascent Industry

The limits of early Argentine industrialization become apparent through the analysis of its structural features. Demand was growing, but still small; mechanization had started, but was limited to a few factories. Firms faced this market and developed optimal strategies for surviving it. With rare exceptions, lack of specialization characterized industrial activities. This feature fostered economies of scope (for instance, some shoe factories produced from three hundred to seven hundred different types), but hindered the development of economies of scale. A similar scenario prevailed in most of the metallurgical industry. With the exception of pins, screws, nuts, and nails, its firms produced a wide variety of articles and resembled the primitive stages of U.S. iron processing.[76] This strategy was nonetheless functional for companies supplying a demand that was insufficient to foster massive production.[77]

In addition, some of the most crucial industrial inputs were missing. Even in those branches with a local supply of raw materials, such as leather, lack of modern technology precluded the production of the highest-quality goods, which were still imported in 1901.[78] As *El País* noted,

> here there are no factories with ample capital like in Europe, which can have large quantities of hides in their storage and tanning pools for two or three months, while they acquire the qualities and degree of maturity that the European product has.[79]

If this was the case in an industry with abundant raw material, it worsened in industries for which the country lacked local inputs. This was especially damaging to the prospects of the metallurgical and textile industries, because Argentina did not produce iron, coal, or cotton. On the one hand, metallurgical firms faced a bottleneck in the provision of inputs and had to rely on imports or on recycled material, primarily from railways and sewer pipes. Not surprisingly, a high tariff on the export of *hierro viejo* (used iron) was one of the main demands of metallurgical industrialists. On the other hand, Argentina developed a textile industry for which cotton yarn had to be purchased abroad. As the *Review of the River Plate* said, it was "about the only country in the world that protects the cotton weaving establishments for which the raw material has to be imported as none is produced in the country."[80]

Prohibitive tariffs on yarn could have promoted the spinning of imported raw cotton. To some extent, this is what happened in the cigarette industry, which purchased most of its tobacco from abroad.[81] The idea of promoting such an activity appealed to some politicians and, in 1903, a law making future cotton-spinning mills tax exempt was passed, prompting the first (albeit doomed to fail) factory of the kind.[82] The possibility of applying a high tariff to cotton yarn, however, died out due to the pressure from the owners of local weaving firms concerned about an increase in the price of their critical input.[83] In addition, until the First World War, even woolen textiles had to face a shortage of inputs.[84]

Most Argentine imports came from Britain, so any development of local industry had a negative impact on British export prospects. Nevertheless, local manufacturing growth diverted rather than reduced those imports in the short term.[85] The British responded to Argentine manufacturing pragmatically, making local industrial growth work in their favor. An examination of Britain's diplomatic sources shows a preference for an adaptive rather than confrontational strategy on tariff issues. The British realized that each new factory in Argentina could be seen as a blessing instead of a curse, since it created a new demand. Thus, local production of soap shrank consumption of coarse British imports but expanded the purchase of caustic soda, soda ashes, palm oil, talc, and resin, an opportunity that the Liverpool company United Alkali did not miss.[86]

This pragmatism applied especially to textiles, Britain's largest export. Although ready-to-wear remittances dropped dramatically, the production of these clothes in Buenos Aires boosted imports of cotton cloth from 11,390,169 kilos in 1893 to 20,688,000 in 1904, while the opening of hosiery factories in Argentina increased the demand for cotton yarn from 298,392 to 4,759,000 kilos in the same period.[87]

Capital-intensive activities simply did not exist in the industrial setup of the late nineteenth century. This development of the Argentine textile industry also created a demand for imported textile machinery, largely provided by Britain. The British strategy of adaptation was successful and allowed it to maintain—in spite of American and German competition—a third of the Argentine imports until the First World War. France was the main loser in this battle, as it lacked such a policy. In 1896, for example, imports of Manchester cloths were 50 percent higher than in 1889, while French textile imports (composed of finished goods) had fallen to a third over the same period. The British government's flexible approach is also reflected in the care with which it investigated complaints by its nationals before making official demands on Argentine authorities to lower duties on imports. Indeed, a reduction in protective tariffs could hurt a domestic industry that demanded significant inputs and, rather than increasing the more expensive British trade, would only lead to an influx of cheaper German goods.[88]

The absence of a local cotton textile industry has commonly been blamed on pressure from Britain. However, the complexities of British interests in Argentina at the turn of the twentieth century made it difficult for that nation to have a single strategy toward local industry.[89] The case of the Ashworth firm, which arrived through a partnership with the Fábrica Argentina de Alpargatas, illustrates this point. In an attempt to enlarge its business, the former opened a cotton-weaving firm of its own in Buenos Aires. Thus, as a British diplomat explained to his superiors, while his country's exporters asked for free trade with Argentina, Ashworth wanted protection for the articles it produced locally through a higher valuation on imported goods at the Customs House:

> Messrs. Ashworth & Co are both importers of British cotton goods
> and local manufacturers of cotton duck, trousers, towels, etc. In the
> former capacity they made no complaints as regards valuation. But as
> manufacturers they were anxious to prevent a further reduction in the
> valuation on Duck etc. and an increase in the valuation of cotton yarns.[90]

This conflict will continue in the following decades, during which British presence in joint manufacturing ventures in Argentina was not uncommon.[91]

Lack of cotton cultivation was a crucial reason for the lack of spinning mills in Argentina, which was facing the same shortcomings as the Brazilian textile industry had initially confronted and resolved only after planting the fiber in Brazil itself. It was no coincidence that Argentine spinning mills started to expand in the 1920s, when the Chaco region in the Northeast experienced the first signs of a cotton boom.[92] Weaving firms defended themselves from accusations of lacking patriotism by using foreign inputs. In a request to the Congress in 1892, they explained

> We employ, it is true, cotton, spun woolen and worsted yarn from abroad because there is as yet no spinning factory in this country; it would be an absurd claim since nobody will take up the task until the weaving industry, which has just started, offers a dependable and profitable application.[93]

Conversely, the woolen textile firm Prat boasted of being a model of industrial patriotism since it did not use any foreign input but only Argentine wool that it washed at its own mills.[94] Adrián Prat, however, had a lot of leeway due to his close relationship with the government, a liaison that allowed him to survive and succeed: his firm produced uniforms worn by the Army and by civil servants.[95] Indeed, all the previously mentioned shortcomings created an industry with so many weaknesses that, had it been left to its own devices, would have barely survived.

State support was crucial for industrial growth, not only in imposing tariffs on imports but also in providing a badly needed demand. State backing in the birth of industry was not peculiar to Argentina; it is a common feature in various cases of countries that began industrialization. However, the size and the nature of the market transformed what was welcome help in most countries into a desperate necessity for most Argentine industrial companies. The national state had been growing in size and strength since the reunification of the country in 1862. For three decades, military campaigns, such as the suppression of internal rebellions and the Paraguayan war, meant a demand for goods that Argentine firms were more than happy to supply. The final victory of the central government over the last provincial challenge in 1880 did not curtail the state's purchases, which diversified as administrative expansion created a demand for civilian goods. A sixteen-fold expansion in national expenses (in constant currency) between 1880 and 1910 represented a large portion of Argentina's relatively small market and encouraged nascent local factories. By then, government consumption constituted around 6 or 7 percent of the GDP. Moreover, the nature of state demand was as important as the volume, since it offered stability in an economy permeated by depressions and recessions.[96]

The success of major companies (not only Prat) was largely linked to state support. Juan Videla's leather factory grew as a result of contracts to provide goods to the Army during the Paraguayan war. With the profit generated, he opened a shoe factory in 1872. Soon, Videla was selling supplies to a state then engaged in suppressing a revolt in 1874, a role that he continued in subsequent peacetime years.[97] Pedro Bercetche, owner of a small bakery, opened a biscuit factory that soon became the second largest in the country thanks to sales to the Navy.[98] Even small confectioners found in the demand of civil servants the steady market necessary to convert themselves into large industrialists. Daniel Bassi, owner of a candy and chocolate factory, recalled a more modest past. "Luck favored me that year [c. 1887] since by then the Noel firm [Bassi's competitor] had stopped its dough production and I soon absorbed all its old clientele, especially in the downtown area where almost all state offices were located."[99]

As the administration grew in size during the 1890s and the first decades of the twentieth century, it became an increasingly important market for industrial goods. In 1895 the Congress passed a National Purchasing Law stating that "[i]n the acquisition of articles that the intendencies [offices of the government in charge of military purchases] require for the Army and Navy, national production will be preferred if of equal price and quality."[100] Not surprisingly, after the inauguration of President Julio A. Roca in 1898, industrialists visited him and the minister of war to remind them of the law.[101] The growth of the state's civilian sector was as crucial as its military needs in providing a substantial demand, as in the case of the government-supported Catholic Church. The UIA mentioned that domestically produced textiles were used in "all the convents of the country so that monks are more patriotic than us, for they want to dress with Argentine cloth, which they found to be better and cheaper than the foreign."[102]

The state bought cloth and hosiery from local producers not only to sew uniforms for the Army and the Navy but also to supply the increasing capacities it achieved in the public sphere at the beginning of the twentieth century. Administrative requirements created a market for locally produced stationery. In the words of a U.S. Department of Commerce specialist, "[t]he Government is perhaps the largest consumer of paper in the country [and] the Government in general uses Argentine paper."[103] Also, the vast campaign of public health and the opening of the gigantic public hospitals that characterized Argentine state activism at that time meant a significant demand of clothes for medical institutions, orphan asylums, and charity associations.[104] In addition, the ambitious educational campaign launched by the Argentine authorities to promote literacy and education for the sons and daughters of immigrants also created a demand of clothing for teachers and, especially, for the uniform adopted in all public schools to "argentinize" the children: the white apron.[105]

The state also tried to involve itself directly in industrial production, but its role as an entrepreneur failed and proved to be short-lived. At the end of the 1890s, it attempted to monopolize spirits production by taking advantage of a temperance campaign. The project aimed at seizing direct control of an activity that usually evaded taxes (since 1891, alcoholic beverages as well as tobacco had paid internal duties). In the end, it was not carried out due to the opposition of private distillers.[106] The state did become a producer of gunpowder for reasons of "national interest." It opened the Fábrica Nacional de Pólvora (National Factory of Gunpowder) in Río Cuarto, province of Córdoba, which became an appalling example of inefficiency as well as the source of an impressive explosion and accident rate. Many attempts were made to reorganize the company, but all of them failed.[107] There was a strong contrast with the private dynamite company Fábrica Nacional de Dinamita (National Factory of Dynamite), which produced dynamite and sulfuric, azotic, and chloridic acids, and was more efficient and prosperous. The government finally limited its efforts to repairing weapons and making part of the military uniforms.[108]

The imposition of the military draft in 1901 had a major impact on manufacturing, and it resulted in a large increase in the need for supplies. As a result, just after the draft law passed, shoe industrialists pressed War Minister Pablo Ricchieri for contracts to provide the large number of conscripts.[109] Clothing producers also found a similar opportunity in the masses of soldiers and viewed with delight any change in uniform style, since that would necessitate a new contract.[110] Local producers succeeded in supplying military needs, and the state eventually left most uniform production in their hands. Indeed, the Army found foreign providers to be troublingly ignorant of needs, a problem that prompted even the Navy—the military branch less prone to deal with local factories—to purchase from Buenos Aires companies.[111]

The favorable evolution of state purchases was greatly helped by the ability of Argentine industrialists to generate an atmosphere that cast them as the victims of a conspiracy. They initiated a propaganda campaign aimed at terminating purchases abroad and preventing any change in the conditions that promoted the expansion of local firms.[112] Moreover, Argentine industrialists' sales to the state were much higher than they cared to admit, a fact unaccounted for by historians who worked with the UIA reports. One episode shows how reality differed from that claim. In 1898, the Argentine government decided to buy uniforms for the Army and Navy from French suppliers. The UIA noisily protested, accusing the government of being anti-Argentine, and eventually forcing it to reverse its decision and purchase the goods from a local firm.[113] Actually, the most prominent of the three members who served on the commission appointed by the Ministry of War to study cloth provision to the Army was Francisco Seguí, involved in leather manufacturing and the incumbent president of the industrial corporation.[114]

Rather than being the result of a conspiracy, purchasing abroad was made attractive to the state by the outrageous rates Argentine producers charged for their merchandise. The so-called "Providers of the State," indeed, sold goods at high prices to a government that repeatedly signed unfair contracts.[115] An emblematic case was that of industrialist Angel Braceras, who opened his firm as a Fábrica Nacional de Confecciones Civiles y Militares (Factory of Military and Civilian Clothes). In 1908, the Army rejected a stock of uniforms made by Braceras. An investigation revealed that the Argentine firm bought the fabric from the English firm Taylor, Yielding, and Co. and made profits of 150 percent just for sewing the uniforms at its factory.[116] The inflated role played by the state in the creation of industrial demand would become an Achilles' heel on the nascent Argentine industry if a more massive market could not replace it. This weakness became apparent in the crisis that began in 1897.

The Crucible of Industry

Chronic economic crisis became one of the main features of turn-of-the-twentieth-century Argentina. After the collapse of 1890, manufacturing was one of the engines of economic recovery; during that decade, industry grew at an annual rate of 11.5 percent, compared to the 5.5 percent experienced by the GDP (see Table 1.3). In 1894, a journalist pointed out

> [I]n 1889, we were the first to proclaim, in the pages of [the newspaper]
> La Prensa, the advent of an industrial period, which would save the
> country from the disastrous effects of the depression. The great number
> of manufacturing establishments that have been founded since then has
> demonstrated the truth of our prediction. In fact, statistics show that
> currently the industrial production is worth more than the production
> of the agricultural and grazing industries, a result which must surprise

all those who consider Argentina to be a mere raw-material-producing country.[117]

Nevertheless, industry's dreams of continuing expansion came to an end in 1897, when its growth stalled and output dropped for the first time since 1881.[118]

Both the existence and depth of the 1897 recession—mainly affecting the domestic economy, particularly commerce and industry—have been ignored by a historiography focused exclusively on the effects of international crises. Contemporaries, however, became keenly aware of its presence and its effects. Consumption decreased, commercial credits dried up, and firm moratoria rose.[119] Economic distress became so acute that the *Centro de comercio* (the association that represented the main merchants of Buenos Aires city) prepared a long report and asked prominent businessmen for their opinions. Responses varied; some blamed the locusts and the loss of crops, but others pointed out that the poor harvest was not the cause because rural merchants were having an easier time paying their debts. There was a drop in exports that year, but it does not fully explain the uneasy atmosphere. The extent of the crisis, indeed, exceeded its impact on the current account (a similar fall in exports in 1893 did not spark any industrial decline). Its causes must be explored further. Most of the responses in that report targeted the dependency of commerce on an unstable credit chain and an excess of industrial production.[120]

The structural features of the Argentine domestic economy, such as its excessive growth for a relatively small market, lay at the root of the slump. The recession was sparked, however, by a political event: the threat of a potential war between Argentina and Chile over territorial disputes. When the menace of war looked real, the public converted its deposits from local pesos to hard currency and withdrew much of it, provoking a contraction in banking. With the financial collapse of 1890 fresh in their minds, Argentines acted as fast as they could to defend their savings. Since banks were the initiators of the credit chain, which continued with merchants granting loans to their customers, the multiplier effects on the circuit were rapidly felt.[121]

In addition, domestic economic recovery in the second half of the 1890s prompted currency appreciation and diminished the effect of implicit protection (import duties as a percentage of total import value/total imports) on domestic goods. This was a source of distress for those who had debts in local money, for exporters who saw a relative drop in their incomes, and for industrialists who faced competition from cheaper imports (see Table 1.9).

TABLE 1.9

Implicit Protection and Exchange Rate Evolution, 1875–1930

	Import Duties/Total Imports	Devaluation of the Argentine Peso		Import Duties/Total Imports	Devaluation of the Argentine Peso
1875	22	1.00	1903	29	2.27
1876	27	1.14	1904	22	2.27
1877	17	1.18	1905	21	2.27
1878	17	1.28	1906	20	2.27
1879	28	1.29	1907	20	2.27
1880	26	1.22	1908	22	2.27
1881	27	1.07	1909	22	2.27
1882	28	1.00	1910	22	2.27
1883	25	1.00	1911	21	2.27
1884	25	1.00	1912	22	2.27
1885	18	1.36	1913	21	2.27
1886	21	1.39	1914	19	2.27
1887	22	1.35	1915	18	2.30
1888	19	1.47	1916	21	2.27
1889	15	1.83	1917	23	2.19
1890	13	2.58	1918	24	2.16
1891	20	3.75	1919	21	2.22
1892	27	3.32	1920	22	2.45
1893	29	3.24	1921	21	3.02
1894	25	3.57	1922	22	2.67
1895	26	3.44	1923	23	2.79
1896	24	2.96	1924	19	2.80
1897	26	2.91	1925	20	2.39
1898	25	2.58	1926	18	2.37
1899	31	2.25	1927	18	2.27
1900	32	2.31	1928	17	2.27
1901	29	2.32	1929	17	2.29
1902	30	2.36	1930	16	2.63

NOTE: During the period 1875–1882, the value of foreign currency is calculated as the price of the peso fuerte versus the peso moneda nacional. Since 1883, after the government approved a law of monetary unification and with the adherence when the gold pattern was applied, it is the price of gold. The conversion to homogenize both periods is 25 pesos fuertes (1875 = 1 peso oro 1883).

SOURCE: For implicit protection, my own elaboration based on Vicente Vázquez Presedo, *El caso Argentino: Migración de factores, comercio exterior y desarrollo, 1875–1914* (Buenos Aires: Eudeba, 1971), p. 211, Table 1.4; and Vicente Vázquez Presedo, *Crisis y retraso: Argentina y la economía internacional entre las dos guerras* (Buenos Aires: Eudeba, 1978), p. 285. For exchange rate, my own elaboration based on Juan Alvarez, *Temas de historia económica Argentina* (Buenos Aires: El Ateneo, 1929), p. 113, for the period 1875–1914; and on Pablo Gerchunoff and Eduardo Salazar, Argentine economic database, 1875–1930, mimeograph, Universidad Torcuato Di Tella, 2002.

As a U.S. report pointed out,

[H]ere all manufacturers and producers are invariably found to be opposed to any plan proposed looking toward the valorization of the paper money of the country. Such persons desire "high gold," i.e., cheap paper money. In the case of manufacturer "low gold," i.e., an appreciation in the purchasing power of paper money, is equivalent to a reduction in the duty on imported goods and his trade is, hence, injured thereby, since, under such a condition, he finds it more difficult to compete with an imported article than he does when the gold rate is "high." [122]

As the crisis deepened, economist Silvio Gesell offered the printing of money as a solution, blaming tight monetary policies in both Argentina and Chile for the rising tension between the two countries. [123] The economic atmosphere also became strained. In Britain, *The Economist* announced a commercial crisis and business stagnation, in a series of reports, while the *South American Journal* described economic conditions in Rosario, Argentina's second largest city, as being "in most branches, by last accounts, in the most depressed state; in fact, in some quarters it may be said to be absolutely paralyzed." [124] Merchants and industrialists became afraid and created a wave of uneasiness by promoting street rallies. Thousands of supporters gathered to lobby for their respective interests. [125] For its part, the newspaper *La Nación* suggested that

> To reflect the real situation of our commerce and industry, it is only necessary to mention that public opinion . . . is getting more bellicose.
>
> This ghost that everybody sees rising on the peaks of the Andes mountains leaves nothing stable, nothing secure, nothing probable, kills any initiative, and freezes any enthusiasm.
>
> Capital withdraws because, what reason is there to expose it if a war can ruin everything? The merchant limits his operations and his stock, the farmer limits his construction and economizes on his labor force, the artisan and the worker see their initiative blocked, when they have to question how long the task they undertake or the job they have are going to last. [126]

One of the experts consulted by the Centro de Comercio about the crisis was the merchant Ireneo Cucullu. He blamed

> national industrial production, born in most cases under the shadow of an exaggerated protection that has grown from day to day, which in some cases has met the needs for consumption and in some others has accumulated stocks. I can affirm that in almost all cases the manufactured products have been expensive and defective, and I believe the time when national industry will have its own crisis is not far off. [127]

Cucullu's prediction was more accurate than he expected; Argentine industry was already facing hardship. As *The Economist* pointed out,

> As for mechanic class the rapid appreciation of the currency at the end of last year gave such a blow to the innumerable small manufacturing industries, whose name is legion . . . that in most of these bogus trades the employers have been forced to reduce their hands from 20 to 50 percent.[128]

In addition to local currency appreciation, the size of the Argentine market put firms under the stress of excess installed capacity. In 1894, soon after the endorsement of protective duties, a Legislative Tariff Commission noted with surprise that in the textile industry, recently established factories have "had to reduce their output and work at one-half of their potential." [129] This problem was not limited to textile factories; candle, spirits, household wares, glass, hat, paper, shoe, pin, undershirt, chocolate, glass, and bag producers also were running at 50 or 60 percent of capacity.[130] A metallurgical factory, which molded iron furniture, was forced to turn off its furnace six days a week.[131] A Chilean businessman, after a visit to Argentina, reflected on the causes of overproduction:

> The future was calculated according to the present, and instead of pursuing industrialization with caution, industrialists took in many cases a furious and exaggerated approach to the task. Industrial establishments were erected as in Europe, with too much power and cost, since it was thought that the country had enough consumption to provide for a prosperous and active life.
>
> The results, however, were somewhat disappointing.
>
> The reason was clear; nowadays, some industries lack enough consumption. If a factory is established to produce 50 and has a consumption of 20 or 30, it is clear that its path will be difficult if the industrialist, as an expert pilot, does not look for new horizons and new markets in order to compete advantageously with European articles. Production is limited by consumption; nobody escapes the consequences of this economic law.[132]

Even people not very knowledgeable in economics, such as writer Manuel Bilbao, could sense what was in the air. He pointed out that "national industry produces the double of what the country consumes." [133]

Excess capacity caused stern battles among firms. These occurred as soon as overproduction became perceptible. The Compañía Conen invested to produce 180,000 candles and 24,000 kilograms of detergent soap daily, but the demand only warranted running the mills at the daily output of 120,000 candles and 6,850 kilograms of detergent in 1899. The same year, the production of pots and pans from the company of Oscar Schnaith was just one third of its capacity for lack of market demand. With a market smaller than imagined, competition became fierce. In pins and textiles, for example, three large companies competed wildly just a few years after their opening.[134] One of the main consequences of these wars was the plummeting of prices, which shrank profits and jeopardized the very existence of many firms. It might look striking that Argentine firms faced overproduction even in branches where imports were still significant, as was noticeable in textiles. But domestic output was limited to the cheapest and simplest goods. In addition, the already described structural productive features restricted the ability to oust imports through market competition, making tariff protection the only alternative. At the end of the nineteenth century, the Argentine market did not offer sustainable incentives for massive production, with the economies of scale that it would bring.

Some industrialists attempted to overcome the market's small size by making a valiant but unsuccessful attempt to export their products. Carlos Lix Klett, a tireless writer on the excellence of Argentine production, made a strong (and, he thought, realistic) call to find new demand abroad. He asked industrialists to keep in mind that "[t]he appropriate markets are Brazil and the other [Latin] American republics . . . only thus will we have population and consumers, the indispensable elements to Argentine progress."[135] Notwithstanding these good intentions, only the smallest neighboring countries would provide an external market for Argentina; the most successful case was Paraguay, whose consumption of industrial goods was paltry.[136] More attractive markets, such as Chile, Uruguay, and especially Brazil, had closed their economies to protect their own industries. Argentine industrial firms were, therefore, forced to open their own mills in those countries in order to do business. The match producer CGF, the textile firm Campomar, and the Fábrica Argentina de Alpargatas invested in factories in Montevideo, Uruguay, and the latter expanded to São Paulo, Brazil.[137] Although this strategy benefited a few Argentine firms, it did not overcome the structural problems created by the small size of the local market. In this sense, Argentina could not duplicate the Canadian experience of finding demand abroad for its manufactured goods. Having a small market, Canada could produce and export certain manufactures to the United States, such as wood pulp and paper, and the potential of the American demand promoted the former country's industry. In addition, Canada was a magnet for U.S. investments as a bridge to export to the rest of the British Empire.[138] In the 1890s, Argentina's scenario looked more similar to that of Porfirian Mexico, which, as Stephen Haber has shown, faced an endemic excess of industrial capacity with the attendant inefficiencies.[139]

The badly needed market had to be created internally if Argentine industry was to avoid (at least partially) the Mexican fate of a small demand. Assistance came, paradoxically, with the aggravation of the conflict with Chile. In 1898, the threat of war prompted the government to place an additional tax of five percent on imports to support the purchase of war materiel. Moreover, the new budget doubled that of 1897, and war-related expenses boosted an industry dependent on state consumption.[140] This relief, however, was transitory and could not sustain continuing growth. Further expansion had to come from an increase in consumption in the private sector. A market large enough to sustain at least a middle-range industrialization if not a deep one developed by the first decade of the twentieth century as major changes occurred in the demand sphere. The country, especially the areas more benefited by the export boom, was experiencing the rise of a consumer society.

Chapter 2

The Market as an Object of Desire:
The Rise of Domestic Industrial Consumption

The Rise of a Consumer Society

Martin Tow arrived in Buenos Aires while the First World War was devastating Europe. This North American had thirty years of experience as a merchant in Brazil and the will to apply his commercial knowledge in a new area. Tow landed in the Argentine capital without any special expectations since, as he pointed out, "[w]hen I left Rio, I thought I was going to another [backward] Latin city." Buenos Aires, however, provided him with various surprises. The first one was an encounter in which "[t]he cop on the corner of Florida and Corrientes, whom I asked for directions to the Avenida de Mayo [in the city downtown], looked at me and answered with the rushed tone of an Irish–New York policeman, in great contrast to the benevolent humbleness of the blacky placed between Rio Branco Avenue and Asamblea Street" in Rio de Janeiro. Tow's wonder (and racism) was enough for him to decide, "That's it. I am in love with Buenos Aires." [1]

The North American was surprised for a second time to find that a commercial shopping mall, Güemes, recently had been inaugurated, with stores selling the most fashionable world trends. Tow opened a store there to sell wallets, shirts, and ties, some made in Argentina and some imported. He was quite astonished when a shipment of bad-quality American shirts was completely ignored by the arrogant *porteño* (inhabitant of the city of Buenos Aires) public because they were in bad taste and had outdated collars (a rejection that extended to the Salvation Army, which did not even want to accept the shirts as a donation). Next, Tow considered the possibility that the Argentines shared some similarities with the people of his own country, to whom "it was easy to sell any flag's color," and that the market might absorb the same fancy goods items fashionable in the United States. Tow imported "[b]lue, pink, and green shirts" in a commercial operation that was risky because "here their novelty may prove to be too unexpected." Notwithstanding the amazement of his Argentine sole employee, he managed to sell them to a public enchanted with wearing the colorful shirts. He continued trying different strategies and soon understood that Buenos Aires was a real market that needed to be exploited with all the modern commercial practices in prevalence throughout the most advanced cities of the world. Casa Tow would, in fact, become a famous and popular shopping destination.[2]

A few years before Tow's arrival, Argentina had celebrated the centennial of its freedom from Spain. The country took these celebrations very seriously. The local aristocracy was especially keen on this effort. It was as obsessed with displaying the wealth and luxury of the city as it was with the Anarchists' threat to spoil the party. This vision, so full of lights and shadows, hides the development of a parallel phenomenon that was taking place at a quieter and more daily pace: the rise of a consumer society that supported larger industrial output by domestic factories.

An internationally accepted definition of a consumer society is a subject of debate. For a long time, a consumer society was associated with changes in the sphere of production, mainly the mass production of Henry Ford's assembly line that made the United States of the 1920s its first example.[3] A more recent approach relates less dramatic changes in the production sphere (mainly the interchangeability of parts in production, the assembly line being its most efficient expression) to the evolution of mass consumption, and credits the transformation in sales strategies, especially the use of extensive advertising and marketing at the onset.[4] It is possible to reconcile both perspectives and to describe a consumer society as one in which fulfillment of demand creates new desires for consumption and fosters dissatisfaction. If this definition is adopted, Argentina had laid the groundwork for this transformation by the turn of the twentieth century.

As described in Chapter 1, Argentine industry still faced the absence of a substantial demand for its products. Some limited specialization existed, although it lacked the large numbers that could make it a more widely used strategy. The new century offered the opportunity to overcome such a formidable shortcoming through the expansion of domestic consumption. Between 1875 and 1913, the country's economy grew annually by 6.7 percent while the GDP per capita grew by 3.7 percent (rates almost unparalleled in the rest of the world).[5] Immigration slowed down in the 1890s due to the post-crisis atmosphere (the net balance reached almost 370,000 people). However, it gathered steam again by the beginning of the twentieth century to the effect that between 1900 and 1913 more than 1,700,000 foreigners, mainly from Spain and Southern Italy, settled in the country. According to the 1914 census, 30 percent of the almost eight million people who lived in the country were foreign-born, and many of the natives were the offspring of new settlers, which meant that probably half of the population lived in immigrant families. Buenos Aires city continued with its traditional 50 percent of foreigners, as it had showed since 1869, but the percentages jumped dramatically in the provinces of the Pampas (Buenos Aires and Santa Fé), where it accounted for more than 30 percent of the population. The peak of immigration corresponded with the country's new production makeup: instead of concentrating exports on wool, as was common until the 1890s, production diversified into beef and cereals, whose large demand from abroad sustained the Argentinian Belle Époque.[6] In the period 1875–1913, Argentina's population tripled and real per capita incomes rose 40 percent. By combining the growth in population and wealth, in 1913 Argentina had a market for consumption almost nine-fold larger than forty years before. (see Table 1.1

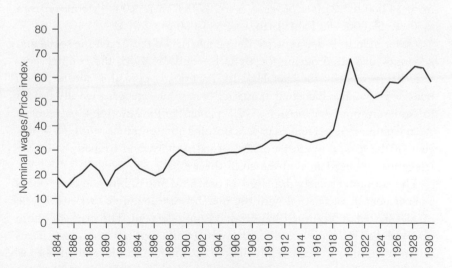

Figure 2.1. Real Wages, Argentina, 1884–1930

SOURCE: My own elaboration based on Jeffrey Williamson, "Real Wages and Relative Factors Prices in the Third World, 1820–1940: Latin America," discussion paper no. 1853, November 1998, Harvard Institute of Economic Research (until 1913) and from the Departamento Nacional del Trabajo for 1914 to 1930.

and Figure 2.1).[7] In the same time period, the British and the Mexican markets—other examples of sustained growth—had not even tripled, while the U.S. economy had increased five-fold.[8] The small size of the Argentine economy in 1875 explains the initial high rate of growth, but it cannot account for the end of the period under consideration. After the interruption produced by the First World War, the economy regained growth but at a smaller rate than before. By 1929, Argentina was one of the richest countries in the world, with a population of almost twelve million people, still relatively modest for its size but with a high GDP per capita.

At the beginning of the twentieth century, not only had population and per capita income risen dramatically, but major transformations in the sphere of commercialization and demand patterns gave these numbers special meaning. The country was experiencing the emergence of a consumer society, which would promote industrial production. The rapidly expanding cities set the stage for this process. On the brink of the First World War, most of the population of this beef-and-grain-exporting country lived in cities that mushroomed between 1869 and 1914. Buenos Aires was the most impressive case; its population increased from 178,000 to 1,576,000 inhabitants (plus another half a million living in the suburbs) during those years. Argentine provincial cities followed this pattern at that time—Córdoba from 34,000 to 121,000, Rosario from 17,000 to 245,000, Mendoza from 8,000 to 58,000, and Bahía Blanca from 1,000 to 62,000.[9]

Other indicators demonstrate the peculiarity of the Argentine social and economic evolution during the Belle Époque. By 1925, the country possessed 16 percent of the overall South American population and territory, but the percentages increased dramatically in some categories usually related to modernization. Argentina had 42.7 percent of the railways, 45 percent of the telephones, 55 percent of paper consumption for publications, 58.4 percent of the cars, 60 percent of the postal activity, and 61 percent of the telegrams produced and consumed in the area.[10]

The consumer society displayed a constant desire to buy goods as well as a permanent dissatisfaction with the merchandise acquired. Once the cycle of sales started, it promoted an ever-increasing demand. The market culture permeated all levels of social life, expanding consumption. This momentous transformation was inextricably linked to modernization and meant, in Argentina and elsewhere, the replacement of traditional values with new ones. One of the leading patterns of social behavior that emerged was emulation. As the middle-class came into focus, this phenomenon became a significant force. Fashion, which channeled the desires provoked by emulation, increasingly influenced the rules of the commercial game. Advertising, for its part, allowed producers to play a crucial role in this contest by persuading customers to buy specific goods. Market values, emulation, fashion, and advertising were not completely new in the Argentine scenario, but they reached a critical level at the period studied in this book, allowing a consumer society to emerge.

The World of Goods

Growth in demand was largely an outcome of the export boom. Despite this, the domestic market gained a dynamic of its own. The two market forces—production and consumption—interacted and created a mutual connection in which, paraphrasing sociologist Pierre Bourdieu, both operated without anticipating or imposing upon the other.[11] A fruitful way to study this field of interaction is to analyze the evolution that occurred in the consumption of some particular and selected manufactured goods. This approach retrieves the social history of goods and makes the consumer a more reasonable object of study.[12] Demand patterns are not linear and not all types of consumption vary the same way at the same time; hence the importance of the study of particular goods at particular times. Because of their significance, the evolution in the consumption of beer, cigarettes, matches, shoes, and ready-to-wear clothes will be analyzed in depth here. Cigarettes represented a long-standing case of consumption and production; matches, shoes, and ready-to-wear clothes had long been consumed but were not manufactured locally on a large scale until the 1890s; beer was, finally, a completely new phenomenon in both consumption and production.

At the turn of the twentieth century, cigarette consumption grew such that it outpassed demographic growth. Smoking was an old habit dating from the colonial era. After independence, smoking grew in parallel with a rise in the number of small workshops, which sold chopped tobacco to stores, and in the number of women who rolled cigarettes at home. The late 1880s, as we saw in Chapter 1, brought about significant changes for the tobacco industry. Higher-quality cigarettes replaced the old ones with their nauseating smell.[13] After the 1890 crisis, tariffs protected the domestic product while the introduction of Bonsack machines reduced the costs. The sale of a cheap product succeeded in making the consumption of cigarettes widespread. In a society eager for refinement, the old *cigarros de hoja* (leaf cigars) came to be regarded as grotesque, while the more expensive *habanos* (cigars) could not be sold in large quantities. This was especially true during

TABLE 2.1

Consumption per Capita, 1891–1930

	Cigarettes (packs)	Matches (gruesas)	Beer (liters)	Coffee (kilos)	Cacao (kilos)	Soap	Writing Paper	Automobiles (cars per thousand inhabitants)
1891	n.d.	0.14	3.6	0.51	0.03	0.02	0.05	—
1895	35.4	0.22	n.d.	0.90	0.08	0.04	0.21	—
1900	n.d.	0.21	n.d.	1.04	0.07	0.07	0.23	—
1905	43.0	0.25	9.1	1.54	0.15	0.10	0.32	0.04
1910	55.5	0.26	14.3	1.78	0.15	0.15	0.49	0.23
1915	57.2	0.25	9.4	2.23	n.d.	n.d.	n.d.	n.d.
1920	49.5	0.21	19.4	2.04	0.34	n.d.	n.d.	1.51
1925	58.3	0.15	18.8	2.09	0.40	n.d.	n.d.	5.42
1930	50.0	0.15	14.4	2.27	0.39	n.d.	n.d.	n.d.

SOURCE: My own elaboration based on the following:

A. For cigarettes, *Boletín de la Unión Industrial Argentina*, September 10, 1897, 18–19; Administración General de Impuestos Internos. *Memoria correspondiente al ejercicio del año 1913* (Buenos Aires: Cía. Sudamericana de Billetes de Banco, 1914), 42; "Industria tabacalera." Cuadro tipeado en el Ministerio de Agricultura. Dirección General de Comercio e Industrias. Sección Industrias, Pesos y Medidas, Warrants, ca. 1917; Piccardo y Cía, *El 43.*

B. For matches, Compañía General de Fosforos. Estadística General. Libro 1, Avellaneda, Paraná, Tucumán y Santa Fé. Resumen de gruesas vendidas. Cigarettes in boxes ★ 1896, 1907, and 1912, 33–34.

C. For beer, República Argentina. *Memoria presentada al Ministro de Hacienda de la Nación por el Administrador General de Impuestos Internos correspondiente al ejercicio del 1 de mayo de 1891 al 31 de mayo de 1892* (Buenos Aires: Imprenta y Papelería "Del Pueblo," 1892), 5; Administración General de Impuestos Internos, *Memoria correspondiente al ejercicio del año 1913* (Buenos Aires: Cía. Sudamericana de Billetes de Banco, 1914), p. 51; Javier Padilla, Datos sobre industria cervecera recopilados por la Sección Industria, Pesas y Medidas, Warrants de la Dirección General de Industria de Javier Padilla, director general a Honorio Pueyerredón, ministro de Agricultura, April 15, 1917, 5; *Monitor de Sociedades Anónimas*. XXII, 1916, 71; Compañía General de Fosforos, Estadística General. Libro 1, Avellaneda, Paraná, Tucumán y Santa Fé. Resumen de gruesas vendidas, 33–34.

D. Coffee, cacao, soap (common and perfumed) and writing paper are import quantities. See República Argentina, Ministerio de Agricultura, *Anuario de la Dirección general de Estadística correspondiente a los años 1893–1915* , "Estadística retrospectiva del comercio especial exterior a cargo del Sr. Ricardo Kleine," in *Anuario de la Dirección de Estadística correspondiente a 1894* (Buenos Aires: Cía Sudamericana de Billetes de Banco), 245–52; República Argentina, *Anuarios del Comercio Exterior, 1910–1925.* Imports of cars, coffee, and cacao and CGF output of matches have been considered a proxy of demand.

E. For the period 1915–1930, *Revista de Economía Argentina*, no. 325, July 1945, pp. 330–32; no. 289, July 1942, pp. 188–190.

the difficult 1890s, when people were compelled to abandon smoking as "the luxurious ostentation of other times."[14] Besides price, the appeal of cigarettes was also due to their great advantage over other forms of tobacco such as cigars and pipes. Cigarette nicotine is released gradually, rather than in one initial and quick hit and remains longer in one's system than other forms of smoking.[15]

Argentines, already heavy smokers in the 1890s, increased per capita cigarette consumption in the new century (see Table 2.1). Cigarettes started to be consumed in large numbers earlier in Spanish America than in the Anglo-Saxon world, where cigars and chewing tobacco prevailed until the late nineteenth century. While North Americans became major cigarette consumers just after the First World War, Argentines already had been heavy smokers for decades. As early as 1890, the French visitor Théodore Child was surprised to find that

> [a]fter the age of ten all men smoke from morning to night. The cigarette is tolerated everywhere, in trains, in houses and on the street, in the ministries and in the public administration, in the entrepôts and in the offices.[16]

In addition, local women started to smoke in huge numbers at an early stage and came to constitute an important market segment—advertisements addressing females, which provoked stern indignation in the United States as late as 1929, were common in Argentina in 1910.[17] Consumption by both men and women jumped from 140 to 400 million packages between 1896 and 1913. By 1913, the average Argentine smoked six times as many cigarettes as did the American pre-Camel consumer.[18] As a result, the most successful cigarette producer, Piccardo, rapidly increased its workforce, a remarkable development for an industry mechanized with labor-saving Bonsack machines (see Table 1.6).

The packaging of matches in colorful small boxes increased their appeal to consumers, while their portability helped spread the habit of smoking. Cooking, heating, and smoking became even less of a problem when production of red *fósforos inofensivos* (harmless matches) replaced the white (and poisonous) ones. Explosions were rare and they were no longer associated with the "romantic method of phosphoric death by intoxication" among women who drank the product dissolved in water to commit suicide.[19] By 1910, match consumption per capita had doubled from the levels of twenty years earlier, a fact that accounted for the success of the Compañia General de Fósforos (CGF) (see Tables 1.6 and 2.1). The sales of the recently merged company had reached 912,000 *gruesas* (twelve dozen) in 1889, but the 1890 depression forced production to fall to 523,000 in 1891, creating a large excess capacity (demand fell from 37 to 21 matches per person). It took the entire 1890s to recover to predepression levels that were only surpassed in 1899, when the firm's sales reached 995,000 gruesas. Between 1900 and 1910, the making of matches took a qualitative jump, and by 1913 the CGF was selling more than 2,100,000 gruesas, which supposed selling 39 matches per capita, not so different from the peak reached by the firm before the 1890 crisis.[20] Price elasticity played a major role in the recovery of the demand. The application of economies of scale led to a thirty percent drop in the real cost of matches. During the 1890s, the company lowered prices to eliminate the excess capacity. Between 1907 and 1913, and in spite of inflation, the gruesa fell from $4.12 to $3.92 paper pesos.[21] Matches gained further favor with the public during the 1920s, when the introduction of the *carterita* (small bag) increased ease of use.[22]

Belief that cigarette paper was not harmful to people's health eased consumption.[23] Moreover, mechanized cigarettes were softer and more comfortable because the ashes did not drop and stain clothes, as often occurred with the handmade products. With Bonsack-made cigarettes and inoffensive matches, smoking did not require the special attention now reserved for pipe smokers. Smoking had been transformed into a worry-free practice that encouraged relaxation and casual chat, one of the cornerstones in the city's growing café culture.[24]

In contrast to smoking, beer drinking was a consumption novelty. National manufacture was, at that time, of very poor quality. The beverage that a few archaic and small breweries were producing by the middle of the nineteenth century did not differ much from the dreadful beer that the coffee-seller in the Buenos Aires *Recova* (old market) had offered during colonial times. A thick and sour liquid, it was disregarded by doctors as well as consumers, who preferred Spanish beverages such as *sangría* and *vinagrada*. In the 1860s, domestic beer improved slightly when the Bieckert firm placed a light brand on the market. Nonetheless, the only good-quality product that Argentine consumers could buy at the time was imported. Since only the "most famous brands of England and Germany had been introduced into the country, its high price excluded all but the wealthy."[25] Everything changed in the late 1880s, when the first large and well-equipped breweries were installed. By then, as shown in Chapter 1, large-scale production allowed Argentine beer to compete with the imported product in price and quality.[26] Local production ousted imports, and beer "was transformed within a few years from a luxurious beverage into a popular one."[27]

Beer consumption increased from 13 to 109 million liters, which more than tripled the per capita index between 1891 and 1913 (see Table 2.1).[28] Heavy investments made by large firms paid off quite soon. Quilmes firm's output increased from three to ten million liters between 1891 and 1898, to thirty five million in 1907, and to eighty million in 1918, while Bieckert production grew from one hundred thousand liters in 1894 to almost fourteen million in 1907.[29] By then, this company had moved to a larger installation in the suburbs of Buenos Aires, ending supply shortages. Machinery facilitated a drop in the production of the coarse *sencilla* (simple) type, "which due to its reasonable price, provides a real service to the working class," in favor of the higher-quality Pilsen-style *doble* (double) beer.[30] A parallel change prompted domestic production: instead of being distributed in bulk to stores, beer started to be sold in bottles, ready to be opened by the final consumer. It only continued to be served by the glass in cheap neighborhood restaurants called *fondas de barrio*, in which a beverage called "5 y 5"—five cents worth of beer or wine and five cents of lemonade— became extremely popular at the beginning of the twentieth century.[31] In addition, beer became incorporated into gatherings of friends and family parties when breweries, trying any strategy to raise their sales, offered to lease elegant barrels with a simple serving device.[32]

The rise in beer drinking was a surprise to those who attempted to correlate it with the population's ethnic origins, since most of the immigrants came from wine-drinking Italian and Spanish backgrounds. As an observer pointed out, "the English and Germans, who are relatively small in number, have imposed their way of life."[33] Moving beyond ethnic customs, Argentines found beer the most effective relief against scorching summers—a time of the year when consumption doubled—as well as a "hygienic" drink for its diuretic value. For a long time, people had been trying to find products that would alleviate the impact of hot weather, and beer was thought to be the solution. As *La Nación* remarked in 1916:

> Beer, softer and less alcoholic than wine, constitutes the beverage of most extended refreshment. For this reason, during the hot season its production must rise considerably, because it will be demanded not only at meal time, but also in the nap hours when perspiration excess clamors for the intake of fresh fluids able to satisfy the continuing thirst that our body announces.[34]

Beer found an ally in ice, which was sold by breweries at an extremely cheap price as an incentive.[35] A description of the demand during the devastating summer of 1900, when temperatures reached 40 degrees centigrade (104 F°) and people in Buenos Aires died in droves because of the weather, underscores the popularity of beer and ice:

> Ice is today an article of absolute necessity. . . . Ice factories were besieged by the continuing demand and, unable to serve even one third of the orders, they decided to close their doors and to isolate themselves by not answering the telephones.[36]

Rise in beer demand went along with a general increase in the consumption of beverages, such as chocolate and coffee, while soft drinks grew in appeal and promoted the rise of some large companies (see Table 2.1). Wine consumption also increased, and it remained the most popular alcoholic beverage. On the eve of the First World War, beer consumption reached between a fourth and a third that of wine, but equaled this beverage during the summer.[37] Such success did not escape the eye of a money-hungry administration that used the excuse of the immorality of drinking to raise taxes on this "widely consumed product."[38]

Ready-to-wear clothing and shoe consumption also experienced notable changes. In the post-independence period, Buenos Aires had one of the largest textile imports per capita rates in the world, and stores were stocked with these items. But until the second half of the nineteenth century, as José Antonio Wilde pointed out, "ladies very seldom employed *dressmakers*; they cut, *assembled*, and sewed their dresses themselves."[39] A major change occurred with the massive introduction of sewing machines in the 1860s, an event that provided dressmakers (and more sophisticated ladies' tailors) with the opportunity to fill part of the market demand.[40] The scenario changed again in the 1880s, with the massive importation of wearing apparel, and especially in the 1890s, when the first large ready-to-wear factories appeared. Dressmakers had to yield a significant portion of the market to the big firms and on occasion to become part of their workforce. A similar evolution took place in the production of shoes. As with clothing, women used to make their own and their family's at home.[41] After the middle of the nineteenth century, the rush to buy the product at stores started. By the 1870s, a number of artisans and small shops supplied part of the needs of the city of Buenos Aires and struggled against imports, as indicated in Chapter 1. Thanks to this change in habits, the shoe industry achieved some success, and by 1887, establishments dedicated to this production were among the few large factories in Argentina.[42]

Meanwhile, there were changes in the kinds of clothes and shoes that the market absorbed. New *camisas a la crimea* (Crimea shirts) replaced *camisas de plancha* (shirts to iron). The former, manufactured in large mills, succeeded thanks to being cheap and wrinkle-free and "achieved a popularity . . . that created serious competition [for workshops] and introduced a real revolution in the market."[43] Changes in taste also allowed domestic production to substitute for imports in a wide range of products beyond the cheapest goods. Casa Zabala explained this point when telling the firm's story in *La Nación*'s 1910 special publication for the centennial of the revolution against Spain: "There was a time when people in Buenos Aires preferred the made-to-order suit, believing that the ready-made article must be inferior, according to common sense." Domestic manufacture "started as a means for people of very limited resources, and for that reason the cloth, as well as the craftsmanship of the low priced suits, left much to be desired." Nonetheless, higher-income customers finally accepted domestic products when "the direct importation of cashmeres, and the cutter's science, made it possible for the ready-to-wear suit to be good quality and perfect cut."[44] Similarly, the preference for handmade shirts (allegedly of better finish) receded.[45] Although some prejudice continued for a long time, by the 1910s, half of the national demand for clothing was provided by ready-to-wear articles produced in local factories.[46] In parallel, a shoe industry that used to supply only the coarsest goods became highly mechanized between 1900 and 1910 (as will be seen in Chapter 3), and industrialists could produce better quality. A lighter and softer Argentine article prevailed over the inferior old one, when nailed shoes started to be replaced by McKay and Goodyear footwear manufactured at local mills.[47] By the mid-1920s, local factories produced sixteen million pairs of leather shoes per year, almost two for each inhabitant.[48]

A market with more numerous and richer consumers increased the demand. But, as in the other cases, reductions in production costs also played a major part. Cheapness, indeed, was one of the main attractions that ready-to-wear domestic production offered. With the new century, price wars among clothing firms became normal. Companies had to compensate for the reduction in profits with high sales volume. Advertising campaigns proclaimed the advantages of one store or brand over another, such as one launched by A. Cabezas. In it, the firm offered a price "no competitor could match" since "our prices are *twenty five per cent lower than in the winter of 1902*. This outcome has been reached thanks to the enormous rise in our production, which is *a hundred and twenty per cent higher than last year*. Costs have dropped to half and the buyer has obtained a significant dividend."[49] The strategy of producing in large scale at lower cost could only have worked in a market of some significant size, such as that developing in Argentina by the beginning of the twentieth century. In 1918, a U.S. Department of Commerce report remarked that "[t]here are in the Republic slightly less than 8,000,000 people, but for the manufacturer of wearing apparel, at least, practically every one of these represents a potential consuming unit."[50]

No institution could do better in these circumstances than department stores (locally called *grandes tiendas*) that based their business on different specialized sections and high turnover. Until the 1880s, stores in the Argentine capital continued to work in the old-fashioned way of waiting for the uncoerced customer. In 1883, Alfredo H. Gath and Lorenzo Chaves opened a small store in the city center that adopted a new strategy: active recruitment of the potential client. The main instruments of the new tactics were window displays and special offers. Tempted by the increasing demand of the late 1880s, the French department store Bon Marché opened a branch in Buenos Aires. The 1890 depression, however, forced the firm to close and sell its monumental building to a railway company.

In the first years of the new century the economic atmosphere was once again encouraging. In 1901, the expansion of Gath y Chaves (by then British owned) prompted the company to move to a four-thousand-square-meter building. Five years later, it had tripled the occupied space and resembled the most famous department stores in the world. In 1913, the London-based Harrods opened a branch in Buenos Aires and transformed its establishment, as did Gath y Chaves, into one of the city's most magnificent. Their structures reached from six to seven stories and employed hundreds of clerks. Seven other, less splendid, companies that also had large buildings completed the scene.[51] Department stores stimulated local manufacturing when they decided to engage in their own production of finished goods, especially clothing. Thousands of workers were employed in their mills. The most notable case was Gath y Chaves, which at the beginning of the century "decided to enter into the industrial field [and] did so resolutely. . . . In their estimation, their optimism was not excessive. Buenos Aires needed . . . a house which could produce many good ready-to-wear clothes." The firm did not make a mistake—their sales rose from paper $738,000 to paper $24,038,000 between 1893 and 1909.[52] This business became so appealing that some of the companies that provided department stores chose to risk commercializing their own brand of finished goods. Textile producer Enrico Dell'Acqua opened nearly forty shops throughout the Republic that sold his products directly to the customer.[53] The firm of Angel Braceras also competed in this market; it moved beyond making clothes for the state to its own "large scale production of civilian" brands. The decision proved successful, and some years later, the company opened its own weaving mills. Risks dropped as the market enlarged. When asked why the firm had waited so long to commercialize its own products, Mr. Braceras explained that the plan could not work without a market that could absorb continuous volume production. But in 1910 it was his observation that "Buenos Aires, and even the provinces, offered a vast horizon, once the scope enlarged."[54]

For a public concerned with prices, easy credit and special sales had a special appeal. Shops opened credit lines that allowed customers to buy merchandise on an installment plan in the belief that accessibility promoted consumption. All sorts of commercial houses supplied customers with credit.[55] Department stores were especially concerned with this issue, since it enabled them to achieve one of their primary objectives: high turnover. This was a strategy that fit well with the variable tastes of the market because there was no point in keeping merchandise that could not be sold in the future. As the department store A la Ciudad de Londres indicated, "[t]he sales aimed at disposing of anything from the last season before the next, since it is known that fashion caprice and taste inevitably vary every year."[56] Willingly or unwillingly, firms were forced to enter the credit system. This was the case with Gath y Chaves, which initially did not want to promote this method of buying but found it had no alternative in order to continue competing in the market.[57] Stores also started to put price tags next to the article to tempt customers.[58] In addition, some firms introduced the tactic of "satisfaction guaranteed." As early as 1891, perfume manufacturer Souëf announced that "[a]ny person who does not feel satisfied with an article bought in this house, can return it, even uncorked."[59] Client comfort was of utmost importance—a store in the resort city of Mar del Plata encouraged visitors not to bother with baggage but rather to buy all the apparel they needed in its shopping district.[60]

The expansion of department stores was largely due to an enlargement of the social range of their targeted buyers. In 1873, A la Ciudad de Londres catered to "the most aristocratic [segment] of the population" with its imported products. In 1910, it offered a variety of goods produced in its own workshops for the engaged couple. The firm was happy to supply them "whether they are going to make their nest in a modest neighborhood apartment, or to inaugurate a new 'petit-hotel.'"[61]

The New Consumers

Traditional scholarship has by and large neglected the development of mass consumption in the early twentieth century in favor of historical descriptions overemphasizing the lifestyle of affluent Argentines. This view is based on the strong association of landed aristocracy with conspicuous consumption of imported goods. This connection is accurate, although luxury, as well as the number of aristocrats, was a limited phenomenon. Shoe industrialist Luis Pascarella pointed out that the landowners satisfied their whims by buying imports; thus "their contribution to the development of the national industry is almost null, and the product of their bullocks and the renting of their land goes from their hands to the pockets of European producers." They were not of much interest to Pascarella since they constituted a small portion of the national consumer market—10 percent according to his reckoning. The industrialist remarked on the fact that domestic industry based its prosperity on another kind of demand. This "consumer class has been totally provided by immigration as it did not exist originally in the country." On the one hand, this group was composed of workers who, in spite of the "incitements that drag them to class struggle," could not resist "the ideas that propel them towards bourgeoisism." Indeed, "whatever his origins, when the worker arrives in the country, he is driven by one sole aim: his economic improvement." On the other hand, consumers included those who "try to imitate what they cannot match in their place of origin. [They are] the social classes of middle pecuniary position, who satisfy their needs . . . and become consumers, stimulating the indigenous production by its own law of gravity and despite all theories." [62] This was especially true after the 1890 crisis, when it was "labor, the paying-teller of this Republic, [which rather than luxuries] claims [the] appliances by which industrial growth and rescue from the present depression may be assured." [63] Thus, national industry found in nonaristocratic mass consumption its actual market as well as a great business. Although the aristocrats targeted luxury, it was the middle- or working-class consumer who secured the success of Argentine industrial firms.

Middle-class consumption was crucial in initiating and sustaining mass production. The concept of such a social group is largely abstract.[64] Defining the middle class is a difficult issue everywhere, but especially in turn-of-the-twentieth-century Argentina, where social mobility was particularly high. The first reckoning of Argentine income, in 1914, showed that the lower participants made up 55 percent of the total population and shared in 30 percent of the income. Rich people—the ones to whom Pascarella referred—constituted only 0.33 percent but represented 11 percent of the total wealth. The ones in between (those whom we may call a middle class) were 39 percent of the population and accounted for 42 percent of the income (see Table 2.2). These numbers—though statistically imprecise and only indicative—reflect a group of people with income comparable to the general idea of a middle class.[65]

TABLE 2.2

Distribution of the General Annual Income in Argentina, 1914

Category $ m/n	% of contributors	% of income
Up to 1,000	54.99	29.8
From 1,001 to 3,000	38.53	41.9
From 3,001 to 6,000	4.42	10.2
From 6,001 to 30,000	1.83	11.5
30,001 and upwards	0.23	6.8
50,001 and upwards	0.13	4.2

SOURCE: My own elaboration based on Alejandro Bunge, *Revista de Economía Argentina, July 1918, I* (1), pp. 65–80.

The members of the working class were consumers and contributors to mass demand as well.[66] Ready-to-wear clothing firms advertised their sale of cheap suits, pants, overcoats, and furniture in working-class newspapers, such as the Anarchist *La Protesta* and the Socialist *La Vanguardia*. Contemporary magazines also offered a graphic demonstration of the phenomenon. In one of many examples, a photograph shows a gathering of the *Federación Obrera de La Plata* (Workers Federation of the city La Plata) calling for the revocation of the social laws. The group of proletarians, proudly holding up a proclamation *Al Pueblo* (To the People) is dressed up in suits, hats, and berets produced by Argentine factories. Not surprisingly, a cigarette producer targeted consumers with a brand called *El Obrero* (The Worker).[67] In addition, factory girls, such as the workers in the cigarette firm Centenario, wore aprons on the shop floor but changed their clothes and cinched their figures with fashionable corsets in the mill's cloakroom before going out onto the streets.[68]

The strategies used in the struggles of the first decade of the twentieth century by Socialists and, particularly, by Anarchists were probably one of the most telling stories about the relation between the emerging working class and the consumer society.[69] One of the main weapons that workers used to wear down the stubbornness of industrialists during a strike was a consumption boycott. Factory owners greatly feared the damage these boycotts did to sales, a fear sufficiently justified by the examination of particular cases. The manifest distributed by the socialist Unión General de Trabajadores (General Union of Workers) urging workers not to buy products of the Fábrica Argentina de Alpargatas had devastating implications for this firm. Indeed, the manifesto led many small merchants, scared of alienating their working-class customers, to stop stocking those products. The importance of the working-class market was so great that on one occasion the powerful brewery Quilmes decided to negotiate with the workers who supported a boycott against its beer. The agreement consisted of a monetary donation to an Anarchist union in exchange for the lifting of the measure. This agreement horrified the Argentine Industrial Union (UIA), and there were some attempts to expel this company, but they failed (in this and in other cases) because business came before loyalty to the industrialists' association.[70]

To suggest that there was a highly different style of consumption for middle and working classes would be misleading. Incomes certainly were a restriction, but the entire world of consumption was steeped in an increasingly middle-class mentality. This environment reached down the social ladder to the less fortunate who, in the land of recent arrival, were eager to climb as soon as possible. In the creation of an expanding middle class, consumption habits played a crucial role in changing social values that fostered a calculated spending. On the one hand, members of the middle class imitated the rich in a Veblenesque way and (to the indignation of the old elite) partially succeeded. As the nostalgic writer Manuel Bilbao said, "the fear of our ancestors that money would triumph over ancestry . . . has been realized."[71] However, these new arrivals created a world of "excess" spending that could only be a short-term strategy. On the other hand, the middle class could impose their own values by giving new meaning to old ones, such as frugality. The ancient idea of discretion, under recent conditions of prosperity, transformed into the concept of saving. Thrift, then, became just a means for further consumption.

Auctions of used goods and firms offering to store furniture and to clean rugs flourished. As one company observed in the advertisement of its services, this "revolution, though slow, is no less secure." It was a recent transformation. "[T]oday . . . we demonstrate stronger and more remarkable tendencies towards economizing; thrift and foresight are no longer unknown, and we take, as a consequence, much more care in the preservation of those objects that . . . may represent for the family long-lasting toils preceding their acquisition."[72] Meanwhile, domestic manufacturing of shirts found a good complement in imported German Mey collars, a cardboard covered with fabric that did not get soft with sweat and, because of its price, was disposable. Shirts could look brand new for a long period, a convenient feature for a group obsessed equally by appearance and cost. Similarly, mobs, as well as a legion of *mecheras* (shoplifters), invaded department stores during special sales that, as an observer recalled in 1918,

> are generally well patronized, especially the annual stock-taking one, and many people of the middle class practice economy for weeks in order to buy more cheaply at the "sale". . . . During these periodic sales the stores are frequently crowded with eager shoppers until 8 or 9 o'clock in the evening and often it will be midnight before the tired sales force can leave the counters.[73]

In 1915, the government created the National Post Office (Caja Nacional de Ahorro Postal) to foster a savings culture. In the years following its creation, the institution launched a campaign to open small savings accounts for a clientele that included children and maids. Not surprisingly, the CGF entered an agreement to distribute saving stamps from the post office in their match boxes, associating themselves with "a campaign that would have a beautiful and charming result, the encouragement of savings."[74]

Mass consumption goods gathered representatives of a broad social rainbow in the marketplace. Already in the 1880s, two writers had observed that "nowadays the use of the [stearine] candle is universal and has penetrated the magnificent lounge, as well as the humble shack in the countryside. Indeed, everybody, rich and poor, uses this modest article and at the same time [that] chic candle can be found at the elegant dressing-table as well as the working table of the humble seamstress."[75] Taste preferences also seemed to blur ethnic differences, such as the acquisition of the beer-consumption habit suggests. This integrating power, however, had limitations; the arrival of gas lighting created a gap between those who could and those who could not afford it, while candle-use was relegated to the poorest groups or to emergency situations for the better off. Likewise, beer, cigarettes, shoes, and ready-to-wear clothes bought by the wealthy and the poor were of such different qualities that one would barely think they were the same commodities.[76] In addition, ethnicity was an important factor in consumption, as shown in the marked preference of ethnic magazines for specific imported goods. Indeed, this was the key to the sale success of Italian cotton fabric, olive oil, cheese, and rice.[77]

In this atmosphere, Argentine factories started to produce the goods of "massive consumption" that, according to Carole Shammas's definition, met the dual criteria of being bought by people of different incomes and on a regular basis.[78] The winners of a contest held in 1901 by a cigarette firm showed how varied consumer background was. They were seven journeymen, three employees, two merchants, two commission agents, two painters, an office boy, a machinist, an attorney, a lithographer, a broker, a shoemaker, a dry goods storeowner, a stevedore, a student, a slag dumper, a bookstore owner, a mechanic, a hairdresser, a cook, and a professor.[79] This list represents the bulk of the male population, although it does omit certain cigarette consumers. First, it was unlikely that a member of the upper class would send a coupon to such a contest. Second, a much larger group was even more reluctant to appear publicly in a newspaper as cigarette consumers: women.

Class distinction became increasingly difficult in a country where mass culture bloomed away visual hallmarks of sets and cliques that characterized the old society one—a phenomenon that is a standard feature of modernization. A visually democratic Buenos Aires was not a new concept. The contrast between Buenos Aires and Santiago de Chile took the future president Domingo Faustino Sarmiento by surprise when he returned from his Chilean exile in 1852. Homogeneity in porteño clothing across the social ladder astonished Sarmiento, who was familiar with dressing social codes prevalent in Chile.[80] This impression became widespread and deeper in the following decades. By then, comparisons were not made with Latin

American but with European landscapes. In the 1880s, an English traveler
believed that social mobility was the key to explaining the lack of distinction among the different classes:

> [T]he case in which the social ladder is climbed [is so familiar that]
> *Padre Pulpero, hijo caballero!* (the father an innkeeper, the son a gentle-
> man!) [is a common saying], but as the lower classes in manner
> and address are so much superior to the corresponding order in
> England, this excites no surprise, and elevated position sits facilely
> on parvenus.[81]

More than twenty years later, a Spanish visitor pointed out the visible results
of that process:

> One of the physiognomic features of Buenos Aires is excessively curi-
> ous; one does not notice ill-dressed people in the streets. The workers,
> though many, do not wear the distinguishing clothing that makes them
> stand out in the roads of our cities. The population presents a markedly
> bourgeois appearance; one does not see the blouses and the caps that
> in Paris and Barcelona give a touch of variety to the mobs that circulate
> in the grand avenues.[82]

Part of the progress toward class invisibility resulted from the quiet, un-
noticed evidence of a large middle class. As *La Nación* indicated, the government addressed working-class problems (and consequently confronted the
"Social Question") but did not pay attention to the stresses on a "more resigned group, which suffers because it cannot protest in loud voice, the name
of which is the middle-class."[83] Class tensions were not expressed dramatically in the consumption sphere. The proindustrialist Manuel Chueco, a
member of the middle class himself, was happily surprised by "how much
workers [and] servants spend on their clothes." This inclined him toward a
vision of a society free of class conflict:

> One does not see workers without ironed shirts, without ties, and
> very few do not have a watch, frequently of gold; and it is common
> to see the young factory girls, as well as family house cooks and
> maids, wearing varnished shoes, and sometimes even showing fish-
> net tights.[84]

In this way, Buenos Aires started to manifest characteristics associated
with cities overflowing with the features of a consumer society. In these
places, the social differences tended to melt visually in the exteriority of the

public world.[85] A parallel, and also apparent, leveling occurred in the space of urban daily life. The coexistence and cohabitation of different groups in the private sphere were not new. The radical novelty was that public space offered not only an area of cohabitation but also an arena of common practice. A sarcastic Santiago de Calzadilla commented about the new times,

> The tramway has turned out to be for the Argentines the *federis Arca [Noah's Arch]*. Many times, one can see in the most intimate elegance a great dame with her wealthy attire next to a scullery maid with her basket and gossip, a factory peon next to a lieutenant general, an austere priest rubbing elbows with a laundress, the seamstress, the market woman, the maid, the ironer, each one with her little bundle, tray or work basket, symbol of her occupation, rubbing together with a bank manager, with a sportsman, with a director or president of the Rural Society, or a charity sister next to the *tenement house impresario*. . . . Oh triumph of democracy![86]

Palermo Park, which used to be the privileged space for recreation in Buenos Aires, became the showplace for the unusual interaction of different social groups.[87] Originally, as Victor Gálvez pointed out in his memoirs, it was the domain in which the well-off rode while "numerous others walked on foot." By 1910, the process of social confluence had reached momentous proportions, and an observer commented, "Palermo democratizes. On certain days there are as many renting as owning luxurious carriages." Sadness rather than surprise permeated Argentine Roberto Gache's description of a park far different from the one of his infancy:

> Going to Palermo, one thousand carriages take the same avenue, with one thousand families equal to each other. Next to the lake, an aristocratic setting in past times, they stop their march and make their carnival. Where are the graceful and refined silhouettes that gave in the morning light such a singular charm of elegance to the very same place?[88]

The distinction had already been dissipating in the 1890s, when a French visitor observed that

> In Palermo, the famous park of which I had heard so much, I did not see more than plebeian families, eating under the trees and dirtying the grass with pieces of greasy paper and empty bottles, reproducing the habits at work in the countries with the oldest and most advanced civilization.[89]

The words of politician Miguel Cané, famous for his attempts to preserve tradition, summarized the feeling of the old elite when he queried,

> Where are the old loyal servants whom I strained to see during my first years at my parents' house? Where are those freed slaves who treated us as little princes . . . without any other concern than to serve us well and faithfully? . . . Today, we are served by a European servant who steals from us, who dresses better than us and who reminds us of his status as a free man as soon as you look at him with rigor.[90]

Dismay at the leveling that was occurring was expressed not only by the old aristocracy but also by early immigrants who saw with horror how later arrivals (of the same origin) behaved. Hence a descendant of Italians complained about the celebrations of Carnival, during which,

> mixed with the most luxurious carriages in the parade, one can see [in] the coarse cart of the immigrant of yesterday the family of the honest son of the Italic mountain; he tilts the demijohn at his will, his wife breast-feeds a child, his daughter seasons the salad, his kids run, fork hoisted and all jumbled up and perturb the wagon in its march.[91]

Although market invisibility might have been a socially equalizing mirage, its massification was clear. The number of consumers expanded to such an extent that it allowed local manufacture, unable to supply luxury articles but capable of providing imitations of more modest goods, to grow in an unprecedented way. With this explosion in consumption a new network of relations between people and things gave birth to a world that was notably different from the old one.

Old Consumption, New Consumption

Transformations in Argentina's demand patterns at the turn of the twentieth century produced "consumption capital," a concept that, according to George Stigler and Gary Becker, describes the development of a taste for particular styles in such a number of individuals that it becomes massive.[92] Being a demand phenomenon, this change prompted standardized supply. Some products, such as the flagons filled with perfumed water for use during Carnival, almost disappeared from the market. Their consumption as "a weapon . . . sovereign in the old Carnival fights" dropped, "vanquished" by the ever more popular paper streamer.[93] Under these circumstances, flexible entrepreneurs could survive by adapting their businesses to the new times, such as the owner of the main flagon factory in the country, who dedicated himself to the vigorous manufacture of cosmetics and perfumes.[94] The future, indeed, seemed to belong to those who took advantage of the new opportunities the market offered. This was the case of the hairdresser who became a successful perfume maker by testing his formulas on his customers. His opportunity came during the 1890 depression, when many could no longer "spend five pesos on a flask of essence." The fragrances he created eventually reached an annual production of almost half a million bottles.[95]

In addition to the ebb and flow of demand as goods went in and out of fashion, the very nature of the market changed. This transformation was so deep that the new scenario was unrecognizable to those who faced the changes in their old age. A series of nostalgic writers (of whose existence no epoch is bereft) illustrated how happy the simple and austere society of some decades previous was compared to the complex, shallow, and ostentatious new times. These writers shared a similar tone, portraying a past that was largely an invention; the old "harmonious" days had been plagued by bloody civil wars.[96] During the late colonial times, Buenos Aires had shown signs of transformation—the city grew from 12,000 to 54,000 between 1750 and 1810—and became an increasing market for imported goods, as visitors and observers noted. A similar trend continued in the post-independence days. The modesty of those changing times, however, can be seen in the memoirs of Mariquita Sánchez de Thompson, who lived between 1786 and 1868 and experienced just the first transformations of modernity, which were enough to shock her.[97]

The way that the nostalgic writers who published between the 1880s and the 1900s developed similar issues defines the nature and depth of the changes to which they refer. In Argentina, these men belonged to a conservative group of thinkers who badly missed the old "less demanding" and "quiet society," in which "[e]verybody knew and respected each other regardless of the appearance." In those times, women had dressed "in the Spanish way" with clothing that was "simple as well as elegant," since gowns were considered "accessories and nothing else." They were "attired loosely," being "enemies of the antihygienic corset," and even high-class females had few clothes, whether they had received them as an inheritance or made them at home from imported fabric.[98] Then, food was simple but healthy because "one did not swallow nor drink . . . so many adulterated substances." Also, silverware was plain since the table "did not hold the bread trays, nor sauce boat, or salad bowl, or mustard pot . . . that are essential today," and it was a "very rare person who possessed more than dozen *teaspoons*."[99] When life was "invaded by the tastes and demands of the ostentatious European life," the old patriarchal peace broke down. "The customs of our ancestors, the

noble sociability without pretense, the Spanish chivalry without duplici-
ties, disappeared in our days as a result of the invasion of the enriched
bourgeoisie."[100]

An American visitor summed up the new situation by saying in 1886 that
a procession in honor of any saint had become a rarity in Buenos Aires. This
was the result of the mental transformation of the people, and "it is asserted
by old residents that people now think of nothing but making money. That
all classes have become infected with the desire to get rich to such an extent
that they cannot take time even for the claims of religion."[101] As a British
traveler noticed, two worlds were living at odds with each other in the 1880s,
the "patriarchal simplicity" of the elder and the "pure money-seeking" of
the younger. This contrast, which provoked nostalgia among the well-off
elderly, elicited the traveler's compassion. As he pointed out, the new generation of women were obsessed by "shopping expeditions," a social feature
that breached former boundaries. In the first half of the nineteenth century,
visitors had observed that mothers and daughters kept to each other's company at social events, followed by one or more servants.[102] By contrast, shopping expeditions at the end of that century involved women friends of
similar social status. Moreover, younger women were more educated and
sophisticated than their mothers, creating "an almost painful contrast . . . in
the manners and conversation of ladies of the same family; the older generation appearing in every way inferior." Thus,

> there is something pathetic in one of these poor old dames huddled
> up with antiquated finery on a sofa in some corner of the room . . .
> dreaming . . . all the while of bright and simpler days when they sat
> surrounded by doughty heroes of Oribe's and Urquiza's levies, proud
> to receive the circling mate in their hands or to listen to the tinkle of
> their guitar.[103]

The new times even prompted women to smoke openly at home (albeit
rarely in public places), a practice previously confined to the bottom of the
social ladder. As José Antonio Wilde bitterly mused, in the old days only
poor women had smoked "without reserve," while "[i]n the middle class
they always employed some pretence" and ladies of the "high hierarchy only
did it in seclusion."[104] Smoking paralleled changes such as the appearance of
women at chocolate parlors and cafés. Instead of making accusations, café La
Brasileña followed the changes and was a pioneer in the welcoming of female customers to its facilities; as a result, within a few years the company
achieved striking success, opened several branches, and increased the number of its employees from 7 to 150.[105]

Some of the most profound changes occurred in the commercial practices of the emerging consumer society. Stores, which in the post-independence period had not been more than rooms overseen by their owners, expanded during the decades of the wool export boom at the middle of the nineteenth century.[106] This commerce, however, paled in comparison to the size and complexity of the department stores that rose between 1900 and 1910. These shopping palaces offered a new world to the customer, a whole new space of socializing in an atmosphere highly different from the street. The main department stores practiced seduction as a major sales principle, attracting customers by offering eating and drinking services plus additional spectacles: in sum, a "land of desire" that eclipsed the bare function of supplying an article.[107] Harrods (copying the practices of its London headquarters) became the leader of the new trend:

> Its third story contains the tea and refreshment salon. It is easily the finest in Buenos Aires and no other approaches it in popularity. Ices and cold drinks of a non-alcoholic nature are served, as well as tea, and an American soda fountain is a pleasing feature. At noon, a regular lunch is served at a nominal price. During the afternoon an orchestra renders classical and popular selections.[108]

Within this cosmopolitan atmosphere, sophistication in commercial practices came together with a new sense of social distance. The imposition of a more pompous and deliberately artificial aesthetic created a new social distance in the private sphere. Well-off households no longer summoned their servants by calling their names but instead rang a bell.[109] This new element also affected the relationship between seller and buyer and ended the times when "honest and well-known merchants [who] sold their own merchandise had in their back rooms a permanent group of gentlemen chatting."[110] The old scenario changed when the fixed price system started to prevail, a practice that saved the time and energy of the bargaining process (more reminiscent of a Middle Eastern market than of an Argentina eager to Europeanize).[111]

The distance, when compared to old customs, was not as profound as in the marketing ambience of the United States. By American standards, Argentine commercial practices continued working on a much more personalized level. Thus, the efficient division of labor that pervaded the world's most advanced department stores did not work the same way in Argentina. A U.S. Department of Commerce commissioner was surprised not only by the size and sophistication of those in Buenos Aires, but also by some of their "primitive" features. Indeed, the same clerk who sold him a paltry piece of fifty-cent merchandise escorted him down various stories to the packaging sector, at a loss of five minutes in which the employee could have served another customer.[112] Moreover, the practice of harassing with questions and product offers the potential customer who entered a store (symbol of the grotesqueness of the old sales tactics) only changed with the arrival of Harrods in 1913. The London-based company (meant to be the most modern and elegant store in Buenos Aires) promoted itself by making its cutting-edge attitude clear. Thus, "what characterizes 'HARRODS' and highlights its singularity with a particular seal, is its invariable custom (adopted since its opening) of not bothering the visitors to its magnificent salesrooms with questions about the article desired." [113]

These changes were not peculiar to Argentina or Buenos Aires, even in the Latin American context. As William Beezley, Michael Johns, and Jeffrey Needell have shown, modernity as a symbol of Europeanization broke out in Mexico and Brazil. Fashion and shopping expeditions fascinated the Mexican and Brazilian elite as they did the Argentine. Emulation of Europe and battles against practices considered primitive, remnants of colonial times (such as the Judas burning in Mexico and Carnival in Argentina and Brazil) were strong everywhere. The victory of "modernity," however, seemed to have occurred deeper and faster in Buenos Aires than in Rio de Janeiro and in Mexico City, as the reports of American commercial experts continuously emphasized (and as the end of Carnival water play, which doomed flagon consumption, showed).[114] A major part of the explanation lies in the fact that Argentina received a large wave of immigration that provided a highly favorable background for change as well as the base for a large consuming market of middle- and lower-class individuals. Indeed, in Argentina itself there was a strong correlation between areas experiencing a high level of economic transformation and the presence of a large number of immigrants, as we will see in more depth in Chapter 4.[115]

One of the major features of a consumer society is the clear preeminence of the market as a driving force in sociability. In Argentina, market values reached this point when they invaded the most sensitive and private ceremonies of private life. Funeral services, traditionally organized by surviving relatives, began to be offered commercially for the paying customer. The carriage-company of Benito Cabral y Cía had derived part of its success from being the standard-bearer of "modernity" in the rituals surrounding death. Cabral had formed an association with a Frenchman, Mr. Garat, with the intent of breaking the traditional colonial Spanish-style ceremonies of mourning and funerals. The idea was to replace "a totally backward ceremonial, not appropriate for cultivated people, with solemn and correct practices such as the open casket funeral, the use of condolence cards, lackeys, closed wagons, candelabra, and the subscription card service."[116] Not surprisingly, the firm was renamed as "La Europea" (The European). Cards, for example, were used to create distance, in contrast to former funerals, in which "condolences were personal" and all attending concluded the ceremony by sharing a savory lunch in a relative's house.[117] China and rag flowers, industrial wreaths, and orchids replaced the crowns of roses and violets made by the family of the deceased in the old times. This change created a demand (albeit modest) for the incipient mortuary industry.[118] Moreover, it demonstrated something much more important for both the industrial and service sector: massive consumption was the key to success.

Market values could only achieve such a position by reaching massive proportions. The new funeral practices, according to which the corpses of notable men were now buried, harbored an inherent weakness: their excessive luxury and cost. The strategy of "La Europea" to "not omit neither sacrifice nor diligence in making the funeral splendorous and magnificent commensurate with the merits of the illustrious dead whom the people honored" gathered many supporters (among them, Argentina's most eminent politician Bartolomé Mitre, president during the period 1862–1868). But this did not secure a mass market for the firm which, to the consternation of the Argentine elite, went into bankruptcy.[119] Far more successful was the production of "populuxe" goods and services, which are, in a term coined by Cissie Fairchilds, cheap copies of aristocratic items, products that are not desired for their own value but as a symbol of a lifestyle.[120] Democratization of death ritual was part of the process. The most successful funeral firm of the twentieth century, Lázaro Costa, adopted a new strategy. It continued to offer luxurious and expensive funerals for a select group, "in order to satisfy the insistent petitions of its distinguished clientele." But it also offered services that, while imitating the luxurious, were inexpensive enough to attract the emerging middle class. The firm's growth indicates the effectiveness of its claims to offer "the best of the best at a minimum cost, while [remaining] loyal to its tradition."[121]

As a mass consumption service, weddings and funerals—two crucial ceremonies in people's lives—lost their religious aura, a feature matching the secularization that the ruling politicians were attempting to impose as part of their modernization program. Manuel Bilbao described the new scenario with dismay. In old-time weddings, the priest was a family friend who did not charge large sums, although his blessing was the peak of the marriage ritual. In the first decade of the twentieth century, weddings had become shows in which there was little expectation of religious solemnity. Rites were laden with wedding marches, flowers, and ornaments, turning the occasion into

> a succession of feasts that start in the atrium, continue in the nave of the temple, stop as if by accident in front of the altar, pass immediately to the sacristy, and then to the bride's house, where the final feast takes place.[122]

Cemeteries also became part of the modern Buenos Aires' *theatrum mundi*, and funerals turned into shallow spectacles. Bilbao regretted that people, instead of keeping silent, laughed so noisily they seemed intent on waking up corpses. Moreover,

> People who take those ambits as spots for amusement and a stroll nowadays profane those sad places, sites of remembrance and grief for the hearts of those who have loved. We have seen in the streets and avenues of the Recoleta [cemetery], parades with women displaying their dresses and critiquing those attending as in any other place of entertainment. There, one can even see pastry and mate sellers, people who crowd around the door of a tomb to see the ornamentation and form lines to observe the relatives' grief without any discretion.[123]

If democratization fostered demand by widening the consumer base, secularization did so by channeling the forces of envy, pride, happiness, and boosterism into the sphere of consumption. Both democratization and secularization eventually created the ambience that allowed fashion to explode into the new society with all its strength. Octavio Battolla was right when he recalled that in the old society people "did not talk about fashion, since few novelties had been introduced before the beginning of the [nineteenth] Century. Rather they conversed about *saints*, whose eulogies were thoroughly known." [124] In contrast, fashion became the obsession of the new consumers.

Although desire for fashion had existed for a long time, its intensity and its nature changed with the rise of a consumer society. The picturesque *peinetones* (large ornamental combs) worn before the mid-nineteenth century were an example of both its existence and confinement to the elite. Fashion changed from an elite to a mass phenomenon at the turn of the twentieth century. Middle and lower classes began to feel its attraction, creating the previously discussed uniformity in clothing. Moreover, the arena for displaying a new dress shifted from churches to the state-managed and highly packed parks, such as Palermo.[125] When Palermo reaffirmed its role as a public space, there were more clothes to sport for the first time and, consequently, more reasons to be seen. There, the idea was "not to breathe fresh and pure air" but to show oneself since "evidently, men go to see women, nothing else, and women to see each other. . . . They go there to exhibit themselves and to watch everyone else."[126] Fashion success was largely due to the fact that the new society converted appearance into one of its foremost concerns. As Richard Sennett has indicated, for modern Western cities public events became a social window display in which sociability was the show. Argentine cities were invaded not only by fashion but also by coquetry, the junction of unsatisfied desire and yet-to-be-obtained possessions.[127] As the *Correo del Domingo* remarked when the phenomenon had just begun,

> It is so nice to wear a dress to keep the attention on oneself! It is so delicious to attract everybody's glance! It is so elegant to dress fashionably! But also, it is so painful not to have enough to buy a dress every eight days! It is so sad to see the other with a lot of luxury and yourself with so much misery![128]

Speed emerged as an important feature of the new society, and fashion was a part of it. In the past, what was in vogue in Europe took so long to arrive to Argentina that variability was reduced (the Louis XVI style was still worn when empire dresses had become the trend in Europe). But in the 1860s, Buenos Aires adopted the crinoline only three years after its success in France.[129] Fashion popularization was crucial for the growth of local industrial production. Although demonized by contemporary traditionalists as the quintessence of European influence on the national character, its mutable and massive nature provided an opportunity to boost the output of Argentine factories. This proved true in both the clothing and shoe industries. Rapid changes in the styles, especially among feminine items, favored local industry since they could respond with high speed to the challenge of changing consumer tastes, whereas importers needed at least four to six months to receive their orders from abroad. Indeed, wholesalers

> determine[d] the probable demand for the coming year and place[d] their orders well in advance in all the producing centers of the world [since] because of the distance from the sources of supply, the difference in the time of the seasons, and the delays in clearing goods through the customs, orders are usually placed a year and a half ahead of the season for which they are intended.[130]

Therefore, a local producer, who could more easily satisfy changing tastes, had an advantage over the importer who needed more time to make his purchases abroad.

Variability further benefited local industry by making space for native fashion innovations. At the end of the First World War, shoe importers found themselves in difficulty since the pointed toe that was popular in the United States was considered "impossible" by the female Argentine clientele. As a U.S. Department of Commerce envoy pointed out, "[l]ocal manufacturers have made the most of the situation by pushing women's lines as aggressively as possible and by changing styles more frequently than ever" but, as a report from the Department of State indicated, "the American manufacturer . . . regards these local tastes as peculiar prejudices which should and will be abandoned." [131] Similarly, imports could not compete with domestic production of pyjamas and bathing suits. Pyjamas had side pockets in which to put tobacco (adapting to the Argentine habit of lounging and smoking at the same time) while bathing suits (more in keeping with local conservatism) covered much more of the body than the American or European articles.[132] The prospect became gloomier for importers as the public's attention increasingly rested on local rather than foreign models, as occurred

> [d]uring the annual cattle exhibition, held at Palermo in September of this year, [when] several women of a prominent family of the capital, who had been in mourning, appeared at the grounds in shoes made of pearl-grey leather. Immediately there was a demand for pearl-gray stock from leather dealers, and this leather, which had been more or less a drag on the market for two years, suddenly became one of the most popular leathers.[133]

The "poison introduced by the European dummy model," as Santiago de Calzadilla described fashion, paradoxically turned out to benefit national industry.

It does not seem to be a coincidence that, in this atmosphere, claims for political democratization took on special strength nor that those claims gained the widest audience in the areas where the economic changes were profound. The rise of a consumer society paralleled the growing challenge to closed politics, which would result in the 1912 law of secret and mandatory suffrage, which was already universal but manipulated by political brokers, and the victory of the opposition Radical party a few years later. This party became a standard bearer of middle-class values and an unbeatable electoral force. Conversely, emulation of the "old aristocracy" had its own flavor in a country where the elite was neither old nor aristocratic and resembled an emerging bourgeoisie intoxicated by hedonistic consumption. To conclude that these transformations meant the end of social clashes would be erroneous. Equality in appearance did not preclude the perpetuation of enormous social differences. As Georg Simmel pointed out, the upper class could always discard and escape any fashion cliché. When the lower classes copy an upper-class fashion "and trespass across the borders that the superior class has marked . . . the select circles abandon it and search for a new one that can set a difference from the rabble."[134] When an item was reproduced in "populuxe" copies, a parallel process took place. Exquisite versions were developed and carefully advertised to generate a demand among the upper class.[135] Buenos Aires department stores offered an expensive made-to-order clothing service clearly different from their cheap standard production, and with a refined style that a neighborhood dressmaker or tailor could not reach. Similarly, the upper class developed a strategy for establishing separation in the public space. As early as the 1880s the *Día de Moda* (Fashion Day) in Palermo was born, a working day—in order to avoid popular presence—in which the wealthy could meet face-to-face without any intrusion.[136]

The same goods could also be worn in different ways; good taste could always be distinguished from an uncouth imitation. With all its implications, this was a strategy of self-reassertion, and the establishment of distinctions was so unilateral that misunderstandings became everyday events. This was, indeed, a society in which not everybody was in "his or her place."

Chasing the Customer

Consumption transformations developed in conjunction with changes in the relationship between industrial firms and their customers. The Argentine economy became complex enough to give birth in 1892 to an *Oficina de intereses comerciales* (Office of Commercial Interests) that sold information on market trends. To promote its services, this office insisted that "more than one deluded person has to become convinced that times have changed; there will be, *in principle*, the same honesty and good faith of long ago, but nowadays there is more supply and there is, therefore, a need to fight for the customer with competitors."[137] Aiming to capture the growing mass of consumers, Argentine and foreign firms used all available strategies to increase the number of buyers.

Massive use of advertising became one of the strategies on which national industry put more emphasis. In so doing, domestic brands shaped part of the Argentine people's daily life, and the existence of industrial firms became apparent not only to workers and masters, but also to everyone else. If sales practices made commerce an intermediary between the factory and the individual, advertising set up a bridge (however abstract) between industry and the customer by imposing the specific brand over the generic name of a product, leading to a decline in bulk sales. The merchant was no longer the sole source of knowledge on product quality. The client now came in with a clear idea of the desired brand. Publicity, indeed, puts the merely commercial relationship that exists between seller and buyer in second place and enhances the links between producer and consumer, who acquired an expertise previously monopolized by merchants.[138] This fact was clear to the CGF when it initiated an advertising campaign that awarded bonuses to its match customers in 1924:

> Variations in the price paid by consumers do not represent for them a real advantage. To increase the consumption of matches produced by this company it is necessary to find a way for the consumer to promote his own interest. This will go against the natural resistance and apathy of merchants who only look out for their own interest and prefer the cheapest article regardless of the brand.[139]

These changes took a long time to develop, but the seeds for the transformation were sown at the turn of the twentieth century.

Although the use of advertisements in Buenos Aires can be traced back to the cries of street vendors in colonial times or to the announcements in the postindependence *Telégrafo Mercantil*, the first advertising campaign had a more recent birth date. In 1864, Melville Bagley—who had seen the effects of publicity in his native United States—kept the city population in suspense with ads announcing *Se viene la Hesperidina* (Hesperidina is coming), without explaining what that strange name meant. The mystery was finally revealed: Hesperidina was a liqueur, whose great success was largely due to advertising. Inhabitants of the Argentine capital made jokes, created songs, and included the word Hesperidina in their vocabulary. But this was just the beginning of a life invaded by local brands.[140]

Little by little, other firms became convinced of the virtues of Mr. Bagley's strategy. Jam producer Noel started to advertise during the Continental Exhibition of 1882. Up to then, the company had sold on a small scale as "the circle of its relations slowly and tediously increased, based on the real value of its products and without the intervention of publicity."[141] In spite of its advantages, industrialists did not adopt advertising very rapidly. In 1891, *La Prensa* found this to be one of the causes of customer preference for imported goods:

> The country's manufacturers are largely responsible for this marked preference. They limit their advertising to merchants and wholesalers when introducing their products into the market and forget to make

them known to the consumer public who are the ones who will finally determine by their demand the acceptance of the article in the
market.[142]

It was not until the twentieth century that advertising campaigns became
significant. Previously, people searching for a specific item looked at the
brief, dry, and boring classified ads in the newspapers. Now, illustrated announcements aimed at attracting the casual reader. The change deepened
when emphasis moved from providing information to persuading potential
customers. Innovative magazines—such as *Caras y Caretas*, *Fray Mocho*, and
PBT—born at the turn of the twentieth century not only included folklore,
humor, and caricatures but also dedicated an ample and unusual amount of
space to advertising. The circular letter announcing the appearance of *Caras
y Caretas* in 1898 promised that the magazine "would be composed of at
least 20 pages, fourteen dedicated to text and the rest to advertisements."
This strategy turned out to be beneficial for the magazines, which found an
alternate means of financing that was more lucrative and stable than the traditional subscription, and for the firms, which discovered a wide receptive
audience in the numerous editions of these publications. In addition, these
periodicals learned how to deal with the market and offered their expertise
to facilitate the task of selling goods.[143]

Advertisements included unrealistic treatments for diseases, tonics against
baldness, and fortuneteller services as well as a wide variety of industrial
goods whose producers wanted to distance themselves from the former.
There was, as in other countries that had experienced the rise of advertising, a cohabitation of the old and false types of announcements for impossible cures with the new ones based on a relationship of trust between
consumer and producer. In this last sense, the ad was allegedly only a way to
sell goods to people in remote areas or provinces.[144] Cigarettes occupied a
special place in industrial publicity. As *La Nación* pointed out, "[T]obacco
manufacture is perhaps one of the industries whose survival depends heavily on the resources of advertising."[145] This was a universal phenomenon due
to the ease in differentiating brands. But in Argentina it was even more
important, since cigarette producers, unlike in the United States, never succeeded in creating a pool that encompassed all the firms. Tough competition and the need to broaden a market that could be smoothly supplied
through the acquisition of more Bonsack machines combined to foster a
commercial war. Company Piccardo started in 1898 in a bedroom with its
two proprietors as the sole workers; in 1910 it had become a large firm with
more than four hundred laborers (see Table 1.6). Asked about the reason for

such impressive success, one of its owners answered with two responses. One was a cliché—they had maintained quality—but the other was more perceptive:

> [W]e have advertised a lot. . . . We have announcements everywhere, in the city, in the countryside, on the walls and in the public spots and, especially, in the newspapers. . . . We are persuaded of the advantage we gained from the public always keeping us present in their view and their memory.[146]

Rather than imposing a culture, brand symbolism usually expressed people's feelings. Potential military conflict with Chile in the early 1900s left a long heritage of bellicose names for several brands: shoes *El Soldado* (The Soldier), textiles *El Patriota* (The Patriot), hardware *Bandera* (Flag), cigarettes *Guerra* (War) and *Marte* (Mars), foodstuff *Lancero* (Lancer), pepper *Escudo* (National Coat of Arms). Brands were also an opportunity to expose manufacturers' beliefs, such as the various names of virgins—the national patroness at Luján being the most popular—for ready-to-wear articles, biscuits, and jams.[147]

The rise of the brand as a phenomenon, in turn, fed back into the process since it needed advertising to sustain consumer loyalty. The cigarette producer Compañía Argentina de Tabacos had an advertising department with draftsmen to design posters and ads. The company believed that, "for advertising to be effective it is necessary, first and foremost, that the article promoted in the announcement corresponds with the excellence proclaimed, otherwise it will be useless."[148] Brand wars (as a particular phenomenon of company battles) were ruthless; some fell vanquished while others became market stars. One of the most successful and long-lasting cigarette brands was the Piccardo company's *43*. Aimed at embracing the largest possible market, the *43* advertised itself as "the cigarette for all ages." Posters included different images to captivate the highest number of consumers. In a complex interplay those images could correspond either to the potential customer's real situation or to a variety of fantasies. One of the *43* posters showed an elegant man to whom smoking added a touch of distinction, an image attractive to the actual rich as well as to those who wanted to copy him; another highlighted a badly dressed worker who found in the cigarette a pause from his long day, while yet another showed a *linyera* (homeless person) who smoked with unrestrained pleasure. And posters were also directed at a market that other sources do not show: the child smoking openly and happily, the relaxed woman who found gender emancipation in a puff of smoke, the elder who looks to the horizon with a cigarette in his lips.[149]

Piccardo's competitors did not lay behind in their advertising efforts. Prizes for customers started to become a common practice in industries that could easily produce on a large scale; such was the case of the soap firm Campana that promoted its bars and cakes of laundry soap by offering to exchange lottery tickets for a certain number of wrappers.[150] Similarly, the Compañía General de Tabacos inserted a number in their *La Popular* brand packages that, if matched with the National lottery, rewarded the fortunate holder with clocks, chains, suits, hats, and berets. Later, it started to give a 20 percent refund to smokers who returned empty packs.[151] Searching for even more appeal, the firm launched a big raffle of lots in new neighborhoods in Buenos Aires, Rosario, and Córdoba. All of them were called Villa Posse, using the surname of the company's owner. This campaign featured a man reaching for the *Gran Premio* (Great Prize) over a big pile of cigarette packages. The firm—which possessed capital assets of paper $1,000,000—spent paper $1,500,000 on a long-lasting campaign reported by the British visitor Reginald Lloyd as "the greatest . . . ever undertaken in South America."[152] At that time, the market looked saturated. A consumer universe in which almost everybody smoked, crossing gender, class, and age barriers, seemed to eliminate the possibility of converting nonsmokers into smokers and therefore fostering a larger demand. Thus, manufacturers had to advertise aggressively to keep a share of the market.

Advertising in general not only aimed at filling a larger portion of the demand, it also strove to enlarge the market itself with new consumers by offering new products, new qualities, or just new announcements. In the case of imported goods, the dealers sometimes had to create a market *ex nihilo*. On occasion, success in selling the article was so great that it prompted import houses to manufacture in Argentina. That was the case of the lens-importing firm Lutz y Schultz, which became the leading local company in its field as Lutz Ferrando. It entered the business of importing antiseptic furniture and surgery implements. The increasing medical activity and the asepsis fever that trendy hygienism brought created a market, in which the state played a crucial role through the building of numerous public hospitals, large enough to prompt the firm to produce domestically the goods it used to import.[153] Other times, importing continued being the only activity. This was the case with the Lepage firm (agent of Eastman Kodak), which promoted its new and still-strange photographic equipment with an announcement in the newspapers. In the advertisement, the goal of which was to show how easy it was to operate a camera,

a young woman takes a photograph in the middle of a gorgeous park, next to a sumptuous chalet. According to the motto of this announcement, house Lepage put this useful and artistic amusement within everybody's reach, simple, easy and cheap. And the official announcement was successful.[154]

By observing cultural trends, advertising recognized the growing importance of the female consumer. Women were a symbol that firms used to create a market; if a woman used a camera, it was assumed all men could. Moreover, women were themselves advertising targets for products like perfumed soap. An ad might address its potential customers by asking: "Girls, do you want a husband? Use liquid soap Gargot."[155] Locally manufactured cooking goods targeted females as decision makers in home purchases. Thus, chocolate brand Aguila-Saint used an advertisement contrasting two women. On one side there was an old, perspiring lady laboriously preparing chocolate using a traditional method in front of an old-fashioned coffeepot. On the other side was a young, shapely, relaxed housewife dropping the product into boiling milk. The print said, "a new fast and economical procedure to prepare chocolate" that portrayed, together with the image, a new woman who had been transformed from a cook into a meal dispenser.[156]

Announcements covered the entire city—outdoor publicity on billboards, in parks, on electrically lighted curtains, in train stations, on tramways, and, in the case of Buenos Aires, on the subway.[157] Around 1920, advertising had reached such a level of sophistication that it surprised a specialist sent to Latin America by the U.S. Department of Commerce. According to the envoy, Argentina was behind his own country (the most advanced in the matter) but well ahead of the rest of the region. Indeed, Argentina was the only place south of the Rio Grande where advertising agencies had a role "in the organization and use of the media in the way the United States is used to."[158] The importance of promotion sales was a widely noticed peculiarity. In a book aimed at increasing the import of Spanish goods, the author pointed out to his compatriots that

> In turning the pages of an Argentine newspaper or magazine, or taking a stroll on a street of Buenos Aires, we realize the enormous sums that are spent on advertising. . . . Advertisements are expensive compared to those of other countries.[159]

Another investigation in 1913 by the same U.S. agency proved the Spaniard's last assertion. This report showed that the prices charged by Argentine newspapers for announcements were double those of their counterparts in Brazil and Mexico, a gap that became a chasm when compared to the most backward countries of Latin America.[160]

Argentines, however, did not follow the same pattern as the American public. Believing they did, U.S.-based International Schools had appealed to the image of the average and anonymous citizen to promote their correspondence courses. This campaign was a resounding failure. The company achieved success only after obtaining local advice and using announcements with the portraits of inventor Thomas A. Edison and former president Domingo F. Sarmiento. Indeed, the Argentine public loved being identified with great men rather than regular people. Thus, use of independence or political heroes became a common practice. No figure was more popular than Bartolomé Mitre, loved to an extreme by Argentines and immigrants, and the longevity of whose life allowed him to see (and to approve with delight) the use of his name and his fame in a wide variety of brands for consumer goods.[161]

In its efforts to influence the potential consumer, advertising includes not only the dissemination of information but also all those practices with "publicity significance" such as window displays and packaging. The obsession with the former reached such a peak that in 1910 the already mentioned Reginald Lloyd noted with surprise that

> London and Paris stores have nothing to teach the window displayers of the Argentine capital. Indeed, the exhibition of electric lights, covering with a multitude of lamps all . . . these large stores that sell clothing, is probably unique in the world of decoration.[162]

Although department stores were at the cutting edge of window dressing, factories also had ample opportunity to use the system, since they usually possessed a downtown sales showroom, such as Singer had pioneered in the United States.[163]

Window displays may have attracted the attention of Buenos Aires visitors in 1910, but that had not been the case twenty or thirty years earlier. In those years, as Aníbal Latino pointed out, the windows of the luxurious stores did not "draw one's attention in the city, especially since some of these shops dim at night for scarcity of lighting." At that time, what "attracted most of the attention of those new to the city were the peddlers with their shouting."[164]

Packaging played a significant role in the new consumption habits. On the one hand, packing was necessary to keep the merchandise fresh. On the other hand, persuasion was at work in the appearance of the product, a new approach that left aside the old times when "form did not influence nor modify the price: only endurance was sought."[165] By the end of the century, presentation became crucial for the success of a product in a competitive market. Thus, when the firm Noel decided to compete with imported goods in the jam market, it made a special effort to offer its product in "luxurious packaging" with a "golden label."[166] A bright presentation was especially important. As a visitor pointed out, "Argentines love the new and whatever attracts the eye," which justified the color and variety of cigarette packs, as well as flint match boxes that, using the portrait of a famous actress on the back side, had surpassed Italian imports in the 1880s.[167]

Firms offered a new commercial instrument—the sales catalogue—that proved to be one of the most effective methods of stimulating consumer interest. The sales catalogue had existed in the nineteenth century, but its sophistication grew enormously when the already mentioned Lepage company led an innovative campaign to transform catalogues from a source of information for the customer into an instrument for improving sales. Soon, firms such as metallurgical producer Vasena followed the trend, publishing a catalogue of two volumes. These were the first to include drawings, with which they took great pains, instead of merely listing prices with article names. Such novelties earned the praise of the UIA, since they "reveal[ed] that our industrialists have begun to understand that merchandise is of no value if it is not well presented in good ads or in good catalogues."[168] Between 1900 and 1910, the department store A la Ciudad de Londres began to prepare special catalogues for each of its new sections: children, ladies, and gentlemen. As a complement, it published the fashion magazine *La Elegancia* (The Elegance), which subscribers received at no charge.[169]

Argentine industrialists used advertising much more effectively and extensively than did foreign producers. A U.S. expert noted the horrible mistakes made by sellers from his country. They included misspelling Spanish words in the ads, offending nationalistic feelings by using the American flag, forgetting the reversal of the seasons in the Southern Hemisphere by promoting clothes for warm weather in July, and violating the Argentine sense of superiority by calling them South Americans.[170] Similarly, the British Consul complained that "advertisements were rarely received from British firms."[171] As a result, a U.S. governmental agent concluded that his country's manufacturers were prisoners of the local merchant who only made an effort to stimulate consumption of imports through advertising when local goods were not available.[172] When there was competition between the domestic and the foreign product, the local merchant often found it more comfortable to deal with Argentine producers, who also had an additional advantage since the same manufacturer was in charge of publicity.

The development of modern methods for publicizing products gave larger businesses a significant advantage. Small Argentine firms could not use the most modern commercial methods and were even threatened by them. Thus, when asking for a *convocatoria de acreedores* (meeting of creditors), haberdasher Ramón Carnota commented on the origins of his failure—the curse of keeping large stocks of out-of-fashion clothes:

> Large houses, with their powerful advertising means and the substantial sums of financial outlay daily invested totally swallow up the clientele of the middle-size houses and put these in grave trouble.[173]

The victory of big business paralleled the unfolding of a consumer society that created a new market. Then, demand gave Argentine industry the opportunity to produce in larger scale and to surmount, albeit only partially, the problem of capacity excess. Major transformations in the supply sphere fostered that triumph.

Chapter 3

The Victory of Big Business:
Industrial Growth in the First Decades
of the Twentieth Century

Renewed Optimism

Argentina had been recovering slowly from the deep depression suffered at the beginning of the 1890s. Pessimism and anxiety cast a pall on the economic atmosphere of the new century. Although a fast recovery had been expected since the short crisis of 1897–98, the turbulence in international financial markets during 1900 and 1901 delayed its arrival. Moreover, the threat of potential conflict with Chile grew, and any good news about economic growth was regarded as fragile as peace. By 1900, the *Review of the River Plate* attempted to infuse a sense of optimism. It reported that

> Capital . . . continues, and will continue, to flow into this country, population is undoubtedly increasing, production will follow suit, and although we shall from time to time suffer temporary checks, such as have happened to us during the past year, nothing can prevent the onward march of civilisation and progress in Argentina except war, which we hope and believe is in the highest degree improbable.[1]

The pact signed with Chile in 1902 changed the general mood. When fear of war ended, it set loose an unexpected tide of affluence. A mood of confidence boosted credit, while bankruptcies and moratoriums dropped from forty-four to ten million pesos between 1902 and 1904.[2] At the end of 1904, a U.S. consular report said, "The Argentine Republic has just completed the *most favorable year in its history*."[3] In 1905, the Italian Francesco Scardin, in an impressionistic but revealing description, observed how much the economic scene had changed. Whereas some years before, "[e]very-where one could only hear discouraging words, as if Argentina were on the verge of an immense universal bankruptcy," now the country "has been rapidly reborn and has recovered, with a youthful impulse, its faith in the destiny of grandeur that once seemed to falter."[4] By 1906, Argentina had finished solving the last remnants of the default declared after the 1890 cri-sis, and a year later the country's bonds restarted negotiation in the interna-tional financial market.[5]

By 1904, the feverish economic expansion of the 1880s had returned, but it was now based upon more diversified activities in both exports (with the boom in cereals and beef) and the domestic market. This boom further es-tablished industry in the Argentinian economy. Growth rates were impres-sive for those times. In the period 1903–1913, the GDP increased at an es-timated annual rate of 7.7 percent, while the per capita ratio rose annually by 3.4 percent. Industrial growth jumped even higher, reaching a rate of 9.6 percent. A recession triggered by a crisis in 1913 slowed down expansion through the First World War, but the country regained its economic spirits in the 1920s. During that decade, the GDP, the income per capita, and the industrial output grew at rates of, according to the more conservative esti-mates, 3.5, 1.0, and 4.3 percent respectively. Immigration regained strength after the war, and in 1922 the net annual balance surpassed the number of 100,000. Net immigration rounded 1,030,000 people in the period 1919–1930, with an increasing number of newcomers from Eastern Europe and the Middle East. By 1930, the country had more than twelve million in-habitants. The export profile of a beef and cereal exporter strengthened; the physical volume of exports in the late 1920s doubled that of 1910, and better-quality and higher-price items, such as chilled beef, began to stand out in the international trade. These were the glory days for Argentina: the coun-try seemed at last to have shed its history and seated itself at the table of the richest nations in the world (see Tables 1.1 and 3.1).

As mentioned in the Introduction, scholars have blamed the lack of industry from the 1870s through 1930 for Argentina's failure to fulfill its promise in the rest of the twentieth century. This is what makes analysis of the evolution of manufacturing during the Belle Époque an intriguing sub-ject. Industry encountered a favorable environment in the first decade of the twentieth century. Most of the protective tariffs passed in 1891 remained in place, while state intervention halted the appreciation of domestic currency that had been ongoing during the 1890s, and the resulting decrease in import

TABLE 3.1

Per Capita GDP, Argentina, Mexico, Brazil, Great Britain,
United States, Italy, and Spain, 1870–1913

(at 1985 $ U.S. relative prices)

	Argentina	Mexico	Brazil	Great Britain	United States	Italy	Spain
1870	1,039	700	615	2,693	2,244	1,216	1,221
1890	1,515	762	641	3,383	4,846	1,352	1,355
1913	2,370	1,121	697	4,152	4,846	2,079	2,212

SOURCE: My own elaboration based on Angus Maddison, "Explaining the Economic Performance of Nations, 1820–1989," in William J. Baumol, Richard R. Nelson, and Edward N. Wolff, *Convergence of Productivity: Cross-National Studies and Historical Evidence* (Oxford: Oxford University Press, 1994), Table 2.1, p. 22.

prices (see Table 1.9). In 1899 the government issued a convertibility law (enforced two years later) that pegged Argentine currency to the gold standard. Because the government also wanted to encourage exports, the exchange rate was established at a level that overvalued gold (and foreign currency), thus benefiting domestic industry since imports became more expensive. This practice lasted until 1914, when Argentina (as did the rest of the world) abandoned the gold standard due to the First World War. Francisco Seguí, the incumbent president of the Argentine Industrial Union (UIA), made this clear in a speech at the First Industrial Congress, declaring that "the convertibility law saved the industries of Argentina."[6]

Although some import substitution existed, the 1903–1913 period contrasted with the 1890s in the fostering of manufacturing output increase mainly through aggregate demand rise. This increase transformed industrial supply by promoting mechanization and, eventually, standardization of production. Industrial growth in the golden decade from 1903 to 1913 and in the 1920s is explained by the expansion of the domestic market, whose consumption features were analyzed in Chapter 2, rather than in tariffs imposed by the government, as occurred after 1876 and 1891. But the firms already born under the protective system continued to produce and even enlarged their output. Tariffs for those items continued, and local firms took advantage of the expansion of the domestic market. As a result of this development, some firms shifted to large-scale production, transforming the realm of supply from 1900 to 1913. If the most salient feature of the largest factories in the late 1880s and 1890s was some mechanization, the new century witnessed (again in only a few mills) the rise of a modest standardization. At times preceding the rise in demand, at others motivated by it, the top firms consolidated labor into larger units, integrated several work processes, and incorporated power-driven machinery, helped by the installation of an electrical

TABLE 3.2

Total GDP, Argentina, Mexico, Brazil, Great Britain,
United States, Italy, and Spain, 1870 and 1913

(at 1985 $ U.S. relative prices, in thousands)

	Argentina	Mexico	Brazil	Great Britain	United States	Italy	Spain
1870	1,866	6,453	6,025	78,937	89,897	33,912	19,715
1913	18,137	16,782	16,491	176,967	472,999	77,439	44,970

SOURCE: My own elaboration based on Angus Maddison, "Explaining the Economic Performance of Nations, 1820–1989," in William J. Baumol, Richard R. Nelson, and Edward N. Wolff, *Convergence of Productivity: Cross-National Studies and Historical Evidence* (Oxford: Oxford University Press, 1994), Tables 2.1 and 2.4, pp. 22 and 27.

network in the largest cities, to produce in previously unknown quantities.[7]

In spite of its achievements, industrial production ran against serious limitations that overcast the future of industrialization in Argentina. The demand side pendulumed between weakness and strength. From 1910 to 1930 Argentina had (as Table 1.1 shows) a relatively high GDP per capita while it transformed into a consumer society. This reshaped the country after the features of a mass market, though not all of them. By 1913, a successful economic year, Argentina's GDP per capita ranked tenth in the world after Australia, Austria, Belgium, Britain, Canada, Denmark, New Zealand, Switzerland, and the United States, but it was higher than France and Germany. Due to the small population, the total size of the market was (as Table 3.2 indicates) not large enough to promote mass production to the full extent of the most industrialized countries. The Argentine total national GDP was 12 percent of that of the British or German; compared to the United States, it was even lower: just 6 percent of the U.S. total GDP. The domestic market was, in cold numbers, lower than the Belgian and the Dutch domestic markets and not much higher than those of Sweden or Denmark.[8] These countries, however, created a well-developed industrial sector through exports. The Argentine experience in that arena was, to say the least, disappointing. Calls to find markets abroad when excess capacity became apparent at the turn of the twentieth century were renewed in subsequent years, but industry could not employ this strategy due to its structural limitations. Nor, incidentally, were improvements made. For example, the importance of investment in human capital, proven so successful in the Belgian, Dutch, and Scandinavian cases, was not grasped by a state more concerned with educating immigrant children for the Argentine nation than establishing industrial schools.[9] In the midst of the growth between the first decade of the twentieth century to the Great Depression, Argentine industry went through booms and recessions, experienced expansion as well as setbacks, and encountered both rising consumption in the sphere of demand and excess capacity in the world of supply. This chapter focuses on that period of industrial development and structural transformation, some of which lasted decades.

An Expanding Supply

"Argentina is one of the best markets in the world," said the Italian visitor Genaro Bevioni in 1910.[10] Such an enthusiastic overstatement held a pinch of truth in that the country, making up only eight percent of Latin America's population, accounted for one-third of all imports into the region. British records from 1919 showed that the Argentine market for British products accounted for more than 42 percent of the Latin American demand; as the Commercial Secretary of His Majesty's Embassy in Buenos Aires said, "The Argentine market is by far the most valuable among the Republics of Central and South America to British manufacturers." By 1928, Argentina was the third largest foreign buyer of British goods.[11] This position had been achieved in the wake of the nation's transformations at the turn of the twentieth century. While the Argentine total GDP in 1870 was a third of that of Brazil and Mexico, it had surpassed them by 1913 (see Tables 3.1 and 3.2).[12] If this was good news for a local industry that was already working with excess capacity in the late 1890s, the expansion of state expenditures from 194,957,082 to 419,639,608 hard currency pesos between 1904 and 1914 was further assurance of a more stable demand from this traditional customer. Local production provided the state needs, as already mentioned in Chapter 1, in the expanding activities of administration, education, and health.[13]

No industrial power wanted to miss the opportunity to sell its goods to the growing Argentine market. Americans and Germans became aggressive and tried innovative commercialization methods.[14] Within their more limited capacities, Spain, Belgium, Italy, and France followed suit.[15] All this interest prompted a commercial war with Britain, the traditional supplier. As an American observed in 1916,

> Buenos Aires is undoubtedly the biggest competitive market in all
> classes of goods in South or Central America. In some lines it is the
> biggest in the world. It is hard for a person who has never visited the
> Argentine market to realize how severe the competition there is in
> normal times. There are probably more representatives of firms of different nationalities concentrated in Buenos Aires than in almost any
> other city that can be mentioned. . . . The United States is new at the

South American game, whereas Germany and England have been doing business there on a large scale for a number of years.[16]

In the light of all this competition, the new century seemed to portend a pessimistic future for British exports to the South American country. What is striking, therefore, is the resilience that enabled Britain to retain a top position (around a third of all imports) in the Argentine market during the first years of the new century, until the beginning of the First World War. One explanation might be the pressure exerted over this "informal colony," in which the former nation was the main investor and the largest commercial customer. The complicated nature of British interests—already illustrated in Chapter 1—in addition to the way the Argentine authorities played the war between imperial powers to their own benefit, as both local and British sources show, suggests otherwise.[17] A better explanation should emphasize those features of the Argentine economy that helped the British to maintain their role as major exporters up to the 1920s. First, their ownership of the railways assured the monopoly supply of necessary equipment, which included a third of capital goods imports. Second, tariffs protected the coarsest goods while British exports were, generally, of the highest quality, especially in textiles. Finally, Britain remained the main supplier for Argentine industry inputs and machinery until the First World War. Although Britain could maintain its preeminence for longer than could be expected, especially in the provision of textiles, equipment, and industrial inputs, these years saw the introduction of American goods, from cars to agricultural machinery, that appeared as a novelty in the nascent consumer society of the early part of the century but finally displaced the role of British articles in the 1920s.[18]

This international competition for the Argentine market made importation of goods easier. The usual scenario that had local commercial houses asking for merchandise from foreign manufacturers was replaced by one in which the latter offered their goods to the importers.[19] To some extent, this change hurt domestic industries because it reduced transaction costs for imports. The economy, however, was growing so quickly that domestic industry could expand together with imports.

The shoe industry faced a supply boom when American firms provided machines for local factories. This was part of a worldwide strategy led by the United Shoe Company under a leasing system that charged Argentine producers according to the output (each device had a counter that marked the number of articles made).[20] In the six years between 1903 and 1909, the U.S. firm installed 1,330 machines. In 1910, *La Nación* observed, "the classic and popular shoemaker has been replaced by the real wonders of mechanical invention, admirable machines, which reveal the inventive genius of the North Americans."[21]

In the following years, the strategy spread and, by the 1920s, 416 of 450 firms rented American machinery. In the meantime, Singer Company followed a similar path and opened local agencies to assist with complementary equipment to sew leather shoes. As a result, local mills started to manufacture fine shoes instead of their former output of the roughly nailed articles.[22]

This leasing system fostered a peculiar mechanization that did not require high investment. Cheap access to technology made the opening of a modern shoe factory easier, as was the case for the Italian immigrant Antonio Uboldi. After working at a shoe factory for eleven years, Uboldi had saved enough money to open a workshop with three workers in 1900. Nineteen years later, he owned a shoe factory that employed 270 people. These factories mushroomed and, as an American observer noted,

> Many cobblers or retail store owners became manufacturers almost
> overnight, by means of the facilities offered by the American shoe-
> machinery company, and amassed fortunes in the business in a
> few years . . . and are at the present competing with the larger
> manufacturers.[23]

Despite the pressure from industrialists to transform leasing into buying, and thus avoid competition from petty producers, the system continued and eventually led to overproduction and price wars. By the First World War, the domestic output provided most of the demand, with the exception of the highest-quality shoes and special items, such as those for sports and babies.[24]

Mechanization also permeated the tobacco industry. Although not as lucky as shoe producers, cigarette manufacturers were making intense use of the relatively inexpensive Bonsack machines by 1900 and beyond. This transformation dramatically increased productivity and boosted the capital-labor ratio. The firm Piccardo, for example, expanded its annual output of 15,000 packages per worker to 189,000 between 1900 and 1912.[25] The growing consumption of cigarettes, described in Chapter 2, underwrote the increasing output of a standardized article. Only the production of *toscanos* (cigars), representing a mere 13 percent of tobacco products, remained a labor intensive and handicraft activity.[26]

Due to the lack of grain elevators, the agricultural boom fostered demand for the burlap bags used to pack cereals and linseed. In 1900–1910 the productive profile of the country had transformed, and agriculture had gained space to the detriment of cattle products. Agriculture products composed

48 percent of exports in 1901–1905 and 57 percent in 1906–1910, from less than 2 percent in 1876–1880 and 18 percent in 1886–1890.[27] The daily output of one large producer, La Primitiva, rose from one hundred to two hundred and fifty thousand bags between 1890 and 1905, while the largest cereal export company, Bunge y Born, opened a mill to manufacture these items in Buenos Aires. In addition, the quality of the bags improved, and they became less likely to break on the way to the port.[28] The development of a cereal economy in the Pampas also increased the demand for alpargatas shoes. By 1910, the Fábrica Argentina produced four and a half million pairs annually. This represented one pair for each inhabitant.[29] As *La Nación* noted,

> The use of alpargatas has become most common amongst the working classes of Argentina, more especially in the rural districts, as many look upon the article as one of essential and habitual use. Workers engaged in the loading and unloading of vessels on the docks and laborers employed in different trades and factories wear nothing else on their feet for six days of the week. In fact, all of the vast number of people engaged in such labors [wear alpargatas], for the flexibility and light weight of the shoe is easier on one's feet, apart from the fact that its cost is within the reach of the poorest.[30]

Firms producing foodstuffs and beverages targeted the expanding domestic market. On the one hand, change occurred in quantity; some companies became larger, such as the chocolate producer Bassi, which invested in building new mills to meet the growing demand.[31] On the other hand, the quality of goods improved and drove out imports. The biscuit producer Bagley, also expanding its factory, hired an English expert to prepare the most refined products, which eventually replaced almost all foreign goods.[32] Soft-drink manufacturers took advantage of the nonalcoholic hygienic trend, advertised their products as healthy items, and benefited from sanitary prohibitions on imports, producing their products for the first time in large factories.[33] The main quantitative transformations of the beverage industry, however, occurred in beer production. To increase its output, as noted in Chapter 2, Bieckert moved to a gigantic factory in a suburb of Buenos Aires. Sales quadrupled in only three years.[34] Meanwhile, Quilmes continued enlarging its already substantial works while labor productivity improved: between 1895 and 1915 the ratios capital to worker and sales to worker rose from 18,444 to 42,832 and from 10,000 to 19,533, respectively.[35]

Greater demand for edibles and drinks prompted the production of pots and pans; one producer, O. Schnaith–Ferrum, began large-scale production with U.S. and German machinery.[36] Rising consumption of food and beverages also necessitated the packaging of items. The local paper industry met forty percent of Argentina's demand in the 1910s and achieved success with colored paper, especially the cheap brown variety known as *papel de estraza* used in stores for wrapping parcels.[37]

Rising supply had some other multiplier effects. The expansion in shoe production fostered the enlargement and mechanization of tanning companies in the period 1900–1913. In 1901, European investors encouraged by a German expert formed a company in Antwerp to acquire an old Argentine tannery. Soon the firm—renamed L'Industrielle Belge—was producing almost half a million leather pieces annually, meeting almost all the needs of the entire local market.[38] With the infusion of fresh capital from Argentine businessmen another tannery, Gaggino-Lauret, mechanized, enlarged, and even began to export leather.[39] Beer expansion fostered the success of the main glass producer, Rigolleau, which moved to a suburb of Buenos Aires, near the breweries of Bieckert and Quilmes, to produce bottles on a larger scale. The firm, however, did not limit itself to supplying breweries. At its new location, it invested in major technical improvements that diversified its production to include table articles and flat glass.[40]

Metallurgical companies experienced significant changes when consumption of iron and steel per inhabitant more than doubled in those expansive years.[41] Transformations mainly occurred in three different areas: (1) bolts, nuts, rivets, nails, and pins; (2) metal structures for construction; and (3) agricultural implements. The production of small hardware items encouraged the standardized production that had had a timid beginning in the 1890s. By the 1910s, the two metallurgical firms that had led this transformation were the largest in the country: Vasena and TAMET (Talleres Metalúrgicos San Martín). A propagandist for the former remarked that "the ultimate feature of the works is the part dedicated to the manufacturing of pins."[42] This comment is indicative of the type of simple goods Argentine industry was producing. Nevertheless, methods used in these "modern shops" surprised a U.S. Department of Commerce expert. In addition, the largest firms were engaged in a strategy to increase the economies of scope through the production of a variety of new standardized items, such as iron hoops and metal sheets.[43]

Construction was especially blessed by the booming economy. As Francisco Liernur has shown, this was the era in which Buenos Aires was transformed from a "fragile" (in terms of building materials) city of wood into a "solid" metropolis built in large part of metal and cement.[44] As a result, Vasena enlarged its business in metallic construction material and TAMET initiated the production of metal pipes. Moreover, building structures prompted both firms to enter experimental steel production in the 1910s.[45]

Steel production had begun in a small workshop in 1896, Pinoges company, later Talleres Metalúrgicos Vulcano. Initially, Pinoges produced pieces of molded steel, then eventually began manufacturing steel building materials.[46] This small company was just producing steel as an extravagance; larger firms needed to take over the task. However, experiments at TAMET stopped when the Luxembourg-based ARBED group seized a large portion of the company's shares in the 1920s. The restrictions on steel production by oligopolistic firms in Western Europe led to the creation of the International Steel Cartel in 1926. Since ARBED was one of the cartel's engines, it prevented the development of local steel production in Argentina. It was not until 1933, when a French consortium that was not a cartel member opened the Hierromat company, that domestic steel production began in a more promising way.[47]

A rise in the production of agricultural implements allowed some establishments to transform themselves into large factories. An old workshop led by Basque entrepreneurs became a large manufacturer of agricultural appliances. In 1904, the firm—renamed as La Cantábrica after the Cantabric Sea that faces the Basque Country—attributed its ability "to satisfy all its orders with desirable punctuality" to the investments made in the previous years. The strategy had proven successful, and the company's sales grew at an annual rate of 7.6 percent between 1903 and 1913.[48] Similarly, in 1904 La Acero Platense, formerly the workshop Schwartz, doubled its output and devoted itself to iron lamination: the key to its success was its concentration on the production of buckles used in the countryside.[49]

A few textile firms achieved particular success. The old company Prat received fresh money from local investors; newer Dell' Acqua multiplied its capital four times between 1900 and 1905; and emerging Campomar invested in new areas: wool spinning, cashmeres, and blankets.[50] A kind of international division of labor was established between Argentine and Yorkshire woolen textile firms, the former producing blankets, a product that Britain sold in large numbers throughout its empire, and the latter still providing all other woolen and especially higher-quality worsted goods.[51] There was some foreign capital invested in textiles. Besides the already mentioned Manchester-based firm Ashworth and Italian Dell'Acqua, the Belgian company Gratry and the Catalan Masllorens opened mills to produce hosiery goods in the Argentine capital.[52] The ready-to-wear industry continued to be the most successful of any textile branch. New suppliers of staggering strength appeared in the form of department stores that produced a large proportion of their commercialized clothing in their own mills.[53]

In 1919, a U.S. Department of Commerce envoy stated that "[i]ndustrial growth in Argentina during the last twenty years has been surprising. Scarcely forty years ago the country was practically without an industry."[54] His observations were quite accurate. As Table 1.6 shows (and the stories of every branch of industry illustrate), industrial firms experienced significant growth in that period. The success of large firms in this almost epic history was, however, far from indicative of a full-fledged industrialization process. Major limits and shortcomings had yet to be overcome.

The Limits of Industrial Production

For all its success, Argentina by the 1920s was not an industrialized country by the standards of Britain, Germany, or the United States. While modern technology and new production methods pervaded some industrial activities, others operated on a primitive scale. In some branches of industry, only the most basic production was made locally; in others, no domestic output existed and all consumption was supplied by imports. Limitations, which had already become apparent in the earliest stages of industrialization, continued unresolved during the first decades of the twentieth century. The lack of energy sources, such as coal or hydraulic power, continued to be a major problem, while experiments with oil—discovered in 1907—had poor results.[55] In the 1920s, the lack of combustibles was a hindrance for the metallurgical activity.[56] Also, access to crucial raw materials remained poor. Iron was not yet exploited nor silk or jute cultivated, while cotton (or fibers to replace it) did not show the expected growth.[57] Finally, the dependence of the Argentine domestic market on the booms and busts of the export economy destabilized demand and encouraged industrialists to keep investments low in order to reduce variable costs in the case of a reducing consumption. The case of the Bagley firm during the period 1905–1926, in which we have complete data of sales and costs, is quite telling, as Figure 3.1 shows. Sales of cookies were tied to the ups and downs of the Argentine market, which was dependent on the performance of exports. Thus, a decline in sales could be faced by lowering variable costs (inputs and labor) but a very different situation would have occurred if fixed costs had been a major part of the company's general expenses.

Lack of raw materials was an impediment to cotton textile production, a sector in which Argentina—in contrast with its other industries—was well behind Mexico and Brazil.[58] It was so underdeveloped that amazed contemporaries were appalled by the dependence of cotton-weaving firms on foreign inputs. Bureaucrat Federico Cibils lamented the fact that while

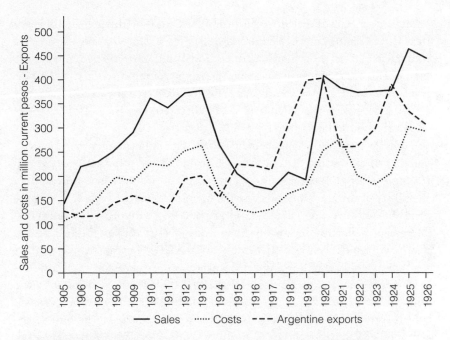

Figure 3.1.   Bagley Sales and Costs: Argentine Exports, 1905–1926

SOURCES: Bagley S. A. Archives and *Anuarios del Comercio Exterior Argentino.*

"[t]he seven woolen textile factories that exist in the capital city each have their own spinning or weaving . . . cotton spinning is missing." [59] Although Lancashire thrived on the importation of raw cotton and efficient production, Argentina was far from playing a similar role in Latin America. Only very high tariffs on cotton yarn would have promoted spinning activity, but duties on that item were low. [60] The first cotton-spinning mill, the stock company Hilanderías Argentinas de Algodón, didn't open until 1905. Its fate was tied to its own cotton plantations in the Northern Chaco region. As a British diplomat observed,

> There is a large demand for yarns, and all that is made is sold without any difficulty. There is a very large consumption for this sort of material in the patterns enclosed in the manufacture for both sexes. . . . The firm three months ago established a spinning mill with 6,000 spindles. This has proved quite successful, and if a sufficient supply of cotton be assured the spindles are to be increased to 20,000. [61]

In spite of all hopes, the outcome was not good. Cotton had to be imported from Brazil since the Northern Chaco plantations had not yet produced enough fiber, and the firm faced prohibitive costs with such inefficiency that, despite being the only spinning mill, it operated with excess capacity utilization.[62] After seven years, it closed down and only reopened during the First World War, due to shortages in the supply of imported textiles.[63] This brief experience shows the dwarfed profile of Argentine cotton activity: whereas the goal of the failed firm was 20,000 spindles, Brazil had 110 mills with 735,000 spindles at the time.[64]

Considering cotton and woolen textiles altogether, Argentine factories were far from meeting the country's demand. Textile imports grew fivefold (from 8,800 to 47,400 gold pesos) between 1876 and 1908; in the meantime, their share of consumer imports into the country increased from 26 to 41 percent. During the same period, food and beverage imports fell from 47 to 24 percent, reflecting heavy import substitution (see Table 1.2). Progress in textiles was much shallower. In those years, the GDP increased elevenfold, so that the fivefold growth in imports indicated some success in local production, but mainly in woolen items helped by the provision of input in the country. As the census of 1908 shows, domestic textile production was valued at seventeen million pesos, supplying just a fourth of domestic consumption.[65] Moreover, this local output was not especially competitive. Lack of integration, applied worldwide, hurt efficiency in Argentina. Thus, factories producing for a market much smaller and less stable than that of the United States, Britain, and Germany could only survive with significant tariff protection. Not surprisingly, it was in the sheltered area of clothing that local industry found its greatest success.[66]

The paper industry could not fully develop due to the failure to produce its main input: wood pulp. Argentine factories had to import it or to use rags and waste paper as in the past. The latter strategy was disastrous in terms of efficiency, for the basic change that had transformed the world paper industry from labor to capital intensive production was precisely the use of pulp instead of rags. Wood pulp production was one of the major goals of La Argentina, the country's oldest firm. For this reason, it was built on the lower section of the river Paraná to obtain power, remove waste, and receive timber. But the company did not have access to cheap hydraulic power, one of the necessary requirements for large-scale paper production, due to the plain surrounding terrain. Nor could it obtain an adequate supply of wood; the quality of timber from the Paraná Delta islands, located in the vicinity of the factory, did not fit pulp production. A more satisfactory raw material could only be found in the distant forests of Paraguay and Misiones on the Upper Paraná, which implied additional cost and outlay of investment. This company's output, then, became limited to experimental products using some native species in the area surrounding the mills. The firm had to find timber abroad, to the notorious shortcoming that lumber was more expensive to ship than paper. Only in 1916, under conditions created by the war, did the firm El Fénix begin to produce pulp from the poplar and willow trees of the Paraná riverbanks, though with a meager output. Moreover, most of its input was still produced from rags and waste paper.[67] As a result, a "gentleman excellently informed on the subject" told the American consul in Rosario,

> The Argentine paper industry subsists at the present time, thanks to a high import duty which alone enables our factories to compete with the foreign product. . . . Suitable raw material is difficult to obtain in the country . . . [and] has to be imported to a considerable extent. . . . Machinery has to be imported at considerable expense. Under such circumstances Argentine paper could not possibly compete with the foreign product manufactured in countries with abundant raw material on a large scale by skilled labor were it not for the high duty. The industry is artificial and is not likely to grow rapidly under present conditions.[68]

Even in a well-developed and mechanized activity such as shoe production, old inefficiencies continued. Lack of specialization was the most blatant remnant. To an American observer, the limits of production in the Argentine factories were reminiscent of the time "before the introduction of machinery, when the work was done entirely by hand [and] it was a simple matter to produce a wide assortment of styles and kinds."[69] When foreign shoe producers visited the Argentine mills in 1916, a production strategy that precluded economies of scale amazed everybody:

> All of them showed great admiration for the fact that in the national factories such a diversity of items were produced simultaneously, and even more by the fact that in the same workshop shoes of different types were manufactured. They could not conceive of the possibility that shoes for women, men, and children could be made at the same time in only one section of machinery. They never attempted it in their own important factories, considering it harmful.[70]

The market features explain again this production strategy. By the mid-1920s, American companies leased no less than 150 different kinds of shoe-making machines in Argentina. Thus, diversification was not a result of entrepreneurial primitivism or even lack of technology (the same machines were used in specialized mills in the United States), but rather was a strategy to cope with the unstable Argentine demand.[71] The same market prompted Mr. Prat, as mentioned in Chapter 1, to run his integrated factory of woolen items, in which his workers washed, sorted, spun, wove, finished, and dyed the product. This risk-avoidance feature typical of integrated woolen textile industry was an appropriate strategy for the Argentine market, permeated by unstable numbers of a demand too dependent on the ups and downs of external trade.

Sometimes mechanization did not exist at all, such as in the furniture industry. In 1919, chairs imported from the United States still flooded the Argentine market. Polish and Russian Jews produced by hand some cheap furniture, while more expensive items were made by Italian and Spanish artisans. Only one cabinetmaking firm operated on a reasonably large scale. As an American observer noted,

> The furniture industry produced by the domestic manufactures is mostly handmade. Very little machine work is done except in roughing out the stock. The cabinet-maker prepares the material and joins it up and completes the place for the finisher. Modern machines such as those for gluing and sanding, and other labor-saving devices, are not used, and the hand labor done is considerable and costly [so that] the local factories producing a good grade of house furniture will not, for the present at least, offer competition to the large, well-organized, machine-equipped, quantity-producing factories of the United States.[72]

The unstable nature of the Argentine economy precluded a steady rate of investment and led to long-term inefficiency.[73] Usually, the purchase of updated machinery was followed by a long period of no replacements. The case of paper production became a symbol of this practice. In 1900, the firm La Argentina introduced a new machine (called "the Monster").[74] By the 1910s, however, this new machinery was out-of-date and the firm had not renewed its installations. In contrast, the emerging paper factory of the Compañía General de Fósforos (CGF) operated, thanks to a recent acquisition, with the most modern machinery.[75] In 1925, nonetheless, lack of further investment made it impossible for the CGF to compete with imports. Needing large investments to survive, it preferred to merge with the largest firm, La Papelera Argentina. The consolidated firm then began a new phase of mechanization.[76]

In many cases, when high investments were required, only major constraints prompted local production. The case of the cement industry, which used domestic clay and lime, is quite telling. The first attempts to open a cement factory dated from 1872 in the city of Rosario, but did not go further than a chancy venture. For decades, other projects—in Buenos Aires and in

Córdoba province—failed.[77] At the beginning of the twentieth century, however, the Argentine construction boom promoted cement consumption and its consequent importation. Shortages in imported cement during the war spurred its production at home. The U.S. International Cement Company opened the first large plant in 1919. Soon the market was large enough to ensure the firm's success and warrant opening a new mill under its name. That was not a bad bet: the construction business, recovering from the war years, tripled between 1919 and 1929.[78]

When the demand mechanism started to work, it was to remarkable effect. Lime production was a success in the province of Córdoba and blanketed the rest of the country. This evolution and the construction in that province of the *dique San Roque*, the largest dam in South America, prompted one of the failures in the cement industry. The constructor of the dam, Juan Bialet Massé, opened the firm La Primera Argentina (the First Argentine) in 1885. But the ambitious project of public works in the late 1880s led by president Juárez Celman, who had been a former governor of Córdoba and had encouraged that construction, ended with the depression of 1890. The president left the government after a revolution, and the Cordobese firm went into bankruptcy.[79] Soaring lime consumption propelled production, as the case of the firm Calera Avellaneda illustrates. The Calera opened in 1919 and had produced, one year later, 3,300 tons in a mill with a potential capacity of 8,000. Originally located in the suburbs of Buenos Aires, the company was forced by rising demand to move to a larger establishment closer to the mines. By 1929, it manufactured 32,000 tons, but its works had a capacity for 100,000. Three years later it was the largest in South America, producing 200,000 tons in an expanded facility. By then, 385,000 of the 812,000 locally consumed tons were produced in Argentina.[80]

Lack of a substantial demand lay at the root of some branches' underdevelopment, as in the case of the machine industry. During the 1910s, this activity was limited to the assembling of imported pieces, while domestic factories built simple machines for themselves. In parallel, extensive repair work supported large workshops, most of them owned by the railway companies.[81] Anything beyond that was considered outstanding; a modest printing machine, manufactured locally for a magazine, was advertised as an amazing triumph of national industry.[82] Though not large enough to promote a local version of National Harvester, the existence of a substantive market encouraged the production of some agricultural machinery production, but again, only those that fit the peculiarities of Argentine consumption.[83] In 1907, the Italian vice-consul explained that the absence of enough domestic production, in spite of increasing demand, was due not only to its size but also to the nature of the market:

> An industrialist who tried to open a firm for the production of agricultural machinery of complicated manufacture in Argentina now, should not count on easy and ready success . . . An establishment of such a kind, however powerful, could not produce more than one type of each kind of machine; the type that would best fit its technical possibilities. But to have the certainty of many and quick sales, it should produce a large variety of types, since the Argentine agriculturist is still very capricious.[84]

As early as 1898, Mr. Worthington, the British commissioner mentioned in Chapter 1, rejected the idea that a lack of technical skills (he considered these quite developed) explained the absence of local machine production, "for the simple reason that although the machinery might be made, it is not worthwhile to turn out only two or three machines after preparing the moulds; and as there would be no market for a greater quantity, those required by the country continued to be imported."[85]

Frequently, local firms exploited opportunities to adapt other country's models to the needs of the Argentine countryside. Technical adaptation proved successful for domestically made scales at Bianchetti company that replaced foreign items and even supplied the railways, which could have imported duty free.[86] But it was the creation of a demand niche that really prompted the production of machines. The firm Fontana Brothers specialized in the construction of machinery for yerba mate mills, since no country outside the River Plate region consumed this product. Fontana made presses to compact this kind of tea, a technique that prevented the incorporation of other products' odors into the yerba, which would make it unfit for a demanding clientele.[87] An even more successful story was that of Italian immigrant Torcuato Di Tella, who became one of the country's leading industrialists.

When the Di Tella family established itself permanently in Argentina in 1905, thirteen-year-old Torcuato found a job with Alfredo Allegrucci, who ran an import-export brokerage firm. Di Tella's transformation into an industrialist took place in 1910, when the municipal government of Buenos Aires prohibited the hand kneading of dough and forced bakeries to mechanize. Alfredo's brother, Guido, had studied the potential market for mixing machines and calculated that Buenos Aires would need around seven hundred of them, a demand that would eventually raise to five thousand if the rest of the country adopted the regulation. The machine Di Tella was in charge of producing was patented under the name of Sección Industria Amasadoras Mecánicas (S.I.A.M.) in 1911. It could compete with imports due to a novel feature that allowed part of the dough to rest while the large mixers moved from one end of the dough to the other. Thanks to aggressive selling strategies, which included advertisements in a baker's trade magazine and the extension of generous credit to the bakers, the firm expanded its capital from 10,000 to 100,000 pesos in 1915.[88]

But not all went well for the new firm. Bakers resisted the elimination of manual labor. As an employee of the company reported in a later interview:

> When mechanization was enforced by public regulations, particularly in Buenos Aires, there was much protest against it and the workers tried to boycott it. They were afraid they would lose their jobs. The bakers' organization was against the machine. The workers frequently were newly arrived immigrants brought by the bakery owners and they were very poorly paid and forced to work long hours. Many bakeries were burned down and many attacks against owners occurred in those days.[89]

The market growth took more time than expected to absorb the new machines. Moreover, renewed state help was necessary since enforcement of the municipal ordinance was less than rigorous; a new and stronger one replaced it in 1922.

Opportunities for capital goods industry did not abound in Argentina, and the cases of Bianchetti, Fontana, and Di Tella were as exceptional as they were notable. The problem, then, was not the lack of entrepreneurial or technical skills but the absence of sufficient demand to sustain large-scale supply. Under these conditions, local firms implemented strategies to cope with this market. In so doing, they helped to change the nature of the capitalist system gaining ground in the country.

The Reshaping of Capitalism

Amidst these achievements and shortcomings, Argentine industry experienced a qualitative transformation. The crisis sparked in 1897 revealed the perils of excess capacity and set up a survival-of-the-fittest scenario. In analyzing the roots of this recession, *The Economist* blamed "competition almost as keen as in Europe." The magazine took special note of the "pressures amongst second-rate [commercial] houses" while "[t]he first-class houses have not, apparently, been affected." In the meantime, the British commissioner Worthington foresaw that, as an outcome of intense competition between firms, "weaker individual factories may have to go." His prediction

proved to be correct. The effect of this competition had profound consequences: the structural transformations occurring within the firms moved
the market toward monopolistic practices and fostered concentration of
capital.[90] The reason for such a concentration, as an American explained in
the case of paper, was that

> Argentina is a big man's country market and there is no room for the
> little fellow unless he is able to combine with other concerns. Competi-
> tion is probably keener in Buenos Aires than in any other paper market
> in the world.[91]

At the end of the nineteenth century, manufacturing and commerce
faced similar challenges. Merchant Federico Portalis proposed dealing with
the market in a different way by creating pools of importers and manufacturers to match supply and demand.[92] Many followed his advice in the first
decade of the twentieth century, during the period of expansion that came
after the crisis. In order to cope with the ghost of overproduction under the
new conditions of increasing demand, concentration of capital strengthened, family firms turned into corporations, trusts flourished, and mergers
became common. In sum, big business emerged, and a dual industrial economy was dominated by either small or very large firms but in any case those
outside the middle-size range.

Argentine industry was highly concentrated from its inception, as the
first disaggregate data available for 1887 suggest. The 130 firms with more
than twenty employees (2.1 percent of the total) accounted for 21.2 percent
of the total workforce. By 1895, after industry had undergone substantial
growth, concentration increased. The fifty-nine largest companies (only
1.5 percent of the total number) employed thirty percent of the workers (see
Table 3.3).[93] Unfortunately, the loss of subsequent census manuscripts—
such as those from the Third National Census from 1914—inhibits the
comparison to other periods through use of market concentration measures
such as the four-firm ratio (CR4) or Herfindahl-Hirschman Index, which
really gain importance when evaluated over a long period of time.[94] The
next available information comes from 1935, when the government made a
detailed industrial census. The numbers, however, are tainted by a process
of deconcentration of capital that started right after the Great Depression.[95]
It is possible, however, to observe the process of concentration through
specific information on particular branches or to compare the sparse data on
individual firms with the aggregate census data.[96]

In some production activities, such as those of beer and paper, an already
high level of concentration was reinforced by these developments. By 1895,

TABLE 3.3

Industrial Concentration in Buenos Aires, 1887 and 1895

		NUMBER OF WORKERS PER FIRM				
		1–19	20–49	50–99	100 or more	Total
1887	Number of firms	5,998	77	25	28	6,128
	% of total	97.9	1.3	0.4	0.5	
	Number of workers	33,242	2,162	1,962	4,865	42,231
	% of total	78.7	5.1	4.6	11.5	
1895	Number of firms	3,569	512	284	66	4,431
	% of total	80.6	11.6	6.4	1.4	
	Number of workers	12,775	6,957	8,197	4,338	32,267
	% of total	39.6	21.6	25.4	13.4	

NOTE: This source has incomplete data, which is why it shows fewer firms in 1895 than in 1887.

SOURCE: My elaboration based on Estadística "Estadística industrial de la Capital Federal encomendada a Angel Ramón Cartavio y Enrique Raymond por el Consejo Directivo de la Unión Industrial Argentina para promover la concurrencia de la industria nacional a la Exposición Universal de 1889 en París," *Boletín de la Unión Industrial Argentina*, June 8, 1889, pp. 1–5; and on Archivo General de la Nación (Buenos Aires), *Segundo Censo Nacional de la República Argentina*, May 10, 1895, Manuscripts, Area Capital Federal. Sección Industrias.

TABLE 3.4

Industrial Concentration: Beer Production, 1895 and 1910 (as a percentage of output)

	FIRMS								
	Quilmes	Bieckert	Palermo	Río II	Cervecería Buenos Aires	Schlau- Santa Fé	Six Largest Breweries	Smaller Firms	Total Number of Firms
1895	49	27	—	2	—	3	88	12	18
1910	52	17	12	7	5	3	96	4	48

NOTES: The total number of breweries was sixty-one for 1895 and forty-eight for 1910. For 1910, percentages vary according to the source, and I have reckoned an average.

SOURCES: My own elaboration based on *Segundo Censo Nacional de la República Argentina*, May 10, 1895. (Buenos Aires: Talleres Tipográficos de la Penitenciaría Nacional, 1898), volume III, pp. 334–38; *Boletín de la Unión Industrial Argentina*, July 15, 1911, p. 41; and Galileo Massei, *La Repubblica Argentina nel primo centenario della sua independenza* (Milano: Arnaldo De Mohr Editore, 1910), pp. 366–67.

the four largest breweries represented 88 percent of the output. By 1910, two new large firms had appeared and the six largest establishments had reached 96 percent of the national production while the rest divided among forty-two small firms (see Table 3.4). Similarly, the concentration of capital, which had characterized the paper industry since its beginning in the late 1880s, continued. By 1916, there were nine firms producing paper, the top four sharing 88 percent of the total output (see Table 3.5).

Metallurgical production evolved toward concentration from a more evenly balanced point of departure; before this activity shifted to the production of standardized articles, a number of middle-size mills, working on a made-to-order basis, had an important presence in this branch of industry.

TABLE 3.5
Industrial Concentration: Paper Production, 1916

Firm	Daily Production	%
La Argentina, Zárate	45	39
Cía. General de Fósforos, Bernal	28	24
El Fénix, Campana	18	16
Fábrica de Papel Casati, San Nicolás	10	9
Smaller mills (5)	14	12
Total	115	

SOURCE: My own elaboration based on Robert Barrett, *Paper, Paper Products, and Printing Machinery in Argentina, Uruguay, and Paraguay,* United States, Department of Commerce, Bureau of Foreign and Domestic Commerce, Special Agents Series, no. 168 (Washington, DC: GPO, 1918), p. 37.

TABLE 3.6
Industrial Concentration: Metallurgical Production, 1907
Monthly Iron Consumption
(in kilos)

Firm	Iron	%
La Acero Platense	700,000	23.7
Vasena	600,000	20.3
O. Schnaith	500,000	16.9
D. Noceti	200,000	6.8
Rezzónico, Ottonello (later TAMET)	150,000	5.1
La Cantábrica	40,000	1.4
Other firms	764,182	25.8
Total	2,954,182	

SOURCE: My own elaboration based on "Establecimientos metalúrgicos en la capital de la República Argentina en 1825 y 1907—Hierro y Acero," in *Boletín de la Unión Industrial Argentina,* February 15, 1908, p. 25.

In 1895, the six largest firms accounted for half of the iron input; in 1907, the same group of top firms consumed 75 percent of this raw material (see Table 3.6). Moreover, it is very likely that this concentration increased in the 1910s, when the Vasena and TAMET firms emerged as the main producers of standardized goods.[97] Hat production also experienced a similar trend toward concentration; when the large firm Compañía Nacional de Tejidos y Sombreros (CNTS—National Clothing and Hat Company) mechanized, its production expanded to sixty percent of the national output, while the other 169 firms manufactured the rest.[98]

The years between 1900 and the 1913 depression witnessed a wave of stock company creation, although some of them (especially in the textile business) went to bankruptcy some years later (see Table 3.7). Sale of shares provided

TABLE 3.7

Founding Dates of the Argentine Stock Companies, 1880–1930

Branch	1880s	1890s	1900–1916	1920s
Alcohol		Devoto-Rocha		
Alpargatas	Fábrica Argentina de Alpargatas			
Burlap sack	La Primitiva, Salinas			
Metallurgic			Anglo-Argentine Iron Co., La Cantábrica, TAMET, Fundición y Talleres La Unión, La Acero Platense, El Eje, Elaboración General. de Plomo, Unión Herradores	Bolsalona, La Metalúrgica Argentina
Paper	La Argentina		Americana, Fábrica de Papel Casati, El Fenix, Cía Fosforera Argentina	La Papelera Argentina
Matches			Rigolleau, Papini	
Glass				
Textiles			Braceras, Cía Argentina de Tejidos, Cía Nacional de Tejidos y Sombreros, Cía Textil Sudamericana, Dell'Acqua, Gratry, Hilanderías Argentinas de Algodón, Moreira	Argentina de Tejidos, Baibieni y Antonini, Campomar y Soulas, Del Sel, Manufactura Algodonera, Masllorens, Sedalana
Foodstuff			Bagley, The Standard	
Beer		Buenos Aires, Fábrica Nacional de Cerveza, Palermo, Río II		
Liqueur			Bilz, Ariza, Cusenier	
Leather			Gaggino-Lauret, Grunbaum	
Cigarettes			Cía Gral de Tabacos, Cía Nac de Tabacos, Piccardo, Ariza, Didiego	
Dairy			La Martona, La Vascongada, La Unión Argentina, Magnasco	
Furniture			Thompson, Cía Nacional de Muebles	
Tin plate			La Cromo Hojalatería	
Pots and pans			Ferrum	
Soap			Conen	
Shoes	Fábrica Nacional de Calzado			
Various	Cía General.de Fósforos		Argentina de Cemento Pórtland, Cemento Argentino	

SOURCE: My own elaboration based on *Boletín Oficial de la Bolsa de Comercio de Buenos Aires, 1914–1930.*

the firms with fresh capital. An increase in size and the introduction of economies of scale accompanied the transition from family-owned establishments to corporations. As the UIA noticed in 1902,

> The concentration of capital in the enormous scale in which it has been taking place over the last years is something that interests all of us for the vital importance it possesses . . . nobody can deny that concentration of capital is rapidly changing the face of commerce and all industries . . . because it is well known that a hundred or a thousand horsepower steam machines used in the same workshop cost less and yield more than the same energy force divided in small units.[99]

In parallel, a rush toward mergers reached into almost every branch of the nascent manufacturing sector. In 1899, the main hat producer—La Actualidad—joined with its principal competitor—Franchini—to create the already mentioned CNTS; eight liqueur firms merged in 1904; the main biscuit factories—Bagley and La Unión—formed one sole company in 1905; and most of the cigarette producers coalesced into the Compañía Argentina de Tabacos (Argentine Tobacco Company).[100] Because the metallurgical industry had been permeated with middle-size firms, its evolution toward concentration is especially telling.

In this sector, the merging process started in 1902, when three middle-size companies—the machinery workshop of Antonio Rezzónico, the bolt factory Ottonello, and machinery producer El Ancla—united with the support of the banking and financial group Tornquist, which already owned the third firm. The merger began in a disorderly way, and, as Table 3.6 shows, by 1907 it still had not become one of the largest companies.[101] But that year money provided by the Tornquist consortium transformed the company into a corporation that later became TAMET. Next, it launched a program of investments such as setting up a forty-five-thousand-square-meter compound devoted to iron founding, nut making, pipe production, and general mechanical work under the direction of a German engineer.[102] One of TAMET's goals was to assemble and modify the implements and agricultural machinery imported by Tornquist.[103] It also specialized in hardware articles and began to compete with Vasena, which was forced to expand its installations to cope with the growth of its adversary. The Vasenas—the same immigrant family who founded the establishment—searched for fresh capital and found investors in London. By 1911, the firm became a British company, but the original owners still held some of the shares and continued to control management.[104] The metallurgical scenario of the 1910s was completely different from that of the 1890s; two large companies led the increasingly oligopolistic production of standardized items, a trend that showed signs of deepening even further in the 1920s.

The first decade of the 1900s saw not only metallurgy but also all other Argentine industry caught up in a global process of profound capitalist transformation: the rise of big business and the trustification of the domestic economy. Concentration is different from big business. A tiny market can be occupied by a small number of producers, as was, to some extent, the case of Argentina in the very first years of industrial growth. Big business, however, is a phenomenon implying monopolistic or oligopolistic control of the market regardless of its size. As soon as they experienced overproduction, large Argentine companies created trusts in order to have a common market policy, especially on prices and output. The process, which had already begun in the 1890s, strengthened in the next decade, a period when demand and concentration both grew. Following this, the formation of trusts occurred in almost every branch of industry, including matches, hats, spirits, bags, pins, paper, textiles, and even ice.[105] In 1894, the UIA declared,

> [W]e have weaving and alcohol factories that surpass the country's consumption; they produce outstanding quantities, which force their owners to reduce the price; in response they unite to maintain prices so that they can obtain high profits in relation to the invested capital. Matches, hats, and other industries are in the same situation.[106]

Concentration of capital, corporations, mergers, and trusts eventually fostered the already mentioned dual industrial complex, mainly composed of large firms and small workshops, which coexisted to the same extent as in the industrialized countries. Nevertheless, the weakness of middle-size establishments, regarded as an intermediate step in workforce, capital, and technology, was especially striking in the Argentine case. The case of alpargatas production illustrates this situation. The bulk of these sandals were made at the large Fábrica Argentina; for a long time this was the only firm that possessed the machinery necessary to produce in massive numbers. A couple hundred sweatshops, which worked "in the manner of the ancient potter's wheel," supplied the rest of the market. For a firm of intermediate size, there was no possibility to succeed between the gigantic mill and the tiny sweatshops. Moreover, small and large companies used different strategies, produced distinct articles, and did not really compete. They were, in fact, two different worlds.[107]

To explain the causes of this transformation as well as to understand the relative importance of productive requirements or the increasing costs of commercialization as the main incentives for the creation of corporations and mergers goes beyond the Argentine case. It leads us to a debate about the role of market forces in the process of capital concentration, stemming from the second industrial revolution that affected the entire capitalistic world following the 1873 great crisis. First of all, the very relationship between firm size and industrial performance is the subject of a debate in which the benefits of economies of scale have been put into question. While some authors continue to support their significance, others have shown—after Kenneth Sokoloff's research—that size and gains in productivity did not rise together as has been previously assumed.[108] The seminal work of Alfred Chandler depicts large firms as necessary for economic development, since they promote not only economies of scale and scope but also economies of speed. Thanks to the latter, Chandler argues, firms can cope with the market by controlling its forces and organizing a "visible hand" in their favor. Placing more confidence in the importance of market forces, the complementary vision of Oliver Williamson finds nothing evil in capital concentration, since transaction costs are the spark that promote larger companies, which attempt to lower these costs with efficiency techniques only permitted by size.[109] Conversely, other authors have disregarded the importance of market forces and stressed that these qualitative processes were strategies to prevent competitors from entering the market rather than a way to ensure efficiency through a better reallocation of resources to eliminate excess capacity.[110] For one of them, consolidation was not inevitable (as Chandler argues) but the consequence of historical crises that caused prices to plummet.[111]

Lack of data precludes a serious discussion of whether reducing competition or the existence of unexploited economies of scale prevailed in the process of capital concentration in Argentina. The sustained growth of Argentine firms suggests that requirements for production and commercialization should not be underestimated as a crucial factor in the formation of corporations and mergers. In addition, as Yovanna Pineda has demonstrated, the top companies showed increasing returns to scale in the period 1895–1935.[112] But capital concentration also occurred in branches with low economies of scale, such as that of burlap bags, or with a specific kind of mechanization that encouraged the rise of smaller units, as in shoe production. A variable demand fostered this process. Beer consumption was an extreme case; linked to the ups and downs of the export economy, the nature of the demand for beer, concentrated in the summer, intensified the variability. Indeed, it was difficult for a middle-size brewery to survive when seasonal demand imposed the constraint of keeping the product refrigerated and unsold most of the year. The only places where this kind of firm could survive were the regions of German colonization, in which consumption stretched

over the entire year. Thus, small breweries flourished in the center of Santa
Fé province, a region in which the German-speaking immigrants first established themselves.[113]

The study of the formative process of a dual economy sheds some light
on the debate if we look at the cases in which this outcome was the result of
a commercial war between large and middle-size firms. In the 1870s and
1880s, a number of modest companies performed quite well in the Argentine shirt market thanks to the production of the *camisas de plancha*. In the
1890s, large factories started the production of *camisas a la crimea* and eventually displaced the former shirts, as explained in Chapter 2. The new shirts
were produced by economies of scale that workshops could not match, and
as a result, most of the latter fell into bankruptcy.[114] In the hat market, a similar process occurred when the large firm La Actualidad and middle-size establishments fought the so-called "boutique war." Again, economies of scale
helped the top company, which had used mechanization to reduce its workforce from eight hundred to five hundred workers between the early 1890s
and 1899, a period when steam power tripled.[115] The merger of the two
main firms, which resulted in the CNTS, sealed the fate of the less powerful units. As in the case of shirts, big business won the hat war, and the largest
company raised its daily output from two hundred to six thousand hats between 1885 and 1900. The remaining eight middle-size firms had an output of between one hundred and four hundred hats per day. One hundred
and sixty "small workshops, with hand-moved machinery," completed the
scenario.[116] From then on, the shirt and hat industries became more and
more clearly divided between large factories and numerous tailors, seamstresses, and small establishments that worked on a made-to-order basis.[117]

The dual economy was evident throughout most of industry. In the production of cigarettes, small establishments did not even possess the machinery to chop tobacco in their own workshops. Small distilleries could not
match the advertising campaigns of the large firms.[118] And as one industrialist observed, in tanning, besides the grand factories, "there are many others that have small workshops in the house of the industrialist and there are
cases where workers labor and tan one or two hides a day and turn it over
to the large factories or directly to the saddlery or shoe store that employs
them."[119] Large companies also tended to absorb units that produced made-
to-order shoes; yet they existed alongside "an important handicraft industry
made up of custom shoemaking establishments and smaller shops."[120]

The existence of a dual economy did not mean that the supply side composed of large factories was closed to newcomers. The example of the already mentioned production of alpargatas shows that a new firm successfully

equipped could soon grow in size. In 1892, the company Adot was producing these sandals by hand at a workshop in a small room. In 1904, it bought its first machine. Thanks to a good entrepreneurial strategy, "primitive MANUFACTURING transformed into a FACTORY. . . . Production multiplied by the hundreds, starting a real invasion of the market."[121] By 1909, Adot possessed a two-story factory, and by 1920 it had added jute-spinning production.[122] By then, it was in the group of the top companies.

Entrance into the club of large firms was possible because the dual economy was primarily the result of market conditions, in which large manufacturing firms were better adapted to the economy, rather than a conspiratorial force. Thus, the search for those factors that made it possible for a firm to become a leading company holds the key to understanding a large part of early Argentine industrialization. To pursue this investigation, areas such as credit and politics will be developed in Chapters 6 and 7. In this section, I will begin the analysis by delving into a factor that made this switch possible and became the main symbol of capital concentration: the economic group.

These groups were conglomerates that included financial and productive activities. Ownership of a bank provided fresh investment capital for the other participating firms. The group founded by the Tornquist family exemplifies the model. Ernesto Tornquist & Cía.—the group's business name—included banking, commerce, cattle ranching, and industry. One firm in this group was an *oficina técnica* (technical office) dedicated solely to the importation of machinery and the installation of factories. This office, the Cía. Técnica e Importadora, "contributed to the foundation of a good number of industrial establishments in the country," as described by one of its publications.[123] The first manufacturing enterprises were in the sugar refining and the brewery business, but the group expanded into metallurgical, textile, and cigar production. Furthermore, association with this group made it possible for some firms to enlarge.[124]

Other economic groups had a structure similar to Tornquist's. The Grupo Italiano (Italian Group), associated with the Banco de Italia y Río de la Plata (Bank of Italy and River Plate), invested in textile, hat, and tannery production while controlling the CGF.[125] Another group, Leng-Roberts, did not have either a bank or the extended economic web of the Tornquist Company. (Mr. Roberts' motto was that "if a business makes paper $1000, we will earn $20 without risking too much.") Nevertheless, the group possessed an advantage; it was a bridge for obtaining loans in the London market, which strengthened its position in the directories and share possession of industrial firms.[126]

The activity of economic groups usually led to the monopolization or oligopolization of the market. That was the case of the consortium headed by Otto Bemberg, the owner of the Quilmes brewery. By the 1920s, he had expanded his business to include a large real estate company specializing in rural property, a tramway firm, and several financial institutions. In parallel, his control over the beer market advanced. As a French visitor observed, "[T]oday it dominates all the production and marketing of beer. . . . One by one, all the competing beer factories . . . have passed into its control." This comment was largely true: the group developed a policy to buy smaller firms, and even the brewery owned by the Tornquist group had ended up as part of the Bemberg complex.[127]

Capital concentration did not secure success. The CNTS that had vanquished its competitors in the "boutique war" went into bankruptcy in 1912. The lack of support from an economic group was at the base of its failure. By the 1910s, five financial groups dominated the scene in Argentina: Tornquist, Bemberg, the Italian (Devoto), and two other groups, one led by the Soulas family and another involved in the paper business.[128]

Many people felt that the old Argentina was vanishing because of the activity of new economic formations. Society at large did not receive big business with open arms. As the *Review of the River Plate* stated, "This country is becoming as fond of trusts as the United States is, and everything should be done to combat them."[129] The new landscape was threatened by the ghost of EL TRUST, a label applied to any form of oligopoly or big business. Major industrialists, bankers, and financiers (some filling each of these roles simultaneously) were the target of a wide variety of attacks, from Socialists defending consumers to Conservatives who viewed the economic giants as too modern and too powerful for traditional Argentina. In January 1918, the Congress conducted an Antitrust Parliamentary Commission, and many of the "fat cats" were subpoenaed, albeit with disappointing results. Farmers pointed at the bag-producer pool as the source of their problems. For newspapers, the paper combine was the cause of expensive newsprint. Even a cigarette producer who preferred to be a freelancer, Piccardo, launched a far-reaching advertising campaign against EL TRUST that comprised most of the competing tobacco companies. In September 1919, the Commission presented the report, and only in 1923 did the Congress finally pass an antitrust law, which did not have any important effect.[130] Not surprisingly, beer czar Otto Bemberg was portrayed as the embodiment of the "evil wealthy" in subsequent years.[131] Angered that the Argentine economy had taken a turn in which he could not find a favorable place for himself, economist

Ricardo Pillado identified Bemberg, along with Ernesto Tornquist, with disdain as being part of "those who are here called the Jews."[132]

Was this scenario so different from that of other capitalist countries? A comparison between disaggregate data and studies on industrial concentration in the leading industrial countries indicates that firm size distribution in Argentina was similar to places such as Germany and France. The average number of workers in firms with more than 50 workers was 176 in Germany and 154 in France, while in Argentina it was 143. The percentage of industry employees in firms with more than 50 workers in Argentina was 39 percent, while in Germany and France it was 38 percent. The main difference was with the United States, in which the average number of laborers in those companies was 185, and the percentage of industry employees reached 83 percent.[133] In these countries, local industrialists also responded to similar challenges, mainly excess capacity utilization and capitalist business cycles, with matching strategies.[134] Naomi Lamoreaux indicated that mergers favored mass production of cheap homogeneous goods over small manufacturing of differentiated and high-quality products, a risky choice for a firm since it had to face the income elasticity of demand.[135] The size of the market, however, gave the term "massive" a very different meaning in Argentina than in the United States or even France, Germany, or Great Britain. In Argentina, concentration of capital faced not only the challenge of standardization but also the problem of coping with a small market, similar to the cases of Mexico and New Zealand.[136]

Moreover, the lack of vertical integration limited the potential of capital concentration. This combination rarely occurred in Argentina and was noticeably absent in activities such as metallurgical, paper, and textile production, as occurred in full-fledged industrialized countries. Vertically integrated firms were crucial for the development of modern capitalism, according to Chandler. In his perspective, their emergence prompted the rise of a group of professional managers who increased efficiency by coordinating and centralizing the different productive processes. This change was so important that countries failing to make it, such as Britain, jeopardized their industrial futures.[137] Whether or not Chandler's assessments are a plausible explanation for success or failure, Argentina was unable to integrate or ignite the movement toward a revolutionary managerial efficiency.[138]

An exception was the CGF, the outcome of a merger between three match firms in 1889. Shortly thereafter, it opened a printing establishment to stamp its boxes and, in 1903, a paper factory to manufacture the cardboard for them. During the First World War, due to a shortage of stearine, the firm bought and refurbished an old factory to make that input, which

eventually produced as well olein and glycerin. The next step was to manufacture cotton snuff for the matches. In 1919–20, the company started a
campaign to persuade colonizers in the Chaco region to grow cotton and
opened a gin in that territory. By 1921, it had its own cotton-spinning mill
in the suburbs of Buenos Aires.[139] This single instance of vertical integration
grew with astonishing success in the 1920s.

A New Crisis, the War, and the 1920s

In 1913, Argentina faced, as one metallurgical firm founded in 1903 recalled
in its annual report, "the most intense crisis in the annals of our Commerce."[140] The depression set off by problems in the Balkans was, indeed,
the most severe for the country since 1890 (and had worse effects, as recent
research has shown, than the one in 1930).[141] Argentina had not yet recovered when the European War started. The effects of the war on domestic industry have been interpreted in various ways. The traditional interpretation
has argued that this war fostered industrialization through forced import substitution.[142] A later position has claimed that it hurt manufacturing growth
due to the halt in imports of vital capital equipment and raw material.[143] Another perspective associates the slow development of manufactories during
the war with structural weaknesses and limitations.[144] The fact was that in
1914 the industrial sector as a whole plummeted 20 percent, a drop similar
to that of GDP, and did not recover the prewar levels until 1918.[145]

The validity of each argument depends on which branch of industrial
production is considered. As has been emphasized here, nothing like a homogeneous industrial sector existed. Rather, there was a wide constellation
of firms and factories, some well developed, others poorly advanced or in
transition from one step to another. On the one hand, those industries that
could get raw materials domestically found war an opportunity to substitute
for imports; wool washing, production of hosiery, furniture building, and
shoe production flourished.[146] The latter was a striking case. Helped first by
the forced import substitution imposed by the war, leather industrialists
were successful in winning tariff protection in the 1918 Congress.[147] Following this, all kinds and qualities of shoes began to be produced, even baby
and sport brands. As an American specialist observed,

> [W]hereas five years ago the factories were turning out a product that
> did not seriously interfere with the sale of imported footwear, today
> a number of Buenos Aires manufacturers are making shoes that are
> such excellent specimens of shoe-factory workmanship that the sale of
> imported shoes is being affected. . . . The shoe-manufacturing industry

has reached a higher state of development in Argentina than in any
other South American country.[148]

On the other hand, manufactories importing crucial inputs faced a hardship.
Paper firms survived only because of Sweden's neutrality, permitting the
continued sale of wood pulp, while breweries were short on malt and hops,
biscuit companies could not obtain imported tin-plate to package their output, and metallurgical firms lacked their critical *hierro viejo* (recycled iron),
which was sold abroad at high price during the war years. The majority of
Argentine industries suffered the scarcity and rising cost of inputs and machinery, plus the labor unrest that emerged in 1917, as we will see in Chapter 5. As a result, there was only a limited expansion in those industries that
already existed and had mechanized before the war, rather than creation of
new firms.[149]

The 1920s witnessed a revival in Argentina's manufacturing growth. Industrial output continued to be domestically oriented. The opportunity to
export, for example, clothes and blankets to the British and French armies,
did not outlive the hostilities.[150] In addition, thanks to the wool-washing
boom, textile mills had, according to an industrialist source, "the opportunity to accumulate enormous profits which allowed them to almost completely replace their machines with the latest models." This development resulted in overproduction and encouraged the opening of new factories by
"inexperienced capitalists," flooding the market, reducing profits, and by
the late 1920s, forcing a restructuring.[151]

After the trouble year of 1919, in which labor unrest was at its peak, 1920
initiated a decade of general prosperity. Argentina even was one of the few
countries in the world that did not suffer in depth the 1921–22 depression.
Industry experienced an annual growth of 4.5 percent in the 1920s, according to the most modest estimates for that period, as a result of aggregate demand increase, new tariffs, and a favorable exchange rate.[152] Those years
have been depicted as a period of booming demand as well as one marking
the emergence of a substantial cultural and economic sophistication. This
assessment is partially true.[153] The features of the rising consumer society,
born in the first decade of the 1900s, virtually exploded in that decade—
advertising became more widespread, commercialization techniques more
refined, productive strategies more apt. But rather than a new world, the
cultural dimensions of the market merely intensified the major transformations that had unfolded at the beginning of the twentieth century.

The positive economic performance of the 1920s, upon which any progress would have to build, is an issue under debate: the so-called "slowdown

controversy." An old interpretation considered the war a lost opportunity for industrial development and the entire decade a waste of time, placing the country's "take-off," in the Rostowian sense, in the 1930s.[154] In a less dramatic tone, some scholars have seen the period as one of a deep deceleration in growth.[155] On the contrary, some others have argued it was a period of splendor, a new Argentine Belle Époque, as glittering as the pre-1913 years.[156]

Between 1890 and 1913, Argentine industry grew at an annual rate of almost 9 per cent, a notable amount that surpassed that of any European country at that time, including Russia. Although the country could not sustain this pace in later years (during the period 1913–1935 it was less than 2 per cent), the 1920s did witness the previously mentioned industrial growth (4.5 percent annually).[157] As Javier Villanueva has pointed out, between 1924 and 1930, investment in the industrial sector reached the pre–Second-World-War high, and in 1930, the consumption of energy by industry was nine times the level of 1920, a growth rate never repeated. By then, industry had experienced a wave of direct foreign investment, mainly from the United States.[158] Expansion of demand fostered this evolution. Consumption, such as can be seen in the case of consumer goods like automobiles, coffee, and cacao, continued growing. The market, however, showed signs of saturation. This occurred with matches, the sales of which went down in absolute and per capita ratios, in spite of price reductions (see Table 2.1).

Betweeen December 1924 and March 1925, Argentine industrialists had an opportunity to show the variety of manufactured goods they produced. In that period, the city of Buenos Aires held a National Industrial Exhibition that surprised visitors for the diversity of items produced locally. The Exhibition displayed woolen, cotton and silk products, boots and shoes, leather items, sports goods, hats, brushes, commercial books, agricultural machinery and its accessories, scales and weighing machines, metallic work in iron, brass and nickel plate, electrical material, bolts, nuts and screws, glass ware, furniture, beverages, parfumes, and soap.[159]

A crucial reason to foster consumption in the 1920s was the notable increase in real wages (see Figure 2.1). According to estimates, from 1918 to 1930 salaries in constant values increased by 7.5 percent a year while the GDP per capita grew at an annual rate of 3 percent. This fact reduced the competitiveness of the Argentine industry by increasing its labor costs, and industrialists pressed for higher tariffs. But better salaries created an attractive domestic market that encouraged foreign companies to open mills in Argentina. Moreover, a more even distribution of income promoted the rise of a strong middle class and allowed for new transformations in the nature of demand in the 1920s. Consumer durable goods, mainly composed by cars and radios, jumped their participation in the total imports from 20 percent to 30 percent during the decade and indicated the increasing purchasing power of the Argentine market (see Table 1.2). The consumer revolution strengthened the features that have been developing since the turn of the twentieth century. Commercialization patterns modernized; an example was advertising, which improved in quantity and quality with the rise of the first creative agencies and the display of sophisticated techniques.[160]

Middle-class consumption grew, to the effect that this social class became the most visible evidence of the Argentine dream of economic upward mobility. Enrique Loncán, who followed in the 1920s the tradition of nostalgic writers, summarized this development in his story "El dulce sueño de Jesús" (The Sweet Dream of Jesús), in which a young Spanish immigrant from Galicia fantasizes about conquering his beloved Dolores by buying a coat in the window-display of a conational store: Fernández Hnos. Loncán would often muse about the horror which dead, old-fashioned aristocrats would have felt, had they come back to life and seen the triumph of the middle class. The new spectacle of Buenos Aires became vulgar for his taste, since the city was invaded by the "*nouveaux riches* of the democracy that completely lack interest, grace and distinction."[161] In 1920, the essayist Juan Agustín García wrote a play called "Los Snobs," a piece in which the characters possess social power only through their newly gained wealth.[162] As Loncán was to state in 1932, a new era had began in Argentina: the one of the "guarangos" (the tacky ones). The guarango was, for Loncán, a person of bad taste and obnoxious manners, a bumptious hunger for life, a figure that indeed stood for the entire destiny of Argentina in the hands of this robustly optimistic new social class.[163]

Working-class consumption followed patterns similar to those developed by the middle-class. The Anarchist–trade unionist newspaper *Bandera Proletaria* showed this behavior in the prizes it offered for the "Gran rifa por presos y jiras de propaganda" (great lottery for the inmates and in favor of propaganda). The trophies demonstrate the dreams of a working-class family: furniture, sewing machines, clothing, watches, women's bags, silver-plate, china. In addition, the main trade unions continued the strategy of consumer boycotts that had been so successfully managed by the Anarchists twenty years before. The Unión Sindical Argentina (Argentine Trade Union), then, did not shy away from announcing, "The working class should apply with decision and intelligence the best and most powerful weapon it has for its struggle: the boycott."[164]

The consumption boom in the 1920s became apparent in the use of leisure time. Buenos Aires and its suburbs had about 170 movie theatres in

1928, and these changed their programs three or four times a week. As the British Commercial Counselor said, "Argentina is insatiable in its demand for films. The consumption per head is probably as high as in any country except the United States." [165]

Tariff issue should not be disregarded in explaining the increase in industrial output. International inflation, in turn, had made the price of imports cheaper. Tariff valuation of goods upon which import taxes were based had been set up in 1905, a process that will be described in detail in Chapter 7; but these fiscal values were unrealistically low in the 1920s. This lag resulted in less protective effects. The peso, however, was depreciated until 1924, when it began a revaluation as a result of governmental efforts to return to the gold standard, dropped in 1914. In 1927, the country reentered convertibility to avoid a higher valuation of its domestic currency that resulted from the economic healthy performance.[166] But before this process started, manufacturing had reached a victory in favor of protectionism. By 1923, new (and higher) duties aimed to reduce the gap between fiscal values of imports and the real prices affected by world inflation. The protective effect on local industry was sufficient to prompt foreign firms to open factories in Argentina to maintain their hold on the market; such was the case of two cotton textile mills, in an industry that had been almost absent: the Belgian firm Algodonera Flandria, which inaugurated on the outskirts of Buenos Aires in 1924,[167] and the large stock company Manufactura Algodonera Argentina, which continued the business of smaller firms.[168] In addition, in 1921 the government exempted from the payment of import duty all the machinery required by new and established industrial firms and reduced to five percent the duty on imported raw materials for manufacturing use.[169]

In addition, lack of foreign currency in the postwar years, plus low exchange rates until 1925, joined with tariffs to help domestic manufacturing.[170] As the British commercial secretary said in his report, "There is no doubt that sooner or later more British firms will have to consider seriously the question of manufacturing locally; some British firms have already taken the lead, while others have the matter well in hand." For this agent, local competition was especially marked in boots and shoes, clothing, furniture, food, beverage, leather goods, electrical fittings, ornamental iron, soaps and parfumes, jute sacks and bags, and glass.[171] However, devaluation was as damaging to an industry dependent on imported inputs as it was helpful in making competition with foreign manufactured goods easier for this same industry.

In a search for ways to improve exports in Argentina, the British government took a survey in 1925 that reported an estimated volume of industrial production two or three times that of prewar output.[172] This was, undoubtedly, an exaggeration. As an economist of those times declared with more precision,

> In the last years, as a result of the European war, we were forced to encourage the growth of our industries, and this fact has mistakenly led us to believe that we are really industrialized.[173]

The war years, by favoring production that would soon overrun the market shortages, looked like the 1890s.

History seemed to be repeating itself. The postwar recovery and the new boom in the Argentine economy in the 1920s increased demand, promoted more mass production, and fostered new corporations and mergers, as had occurred between 1904 and 1913. The tendency toward merger, halted in 1913, regained strength in the 1920s, as became apparent in the paper and metallurgical industries. In this decade, local mills supplied 70 percent of wrapping papers, thanks to the tariff and in spite of their excessive weight and weakness. Production of high quality printing paper, however, continued to be imported.[174] Being keenly competitive, the paper market propelled the signing of a gentleman's agreement among old enemies, such as La Argentina, the CGF, Casati, and El Fénix, to establish output quotas and prices during World War I. Later, they blended to create La Papelera Argentina, which wholly dominated the market and began a standardization program.[175] The textile industry also faced the merging of Masllorens and Campomar in 1919, a negotiation backed by the finances of the Soulas economic group.[176]

The market for metallurgical goods became more concentrated when the company La Acero Platense went bankrupt in 1911. Competition between TAMET and Vasena became wilder, but it ended in favor of the former due to management problems in the latter in 1921.[177] This was a difficult year for that industry beset by the international crisis in iron and steel production. TAMET, with profits of 4.6 percent and 17.6 percent in 1919 and 1920, suffered a loss of 24.5 percent in 1921. The fate of Vasena was worse, and drove its British partners to get rid of the business.[178] The two companies eventually merged in 1926 when the more successful firm bought out its failing competitor. In 1928, a modernization plan was completed, and the outcome was the largest metallurgical mill in South America.[179] With the participation of Luxembourg-based international ARBED group, the new TAMET had two plants (one from each of the original companies) occupying an area of 147,000 square meters, with two Siemens-Martin units and three lamination trains plus four hundred people employed in the management and technical division and eighteen hundred workers in production. The more modern mill produced cast-iron pipes, sanitary wares, screws, bolts and nuts, general iron foundry products, and galvanized iron sheets. The more primitive one manufactured nails, wire (plain and barbed), and metal-frame structures.[180] In 1928, the already modernized company provided a dividend of 6 percent for stockholders; the year 1929 provided more handsome profits, and dividends rose to 8 percent.[181] Although the new facilities had a steel production capacity of twenty thousand tons, control from the ARBED group prevented its full use. The consortium had barred TAMET from developing steel production. After TAMET bought Vasena, the latter's undertaking of steel production stopped, and that kind of input for metallurgical manufacturing was imported from the international group. The steelmaking facilities acquired from Vasena remained idle until the consortium collapsed with the onset of the Second World War.[182] Actually by 1928 consumption of iron and steel increased importation, since there was no other local source than scrap.[183]

Merging seemed to be the natural process in a relatively open and highly competitive economy such as Argentina in the 1920s. The furniture manufacturing spread among various small firms in the hands of Polish and Russian Jews who had reorganized in the new decade; the competition became fierce enough to encourage the creation of a stock company in 1926 integrated by the number of small producers who had been in informal agreement in the previous years: the Cooperativa Israelita de Fabricantes de Muebles (Jewish Cooperative of Furniture Producers).[184]

During these times of fusion the CGF, which had grown to employ six thousand workers, a very large number for an Argentine company, decided to divide up management and property.[185] In the late 1920s, the CGF split into three new firms involved in the main productive activities: paper, matches, and textiles. The paper company merged with competitors (as already mentioned), responding to obstacles in production. Challenges created by both the production and commercialization of matches had been enough to provoke losses for its main local competitor—Compañía Fosforera Argentina—in 1924.[186] Continuing competition fostered an association between the CGF, the Swedish Match Company, and the British Bryant & May to form a new firm, the Compañía General de Fósforos Sudamericana (South American General Matches Company).

The foreign companies, which provided technical assistance and capital, received a handsome portion of the new firm's shares.[187] Market challenges prompted the remaining CGF to concentrate on textiles, under the name of

Fabril Financiera. Before the division, the CGF had already developed a triple-activity cotton business: burl, oil, and spinning.[188] However, the effects of the tariff were not yet felt in 1925, and cotton spinning was not a good business for the CGF. Only in 1927 did demand became substantial; a year later the company decided to increase its number of spindles from 10,600 to 20,000. The business was so successful that in 1929 it decided to integrate vertically by buying cotton gins in the Chaco region.[189] This business was an important achievement; there was a hosiery and fabric production boom following 1924, which increased demand for imported cotton yarn, mainly from Italy, the United Kingdom, and the United States. By 1927, there were five spinning mills with forty-one thousand spindles, producing almost four million kilos of yarn.[190] In addition, the Fábrica Argentina de Alpargatas opened a cotton-spinning mill in 1923; it became such a good business that the firm issued additional stocks in 1924 to back new investments in that activity.[191] In spite of all this growth, in 1930 Argentine cotton textile output met only 9 percent of the national consumption. The years after the Great Depression would bring the final development of the activity.[192]

In the 1920s, Argentina experienced a boom in car consumption; in 1910, annual imports had reached 1,600 vehicles, by 1920 they had jumped to 13,500, and after 1922 they were never lower than 30,000. By 1929, the estimated number of cars in the country reached 260,000, transforming Argentina into a country with one of the highest ratios of vehicles per capita in the world.[193] By 1925, already 70 percent of industrial rubber goods consumed in the country were manufactured in Argentina. Three years later, local suppliers had improved so much that they produced all classes of mechanical rubber goods at only five percent above the English trade prices.[194] Responding to the potential market for car-related activities, in 1923 Torcuato Di Tella signed a licensing agreement with the U.S. Wayne Pump Company to manufacture assembly parts for the imported gasoline pumps. This association lasted until 1927, when the local firm made another deal, this time with the state petroleum company Yacimientos Petrolíferos Fiscales (Public Oil Fields). With the signing of this agreement, it became the almost exclusive supplier of gasoline pumps in the country, in addition to the contract Di Tella already had with the municipality of Buenos Aires. Soaring pump activity plus the continuing expansion in the bakery machinery business made the sales of Di Tella's company S.I.A.M. rise from one to almost five million pesos between 1924 and 1927. Encouraged by this growth, Di Tella built a new large factory in the Buenos Aires suburb of Avellaneda.[195]

By 1929, S.I.A.M. was supplying about 90 percent of dough machines, 60 percent of gasoline pumps, and 50 percent of the service station equipment sold in the country, and it expected to increase its market share. Di Tella was the owner and the leading presence at his works, where he provided administrative and technical skills. As one of the managers later recalled,

> Activities started at Avellaneda [suburb] in July 1929. Di Tella wanted to move from Córdoba [street, in Buenos Aires downtown] to Avellaneda as quickly as possible and start making new models of pumps for filling stations, because in all parts of the world there were new types and Di Tella was afraid of being left behind. The model of the pump they started to manufacture was wholly Mr. Di Tella's idea. He would stay beside the project designer and give him instructions. As an engineer Di Tella was very good . . . he had a very good eye.[196]

Di Tella was also modernizing commercialization strategies. He returned from a trip to the United States in 1928 with the idea of expanding sales on credit paid for in monthly installments. This caused the firm's activities to soar.[197]

Di Tella exemplified the rise of a new kind of industrial entrepreneur. In a 1907 funeral eulogy for Ernesto Tornquist, a former finance minister called him "the first merchant, the first industrialist, and the first financier of the country."[198] This, in many ways, was an accurate depiction of the type of entrepreneur leading Argentine industry at that time. But in the 1920s, the title of the leading industrialist could best be borne by Torcuato Di Tella, who had become the "Henry Ford of Argentina." If Tornquist was a businessman involved in industry, Di Tella was closer to a pure industrialist, a man obsessed by his mill who foreshadowed the new type of entrepreneur who would be the engine of industrialization after the 1930 Depression.

When the depression arrived, Argentina already had a growing manufacturing activity. Industry further expanded in the 1930s, first in the cotton textile branch and later in the durable consumer goods. The annual rate of growth of all industrial activity between 1930 and 1934 reached 8 percent, similar to the 7.8 percent growth rate that had characterized the 1900–1910 decade, lower than the 11.5 percent rate of the 1890s and higher than the 4.5 percent rate of the 1920s.[199] The structural features of local industry (in the spheres of both production and consumption) showed, in the postdepression era, a noticeable continuity.[200]

In defiance of its own shortcomings, local industry had made remarkable progress in the short time that had elapsed since the 1870s. Demand had played its part in this expansion. Changes in consumption occurred mainly in the more dynamic cities of the Pampas, Argentina's major exporting region. Buenos Aires is the best example. There was, however, another

Argentina in which these changes were not experienced in the same way. As James Scobie asserted, perhaps with exaggerated emphasis, in places like the northern cities of Salta and Corrientes, modernity solidified old social structures and increased class distinction.[201] Whatever the geographical variations in the degree of social modernization, Argentina as a whole became a national market for manufactured goods at the turn of the twentieth century. Buenos Aires factories benefited from the market's emergence because it ensured a larger demand, as the next chapter will show.

Chapter 4

Only One Argentina:
The Creation of a National Market
for Manufactured Goods

The Geographical Concentration of Argentine Industry

In the first decades of the twentieth century, Expreso Villalonga became a large transport firm due to its efficiency in delivering goods to any part of the country. Rather than competing with railways (Mr. Villalonga was himself a railroad manager), it complemented them in the transportation of merchandise. The secret of the company's prosperity was its completion of the commercial distribution chain between producer and consumer—it took the goods from the train station to the buyer's address and charged the service to the sender.[1] In 1910 the company employed 795 people, 375 in the city of Buenos Aires and 420 in its branches. By the 1920s, the delivery system had improved so much that

> Today any inhabitant of the interior [inland provinces] . . . can place an order with the capital's great firms, with the assurance that they will be served without delay. . . . Nowadays, within the complex mechanism of Expreso Villalonga, the remittance of merchandise based on the cash delivery system constitutes a section of exceptional importance. In other times, merchant houses frequently encountered trouble in serving their customers in the interior. Of course, it was easy to take care of a letter request by sending a postal package, whether through Villalonga or the railway companies. The real difficulty was to assure payment for the merchandise. Besides, whatever the respect inspired by the seller,

the system of demanding payment in advance of shipping restricted transactions so that the introduction of the service created by "Expreso Villalonga" came to satisfy a real need.[2]

Expreso Villalonga's success was not an isolated experience but rather part of a broader phenomenon that was taking place at that time: the construction of a national market for services, goods, and production factors: land, capital, and labor. In the case of manufactured items, the formation of this market reshaped regional economic relations by generating winners and losers in a battle from which, most of the time, Buenos Aires emerged victorious. With few exceptions—the most well-known cases being agro-industries such as wine and sugar—industrial firms based in the country's capital city prevailed over their inland competitors. Among these porteño companies, big business led the process and benefited from its outcome, while drawing an ever larger area into its sphere of influence. The crystallization of such an economy occurred in parallel with state efforts to create an Argentine nation by defeating two threatening forces: the original provinces' desire to maintain their autonomy and the ethnic allegiances of new European immigrants.

The war of independence against Spain lasted from 1810 to 1820. This conflict was replaced by a civil war that lasted for decades and in which new entities grew as small states: the provinces. Each city that had collected taxes in colonial times gave birth to a new province. As a result, each of the new fourteen provinces—with the exception of Entre Ríos—took the name of its capital city. In the period from 1852 to 1880, a central state strengthened its authority over the provinces. The final stage of this process occurred in 1880, with the last provincial rebellion, when the national army defeated the troops of the powerful Buenos Aires province, which did not want to surrender its main city to become the federal district capital of the country. After the creation of a central state that monopolized the use of violence, Argentinian leaders undertook the task of creating a nation, in which all inhabitants believed they shared the same destiny. Efforts to "nationalize" targeted both provincial old allegiances and immigrant offspring. This campaign began in the 1880s and strengthened in the first decade of the twentieth century through the educational plan already mentioned (in Chapter 1), which created the market for the white aprons used by all public elementary school pupils. A national market arose from the economic and cultural integration of the different provinces and regions that formed Argentina. Every firm's "patriotic" desire for its product to reach the nation's borders was as compelling as any commercial interest.

TABLE 4.1

Relative Distribution of Population in Argentina by Census Year and by Region, 1869–1914

(in percentages on the total population)

	Buenos Aires City	Buenos Aires Province	Pampas	West	Córdoba	Northwest	Other
1869	9.7	17.3	39.2	9.7	11.5	19.8	19.7
1895	16.8	23.3	58.1	7.1	8.9	13.7	12.3
1914	20.0	26.2	64.3	6.5	9.3	9.2	10.7

NOTE: The Pampas region includes the provinces of Buenos Aires, Santa Fe, Entre Ríos, the city of Buenos Aires, and the national territory of La Pampa. The West includes Mendoza, San Juan, and San Luis. The Northwest includes Catamarca, La Rioja, Tucumán, Salta, Jujuy, and Santiago del Estero.

SOURCE: My own elaboration based on Primer censo de la República Argentina verificado en los días 15, 16 y 17 de septiembre de 1869 (Buenos Aires: Imprenta del Porvenir, 1872); *Segundo Censo Nacional de la República Argentina*, May 10, 1896 (Buenos Aires: Talleres Tipográficos de la Penitenciaría Nacional, 1898), volume II, p. CXLIX; and *Tercer Censo Nacional levantado el 1° de junio de 1914*, (Buenos Aires: Talleres Gráficos de L. J. Rosso y Cía, 1916), volume 3, pp. 109–111.

Argentine industry concentrated increasingly in the city of Buenos Aires. Visitors to the 1871 Industrial Exhibition in Córdoba described a collection of items in which those from Buenos Aires were an exception. By 1910, in a similar display in the capital city, industrial goods produced in the inland provinces were difficult to find, while those produced in porteño factories overwhelmed the visitors.[3] Many causes, some economic, some political, must be considered to explain why the country did not develop more regional manufacturing centers in secondary cities beyond that of the agro-industries cases. The Argentine capital and its surrounding region had a relatively large population; in 1895, the area encompassed 40 per cent of the country's total, and by 1914 this had increased to 46 per cent. Industrial concentration, whether considering labor or capital, greatly surpassed these percentages, especially in those branches of manufacturing in which large factories rather than handicraft output prevailed (see Tables 4.1 and 4.2). Other factors, then, must also have been at work to foster this geographical concentration.

The population of Buenos Aires was richer than the Argentine average. This would partially explain the difference between population percentages and industrial capacity. Other rich and populated parts of the country, however, did not enjoy the same good fortune. The most notable case was Rosario, the second-largest city, a major grain port and booming economic center of the Littoral (the richest region of the country, which includes the Pampas alongside the Paraná River) that could have been an Argentine version of Mexico's Monterrey. In 1919, Juan Alvarez, a famous economic essayist and Rosario native, commented with bitterness on the lack of

TABLE 4.2

Buenos Aires Share of Industrial Labor and Capital, 1895 and 1914

(as a percentage of the national total)

| | INDUSTRIAL LABOR | | | | INDUSTRIAL CAPITAL | | | |
| | BUENOS AIRES CITY | | BUENOS AIRES CITY AND PROVINCE | | BUENOS AIRES CITY | | BUENOS AIRES CITY AND PROVINCE | |
	1895	1914	1895	1914	1895	1914	1895	1914
Cooking oil	40.9	61.7	55.7	70.9	51.6	55.8	62.0	63.1
Biscuits	79.1	62.4	82.3	75.4	80.6	85.3	83.2	93.2
Alpargatas	83.1	63.0	92.7	74.4	77.3	68.8	88.4	75.3
Beer	21.3	21.4	76.1	77.2	21.2	8.9	76.6	77.9
Tobacco	66.3	61.9	72.1	70.8	73.8	91.0	78.5	95.0
Shirts	91.6	93.9	93.0	95.3	92.9	93.7	93.9	93.9
Textiles	81.1	61.7	90.3	75.2	84.5	84.3	98.5	97.6
Shoes	56.7	81.8	73.8	86.2	53.3	80.4	74.1	86.6
Hats	84.7	77.7	92.3	96.3	89.1	84.7	92.3	98.1
Bags	53.1	67.2	54.2	71.3	67.3	90.9	67.8	92.7
Furniture	80.6	61.4	88.7	77.2	80.8	53.8	89.7	74.5
Foundries	65.5	41.1	86.0	48.8	56.7	65.6	72.6	91.5
Tin–plate	56.0	81.8	75.5	95.7	52.4	82.7	73.4	90.9
Soap–candles	22.7	18.2	78.2	70.9	27.9	26.6	79.1	81.2
Chemical	69.4	31.2	92.7	80.9	80.1	28.7	96.5	90.1
Tanneries	52.2	44.4	63.0	65.8	61.3	38.9	70.3	51.0
Glass	n.d.	7.5	n.d.	97.1	n.d.	7.5	n.d.	97.1
Matches	n.d.	18.7	n.d.	80.6	n.d.	16.8	n.d.	89.6
Paper	n.d.	n.d.	n.d.	94.4	n.d.	n.d.	n.d.	96.4
Total of industrial workers and capital on the national labor force and investment	48.4	36.4	66.8	60.5	50.6	30.6	71.4	57.0

SOURCE: My own elaboration based on *Segundo Censo Nacional de la República Argentina*, Mayo 10 de 1895, Vol. III (Buenos Aires: Talleres Tipográficos de la Penitenciaría Nacional, 1898); 270–75 and 334–39; and *Tercer Censo Nacional levantado el 1° de junio de 1914* (Buenos Aires: Talleres Gráficos de L. J. Rosso y Cía, 1917), Vol. VII, for Buenos Aires City and Buenos Aires Province Industrial Capital, pp. 115–26, for total industrial capital in Argentina, pp. 186–92, for Buenos Aires City and Buenos Aires Province Industrial Labor, pp. 313–26, and for total industrial labor in Argentina, pp. 395–403.

substantial industry in his town despite its comparative advantages in labor supply and levels of consumption, an outcome he linked to political conspiracy.[4] The nature of Argentine industry and industrialists, however, provides a more plausible explanation of the localization pattern.

On the one hand, microeconomic features were at stake. Industrialists not only bought raw materials and inputs for their production from abroad but also imported and traded finished goods of the same type. As a result, sales of imports and manufactured goods became mutually reinforcing. The vast majority of import activity was concentrated in Buenos Aires, due to its long-standing position as the area's main entrepôt, dating to colonial times.

Therefore, establishing their factories in the capital city enabled these industrialists (and merchants) to develop their dual enterprises in the very same place. On the other hand, this type of combined business promoted a peculiar macroeconomic effect. Being both industrialists and importers, these entrepreneurs could not promote a well-defined tariff policy. Instead of supporting a clear free trade or protectionist policy, they evaluated their interest on a case-by-case basis. As import tariffs were voted on every year until 1905, they had to lobby constantly. Physical proximity to the Congress and the Executive Power was essential to this effort. All roads, then, led to Buenos Aires.[5]

Michael Johns underscores the strong financial and commercial position of Buenos Aires as a contributing factor to the primacy of Buenos Aires. This precluded the industrialization of Rosario and prevented it from even becoming a major site of internal trade. As Johns has shown, it was not market attraction but the advantages of controlling production and commercial circuits from the national capital that hindered the industrial development of Argentina's second city. Indeed, some firms opened branches in Rosario when its boom started at the end of the nineteenth century, but soon backtracked and closed them to concentrate on their original Buenos Aires installations.[6] A crucial element in explaining industrial localization was Buenos Aires' control of a well-developed commercial and distribution system extending throughout the country. The achievement of this network, however, had proven to be more difficult than had been anticipated, as this chapter will describe.

Once established in Buenos Aires, big business strengthened itself through geographic expansion. The dual economy that was first evident in this city came to characterize the rest of the country. As a result, industrial supply was concentrated in two complementary ways: financial capital and location. Interior middle-size establishments fought against two imposing forces and fell vanquished. This battle tells us much about the transformation of Argentine capitalism mentioned in the previous chapter.

From Buenos Aires to the Conquest of the Country

The existence of a national market without internal trade barriers became more critical when firms in Buenos Aires began to produce domestic manufactures and the city not only was the commercial gateway of imports but also the manufacturing engine of the country. This market was created over a long period in which politics played a crucial role. The integration of Buenos Aires and the interior started during the colonial era and continued after independence from Spain in the 1810s. For decades the area that later became Argentina was divided into fourteen provinces participating in a loose confederation (when not at war); each one had its own laws, currency, customs house, and even flag.[7] As the major import trade site for the territory, Buenos Aires controlled the commerce of foreign goods into the provinces. Overseas imports arrived inland with prices inflated by taxes levied at the point of entry and by the high transport costs of the prerailway era. This provided some protection for domestic production. In addition, local authorities imposed their own tariffs on these goods at will. Provinces also could collect duties on items produced in other areas of the Confederation. The combination of these factors created obstacles for trade. Following years of civil wars, by 1862 all provinces had accepted the National Constitution promulgated in 1853, which clearly banned any interference with internal trade and prohibited local customs houses. But the victory of a centralized state, which could enforce constitutional aims everywhere, was not achieved until 1880, with the already mentioned victory of the national authority over the last provincial rebellion. Prior to this year, Buenos Aires had been bogged down in a struggle between forces desiring provincial autonomy (and even a seceded state) and those who wanted to tie Buenos Aires to the interior. The latter group finally prevailed, and the construction of a national market became one of its aims, which required overcoming impending forces.[8]

First and foremost, the country needed to eliminate the legal barriers to internal trade. This was a difficult undertaking since provinces depended on commerce taxes as one of their main revenue sources. The national government made efforts to unify the system of weights and measures, and by 1878 had established penalties for those who did not use the metric standard. In 1881, it took a new step with the creation of a national monetary system, eliminating the multiple forms of currency used all over the country.[9] Obstacles to internal trade were, however, still rife. Outlawed by the Constitution, provincial customs houses, more or less disguised, continued to exist for several years. In 1877, *La Nación*, the newspaper that supported the nationalists or *Mitristas*, followers of former president Bartolomé Mitre and the faction who had worked the hardest to unify the country, voiced their displeasure in an article titled "Internal Customs Houses: A Regression to Barbarism." For the newspaper, the time before the Constitution constituted the local version of the Dark Ages:

> Every province had a cacique [local political and military leader, a pejorative term] for life . . . each cacique had his army [and] the only revenue was confiscation, the only commerce was transit, the only industry was that necessary to provide for local needs.[10]

After a period of successful commerce (especially, as the newspaper high-lighted, during the Mitre administration from 1862 to 1868), money-starved provinces tried to return to the times of anarchy by once again imposing tariffs on internal trade:

> The first province that challenged the Constitutional order was San Luis, in imposing export duties by a Legislative law . . . San Luis was followed by Córdoba, Corrientes, and Entre Ríos, which proposed to establish duties on exports and imports under diverse names and forms.
>
> Provinces involved in commercial wars applied tariffs on internal trade. Only the intervention of the Nation's Supreme Court eliminated these duties. But new ways were found. A commercial war between the provinces of Tucumán and Salta to protect their own wine industries from each other's 'exports' ended with a *derecho de patente* [licensing] on products coming from the rest of the Argentine territory.[11]

In spite of Supreme Court intervention against various attempts to impose taxes on internal trade, provinces found other ways to obstruct it, such as the creation of *oficinas químicas* (chemical offices), which set standards for any article potentially damaging to public health.[12] These offices functioned as a barrier against products from other provinces and became a focal point of protest by industrialists and importers, who complained about the restoration of colonial *Aduanas Secas* (customs houses used by the Spanish crown in non-port towns to control contraband) in a new form.[13] As late as 1915, the merchant association *Liga de Defensa Comercial* (League of Commercial Defense) was lamenting the impediments to internal trade of foodstuffs:

> With the aim of defending public health against possible product adul-terations, various provincial governments have created chemical offices, which operate independently from the federal government [forgetting that] the provinces . . . constitute one and the same nation and . . . must develop their rights harmoniously.[14]

Even by 1929 the issue was continuing to cause trouble between provinces.[15]

The existence of a *patente* (license) that each province charged merchants to trade within its borders was also considered a hindrance to the internal circulation of merchandise. British merchants complained that

> Commercial travellers, proper, pay a fixed license fee of fifty dollars, which covers all their operations *here* [city of Buenos Aires] and in the national *territories* [the land most recently conquered from the natives and directly controlled by the federal government] as distinct from

the other *Provinces* of the Confederation. Should a traveller proceed to the latter, in the prosecution of his business he is at once subject to a further impost, which is fixed by the local Authorities at a much higher rate.[16]

Provincial licenses represented a sizeable expense for merchants. They were so high that a merchant who wanted to sell in every province had to spend paper $10,000 annually, a significant sum of money that only large firms could afford (a middle-size industrial company had, roughly, capital assets of paper $100,000). Fees varied from one place to another. While the charge for trading in the city of Buenos Aires was three pounds and three shillings, in the Northwest provinces of Tucumán and Salta it was as much as seventy pounds.[17] *La Nación* explained the logic of these differences:

> The poorer the trade of a province is, the smaller the number of trans-actions, the slighter the importance of established houses, the more reduced the population and the number of consumers, the larger are the efforts that must be made to prevent competition from the capital city from absorbing the mercantile transactions of the locality and becoming the owner and master of the market.[18]

The Argentine Industrial Union (UIA) supported these complaints and dwelt on the lack of national consciousness, accusing that "[e]ach province proceeds in its own way and charg[es] whatever it wants."[19]

The interior was an attractive market for manufactured goods, both those produced in Buenos Aires and those produced abroad. In the case of foreign firms, trade in the interior was important enough to become the main target of some import houses and to concern the British consul, who made a trip to the provinces in 1907 to study his country's commercial activity there.[20] For industrial items produced in the Argentine capital, the interior became increasingly important as a market badly needed to overcome excess capacity. In the early 1880s, as a general rule, nascent Buenos Aires industrial firms confined their sales to the city.[21] At the beginning of the twentieth century, most of these companies had started promoting sales in two columns, *A nuestra clientela de la capital / A nuestra clientela del interior* (To our customers of the capital / To our customers of the interior) as trade with the interior became widespread. When narrating its success, the varnish and painting firm Bacigalupo told a typical story: "Buenos Aires was not the only market. Rosario first, and later the rest of the interior cities, became aware of the convenience of getting rid of the foreign product" (and buying the articles of this factory).[22]

The industrial goods of Buenos Aires took hold rapidly on the Pampas. This fact surprised a French observer, who noted that in little *ranchos* (country huts) some flowers "have been planted in a box from Gruget [a canned-food firm in the capital], the content of which had been served as the lunch of some traveler."[23] Also, the sale of locally made varnished products in Buenos Aires at a cheaper price than the imported article fostered a fashion revolution and could be seen in the popularity of

> country clothing, with the ousting of the traditional *bota de potro* [riding boot made of the skin of a horse's leg] by the polish and elegance of *cuero de lobo*, as it was then called, and of buffalo, as it is called nowadays, which is in actuality no more than cow or young bull leather from our prairies elaborated in establishments of the capital.[24]

The already significant rural demand in the region soared when the agricultural boom, especially noteworthy since the 1890s, changed the landscape of the cattle-raising country, and members of farm colonies and sharecroppers, also potential consumers, established themselves on the prairies.

The settlement of foreign colonists occupied in cereal production and export in the Littoral province of Santa Fé and the southeast region of Córdoba created a growing consumer market. Named as *las colonias* (the colonies) by Buenos Aires' industrial firms, this market became an early target in their expansion outside the city. The colonists, far from being self-sufficient farmers who made their own clothes, were market-oriented and demanded a wide variety of goods that companies in the capital sought to provide.[25] Since these goods were similar to those consumed in Buenos Aires, this city's companies did not need to make changes in production or packaging to supply them and usually kept, as in the case of chocolate and packaged coffee producer Saint, sizeable stocks in the neighboring cities of Santa Fé and Rosario "largely to provision the agricultural colonies."[26] (See Figure 4.1)

By then, the winds of modernity were penetrating parts of the interior, albeit less smoothly than on the Pampas.[27] The Northwest was the area of earliest Spanish settlement, and it had been the richest region during the first centuries of colonial rule. But the absence of a staple for export turned the region into the most backward of Argentina during the economic boom.[28] The reaction of the population to the advent of "modern" consumption habits illustrates how different the area was from the Littoral. In the Northwestern province of Santiago del Estero, the replacement of the traditional Spanish *manzanilla* by beer created a scandal, far from the smooth diffusion of the beverage in Buenos Aires. Notwithstanding such collisions, in the late 1880s an observer noticed major changes in town life, which advanced in the

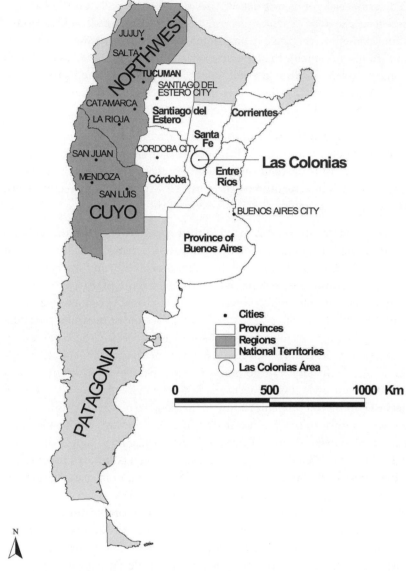

Figure 4.1. Argentina, provinces and regions, c. 1910. Christian Scaramella's own elaboration based on Punzi (1997) and Walther (1970).

next decade when the railway reached the main provincial centers and the interests between local merchants and the city of Buenos Aires merged:

> I see in the streets and public promenades highly imitative portrayals of those who are admired in the Littoral cities, where one observes a taste

and hygiene in clothes based upon models that are received directly from the European capitals. I see in the stores an infinite variety of articles that prove the importance of our import trade, and all the products of the first national industries that are beginning to be produced in the emporiums of the Plata and Paraná [rivers].[29]

Demand in part of Córdoba and the entire Northwest differed from that in the Littoral area.[30] The poverty of the former region limited most of its purchases to products whose low quality and out-of-fashion nature made their sale in Buenos Aires impossible, items such as the out-of-fashion flagons for Carnival and the coarse *sencilla* beer.[31] The commentary of the Leroux chocolate firm upon introducing machinery reveals such a difference in expectations:

> [W]ith hand elaboration, always faulty, it is possible to obtain only an inferior quality product, similar to that which the Bolivians peddle in the Northern provinces, good only for the Indians and unfit for the delicate stomach of an elegant porteña.[32]

The creation of a rail network and the subsequent reduction in transportation costs helped to introduce Buenos Aires goods into the interior. Market control, however, did not always follow the railroad track. One of Córdoba's newspapers, *El Progreso*, announced that the new stocks of Buenos Aires–based department store A la Ciudad de Londres could be found at the train station. Yet, the communication showed that the house could not stop regional producers from forging its articles. Addressing *nuestros favorecedores* (our shoppers), the firm warned its Cordobese customers that

> It has no branch and has nothing in common with the small town or city houses, which here and in some other provinces have taken the same name. It urges the Ladies and the general public to be alert against the merchants who take advantage of the label "A la Ciudad de Londres" with the aim of creating confusion between [their items and those of the store].[33]

Some firms opened branches in provincial spots to avoid such a problem, a process aided by the desire of most secondary Argentine cities to become microcosms of Buenos Aires' consumer society.[34] No place was more successful in doing this than Rosario, which reached a population of 226,000 by 1914. Tiendas La Favorita, a large department store founded in 1897, paralleled in growth—albeit on a smaller scale—its counterparts in the Argentine capital. By 1910 it employed 210 clerks plus 212 workers to manufacture its own goods (still far from the one or two thousand of a major store in Buenos Aires) and had branches in Santa Fé, Tucumán, Córdoba, Paraná, San Nicolás, Mendoza, San Juan, Río Cuarto, and Santiago del Estero.[35] As occurred with the "land of desire" offered by Harrods in Buenos Aires,

> Dames and ladies of the most prominent families of Rosario frequently parade through the various departments of "La Favorita." The site customarily projects the appearance of a social gathering and the distinctive atmosphere created by the congregation of such a select clientele makes it difficult to imagine one is in a house of commerce.[36]

Other department stores opened in Rosario, while the rest of the secondary cities had even smaller copies of the Buenos Aires palaces. They used foreign names from the small selection still available; A la Ciudad de Roma appeared in Rosario, and A la Ciudad de Messina in Chacabuco and Mar del Plata. Copying from Buenos Aires models, as was the open aim of La Marina in Bahía Blanca—a booming city in the wheat region of the Southern Pampas—also meant purchasing most merchandise in the capital city.[37] Very little importation was done directly, even in the case of Rosario, and the vast majority of stores in the Argentine interior relied completely on those of Buenos Aires.[38] Efforts to avoid the latter's influence resulted in failure. To redress the balance of the import trade in their favor, in 1913 merchants from the provinces of Mendoza, Córdoba, and Tucumán attempted to levy taxes at their destination on foreign goods in transit to the interior, but the idea was never instituted.[39] One of the most successful stories (that of the Compañía Importadora Tucumana) resulted from a merger among several commercial houses in Tucumán, but it had only twenty-one employees.[40] In addition, Buenos Aires companies had the advantage of attracting well-off people from the provinces whose frequent visits to the capital city turned into shopping trips. The department store A la Ciudad de México expanded its circle of customers because

> Our customers are, besides the elegant clientele of the city [of Buenos Aires], the people of the diverse points in the republic, an enormous public of travelers who, when coming to the capital for pleasure or business do not forget to make considerable purchases in our houses of undisputed reputation.[41]

With the geographical expansion of changes in commercialization, industrial and merchant firms of Buenos Aires were able to exert further control over the interior market. The use of mail orders accompanied the success of catalogues and could fully develop thanks to the rise of such companies as the

aforementioned Expreso Villalonga. The widespread acceptance of catalogues, with precise instructions for how to buy the exact size and model the
customer needed, improved the system. Already in 1900, a clothing store was
advertising its summer articles to customers outside Buenos Aires:

> Important
>
> Our shipment to the provinces has been notably improved, making
> it faster and more exact provided the indications of our Catalogue are
> followed.
>
> More than five thousand letters from our customers confirm the
> seriousness and precision of our services to winter season requirements.
>
> Expreso Villalonga has established an exclusive service for our cus-
> tomers in the main towns of the Republic.
>
> For any inquiry about our men's and children's items, consult our
> Catalogue.[42]

As we have already seen, by the 1920s this strategy was fully operational.
The parallel development of a credit system further fostered the activity of
the firms in the Argentine capital. As an article in a La Rioja (Northwestern
city) newspaper explained,

> The purchaser from the provinces finds in the commissioner [from
> Buenos Aires] large advantages. The latter puts the former in direct
> contact with the best and the biggest wholesale houses of the Republic,
> and the use of catalogues provided by these large houses helps [the pur-
> chaser] choose the most advantageous item. Being the commissioner
> responsible for commercial operations, he IMMEDIATELY GIVES
> credits that otherwise would have been very difficult to obtain.[43]

Sales in the interior grew further with the full development of a network
of salesmen by Buenos Aires companies. Introduced on a large scale by German commercial firms, the system was rapidly adopted by many Argentine
houses. By the 1910s, the number of salesmen for the provinces had increased
and outstripped those working in the capital city. Buenos Aires shoe-pro-
ducing firms had four, five, and even up to sixteen of them visiting the most
populated centers of the interior. In addition, the system worked with youthful energy—selling in the interior, albeit more tiresome and less profitable
than in the capital city, proved to be a good opportunity for a beginner who
wished to start a career at a company.[44] In conjunction with salesmen, stores
in the interior announced the arrival of the "latest creations" from Buenos
Aires. Moreover, the most successful companies of the Argentine capital
opened commercial offices and filled the columns of provincial newspapers

with their advertising.[45] With a well-developed distribution network, A la Ciudad de Londres could breath more easily as

> [T]he orders from the provinces are more numerous all the time. This growth has forced the creation of a special department exclusively dedicated to serving the daily shipment, in which many proficient people are engaged. The limitless purchases that the public has made are packaged and bundled there, either for delivery the same day within the capital, or to the interior, where they are sent without delay, taking advantage of the fastest transportation means available.[46]

Its increasing accessibility to Buenos Aires manufactured goods impeded the interior from developing a significant industry of its own.

Many Dreams, Few Deeds: The Industry of the Interior

In the interior, business was limited to finding niches for industrial production. Córdoba was the province that offered the most significant possibilities based on its central key location between the Northwest and the Littoral and its potential hydraulic power. Whereas the first advantage was neutralized by capital-city control of the commercial network, the second continued to attract industrialists' interest, albeit without major results. The demand for calcium carbide and acetylene used for lighting public places in Argentina's thriving cities gave rise to a project in which the installation of Union Carbide next to Niagara Falls would be replicated in Córdoba with the energy of the Río Primero dam. Problems, however, outnumbered results, since hydraulic capacity did not develop as planned. By 1905 the production of two factories in Córdoba was about 120 tons per month, well below the demand of 300–350, which was rapidly increasing.[47]

Córdoba did not have a large handicraft tradition, and most of its manufactured goods had long been imported. As early as 1855, the province had passed laws offering concessions for the establishment of brick, saw, and flour mills. In the 1870s, Córdoba's government abolished these privileges and replaced them with the distribution of premiums; in 1893 the legislature even exempted factories from taxes. Privileges continued to be granted in subsequent years, and some local industry benefited. But despite all its efforts, Córdoba did not develop a significant industrial base. Competition from Buenos Aires killed the Cordobese biscuit and woolen hat industries and seriously affected the production of furniture, carriages, leather, soap, candles, and cigarettes.[48] Attempts to open a cement factory in Córdoba dated from 1872 and went unsuccessful between 1885 and 1892, when the construction of the

San Roque dam seemed to provide a market for a company just created by its constructor. After the opening in 1919 of the long-lasting Compañía Argentina de Cemento Portland (Argentine Portland Cement Company) in Olavarría (province of Buenos Aires), attempts to foster a similar firm in Córdoba gave birth to the Fábrica Nacional de Cemento Portland in Córdoba. But this undertaking ended in a failure. The first flourishing cement company in the province—Corcemar—was not inaugurated until 1931.[49]

The few positive outcomes proved to be exceptions to the rule. Cordobese industry successfully resisted the control of Buenos Aires in flour milling, brewing of beer, and shoe production. The milling firm of Minetti, drawing on contacts with local financial sources, exhibited an impressive capacity to resist the efforts of the Buenos Aires–based cereal exporter Bunge y Born to monopolize this activity.[50] Cordobese breweries remained protected because beer distribution to distant places required expensive refrigerated wagons. As a result, large Buenos Aires firms, such as Quilmes, distributed beer in the interior through cold storage facilities built in Córdoba, Tucumán, and Bahía Blanca. Eventually Quilmes opened breweries in some of these and other interior towns.[51] Córdoba was particularly successful in carving out a niche in a relatively broad market. Its brewery Cervecería Río Segundo adopted a strategy of specialization; it concentrated on the production of the cheap *cerveza negra* (black beer) that was consumed in ample quantities in the Northwest—"the main market for Cordobese beer"—and to a small degree in the Littoral. A national division of labor took place, and Buenos Aires firms preferred to focus on the pilsen and lager varieties. As a result, Río Segundo made investments to double its productive capacity in 1904. In 1905, the bulk of its 1,190,000-liter output was consumed in Tucumán (460,000), Córdoba (300,000), Santa Fé (200,000), the city of Buenos Aires (90,000), Salta (90,000), and Jujuy (23,000), with the remainder consumed in other Western and Northern provinces.[52] The selling of ice, the same strategy used by Buenos Aires firms, assisted its commercialization in the branches that the company possessed in the provinces of Tucumán, Salta, Santiago del Estero, and the secondary Cordobese city of Villa María.[53]

The success of the Cordobese shoe industry—the most developed manufacturing activity in the city, employing a thousand workers by the first decade of the 1900s—was as striking as it was exceptional. The five steam-powered factories sold fifty percent of their output in other provinces. They also won a commercial battle in which "Córdoba's factories had to compete tenaciously with those of the Littoral, especially from the capital of the Republic, for the Northern markets, [now] open to the latter because of the direct railway lines."[54] Céspedes, Tettamanti & Company was the largest firm in the interior by the 1910s and supplied a great portion of the retail trade in the Northern Provinces. Like the firms in Buenos Aires, Céspedes, Tettamanti found an ally in "the Villalonga Express Co [which] is utilized a great deal by retail shoe stores in the principal cities for delivering shoes to customers in the interior or distant sections of the Republic, the collect-on-delivery method being used." [55] The firm's success did not lay in Córdoba's energy potential; ironically it was the only large factory in the country using steam power, while the rest used electricity. Rather, a good part of its performance was due to its connections with local merchant circuits, a wise management strategy, and the ease with which a shoe factory could rent machinery, as explained in the previous chapter. [56] Successful shoe production even had a multiplier effect on the provincial economy. Members of the Tettamanti family were important shareholders as well as the main customers of a new large tanning factory. [57] But overall, Córdoba could not match Buenos Aires performance (however limited this may have been) and became, as Waldo Ansaldi has coined, a case of failed industrialization. [58]

The interior's hope of becoming part of the industrial network was strong in the poor Northwestern provinces, which tried to find an economic alternative to replace state subsidies or special tariff protection to finance their budgets. These regions met with even more disheartening results than did Córdoba. The Northwest wanted to produce raw materials for the factories of Buenos Aires and, if possible, to have their own mills. One example is Catamarca, a province that had enjoyed some importance during colonial times in handicraft textile activity. Glory days (and textiles) were gone by the turn of the twentieth century. [59] In response, Catamarca's governor, Guillermo Correa, transformed himself into a champion of protectionism, under the illusion that his province could renew its growth. A potential source of wealth was seen in an unexplored mineral reservoir in the Andes. For Correa, however, these hopes were only a small piece of the future. In his words, "mining in Catamarca is nothing compared to its textile capacity, since in chaguar [a fiber that could replace jute for alpargatas] alone the province has enough to provide what the most demanding trade would require." [60] In spite of some effort, experiments with chaguar failed. Another illusion was cotton. Santiago del Estero hoped to sell it to the future spinning mills (not yet founded) in Buenos Aires, and Tucumán thought that a cotton era would follow the sugar fever, as its production was already reaching its limits at the end of the nineteenth century. [61] As a result, in the province "there now reigns, with truly epidemic features, another enthusiasm, the one for cotton plantations. Everybody prepares to plant cotton, and the benefits of textile will be the salvation of the province."[62] Nevertheless, harvests did not reach significant levels in Argentina until the 1920s, when the Northeastern Chaco region, not the Northwest, emerged as the leading producer of the fiber.[63]

Failing as a provider of raw materials, the Northwest engaged in another deception in its effort to develop its own factories. The region's provincial governments granted licenses to open paper, glass, and textile mills, but with few results.[64] Tucumán made plans to establish textile factories, a dream that fed other illusions in the region. Indeed, there was a belief that Catamarca's poverty would be alleviated if the province could produce raw material for those mills.[65] Manual rather than mechanical industry was the result of Tucumán's aspirations; its main textile establishment was based on the labor of internship girls who wove cashmeres and blankets by hand.[66] In spite of the efforts to infuse optimism, as was the case of the Ministry of Agriculture reports, for the rest of the Northwest, the scenario was even gloomier.[67] Its greatest achievement, due only to the constant pressure of its senators, was the governmental acquisition of four hundred refined sheep. They were sent to the remote Andean Puna region of Catamarca and Jujuy, together with an instructor to teach the indigenous population new methods to produce cloth of better quality than they had been manufacturing for centuries.[68]

By no means was the interior a homogeneous market, but rather a scattering of provinces and regions with different economic and social traits. Generally, the economic prosperity of each area corresponded to its ability to provision the growing domestic consumer market in the Littoral. Wine production in the Western region of Cuyo and sugar in the Northwestern province of Tucumán (and, to a lesser extent, Jujuy and Salta) thrived. For the rest, there was not much more than reliance on federal state subsidies.[69]

Integration into the national market had a double meaning for the interior: opportunities for some and overwhelming competition for most. Seizure of the inland provincial market, however, proved to be surprisingly difficult for Buenos Aires firms. In the face of these difficulties, the companies of the capital city used any available mechanism to control the Argentine market.

To Reach the Borders with Our Products

Sometimes market rules, with the help of economies of scale, were enough for Buenos Aires' firms to eliminate competition in the interior. Until the 1870s, the Northwestern provinces of Tucumán, Jujuy, and especially Salta had enjoyed a flourishing industry in shoe soles, some of which were even sold in the Littoral. In that decade, nascent Buenos Aires tanneries started to compete seriously with the Northern producers and, by the 1890s, undertook the entire process of tanning cattle hides instead of just finishing soles bought in the North. This forced three large establishments in Salta to close.[70] By then, the imbalance in production had become apparent—in 1892 the largest Buenos Aires factory had the capacity to manufacture one hundred thousand soles a year, whereas the entire province of Salta produced only fifty thousand and Jujuy twenty-one thousand.[71] Buenos Aires expanded its sales into the interior and had, in the estimation of one of its firms, "the Federal Capital [the administrative name of Buenos Aires city], the provinces of Buenos Aires, Santa Fé, Córdoba, Salta, and in general the entire republic as a market for these products."[72] One large porteño tannery, which had initially confined the sale of its harness products exclusively to the city of Buenos Aires reached out to "the most distant regions of the country."[73] In 1893, the UIA explained the success of these tanneries:

> [A]s a result of the strong capital they possess, they can produce the article at a lower cost than those of the interior, and as a consequence they can sell their output more easily in the internal trade. . . . Nowadays, the large surplus of soles that exists on the market only represents the items from the interior that have to compete in price with those of the local factories. It is true that the interior sole offers our markets a superior quality that should give it an advantage over local production, but instead, it comes with higher costs. This is the source of the current glut of provincial soles whereas the porteña article, by contrast, enjoys brisk sales, allowing the factories to continue operating with the security that under no circumstances will their product remain unsold for lack of demand.[74]

This process continued in the following decades—between 1895 and 1914, the three Northwestern provinces' share in the total energy consumption of Argentine tanneries dropped from 15 to 9 percent. While Buenos Aires firms mechanized and adopted the latest chemical advances of the time, the Northwestern workshops continued working "with primitive procedures, the same as inherited from colonial times."[75] Nonetheless, there was still a niche that allowed provincial industry to survive in the face of capital city encroachment. The Talabartería y Lomillería [Saddlery and Harness Shop] Junco Hnos. endured by producing artisan articles. Its advertisements claimed that the house was dedicated to the

> manufacture of every kind of refined and made-to-order based mount. Reins on muff and braided in all forms. Harnesses in general. One does

not acknowledge any superiority in elegance, strength and price in those imported from Buenos Aires.[76]

While Buenos Aires tanning firms displaced the interior manufactures simply by using technological advances and economies of scale, the production of biscuits was a different story. By the end of the nineteenth century, the market for biscuits was divided into two regions supplied by different firms: the Pampas and its zones of influence (including the East and the West) and the Córdoba-Northwestern area. As with other goods, the first territory featured a concentration of the wealthiest customers who demanded the highest quality, while the second had poorer consumers who purchased the coarsest articles; thus, supply division reflected parallel demand segmentation. The former region was served by the large Buenos Aires companies Bagley and La Unión and by two middle-size establishments in secondary cities in the Pampas that had opened in the 1890s (La Julia in La Plata and La Aurora in Rosario).[77] The latter area was only partially supplied by Buenos Aires, while a group of local firms—mainly the S.A. Fábrica de Galletitas in Córdoba and La Tucumana in Tucumán—accounted for a significant part of regional production.

The four firms in the Littoral market competed fiercely, forcing a reduction in prices (a scenario repeated throughout Argentine industry in response to excess capacity, as noted in Chapter 3). In order to end price wars, in 1902 they created an organization called *Fabricantes Unidos* (Unified Manufacturers) that negotiated prices and established output quotas.[78] After the agreement, this pool undertook the conquest of the national market, which meant the seizure of Córdoba and the Northwest. Economies of scale and access to railway transportation were a major help, though not enough to accomplish this goal, since local factories showed a remarkable ability to stay in business. The main Córdoba company, the S.A. Fábrica de Galletitas, was the heir of a small firm that had opened in 1888 with the name of its founder Gabriel Olivé and provided the local and the Northern markets. By 1896, the construction of a railway line to Salta and Jujuy allowed for the arrival of goods from Rosario and Buenos Aires at cheaper prices, and the Córdoba factory reduced its sales in the Northwestern market. The company, however, remained in the market through reduction of profits, receipt of subsidies, and tax exemptions from the provincial government (although the municipal authorities taxed it).[79] Because the Córdoba biscuit establishment showed surprising resilience, the consortium of the Pampas tried a new strategy and agreed to create "a general fund to subsidize the small factories provided that they stop working" in the cities of Córdoba and Tucumán. In 1903, the group made an offer that the Córdoba firm accepted: payment of an annual subsidy in cash that surpassed its profits, in exchange for turning off the ovens.[80]

The commercial conquest of Córdoba and the Northwest was a much more difficult task than the Fabricantes Unidos had foreseen. Ending production at the main regional firm did not mean that the market fell like a ripe fruit into the hands of the consortium. Interior middle-size establishments proved to be more resistant to trustification than their counterparts in Buenos Aires, using a variety of strategies such as lowering profits and overexploiting the family workforce. Big business had to employ different strategies from those applied on the Pampas. In Córdoba and the Northwest, economies of scale alone did not ensure market domination.[81]

In part, the success of local firms lay in their adaptive commercial strategies, which responded to the demand patterns of a market poorer than that of the Pampas. According to an assessment by Bagley company, "the small biscuit factories in Córdoba and Tucumán hurt our sales in those areas [because they] sell inferior quality products at very low prices."[82] In addition, these firms sold biscuits to merchants in 17 to 18 kilo bundles instead of the 22 kilo size that the Fabricantes Unidos traded in the richer Littoral and attempted to impose everywhere. As the main firm of the pool remarked, "[t]his weight difference is very appealing in the interior so that [the manager of Bagley] thought we should defend ourselves using the same methods."[83]

To cope with lower incomes and purchasing habits that differed from those of the consumers they were used to supplying, the consortium designed new merchandise and created new brands, both specifically for the area they were attempting to penetrate. Following the elimination of Córdoba's main factory, the chief source of competition came from Tucumán's largest producer, which was selling its biscuits at lower prices than Fabricantes Unidos. The suspicion was that Mr. Cremades, the owner of La Tucumana and of a smaller factory in Córdoba, had launched a dumping strategy in the provinces of Tucumán, Salta, Jujuy, and Santiago del Estero in order to undermine the influence of the firms in the association.[84] The struggle reached a stalemate and negotiations started. First, Cremades "insinuated to one of [Bagley's] salesmen that he was eager to sell the machinery of his factories in Tucumán and Córdoba for paper $40,000," but the consortium considered this excessive and "having no interest in the acquisition of the installations decided not to consider this offer."[85] Indeed, they only wanted the interior factories to stop producing. Second, Cremades offered to limit production to almost a fourth of the group's sales, and to give them control over his firm's management. Finally, an agreement was reached in 1910 through the payment of a subsidy in exchange for the closing of La Tucumana and the restriction of the Córdoba branch to the production of the coarsest articles, completely eliminating a higher-quality item. As a result of the pact, the pool was able to increase the price of its biscuits in Tucumán.[86]

Despite the deal, coexistence between Cremades and Fabricantes Unidos was not easy. The latter accused its competitor of producing biscuits not included in the agreement, and new negotiations began in 1911. These resulted in the sale of most of the equipment used in Cremades's factories in Tucumán and Córdoba, limiting production to only very coarse goods destined to be sold in Córdoba and the poor provinces of La Rioja and Catamarca. Yet, Cremades and his extremely reduced installations continued to compete in Córdoba thanks to a provincial tax on "imported" goods from other Argentine districts. Finally, in 1912 Bagley's directors "persuaded of the advantage inherent in eliminating this competition [decided] that it is necessary to bring such an unsatisfactory situation to a conclusion, and to liquidate this factory by buying it, because in this way all the Northern region would be free."[87] In the meantime, a new arrangement was made for the final closure of the S.A. Fábrica de Galletitas de Córdoba, whose recovery had been limited but was still a threat. As a result, the prices of Buenos Aires biscuits in the area increased anew.[88]

By 1912, the Buenos Aires consortium finally controlled the market. The biscuit factory of El Globo, which opened in 1903, went into bankruptcy two years later. Moreover, a new company created to follow the steps of the one associated with the cartel (Fábrica de Galletitas Sociedad Anónima) in 1908 dissolved in 1912.[89] The consolidation of the Littoral producers meant equalized profit rates, previously distorted by promotion policies, all over the country—the largest variance was reduced from paper $1.22 to $0.72. Prices began to converge (the gap narrowed from paper $1 to $0.40 between neighboring areas) when the company reduced prices in old settlement areas and increased them in the new ones. Thereafter, the different geographical areas of Argentina started to exhibit similar prices and profits. For some time, promotion prices still applied in the Southern and distant Patagonia regions due to their connection to the Chilean market. Yet by the late 1910s, the situation had started to change even there. Market prices, then, became the sum of outlet values plus transportation costs, one of the most significant indications of a national market control.[90]

Bagley, which employed 18 percent of the national workforce engaged in the biscuit industry in 1895, reached 39 percent by 1914. In the meantime, the participation of Córdoba-province firms had fallen from 5.5 to less than 1 percent.[91] Victory in this long-lasting battle had significant consequences for the pool's main firm; by the 1920s, between 15 and 20 percent of its sales were made in the Northwest and another 5 percent in Córdoba.[92] The nature of the market remained stable, and biscuits sold there were the cheapest and of the lowest quality. This proved to be a wise strategy. Indeed, the extreme income-elasticity of this market became apparent during the 1930 Depression, when sales dropped two-thirds in the region but halted only in the Littoral.[93]

The buy-out strategy was limited to conquering a market that could only be penetrated with the application of nonmarket policies. In an area where the consortium was already well established, tactics were different, and small factory production was tolerated. When a biscuit firm of Gualeguaychú, in the Littoral province of Entre Ríos, expressed interest in an arrangement to close its ovens similar to that made in Córdoba, the pool rejected its offer. A year later, salesmen reported that

> the Factory of Gualeguaychú is giving us some competition [but the Board of Directors] decided not to take these small firms in the provinces into account, recommending, however, that our salesmen continue to watch them and communicate any change in the matter.[94]

Meanwhile, as occurred with most industrial activity, the pool itself changed and altered biscuit supply under trustification. In 1905, the two main firms of Fabricantes Unidos, Bagley and La Unión, merged and continued under the name of the former. This altered the internal structure of the consortium, which was now dominated by one company.[95] Then, the middle-size firm La Julia, understanding that its power would become insubstantial in a pool largely controlled by one sole entity, offered to close its factory for a large sum of money. Bagley, however, saw the offer as unacceptable, not to mention useless.[96] By then, it felt strong enough to fight using open-market strategies. When another middle-size firm, Maneffa, entered the market and began producing a cheap and good-quality biscuit, Bagley chose to engage in a price war. Thanks to new investments, reduction in salaries, and advertising resources, it succeeded in producing a similar item at a cheaper cost: it could sell at paper $11.50 a biscuit comparable to the one that Maneffa offered at $15. This was a wise strategy, as Bagley's success in the following years proved, for entrance into the biscuit market was not difficult. After big business consolidated, market strategies seemed to be more suitable mechanisms for capturing demand.[97]

Companies successfully used monopolistic strategies to gain control of the national market and to concentrate production in the city of Buenos Aires. Yet, provincial states could reverse the trend, as they did in a few cases. The provinces collected direct taxes over the production of matches to meet their budget needs. In 1906, the largest match producer, the Compañía General de Fósforos (CGF), opened a branch in Paraná (Entre Ríos) as part of a decentralization strategy uncommon among Buenos Aires firms. This factory was not small; it employed three hundred workers, a fourth of its labor force in the Argentine capital, and contributed, by 1920, around 25 percent of the CGF's total output.[98] According to the firm's official history, the Paraná opening was "undertaken in response to the continuing rise in consumption and the possible inconveniences of concentrating in one sole factory the production of an article destined for the entire population of the Republic."[99] Provincial tax exemption, however, was a more compelling force, as the more reserved board of directors' minutes makes clear. In the 1920s, provincial state intervention prompted the company to open factories in Tucumán, Santa Fé, Córdoba, and Corrientes, where provincial laws concerning tax collection on matches became overtly favorable to local firms.[100] More than half of the company's sales were channeled through the Buenos Aires–based system of Almacenes and Depósitos (Warehouses and Storage). Commerce in the interior, however, was significant enough for the company to defend its position. Especially important was the Santa Fé province market, concentrated in Rosario, and the prosperous immigrant market of *las colonias*. By 1917, sales in Santa Fé had reached 420,970 gruesas (32 percent of the CGF's total), while those in Córdoba were 4 percent and in the entire Northwest just 3.8 percent.[101]

By 1925, the CGF felt its market position was jeopardized by the benefits that local companies obtained through provincial tax-exemption privileges. The firm's strategy to counterattack this threat varied—it reduced sale prices to foment a higher demand, increased the production of cheap paper matches (more suitable for the interior market), railed against the unconstitutional features of those privileges, and solicited direct political intervention. In Corrientes, a representative of the Buenos Aires company started lobbying "the political authorities in that city and received ample indication that the opening of a match factory in the province would be welcome and would enjoy the same privileges obtained by its [local] competitor."[102] In Santa Fé, the company had received similar words of encouragement from provincial authorities. Not surprisingly, the opening of a factory in that city was organized as a big event in order to focus public attention.[103] Since the local competitors in most of these provinces were controlled by the company Demarchi and Ferreira, the CGF reached an agreement with them to rent their factories in Santa Fé, Córdoba, and Corrientes, and share their privileges not only in these provinces but also in Salta, where the CGF had no mill.[104] By

1926, the CGF had opened branches in Santa Fé and Tucumán; by 1928, it had added two more in Córdoba and Corrientes. Output in Paraná (and more slightly in Buenos Aires) was reduced to favor these new factories, each of which reached around 5 percent of total production. The Buenos Aires firm avoided the construction of a new mill when possible and also resisted pressure from the provincial states—in San Luis, despite legislative efforts to tax matches, no factory was opened.[105]

As in the case of Bagley, in places where the CGF enjoyed a secure hold, it preferred to face competition with open-market strategies. This was the case of a match firm in Bahía Blanca; it offered to sell itself to CGF. Since no privilege was at stake, the CGF rejected the offer as had Bagley in the cases of Gualeguaychú and Maneffa, and preferred to work improving its competitive potential. It spent more on advertising, including the exhibition of a film describing the firm's production process called *La Caja Misteriosa* (The Mysterious Box), shown in cinemas all over the country. Thanks to these campaigns, in the firm's own words, "the market of this republic was seized back and reassured."[106]

The Countryside in the City

Control of the national market by Buenos Aires firms changed life in the interior, although these transformations were not as beneficial as some of the provinces would have desired. It also meant changes for Argentina's main city, which started to feel that the entire country was a part of its life. The interior relinquished part of its production to the country's capital. Conversely, Buenos Aires and its surrounding area abandoned some production for the benefit of the interior, as was the case with wine production, where the port region could not compete with Mendoza and San Juan.[107] If some natural wines remained (the so-called *vinos de la costa*), the production of coarse *vinos de pasa* (artificial ones made by adding alcohol to raisins) in Buenos Aires languished with the arrival of products from Cuyo and the enforcement of ordinances prohibiting the consumption of that "unnatural" article. To ensure enforcement, Mendoza's legislators were especially vigilant. In addition, a proposal to produce beet sugar on the Pampas was never undertaken due to the pressure from Tucumán and Salta's sugar cane interests.[108]

Buenos Aires' gains were greater than its losses, as explained in previous sections. Moreover, during the process of industrial concentration, it absorbed not only manufacturing previously carried out in the provinces but also some production previously developed in its own rural sector on the sheep-raising plains. Some woolen textile factories had opened in such small towns as Roque Pérez and San Nicolás in the 1890s. In the following decade, however, this localization strategy proved to be a failure, and the vast majority of this activity gravitated towards Buenos Aires.[109] In addition, the city began to control the processing of food even in its simplest forms. Flour milling was concentrated in the establishments of Bunge y Born in Buenos Aires' new port, while meatpacking houses, yerba mate, and rice mills clustered in the city and its outskirts.[110]

As David Harvey has indicated, the urbanization of rural activities is crucial to the development of capitalist cities; Buenos Aires in the 1900–1913 period is a case in point.[111] Traditionally, it had obtained its milk from small countryside dairy farms. But by 1913 this accounted for only a third of the city's milk supply, while two large firms, La Martona and La Vascongada, provided the rest.[112] The increasing upholding of capital in a few hands in milk production was part of the broader process of industrial concentration discussed in the preceding chapter. A major change was La Vascongada's location within the city of Buenos Aires itself, a pattern that was repeated to an even greater extent in the butter industry.[113]

Along with increased capital concentration in Argentine capitalism, the urbanization of food production led to the already discussed physical location of most firms in Buenos Aires. Some characteristics of modernity, such as consumers' obsession with much touted cleanliness, helped this process. Yerba mate firm Matte Larangeira switched from processing the products at the harvest location to a site in Buenos Aires that became famous (and successful) for its hygiene. Packaging of yerba in cylinders or wooden boxes was done automatically,

> without the intervention, as occurred before . . . of the peon with his hand, inevitably sloven . . . and without the incorporation of the cigarette stub that had inadvertently fallen, swelling the merchandise weight contrary to the will of the proprietor and the consumer.[114]

Fear of rural conditions prompted the *Revista Municipal*, a magazine sympathetic to hygienism, to assert

> In general, the dairy farms of the province, the main source for the provision of milk to Buenos Aires, are unscrupulous about the hygienic treatment of the product. Starting with the milking that is generally done in conditions of untidiness that are appalling and concluding with the packaging that barely receives a superficial washing before use . . . all [of which] imply a severe danger for the consumers' health.[115]

The rise of big business changed the scenario. La Vascongada, which received two milk trains daily in its Buenos Aires mill, had succeeded in enhancing the sanitary conditions of the product through pasteurization. As a result, "over time, the large firms dedicated to milk production have notably improved the condition of a substantial quantity destined for consumption."[116] The fact that the Argentine capital had one of the world's highest per capita demands for the pasteurized product exemplifies the nature of consumption in the city.[117] Unsurprisingly, a new company—Kasdorf—specializing in high-quality items such as pasteurized milk goods for babies, steadily grew from its opening in 1915.[118] Large firms competed with (and to some extent displaced) Buenos Aires street vendors who bought directly from producers and reduced the clientele of neighborhood *tambos* (dairies), where people went to obtain fresh milk and butter. These products were by nature suspected of being dirty and mixed with water (*aguados*). The other large dairy, La Martona, was as active as its main competitor; although it had its headquarters in the countryside, it promoted the purity of its products through twenty branches in Buenos Aires.[119]

In a rural context in which hygiene was often lacking, industry gained public acceptance through its association with conveniences and the benefits of urban modern life. This battle took place against a rural backdrop that elicited mixed feelings in Argentina, as it did worldwide. It provoked nostalgia for a corruption-free society, of which literature became a mouthpiece. A popular play by Nicolás Granada, *Al campo* (To the Countryside), depicted the indignation of a country family witnessing the dissolution in the capital town. Granada's solution was to return home, which meant to the quiet life of the prairies. In the most famous bestseller of the early twentieth century, *Stella*, a pure Alex Fussler, troubled by a city riled with envy, finds her salvation in teaching children in the clean atmosphere of the Pampas.[120] For all these rustic paeans, however, urban dwellers remained mistrustful of the backward customs of rural Argentina.

With their control of the national market, Buenos Aires' industrial firms could enlarge their circle of consumers. Although the interior was important for these companies' sales, its significance went beyond the making of profits. Every corner of the country was worth supplying with local merchandise, regardless of the size of demand. Even markets that were left aside by importers were meaningful to Buenos Aires companies. The provinces of San Luis and Catamarca, to which the British merchants did not bother to send travelers since "it seems that it has not been worth while," were of interest to the establishments of the capital city.[121] In this effort, the state helped the private sector by building railroad lines to areas where traffic was not profitable, such as some parts of the Northwest. Having the necessary transportation network, industrial firms made every possible effort to reach the borders of the country with their products, their brands, and their names. The explanation for such an effort goes beyond the sphere of economics.

The construction of a national market was the economic equivalent of building the Argentine nation. After the victory of the central state in 1880, this process became one of the main goals of the country's ruling group. Education, the military draft, patriotic celebrations, and merchandising were part of the same process. Industry was one of the many forces in the nationalization process, an instrument that created a sense of community between a consumer in Catamarca and another in Buenos Aires when buying a can of Saint coffee, eating a slice of Noel quince jelly, or drinking a bottle of Quilmes beer. As the nation was constructed, there were winners and losers. Interior residents consumed the output and absorbed the advertising of the capital city in an atmosphere of coercion and persuasion. Indeed, the sense of belonging generated by the creation of a national market was fraught with tensions. This strain, however, appeared minimal when compared to the conflict between industrialists and workers, the two social actors in the production sphere and the topic of our next chapter.

Chapter 5

Tension and Harmony in the Industrial Family: Entrepreneurs and Workers in Argentina's Factories

Transforming Relationships

In 1919, while the world was living in a postwar atmosphere of radical changes and social turmoil, a wave of strikes hit Argentine industry as never before. Hysteria, fear, and uneasiness pervaded the social scenario. The unrest, building since 1917, had reached its peak in January during the "Semana Trágica" (Tragic Week), known thus for the high number of strike-related casualties incurred in those few days. An intense repression followed, with significant participation by vigilante groups who eagerly helped the police confront what they regarded as a Bolshevik uprising. Tension remained during the rest of the year.

Strikes were not unknown in Argentina—the first decade of the 1900s had witnessed the emergence of the "social question" as a consequence of workers' upheaval in the largest cities. Then, however, the unrest had had a lesser impact on some firms; the wave of strikes passed over most of those companies whose owners had adopted a paternalistic model with their workers. Conflicts (if at all) had been settled in direct negotiations between masters and laborers, as was the case of jam producer Benito Noel with his workers. The days of 1919 brought unaccustomed distress to this and many firms like it. For the first time, Noel's workers asked for union help from the *Sociedad de Confiteros* (Confectionery Society) in battling for improvements in labor conditions and went on strike. The company's owners angrily rejected

152

any possibility of holding talks with what they considered an interloping organization in the "industrial family." When the workers insisted, Mr. Noel fired them all and started a new hiring process, a strategy that forced an end to the strike. Most of the new workers were previous employees who now presented themselves at the counter presided over by the firm's vice president, Mr. Damián Bayón. One of the episodes—related with pride in a company apologia—reveals the very meaning of the conflict for industrialists. A former worker in line at the hiring place finally reached Mr. Bayón, who

> exhibiting the strain, which is an expression of sadness and energy at the same time, waits for them [the workers] at his desk. They pass by, one by one, holding their hats in their hands.
>
> What is your name?
>
> But . . . Damián, don't you know me?
>
> No, sir.
>
> That is not possible, Damián . . . I have been working at the company for twenty years . . . you know that.
>
> I know nothing . . . Or what I do know is that the House did not deserve this strike.
>
> Yes, Damián, we all understand. But the Workers' Federation imposed the strike upon us for solidarity.
>
> Your solidarity should have been with the House. But we have nothing to discuss. Do you want a job? What is your name?
>
> And the same dialogue is repeated over and over again. The workers feel ashamed of having treated the firm unfairly. And they go into the workshops, after filing a form, crest-fallen . . . .[1]

In facing the increasingly complex relationship between masters and laborers, industrialists were by no means a homogeneous group. The first so-called industrial associations arose in the 1870s, and in 1887 the Argentine Industrial Union (UIA) was born, an institution that still claims to represent industrialists. At the turn of the twentieth century, Argentina experienced the simultaneous creation (or invention) of both an association and the group it was supposed to represent. The UIA built its own identity before being recognized by the state and other social entities.[2] The traditional narrative has assumed that industrialists were a self-conscious group in search of a voice, which was finally found in the UIA corporation. By its own account, the UIA's first years of existence were a struggle in defense of industry against an indifferent society and a hostile state.[3] Representation, however, was reached only after a great effort, a process that has been neglected up until now by scholars.

This chapter investigates the origins of the industrial corporation and explores why factory owners in Argentina came together. In examining this question, we will discover that Argentina took a different path than that of most industrialized countries. Only when workers seriously threatened their interests did Argentine industrialists unite. Because labor agitation was a major concern of entrepreneurs and gave birth to their first collective action, the study of those issues to which the industrialists were most sensitive is the key to understanding the emergence of the institution that came to represent them. The industrialists needed to justify the employment of women and children in the mills, which Argentine society condemned, and to deal with the "evils" of strikes that disrupted their idea of harmonious environment governed through paternalistic strategies. Labor conflicts drove entrepreneurs to join forces and made it possible for the UIA to become a representative institution. In more developed countries, industrialist associations were born with the aim of pressuring the state for protective tariffs and only later faced labor problems as a field of collective entrepreneurial activity.[4] In Argentina, the reverse trajectory created a scenario that deeply influenced the country's social relations.

The depiction of turn-of-the-twentieth-century industrialists in Argentina has been a controversial issue. For some time, scholars regarded them as embodying the traits of an industrial bourgeoisie composed of factory owners solely dedicated to manufacturing. According to this interpretation, they were impotent actors in an economic and political atmosphere dominated by agriculture and cattle-ranching interests that influenced the state at whim.[5] The influential work of Adolfo Dorfman, challenging this account, was later clarified by more complex explanations of the Argentine bourgeoisie's behavior. Milcíades Peña and Jorge F. Sábato disputed the existence of divisions based on economic activity and proposed in their place the presence of a "dominant class." According to these scholars, this "class" was able to dominate society because it had diversified interests throughout the entire economic realm, including land, finances, commerce, and industry. This group's strategies followed a commercial pattern rather than the logic of entrepreneurs investing heavily in a sole productive activity.[6] This entrepreneur figure fits well into the depiction we have made in previous chapters about domestic demand volatility in Argentina. Indeed, economic cycles and changing relative prices would have encouraged the possibility to bank on the most beneficial investment opportunity year by year. To profit from changing business opportunities in an unstable economic environment, entrepreneurs strove for high liquidity by lowering fixed costs as much as possible.

Some of the top manufacturers, those belonging to the kind of "economic group" described in Chapter 3, would fit well into the "class" depicted by Jorge Sábato. Other major industrialists, however, did not have diversified investments.[7] Yet, they would follow the commercial pattern of the "dominant class." As mentioned in the previous chapter, most factory owners imported and traded finished goods in the same branch in which they operated. If this feature promoted the concentration of factories in Buenos Aires, it also created a social actor who worked in a peculiar way. Production and importation were as microeconomically compatible as they were macroeconomically at odds. This was the case for those industrialist-importers who ran both businesses. With harmony and efficiency, this double activity diminished the risks of relying solely on one production in a market characterized by ups and downs. By operating with a microeconomic logic that maximized benefits for themselves, industrialist-importers performed in a way that differed from the alleged and traditional model of industrial entrepreneurs.[8] The UIA members were this type of entrepreneur; with them, the industrialist corporation had to create a basis for representation and legitimacy.

By the 1920s, however, the social reputation of industrialists had changed from the early period of the first factories. As already discussed in Chapter 3, the symbols of industrial power were no longer such figures as businessman Ernesto Tornquist but rather others like factory-obsessed Torcuato Di Tella. Models for economic policies were also changing. The role of industry, which had been previously considered merely one of a number of economic forces necessary for balanced progress, as supported by Carlos Pellegrini in the 1890s and into the 1900s, was transformed into the very engine of development, as Alejandro Bunge advocated beginning in the 1910s. By the 1940s, the movement was complete and Peronism had made industrial growth one of its cornerstones, no matter the cost to the rest of the economy. The seeds of this process existed long before Peronism, and the development of an industrialist identity was a crucial factor in its unfolding.

The Search for Representation

The predominance of industrialist-importers shaped the landscape of Buenos Aires. At the turn of the twentieth century, people associated industrial neighborhoods with the city's southern districts, where factory mills were easily distinguishable from neighboring buildings. Although it had an equivalent concentration of mills, the presence of industry in the commercial and more downtown neighborhood of Once escaped notice.[9] Part of the explanation for this misperception lay in the residential facades of Once factories (also dedicated to commerce), which suggested nonindustrial activities. The illusion was based solely on observation—the rear part of these buildings, some of them adorned with artistic ornamentation, housed hundreds of workers engaged in manufacturing, while the sale of merchandise occurred in the front.[10] The complex behavior of the entrepreneurs who built these peculiar factory-stores gave the industrialists' associations a special meaning. Was it possible for an association defending exclusively manufacturing interests to be successful?

In 1876, a group of people with different interests and experiences (politicians, landowners, merchants, liberal professionals, and artisans) founded the first so-called industrialist association, the Club Industrial (Industrial Club). Later in the decade, when those who were actually involved in manufacturing (artisans and small-shop owners) took the lead in the association, a split occurred. Those partially engaged in manufacturing formed another organization, the Centro Industrial (Industrial Center). In 1887, both the Club and the Centro reunited and formed the UIA.[11]

In its effort to create a recognizable collective representation of industrialists, the UIA first had to persuade its own constituency. Since nothing like an industrialist identity existed, this struggle turned out to be complicated. Soon after its creation, the UIA established an "Industrial Commission" to study tariffs, a crucial issue for industrialists. This commission had weekly meetings, to which industrialists had an open invitation. Attendance, however, was disappointing. As an association report said in 1889,

> [D]ue to the considerable number of industrialists that were summoned in the different branches, we [the UIA] assumed that all of them would be well represented in the session. Nevertheless, the contrary happened and only three out of twenty-seven people called to collaborate on such an important issue had the courtesy to come.[12]

This comment highlights the lack of success of the UIA's early attempts to become a representative corporation; for some meetings, not even one industrialist showed up. The crisis of 1890 prompted a few factory owners to channel some requests through the industrialist association, albeit without major changes in the overall scenario. In 1902, the UIA still complained about the "lack of attendance at sessions [to discuss] issues in which the Association might develop its efforts on behalf of industry." Complaints went as far as accusations against "the majority of the Council [of Administration] members [who because they] do not attend or do it very seldomly, make it impossible for the Association to get the work done the proper way."[13] In the meantime, the UIA suffered a split that led to the creation of the *Sociedad de Industrias Fabriles Confederadas* (Confederate Association of Manufacturing Industries) in 1897. The new organization, which grew out of minor misunderstandings within the UIA, lasted only until 1900, when both branches reunited but found themselves no closer to accomplishing their objectives than previously.[14]

To achieve its goals—and in response to the indifference of the Congress, newspapers, and common people—the UIA decided to take action in the public sphere.[15] Popular rallies and festivals were part of the new strategy, among them the "industrial meeting" of 1899 to ask for the maintenance of tariffs and the "peace meeting" of 1903 to express the solidarity of Argentine industrialists and workers with their Chilean counterparts.[16] In those street gatherings, in which the demonstrators were mainly factory workers, the goal was to show the entire "industrial family" at work. In 1899, both the president of the House, Emilio Mitre, and the president of the Republic, Julio A. Roca, addressed the multitude, visibly moved by their emotion at the size and composition of the crowd (a cross section of age and gender). Conversely, the impressive turnout prompted the socialist newspaper *La Vanguardia* to publish the following editorial:

> We write these lines painfully, after having viewed the degrading and monstrous spectacle of thousands of workers, men, women, boys and girls of four to ten years of age, blindly swarming in the streets, demanding with their presence privileges and rights which they do not understand and which are not intended for them; that is, rights and privileges for their masters, who daily mistreat and exploit them; rights that are frankly antagonistic to the most elemental rights of the worker.[17]

In spite of worker support on these occasions, later labor agitation would eventually unite their masters and create the kind of constituency the UIA was attempting to represent.

The UIA usually complained about the lack of labor, a comment that should be carefully examined. Labor shortages presented a problem for some firms, most clearly in the metallurgical industry, which had to hire technicians and skilled workers from Europe.[18] The situation in woolen textile firms was quite different. On the one hand, a country so full of immigrants was not devoid of skilled workers, as producer Mr. Bozzala pointed out in an interview. For him, the vast number of experienced laborers—mainly from Italy, a country with an extensive textile artisanal experience—constituted a valuable pool.[19] On the other hand, labor training was not a difficult task (as in metallurgy), and it proved to be a successful strategy. Adella Baranzelli, who ran the weaving factory of Mendonça and Baranzelli, after this Milan firm opened a branch in Buenos Aires, "had to start training *nuestras criollas* [our creole women]" with good results.[20] In the town of Roque Pérez on the Pampas, almost a hundred workers of both sexes and from a rural background, such as "*los hijos de un puestero de la localidad*" (the children of an overseer of the locality), formed the labor force of the knitted-goods factory of Mr. Combelles. They were

> mainly indigenous people, who in our cities are called *gauchaje* and who demonstrated in Roque Pérez outstanding and uncommon qualities of intelligence and dexterity [The factory worked on a piece system and] a smart *morocha* [dark skinned woman] interviewed by us stated that she had worked in the factory for three months obtaining in the last month 58 paper pesos thanks to her outstanding dedication and intelligence for her work.[21]

Industrialists also lamented the high costs of labor, which again must be considered in relative terms. Salaries in Argentina were high enough to attract European immigration but lower than those paid in the United States, as indicated by differences in the effort that local manufacturers made to use labor-saving technology.[22] Mechanization in the Argentine cigarette industry, for example, resembled England rather than North America. Indeed, it was fully developed in the production sphere with the Bonsacks but did not extend to cigarette packaging, which was still handmade (mainly by women and children) rather than machine-produced as in the United States. This situation would continue as long as labor was cheaper than capital. Industrialists favored employing ill-paid women and children over buying more machinery. However, by the 1920s—a decade of significant improvement in working conditions and the raising of real wages—salaries were high enough to prompt some firms, such as biscuit producer Bagley, to undertake a program of mechanization substituting capital for labor. Persuaded by the strength of the demand, the firm became obsessed with the idea of replacing hand labor with machines. This strategy increased fixed costs and proved to be too optimistic given the instability of the Argentine market. If the firm could easily reduce its variable costs (mainly workforce and raw materials) during the depression of 1913, the inflexibility of fixed costs almost sent it into bankruptcy in the bleak years of 1929–30. Not surprisingly, recovery during the 1930s was based on a decline in the purchase of machines and the massive hiring of female workers.[23]

The peculiarities of Argentine industrial evolution had an impact on the labor market. Modern and traditional operated under the same mill roof and the putting-out system grew together with mechanization. Shoe production was one of the industries in which the former was most evident; workers made and fitted the upper part of the shoe at home while the use of modern machines, leased by the United Shoe Company, increased. According to a U.S. expert,

> The chief reason for preparing uppers outside the factories appears to be the difficulty experienced in obtaining women to perform such operations in the factory where the work has been done regularly during certain hours. It is much easier to obtain women who can be depended on to do this work in their home at odd moments during the day, many times with the assistance of children or other members of the family.[24]

As in the case of cigarette making, the evolution of the Argentine shoe industry differed from its counterpart in the United States, where the manual putting-out system gave way at an early stage to machine production. Instead, it resembled that of Europe, where a cheaper work force enabled the shoe industry to remain a more labor-intensive activity.[25]

Putting-out was more functional than primitive. Those who support its adaptability and efficiency in the context of European industrialization have challenged the traditional view of this system as backward, transaction-cost heavy, and nothing more than a transitional organizational form when compared to the factory method.[26] Operating at high risk, the system was well adapted to the Argentine case. It included, by 1908, as much as 20 percent of the total industrial work force (a percentage that rose to more than 50 percent in the textile and garment branches).[27] This system further reduced labor costs for industrialists and allowed the collaboration of relatives, mainly children, to provide "invisible" labor. This lowered the price paid for the piece produced at home and resulted in a net benefit for the manufacturer.[28] The end of the system in a particular branch or company did not necessarily accompany a technical improvement, but more often followed changes in consumption patterns. For example, in the 1880s, one of the largest producers of burlap bags had only five sewing machines at its works, while more than a thousand seamstresses sewed bags at home. In response to the boom in agriculture and a steadily increasing demand for these bags, the firm bought 50 machines from the United States in 1888 and 120 more in the early 1890s, and reduced the number of workers under the putting-out system to 250. The machines used at home and in the factory were of the same type, but the gain for the company came from its additional control over the pace of output when facing a steady demand.[29]

The poor quality and the misleading character of census information place major restrictions on analysis of industrial workforce evolution in Argentina. Besides the problems of aggregation, different methods of collecting information limit such a study. The diverse criteria used in the censuses, indeed, preclude some of the most interesting comparisons. The 1904 survey discriminated between adults and children but not between those who worked in mills and those who worked under the putting-out system. For its part, the 1908 census did the latter but not the former. Finally, none of the other censuses considered these features.[30] Rather than a continually unfolding story, only a series of unrelated snapshots could be drawn from these data, assuming they are correct. A study of the original census manuscripts could provide a more accurate basis for analysis. However, with the exception of the 1895 survey, these documents have been lost. This is unfortunate, since examination of the surviving data from this one census leads us to conclusions very different from those suggested by the aggregate numbers.

Standardization, Skills, and Gender

The increasing standardization of production from the late 1880s on signaled a major shift in the history of Argentine labor. Not surprisingly, this was a subject of contemporary criticism from the left. Argentina did not possess a large handicraft tradition, as explained in Chapter 1. But these critics dreamt about some arcadian artisan past that had vanished before the onslaught of capitalism. For them, standardization had destroyed individual skills (as Karl Marx had described), while male workers faced competition from women in the job market for the first time. As elsewhere, employment of women further reduced labor costs, since they received lower salaries than males. Pablo Storni, who produced a report in 1909 for the government calculating these differentials, concluded that "[m]en have actually in women their most serious competitor, not only because the latter are destroying the monopoly reserved for the former in some activities but also because of their lesser needs, which are translated into lower salaries."[31]

Between 1855 and 1895 there was a substantial drop in the level of female participation in the Argentine workforce (from 37 to 22 percent). This phenomenon—described by scholars as the descending part of a U curve—was due to the fall in women's provision of visible labor in the initial stages of modernization. Women became invisible in the labor market but continued performing tasks at home, which were not counted in their

TABLE 5.1

Gender and Age Participation in the Industrial Workforce of Buenos Aires City, 1895–1914

(aggregate data)

		Food	Textile-Garment	Metallur-gical	Chemical	Other Industries	Total
1895	Men	8,978	12,629	5,891	1,716	27,078	56,292
	Women	1,171	8,716	351	518	3,268	14,024
1904	Men	6,184	10,711	7,936	1,647	28,897	55,375
	Women	236	4,739	96	849	7,157	13,077
1914	Men	13,184	17,176	8,693	1,474	36,121	76,648
	Women	574	4,411	129	204	4,068	9,386
	Children	141	281	103	109	610	1,244

SOURCE: My own elaboration based on *Segundo Censo Nacional de la República Argentina*, May 10, 1895 (Buenos Aires: Talleres Tipográficos de la Penitenciaría Nacional, 1898), volume III, pp. 272–73; *Censo general de población, edificación, comercio e industrias de la ciudad de Buenos Aires, levantado en los días 11 y 18 de septiembre de 1904* (Buenos Aires: Compañía Sud-Americana de Billetes de Banco, 1906), pp. 176–87; and *Tercer Censo Nacional levantado el 1° de junio de 1914* (Buenos Aires: Talleres Gráficos de L. J. Rosso y Cía, 1917), Vol. VII, pp. 313–320.

participation rate. Finally, with structural changes in production, women regained their weight as workers in the visible market.[32] The pioneer research of Donna Guy analyzed female labor from the perspective of the type of final product rather than from the nature of the work site: producers of alpargatas, burlap bag producers, shirt and hat factories, tailors' shops, and commercial laundries.[33] Nevertheless, as previous chapters have shown, nothing like a homogeneous "industrial sector" existed in turn-of-the-twentieth-century Argentina, and one wonders in what kind of production units—large or small—women predominated.

In the past, analysis of female participation in the industrial labor force and the presence of females in the economically active population has been based on the aggregate census data. In 1895, both figures—20 and 22 percent respectively—are similar (see Table 5.1). This aggregate data is disputed by research at a micro level, such as that based on the forms filled out by individual respondents in the 1895 census. By investigating census manuscripts at this level, it is possible to classify workers according to firm size. The results are revealing. Women's industrial presence encompassed a third of the workforce in the largest factories and an even higher proportion in the cases of the textile and garment industries (see Tables 5.2 and 5.3).[34] These results show that female incorporation into the visible workforce took place in the newest and most modernizing sector of Buenos Aires industry, "big business." As a result, concentration of capital and participation of women in the industrial labor market became two sides of the same coin.[35]

Women were both pulled and pushed into the labor force of Buenos Aires industry. With standardization of production, large factories turned to

TABLE 5.2

Workers in the Largest Factories of Buenos Aires, 1895

(disaggregate data)

	Number of firms	Men	Women	Women as % of Total
Food	2	241	40	14
Shoes	7	1440	284	16
Alpargatas	1	100	450	82
Weaving	4	211	1020	83
Jute Bags	2	140	460	77
Hats	1	164	156	49
Clothing	3	30	608	95
Tailor shops	1	63	37	37
Tobacco	5	707	438	38
Printing	6	1177	470	29
Tanneries	5	983	30	3
Leather	5	476	50	10
Sawmills	3	690	—	0
Metallurgical	6	1065	14	1
Glass	4	549	24	4

NOTE: The largest factories are those employing one hundred or more workers.

SOURCE: My own elaboration based on Archivo General de la Nación (Buenos Aires), *Segundo Censo Nacional de la República Argentina*, May 10, 1895, Manuscripts, Area Capital Federal, Sección Industrias.

TABLE 5.3

Gender of Industrial Workers in Buenos Aires, 1895

Number of workers	Number of firms	Men	Women	Total	Women as % of Total
1–9	3569	11050	1605	12655	12.7
10–19	512	5886	1058	6944	15.2
20–49	284	7276	901	8177	11.0
50–99	66	3768	935	4703	19.9
100 or more	57	9084	4349	13433	32.4
Total	4488	37064	8848	45912	19.3

SOURCE: My own elaboration based on Archivo General de la Nación (Buenos Aires), *Segundo Censo Nacional de la República Argentina*, May 10, 1895, Manuscripts, Area Capital Federal, Sección Industrias.

cheaper female labor. In addition, the labor of women was more convenient for industrialists; family and home responsibilities resulted in a high turnover rate that was well adapted to the variable nature of industrial output in Argentina.[36] At the same time, changes in the household economy, prompted by the severe recession of the 1890s, visibly forced women into the labor market.[37] *La Prensa* noted this new feature in 1901:

> Not many years ago, few women looked for a salary to increase household incomes, since the head of the household obtained remunerations that allowed him to take proper care of the family's expenses. [Now],

even the least pessimistic spirits realize exactly what [salaried work] represents to the moral as well as the physiological condition of the unhappy females who toil for ten hours a day in the factories to gain paltry wages.[38]

At the beginning of the twentieth century, the predominance of foreign-born proprietors and workers led some Argentines to attack Buenos Aires industry as "unpatriotic and alien."[39] The aggregate data of the 1895 census supported their claims (72.5 percent of industrial laborers were foreigners).[40] Similarly, a look at Buenos Aires demography would suggest high percentages of foreigners among female industrial workers, since foreign women greatly outnumbered Argentines in the 18–39 age bracket in which we would expect to find most laborers. Beef-exporting activities confirm this idea, since a high percentage of female workers in the meatpacking houses of the Buenos Aires suburbs were foreigners.[41]

This conclusion, however, does not apply to women working in large mills producing for the domestic market. In those mills, unlike their male counterparts, factory girls were largely Argentine-born. The disaggregate data shows that the percentage of women in these factories reached 77 percent and the percentage of Argentines 51 percent. Moreover, the coefficient of correlation between women and Argentines is positive and relatively high ($R = 0.7141$ and $R^2 = 0.5100$).[42]

Who were these women and where did they come from? Nativism in female workers can be explained by two factors. One is internal migration from the poor Argentine provinces to the city of Buenos Aires, a topic much talked about in the newspapers of the day.[43] But perhaps the most important feature of female workers is their youth, which could mask foreign ethnic origins. Factory women used to be younger than their male counterparts because many left the factory after they married. Then, the possibility of being the young offspring of recent immigrants increases. Their early age is suggested by the fact that most women working in factories were single. The demographic structure of the female population points in the same direction: Argentine women outnumbered, if only just barely, foreign females in the 14–17 age bracket and more substantially in younger age groups.[44]

Employment of women and children in mills was part of the overall strategy used by industrialists to reduce labor costs. As the unionist leader Carlos Mauli affirmed,

There are many factories, especially the textile ones, where only women are employed. The machines do almost all the work and these are so perfected that even a kid can deal with them. The industrialists have taken advantage of this advancement in modern machinery. Before they employed women at paper $2.50 and $3 daily. Now, they employ children of 10 to 14 years of age whom they pay 80 cents to $1: and in this way, industrialists reap a considerable saving, without regard for the children's health.[45]

It was with sadness that the socialist Adrián Patroni depicted similar changes in the production of cigars. According to him, "machines have displaced an enormous number of workers [and] nowadays only 20 percent of the old number of workers who dealt with the manufacture of cigars are employed, because in many factories they have been replaced by women."[46]

Both *El País* and the census of 1904 indicated that children composed more than 10 percent of the work force; the 1894 estimate of *La Nación* was even larger, between 13 and 16 percent for females.[47] The percentage of child labor was, however, relatively small for a country just beginning to industrialize—the number of children employed was close to the percentages in contemporary Britain and the United States.[48] From the inception of standardization, females and children filled the labor demands of Argentine industry, showing that, in this aspect, Gerschenkron's pattern for backward countries worked (the country, indeed, started industrializing from an intermediate phase rather than repeating the evolution of the early stages of the developed nations).[49]

The incorporation of women and children into the industrial workforce significantly shaped the perception people had of rising manufactures. Most contemporaries rejected, to various degrees, the idea of females working in factories.[50] The sentiments expressed by the socialist representative Alfredo Palacios were commonplace when he said at a Conference given in 1904, the year he was elected, "I dream of the day that not one woman will go to the workshop, but will be able to concentrate instead on their real and noble task, that of being mothers."[51] Similarly, the Buenos Aires press noted and denounced child labor. When describing the 1899 industrial meeting, *La Nación* found that

> [f]or many it was a revelation and a surprise to learn that there are thousands of children who, instead of attending school or playing games appropriate to their tender years—some apparently of pre-school age— are working in the factories.[52]

For its part, *La Prensa* lamented that

> [i]n spite of their hard work, their wretched parents cannot obtain a sufficient salary to feed their families. [This shows] that there are a large

number of teenagers among us who go to work prematurely when they have not yet acquired the proper physical growth.[53]

In contrast, industrialists and their supporters considered female employment in large mills an opportunity of a modernizing society, far more desirable than employment as a household servant. For *El País*, those factories offered

> a moral action on behalf of the modest classes of our population, for there are no men in their workplace, and young women are removed from laziness and vice and given the necessary means for an easy life without the difficulties and hazards of the daily work of washing, ironing and other domestic labors.[54]

Moreover, defenders of protectionism used women (as well as children) to justify import duties. This was the case of the high school professor Alberto Cassagne Serres, who said that tariff protection was an "act of justice" to help women to "support their families with the work of their needles."[55] But in spite of this professor's words, factory owners were a lone voice in favoring female work outside the home. Their discourse made sense only in the context of their claim that the "industrial family" was a refuge from the uneasiness of modern times.

Paternalism, Workers, and the State

Paternalism was a common feature of nascent Argentine industry, during both tranquil and troubled times. As Richard Sennett has pointed out, paternalism was a phenomenon of late capitalism embodying the idealization of an allegedly peaceful past that had been destroyed by the industrial revolution. As an ideology, practice, or program, it focused on the traditional family, an institution that modernity was dissolving, and placed the father-child relationship in a moral context, in which duty and loyalty reinforced each other. Paternalism found fertile ground in Argentina as much as the nostalgic rose-tinted remembrance of a harmonious preconsumer society, rural life, and artisan tradition.[56] Notwithstanding its various meanings and the differences from country to country and firm to firm, paternalism implied, as Mary Jackman has pointed out, "a powerful ideological mold that offers the most efficient and gratifying means for the social control of relationships between unequal groups."[57] As in traditional families, democracy and egalitarianism did not prevail; in the industrial sphere there were parents and children, men and women. The strong had not only the right to lead but the duty to protect the weak as well. Studying the response of paternalism to "disharmonies" in the "industrial family" allows us to examine industrialist attitudes. In bad times, the factory owners' image of the workers reveals itself with clarity.

In the long run, paternalism's shortcomings encouraged the new relationship between state and workers that Peronism erected in the 1940s. In the shorter term, however, it demonstrated as much success as failure in coping with labor conflicts. Many firms launched welfare policies to provide workers with limited health care, sick leaves, and retirement pensions. This strategy, many times linked to the Social Doctrine of the Catholic Church, was applied at the discretion of industrialists, much as a father gives a gift to a child.[58] The UIA praised paternalistic strategies, since they fostered harmonious relationships in the industrial sphere. It was customary to congratulate a company, as in the case of hospital implement producer Lutz y Schultz, for building houses for its laborers. From the UIA perspective, it allowed the industrialist "to educate the worker, to inculcate family love, and to take him out of the environment of misery and irresponsibility in which bad habits and teachings take root."[59]

In the late 1880s, the first major signs of strife arose in the manufacturing sphere when workers asked for higher salaries, paid holidays, and fringe benefits. The response of firms went, unsurprisingly, in the direction of preserving paternalism.[60] The decade following the 1890 depression was relatively quiet in labor matters and allowed discussions of issues to occur without the urgency of a threatening conflict, such as that over the creation of "company unions" similar to those promoted by the reform movement in the United States.[61]

The social clashes of the first decade of the 1900s prompted industrialists to switch strategies. For the first time, fear reached sufficient levels to support the organization of a unified front against workers and unions, a transformation in which the UIA would play a major role. As elsewhere, industrialists in Argentina did not view strikes with sympathy. Labor discontent was not itself dramatic, but became so when unions interrupted the paternalistic dream of a "happy family." Industrialists, indeed, were not unreceptive to workers' demands so long as labor's claims could be met with charity. Industrialists labeled unions as resistance societies and considered them— with the exception of the few labor organizations they patronized—as nefarious bands lacking juridical status and acting in an illegitimate (and illegal) way. For the UIA, unions were "instruments of sectarian propaganda that fight with completely unacceptable and frequently criminal methods."[62]

Not surprisingly, the intervention of a union was usually reason enough to reject a request. In a 1904 tannery strike, the owners of six large firms posted a telling proclamation outside the mill doors:

> To our workers
>
> Due to the continuing hindrances and obstacles posed by the Resistance Society, which unceasingly harasses the good harmony between masters and workers, we are forced to disavow completely that Resistance Society as of today and to come to an agreement directly with our workers.
>
> Any fair claim will be attended to immediately by the owners who, led by the same interest, desire the welfare and the prosperity of their workers, and will pay equitable salaries.[63]

The memoirs of chocolate producer Daniel Bassi lay bare the typical industrialist mind. Bassi's awkward and contradictory account of a workers' strike at his factory reveals a great sadness on his part:

> I cannot be sure whether it was in 1904 or 1905. . . . In other industrial activities strikes had already started, and in our mill a committee with personnel from other factories had been created. Since I was certain that no one from my factory was on the committee, I remained calm. But during a meeting of the leaders, the idea that the first strike should be at my company, the bedrock of chocolate production, arose; because once the firm Bassi came to terms, all the rest would follow as a block. All at once, they set out to persuade the most susceptible [of my workers] and suddenly one day a numerous committee, which did not include anyone from my Company, prevented my personnel from getting to work and succeeded in attracting the youngest element to the meeting, although the majority went back home. The committee gave me the conditions, which I returned unread. . . . My personnel, after ten days of strike, were tired of being lazy and clashed with those who wanted to continue supporting the union, resulting in a fight in which two people [were] injured.

The story continues with the intervention of the police, who incarcerated "the most over-excited" workers. The commissar, "an excellent gentleman" according to Mr. Bassi, was in direct contact with him and asked for a note with his signature to liberate those in prison. After agreeing to go back to work, all were freed and the factory was ready to restart its activities. As Bassi recalled, "there were some other strikes, but in none of them did I accept any imposed specifications, and we even succeeded in expelling those that promoted them."[64]

Industrialists' dislike of strikes engendered a variety of responses to labor troubles. Divisions were sharp, which worked to the benefit of the UIA in its search for representation. The association, indeed, could transform into the privileged field to negotiate a number of different perspectives. At the peak of the conflict, it succeeded in becoming the locus of confrontations between moderates led by glass producer León Rigolleau and advocates of heavy-handed strategies embodied by metallurgical industrialist Pedro Vasena.[65] Industrialists who dealt directly with unions were not unheard of, as in the case of the feared consumption boycotts already mentioned in Chapter 2. When this occurred, the UIA threatened to oust them from the organization since "the sinful weakness of proprietors, entangled in their anachronistic egotism" fueled workers' activism.[66]

The case of Mr. Bassi comes to our attention again as an illustration of the divisions among industrialists. When he received the committee's specifications,

> I was decided not to take them into account, but the fact that other Houses continued production bothered me so much that I initiated a plan to make their personnel also join the strike by organizing a meeting. . . . All the main [industrialists] attended. . . . I immediately told them that I had no problem in bearing the strike and resisting union claims, provided that each firm's personnel obtained a daily salary instead of a monthly one, adding with energy that, unless my proposal was embraced, I would accept all the strikers' conditions, which would force everybody to submit to the committee's will.[67]

The threat of social conflict combined with the division among industrialists to provide the UIA with the opportunity to legitimize its role. Its program to unite factory owners in their response to workers' claims won praise from factory owners. Industrialists began to take the association more seriously, to attend its meetings, and to undertake its reorganization by dividing members into guilds, according to their product. Due to their strict labor regulations, metallurgical firms were especially vulnerable to conflicts with their workers. Not surprisingly, their guild, the Sección Industrias Metalúrgicas, was the first one created. On its first anniversary, speakers underscored what prompted its creation:

> Precisely a year ago, when we were harassed by claims, outrageous in their content and unacceptable in their form, of entitled workers'

groups composed and led by professional agitators, we felt the impera-
tive need to unify . . .

Truly exceptional circumstances were needed to make us abandon
our apathy and our reciprocal isolation.[68]

As a result of the UIA's growing importance, an industrialist guild could
impose the same regulations on most factories. Those for metallurgical
firms were severe and designed to disrupt the private life of workers, which
prompted frontal attacks by Anarchists, who saw them as the symbol of industrial exploitation. Although especially harsh in these factories, internal
regulations to exert control prevailed in most of the large companies—
government investigators were appalled to discover that workers were pun-
ished just for talking to fellow laborers. Finally, the strength gained by
acting in concert encouraged industrialists to use more extreme strategies in resisting strikes, such as the lockout, the mirror image of consumer
boycotts.[69]

A similar ideological approach shaped the industrialist assessment of the
emerging left. From 1900 to 1910 the Anarchists were the most threatening
force. The very nature of Anarchism makes it impossible to apply a single label to a homogenous group. Historians have lumped a vast array of groups
variously rejecting the state, the church, and capitalism under the heading of
"anarchist culture." It was the most successful ideology among working-class
activism, through the promotion of traditional strikes against production
and the already mentioned consumption boycotts. There was no Anarchist
party nor any attempt to compete in the elections. In contrast, the Socialist
party (founded in 1896) soon entered the bias of European social democracy
and participated in the ballots. In 1904, Alfredo Palacios was elected as the
first Socialist representative for the Congress in Latin America. The industrialist view of the left diverged from the reformist side of the governing elite
which, while rejecting an anarchism that challenged the very existence of the
state, attempted to work with a socialism that accepted the rules of the political game. Liberal reformists, influential in politics at the beginning of the
twentieth century, faced the "social question" with the idea of making limited changes to avoid further workers' unrest.[70]

But industrialists did not make a distinction between these two since both
"poison the relationship between workers and masters and tend to hopelessly
separate interests that should be discretely strengthened."[71] Their reason for
putting all the left in the same sack was simple: the two ideologies differed
significantly over the role of the state, but they both viewed industrial paternalism as an evil. In addition, industrialists disliked the governmental

reform movement that proposed long-term solutions to the "social question," such as those embodied in the Labor Code voted by the National Congress in 1905. There were fears of both rising labor costs (for example, the Sunday Rest Law required payment of salaries for a day on which no work was performed) and intervention in contractual freedom. Reforms were, for the UIA, working against market forces and tradition and were destined to fail since they had been "silently prepared by people, who although very worthy of esteem, were notoriously addicted to the most advanced theories and visibly ignorant about our working methods." Their naiveté could cause reformers to lead the country into the "state socialism" fashionable in Australia and New Zealand, but only suitable (if at all) for Anglo-Saxon workers.[72] After the Labor reforms passed the House, the UIA successfully lobbied the Senate to reject them. The political influence of the industrial association, however, should not be overemphasized. Both industrialist and worker opposition defeated the Labor Law. Moreover, thanks to the efforts of the sole Socialist representative Palacios, a law limiting working hours for women and children was approved in 1908, despite the UIA's protests.[73]

As long as the Argentine state continued with the idea of launching reforms, the UIA showed active opposition. President Manuel Quintana's inaugural address in 1904, which accepted some points of the minimum Socialist program, was not a good sign for industrialists. Nor was the perception that social reformism was an ever-expanding force. The evolution of the proindustrial newspaper El País on labor issues, for instance, left the UIA without one of its main allies. In 1902, this newspaper had broken with the political sector led by the proindustrialist leader Carlos Pellegrini and shifted its support to the incumbent president, Julio A. Roca—who governed from 1898 to 1904 and had a reformist minister of interior, Joaquín V. González—discussing his efforts for labor reform in a positive way. El País even introduced a permanent section called Movimiento obrero (Workers' Movement), in which they regarded Socialist and even Anarchist unions with sympathy.[74] The creation of the National Department of Labor, in 1907, opened a new area for industrialist criticism. At first, the UIA welcomed the new bureaucratic office, but as soon as it revealed the will to enforce reforms, these sentiments turned to anger. The industrialist association, then, attacked it as a useless and dangerous interloping force that could shatter the harmony of the industrial family. Now it was the Labor Department that suffered from the presence of "distinguished citizens who deserve respect, but were totally alien to the environment in which they have to act."[75]

A Created Identity

Industrialists were receptive to certain types of state interference, such as police intervention when a conflict went too far.[76] In 1917, when social unrest returned, repressive help was even more welcome. Nevertheless, the state (in the hands of the populist Radical Party since 1916) was not as responsive as industrialists hoped, and UIA efforts to meet with incumbent president Hipólito Yrigoyen were unsuccessful. On December 2, 1918, a strike at the Vasena metallurgical firm unleashed the storm that in January 1919 culminated in the "Semana Trágica."[77] It was not surprising that strife arose in that company. Metallurgical mills imposed especially harsh working ordinances from Mr. Vasena himself, who advocated a "strong hand" in dealing with workers. Relationship between labor and management was tense. The factory itself was a massive Central European–style building that instilled fear in those who entered. More intriguing, however, was the expanding wave of social turmoil beyond this mill.[78]

Conflicts continued throughout 1919 and moved to paternalistic companies that had previously enjoyed relatively harmonious labor relations with their workers, as in the case of the Noel firm, mentioned at the beginning of this chapter. By April, biscuit producer Bagley, who had instituted welfare policies and had not faced dramatic strikes in the past, noticed uneasiness among workers who threatened to walk out in protest. To avoid this, his firm posted an announcement offering a holiday with full pay for May 1, a 10 percent increase in all salaries, and a raise in the interest paid to workers on their savings accounts. However, on April 20 the feared strike was declared. Only then did the firm understand the indifference to its offer, having learned, according to the board of directors minutes, "that the [Labor] Confectionery Association had been toiling to unionize them." An aggressive conflict began; in some sections, workers closed the installations and took the keys to their homes. The union asked for an increase in salaries and an eight-hour workday, a demand that, for the company, included "a number of conditions that are impossible to discuss if we want to keep authority and discipline at the mills." The board of directors decided to post another announcement acknowledging the demands "without accepting the Confectionery Society nor the appointment of sectional delegates, because it understands that this would mean relinquishing the authority that *each one has in his house*, which is the basis of Order." Again, the offer was "ignored and nothing happened." Ultimately, the firm decided to call the police, who efficiently dispersed strikers around the mills with the help of the vigilante Asociación del Trabajo (Labor Association). After the repression, the firm announced that, "[g]iven the abandonment of labor by our workers, our *Improvements*, offered to conciliate but rejected, will *be cancelled.*"[79] Strike leaders (labeled as agitators) were fired, and "to maintain discipline . . . those people who have shown through their activities that they did not deserve our trust, are going to be suspended for an undetermined period." A rehiring process, including all the formalities and symbolic use of power, similar to that which occurred at Noel, took place.[80]

In the minds of factory owners, the "industrial family" needed to survive any conflict. This was to be accomplished through long-term strategies involving the state, the workers, and industrialists. While the UIA rejected the Reform Laws in the first part of the century, it promoted a more interventionist legal system when conflicts seemed to be out of control. In 1919, as strikes continued, the industrial association asked for a law enforcing labor discipline and declared that

> [t]o think of the law as the last word in worker legislation would be absurd . . . . Thus we march, always forward, progressing, not by spasmodic reaction characterized by virulent emergency laws saturated with ill-considered passion, but by the just reflection that makes human efforts good and lasting.
>
> Our Association has seen in the last fifteen years what eventually had to come if measures were not issued on time. [This was] something that everybody only now discovered, after experiencing a period of ongoing striking and as a result of a bloody and unprecedented scandal for our country.[81]

On the eve of 1922, fear of strikes was still high. In an editorial titled "The Industrial Peace," the UIA urged the national government to issue social legislation dealing with conciliation and arbitrage, professional associations, and collective contracts; it even supported the idea of a labor code. In 1921, the institution had been summoned by the Budget Commission of the House of Representatives and wrote a memorandum asking to end the period of "digressing" that had evolved since the frustrated Labor Code project of 1905, which did not find presidential approval, and to develop instruments that could avoid "the use of the well-known weapons favored by workers and proprietors in their blind battles." This document was almost comical, given that the failure of the original project to become a law was partly due to the opposition of the UIA. The words of warning about "other" ideas for legislation was clear; those dealing with the issues not included in the industrialist plan were suspicious. The main threat was the retirement program that was taking shape in the Radical administration. Reasons for opposition echoed those against the earlier Reform plans; the new plans of the 1920s "follow, in theory, noble aims for justice. We are not going to give an open opinion of them; we will just say that, in general, they commit the sin of an exaggerated optimism, based on the short experience shown in some nations that, due to their culture and their wealth . . . cannot be compared to ours."[82]

Suspicion became resistance when the administration of President Marcelo T. de Alvear—elected in 1922 as the Radical successor to Yrigoyen —attempted to issue the frightening retirement law (opposed as an interference) in 1925. Just as it had earlier, the UIA followed the lead of the unions. The main central labor organization—the Unión Sindical Argentina, the same that promoted consumption boycotts—rejected the law just as fiercely. In addition, it called for a demonstration protest on the steps of Congress in June 1925, attended by fifty thousand people, most of them workers. In the face of entrepreneurial and labor opposition, the law was revoked in 1927.[83]

Worker support for the industrialists' agenda is not surprising. It occurred in 1899, when asking for tariffs, in 1925, and on any occasion in which management considered manufacturing activity to be in danger. Moreover, rather than fostering a passive attitude, industrialists sought to steer their laborers' activism. During its proindustrialist era, *El País* proclaimed that "workers and masters should be the united hand that holds high the symbol of the Republic in the national coat-of-arms" as the industrialists are "the natural protectors of their subordinates."[84] Industrialists took this task seriously. A meeting of 1915, organized by shoe manufacturers, embodied their dreams:

> Argentine flags and banners and slogans were indicating the aims of
> the meeting. One said: "the 60,000 families who live from this activity
> claim protection. People should consume articles of national produc-
> tion." Another: "The tariff paid on foreign shoe is at odds with article
> 13 of the Customs law" . . . And a fourth banner proclaimed in syn-
> thesis: "Down with free-trade."[85]

No less was the enthusiasm promoted among industrialists by the discourse of Mr. Savazzini, leader of a patronized union. He remarked on the unity of workers' and proprietors' interests and finished by saying: "We want the Argentine flag to always fly over the fertile national industries and not the sterile market of imports."[86]

In the meantime, industrialists changed from quick action to long-term strategies to keep paternalism alive. The relatively peaceful social period in urban working life after 1922 provided a basis for such a transformation.

Vigilante groups—such as the already mentioned Asociación del Trabajo and the Liga Patriótica Argentina (Argentine Patriotic League)—were crucial in strengthening factory owners at the conflict's peak and in fostering their intransigence in 1919.[87] Moreover, the Liga was ready to make a rapid and tough response whenever any sign of "bolshevism" appeared, as was the case in the infamous attack on strikers in 1921.[88] When strikes declined in the cities, these associations changed their strategy. In the rest of the 1920s, the Liga launched the opening of factory schools to "Argentinize" workers, especially women, who were taught how to be good mothers.[89]

Paternalism prevailed over labor strategies, promoting a more "rational" and "modern" relationship with workers. New methods to organize labor were limited to export-oriented industries, such as the branches of American meatpacking houses.[90] The call for a crusade in favor of Taylorism by the magazine *La Ingeniería* in 1922 did not receive a strong response. In the 1930s, a textile firm founded by the economic group Bunge y Born introduced Taylorism, but only as a novelty.[91] Moreover, new industrial firms opening mills in the 1920s applied paternalism as an unquestioned strategy.[92]

How exceptional was the behavior of Argentine industrialists compared to the rest of the world? Industrial paternalism has been considered a unique feature of the Argentine case: a relationship parallel to that established between a master and his sharecropper in an economy dominated by landowners, a "noblesse oblige typical of a self-confident aristocracy."[93] Paternalism was, however, common in well-developed nations, even in the United States, where new methods of labor organization found the most intense expression.[94] In Argentina paternalism would have still a long life. The state did not have a substantial presence in the master-worker relationship until the arrival of populist Peronism in the 1940s, notwithstanding the effort of profascist Buenos Aires governor Manuel Fresco in the late 1930s to establish a corporate state with a direct relationship between government and workers.[95]

In the meantime, labor conflicts gave the UIA long-sought legitimacy by providing the association with a role in unifying industrialist discourse and practice. In so doing, it represented industrialists as a unique social actor. This process of invention was helped by changes in the institution itself. In 1920, a conflict arose between small and large industrialists in which the latter gained more control of the association.[96] In the years that followed, the UIA launched a campaign to foster an industrialist identity, which resulted in its own growth as a corporate actor.

The attitude of the UIA toward landowners—represented by the Sociedad Rural Argentina—had been traditionally harmonious. Industrialists

believed their activity should develop within a balanced program that included the "mothers of economic activities," as agriculture and cattle ranching were called. The postwar scenario changed this relationship. In the
1920s, the UIA moved from selective to open protectionism in a world that
did not want to return to the laissez-faire previous to World War I.[97] Under
the leadership of its long-term president, Luis Colombo, the institution began to attack landowners as the enemies of industrial development. Industrialists who became more exclusively dedicated to manufacturing rather
than importation considered themselves the most appropriate leaders of modernization and advocated a break with any remaining backwardness, the
most notorious examples of which were absentee landlords. The UIA even
leaned toward Georgism and its idea of renewing capitalism by doing away
with landowners' rent. Long-standing good relations between the UIA and
the Rural Society broke down.[98]

Not surprisingly, anti-industrialism gained support in the Rural Society,
which reexperienced the old fear that industrialized countries—and especially Britain—would stop buying Argentina's primary products if their
own manufactured goods were not sold in the country because of tariff
protection. The rural strategy was twofold. On the one hand, local industrial growth should be limited. On the other hand, U.S. imports (since this
country traded in only a few Argentine goods) should be discouraged in
favor of British, under the slogan "To buy from those who buy from us."[99]
By 1929, the conflict had become an open wound. Luis Colombo was writing in the newspaper *La Nación* in favor of protectionism as a means to
support patriotism.[100] In addition, he sent an institutional note to President
Yrigoyen, reelected in 1928, called "The Defense of Cattle and Agricultural
Interests Cannot Be Made at the Cost of the Argentine Manufacture." This
document was a response to one conveyed by the Rural Society, asking
for a direct treaty with Britain in which tariffs would be lowered.[101] Not surprisingly, the UIA wrote a special note showing a pro-British attitude but
warning of any anti-industrial action when Lord D'Abernon visited the
country as a Board of Trade commissioner to sign a treaty between his country and Argentina.[102] As a result, dividing lines between industrialists and
landowners became unusually clear, foretelling future battles in Argentine
history.

By the 1920s, after more than thirty years of effort, the UIA had become
a social actor. It had won legitimacy among industrialists, and in the process
created a corporate identity for its constituency. In the first decade of the
twentieth century, identity resulted from unification before the labor unrest.
In the 1920s, with the labor scenario in peace, the association attempted

to gain legitimacy with the rest of society by casting industrialists as the primary modernizing force in the country. As the UIA was gaining strength and legitimacy, its platform was becoming widely accepted, first among industrialists, and second, in public opinion. In this discourse, the Argentine state was portrayed as an enemy of local industry. The two areas in which this hostility manifested itself most intensely were the world of finance and the sphere of tariffs, as the next chapters will explain.

Chapter 6

Money and Factories:
The Myths and Realities of
Industrial Financing

Workers, Industrialists, and Banks

In 1900, Francisco Grandmontagne, a journalist sympathetic to industrialists, described a Saturday evening at a British bank in Buenos Aires. Grandmontagne noticed with surprise that "[a]ll the depositors are Italian and Spanish workers" and with joy a scene of burgeoning capitalism:

> seeing the workers depositing their small savings . . . The satisfaction
> and the pride of a worker who manages to reach the counter of a bank
> is something that surely escapes the majority of those reading this article. I did see them, approaching the golden grating, with the joy of
> my spirit that loves all that is humble. Shy and bashful those who came
> for the first time, more confident and haughty the others, those who already had business with the bank. And all of them felt the pride of rubbing elbows with those superior forms of economic life: they felt, when
> releasing the money, the vanity of being creditors.

The story continues to the next step, the process of opening an account. To do so, the bank clerks asked the workers to record some personal particulars in order to avoid fraud if their savings books were stolen. An Italian worker

> approached the window to keep the other depositors from hearing him
> and confessed to the employee that under his left nipple he had the scar
> of a stab wound, pointing towards his heart, obtained in the confusion

of a strike day in which he did not want to relinquish the right to carry
the flag of Karl Marx in the procession.

Grandmontagne's depiction may be true or may not (although bank advertisements in Anarchist newspapers suggest it was not far from reality).
Whatever its accuracy, it shows the industrialists' desire for social harmony—
analyzed in the last chapter—through the eyes of one of its supporters. A savings account could establish a tie uniting workers and factory owners in the
world of capitalism. Frequently, firms opened these accounts for their laborers that held their life's reserves; not surprisingly, an increase in the interest
rates was a standard strike demand. One of the goals of this entrepreneurial
strategy was to create an atmosphere such as that described by the journalist
watching the workers "[l]eaving a bank with the satisfaction of those who
have skipped some steps in the elevated slope of life." [1]

When it came to raising their own financial resources, however, industrialists described the capital market as an evil force. The historical evidence
supporting this aversion cannot be taken for granted and needs exploration.
To delve into the ways manufacturing obtained capital means debunking the
well-accepted canonical argument explained in this book's introduction.
Created by the Argentine Industrial Union (UIA), the version's bottom line
was that industry could not obtain credit, suffered constant capital shortages,
relied on the meager personal savings of industrialists, and barely survived
due to negligible profits. Lack of financing, therefore, would have precluded
manufactures from making the investments necessary for growth and was at
the root of the country's failing industrialization. This chapter will question
these conclusions (or assumptions). In so doing, it will suggest the value of a
new explanatory scheme for industrial financing. [2]

The alleged failure of the banks to support industry is hardly an argument
confined to the Argentine case. The relative lag of British manufacturing
during the second industrial revolution, just to mention an example, has also
been attributed to the inaccessibility of long-term loans. In Britain, a debate
raged around this issue. Those who supported a structural approach blamed
the supply side and targeted the financial institutions, which they accused of
not being flexible and responsive enough to the financial needs of industry.
Advocates of a neoclassical analysis found the accusation that the banks
would not meet demand for such loans to be irrational. [3] In Argentina, the
first position has prevailed. The state was the *bête noire* of this narrative, since
it had allegedly neglected to assist industry through the banks it controlled.
The main state banks were two institutions, the Banco de la Provincia de
Buenos Aires (Province of Buenos Aires Bank) and the Banco de la Nación

Argentina (Bank of the Argentine Nation), which represented almost half of the system's transactions during the period studied in this book. The next pages will analyze information from these banks, those assumed to voice the anti-industrial bias of the entire economy, in order to evaluate and challenge this well-accepted story.

Imagined Enemies

On the brink of the First World War, the Argentine banking network was far less sophisticated than its counterparts in developed nations. The problem was the absence of a well-established financial system rather than the lack of strong banks.[4] The reconstruction of the financial system after the 1890 collapse was based on conservative, precautious institutions that did not want to repeat the experiences after the credit generosity of the late 1880s that sent most banks into bankruptcy. But, as the *Anuario Comercial y Bancario* pointed out in 1913, there are "powerful credit institutions that, on the basis of their capital and the well-deserved confidence they inspired in the public, can easily be compared to the best in the world [but] rediscount is not generalized because our banks, which are models of activity taken in isolation, resist anything that involves the idea of mutual dependence or putting limits on the operation of each one of them, even for the benefit of their increased activity."[5] For instance, only in 1912 did the banks of Buenos Aires establish a clearing-house system—limited to checks—while jealously continuing to guard credit information from one another.[6] In a nutshell, Argentina had individual good banks in the first decades of the twentieth century but lacked a well-developed banking system.

In spite of their shortcomings, state banks played a crucial role in industrial growth, providing firms with money for working capital and investments. This conclusion is drawn from applying a new methodology, already employed in other sections of this book, to analyze industrial financing: the micro approach. This method, which considers each unit of production instead of the aggregation data, does really improve our knowledge on how industrial financing worked. The sources for tracking the credit given to each of the industrial firms are the banks' archives. By checking the names of all firms and persons who received credit from those banks, it is possible to reconstruct a scenario closer to reality than what plain aggregate data offer. This tiresome strategy proves to be worth the effort.

The Banco de la Provincia de Buenos Aires, founded in 1822, was the main financial institution of the Argentine economy until the 1890 crisis sent it into bankruptcy.[7] Not surprisingly, the UIA picked it as the fallman of its campaign to demonstrate bank anti-industrialism.[8] As Appendix 1 shows, however, the bank did extend credit to the nascent industrial firms, primarily through note discount and later through operations in current accounts. Neither the amounts lent nor the number of loans was enormous, an understandable outcome given the small size of the manufacturing sector at that time. The institution did not reject requests made by industrialists, thus indicating an absence of demand by factory owners rather than any anti-industrial bias.[9] On the contrary, the bank was receptive to the requests of manufacturers. For instance, the Fábrica Nacional de Dinamita (National Factory of Dynamite), a stock company founded in 1888, successfully applied for a loan of one hundred thousand gold pesos (roughly 150,000 paper pesos), quite a large sum of money since it was the average capital of a large firm.[10]

Information from the Club Industrial and the Centro Industrial, the two corporations that preceded the UIA, confirms this assertion. Written correspondence between the first association and the bank provides a wealth of insights. The club had created a *Consultorio Industrial* (Industrial Information Bureau), "with the aim of providing data on credit to the Republic industries," for applicants seeking loans.[11] The Centro Industrial was even more explicit in its acceptance of banks' predisposition to give loans to manufacturers. It offered to be the guarantor of credit applications and organized internal regulations to accomplish this. The candidate was expected to be honest, keep commercial books, and have sufficient assets to support the request.[12] In a letter to the bank, the president of the Centro signaled that

> [t]he beneficial cooperation of official banks has already been felt, with the mediation of our association in many of the industrial establishments, providing the producer with convenient loans without which the work of national production could not have continued.[13]

During this allegedly "anti-industrial" period, the *Centro Industrial de La Plata* sent a telegram "congratulating the Directory [of the bank] for the attitude adopted in the current circumstances and offering our humble collaboration."[14]

Belief in an anti-industrial Banco de la Provincia, however unsustainable, prompted the UIA to launch the creation of a Banco Industrial (Industrial Bank) in 1888 in order to "[p]rotect especially industrialists and farmers, facilitating their loans with the sole guarantee of their signature, merchandise, property, etc." [15] The potential beneficiaries of the new bank were not well established firms, since its aim was

> to put above all within the reach of the small industrialist and of the artisan the necessary capital for their work . . . and thus they will avoid the production doldrums in which they find themselves, most of the time, for the relatively insignificant sums they need. [16]

Nevertheless, the project was never carried out and died in the 1890s from the same lack of interest among the industrialists that accounted for the failure of UIA efforts to achieve recognition as a corporation. The association declared

> If the collective effort is not enough to raise the small sum needed to concretize the "Industrial Bank" in exceptionally advantageous conditions, we will actually desist from any effort . . . . The indifference, the apathy, the inertia in which [industrialists] are nowadays, cannot last if the Industrial Union is going to survive. [17]

The Banco de la Provincia and the Banco Nacional launched a generous loan program, in which all economic sectors participated in the 1880s. This strategy eventually led them to bankruptcy in 1891. The new banking system was reconstructed along conservative lines, and institutions only granted credit on a selective basis while maintaining a high level of reserves. The UIA criticized this conservatism and targeted the state-owned Banco de la Nación Argentina, created in 1891 to regain state power on the financial system and meant to be one of the driving forces of the renewed banking network. The new institution was part of a "regeneration" program that established its independence from governmental needs (the old Banco de la Provincia was known as the financial backer of the political party in power) and stipulated a level of reserves comprising twenty five percent of its capital. [18] Criticism about the Banco de la Nación's credit policy—restrictive according to the industrial association, prudent according to bank sources—centered on the supposedly burdensome requirements that a loan concession implied. Actually, these demands were far from immense, since a guarantee only needed two signatures. This requirement, the UIA said, "is repugnant to the worker [for industrialist, FR] who is forced to beg from one door to the other for that guarantee which, in the majority of cases, results in a rejection." [19] By 1894, this bank's note discount distribution gave commerce—whatever the final destination—the bulk of extended credits, while industry received 11.7 percent, slightly higher than agriculture (10.7 percent). This was inferior to that of cattle-ranching (19.2 percent), but significant when measured against the real importance of Argentine manufacturing.[20]

In 1895, the bank explained the reasons for its conservatism. The institution was at a disadvantage relative to private banks that "deny any loan" requested by an unknown petitioner. According to its own reports, this was a policy

> which the Banco de la Nación could not follow without bringing upon itself a sour and, perhaps, a fair condemnation. When a person introduces a petitioner who deserves faith, and when he claims to have the goods that can be enumerated and guarantee his responsibility, a rejection is not possible, even without personal knowledge.

Nevertheless, the bank saw an increase in its default portfolio that could only be reduced by confining the extension of credit to safe operations, something that could not happen, since "its purpose would be transformed into giving loans to rich people. That was not the aim of this bank at its creation, as its Directory understands it, rather it was to help and favor the small as well as the large landowners, industrialists, and merchants."[21] With the goal of reaching more customers, in 1899 the bank made the decision to dedicate, especially in the provincial branches, "[a]n important part of the discounted sums with trimonthly redemptions of ten percent, mainly to favor small industrialists and agriculturists."[22]

Two discourses, the industrialists' and the banks', were at odds. The evidence from 1892 to 1896, a period in which loans were supposedly difficult to obtain because of the 1890 economic depression and the collapse of most of the banks, is striking. In 1895, there were seventy industrial firms in the city of Buenos Aires, each employing more than one hundred workers (the units of production one might call large), plus eighty firms with between fifty and one hundred laborers (the ones that can be labeled middle-size). I was able to identify forty-eight instances in which the head office of the bank in Buenos Aires extended credit to middle-size or large industrial firms or directly to the industrialists who owned them during this five-year period. A third of the industrial companies received loans from the sole state bank in a period of credit restriction. In sum, the picture was far from the anti-industrial bias signaled by the canonic version (see Appendix 2).

The bank granted short-term loans through note and promissory note discounts, which was, in principle, short-term credit. But in practice, the term was much longer than it seemed. As Andrés Lamas pointed out in 1886, the loans were converted into middle-term or even long-term investments through consecutive renewals. This mechanism, which worked well for wool producers, was generously used in the case of industrial firms.[23] A closer look at the alleged "overwhelming" guarantee requirements reveals a reality that was far from this gloomy depiction. Actually, the two required signatures were only one, since the other was the petitioner's, and many times industrialists backed each other to obtain credit.[24] Finally, the money received provided considerable working capital and even funds for investments; some credits exceeded paper $100,000, a sum that represented in itself the capital of a company of considerable size. In addition, it is noteworthy that some firms were allowed to draw on the entire amount of this credit in one sole operation, as in the cases of textile manufacturer Dell'Acqua and paper producer La Argentina (see Appendix 2).

Although its discourse highlighted the indifference of state banks toward industrialists, UIA contradicted itself in its official publication. When narrating the evolution of tin-plate firm Molet, the industrial corporation admitted that

[w]ith the product of sales and small savings, Mr. Molet created his capital base, building the firm with the opportune collaboration of the state bank loans, albeit on a small scale, thanks to which he could enlarge the workshops that today we admire for their capacity to fill any order. Molet will never forget the protection that those state credit institutions provided to him.[25]

The UIA's memory was worse than Molet's, and the association soon forgot it had previously praised the ability of the Sánchez shoe factory to move "with unlimited credit in this commercial center."[26] Proindustrialist essayist Juan S. Jaca in 1899 admitted that "[i]t is true that many of the industries I have mentioned and that you are familiar with, have had a more or less determined protection in terms of the Customs House and in credit concessions that the official banks have granted, a credit that they have honored."[27]

The virtual absence of denied applications suggests that potential demand for credit went no further than the actual concessions. Moreover, an atmosphere favorable to manufacturing in banking institutions makes it impossible to conclude that industrialists (imagining they were not easy to obtain) did not ask for credits if necessary. *El País* pointed out with indignation that the directors of the Banco de la Nación had declared publicly that since "there is no one to whom to lend more money there is no reason to raise the capital of this establishment."[28] According to the proindustrialist newspaper, the bank had not contemplated a hidden potential demand that always existed. This assertion did not take into account that the same industrialists were afraid of contracting debts in an unstable economy such as that of

Argentina. Excessive indebtedness, indeed, hit import commerce harder than manufacturing in the 1897 crisis described in Chapter 1. This demonstrates that an industry less dependent on credit could better overcome the recession.[29]

In the new century, the Banco de la Nación remained a cornerstone of the Argentine banking system. Following its reorganization in 1904, the bank placed more emphasis on cattle ranching, although industrial loans continued to match those of agriculture.[30] In parallel, new private banks appeared and old ones were consolidated with the infusion of local and foreign capital.[31]

Increasing deposits and confidence in economic growth prompted banks to lend money more liberally, reducing their cash reserves and augmenting their lending potential.[32] Nevertheless, the memory of the 1891 financial collapse as part of the 1890 crisis was so vivid that credit liberalism had its limits, a strategy that proved to be wise in the face of the 1913 depression, which did not hurt financial institutions too deeply thanks to their conservatism.[33] In 1906, the former Banco de la Provincia de Buenos Aires reopened its doors with a new managerial structure. Its rebirth was based on solid foundations and, just four years later, it possessed 10 percent of the nation's deposits and granted 12 percent of the loans.[34] The aim of the resurrected bank was to lend money in modest quantities to "promote small industry, agriculture, cattle ranching, and other types of firms."[35] In order to ease credit, it lent money *a sola firma* (with the sole signature of the petitioner). But, aware of its history of being too generous a lender in the 1880s, it reiterated that speculation should be avoided, since

> to promote the liberal concession of credits in those businesses or industries is to conspire against the interests of all of us, it damages general prosperity, and contributes to the ruin of those unwary people who, deceived by the apparent results obtained by others, risk all their own as well as other's capital in those undertakings.[36]

At least eighty-five middle-size and large industrial firms received Banco de la Provincia credit during the period 1906–1916 (see Appendix 3). They included promissory note discounts and loans in current account for a term that spanned from 90 to 180 days.[37] Renewal was almost automatic, even more than in the Banco de la Nación, if industrialists desired it, and loans easily became middle term. Moreover, there was almost no denial of credit for this type of business. Some firms received considerable sums of money— the metallurgic companies Vasena, La Cantábrica, and Spinola; the textile company Campomar; the bag producer Salinas; and the paper company

La Argentina obtained credit that surpassed paper $900,000 apiece (a handsome amount considering that a company with capital assets of $500,000 could be considered large). These sums turned out to be of great importance in providing funds for working capital and investments. For instance, biscuit producer Bagley could finance a substantial portion of new and modern oven construction thanks to this bank's loans, while the textile company Angel Braceras could enter weaving production without monetary constraints thanks to this and other banks' credit.[38]

Although not analyzed here, there is no sign of anti-industrial bias in private financial institutions.[39] On the contrary, immigrant banks seemed to have been generous with petitioners from similar national backgrounds.[40] Individuals and associations used them extensively, and they helped the success of some foreign firms. The case of the Banco de Italia and Río de la Plata, which became the hub of the so-called Italian Group, is a notable example of how immigrant banks supported the growth of industrial companies such as the gigantic Compañía General de Fósforos (CGF).[41] The presence of industrialists on the directorates of various private banks repeated a pattern followed by the United States and continental Europe, making an "anti-industrial" policy in those institutions unlikely.[42]

All this does not mean that manufacturing was facing the best possible capital market. Longer terms without renewal, lower interest rates, or straight credit subsidies would have made industrial life easier. Although not anti-industrial, the Argentine state was far from giving more support to an economic activity said to be "artificial" (for being the result of protective tariffs). The importance of bank loans for industry varied according to the company, as banking debt ratios in Table 6.1 show. Rates ranged from 0.05 to 0.78 in the booming decade that began in 1903 but lowered significantly (in some companies it was even negligible to count) in the 1920s. Without being the engine of financing, bank loans played their part in meeting the companies' financial needs in the early twentieth century. In the Latin American context, and especially during the period 1903–1913, the Argentine situation *seemed* more similar to the Brazilian textile industry (with rates of around 0.50) than to that of Mexico, which never surpassed 0.12 and usually hovered around 0.03. A look at the larger context gives us more insights into the Argentine case, especially against the background of comparative research on Brazil, Mexico, and the United States. Stephen Haber, for instance, considers the main elements obstructing the working of the capital market to be the political involvement of the banking system, the small size of the demand, and the decrepit legal system.[43] Let us examine the Argentine case within this explanatory framework.

TABLE 6.1
Debt to Equity Rates, 1903–1930

Firm	1903–1916			1920–1930		
	BD to Equity	OD to Equity	TD to Equity	BD to Equity	OD to Equity	TD to Equity
A. Braceras	0.78	0.45	1.23	—	—	—
Bagley	0.10	0.15	0.25		0.10	0.10
Bilz	0.18	0.23	0.41	0.01	0.12	0.13
Cervecería Buenos Aires	0.06	0.26	0.32		0.68	
Cervecería Palermo	0.56	0.22	0.78		0.41	0.40
Cervecería Río II	0.23	0.02	0.25		0.19	0.19
Cía.Gral. de Fósforos	0.05	0.02 (1)	0.07		0.12	0.12
Cía. Nacional de Tejidos y Sombreros	0.07	0.26	0.33	—	—	—
Cristalerías Rigolleau	0.14	0.78	0.92		0.34	0.34
Elaboración General de Plomo	—	—	—	0.15	0.29	0.44
Fábrica Argentina de Alpargatas	0.48	0.20	0.68	0.02	0.10	0.12
Fábrica de Papel Casati	0.06	0.10	0.16	—	—	—
Fundición y Talleres La Unión★	0.11	0.25	0.36		0.10	0.10
Gaggino-Lauret	0.04	0.30	0.34	—	—	—
Hilanderías Argentinas de Algodón	0.20	0.20★★	0.20	—	—	—
La Acero Platense	0.15	0.43	0.58	—	—	—
La Argentina★	0.33	0.33★★	0.33		0.18	0.18
La Cantábrica	0.16	0.16★★	0.16		0.13	0.13
La Martona	0.07	0.52	0.59			
La Primitiva	0.16	0.22	0.38		0.13	0.13
La Unión Argentina★	0.22	1.57	1.79		0.34	0.34
La Vascongada	0.13	0.02 (2)	0.15		0.78	0.78
Salinas	—	0.05	0.05	0.22	0.01	0.23
TAMET	0.14	0.62	0.76		0.71	0.71
The Standard	0.05	0.01 (3)	0.06		0.06	0.06

NOTES: OD = outstanding debt; BT = banking debt; TD = total debt (outstanding + banking debt)

★ For Fundición y Talleres La Unión data correspond to the period 1920–29; for La Unión Argentina to the period 1921–1930; for La Argentina to the period 1920–24.

★★ Corresponds to total debt since balance sheets do not specify the following (1) data on long-term debt is only available for 1906–1907 with a rate of 0.13; (2) data on long-term debt is only available for 1915–16; (3) data on long-term debt is only available for 1913–15.

SOURCE: My own elaboration based on *Boletín Oficial de la Bolsa de Comercio de Buenos Aires: Balances de sociedades anónimas, 1904–1916.*

Haber finds the very high level of politicization in Mexican banking to be less evident in the Brazilian model, and low in the United States. Analysis of this issue for Argentina requires that a temporal division be made between the pre- and the post-1891 financial collapse years. In the years before this depression, the politicization of the Argentine state banking system resembled that of the Mexican Porfiriato. The main official bank (the Banco de la Provincia) was in the hands of the political group who controlled the province of Buenos Aires and had made credit expansion one of its banners. The other major state bank was the Banco Nacional (National Bank), which mirrored its provincial counterpart in every practice and strategy. The administration of president Miguel Juárez Celman (1886–1890), a former governor of the inland province of Córdoba, broadened the liberal approach. His political plan was to take power from both the city and the province of Buenos Aires by expanding credit to the rest of the country. The issuing of the "Ley de Bancos Garantidos" (National Guaranteed Banks Law) basically allowed any province to distribute credit on an unprecedented scale. The provinces managed to break the banking monopoly of Buenos Aires, and money flooded the country. Consequences were devastating, since this strategy took place in conjunction with an expansive fiscal policy and in the absence of a competitive banking system and transparent capital market rules. The crisis meant almost the outright dissolution of the existing banking network.[44]

In the 1890s, the government reconstructed the state bank system on a different foundation that stressed conservatism in a way comparable to the post-Encilhamento (a contemporary critical period) policies in Brazil. At that time, the differences with the Mexican Porfirian style became apparent. The shock suffered in 1890 was so strong that no effort was spared to avoid a repetition of such an experience. For some months, President Carlos Pellegrini attempted to keep the dying state banks afloat, until the endless withdrawal of deposits by clients finally forced them to close by March 1891. After the collapse, Pellegrini veered toward the idea of creating a new system by opening the Banco de la Nación Argentina. He said to the members of its first board of directors, "[t]his bank is not based on any political interest."[45] These were not mere words; the operating rules of the new bank contained restrictive clauses, such as one that precluded it from lending more than twenty percent of its capital and reserves to the government. This rule was strictly followed. In 1901, when the national government attempted to force the bank to issue a credit in its favor, the board of directors denied it with open indignation and threatened to resign. The Executive Power abandoned the idea.[46] This did not mean that political figures did not lobby to obtain personal credits. A survey of the loan beneficiaries of the bank shows a substantial number of prominent figures such as Senate leader Benito Villanueva (of the party in power at that time) as well as Hipólito Yrigoyen (the Radical leader, by then in the opposition) and even the *caudillo de barrio* (local boss) Cayetano Ganghi. But this was not mainstream bank business. A similar situation developed when the Banco de la Provincia de Buenos Aires was resurrected in 1906. It reopened under the auspices of the notorious politician Marcelino Ugarte, leader of the electoral machinery of Buenos Aires province. Bank property was divided in half (fifty percent being provincial, fifty percent private), but management was kept in the hands of the private partners (the Banco de Comercio Hispano Americano), which implied severe limits on its use for political clientelism.[47]

In terms of market size, Argentina could claim to be larger than Brazil or Mexico (see Table 3.2). This fact provided the basis for a higher number of operations and a more fluid capital market, as comparative analysis of industrial firm debt rates shows. Yet, it was small relative to the most developed countries and followed, as in other aspects of its industrialization, a middle-ground evolution. No applications for additional industrial credit reflects the lack of incentives for further expansion; the increasing sophistication of consumer demand was not enough to overcome the limited numbers of the Argentine market.

In addition, shortcomings in legal institutions were a source of problems at the beginning of the twentieth century, although, in the end, market forces seemed to prevail over legal incentives or barriers.[48] Conservatism on the banking side in granting loans matched prudence on the industrialist side in requesting them. The ups and downs of the Argentine economy suggested the wisdom of a more sober form of production, one least susceptible to excess capacity, as demonstrated by the 1913 and 1930 depressions, which each halted a decade of continuing expansion and illusions of nonstop growth. Those decades saw a major lowering of institutional barriers, especially regarding the possibility of listing shares on the Stock Exchange, an issue that requires more explanation. In conclusion, the Argentine situation might be considered closer to Brazil than to the United States in Haber's scheme. An imperfect but not disastrous—in Latin American standards—capital market paralleled the kind of midway—in world standards—industrialization that Argentina experienced before the 1930 Depression.

Industries and the Stock Exchange

The role of the *Bolsa* (The Stock Exchange of Buenos Aires) in industrial financing during the period of the export boom is still a puzzle. The few authors dealing with the subject have concluded that the institution played no part in providing money to the nascent mills.[49] References to this institution go back to its role in unleashing the 1890 crisis, a vision fostered by a body of novels, called the Bolsa cycle, which targeted the Stock Exchange as the embodiment of the speculation and corruption that supposedly lay at the roots of the slump.[50] The story of the institution after the crisis is becoming less mysterious. Our knowledge comes solely from a "general feeling" that the share market was merely a formality until the 1940s. This "feeling," however, is not based in reality. Empirical evidence, as will be presented, not only shows that some industrial firms found in the Stock Exchange a supplemental, albeit limited, alternative source of capital, but also indicates that it offered a means of acquiring money that was not used to its maximum potential. Therefore, this section will not approach the Stock Exchange as a defective institution but rather will address the reasons why industrialists did not use this mechanism more effectively.

After the collapse of 1890, the Bolsa plummeted and it took more than a decade to regain a significant level of activity.[51] Even in 1903 the young broker Alejandro Tornquist, when borrowing money from his powerful uncle Ernesto, justified his financial needs by explaining,

> Commercial houses give little due to the abnormal situation we are going through and although I insist and worry, I am a voice crying in the desert. Patience! In the Stock Exchange there is little, or I should rather say, nothing that has been done.[52]

While Alejandro Tornquist was writing his mournful letter (perhaps exaggerating in order to elicit sympathy), the foundation of the institution's recovery, as well as of the entire Argentine financial system, was being laid. The peace treaty signed with Chile in 1902, referred to in Chapter 3, cleared the way for renewed economic expansion. A sign of this revival was the Stock Exchange's official publication, which in 1904 shifted its focus from general economic information to stock companies and their balance sheets. This was a significant alteration, since it provided, for the first time, detailed company information to actual and potential stockholders.[53] The Bolsa had become notorious because of the speculation on gold in the 1880s. And the institution was a gauge for the country's financial mood measured in gold price variations. After its recovery, the Bolsa returned to its position as the best measure for market sensitivity. The newspaper *El País* encouraged the Banco de la Nación to operate with bonds and shares like the other banking institutions because of the influence that stock exchange transactions exercise over the development of the spirit of national association, whose existence (in spite of a period of abuse) is essential to the resolution of public works and industry to avoid their exclusive dependence on silent partnership.[54]

There were two different types of transactions at the Stock Exchange: the safest investments made *al contado* (for cash) by small investors; and the more volatile ventures in public bonds and company shares made *a plazos* (on credit).[55] Industrial shares faced competition in the capital market from real estate investment opportunities (an attractive alternative due to rapidly increasing land value) and in cédulas hipotecarias (mortgage warrants) for

TABLE 6.2

Negotiated Industrial Shares in the Stock Exchange, 1911–1921

	Accumulated Negotiated Shares	Issued Capital in 1915	% Shares/ Capital
Bagley	2,904	15,000	19.4
Bilz	18,120	6,000	302.0
Cervecería Buenos Aires	1,153	10,000	11.5
Cervecería Palermo	2,462	15,000	16.4
Cervecería Río II	134	19,995	0.7
CGF	7,408	51,000	14.5
Cristalerías Papini	1,490	14,000	10.6
Elaboración General de Plomo	926	5,880	15.7
Fábrica Argentina de Alpargatas	2,753	8,325	33.1
Fábrica de Papel Casati	1,407	8,000	17.6
Fundición y Talleres La Unión	3,891	7,000	55.6
La Argentina	33,507	40,859	82.0
La Cantábrica	3,970	15,000	26.5
La Martona	1,065	13,500	7.9
La Primitiva	44,822	15,000	298.8
La Unión Argentina	2,789	5,213	53.5
La Vascongada	196	5,830	3.4
Salinas	28,983	16,000	181.1
TAMET	220	13,000	1.7
The Standard	2,250	2,500	90.0

SOURCE: My own elaboration based on *Boletín Oficial de la Bolsa de Comercio de Buenos Aires, 1911–1921.*

rural properties, plus the crowding-out effect created by the issuing of government bonds.[56]

By the 1910s, a handful of industrial corporations offered good opportunities for investment (see Tables 3.7 and 6.2). Sales of industrial shares through the stock exchange gained momentum during periods of stability and strongly diminished in times of trouble for two reasons: instability reduced long-term investments and accentuated crowding-out by government bonds, which already constituted the bulk of operations.[57] During the First World War, the Tornquist group observed,

> Our Stock Exchange, as could be expected, has been influenced very unfavorably by the war. The shares of industrial concerns have scarcely been dealt in and business has been practically limited to cédulas [Warrants], government bonds, and a very small number of other securities.[58]

Conversely, Stock Exchange performance during the periods 1905–1912 and 1924–30 (which leaves out the disruption of the First World War) shows returns above 7 percent annually.[59]

Why did an industrial company trade on the Bolsa? The number of shares negotiated during the 1910s and the 1920s, though highly affected by the 1913 crisis and war troubles, made up a significant amount of their capital for some firms (see Table 6.2). This indicates that industrial companies found a potential alternative source for financing capital needs in the share market, and their presence there was not merely a formality. These transactions could have been merely speculative, as occurred with shares sold without issuing new capital. A micro perspective forces us to scrutinize this issue, since each firm represents a different case. Speculation permeated the volatile stock of the bag firms, which reached amounts between 200 and 300 percent of the value of shares negotiated over their capital. But productive needs were at stake for alpargatas, paper, and biscuit firms, in which this percentage rose to more modest numbers (between 20 and 80 percent). Metallurgic activity provides a telling case. La Cantábrica and Talleres La Unión firms had percentages of 26.5 percent and 55.6 percent respectively of negotiated shares/capital, but TAMET, owned by the Tornquist economic group, only reached 1.7 percent. This was one of a score of companies whose backing by an economic consortium meant that it did not have to turn to the Bolsa as a source of capital. Moreover, in an economy dominated by large companies, it is remarkable that middle-size firms like soft-drink maker Bilz or confectionery producer The Standard were active participants in the Stock Exchange. In the first decade of the twentieth century, commercial legislation reforms made it easier for firms to quote—they could do so when at least 40 percent of the capital was subscribed and paid or when the share issuing plus the reserves reached the same percentage. Thus, it is surprising that companies did not use share negotiation more extensively. To delve into this issue it is necessary to investigate how attractive industrial shares were to potential investors, an analysis that leads to the matter of profitability.[60]

The canonical version has insisted that industry was not a profitable activity during the export boom since it faced a hostile political and economic environment. Consequently, it would not have attracted investors' attention, hence, the alleged lack of manufacturing activity. Empirical evidence shows otherwise, as Table 6.3 demonstrates. In addition, profitability crossed all industrial branches and not only agro–industries, as the staple theory supported. The high variability in profit rates might, *prima facie*, be surprising. If the Bolsa worked with the fluidity described earlier, one would expect differences to even out through arbitrage confluence. A calculation of profits based on share prices (nominal capital multiplied by quote price) shows that this was exactly what happened. If profits are adjusted according to the quote

TABLE 6.3
Profits of Industrial Stock Companies Quoting in the Stock Exchange
(Profit/Equity), 1901–1930

Firm	1901–1916		1920–30★
	Profits/Equity	Profits/Equity Adjusted to Share Prices	Profits/Equity
A. Braceras	15.3	13.7	
Bagley	11.6	9.0	17.45
Bilz	18.8	13.4	15.52
Cervecería Buenos Aires	7.1	8.2	
Cervecería Palermo	5.8	5.0	
Cervecería Río II	9.0	9.6	
Cía.General de Fósforos	19.2	9.2	
Cía. Nacional de Tejidos y Sombreros	6.3	10.8	
Cristalerías Rigolleau	2.4	2.7	5.87
Elaboración General de Plomo			5.42
Fábrica Argentina de Alpargatas	16.0	13.7	6.01
Fábrica de Papel Casati	12.0	11.1	
Fundición y Talleres La Unión	9.9	8.7	11.23
Gaggino-Lauret	0.1	−4.6	
Hilanderías Argentinas de Algodón	−7.8	—	
La Acero Platense	6.9	5.6	
La Argentina	11.0	9.1	4.80
La Cantábrica	9.4	10.8	10.13
La Martona	6.3	6.3	
La Primitiva	20.6	12.9	13.51
La Unión Argentina	0.3	5.3	5.81
La Vascongada	17.5	—	3.91
Salinas	23.9	20.7	7.23
TAMET	5.8	—	
The Standard	9.9	9.7	9.30

NOTES: Equity is the sum of the total capital stock and retained earnings.

★ For Fundición y Talleres La Unión, data correspond to the period 1920–1929; for La Unión Argentina to the period 1921–1930; and for La Argentina to the period 1920–1924.

SOURCES: My own elaboration based on *Monitor de Sociedades Anónimas*, 1901–1916; and *Boletín Oficial de la Bolsa de Comercio de Buenos Aires*, 1904–1916.

price of the stock, they show much less variation than originally reckoned (see Table 6.3).[61]

The use of the yield[62] (dividend/share market price) indicates how attractive industrial shares were compared with other possible alternatives. As Table 6.4 shows, industry usually looked like a more appealing investment than putting the money in the bank, at a rate close to the discount one of 7 percent, or buying government bonds, with an interest ranging from 4.5 percent to 7 percent. But if we take the two large bag producer firms out of the picture to avoid the blurring effect that direct speculation in these shares had on the overall landscape, return ratios are quite similar. A further

TABLE 6.4
Yield, 1906–1919

Firm	Percentage
Bagley	6.4
Bilz	7.6
Cervecería Buenos Aires	8.3
CGF	7.9
Fábrica de Papel Casati	9.3
Fundición y Talleres La Unión	8.3
Fábrica Argentina de Alpargatas	7.5
La Argentina	8.6
La Primitiva	13.4
Salinas	18.3
The Standard	6.2
Discount rate	6.9
Government bonds	4.5–7

SOURCES: My own elaboration based on *Boletín Oficial de la Bolsa de Comercio de Buenos Aires*, 1906–1919. For the discount rate, see Instituto de Economía Bancaria, *Análisis estadístico y económico de algunas series bancarias y afines en el período 1901 a 1927*, Primera parte, p. 38. For government bonds, see Roberto A. Ramm Doman, *Manual de la Bolsa de Comercio de Buenos Aires* (Buenos Aires: n.p., 1912).

attraction to invest in industrial stock was that its purchasing generally implied tremendous capitalization. The vast majority of the shares quoted above par, which means they have a market price above face stock value. Sometimes, as in the first stock quote of the Fábrica Argentina de Alpargatas, shares opened at 40 percent over the nominal price. Capitalization, however, was the Achilles' heel of these transactions. The small size of the market drove prices well above the nominal value and restrictively beyond the reach of new investors. In an industrial asset market such as this, a small number of operations could send prices skyrocketing, and these overvalued stocks were unattractive for new investors—a purchase of 1,480 shares of La Cantábrica raised stock prices from paper $148 to $220. When the company was well-established, even meager operations could produce an upheaval in the market. The sale of just 326 shares of the CGF drove their value from paper $280 to $400, while a similar transaction of 224 stocks of the Fábrica Argentina de Alpargatas pushed values from paper $165 to $250.[63]

Thus, the scenario is different from the one traditionally assumed. The failure lies not in the lack of interest in industry but in the few opportunities it provided to investors. This fact, more than other constraints, created the contrast between the Argentine Bolsa and its counterparts in the industrialized nations. On the Paris Stock Exchange, for instance, daily negotiations ranged from 1 to 3 percent of the potential assets, while in Buenos Aires it required a month to reach this level. The transformation of the former into a place mainly dedicated to negotiating company shares was, however, a later phenomenon. In addition, until the First World War, the definition of an investor was associated worldwide with the purchaser of government bonds, whereas those who bought company shares were considered speculators.[64]

No special aversion to industry existed. This compels us to examine industry itself rather than a capital market conspiracy to explain why firms did not issue more shares to obtain fresh capital. An analysis of alternative methods of financing available to firms provides an answer to this question— firms found a source of capital in the issuing of long-term debt and especially in self-financing.

Long-Term Debts

Industrial companies successfully used the issuing of long-term debt, usually as debentures.[65] Table 6.1 considers firms' long-term debts through the outstanding debt to equity index. This rate—less than one—was low compared to modern firms, for which values go from one to five, but quite high compared to the Mexican case, in which the capital market worked with more restrictions than in Argentina.[66] The metallurgical firm La Unión, for instance, assumed a liability of paper $200,000, which represented a third of its capital. The conditions of the transaction were favorable to the company— the interest rate was seven percent with a ten-year waiver before capital redemption. As a result, La Unión could enlarge its mills and achieve a better position in the market for iron and bronze products. Even more impressive was the case of glass producer Rigolleau, which issued debentures for an amount equal to its capital. This allowed it to strengthen its traditional bottle output and to enter flat-glass production. These issues generally were sold in Buenos Aires, London and, to a lesser extent, in Paris, markets that preferred the lower but safer rates of these debentures to the higher but more volatile dividends that a share could offer.[67] For smaller companies such as Bilz or the Compañía General de Envases, debentures that would allow them to enlarge their mills could only be issued in Argentina, forcing these companies to assume liabilities with rates higher than those of the European market.[68]

Negotiations on the Stock Exchange and the issuing of long-term debt took place in parallel with the twentieth century cartelization process described in Chapter 3. Moreover, easier access to financing boosted the creation of these conglomerates.[69] The first wave of stock-company formation had taken place in the late 1880s. Prompted by the unprecedented expansion of the Argentine economy, a handful of firms transformed themselves into corporations, joined by others that were initiated during this period.[70] With few exceptions, the 1890 depression halted this incipient process. Finances are extremely sensitive to market expectations, and only the lure of long-term stability could attract large investments into the capital market. The corporate rush only regained strength after 1904 and through the following decade of sustained growth.

In the new wave of rising corporations, the role of economic groups (also described in Chapter 3) became crucial. As the previously mentioned Juan S. Jaca, a supporter of small industries, noted,

> Just when [industries] achieve some development, the absorbing and monopolizing tension of capital, often anonymous, begins by oppressing the working guilds [for industrialists, FR] and by limiting the horizon of their aspirations and perspectives.[71]

The transformation of an industrial firm into a stock company often signaled its takeover by a powerful financial group. Later, scholars considered this to be a major impediment to full-fledged industrialization in Argentina.[72] However, Jaca had pointed out a reality that this analysis did not take into account: in the intervention of these groups in the economy, Argentina was not an exception but an example of a "universal vice"; the United States and Germany were experiencing the same phenomenon with particular strength.[73]

As the examination of specific cases shows, links between economic groups and industry were more complex than usually thought when becoming stock companies. Industrial firms followed different paths. One of them was the acquisition of fresh capital without major changes in company control. In this case, the old owners kept most of the shares and served on the board of directors, usually as chairmen. A number of firms followed the example of the paint producer Bacigalupo, which transformed into a corporation with Ireneo Bacigalupo as president. The change in status was sought because

> Four years ago, the size attained by our business in relation to the scarce importance that it had at first made it clear that the company had an opportunity to enlarge the sphere of its activities with an increase of capital. At that time, the stock company that took charge of the old firm was formed and elements of unquestionable experience and profound knowledge in the production of articles came together by that means.[74]

When companies needed large sums of capital in regard to their assets, the original owners gave up ownership, albeit rarely management, whether at the hands of an economic group or through property diversification of shares.

The Tornquist group played the leading role in backing this kind of transformation. Sometimes an initial investment was the springboard for further control. At other times the group provided capital but did not control the majority of the new company's shares.[75] Finally, the formation of a stock company could simply be a "modern" way to begin an industrial business.[76]

Once a new stock company emerged, it satisfied its need for further money by issuing equity capital. This mechanism was especially popular, as expected, in the oldest corporations. The paper firm La Argentina doubled its capital between 1888 and 1908, and the match company CGF almost tripled its own between 1905 and 1912.[77] These corporations were usually in the hands of local capital, as was the general case in manufacturing. Foreign participation in industrial stock companies was small. British investment started in the 1880s, stopped after the 1890 depression, and experienced a mild resurgence in the new century—the largest British operations in local industry were the purchase of the Bieckert brewery in 1889, the metallurgical firm Vasena in 1912, and the Cía Nacional de Tabacos in 1913.[78] The limited amount of foreign investment in industrial activities, which also included some Belgian, German, and Italian money, was related to the lack of both push and pull incentives. It was well known that investments in the country were monopolized in Britain by a group of financiers known as the "Argentine circle," who preferred to concentrate in railways. More decisively, Argentine entrepreneurs were enthusiastic about funneling their money into manufacturing, thus limiting opportunities for foreign investors.[79] It was not until the 1920s, when business opportunities became more numerous, that foreign investment in Argentine industry, primarily from the United States, began to grow, as explained in Chapter 3. By then, a market for new products, mainly chemical, metal, electrical, and cosmetic appliances propelled the opening of more than forty foreign companies in the industrial area.[80]

Stock companies' importance in the industrial area was not due to their number, which was small, but to the capital, workers, and output they implied. Stock companies composed the majority of firms in almost every branch. Moreover, more large industrial firms, especially in the textile activity, became stock companies in the 1920s (see Table 3.7).

The variety of cases and scenarios demonstrates that there was not a singular or predominant process in the creation of industrial corporations. Possibilities, as well as consequences, varied widely. Furthermore, formation of corporations was not exclusive to the largest firms but indeed included a few middle-size companies. Limited use of bank loans (and even more so of stock operations) and a broad strategy of capital concentration combined with self-financing to ensure the growth of industrial firms.

Self-Financing and the Argentine Dream

Self-financing was a mechanism of extreme importance for manufacturing firms' performance, and it was recognized as such at the time. For industrial apologias, this strategy was the result of pioneer efforts to create a large firm through hard work, obsessive saving, and a driving passion for success. Italian Francesco Scardin, wishing to show the triumph of people from his native land, said,

> [I]n what refers to the development of an industry from its primitive origin, the case is almost always the same. I mean, the story of an industry that feeds on itself to achieve, with the passage of time and with the help of circumstances, the growth, improvements, and perfection, the grandiosity that many workshops display nowadays by taking full advantage of the firm's profits.[81]

Similarly, J. S. Jaca pointed out that reinvestment was the growth engine of most industrial establishments because

> with few exceptions, besides being national they are the product of the industrialists' intelligence and personal thrift. Many of the foundries and the small metallurgy workshops that employ hundreds of workers have had as a base a poor blacksmith shop and as a director the modest artisan who, with the savings of the salary he obtained through apprenticeship, founded the workshop that slowly grows and in the end blossoms into a beautiful factory.[82]

For profit reinvestments to play a crucial role in industrial growth, two prerequisites must have been met: (1) that industries were profitable, and (2) that a substantial part of these benefits were kept as a reserve instead of being distributed among proprietors. The presence of the first condition has been demonstrated in previous pages. To assess the second, I have constructed Table 6.5, which shows that the level of reserves (calculated as a percentage of the equity) was, in general, quite high. The undistributed profits line in balance sheets could reach handsome sums—in the paper firm La Argentina, it was 70 percent of the profits, in bag producer La Primitiva 60 percent, and in Piccardo tobacco company almost 40 percent.[83]

Firm policies with respect to accumulation of reserves were especially conservative. Companies took advantage of years of exceptional profits to increase those funds and did not use them to compensate partners' losses if bad years followed. Thus, when the Centennial celebrations of 1910 implied higher construction demands for the metallurgical company La Unión, the

TABLE 6.5
Reserve Levels (Reserves/ Equity) in Industrial Firms, 1903–1930

Firm	1903–1916*	1920–1930**
A. Braceras	3.8	n.d.
Bagley	23.2	15.49
Bilz	22.2	23.40
Cervecería Buenos Aires	19.2	n.d.
Cervecería Palermo	41.6	n.d.
Cervecería Río II	14.6	n.d.
Cía. Gral de Envases	50.0	n.d.
Cía. Gral de Fósforos	33.3	n.d.
Cristalerías Rigolleau	16.8	11.30
Elaboración General de Plomo	n.d.	8.06
Fábrica Argentina de Alpargatas	31.6	12.93
Fábrica de Papel Casati	8.8	n.d.
Fundición y Talleres La Unión	15.9	25.57
Gaggino-Lauret	8.0	n.d.
Hilanderías Argentinas de Algodón	0.8	n.d.
La Acero Platense	1.7	n.d.
La Argentina	13.4	11.49
La Cantábrica	22.3	7.26
La Martona	13.2	n.d.
La Primitiva	37.0	6.59
La Unión Argentina	28.6	19.66
La Vascongada	34.5	9.62
Salinas	23.9	8.39
TAMET	16.3	n.d.
The Standard	6.1	8.72

NOTES: *The periods considered are A. Braceras, 1911–15; Bagley, 1909–1916; Bilz, 1907–1916; Cervecería Buenos Aires, 1905–1916; Cervecería Palermo, 1903–1916; Cervecería Río II, 1905–1916; Cía. General de Envases, 1915; Cía.General. de Fósforos, 1906–1916; Cristalerías Rigolleau, 1908–1916; Fábrica Argentina de Alpargatas, 1911–16; Fábrica de Papel Casati,1912–16; Fundición y Talleres La Unión, 1906–1916; Gaggino-Lauret, 1906–1911; Hilanderías Argentinas de Algodón, 1906–1911; La Acero Platense, 1904–1909; La Argentina, 1905–1916; La Cantábrica, 1906–1916; La Martona, 1904–1916; La Primitiva and La Unión Argentina, 1905–1916; La Vascongada, 1911–1906; Salinas, 1914–16; TAMET and The Standard,1913–16.

**For Fundición y Talleres La Unión, data correspond to the period 1920–29; for La Unión Argentina to the period 1921–1930; for La Argentina to the period 1920–24.

SOURCES: My own elaboration based on *Boletín Oficial de la Bolsa de Comercio de Buenos Aires: Balances de sociedades anónimas*, 1904–1930. Data on Cía Gral de Envases is taken from *Monitor de Sociedades Anónimas*, XX, 1915, p. 70.

firm decided not to squander the money by distributing higher dividends but instead chose to strengthen reserve funds.[84] If a problem in the economic or political environment was anticipated, caution increased. As soon as the war broke out, the brewery Buenos Aires declared that, although having high profits, it had preferred not to distribute dividends "in anticipation of the contingencies that could occur as a result of the situation in Europe."[85]

Firms usually had an extra source of financing through the deposits of their own workers, a part of the companies' welfare policies mentioned in

Chapter 5. Amounts involved in these internal savings programs are not known, but the fact that the issue is never mentioned in firms' financial discussions suggests that this policy was adopted for paternalistic reasons rather than profit. Finally, there were informal ways to provide money: through friends, relatives, and neighbors. This mechanism worked smoothly among immigrant groups, which constituted a large portion of the factory owners.[86] But in a market that provided credit with some generosity, this help could be related to cultural rather than economic issues. Tables 6.1 and 6.5 taken together indicate that different means of financing operated in every firm according to debt scenarios. It is noteworthy that most companies with a low outstanding debt level had high reserve rates. Conversely, some of those establishments with a low self-financing profile found their main source of obtaining fresh money in banks.

In the 1920s, the behavior of industrial firms revealed some signs of continuity. The profit level of the twelve firms with data to compare the periods 1901–1916 and 1920–1930 showed a slow decline: from 10 percent to 9.2 percent. The difference is not significant. This reduction was, indeed, influenced by the less successful performance of the highly profitable bag producers—La Primitiva and Salinas; the latter even suffered a three-year period of losses in the late 1920s. This evolution was the result of a ruptured commercial agreement between the largest producers, which promoted stern competition.[87] Debt rates tended to be lower, with the exception of companies with more modest results in the decade: Salinas (which obtained bank loans) and the dairy La Vascongada. Actually banking debt ratios were lower than in the previous decade (see Table 6.1). This fact did not mean lack of investment: companies issued stocks to increase their capital to back the new projects or obtained the help of the economic groups where they belonged. The Fábrica Argentina de Alpargatas rose its authorized stock capital from 3,500,000 to 7,500,000 gold pesos (roughly 9,800,000 and 21,000,000 paper pesos) in 1923, a more than 100 percent increase, to strengthen its newly started cotton-spinning and weaving concessions. The glass company Rigolleau followed the same pattern to give impulse to production of flat glass for windows and ceilings during the boom construction in Argentina in the 1920s. The company bought machinery from the United States in 1924 and paid the investment by issuing new shares.[88] That new investments did not always involve bank debts, however, is no sign of poor functioning in the financial system. The Alpargatas firm obtained loans in 1924 and 1925 that were 15 percent of its equity as a complementary source to back its investments.[89] The result was that the firm had a bank debt ratio of 0.10 in the decade, high compared to other stock companies (see Table 6.1)

Conservatism continued in the distribution of dividends. In 1925, for example, the company TAMET had its best year in a decade; after reporting dividends of from 3 percent to 6 percent in the tough years of 1919–1921, the rate reached almost 20 percent. Instead of dividing the money among shareholders, the firm decided to continue pursuing the plan it had in place, "strengthening the amortization account and the reserves." Indeed, the company directed seventy percent of the benefits to amortization and a third of the remaining money to the reserve account, quite an extraordinary sum. These funds grew in the following good years and were set aside for the modernization plan that began with the purchase of its main competitor, Vasena, in 1926 and was completed by 1928.[90] After four years of maintaining high reserves, the textile Manufactura Algodonera Argentina could invest them to enlarge facilities in the cities of Buenos Aires and Resistencia (in the Chaco cotton region).[91] Similarly, reinvestment of nondistributed profits allowed the jam producer Noel to open a new three-story building in 1924, where it could achieve one of its owners' dreams: bringing together the mill, the warehouse, and the administration under one roof.[92]

The Stock Exchange enhanced its presence with the increasing number of textile firms that began to quote their shares (see Table 3.7). The Bolsa itself was surprised by this situation, which called their attention to "the small movement of corporation shares when measured against the wide variety of activities in which capital could be invested."[93] Nevertheless, as Leonard Nakamura and Carlos Zarazaga have shown, a more accurate estimation would make Argentina's capitalization in 1929 around 20 percent of GDP, a substantial share for an emerging market (the stock bubble of New York reached 60 percent of GDP while the Italian counterpart was less than 15 percent). As they have reckoned, real rates of return were higher in the 1920s than during the period 1906–1913. This fact suggests that returns on capital investment in Argentina did not differ significantly from those in the most developed countries. Let it be stressed, however, that even in the golden years 1926–1929, only 11 percent of transactions corresponded to corporate stocks and debentures in Argentina, the rest being bonds and warrants.[94]

Limits to investment in industry came from the opportunities the manufacturing sector was offering itself. Analysis of a specific case illustrates the actual functioning of the credit system from a firm's perspective. Daniel Bassi began with little money and eventually came to own a large chocolate and sweets factory. His story evokes how financing mechanisms worked in the evolution of a successful industrial firm. Mr. Bassi was an Italian Piedmontese immigrant who moved with his family to Buenos Aires in 1870 at the age of fourteen. In the Argentine capital, he worked first at a bakery, then in a confectionery, and, as Bassi says in his own memoirs, "not desiring to continue being an apprentice for all my life, I went [to work] in the only candy factory with steam power."[95] Around 1882, a confectionery owner, impressed by his skills, hired Bassi to be in charge of his store. Using a strategy of thrift and savings, Bassi employed only one boy who cleaned the store and helped him in the sale of merchandise. At the end of the first year, profits were twice the costs and Bassi obtained part of them as a reward. It came at great personal deprivation. In his own words: "I had not enjoyed an hour of stroll or amusement, having dedicated the entire year to the business, which I was not eager to repeat. In spite of the benefits, at my age I was not fond of slavery and I dreamt of future factories instead of the indoor life behind the counter." As a result, Bassi left his job and joined the dispatching section of the Godet chocolate factory—founded by a French immigrant in 1864—as a salesman, where he created "immaterial capital" through growing contacts.[96] While there, he was able to save enough money to buy the necessary elements for a pastry shop, "an oven, cans and molds, some metal bowls and copper casseroles, and an iron heating hole." Bassi's savings came to only paper $500 and the price of these tools was $1,900. But he reached an agreement with the seller to substitute three promissory notes for the rest of the money. Highly indebted but happy in his own pastry store, Daniel Bassi proudly wrote that on the 1st of July of 1886 "I gave a final complete stop to my proletarian life of 16 years."[97]

The personnel in the pastry shop included Daniel's brothers (who worked as bakers and deliverymen), a cook, and another peon, both also Italians. Bassi found his initial customers among the people he had met as a salesman, but faced difficulties in the first month paying the employees and the store rent. An Italian blacksmith saved the enterprise, lending Bassi money he was able to repay in two months. "As soon as [the customers] started to pay their monthly bills, I never faced any lack of money because I could manage to collect everything before the 15th of each month and, since I applied the [Argentine] adage 'quien no llora no mama' [who does not cry does not suckle], I always managed to get them to pay me." The next year, Bassi had paid off all his debts and his store enjoyed a healthy financial outlook "that still I do not understand . . . with such a small place and scarce tools." The success of the pastry store was partially due to sales to the employees of the nascent central state, substantial enough to allow Daniel's sisters to stop working as seamstresses. In the early 1890s, Bassi's business increased, and "as all the profits were for myself, I had a small deposit at the Banco de la Provincia and I thought that the time to achieve my old ambition of having a complete factory had finally come."[98]

In 1893, Bassi bought a lot where he installed a workshop with steam-powered machines to produce candies, glazed fruit, and the specialty of the house: confetti. In 1897, Mr. Guillot, owner of the Godet firm, offered Daniel Bassi the opportunity to become his silent partner. In spite of the high sum required (the company would have a capital of paper $100,000), Bassi accepted and became one of the owners of the mill in which he had once been a blue-collar worker. As he observed with pride "to attain ownership of the country's most important company in our field was the height of my aspirations." By 1898, Guillot's Parisian lifestyle, according to Bassi's Italian hardworking flavored account, had placed the Frenchman in financial straits, and he offered Bassi sole ownership of the Godet firm. Bassi's main challenge was the debt that Guillot had contracted with Banco Francés (French Bank), especially since this institution was reluctant to support clients of other nationalities. A loan from the Banco de Italia (Italian Bank) plus high profits helped Bassi solve his financial problems in a short time, and "with that operation we put an end to our struggle for capital, paying everything in cash." In 1898, his hefty debt of paper $258,000 had been transformed into a credit of $138,000.[99]

Bank support was crucial not only in paying this debt but also in sustaining further growth of Bassi's factory. In 1905, he held paper $80,000 in notes deposited in the Italian, French, and Spanish Banks. This was because each year "whether by coincidence or my lucky star, was even better and allowed me to divert funds to invest in notes, since I began being the sole owner." Bassi took full advantage of both the consumption explosion of the early twentieth century and the consolidation of the national market by organizing a sales network. Indeed, he sold a substantial amount to the interior provinces. With high profits sustained over several years, Bassi began the construction of a large factory in 1911, an undertaking not completed until 1918 due to its magnitude.[100] Similarly, the soap firm of Alejandro Llauró, established as a small mill in 1878, could expand without credit constraints by reinvesting profits into buying simple machinery. It expanded between 1900 and 1920, at the same time Bassi did. By the 1930s, it was a large company exporting glycerin, advertising with the motto "Before Buenos Aires had electric power or gas, it already had Llauró soap."[101]

To what extent was Bassi's case unique? Probably, as the evolution of capitalism has shown all over the world, self-made, large entrepreneurs were a minority. The industrial environment in a capital concentration process did not seem to be the best for small players. The middle-size beverage company Bilz is a case in point. It had sufficient capital to negotiate its shares at the Stock Exchange, it had credit with the banks, and it was profitable. Yet, it was forced to become part of an economic group, in this case the Bemberg. The whole world and the nature of the Argentine economy would have to change to halt this process; it was not until the Great Depression of 1930 and the restriction of the economy to international trade that capital concentration reversed.[102]

Data on the financing of small workshops that did not have the potential to jump to a larger scale are not available. Indirect evidence suggests their relatively solid performance. The tiny number of industrial workshop failures noted in *Tribunales de Comercio* (Commercial Courts) indicates a generally healthy outlook. Moreover, when bankruptcy did occur, credit was not identified as a problem, perhaps also a reflection of the cultural background of immigrants who took pride in their reputation as good payers. That was the case of Carlos Cermesoni, the owner of an *herrería de obras* (blacksmith's shop). According to the state accountant, Cermesoni "obtained the credit [to buy] the machinery that the workshop required, and the merchandise for the first works . . . . The volume of the orders accepted made new machinery necessary, and the credit was facilitated without difficulty."[103] Similarly, a small manufacturer of belts and ladies' handbags, Moisés Chaim Vino,

> started to work in a modest way in 1917 and managed to give some boost to his business by benefiting from the credit that in a relative way banks and some stores of the branch granted him . . . because if we refer to credit, this was granted in a way that we could call generous in relation to the turnover of his business, an assessment that the number and sum of the verified loans supports.[104]

Cermesoni and Chaim Vino went into bankruptcy as a result of personal problems.

The relative health of small workshops in the emerging dual economy is not surprising. In spite of the strength of financial groups over the market played by industrial firms, a company nonallied with big business was not necessarily doomed to fail. Algodonera Flandria, Bassi, The Standard, and other middle-size companies could maintain their portion of the market. Moreover, after the 1930 Depression a deconcentration of capital process took place and gave more room to workshops and middle-size companies. In the 1930s, small scale and inefficiency became assets rather than liabilities.[105] But even before the depression, many perils to industry lurked in the economy. Lack of credit was not the most significant. The financial market was far from perfect, but one thing it did not have was an anti-industrial bias. The canonical version lays the responsibility of Argentina's failure to industrialize not just on credit but also on politics, an issue I will examine in the next chapter.

Chapter 7

The Empire of Pragmatism:
Politics and Industry in the Period
1880–1930

The Issue of Protectionism

Amidst the commercial wars over the Argentine market between industrial powers at the beginning of the twentieth century, the Briton N. L. Watson observed,

> Argentina is professedly a protectionist country. . . . Curiously enough, the vital industries of the country have not been favoured in any way [by] the fiscal system, which has been used to foster exotics [goods] and economic growth hardly suited to the conditions of the country. . . . With the exception of railway material, which for the most part comes in duty free, all manufactured articles pay a very heavy duty indeed.[1]

At nearly the same time, the Argentine economist Emilio Frers authored a work analyzing the alleged protectionism prevalent in the nation's economic policies. According to his study, customs duties totaled up to 30.5 percent of the cost of all imports, which was comparable to the United States (26.9 percent), yet higher than France (9.4 percent), Germany (8.6 percent), and Great Britain (5.0 percent).[2]

Watson's and Frers's depictions of the Argentine economy are shocking in light of the traditional understanding of economic policies during the export boom period. Indeed, the canonical version established as an article of faith that, before the 1930 Depression, Argentina took a free-trade stance that was at odds with (or at least indifferent to) its own industrial activity. One of the alleged signs of this anti-industrial bias—the state credits system—has been challenged in the last chapter. Now, it is time to question the other pillar of the canonical version: the lack of tariffs to protect domestic industry.

This chapter addresses this issue by showing that the relationship between the Argentine state and industry was far from this straight-forward antiprotectionist assertion. Rather it was part of a complex and quite chaotic interaction. Discussion of the topic in the country's main political institutions provides an insight into this connection, which intertwined economic interests, political practices, and ideological stands. This chapter first discusses the role of the Congress, an institution poorly researched in Argentine history. Then it analyzes the role of the Executive Power, especially in its aim to create the bureaucracy of a modern country. The resulting picture will differ significantly from the canonical version's depiction.

The question of just how protectionist Argentine policy was before the 1930 Depression is difficult to answer. Protection might have different effects: on production, consumption, resource distribution, international trade, and fiscal balance. State action toward industry was, during the period studied in this book, an outcome of general economic policies rather than specific strategies for manufacturing. Moreover, it is an intricate task to separate the original goals and the resultant effects in each of the areas just mentioned.[3] For the period analyzed here, the odds against arriving at trustworthy conclusions on this issue are appalling. A major reason was the structure of the Argentine tariff.

The tariff consisted of two elements: (1) the duties, a percentage applied as a tax on the imported article, and (2) the *aforo*, the name given to the valuation. The aforo was assigned by the state, and it meant market price, plus freights, insurance, and shipment. Duties were applied upon aforos; thus any distortion in the latter's valuation significantly altered the sum paid by the importer. If the aforo value was lower than the market price, duties (as a percentage) were not as high as originally planned. For example, there was a great difference between paying a duty of 25 percent upon a product valued at paper $100 and one valued at $200. Conversely, a higher aforo meant a larger duty protection. It is not surprising that importers complained incessantly about higher aforos whereas industrialists did the same for low ones.

To answer the question about the degree to which Argentina supported protectionist or free-trade policies involves looking at the implicit protection set by the percentage of import duties on the total import value (see Table 1.9). These rates were similar to those between 20 and 30 percent

TABLE 7.1
Implicit Protection and Exchange Rate, 1876–1930

Period	Implicit Protection	Implicit Protection/ Exchange Rate
1870s	22.14	26.06
1880s	22.58	27.73
1890s	24.55	74.97
1900s	24.62	56.43
1910s	21.14	47.52
1920s	21.30	54.53

SOURCE: Table 1.9.

of the Mexican Porfiriato. However, as Edward Beatty has demonstrated for this case, this rate says little about specific protection and much more on the level of economic openness toward world trade.[4] A crucial variable to consider in evaluating the degree of protectionism is the exchange rate. If we take into account its variations, we observe how the devaluation of the peso protected domestic manufacturing production. This is especially evident in the 1890s and coincides with the rest of the evidence presented in this book. In addition, this exchange protection lessened in the twentieth century but not to the pre-1890 levels. On the contrary, it continued to be one of the forces in favor of industrial growth from 1900 to the 1920s (see Table 7.1). Regarding the accuracy of the aforo value, another issue crucial to analyzing the protectionism level, we know that the aforo values went down due to international prices inflation after it was set up in 1905. But the war worked as a hindrance until 1919. After that, the pressure of industrialists to raise aforos increased. Nonetheless, the peso devaluation worked in their favor. When the domestic currency began to revaluate in 1924, the Congress had already passed the law that increased the aforo values, as we will see in the following pages. A look at the duties applied to specific items after 1890 suggests a cascading tariff system: while clothing had duties from 50 percent to 60 percent, fabrics were from 20 percent to 30 percent, and cotton yarn was from 5 percent to 7 percent. In addition, inputs such as wood pulp or iron paid very low or no duties, while machinery and combustibles were exempted from paying taxes (see Table 1.7).

Analyzing the composition of imports according to their productive nature can make a more interesting study (see Table 1.2). Decline in the relative importance of some durable goods imports, and especially the increasing weight of industrial inputs, indicates a more suggestive dimension of manufacturing domestic output and protection. A more disaggregated outlook at the evolution of the tariff duties illustrates the changes in favor of protection in 1876 and 1890, a trend that stabilized in 1905 (see Table 1.7). In 1900–1910, however, specific duties became increasingly important. The contemporary estimates made by the bureaucrat Francisco Latzina for 1900 show a high degree of protection for the items—usually products manufactured domestically—covered by this kind of tariff. These levels, expressed as an E in Table 1.7, were basically prohibitions for goods produced in Argentina, with usual duties above 60 percent or 70 percent and even more than 130 percent.[5]

As already indicated, other forces influencing protection (such as exchange rate) should be taken into account. However, the convoluted industrial policy applied by the Argentine administrations during the period under study leads us to respond to the question about the extent to which Argentina supported protectionist or free-trade policies by reviewing the outcome achieved in domestic manufacturing. The disappearance of imported matches following the 1880s indicates an effective protective tariff on them. To evaluate how protectionist the so-called protective policies were, we must refer back to Chapters 1 and 3 and look at how much import fell and local production grew. The substitution rates, which means the percentage of the consumed industrial items produced domestically, rose from 40 percent in 1900–1910 to 49 percent in the 1920s.[6] The intricacies of the web we are studying force us to check, case by case, the rationale of industrial policies. In so doing, we will get a glimpse of the prevalent approach to manufacturing.

The Realm of Interests

During the time of the Argentine Confederation, the provinces applied tariffs to articles competing with those produced on their home turf. In 1835, the governor of Buenos Aires, Juan Manuel de Rosas, prohibited importation of foreign manufactured items in the inner provinces and raised duties to as much as 50 percent with the aim of appeasing his allies in those districts. This strategy was short-lived and tariffs soon dropped, but the hostilities with France and Britain, and the subsequent blockade of the ports, resulted in nearly total protection of the meager artisanal production from the inland provinces. Conversely, the fall of Rosas in 1852 sparked efforts to lower duties. The following years were a liberal era, and supporters of free trade prevailed. Among them, the Mitristas (already mentioned in Chapter 4) were especially adamant in defending that principle. In 1863, a year after Mitre inaugurated his presidency, tariffs reached a general level of only 15 percent by a general Customs Law.[7]

But the glory days of this kind of liberalism did not last for long. In 1870, duties on imports grew from 15 to 20 percent. As discussed in Chapter 1, when the 1873 depression hit the country, a different political atmosphere prevailed, one in which the new rulers were much less confident of commercial freedom's benefits. The government raised customs duties in order to cope with the crisis, and these reached a general level of 40 percent (see Table 1.7). At that time, the House of Representatives became involved in an intense debate over the issue of protectionism versus free trade. In contrast to what had occurred in previous discussions, such as during the debate over the 1835 customs law, the most fervent defenders of protectionism were from Buenos Aires, while representatives of the interior provinces opposed it. This switch was the result, as we have seen, of the province's landowners, who wished to promote domestic textile industrialization in order to create a demand for their wool, by then in less demand on the world market. There is a general consensus among historians that the regularization of the world economy put an end to protectionist ideas.[8] Protectionism, however, continued and even intensified in the following decades for a variety of reasons, as more recent scholarship has shown.[9]

The kind of protectionism Argentine authorities displayed in the period 1880–1930 was nowhere near being overall prodomestic industry policy but rather was a result of lobbying activities on specific items. Actually, as the following pages will show, commercial policies were not even closer to the idea of industrialism that Edward Beatty had found in Porfirian Mexico between 1880 and 1910.[10] Protectionism, like any economic variable, is a relative issue. If we compare the commercial policies before the 1930 Depression with the ones undertaken by Perón in the 1940s and 1950s, which meant the eventual closure to all imports that could be manufactured domestically, the degree of protectionism could seem low. But if we take into account the number of industrial firms that opened in the predepression years, which came to account for one fourth of the Argentine GDP, the accomplishment seems enormous for a country with no previous artisanal activities. Thus, the history of this commercial policy deserves some exploration.

First of all, the assumption that industrialist and landed interests were by nature at odds is false: both favored, for example, an undervalued domestic currency. In addition, the tariff issue (about which most of the controversies between landowners and factory owners allegedly took place) should be regarded carefully. Indeed, duties on imports provided the bulk of fiscal income, and any decrease would have meant a necessary replacement for other taxes, such as direct ones, that would have hurt landowners' interests. The fiscal readjustment of 1884 illustrates this situation. Until then, the taxation structure of Argentina had been based on duties on imports and, to a lesser extent, on exports. Landowners had long pressed for an elimination of all taxes on their sales abroad, when the government decided to promote those sales by abolishing the remaining duties on cattle-ranching export products.[11] This change meant the loss of paper $1,000,000 in revenue, a gap in the state's budget that had to be filled. The idea of taxing income or capital was unthinkable due to the inevitably fierce opposition by members of the elite and the unfeasibility of applying such a system in a country with an infant bureaucracy.[12] Since the provinces controlled the *contribuciones directas* (direct taxes, mainly on urban property), the national state could not turn to this as a source of revenue. There was a third alternative: to increase the duties on imports. This was, in the words of one senator, the best solution since "taxes on imports offer the simplest means because they are less difficult to collect and people are already used to them."[13] As a result, the Congress raised tariffs on tobacco goods, liqueurs, beer, and wine. Landowners and domestic producers of these items were happy while importers proclaimed their serious opposition. The importers' association, the *Centro de Comercio* (*Commercial Center*), complained about a "prohibitive fiscal regime":

[V]ery high Customs duties have ruled us since 1876, duties that in any other country of the world of population less scarce than ours, would have been enough to develop a vigorous and active national industry. With the exception of a couple of industrial branches . . . national production has not succeeded, in spite of these duties, to wholly dominate the market in its consumption needs.[14]

Tariffs on imports were not only, as is commonly assumed by historians, the mere outcome of fiscal needs; they were also governed by political interests wherein local entitlements were at stake. In 1880, the national authorities vanquished the last provincial rebellion and a victorious national coalition, the *Partido Autonomista Nacional* (PAN), set the formation for political stability. This party, in contrast to the liberalism of *Mitrismo*, promoted a more active role for the state in economic matters. Julio A. Roca, the leader of PAN and president of Argentina from 1880 to 1886, embodied this shift.[15] In 1885, at an industrial exhibition in the wine-producing city of Mendoza, Roca received enthusiastic applause from the audience when he "declared [himself] to be an open and definite partisan of the protectionist system covering the products of the national industry."[16] His pronouncement scared foreign diplomats; those who questioned the president about his intentions received a response that demonstrated his political skills. According to the French Consul,

> General Roca has told me confidentially that he does not believe that the program he designed would be applied for many years. But, since protectionism is so popular, he had incorporated that idea into the electoral platform, [at the same time] alleviating the spirit of political uncertainty prevalent at the time. . . . It is really difficult to protect an industry that does not exist. . . . Nevertheless, it is not possible to hide the fact that protectionist ideas are more and more part of the life of the Argentine Republic.[17]

Roca's speech was timely since 1886 was the year in which his successor would be elected. The fact that he used protectionism as an electoral banner reveals the general attitude toward this issue (or at least that of those who controlled the electoral machine). A protectionist coalition was forming, an alliance that would come into its own by the 1890s, when industries became a visible element of the Argentine economy. By then, tariffs on imports were raised, which led to the growth in manufacture under an import-substitution scheme as described in Chapter 1 (see Table 1.8). At this time, perhaps, do we find the closest similarities with Mexican Porfiriato. During his short-term presidency (1890–1892), President Pellegrini fostered a commercial policy that looked for a balanced economic growth of the country, one that took into account both agriculture and cattle ranching, and also industrial activities. Industrial protectionism, however, did not have the meaning it does nowadays. To a large extent, it was a desire to manufacture simple raw material; what is called in Argentina Manufacturas de Origen Agropecuario (Manufactures of Agricultural Origin).[18] In the import-substitution process that followed the 1890 depression, the raising of duties on imports, and the collapse of the domestic currency, there was a "cascading" tariff structure that allowed the imports of industrial inputs and precluded that of finished items.

The year 1890 was a watershed not only in economics but in politics. Although the July Revolution led by the opposition to the government of Juárez Celman was crushed by the military, Congress forced the president to resign. Pellegrini, his vice president, replaced him and had to deal with the financial crisis that left him little attention for other projects. But the successor of Pellegrini, Luis Sáenz Peña, became a clear symbol of the time of troubles ushered by the Revolution of 1890. Although the heavy-handed President Roca had set up a presidential-centered style of governance following the military victory of 1880, the 1890s were characterized by a weak Executive Branch and a relatively more powerful Congress. Luis Sáenz Peña was elected in 1892 with feeble political support and as a compromise candidate for troubled times. He decided to cede power from the presidency over to Congress. The years 1893 and 1894 (until the resignation of the president in January of 1895) witnessed this new political balance. Congressional concern regarding industrial policies was an example of a new era in which parliament wanted to be more active.[19] This activity included increasing support for some protectionism among most lawmakers, a wave of enthusiasm that free-trade defenders considered a mere embodiment of particular interests. The newspaper *El Diario*, defending laissez-faire, published a reader's letter that delighted the editors. The reader wrote, "[C]an some legislators who fill a seat in the Congress while they are at the same time associated with an industrial establishment legally give their vote on various items of the Customs law? [He also hoped that] the Congress would not become a syndicate of manufacturers or their managers."[20]

A more refined version of the depiction of Congressional protectionism did not view lawmakers as personally tied to industrial interests but considered them to be the instruments of a manufacturing lobby. The newspaper *El Argentino*, also sympathetic to free trade, remarked,

> We are not talking hypothetically but based on events that take place daily, in the lobbies and salons of the Congress, in the private homes of the members of the Parliament; everywhere, in short, where the representatives and senators of the Nation meet, collectively or in isolation.[21]

This lobby, according to *La Nación*, had created a "Third Argentina"— after cattle ranching and grain production—that had been extremely successful in fostering an "official industrialism" in which

> the industrial corporations court the government and exact satisfaction in return. . . . We knew and complained about the evils of bureaucracy, about *empleomanía* [mania for holding public office] that looked like one of the most ruinous symptoms of official politics; but this is reduced to the least importance when compared to the official industrialism.[22]

Industrialists did, indeed, lobby the Congress. A senator from Catamarca described this process:

> Industrialists, those protectionists, generally besiege the Finance Commission the same way that Petitions and Military Commissions work

on the issue of pensions. There is not even one industrialist who does
not come asking for protection.[23]

Industrialists were not the only interest group using lobbies. When serious
discussion on the protection of wine took place, the *Cámara de Comercio
Española* (Spanish Chamber of Commerce) pressed the Argentine Congress
to lift tariffs that hurt wine sales from Spain. *El Correo Español*, the leading
newspaper representing Spanish interests in Buenos Aires, pointed out,

> [V]otes are triumphs. . . . This is the time to act. . . . The national pro-
> ducers work tirelessly; we know they are preparing a presentation for
> the Congress, in which mistaken and incorrect data about Spanish
> wines will probably abound; it is necessary, therefore, to neutralize
> them, because it is known that Congressional opinion is easily swayed.[24]

Direct connections between industry and the Congress did exist. Some
industrialists, such as Argentine Industrial Union (UIA) presidents Antonio
Baibiene, Alberto Demarchi, and Francisco Seguí, became lawmakers.[25]
Nevertheless, neither lobbyists nor the presence of representatives with direct interests in industry can explain why the majority of the legislative body
voted in favor of protectionism. To examine this question, it is necessary to
analyze the peculiar formation and functioning of a protectionist alliance.

The Congressional protectionist alliance was neither permanent nor the
main coalition at work in the Congress.[26] On the contrary, it was quite pre-
carious. But its study reveals a good part of the relationship between political power and industry. This alliance was, in part, the result of a regional consensus. And this was an important issue for Argentina, a country with a
federal constitution where a powerful Senate guaranteed two seats to each of
the fourteen provinces (regardless of its population). Some provinces played
a crucial role, mainly sugar-producing Tucumán and winemaking San Juan
and Mendoza. All of them lobbied to hinder the introduction of cheaper foreign products.[27] In 1894, *La Nación* noted that the issue of protectionism had
become of such importance in the election of representatives that

> some provinces have influenced the election of their representatives to
> an effect that favored citizens who were admittedly protectionist. The
> sons of Tucumán, since she is the most interested, are the ones who
> have exerted the most influence, looking for adherence to the triumph
> of the tariffs that favor them.[28]

By then, representative Eliseo Cantón, a fanatic defender of protectionism
as a representative of the sugar-producing (at a high cost) province of Tucu-

mán, attempted to push the favorably inclined House toward a clear policy on tariffs by stating that

> [t]he country cannot live eternally within uncertainty and doubt, without knowing whether free trade ideas will triumph in the Argentine parliament or if the latter, honoring its tradition, experience, and foresight, will continue developing a protective policy toward industries.[29]

To champion the cause of its own protection, any given province had to prove that protectionist policies would be beneficial for the entire nation and not just a matter of regional interests. The representatives of sugar and wine-producing provinces, therefore, supported protectionism as a general principle to be applied across the country. Industry in the city of Buenos Aires benefited particularly from this effort. *El Diario* considered protectionism a minority opinion and attributed the success of the alliance between Buenos Aires and the provinces to *compañerismo criollo* (Creole comradeship) between

> a few sugar producers in Tucumán, some wine manufacturers in Mendoza, and thirty or forty industrialists constituted in legion [referring to Buenos Aires city] cloaked by their representation of national progress.[30]

On his part, the representative from Buenos Aires province, Rufino Varela Ortiz, a conspicuous member of the ruling PAN, captured the significance of the alliance:

> [T]his chamber might allow me to incorporate these primordial industries. . . . all the others, which I will not always specify—tannery, shoe-producing, etc.—because all of them are also industries that transform products of our soil. . . . Please acknowledge that when I talk of these great industries—wines, sugar, etc.—I am talking about the economic system that should prevail in the nation.[31]

Therefore, it was understandable that Representatives Agustín Alvarez, from Mendoza, and Eliseo Cantón, from Tucumán, took up the defense of factories in the city of Buenos Aires while Senator Rafael Igarzábal, from this city, defended manufacturing production in the interior.[32]

Supporters in those districts dreaming of industrial development strengthened the alliance formed by the provinces with actual production interests to protect. This was the case for Salta, one of whose representatives promoted the installation of a cotton-spinning firm, hoping his province would play a role in the harvesting of the fiber. The same was true of Cata-marca, whose industrial aspirations have been discussed in Chapter 4.[33] The relationship between the state and particular interests is even more complex than has already been portrayed. With the exception of Tucumán and Men-doza, district representatives were divided on the issue of protectionism. Indeed, issues unrelated to their own provinces' interests, real or imagined, determined the position of some lawmakers on protection.

Protectionism as a Passion

The protectionist coalition proved to be more than an expression of regional self-interests; it became a strategy for nation building. The senators were supposed to represent their provinces and not the entire country, unlike the representatives. Nevertheless, they formed a coalition based on a broader idea. Both of the senators from the province of Jujuy, Domingo Pérez and Eugenio Tello, became strong defenders of soap and pin factories in the city of Buenos Aires. When a representative from the province of Buenos Aires advocated a milder protectionism, Senator Tello responded,

> It is worthwhile to know one establishment of this kind [a metallurgic factory]; but unfortunately it happens that those who have been born in Buenos Aires do not care about the South [a section of the city where many factories had risen]. They do not even know the public promenades. We, the ones who come from the interior, try to notice everything and thus it happened that I visited that factory twice.[34]

Pérez turned out to be one of the strongest voices in favor of protec-tionism. This representative of a province with a promising sugar industry, which needed high tariffs to survive foreign competition, advocated high taxes on hats and tin-plate articles produced in Buenos Aires, one piece of the national discourse in favor of all protection.[35]

But support for industry as a national cause went beyond this, involving lawmakers from regions with neither industry to defend nor dreams of de-veloping one in the near future. A representative from a district with no special interests in the issue explained the rationale of his protectionist position:

> I have no reason to take up the pro-industry banner under discussion in this chamber. As a national representative, I represent the interests of the nation. Elected by the district of San Luis, it is not my links to this

province that prompt me to support advantages for industries that my province does not have, but the consideration of the national as the common interest of all provinces.[36]

A midway version of protectionism, seen by many legislators as an important aspect of economic development and modern nation building, found its stronghold in the Senate. Senators could be divided between mild and fervent protectionists, while free trade did not find a voice until the election of Lorenzo Anadón in 1892. Anadón's arrival from the agriculture-exporting (at cheap prices and without any need of protection) province of Santa Fé was nothing less than a spark put to an open flame. He had three passions: the PAN, Catholicism, and free trade. The last stand made him a *rara avis* in the Senate. Perhaps this is why he campaigned for low tariffs with a crusading fervor, made clear from his very first speeches.[37] Anadón's efforts—usually clashing with those of Pérez—were in vain. Finally, the inclusion in 1896 of Carlos Pellegrini (the former president openly supportive of industry) to the Senate gave protectionists an influential leader that ended Anadón's hopeless crusade.[38] The analysis of the House reveals a political reality in which protectionist coalitions were less easily created than in the Senate. Moreover, friction between the two chambers regarding this issue was not uncommon.[39]

In the 1880s, the political map of Argentina had been roughly divided between a party in power, the PAN, and another one in opposition, Mitrismo. In the 1890s, this map changed, at the same time that protectionism became a disputed issue. A new political party named *Unión Cívica*, composed of former *Mitristas* and other opponents of the PAN, led the failed revolution of 1890. In 1891, the *Unión Cívica* split between the Mitristas, who signed a pact with the PAN and became the *Unión Cívica Nacional*, and those who did not want any agreement with the forces in power and developed their own party, called *Unión Cívica Radical*. Thus, in the 1890s the Argentine political landscape fell into three major "parties": the PAN, which was in power and controlled the Congress, the Mitristas, and the Radicals.[40]

One of the hopes of free-trade supporters, such as the newspaper *El Diario*, was that the Unión Cívica (before it split into Nacional and Radical) would resurrect the liberal tradition in commercial matters, which had vanished following the 1870s.[41] The election of Radical representatives in 1894 brought the issue of protectionism to the forefront in the House. In these debates, the PAN supported protectionism while the nascent Radical Party defended free trade, mainly through representative Francisco Barroetaveña.[42] Barroetaveña embodied, rather than an antistate position, the idea of a consumer party. Mitristas, labeled the "party of merchants," also supported free trade, though their enthusiasm diminished when they established political alliances with the PAN. When these alliances later broke down, they resumed their historical stance.[43] Thus, Emilio Mitre, the son of Bartolomé, offered some opposition (short-lived in a House so prone to high tariffs) to the extreme protectionism of Tucumán's representative Eliseo Cantón.[44] In 1904, during the senatorial campaign in the city of Buenos Aires, Emilio Mitre and his *Partido Republicano*, a new name for Mitrismo, defended free trade as an electoral banner against the two candidates of the then divided PAN, Benito Villanueva and Carlos Pellegrini. In addition, that very same year the Republicans made an appeal to merchants and tried to obtain their vote by showing how deeply protectionist the PAN was. By then, the former Mitristas had launched a strong attack against foreign capital, which was well suited to an atmosphere poisoned by the threatening rise of trusts.[45] Conservatives, the name used by the old PAN's followers since 1908 (after the creation of the Conservative Party in the Province of Buenos Aires), continued with their traditional support for local industry. Moreover, when a new force, the Partido Demócrata Progresista, attempted to modernize politics from the top down in the 1910s, protectionism, as "respect for the current situation of industry" and promotion of import substitution, became one of its banners.[46]

The free-trade position defended in the House by Barroetaveña languished, as did Anadón's defense in the Senate. By 1895, the House of Representatives was considered to be completely in the hands of protectionist representatives, a feature that persisted in the following years.[47] Not until the arrival of Socialist representative Alfredo Palacios in 1904 did the debate on protectionism regain strength. By supporting free trade (and the resulting lower price of imported consumer goods), this emerging force carried forward the idea of the "party of the consumers," which early radicalism had followed, and was met with the same lack of success.[48]

The Radical Party continued to support free trade in the 1890s. Partisan leaders reinforced the free trade position, such as the case of José Bianco in 1894.[49] But the party switched position at the beginning of the twentieth century, accepting a midway protectionism under the leadership of Yrigoyen, more inclined to create a wide national constituency than to follow principles that could alienate adherents in the provinces. The issue surfaced in 1909 when a prestigious leader from Córdoba—the former director of the local partisan newspaper *La Libertad* and president of the Radical National Committee, Pedro C. Molina—resigned from the party because *La República*, its official publication, supported protection for the wine industry. In a letter challenging Molina, Yrigoyen took a stand against someone who "proceeds in this way because a newspaper written by radicals has given space to an economic thesis which is different from his." For the Radical leader Yrigoyen, the party could not "formulate or justify partisan trends nor singular propensities; because all these interests must shut down in order to back those of the Nation." By stating that the ideology of the radical party was "the cause of the same Nation," Yrigoyen was leaning toward the pragmatism that had guided the relationship between state and industry since the 1870s.[50]

The Synthesis of Rational Protectionism

The degree to which the state should and did get involved in the economy and society was an issue of great discussion in the Argentine parliament. Defenders of protectionism supported a larger degree of involvement, such as this representative from Mendoza, who responded to a colleague by saying,

> I can tell this to the representative: since he was born, the state has been watching and taking care of him; it has provided him with the doctor, with the wet-nurse, (laughs). He has been taught by the state. Humanity is constituted by a large society of mutual assistance: from the time the individual is born and until he dies he is sheltered and protected by society.[51]

Protectionism and state activism were, from this perspective, intertwined. In the 1880s, the central state amplified its power by declaring as public certain activities formerly deemed private: education, plus the record of marriages, deaths, and births. Such activism met with opposition from the Church, the institution formerly responsible for those tasks. Anadón's free-trade position in the 1890s was related to a militant Catholicism that wanted to limit governmental activity. In this battle, he found support in early Radicalism and the erratic Mitrismo.[52] Both parties supported the idea of a passive government in the economic sphere, whereas the PAN advocated a more active state role.[53]

The perils of state intervention were clear to those who opposed it. Anadón, for example, thought that the state was promoting a dangerous activity in fostering industrial growth and called the attention of his contemporaries to the social problems that, in his view, were caused by factories:

> [W]hy am I going to enumerate all the inconveniences that protectionism has brought to this Republic? . . . We are laying the groundwork for our first labor crisis. We have already had two or three thousand

workers of a single industry, shoes, on strike, and if we continue this trend, within four or five years we are going to have many thousands of workers on the streets asking for jobs from the public powers such as they do in Europe. This is what the tariff is portending.[54]

In this battle of extremes between supporters of a providential state and adherents of an absent state, a middle position finally triumphed in the sphere of industrial policies: "rational protectionism."[55] This strategy adopted import tariffs as a good instrument of economic policy, but opposed the extremism of some lawmakers such as Tucumán's Eliseo Cantón or industrialist Francisco Seguí. The difference resulted in the encouragement of factory production by means of protection, but confined itself to a few goods, accepting the limitations of the Argentine economy to foster a deeper industrialization. Representative Lucio V. Mansilla—an elderly general, skilled politician, and superb writer noted for this ability to capture the essence of an issue—defined the midway position. In opposing import duties in paper currency that would favor imports and supplied tariff in more expensive gold pesos, Mansilla declared, "I am not going to oppose it because I am a protectionist or a free-trader, as I have already said; nor am I eclectic, except in specific cases. I am the only way one should be: 'possibilist'."[56]

Rational protectionism was a mix of different approaches toward industry. It melded the defense of particular interests with some general principles, such as regional equilibrium. Supporters of extreme tariffs, such as representative Cantón, lamented the alleged lack of attention to the Northwest by a Congress that, he insisted, should endeavor to unify the varying regional interests. As he said,

> The interests of the North and the West of the Republic come sparingly and to a cold reception in the Argentine Parliament. . . . This is not the case for the local interests of the Federal Capital that are daily and constantly lobbying on the Congress.[57]

Conversely, Enrique Berduc, a prominent representative of rational protectionism, emphasized that favoring regional production might mean imbalances for the rest of the country. This representative from the Littoral (and jerked beef exporting, with no industrial forces) province of Entre Ríos accused a colleague of "speaking as a *Mendocino* [resident of the province of Mendoza] rather than as an Argentine protectionist" and pointed out that the country was a whole unit, not a conglomeration of parts:

> that many representatives from the Littoral are part of the Argentine Congress; these men, in all cases, have shown their patriotic good will

in favor of national industries, especially towards sugar and wine production. By conceding protection precipitously, they have endangered the interests of the Littoral provinces.[58]

The potential for retaliation by foreign governments was the basis of this complaint. Indeed, Spain threatened to stop importing jerked beef if Argentina protected wine.[59]

For defenders of rational protectionism, regional balance was critical to the very building of the Argentine nation. A representative from Mendoza made it clear that if equity among regions was lacking, the issue of tariff protection could spark a civil war. In his words, the evils of the past could return if one region was helped by the national state and another was not.[60] On this basis, a lawmaker from the province of Corrientes, which had nothing to protect, supported some protectionism as a precautionary measure against renewed civil warfare in the form of regional parties:

> [W]hy do we look for new reasons to quarrel in the Argentine family when we should be fed up with the ones we have and cannot yet solve? What reason is there to promote geographic parties? Why should we raise regional resistance?[61]

The PAN accused the Socialists of being against national unity because of their support of free trade. Representative Miguel Padilla, from Tucumán, reacted to one of their proposals to end any protectionism by saying,

> I am not surprised that the Socialist representatives who subscribe to the project do not consider this law a law of national solidarity, since they are lacking in the very concept of nationality; they are internationalists . . . and since they prefer the red flag to the white and blue [the colors of the national flag], which is the standard of Argentine nationality, it is not surprising that they do not share this principle with us.[62]

In the minds of some politicians, some degree of protectionism could save Argentina from the perils of the social explosion feared by senator Anadón. Industrialists petitioning the Congress commonly used the threat of massive unemployment if protection ended. They invited lawmakers to their factories in order to evoke a strong emotional response. The factory owners proudly showed their best machinery and their production methods. Their tours concentrated, however, on the masses of people, especially women and children, who were employed. To highlight this point, industrialists packed their factories with extra workers. For instance, in preparation for one of these visits, the textile factory Enrico Dell'Acqua, which did not employ more than five hundred people, suddenly became twenty-six hundred strong on the day Congressional lawmakers toured the place. The lawmakers were impressed to see a range of workers "from little girls of 10 to 12 years of age . . . to experienced women who watch the large machines."[63] Congressmen visiting the Fábrica Argentina de Alpargatas saw twice the usual number of female laborers. During a tour to the CGF, Senator Pérez was surprised to see "close to a thousand workers, 600 of them women, children, and young girls, presenting an edifying spectacle."[64] A representative from the Northwestern province of La Rioja, with no factories to protect, referred to the delicate issue of unemployment:

> We must keep in mind that those industries employ an immense number of women and children, contributing in this way to the resolution of one of the most far reaching of our social problems, which is to bring occupation to the woman and to the child, because a woman and a child with a job are a guarantee against immorality.[65]

Recognizing the emotional impact of factory field trips, Senator Anadón preferred not to be involved in any

> of those visits that predispose [lawmakers] in favor of factories. That is why, on purpose, I do not want to visit them, because anybody's sense is overwhelmed . . . when one sees a vast factory, with many machines, with big engines, and in which three hundred women and four hundred children work.[66]

There was a political stand that was far from all-out protectionism yet pragmatically intent on keeping the Argentine divergent social and economic forces at peace. Rational protectionism was, for most of its supporters, the necessary and pragmatic course for those who were in power. Minister of Finance José Terry explained that "one thing is to be a free-trader on the street, in the clubs or in the academies, and it is another to be a free-trader when one has the burden and the responsibility of the tasks you will fulfill." The influential representative Berduc, for his part, made the role of the administrator clear. "We must examine, in every case, to what extent the government must come to the aid of any production."[67] Therefore, it was understandable that Mitrismo, which had been in the opposition since 1868, sustained free trade.[68]

Rational protectionism rejected doctrinaire positions.[69] No one explained this point better than incumbent president Julio A. Roca in an 1899 industrial rally:

We are not in the position of one of the oldest and richest of monar-
chies, which, having arrived at its last economic evolution, may boldly
proclaim free trade. Nor are we in the same position as the richest and
most powerful republics in the world, which, having given great impe-
tus to its industries, can afford to liberate themselves from foreign demand, and hunker down behind absolute protectionism. In this respect
our condition must be that of the other nations of the earth. We have
our own traditions and an economic system, which we cannot suddenly
renounce because under its influence very valuable interests have sprung
up, and because one million people earn their living under that regime.
National industry, which is mainly the result of protection laws that
have been in force for years, is today a great power. It represents considerable capital and labor, both of which the Government must respect
because they are incorporated into the life and development of the
country. But, as you yourselves recognize, it will be necessary to moderate the system and to remove whatever is exaggerated therein. Protection should be reasonable and fair, otherwise interests equally worthy of
respect would be injured, and industry would be driven into erroneous
channels to its own detriment.[70]

Roca's rational protectionism was the extension of his pragmatic approach
toward economics to the industrial sphere.[71] During the debate on the convertibility law in 1899 the president was, according to his own party newspaper, "positioned in the middle-ground between the extreme schools."[72]
The *oristas* (gold standard backers and free trade supporters), such as Lorenzo
Anadón and Victorino de la Plaza—who would become vice president in
1910 and president in 1914—rejected any state intervention in the monetary market. Conversely, the *papelistas* (paper currency backers and sustain-
ers of protectionism) advocated state intervention but only after fixing a very
low local currency rate, converted to 0.25 gold pesos. Roca's position, which
finally prevailed, was to support state intervention in the monetary market
by fixing the Argentine peso to a gold value, but with a lower exchange rate:
0.44, a little higher than that signaled by the foreign currency market but
much lower than the papelistas advocated.[73] As in the case of industry, the
resolution was closer to state intervention than to free trade, which outraged
the *Centro de Comercio* as a "sudden intervention of the state" in the monetary market.[74]

During the same period, certain groups became increasingly interested
in redefining the political map. Attempts to change old methods of poli-
ticking gained strength, despite the efforts of the PAN electoral machine to

undermine them. Some promoters of change thought that the system of traditional parties, based on personal loyalties, was close to collapse and that,
after its death, entities representing economic interests should fill the new
political situation. Against this backdrop, the influence of university students
and faculty on political affairs rose to unprecedented levels.[75]

Defenders of free trade represented a group of unheard voices. Alejandro
Gancedo, a preacher from the province of Santiago del Estero and a professor of economics at the University of Buenos Aires, wrote a pamphlet in
1901 called ¡Despierta Argentina! (Argentina. Wake Up!) and proclaimed that
the real division within politics should be between protectionism, representing colonial times, and free trade, embodying a modern economy.[76] In
1903 Gancedo wrote an article on protectionism and free trade in which he
attempted to encourage free-trade defenders as real thinkers and not mere
dilettanti, as their critics labeled them. But his preaching did not find much
of an echo.[77]

Student activism went beyond university walls and turned into riots,
amidst a revival of street demonstrations that were—whether violent or
peaceful—a sign of the new political strategies. Among the increasing number of rallies that took place during these years, industrialists organized the
famous one of 1899, which reached grandiosas proporciones (enormous proportions) according to the anti-industrialist newspaper La Nación.[78] This
meeting was, as indicated in Chapter 1, a response to the perils of the end-
of-the-nineteenth-century economic crisis and a weapon that the UIA used
in its struggle to gain representational power. Emilio Mitre, the incumbent
vice president of the House, asserted before the industrial gathering that it
differed

> from the old deliberative congregations of the public square that
> seemed to assume for themselves the right to rule [and were instead]
> citizens in the most modern assertion of the concept. Those who have
> an exact notion of the state and who understand that the needs of the
> people and justice are linked in a modern society: contribution and
> revenue, revenue and the very existence of the state indicate a happy
> evolution in the national life, a real progress in our education as civi-
> lized people and of our organization as a force able to make the banner
> of our national destinies victorious in the universal struggle of eco-
> nomic interests.[79]

At that time, industrialists felt that the country was ready for the creation of a political party organized around the interests of manufacturing.
Rural producers, in fact, went in the same direction by creating the Unión

Provincial and the *Defensa Rural*.[80] The strongest effort to this end was the formation of the *Gran Comité de la Producción Nacional* (Great Committee of the National Production), engendered by the uneasy times that closed the nineteenth century. In November 1899, a group of industrialists gathered together to defend themselves against the campaign of free-trade supporters and to "counterattack the movement attempting to eliminate the protectionist policy that, in the last fifteen years, has dominated our legislation." In January 1900, some followers of the Gran Comité asserted that, "[t]he formation of this party is the sign of a revolution in the political divisions among those aspiring to power: the old parties will disappear and the new, those belonging to the future, the economic parties, will be the basis for divisions in public opinion."[81] The Gran Comité launched a call *Al Pueblo de la República* (To the People of the Republic) to end their ties with old politics. It selected a *junta ejecutiva*, in which well-known industrialists were predominant, and built its organization from networks already in existence at the municipal level. The main area of operation was in Villa Crespo, a neighborhood in Buenos Aires city where a couple of large industrial firms had substantial influence. This importance was localized and it did not extend to other areas of the city or the rest of the country. The message of the Gran Comité was ignored, and the party eventually disbanded due to a lack of support. The limits and the failure of the Gran Comité are, to a large extent, symbolized by the fact that only the proindustrial *El País* made note of its existence.[82]

In 1908, during a profound crisis in the PAN between the leadership of Roca and the incumbent president José Figueroa Alcorta, who began his term in 1906 after the death of his predecessor Quintana, industrialists believed that the collapse of the old political parties had finally occurred. The shoe producer Luis Pascarella attempted to launch a pro-manufacturing party, since "[t]he politics of the present, and even more of the future, will be in the movement of economic forces in the distinct forms that the economy presents to them."[83] But this attempt also failed, even more so than the landowners' efforts to create a party to represent them politically.[84] Argentine politics was not well adapted to the formation of parties representing specific economic interests.

In 1914, the UIA faced a dilemma. After the electoral reforms of 1912, the Socialist Party won two successive elections in the city of Buenos Aires. This led many to believe that the party was going to expand across the entire nation.[85] The success of Socialism, according to the UIA, was due to the growth in the number of blue-collar workers that accompanied the rise of factories. Industrialists, however, did not have their own political party. The dilemma, therefore, was over whether to hand over the Radical Party, whose economic program is still a mystery . . . or to adopt traditional politics, which by virtue of an historical law are doomed to disappear. In the first case there is the danger that the representatives will turn against the represented; in the second case it is a losing battle.[86]

The Radical Party won the elections of 1916, and contrary to the worst fears of industrialists, it did not break with the past in economic matters. The verbal battle of 1909 between Yrigoyen and Pedro Molina had foreshadowed the transformation of the Radical Party's economic policies from a clear stance in favor of free trade to the lack of definition, as the latter had suspected. The new administration did not change the basic features of the relationship between state and manufacturing. Industrialists pursued the traditional lobbying strategy, which continued to show good results. Representative Berduc had said that rational protectionism was the destiny of those in power, and it appeared that he was correct. One sign of this was the stance of the main Radical newspaper, *La Epoca*, which engaged in an open campaign in support of national industries. Another was the appointment of protectionist Javier Padilla as Director of Commerce and Industries. Moreover, Alfredo Demarchi, an industrialist and former president of the UIA, became Yrigoyen's Minister of Agriculture, a position which also overlooked all industrial matters.[87]

There was, however, some realignment in the Congress, in which sectional voting started to divide legislators as never before, and fears of parties aligned by regional interests seemed to be realized. The system of a fixed valuation on each imported item had left the aforo undervalued after the international inflation that accompanied the First World War. In 1918, 1920, and 1923 three crucial votes on industrial tariffs (the first was specifically on shoes while the second and the third dealt with duties in general) made this shift apparent. Unsurprisingly, Socialists supported free trade and Conservatives defended protectionism. But a more complicated dispute arose within the Radical Party, whose legislators from the Littoral were becoming less enthusiastic about protecting industry at the cost of their constituency's living standard. This division created serious problems within the incumbent party, whose Northwest supporters protested against the new challenge to their well-being. The case of the province of Jujuy provides a good example. In 1920, the national government sent a project to the Congress to expropriate two hundred thousand tons of sugar, which would be bought at a price lower than market value and sold to the consumer at the same rate. The project never passed Congress, but this prompted the Radical leader of the province—Benjamín Villafañe—to form an alliance with the Conservatives, which won him the gubernatorial election in 1924, and eventually to abandon his original party. By then, the new Radical administration, led by Marcelo T. de Alvear since 1922, had allowed the importation of sugar, outraging domestic producers. Villafañe (who during Yrigoyen's term described him as "basically a socialist") went to Buenos Aires in a failed attempt to stop imports; in 1927, the Jujuy governor organized a conference of Northwest governors to defend regional interests.[88]

Shoe producers had been especially successful in lobbying Congress for increased protection for their products in 1918. Since then, world inflation had made the aforo values (on which the percentage of import duties was reckoned) too low. This hurt local industry and fostered imports. Industrialists began to plead for help. When Alvear's presidency began, his attitude appeared favorable; in his inaugural speech he supported local manufactories.[89] In addition, his first minister of finances, Rafael Herrera Vegas, took a proindustrialist stand and sent a project to Congress to reorder aforos and duties.[90]

The aforos in force were those calculated in 1905. Everybody agreed that the old values had been surpassed by international and domestic inflation, which damaged local production in spite of forces that restricted imports, such as lack of foreign currency in the postwar years, plus low exchange rates.[91] The House of Representatives modified the aims of the original project, which proposed a general increase of 80 percent in the aforo value. The growing awareness of consumer interests among Radical representatives led to a compromise position, the revaluation of aforos at 60 percent rather than 80 percent. After fixing the new aforos, the Congress voted new duties on goods, ranging from 50 percent to 5 percent ad-valorem. The rationale of pragmatic protectionism continued, but instead of item-by-item rates a single tariff was applied to each group of items. Silk articles provide a good illustration of this new application of the traditional pragmatism of Argentine tariff policy. All ready-to-wear silk goods (a recent domestic undertaking) carried the same protective duty of 50 percent, all woven goods paid 15 percent, while the raw silk, not produced in the country, entered almost duty free and continued the trend in favor of a cascading tariff structure. The key to understanding this tariff lies in the specific duties on locally manufactured goods—cigarettes, beer, matches, paper, pins, hats, candles, pasta, biscuits, and so on.[92] The protective effect of this tariff was significant and prompted a number of foreign firms to open factories in Argentina, as already seen in Chapter 3.

The threat imposed by a less protectionist lower chamber added to the one created by the appointment of a new minister to replace Herrera

Vegas in 1923. The new minister was Victor Molina, an advocate of laissez-faire economic policies.[93] As a sign of his new "anti-industrial" bias, one of Molina's first measures was to cancel the Counseling Commission recently created to help the Executive Power in economic affairs. The commission was, in the eyes of the UIA, merely a ploy to influence the administration. Molina did not further reduce tariffs. A laissez-faire minister could not do much given the working political network of pragmatic protectionism.[94]

This outcome was in part due to the limited options created by the necessity to finance the Argentine state. If tariffs on imports were lowered, the fiscal gap must be filled, as occurred when taxes on exports ended in 1884. The message of minister Molina in 1923 was clear:

> The current contributions . . . looking to consumption as the principal fiscal source, weigh disproportionately on those who bear it. Taxing income means a new orientation in economic and social policy, since its implementation will eliminate many duties that today provoke the high cost of living . . . What are the taxes that increase the cost of living? . . . The president of the Republic himself says it: they are the taxes on consumption.[95]

The solution was the income tax, a project undertaken by the administration of Alvear but which did not find support in the Congress. Only with the onset of the 1930 Depression was national direct taxation seriously considered, and subsequently applied. But by then the role of the state had transformed.[96]

The Autonomy of the State

The Executive Branch adopted a twofold strategy in regard to industrial matters. On the one hand, it acted like the Congress, listening to the particular interests of industrialists and supporting some policies according to the fairness (or lobbying power) of their claims. On the other hand, it attempted to become autonomous from the civil society and to behave as an independent entity. This last approach, which grew in importance with the effort to bureaucratize the state, met resistance in the Congress, which considered itself the arbiter of conflicting societal demands.

At the turn of the twentieth century, Argentina lacked a civil service comparable to that of the United States. A career in the bureaucracy was heavily politicized, since parties claimed to be the school of administrators and positions were typically obtained through contacts with party associates, friends, or relatives. The case of Carlos Guido y Spano, a well-regarded administrator, is paradigmatic. In 1872, he was appointed to the newly founded *Dirección Nacional de Agricultura* (National Agricultural Department). Guido y Spano knew nothing about agriculture, but he did educate himself about it while serving as director rather than simply using his position as a source of income, as was the standard.[97] At that time, any attempt to take politics out of an institution meant turning it over to private management, as occurred with the Banco de la Provincia in 1906.

Some degree of bureaucratization was achieved, not because of a well-developed plan but through the haphazard sum of increasing needs and demands on the central state that required technicians and well-established officials.[98] One of the main efforts to set up professional standards in the bureaucracy came from the incumbent Conservatives, who aimed for the "stability of a civil service" in 1916. Their attempt was doomed by its opportunism. With the victory of the opposition Radical Party in the national election that year, the lame-duck officeholders had indeed adopted this position to protect their cronies. The Radicals, for their part, were not enthusiastic about any kind of independent administrative career development and continued using the state apparatus as a patronage system.[99]

The dual realities of a state trying to cater to particular interests and maintain autonomy at the same time fostered a complex mode of operation. Eusebio García's appointment to *Sección Industrias Fabriles* (Section of Manufacturing Industries) in the newly created Ministry of Agriculture exemplifies the contradictory nature of the Argentine state. García was a civil engineer who became part of the country's nascent and small bureaucracy, but he had also been an industrialist and a manager of the UIA before his appointment. Moreover, his designation was part of an agreement between the free trader Federico Cibils, the first director of the Division of Commerce and Industry, and the industrialist association.[100] Therefore, García was at the same time a bureaucrat who was supposed to defend state interests and the UIA's voice in the government.

We can detect a more decisive trend toward state autonomy in the bureaucracy that dealt directly with tariffs. According to the Constitution, the Congress was in charge of all taxes on imports, but their intricate nature gave the Executive Branch a role that went far beyond Constitutional prescriptions. The Congress, which should have arranged every aspect of the tariff, voted only on the duties. Since it did not feel that setting the aforo was a political task, responsibility for this valuation and all its implications on industrial policy fell on the Executive Branch.[101]

The accuracy of the aforo valuation created bitter controversies.[102] Scholars have usually taken the side of industrialists who claimed that aforos were always lower than market prices, leaving domestic production unprotected.[103] Importers, however, cried just as loudly that the opposite was true.[104] There are indications of a confusing setting that would fit well with the rational pragmatism prevailing at the time. A study made in the 1890s by the customs expert Eduardo de Ezcurra showed tremendous inaccuracies (reaching levels of 40, 50, 60, and even 80 percent of difference) in both over- and undervaluation. Other confidential, detailed, and extensive studies led by the British authorities and Chambers of Commerce support Ezcurra's argument: both industrialists and importers had legitimate complaints. For the most part, this is unsurprising given the pragmatic policy of government toward industry in those years.[105]

The *Dirección General de Rentas* (General Direction of Revenues-DGR) was created in 1876 to deal with revenue issues, including aforo valuation.[106] For its part, the Customs House was in charge of implementing this valuation through its employees, known as *vistas de Aduana* (customs valuators). The vistas had to classify each imported item and assign it to the proper *partida* (category of merchandise), with the consequent aforo and duty. The Customs House was an old institution because, following independence, most taxes came from import duties. To improve revenue collection, it had to undergo major organizational changes at the end of the nineteenth century. The Customs House had long been involved in politics, and the institution was well known for transporting peons to the election spots. This impaired its ability to monitor trade efficiently.[107] In the 1890s, the administration made serious efforts to establish professional standards at the institution, which was—in terms of number of employees and tasks involved—at the forefront of the country's bureaucracy. The outcome was a more complex network but one experiencing the growing pains that accompany the emergence of a modern state.[108] Bureaucratization made commerce faster, but the Customs House continued to be spoken of as a chaotic place of incompetence and inefficiency.[109] In spite of this criticism, some changes were noticeable.

In the 1880s, the UIA complained that Customs House valuators lacked technical knowledge. This hurt domestic production because Customs House's employees favored imports by confusing *partidas* and giving items a lower-quality marking.[110] A decade later, reorganization of the institution transformed the more skilled vistas into allies of "rational protectionism," especially since the government had decided to keep the salaries of customs officials low and pay them a percentage of the irregularities they found.[111] Not surprisingly, this strategy resulted in an outcry from merchants, who accused the office of harassment. In the words of *The Review of the River Plate*, the administration treated them as mere smugglers, when "importation is after all an honest industry."[112] The classification of imports became a source of bitterness for importers, who felt that the Customs House put their merchandise into a finer category, which meant a higher aforo.[113] Amidst all these conflicts, a new proposal emerged—abolish the aforo and apply a valuation ad hoc with every shipment. But, as Eduardo Ezcurra put it, "[in this] Republic, which is not the one imagined by Plato," the ad hoc system would create rather than solve problems, for "it would bring a consequent seedbed of difficulties, disputes and claims, always damaging for the Treasury . . . since more than a few would try to cheat on the real value of the articles."[114]

As the number of bureaucrats and their influence grew, the idea of a state independent from particular interests became increasingly attractive. Ever since political independence in 1810, the government had created commissions to consult with the private sector in setting the aforos. The first one was formed in 1822 by the province of Buenos Aires and included representatives of cattle ranchers, exporters, and importers, in addition to Customs House officials, a representative of the Ministry of Public Treasury, and a member of the Budget Commission from the House. The fall of Governor Rosas in 1852 inaugurated a period of commercial influence over tariff issuing. According to a law passed in 1857 in what was then the autonomous state of Buenos Aires, each commission would be composed of four Customs House valuators and five merchants appointed by a corporate merchant institution called Commerce Tribunal.[115] The consolidation of the central state in 1880 changed this setting. Customs House representatives took their jobs more seriously and considered it completely legitimate to ignore private interests in making decisions. This zealous approach drove the recently created DGR, which decided to double-check any decision made by the Tariff Commissions before enforcement. This resulted in a process of negotiations and mutual concessions between merchants and civil servants. In 1883, the merchant association *Centro de Comercio* recalled with nostalgia the old times when "the government never took the opportunity to review the tariffs prepared by a Commission dominated by merchants rather than representatives of the Treasury."[116] Mitrista rule had been the happiest time, when, according to the association, the administration's involvement had been much more limited. Once the PAN came to power in the 1880s, the reduced role of civil society in the setting of tariffs was only one part of their program to create a strong central state.[117]

A major breakthrough in the formulation of industrial policies took place during the presidency of Luis Sáenz Peña. In 1893, he launched a series of original (if short-lived) reforms in the country's governance, such as the creation of a position similar to that of a prime minister.[118] In 1894, Sáenz Peña appointed a Special Tariff Commission that was to be more sophisticated than its predecessors since it would seriously study all issues and consult with all relevant associations and groups.[119] The idea behind the creation of this special commission was twofold. First, it would stress the role of the state as arbiter between interest groups. In so doing, the administration attempted to take into account all demands, including those of consumers. As the message explaining its creation said, "it is the duty of the rulers and lawmakers to distinguish between particular and general interests in their varied and multiple forms and in their relationship with the interests of the state."[120] Second, there was a revolutionary attempt to grant the Congress more power, which meant returning its constitutional power over tariffs and its right to intervene in the fixing of the aforo. But the number of new industries springing up under the umbrella of official "rational protection" made tariff reckoning a complex issue, one with which the parliament did not want to be involved. As one representative explained, "[t]he Congress is not going to reckon the valuations; it leaves this to the administrative power: as it constitutes an administrative function."[121] The government felt that the rush of claims and lobbies created by new interests (and those trying to silence them) was in itself intolerable without undertaking a review of the entire process.[122] To resolve conflicting aims, the president created a commission composed of Congressional members to act as an arbiter between the particular interests of merchants, industrialists, customs valuators, and other groups. Those who attended its sessions looked like a parade of witnesses at court. For the commission, this innovation was nothing less than the dawn of a new era. In its concluding report, it referred to it as "the first investigative administrative summary" in Argentine history. If it had taken such a long time to accomplish this point, it was because of

> the context of universal and administrative ignorance. . . . If, on condition of their very existence, our governments had not been forced to defend or attack perpetually, it would be impossible to explain the passivity of the predecessors of Your Excellency on this issue.[123]

The fact that a lawmaker led the commission helped give the legislative branch more political space. But since this man was Senator Anadón, suspicions arose among industrialists. There was also distrust of the institutional setting. The two objectives—arbitration of private demands and pleasing the Congress—were at odds with one another. Congress felt that the embodiment of particular interests was a legitimate role for the state, while it did not trust the bureaucrats, whom Congress members considered to be mere *empleaduchos* (petty civil servants). Indeed, in 1894 the Senate insisted that Customs House officials participate only as consultants, while most of the commission members were representatives of the private sector.[124]

It was widely recognized that the Special Commission operated with unprecedented professionalism. As one representative asserted, while former commissions took twelve or fifteen days to analyze the aforos, this commission conferred for months and "has gathered information from competent people and from all Customs House vistas."[125] The job was, in fact, monumental. The commission worked five days a week from March 15 to June 1, and often on the weekends as well. It had three main areas to review: sugar, wine, and the other industries that had sprung up in the city of Buenos Aires. Divided into subcommissions, it reviewed a total of 3,567 *partidas*, studied 101 claims from merchants and industrialists, and spoke to them personally searching for information.[126] Most of its members were sympathetic to lowering tariffs, albeit at different levels. Anadón, given his well-known stand, abstained from voting.[127] The only manifestation of the antiprotectionist bias was an anti-industrial discourse in a final report that did not initiate any major changes in the actual tariffs. Unsurprisingly, the results appalled defenders of free trade.[128]

The explanation for such an outcome can be found in both the effectiveness of lobbying efforts and the institutional setting in which the commission worked. Whether allied with sugar and wine producers or by themselves, Buenos Aires industrialists were successful in pressing the administration. Such pressure led to a revision of claims, as occurred with hat producer Cayetano Dellachá. The commission had decided to reduce the aforo for hats from paper $0.50 to $0.30. But Emilio Hansen, one of the members who proposed that change, agreed to reconsider after he received a visit from

> Mr. Dellachá who, before talking to the President, visited me and made a long exposition of the critical situation in which his industry finds itself, because importers have been smuggling felt for hats. . . . The main reason for asking for this reconsideration is that wool, a product of this country, is the primary raw material in the manufacture of hats. Although some of the commission members are not favorably inclined toward protectionism, I understood that it was convenient not to radically alter the aforo.[129]

The commission recognized its restrictions and proposed only limited reductions on a few items such as coffee, cacao, yerba mate, and raw tobacco, none of which hurt local industries, since these items were imported. Any major change would have incited the opposition of Congress or even the Executive Branch (for instance, the president vetoed a minor reduction made in 1894 in the shoe aforo). The UIA, originally concerned about the free-trade stance of many of the commission members, applauded its conclusions in later years as "a brilliant and extensive report."[130] The best the commission could hope for, according to free-trade supporters, was to create an "atmosphere" sympathetic to lower tariffs, a climate that would influence the debates of 1894 in Congress but result in no major changes in protectionist policy.[131]

The 1894 appointment of a commission was repeated in 1899 and 1902; Congress finally reached an agreement in 1905 to pass a "definitive" tariff that set all aforos and duties. The appointment of a commission in 1899 was prompted by the impending economic crisis and was similar in its intent and membership to its predecessor. This time, industrial interests were more active. According to the *Review of the River Plate*,

> This immediately brought forth an energetic protest from a number of our embryo industries, the owners of which declared that they would be ruined if the proposals were accepted. About a fortnight ago it was stated that the report was ready for the signature of the Minister, who had accepted it, but apparently, the 'Industriales' have managed to get a word in, for the decree has not appeared to date, and great pressure is being applied to hold it.[132]

In 1902, the new commission set a departure from the previous trend. Most of its members were bureaucrats who attempted to keep a distance from particular interests. The already mentioned Eusebio García, for example, represented the UIA. The commission president refused him permission to take notes in shorthand, because most of the members wanted to keep meetings secret "with the aim of not alarming commerce and industry and forestalling the rise of any resistance against the work of the commission." The private lobbying at work during the open-door discussions in 1894 and 1899 would not be repeated. This time, appeals to private interest groups were rare, since "the commission declared that it had nothing to do with guild interests and did not consider it necessary to consult merchants and industrialists."[133] The increasing desire to create a distance between the bureaucracy and civil society worked in parallel with changes in the nature of the import business at the beginning of the twentieth century. On the one hand, many importers were now industrialists, so their aims were more complicated than merely facilitating sales abroad. On the other hand, the remaining trade became concentrated in the hands of a group of large houses that mirrored the cartelization that was taking place in the manufacturing sphere. Importers lost their merchant identity and the interest in everyday politics that had characterized them in the glory days of Mitrismo.

The "definitive" tariff of 1905 appeased but did not end the special-commission mania. New ones were appointed in 1907 and 1909 to review minor issues.[134] A major step toward distancing the state from civil society occurred in the 1910s. The lame-duck government of Figueroa Alcorta, as part of an agreement with incoming president Roque Sáenz Peña, who won the national elections in 1910, appointed a *Comisión Revisora de funcionarios públicos* (Review Commission of Civil Servants) to handle tariffs without any intervention from the private sector. The state-centered drive elicited broad opposition. *La Nación* commented with indignation that this method of determining tariffs

> should be studied together with the interested guilds, such as the Liga de Defensa Comercial and the UIA, in conjunction with the Treasury, to look for a solution that conciliates all aspirations for they affect not only state revenue but also the general interest, which is worth taking into account.[135]

The victory of Roque Sáenz Peña in the election of 1910 seemed to offer gloomy prospects for industrialists. His government meant the rise of the circle of Catholics (including Lorenzo Anadón as Finance Minister), and the accession of financier and free-trade supporter Victorino de la Plaza to the vice presidency. Sáenz Peña calmed the anxieties of industrialists in an interview sponsored by the newspaper *La Razón*, an outspoken protectionist publication, while still a candidate. The future president praised the protectionism of former president Carlos Pellegrini and stated:

> I cannot and should not hide that I am not protectionist in principle, but I conceive of the government as having to adapt to the economic process of every state, and never as a subject for the theoretical rehearsal of extreme doctrines. We will, then, protect the existing industries, which represent substantial capital, and promote those that could take form and develop with moderate help from the state.[136]

Roque Sáenz Peña's government introduced a plan of political transformation that included, besides electoral reform, a redefinition of some of the state's capacities, such as a more interventionist Department of Labor, an issue Catholics cared much about.[137] In the area of industrial policy, this administration attempted to give final shape to the bureaucratization of the tariff discussion. In 1911, the president fostered a Junta de Aforos (Aforos'

Committee), a permanent body to investigate merchandise valuation. The idea, however, was not applied until 1916, when the war prompted the government to appoint a commission to carry out the Junta's goals. All of its members were bureaucrats, while representatives of import commerce, the UIA, and the Rural Society would advise the commission without having a vote.[138]

The idea of reducing tariffs came back to the political discussion in 1913. But it was soon disregarded due to opposition, and a new set of taxes on alcoholic beverages replaced it. This evolution gained the opposition of the Liga de Defensa Comercial that faced with dismay the impossible task of shrinking duties on imports. By then, the war had interrupted tariff discussions and placed a parenthesis around the discussion of aforos.[139] But the idea of having a permanent bureaucratic mechanism to fix them reappeared during Alvear's administration. The idea was to stop using the aforos as an instrument of industrial policy (this was to be confined to duties) and to respect their original purpose, that of expressing market values. To accomplish this, the national government proposed the creation of a *Junta Permanente de Aforos* (a permanent committee) composed of official representatives and with the participation of interested corporations, who would have a voice but no vote. Corporations that wanted to be decision makers resisted the role of adviser and wanted to vote in the process. Neither the proposal to create the Junta nor the corporate desire were ever considered; the Lower Chamber found the 1923 law to be sufficient framework for dealing with aforos.[140]

The UIA had proposed a solution that could not easily be implemented, and as it transpired, was unable to solve the problem either; it was impossible to set up the real market value for the aforo every year:

> Let's suppose that a retail merchant buys in a foreign factory 5,000 units of article X for a price of $1 m/n per unit. When the product is introduced in our country, it will pay duties for paper $0.32 per unit. But another merchant, a wholesaler, has obtained a bonus of 10 percent or more for having bought 500,000 units of the same article, and has paid only $0.90 per unit. When the product is introduced in our country, it will only pay duties for $0.28. Although the procedures of the Customs House have been completely correct, a flagrant injustice has occurred due to a flaw in the system.[141]

The industrialist group, which waved the unpopular figure of the trust to support its claims, began to make use of a greater threat: the new trust, under the figure of "El Dumping," was arriving from abroad. A difficult problem needed a more complex solution. In the 1920s, the UIA started to petition for a well-defined program of protectionism. The corporation asked Minister Victor Molina to reinstate the project of the Junta Permanente and to support a nonfiscal approach to tariffs. Spurred by the essays of Alejandro Bunge, who had forecasted a crisis resulting from high imports, the UIA set up a classification system for imported goods based on the goals of the new economy. For goods whose consumption should be promoted, such as machinery, duties should not surpass 25 percent; for those whose consumption should be discouraged, such as luxury items, duties should be over 50 percent. The industrialist project should focus on the items whose local production the state should encourage, and the range of duties should be from 25 to 50 percent.[142] This project remained only an idea, but it set up the basis for future claims in favor of a more protectionist industrial policy.

The scenario of the 1920s looked completely different from that of the early stages of central institutional construction. The state had formally distanced itself from particular interests. Bureaucrats, instead of merchants, defined valuations. Despite the changes in the role of the state, its ability to transform the economy remained limited. The bureaucrats had their hands tied and could do nothing more than prepare speeches. Commissions that supported free trade could change nothing without incurring the fury of the Congress or even the Executive Branch. As a result, very little came of the efforts put forth by the commissions. Rational protectionism prevailed. The trend toward an autonomous state might have meant a lot in the sphere of representation, but its impact on economic realities was inconsequential.[143]

Neither a protectionist nor a free-trade orientation, but rather a midway position based on a complicated case-by-case approach, explains the Argentine tariff. It looked like the product of a "patchwork state," similar to the prebureaucratic stage of governmental evolution in the United States.[144] Indeed, some products were protected; others were not. For contemporaries, such as the UIA, this tariff "lacked any rational and methodical plan; [and] it is a mere sieve."[145] A state-centered approach does not explain the construction of such an intricate web. The explanation lies in the transformation of interests into specific policies and in the institutional setting of the country. In addition to allowing for negotiation between the central authorities and the provinces, the Argentine Constitution established a system of multiple checks and balances between the Executive Branch and Congress.[146] This complicated intersection of interests and institutions was mirrored in an industrial policy that resembled the current United States' "Swiss cheese" tributary system, full of particular exemptions. The Argentine tariff, by contrast to other countries, was highly particularized, whereas in wholly protectionist cases (such as the United States) the tariff system was a much more solid

and organized front. The presence of a peculiar industrialist social actor provides a partial explanation. Those who were simultaneously producers and
importers of manufactured goods or who had diversified interests in different economic activities promoted this kind of policy. Indeed, rational protectionism, if controlled, was the best way to support their business.

In summary, let us return to the question that opened this chapter about
the makeup of protectionist Argentina. The tariff setting was badly organized
but not random. Rational protectionism was the outcome of intertwined
interests, ideas, fears, and promises. It promoted the growth of industry but
considered it to be ancillary to the economic powerhouse of the country,
which was the agricultural riches of the Pampas. In the sixty years that preceded the 1930 Depression, Argentina became a country with industries but
without an industrialization project. This project waited until the 1940s to
become the center of political preoccupation. However, by then, the idea
that Argentina had just a meager industry not only was false but also had bad
consequences for the issuing of the most efficient economic policies for the
country.

A Midway Industrialization:
Concluding Remarks

Industry was one of the leading forces in Argentina's transformation during the Belle Époque, the sixty years that preceded the Great Depression of 1930. Visitors, natives, and foreign residents shared a growing awareness that such a shift was occurring and took note of it during the Centennial year of 1910, as the country celebrated the anniversary of its revolution against Spain. Visitors were amazed by the material achievements before their eyes. Those living in Argentina were captivated by their own progress and measured it with the authority of those who can appraise past and present. There was a general agreement that the growing shape of Argentina differed from the old one. For the residents of a country with troubled precedents, the desire to change heightened the perception of the transformation, giving it an exaggerated sense of drama. In Argentina, political leaders considered the past as a burden.[1] Immigrants also partook in the sense of accomplishment, comparing their present lot to their origins. Some of the perceived ruptures were real, while others were imagined; some trends were new, others intensified old ones. The transformation not only generated confidence among contemporaries but also sparked anxieties toward the new social forces. Industry played a role in all these developments and made it clear that the country had set out on a new course.

Change first became apparent when Argentina successfully reversed its history of commercial marginality and civil wars, and emerged as a rising economic star and model of political stability. In these years, the country became a magnet for a growing number of immigrants, whose presence seemed to prove (with every ship arrival) that it was on the right path. An ambience of social mobility set Argentina apart from the Latin American model, especially when a new group emerged from the heart of Argentine society: the middle class. A land of opportunity had been created in the Southern Cone. The bright lights of these new realities, however, had their dark linings. Economic growth, political stability, and personal opportunities coexisted with trustification, corruption, and social unrest.

The development of local industry was one of the major innovations in modern Argentina. Since the country did not have a large handicraft tradition, almost every manufacturing effort began from scratch and had the impact of a hurricane. By the beginning of the twentieth century, following a period of rapid growth, industry constituted around a fourth of the national income and had become one of the driving forces in the domestic market, which was itself experiencing major changes.

Industrial growth was the result of a twofold force. On the one hand, international economic depressions set off a flurry of factory openings as part of an import-substitution process. On the other hand, domestic prosperity magnified demand, prompting the enlargement of already established manufacturing companies and enhancing the drive to open more.

The depressions of 1873–77 and 1890–91 played a crucial role in fostering the rise of industry. Timidly in the 1870s and more decisively in the 1890s, industry grew with each crisis in response to the need of a damaged economy to improve its trade balance through import-substitution. Tariffs were as important as exchange-rate variations in propelling industrial development. The effects of the 1913 depression on manufacturing are impossible to evaluate—the First World War immediately followed this blow to economic prosperity and growth. This dramatic and disruptive event had a more mixed effect than would a depression. Some import substitution took place in production that found inputs within the country, as occurred with woolen and leather activities. Stagnation, however, slowed down the kind of manufacturing dependent on imported raw materials or intermediate goods, especially those from countries at war. Since industry dependent on foreign inputs comprised the majority of factories, the overall effect of the war was negative. Finally, the 1930 slump proved to have an effect similar to that of 1873 and 1890. The Great Depression deepened the import-substitution process but did not initiate it. More goods were added to the domestic industrial realm while the remaining gaps were just awaiting a future opportunity.

The other side of this dual movement in favor of industrial growth was the rise of consumption. The cycle of rapid increases in demand that fostered the opening of new factories began in the 1880s; by the end of the decade the economic boom was deep enough to promote the opening of the first large mills to incorporate mechanization. After the interruption of the recessive 1890s, a new spurt in demand brought on the golden decade of 1903–1913, which witnessed some standardization. After the First World War, the 1920s faced a repetition of this trend—more demand, more large factories—but with the beginning of a new process: the arrival of foreign investment in domestic manufacturing, led by U.S. firms.

Some large factories began to produce a high volume of goods and hired hundreds of workers. By the 1910s, a group of mills in the leather, metallurgical, textile, burlap bag, beer, glass, cigarette, paper, match, and shoe industries employed more than one thousand workers (and some of them almost double this number). With the emergence of these large factories and the expansion of the cities where they were erected, the term *massive* could be applied for the first time to the economy and society of a country associated with the image of a vast desert. The response to these developments was ambivalent. Argentines found it to be both appealing and appalling. If the flood of immigrants was attractive to a country with a paltry population, they were also a threat to public stability. A greater concentration of wealth, pollution, and the employment of women and children toiling long hours in closed quarters accompanied large factories. Leading groups feared that alienated social constituencies laid the country open to the preaching of Anarchism. This trend, in fact, inspired the members of the Special Tariff Commission of 1902 to issue the condemnation of industry with which this book begins.

Industry appeared most dangerous when associated with conspiratorial forces, as occurred with the rise of trusts. The process of capital concentration and cartelization that peaked at the beginning of the twentieth century transformed market rules through the creation of pools, gentlemen's agreements, mergers, and corporations. The criticism not only addressed conservative concerns but was also the seed of future populism. An idealized pastoral society of the past was conjured up to highlight the dark side of modernity that threatened to engulf homegrown national values. It is not surprising that an industrialist (the beer producer Otto Bemberg) rather than a landowner was targeted as the embodiment of the evils of wealth at that time. Nor did he stop playing this role in the 1930s and 1940s, continuing to feed a rising populist animus. The target of José Luis Torre's pamphleteer literature and Aníbal del Valle's political poetry, the "old German" was accused of all possible sins.[2]

The rise of big business was the result of the reshaping of industrial production and the introduction of new commercializing practices in response to both negative and positive circumstances. Ill times came in 1897, when the threat of war with Chile sparked a recession that halted the growth of activities based in the local economy, such as industry and commerce. Structural problems in manufacturing became apparent; excess capacity confronting a relatively small market was the most evident sign. Inefficiencies that precluded the displacement of imports or the pursuit of sales in foreign countries were a more serious restraint on industrial growth. In any case, Say's law did not work as industrialists wished, and the structural weaknesses turned into price wars between producers. This had various consequences. Some firms closed, others embarked upon a cartelization process, and the few remaining barely survived on the old rules. As a result, a small number of large firms, in which most production was concentrated, and a sizable number of workshops coexisted and filled the industrial landscape. In spite of the risks that capital concentration posed for contemporaries—a nightmare that became reality when cartels gained control of the market and set new rules—the outcome was a more efficient industrial output. Production did not become competitive enough to transform Argentina into an industrial power, nor was the range of goods subject to new productive techniques very large. The country, indeed, standardized the manufacture of pins, biscuits, and clothes rather than machines or automobiles. But this transformation was enough to sustain the supply side in the rise of a consumer society in the richest and most dynamic areas of Argentina.

Cheap goods resulting from economies of scale met with changes in the demand side to generate an insatiable desire to consume. Revolutionary changes in commercialization eased the magical encounter between supply and demand. For its part, greater consumption propelled more standardization and economies of scale. Moreover, the consumer society that manufacturing promoted turned out to favor industry in an unexpected way— Argentine producers could match the demand generated by fashion changes faster than could importers, while domestic industrialists enjoyed the benefits of local market expertise in advertising. Qualitative changes accompanied a quantitative increase in demand. Life seemed more sophisticated under the charm of window displays, the allure of department stores, the glamour of fashion, and the spell of advertisements. These elements put Argentina (and primarily its capital city) at the center of a momentous transformation in the cultural meaning of the market. Market values replaced traditional standards in social and economic behavior. In effect, economics became a driving force in the creation of social values. In parallel, a more secular and more democratic time and space set the stage of everyday life, matched by pressing demands for political openness. To some extent, secret and mandatory suffrage in 1912 (which made effective the already universal vote) and the victory of the Radical party four years later were the logical political outcomes of the changes that had occurred in the socioeconomic spheres.

The evolution of the consumer society, however, was more complex than has previously been assumed. Some changes in the area of demand pointed toward more equality: access to goods and services was eased by credit, and more public spaces opened to leisure. The sphere of commercialization itself was experiencing a process of capital concentration parallel to that of industry. Department stores were the most striking example. At this point, one wonders to what extent the massification of the market transformed Argentina into a more democratic economy, since the era of trusts, strange as it might be, coincided with the rise of democracy and the victory of middle-class values.

Shifts in production, commercialization, and consumption followed the establishment of a central state. The bloody and interminable civil wars of the past had at long last ended. But the leadership undertook building a nation out of the disparate provinces, an endeavor that became an obsession, just as an influx of immigrants challenged the tenuous notions of national identity for the present and the future. The aims of the private sector complemented those of the state, and industry played a major role in the social construction of the nation. Ever on the lookout for more customers, manufacturing firms treated the entire country as a market. With their drive to sell throughout the country, their salesmen, mail-order systems, and catalogues, as well as their monopolizing strategies, helped transform a domestic market into a national one. Certain brand names became part of everyday consumer life in every part of the country. There were regional winners and losers in the struggle over this market. There is little doubt that the city of Buenos Aires, where most domestic industry concentrated, was on the victorious side. Beginning late in the first decade of the twentieth century, at the same time that all Argentine school children were reciting with exultant patriotism the *Oración Cívica* (Civic Oration) that praised Argentina as the best country in the world, the products of Buenos Aires factories reached all far-flung corners of the country.

Concentration of capital and production in Buenos Aires also meant a concentration of industrial workers. A coexistence of harmony and conflict characterized the relationship between industrialists and workers, many of them women who were incorporated into the formal economy as *fabriqueras*. In most firms, paternalism was as pervasive as modern labor organizational strategies were absent. Factory owners wanted to keep the relationship with their employees under private control in which, unsurprisingly, strikes were anathema. At the beginning of the twentieth century, when the labor menace grew into something of a nemesis, industrialists felt the need to fashion a corporate identity for themselves. This development benefited the Argentine Industrial Union (UIA), the association that had been unsuccessfully trying to coopt representation of industrialists since 1887. By the first decade of the twentieth century, it had started to enjoy some success, at the cost of changing its very nature. Although the UIA was originally founded by a wide range of industrialists, the shift went a long way toward placing it in the control of the most powerful firms. The process ended in the 1920s, when the UIA found itself in an unanticipated confrontation with other economic actors. By then, factory owners had changed their microeconomic strategies. After a long history as industrialists and importers of manufactured goods, they strengthened the manufacturing side of their activities, a trend initiated by disruptions during the First World War and more opportunities to invest in the following decade. In parallel, the cooperative relationship between factory owners and landowners that characterized the harmony between the city and the countryside broke down. The former advertised their importance as the engine of production and referred to cattle ranchers as parasites. It was then that something resembling an industrialist "identity" started to take shape.

This "identity" helped industrialists influence the national administration, an effort that grew with time and reached its peak with the arrival of Peronism in the 1940s and lasted until the 1975 depression. This depression was a local slump originated by the breakdown of import substitution, augmented by the impact of the world oil crisis and continued by a tragic political period after the military seized power in 1976. The industrialists' success went together with the increasing appeal of a "canonical version" of Argentine economic history that depicted industry as a long-standing victim of a hostile state. According to this interpretation, manufacturing would have needed state involvement in the form of credits, tariffs, and government purchases for industry to grow (and, subsequently, for the country to develop). Although this may have been a legitimate tactic in the promotion of their supporters' interests, this version—as this book has shown—was largely an invention. First, the financial environment that industry faced in the period of the export boom was not as hostile as argued. Firms could obtain money for working capital and investment through a variety of sources, including the state banks. Second, the state had been setting tariffs since the 1870s without major interruptions, slowly and selectively increasing duty protection over the years. Finally, the government had been one of the main customers of local industrial goods since the early growth of manufacturing.

Moreover, this trend deepened in 1895, after Congress passed the National Purchasing Law.

The result of the incorrect diagnosis was nothing less than a mistaken solution. If only credits, tariffs, and governmental purchases were needed, a state aiming to industrialize the country in the 1940s would just provide more of the same. Unsurprisingly, the outcome was frustration. Argentine industry during the export boom had barely surmounted part of its inefficiency thanks to state intervention. Before the 1940s, this governmental activism had been restricted—loans were not given within a program for development nor were import duties a response to a general design, not to mention the discretionary nature of state contracts with specific firms. Import duties were an example. Once working factories were protected, it became impossible to disassemble them. Every new product created a lobbying interest and became a Frankenstein's monster with a life of its own. These interests appealed to the government through a wide variety of strategies, but especially by playing on fears of social unrest. The government responded with a policy that looked at each case piecemeal outside of any overall design. At that time, this policy was labeled "rational protectionism," a combination of lobbying interests, dreams of manufacturing growth, concerns about regional balance, and alarm over the possibility of unemployment and social unrest. As a result, "pragmatic disorder" became the industrial face of the "conservative order" (adopting Natalio Botana's concept) that reigned in the political sphere, a policy that the Radical administrations continued in the years from 1916 to 1930.[3]

In addition, the canonical version diverted attention from certain structural problems that industry faced and that should have been the target of state intervention, if this was supposed to be a worthwhile effort. These troubles were at the roots of Argentina's middling industrialization, and any attempt to enhance the manufacturing process should have considered them. First, the lack of market demand and chronic excess capacity bottlenecked the growth of Argentine industry. By the 1920s, Argentina had a high GDP per capita, but the population was still small and, as a result, the total demand was much more modest than imagined by a visitor to Buenos Aires. By 1914, the city and its suburbs had already surpassed two million inhabitants; but there was no equivalent elsewhere to the capital city, which concentrated one fourth of the entire country's population. Rosario and Córdoba, the second and third largest cities, had 245,000 and 121,000 inhabitants, respectively. Thus, the overall size of the economy was similar to a small European country. Exports of manufactured goods, one of the keys to the success of countries with limited domestic demand, was not possible for an industrial complex working inefficiently, even with all the improvements made in the early twentieth century. Lack of crucial inputs, such as coal and iron ore, a discrete rather than a continuing rate of investment, and a relatively expensive and unskilled labor force were all serious and unresolved flaws that could be addressed. These restrictions hampered a more efficient industrialization and resulted in bumpy development patterns. Some goods were produced with the most modern techniques, some were still the products of a backward technology, and others were not produced at all.

This study does not delve into the debate surrounding the "Argentine riddle" and is limited to the world created by industry. Nevertheless, it does make sense to address the eternal query as to why the country did not fully industrialize, a question that is part of the search for the roots of Argentine economic decline in the second half of the twentieth century. Assessment of the country's industry depends on the frame of reference. Compared to the most developed countries—such as Great Britain, the United States, Germany, or even Italy—its progress was poor. Compared to its own past, manufacturing growth was significant. Indeed, within the context of the history of Argentina, industry made remarkable strides in a few short decades. In the early 1870s it was of insignificant proportions; by the 1920s, it was a major component of the country's economy. If further growth was not enough to fully industrialize the country, it was because its structural problems, referred to earlier, were never resolved. As a result, Argentine industry could be considered a case of mid-level success.

Comparison with Brazil, Mexico, and the United States underscores the idea of Argentine exceptionalism in the Latin American setting. The country that was supposed to replicate the United States in the Southern Cone faced, as we have seen, an industrial experience closer to the Brazilian and Mexican cases. The capital market, the lobbying interest, the presence of powerful economic and financial groups, a state porous to particular petitions—all these features made Argentina a successful case of an export economy. The facts that this boom was based on agriculture and cattle rather than on mining, and that the Argentine population was slender before massive European immigration, gave some specific features to a country otherwise steeped in the Latin American experience.

A history of a state supporting industry does not fit into the traditional interpretative framework that has linked that role to the post–1930 Depression and Peronist Argentina. Continuity in a policy that started in the nineteenth century was, however, the historical reality. The import-substitution of the 1930s and 1940s did not completely differ from the industrialization process that had begun timidly after the 1873–77 crisis and gained strength after the 1890 collapse. The passing of the years added more goods to the list of tariffs, and the degree of protection and state activism increased. The zeal with which textiles were protected in the 1930s, durable goods during Peronism, and heavy industry in the 1960s did not differ from the fervor with which ready-to-wear goods, cigarettes, matches, screws, or pins were defended in the 1890s.

Argentina's economy experienced a profound economic transition in the 1990s, from state interventionism to free-market policies, when the strategies to open the domestic market to international trend took the final shape that had begun with the strategies implemented in 1976 after the failure of the import-substitution process. The convertibility plan, which launched this process in 1991, continued this trend and ended the remaining tariff protection. But this plan came to an end in 2002, when a deep depression hit the country after years of recession begun in 1998. Economic recovery in 2003 was surprisingly fast and high, and up to the year 2005 looks also promising. But the country still faces many economic, social, and political problems that make the future quite unpredictable. At any rate, after reading this book, we can see that the first commercial policies to end protectionism—in 1976 and later in 1991—ended a process that had started in the late nineteenth century with an active state and a protected economy. Evidence of continuity between the period of the export boom, the Depression, and Peronist years becomes apparent just as the long-running period of state interventionism comes to a close. This is probably because, as Charles Maier has said, the historian usually sees "the outlines of an era precisely as it is ending."[4]

Reference Matter

Appendix 1

Credit Granted to Industrial Firms by the Banco de la Provincia de Buenos Aires in the 1880s

Saturnino and Secundino Salinas: $5,000
Aquiles Maveroff: $70,000
Fernando Martí y Cía: $19,600 m/n and 14,400 o/s
Juan Videla: $200,000
C. Rezzónico: $4,000
José Ottonello: unspecified
Juan Bercetche: $17,100
Egidio Colonelli: $5,000
Leandro Coy: $2,850
Santiago Massalin: $18,680 and $5,000 o/s
José Daumas: $10,000 and $5,000 o/s
A. Daul y Cía: $34,596
Santiago Baibiene: $6,000
Ventura Martinez: unspecified renewal
Fábrica de fideos La Rivadavia: $180,000 in 1877 (ABP, 015–2–F)
Fábrica Nacional de Dinamita: $100,000 (ABP, 015–2–F)
Fábrica de ladrillos La Quilmeña: $7,000 (ABP, 015–2–F)

SOURCE: Libros de Actas del Directorio del Banco de la Provincia de Buenos Aires (Minutes of the Board of Directors' Meeting) 1880–1889. The loans correspond to note discounts.

Credit Granted to Industrial Firms by the Banco de la Nación Argentina in 1892–1896

Above $100,000

Bemberg, Otto: $158,000
Cía Gral de Fósforos / Cayetano Dellachá: $610,567
Cremona, Andrés: $141,000
Dell'Acqua: $282,395
Fábrica Argentina de Alpargatas / Ashworth: $145,000
Fábrica Nacional de Calzado: $219,874
Gaggino–Lauret: $385,000
Huergo, Joselín: $172,750
La Argentina: $122,019
La Primitiva: $234,698
Martí Hnos.: $110,000
Molet, A. y Cía: $238,000
Pini: $100,268
Seré y Cía: $180,000
Spinola, Pablo: $324,750
Vasena, Pedro: $105,000
Videla, Juan: $356,259
Zambrano, Pedro: $149,217

Below $100,000

Antonini y Baibiene: $15,000
Ariza, Francisco: $10,000

Bonfanti, Miguel: $70,000
Canale, S.: $45,000
Chientelassa: $20,000
Destilería Franco-Argentina: $80,000
Didiego: $11,500
Egidio Colonelli y Pedro Merlini: $34,000
Fábrica de Cales Cerrano: $40,000
Fábrica de Conservas El Cazador: $5,240
Fábrica Nacional de Dinamita: $80,000
Fábrica Nacional de Tabacos: $52,161
Fusy, E. y Cía: $76,919
Gómez, Casimiro: $20,000
Gruget, Amadeo: $73,745
Hellmuth y Cía: $10,000
Maveroff, Aquiles: $20,000
Mitau y Grether: $22,030
Moreira, José: $5,000
Noel, Benito: $40,000
Ottonello y Cía y Luis Huergo: $20,000
Petit y Piria: $45,000
Posse, Juan: $15,000
Praudina y Cía: $15,000
Sackmann, Carlos: $20,000
Saint, A.: $45,000
Salinas: $32,009
Seeber, Carlos y Francisco: $25,000
Seminario y Cía: $30,500
Vetere, Nicolás: $11,000

SOURCE: Libro de Actas del Directorio del Banco de la Nación Argentina (Minutes of the Board of Directors' Meeting), Libros no. 2 to no. 18.

Appendix 3

Credit Granted to Industrial Firms by the Banco de la Provincia de Buenos Aires in 1906–1916

Above $500,000

Bagley: $680,000
Campomar: $1,285,000
La Argentina, fábrica de papel: $1,375,000
La Cantábrica: $910,000
La Martona: $535,000
Pagola, Martínez y Cía: $570,000
Reta y Chiaramonte: $554,309
Salinas Hnos: $1,210,000
Spinola, Pablo: $955,000
Vasena Pedro e hijo: $1,400,000

Between $100,000 and $500,000

Aquiles Maveroff: $148,000
Azzaretto Hnos: $323,000
Baibiene y Antonini: $110,000
Balbiani Hnos: $110,000
Cerv. Arg. Quilmes: $300,000
Cía Fosforera Argentina: $145,000
Cía Gral de Fósforos: $200,000
Cía Gral de Tabacos: $290,000
Dell'Acqua: $100,000
Del Sel, R y N: $150,000

Elaboración General de Plomo: $495,000
Fábrica Argentina de Alpargatas: $150,000
Franchini, Guillermo: $320,000
Gaggino-Lauret: $436,137
Grandes Destilerías de Bs As: $140,000
Grimoldi Hnos: $100,000
Grunbaum y Soulas: $100,000
Inchauspe: $221,300
Kulcke, Frankel y Cía: $188,000
La Acero Platense: $230,000
La Cromo-Hojalatería: $100,000
Larraechea: $320,000
Magnasco, Luis y Cía: $180,000
Merlo, Viuda de Francisco: $200,000
Peters Hnos: $200,000
Piccardo y Cía: $100,000
Pini, A y Cía: $220,000
Rigolleau: $450,000
Sauveterre, R.: $220,000
The River Plate Dairy: $175,000
Zimmermann, Noé y Cía: $160,000

Below $100,000

A la Ciudad de Londres (J. Brun y Cía): $50,000
Angel Braceras: $82,750
Ariza: $10,000
Ashworth y Cía: $50,000
Bilz: $8,885
Cerv. Palermo: $10,000 oro
Céspedes, Tettamanti y Cía: $10,000
Cía Argentina de Productos Tartáricos: $30,000
Cía Nacional de Aceites: $30,000
Cía Nacional de Ladrillos: $50,000
Cía Nacional de Tejidos y Sombreros: $30,000
Colonelli, Egidio: $35,000
Coy, Francisco: $50,000
Cristalerías Papini: $10,000
Curtiembre La Argentina Grunbaum Soulas: $80,000
Dasso: $85,000
Fca de Papel Casati: $27,000
El Fenix, Fca de Papel: $50,000
Ferrum, Industria Argentina de Metales: $50,000
Fontana Hnos: $26,000

Gerino Hnos: $5,000
Hornos de Ladrillo La América: $40,000
La America, horno de ladrillos: $10,000
La Destiladora del Norte: $15,000
La Fosforera Argentina: $10,000
La Refinadora de Aceites: $8,000
José Moreira e hijos y Cía: $57,000
Noé, Eugenio y Cía: $25,000
R Papini y Cía: $35,000
Seguí, Francisco: $10,000
Sternberg, H y Cía: $60,000
Taller Universal, Fábrica de ladrillos: $10,500
Uboldi Hnos: $15,000
Viuda de Seminario: $15,000
Zamboni, José: $31,225

SOURCE: Libros de Actas del Directorio del Banco de la Provincia de Buenos Aires (Minutes of the Board of Directors' Meeting) 1906–1916. Unless otherwise indicated, they correspond to a current account for 90 or 180 days with all their subsequent renewals.

Appendix 4

Manuscripts of the 1895 Second National Census

The manuscripts of the 1895 census are of special value, since the 1914 forms (Third National Census) have been lost and the next census was not held until 1947 (Fourth National Census). The census aggregate results comprise a substantial number of repetitions and a large group of establishments that were included by mistake or in an unclear classification standard, such as barbers, grocery stores, and even dentists, all of which I eliminated from my study. Unfortunately, the material from some jurisdictions has disappeared, but I was able to consult the complete data for 80 percent of the sections of Buenos Aires city. In total I have worked with 6,100 of 8,439 manuscripts, of which 4,500 are accurate to use, the other 1,600 being repetitions of establishments already surveyed or professional and commercial activities. This last fact and my "purification" of the data render meaningless any comparison between the tables of this paper and the aggregate results of the census. The material available is from sections 1, 2, 3, 4, 5, 6, 7, 8, 9, 12, 13, 15, 16, 18, 19, 20, 21, 22, 24, 25, 27, 28, and 29. Sections 10, 11, 14, 17, 23, and 26 have been lost.

Appendix 5

Source Information for Table 1.6

Circa 1877

For data on Godet, Bieckert, Luppi, Prat and Zamboni, see Club Industrial, "Movimiento industrial habido en la República Argentina desde el año 1874 hasta el presente: 15 de Septiembre de 1880," Para nuestro socio honorario Dr. Victorino de la Plaza, in Archivo General de la Nación, Buenos Aires, Archivo Victorino de la Plaza 5–6–12, pp. 18–25.

Circa 1887

For data on Godet, Saint, Bieckert, Prat, Vasena, and La Primitiva, see "Estadística industrial de la Capital Federal encomendada a Angel Ramón Cartavio y Enrique Raymond por el Consejo Directivo de la Unión Industrial Argentina para promover la concurrencia de la industria nacional a la Exposición Universal de 1889 en París," *Boletín de la Unión Industrial Argentina*, June 8, 1889, pp. 2 and 5.

For data on Noel, see *Boletín de la Unión Industrial Argentina*, January 11, 1888, p. 1.

For data on Fábrica Argentina de Alpargatas, see *Censo General de Población, edificación, comercio e industrias de la ciudad de Buenos Aires levantado en los días 17 de agosto, 15 y 30 de septiembre de 1887* (Buenos Aires: Companía Sudamericana de Billetes de Banco, 1889), volume II, pp. 316–17.

Circa 1893

For data on Godet, see Dr. Moorne, *Las industrias fabriles en Buenos Aires: Colección de artículos publicados en "El Nacional," Vol. I* (Buenos Aires: Librairie Française de Joseph Escary, 1893), p. 110.

For data on Noel, Quilmes, Gaggino-Lauret, and Vasena, see *Boletín de la Unión Industrial Argentina*, March 1, 1893, p. 1; February 6, 1889, p. 1; October 23, 1890, p. 2; and October 15, 1891, p. 1.

For data on Bieckert, see *La Nación*, November 5, 1894, p. 6.

For data on Fábrica Argentina de Alpargatas, see Dimas Helguera, *La producción Argentina en 1892* (Buenos Aires: Goyoaga y Cía, 1893), p. 46.

For data on Sternberg, Fábrica Nacional de Calzado, and La Primitiva, see Dr. Moorne, *Las industrias fabriles en Buenos Aires: Colección de artículos publicados en "El Nacional."* (Buenos Aires: Librairie Française de Joseph Escary, 1893), pp. 125, 139, and 123.

Circa 1895

For data on Godet, Bagley, Noel, Saint, Bieckert, Luppi, Casimiro Gómez, CGF, Fábrica Argentina de Alpargatas, P. Merlini, Sternberg, Dell'Acqua, Vasena, Fábrica Nacional de Calzado, Martí, Rigolleau, La Argentina, FERRUM-Schnaith, Barolo, Gath y Chaves, and La Primitiva, see Manuscript Census, República Argentina, Area Capital Federal, Sección Industrias, *Manuscritos del Segundo Censo Nacional*, 1895, Legajo 104, Sec. 1, p. 306; Sec. 2, pp. 75 and 113; Sec. 4, pp. 69 and 160; Legajo 105, Sec. 8, pp. 57 and 125; Sec. 9, pp. 106 and 240; Legajo 106, Sec. 12, pp. 5 and 68; Legajo 107, Sec. 19, pp. 1, 38, 62, 168, 188, 189, and 223; Sec. 20, pp. 6 and 94; and Legajo 108, Sec. 24, pp. 148 and 151; Sec. 28, p. 108 and 134.

For data on Franchini, see *Boletín de la Unión Industrial Argentina*, January 1, 1894, p. 2.

Circa 1898

For data on Gaggino-Lauret, Luppi, CGF, Merlini, Dell'Acqua, Vasena, Fábrica Nacional de Calzado, and Zamboni, see T. Worthington, The Special Commissioner Appointed by the Board of Trade to Inquire into and Report upon the Conditions and Prospects of British Trade in Certain South American Countries, *Commercial Mission to South America, Third Report: The Argentine Republic* (London: Eyre and Spottiswoode, 1898), pp. 560, 562–64, 567.

For data on Godet-Bassi, see *La Argentina monumental en la exposición de París de 1900* (Buenos Aires: Da Costa y Cía, 1900), p. 188.

For data on Saint, see *El País*, June 13, 1900, p. 6.

For data on Quilmes, see Finanzas, comercio e industria en la República Argentina. Editado por la "Oficina de Informes Comerciales" de Papke & Dankert. Buenos Aires: Imprenta Roma de Juan Carbone, no. 1, 1898, p. 101.

For data on Fábrica Argentina de Alpargatas, see *El País*, January 7, 1900, p. 7.

For data on Franchini, see *La Nación*, October 9, 1898, p. 2.

Circa 1905

For data on Godet-Bassi, Saint, CGF, Prat, Vasena, Fábrica Nacional de Calzado, Martí, La Argentina, and Ferrum-Schnaith, see Francesco Scardin, *La Argentina y el trabajo* (Buenos Aires: Jacobo Peuser, 1906), pp. 552–53; 584; 536; 583: 587; and 525–26.

For data on Piccardo, see *El 43* (Buenos Aires: Manufactura de Tabacos Piccardo y Cía, 1914), p. 112.

Circa 1910

For data on Godet-Bassi, Bagley, Noel, Saint, Luppi, Casimiro Gómez, Piccardo, Merlini, Vasena, Fábrica Nacional de Calzado, Rigolleau, Gath y Chaves, and La Primitiva, see *La Nación: Edición conmemorativa de la revolución del 25 de mayo de 1810* (published in 1910), pp. 12, 175, 131, 147, 328, 197, 87, 217, 325, 226, and 192.

For data on Quilmes, Fábrica Argentina de Alpargatas, Sternberg, and Dell'Acqua, see Reginald Lloyd, *Argentina in the Twentieth Century*. (London: Lloyd Greater Britain Publishing, 1911), pp. 418, 423, 417, 426.

Circa 1916

For data on Godet-Bassi, Casimiro Gómez, and Rigolleau, see *La Nación, Edición aniversario de la independencia, 1916*, pp. 49, 109, and 201.

For data on Quilmes, see "Las industrias nacionales. Producción de la cerveza. Un modelo de las fábricas de Quilmas," *La Epoca*, August 31, 1918, p. 2.

For data on Piccardo, see *El 43* (Buenos Aires: Manufactura de Tabacos Piccardo y Cía, 1914), p. 112.

For data on CGF, see *Almanaque La Razón 1917*, p. 175.

For data on Fábrica Argentina de Alpargatas, see *Boots and Shoes, Leather, and Supplies in Argentina, Uruguay, and Paraguay* by Herman Brock, U.S. Department of Commerce, Bureau of Foreign and Domestic Commerce, Special Agents Series no. 177 (Washington, DC: GPO, 1919), p. 61.

For data on Vasena, see *Fray Mocho*, May 5, 1916, p. 46.

All translations of Spanish, French, and Italian are my own unless otherwise indicated.

Introduction

1. See Roberto Cortés Conde, *La economía Argentina en el largo plazo (Siglos XIX y XX)* (Buenos Aires: Sudamericana/San Andrés, 1997), chapter 7; and "Estimaciones del producto bruto interno de Argentina, 1875–1935," working paper, Universidad de San Andrés, Victoria, Buenos Aires, October 1994. Along with Cortés Conde, the Economic Commission for Latin America (CEPAL) also estimated the total and the industrial GDP for the period starting in 1900. See United Nations, CEPAL, *Análisis y proyecciones del desarrollo económico. Vol V: El desarrollo económico de América Latina* (Mexico City: CEPAL, 1959). For the main differences between both estimates, see Table 1.2. For social history studies, see Mirta Lobato and Juan Suriano, *La protesta social en la Argentina* (Buenos Aires: Fondo de Cultura Económica, 2003).

2. "El informe de la Comisión Revisadora Aduanera de 1902: Las reformas aconsejadas y sus fundamentos" in *Sumario de los pormenores y antecedentes que se refieren a la reforma aduanera y a los tratados que la Liga de Defensa Comercial ha presentado al Honorable Congreso de la Nación*. Datos acumulados por José Praprotnik (Buenos Aires, 1903), CXCIV.

3. See, for example, Pablo Storni, "La industria y la situación de las clases obreras en la capital de la República," Informe presentado al ex ministro del interior Dr. Joaquín V. González como antecedente para la preparación del Proyecto de Ley Nacional de Trabajo, *Revista Jurídica y de Ciencias Sociales*, 25(3), July–September 1908, 237–321.

4. Victor Bulmer-Thomas, *The Economic History of Latin America Since Independence* (Cambridge, MA: Cambridge University Press, 1994); and Rosemary Thorp, *Progress, Poverty and Exclusion: An Economic History of Latin America in the 20th Century* (New York: Banco Interamericano de Desarrollo, Johns Hopkins University Press, 1998).

5. See Mirta Zaida Lobato and Juan Suriano, "Trabajadores y movimiento obrero: Entre la crisis de los paradigmas y la profesionalización del historiador," *Entrepasados*, 1993, III(4–5), 41–64.

6. See John Fogarty, Ezequiel Gallo, and Héctor Dieguez, *Argentina y Australia*, Serie Jornadas, Instituto Torcuato Di Tella, 1979; D.C.M., Platt (ed.), *Argentina, Australia and Canada: Studies in Development, 1870–1965* (Oxford: Macmillan, 1985); and Guido Di Tella, *Rentas, cuasi-rentas, ganancias normales y crecimiento: Argentina y las áreas de colonización reciente* (Buenos Aires: Instituto Torcuato Di Tella. Centro de Investigaciones Económicas, 1986).

7. Dante Alighieri, *The Divine Comedy*, trans. Charles Singleton (Princeton: Princeton University Press, 1980), 55.

8. Carlos Díaz Alejandro found the roots of the decline in the Peronist economic policies implemented in the 1940s, David Rock in the structural features of Argentine economy and society, Carlos Waisman in the overreaction of the elite to a supposed Communist threat and Alan Taylor in the demographic burden caused by immigration, with its consequent troubles in saving rates and capital formation. See Carlos Díaz Alejandro, *Essays on the Economic History of the Argentina Republic* (New Haven and London: Yale University Press, 1970); David Rock, *Argentina 1515–1987* (Berkeley and Los Angeles: University of California Press, 1985); Carlos Waisman, *Reversal of Development in Argentina* (Princeton: Princeton University Press, 1987); and Alan Taylor, "External Dependence, Demographic Burdens, and the Argentine Economic Decline After the Belle Époque," *Journal of Economic History*, December 1992, *52*(4), 907–936, and "Argentine Economic Growth in Comparative Perspective," Ph.D. dissertation, Harvard University, 1992. David Landes has recently recovered this issue by including Argentina as the only possible (albeit failed) case of a Latin American way to development. See his *The Wealth and Poverty of Nations* (New York and London: W.W. Norton, 1998), chapter 20.

9. Adolfo Dorfman, *Historia de la industria Argentina* (Buenos Aires: Losada, 1942). Moreover, Argentine industry has not found the appeal that other national cases in Latin America did in the last years. See Colin Lewis, "Industry in Latin America before 1930," in Leslie Bethell (ed.), *The Cambridge History of Latin America*, Vol. IV (Cambridge: Cambridge University Press, 1986), 319–23, and "Industry in Latin America," in Patrick O'Brien (ed.), *Industrialization: Critical Perspectives on the World Economy* (London, Routledge, 1998); Stephen Topik, *The Political Economy of the Brazil State, 1889–1930* (Austin: University of Texas Press, 1987); and Stephen Haber, *Industry and Underdevelopment: The Industrialization of Mexico, 1890–1940* (Stanford, CA: Stanford University Press, 1989).

10. *Boletín de la Unión Industrial Argentina* (hereafter cited as *BUIA*), Buenos Aires, August 8, 1888, p. 1.

11. Alejandro Bunge, *Los problemas económicos del presente* (Buenos Aires: n.p., 1920); and *Una nueva Argentina* (Buenos Aires: Kraft, 1940). For Bunge's career, see Juan José Llach, *La Argentina que no fue. Tomo I* (Buenos Aires: IDES, 1985).

12. Américo Guerrero, *La industria Argentina: Su origen, organización y desarrollo* (Buenos Aires: Establecimientos Plantié S.A., 1944). For the 1940s atmosphere, see Gisela Cramer, "Argentine Riddle: The Pinedo Plan of 1940 and the Political Economy of the Early War Years," *Journal of Latin American Studies, Journal of Latin American Studies*, October 1998, *30*(3), 519–50. For the Peronist experience, see Hugh Schwartz, "The Argentine Experience with Industrial Credit and Protection Industries," Ph.D. dissertation, Yale University, 1967; Pablo Gerchunoff and Lucas Llach, *El ciclo de la ilusión y el desencanto* (Buenos Aires: Ariel, 1998); and Marcelo Rougier, El Banco de Crédito Industrial Argentino y la política económica del peronismo, 1944–1949, master's dissertation, University of Buenos Aires, 1999.

13. Dorfman, *Historia de la industria Argentina*. See also Ricardo Ortiz, *Historia económica Argentina* (Buenos Aires: Raigal, 1955).

14. For the Structuralist perspective, see Aldo Ferrer, *La economía Argentina* (Buenos Aires: Fondo de Cultura Económica, 1964). The Marxist analysis shared a similar view. See Mónica Peralta Ramos, *Etapas de acumulación y alianzas de clase en la Argentina, 1930–1970* (Buenos Aires: Siglo XXI, 1973).

15. Guido Di Tella and Manuel Zymelman, *Las etapas del crecimiento económico Argentino* (Buenos Aires: Eudeba, 1967).

16. Roberto Cortés Conde, "Problemas del crecimiento industrial Argentino, 1880–1914," in Torcuato Di Tella, Gino Germani, et al. (eds.), *Argentina sociedad de masas* (Buenos Aires: EUDEBA, 1967).

17. For a discussion of this approach, see M. H. Watkins, "A Staple Theory of Economic Growth," *Canadian Journal of Economics and Political Science*, 1963, *29*, 141–58, and Morris Altman, "Staple Theory and Export-Led Growth: Constructing Differential Growth," *Australian Economic History Review*, 2003, *43*(3), 230–55.

18. Ezequiel Gallo, "Agrarian Expansion and Industrial Development in Argentina, 1880–1930," in Raymond Carr (ed.), *Latin American Affairs St. Antony's Papers*, no. 22, Oxford, 1970; Lucio Geller, "El crecimiento industrial Argentino hasta 1914 y la teoría del bien primario exportable," in Marcos Giménez Zapiola (ed.), *El régimen oligárquico: Materiales para el estudio de la realidad argentina (hasta 1930)* (Buenos Aires: Amorrortu, 1975); and Armstrong Warwick, "The Social Origins of Industrial Growth: Canada, Argentina and Australia, 1870–1930," in D.C.M. Platt and Guido Di Tella (ed.), *Argentina, Australia and Canada. Studies in Comparative Development, 1870–1965* (London: Macmillan and Oxford: St. Antony's College, 1985).

19. Díaz Alejandro, *Essays on the Economic History of the Argentina Republic*, 208–214. For a similar approach, see Paul Lewis, *The Crisis of Argentine Capitalism* (Chapel Hill and London: The University of North Carolina Press, 1990), 30–32; and Alfredo M. Irigoin, "La evolución industrial en la Argentina (1870–1940)," *Libertas*, 1984, (1), 247–88.

20. Díaz Alejandro, *Essays on the Economic History of the Argentina Republic*, 40–42 and 215. For this historiographical evolution in the long-run, see María Inés Barbero and Fernando Rocchi, "Industry," in Gerardo della Paolera and Alan Taylor (eds.), *The New Economic History of Argentina* (Cambridge, MA: Cambridge University Press, 2003).

21. Juan Carlos Korol and Hilda Sabato, "Incomplete Industrialization: An Argentine Obsession," *Latin American Research Review*, 1990, *25*(1), p. 24.

22. For the business history approach, see María Inés Barbero, "Grupos empresarios, intercambio comercial e inversiones italianas en la Argentina: El caso de Pirelli (1910–1920)," *Estudios Migratorios Latinoamericanos*, 1990, *5*(15–16), 311–41; Leandro Gutiérrez and Juan Carlos Korol, "Historia de empresas y crecimiento industrial en la Argentina: El caso de la Fábrica Argentina de Alpargatas," in *Desarrollo Económico* (hereafter cited as *DE*), October–December 1988, *28*(111), 401–424; and Donna Guy, "Refinería Argentina, 1888–1930: Límites de la tecnología azucarera en una economía periférica," *DE*, October–December 1988, *28*(111), 353–73. For a critical balance on entrepreneurial studies, see María Inés Barbero, "Treinta años de estudios sobre la historia de empresas en la Argentina," *Ciclos*, First Semester 1995, *5*(8), 179–200. For a long-term study of industrial evolution, see Jorge Katz and Bernardo Kosacoff, *El proceso de industrialización en la Argentina: Evolución, retroceso y prospectiva* (Buenos Aires: Centro Editor de América Latina, 1989). For an original analysis of industry and space, see Graciela Silvestri, "El paisaje industrial del Riachuelo: Historia de una forma territorial," Ph.D. dissertation, University of Buenos Aires, 1996.

23. This approach has been taken in some major works on economic history, such as Alfred Chandler's *The Visible Hand: The Managerial Revolution in American Business* (Cambridge, MA: The Belknap Press, 1977), and *Scale and Scope: The Dynamics of Industrial Capitalism* (Cambridge, MA: Harvard University Press, 1990).

24. See Censo Industrial de la República Argentina levantado por la Dirección de Comercio e Industria del Ministerio de Agricultura, 1908, Boletín no. 1, in Pablo Storni, "La industria y la situación de las clases obreras", p. 239. Census deficiencies were highlighted at the time. See *BUIA*, August 15, 1907, pp. 1–3.

25. Alexander Gerschenkron, *Economic Backwardness in Historical Perspective* (Cambridge, MA: Harvard University Press, 1962).

26. Javier Villanueva, "El origen de la industrialización Argentina," *DE*, October–December 1972, *12*(47), 451–76. See also his *Industrial Development in Argentina: The Process Up to the 1960s* (Buenos Aires: Instituto Torcuato Di Tella, 1987).

27. See, for example, Barbero, "Grupos empresarios"; Gutiérrez and Korol, "Historia de empresas"; Guy, "Refinería Argentina"; Jorge Katz and Bernardo Kosacoff, "Multinationals from Argentina," in Sanjaya Lall (ed.),

The New Multinationals: The Spread of Third-World Enterprises (New York: John Wiley, 1984); and Jorge Schvarzer, *La industria que supimos conseguir* (Buenos Aires: Planeta, 1996).

28. Roberto Cortés Conde, "The Vicissitudes of an Exporting Economy: Argentina (1875–1930)," in Enrique Cárdenas, José Antonio Ocampo, and Rosemary Thorp (eds.), *An Economic History of Twentieth-Century Latin America, Volume 1: The Export Age* (Oxford: Palgrave-St. Antony's College, 2000), and Cortés Conde, *La economía Argentina en el largo plazo*.

29. One exception is the brief reference made by Luis Roque Gondra in *Historia económica de la República Argentina* (Buenos Aires: Sudamericana, 1943) and, for more recent examples, Carlos Mayo, Julieta Mirand, and Laura Cabrejas, "Anatomía de la pulpería porteña," in Carlos Mayo (ed.), *Pulperos y pulperías de Buenos Aires, 1740–1830* (Mar del Plata: Universidad Nacional de Mar del Plata, 1996); Aníbal Arcondo, *Historia de la alimentación en la Argentina: Desde los orígenes hasta 1920* (Córdoba: Ferreyra Editor, 2002); and my own work "Consumir es un placer: La industria y la expansión de la demanda en Buenos Aires a la vuelta del siglo pasado," *DE*, January–March 1998, *37*(148), 533–58. Ricardo Salvatore analyzes cultural implications of market changes in "Repertoires of Coercion and Market Culture in Nineteenth-Century Buenos Aires Province," *International Review of Social History*, 2000, *45*, 409–448. For Latin America, see Arnold J. Bauer, "Industry and the Missing Bourgeoisie: Consumption and Development in Chile, 1850–1950," *Hispanic American Historical Review*, May 1990, *70*(2), 228–53; Arnold J. Bauer and Benjamin Orlove (eds.), *The Allure of the Foreign: Imported Goods in Postcolonial Latin America* (Ann Arbor: The University of Michigan Press, 1997); and Arnold Bauer, *Goods, Power and History* (Cambridge, MA: Cambridge University Press, 2001).

30. See, for example, Neil McKendrick, John Brewer, and J. H. Plumb (eds.), *The Birth of a Consumer Society: The Commercialization of Eighteenth-Century England* (Bloomington: Indiana University Press, 1982); and Daniel Miller (ed.), *Acknowledging Consumption* (London and New York: Routledge, 1994).

31. This research will not delve into consumption by drawing upon sources similar to the "probate inventories," such as done by some scholars. See Jan de Vries, "The Industrial and the Industrious Revolution," *Journal of Economic History*, June 1994, *54*(2), 249–70; and Carole Shammas, *The Preindustrial Consumer in England and America* (Oxford: Clarendon Press, 1990).

32. This evolution was already noticed by Gondra, *Historia económica*; Ortiz, *Historia económica Argentina*; and Eduardo Jorge, *Industria y concentración económica: Desde principios del siglo hasta el peronismo* (Buenos Aires: Siglo XXI, 1973). Usually, trustification had been associated with foreign capital. See, for example, Jaime Fuchs, *La penetración de los trusts yanquis en la Argentina* (Buenos Aires: Cartago, 1959); and Luis V. Sommi, *Los capitales yanquis en la Argentina* (Buenos Aires: Monteagudo, 1949).

33. Cliometricians take the qualitative readjustment stance while "Regulation theorists" support the idea of qualitative transformations. See Naomi Lamoreaux, *The Great Merger Movement in American Business, 1895–1904* (Cambridge, MA: Cambridge University Press, 1985), 8–9; and Michel Aglietta, *A Theory of Capitalist Regulation* (London: New Left Books, 1979), 218–19.

34. See Emilio Sereni, *Capitalismo e mercato nazionale* (Rome: Editori Riuniti, 1974); Edelberto Torres Rivas, "La Nación: problemas teóricos y políticos," in A.A.V.V., *Estado y política en América Latina* (Mexico City : Siglo XXI, 1983); and Waldo Ansaldi, "Notas sobre la formación de la burguesía Argentina, 1780–1880" in Enrique Florescano (ed.), *Orígenes y desarrollo de la burguesía en América Latina* (Mexico City: Ed. Nueva Imagen, 1985), 596–98.

35. Roberto Cortés Conde, *El progreso Argentino, 1880–1914* (Buenos Aires: Sudamericana, 1979). In the Latin American field, some major works pointed out the importance of studies of national market construction in the region's economic history. See Steven Topik, "The State's Contribution to the Development of Brazil's Internal Economy, 1850–1930," *Hispanic American Historical Review*, 1985, *65*(2), 203–228; Stephen Haber, "Assessing the Obstacles to Industrialization: The Mexican Economy, 1830–1940," *Journal of Latin American Studies*, February 1992, *24*(1), 1–32; and Orlove and Bauer, *The Allure of the Foreign.* In addition, new studies have insisted on the need to reexamine the links between national borders and market frontiers. See A.A.V.V., Comité Internacional de Ciencias Históricas, Comité Argentino, Historiografía Argentina, 1958–1988, "Historiografía de la historia regional," in *Una evaluación crítica de la producción histórica Argentina*, (Buenos Aires: Palabra Gráfica y Editorial, 1990) pp. 87–147; Erick Langer, *Economic Change and Rural Resistance in Southern Bolivia, 1880–1930* (Stanford, CA: Stanford University Press, 1989), and Erick D. Langer and Viviana E. Conti, "Circuitos comerciales tradicionales y cambio económico en los Andes centromeridionales (1830–1930)," *DE*, April–June 1991, *31*(121), 91–111.

36. See William Fleming, *Region vs. Nation: Cuyo in the Crosscurrents of Argentine National Development, 1861–1914* (Tempe: Arizona State University, Center for Latin American Studies, 1988); and "Regional Development and Transportation in Argentina: Mendoza and the Gran Oeste Railway, 1885–1914," Ph.D. dissertation, Indiana University, 1976; Susana Bandieri, "Espacio, economía y sociedad en Neuquén: El auge del ciclo ganadero y la organización social del espacio (1880–1930)," *Entrepasados*, 1991, *1*(1), 35–79; and "The Argentina-Chile Frontier as Social Space: A Case Study of the Trans-Andean Economy of Neuquén," in Paul O. Girot (ed.), *The Americas: World Boundaries*, Vol. 4 (London: Routledge, 1994); and James Brennan and Ofelia Pianetto, *Region and Nation: Politics, Economy, and Society in Twentieth-Century Argentina* (New York: St. Martin's Press, 2000).

37. Tulio Halperin Donghi, *Proyecto y construcción de una nación, 1846–1880* (Buenos Aires: Ariel, 1995); and "¿Para qué la inmigración? Ideología y política inmigratoria en la Argentina (1810–1914)," in *El espejo de la historia: Problemas Argentinos y perspectivas Latinoamericanas* (Buenos Aires: Sudamericana, 1987). For the formation of an Argentine nation as a topic, see Adolfo Prieto, *El discurso criollista en la Argentina moderna* (Buenos Aires: Sudamericana, 1988); and Lilia Ana Bertoni, *Patriotas, cosmopolitas y nacionalistas: La construcción de la nacionalidad Argentina a fines del siglo XIX* (Buenos Aires: Fondo de Cultura Económica, 2001).

38. Eugene Sharkey, "Unión Industrial Argentina, 1887–1920: Problems of Industrial Development," Ph.D. dissertation, Rutgers University, October 1977.

39. See María Inés Barbero and Mariela Ceva, "El catolicismo social como estrategia empresarial: El caso de Algodonera Flandria," *Anuario IEHS*, 1997, (12), 269–89; Mirta Lobato, *El "Taylorismo" en la gran industria exportadora, 1907–1945* (Buenos Aires: Centro Editor de América Latina, 1988); and *La vida en las fábricas: Trabajo, protesta y política en una comunidad obrera: Berisso, 1904–1970* (Buenos Aires: Prometeo libros/Entrepasados, 2001).

40. Cortés Conde, *El progreso Argentino*, chapter 4.

41. For women as a concern of policies and discourse at turn-of-the-century Argentina, see Donna Guy, *Sex & Danger in Buenos Aires: Prostitution, Family, and Nation in Argentina* (Lincoln: University of Nebraska Press, 1991); and Karen Mead, "Oligarchs, Doctors, and Nuns: Public Health and Beneficence in Buenos Aires 1880–1914," Ph.D. dissertation, University of California, Santa Barbara, 1994.

42. See, for example, María del Carmen Feijóo, "Las trabajadoras porteñas a comienzos del siglo," in Diego Armus (ed.), *Mundo urbano y cultura popular: Estudios de historia social Argentina* (Buenos Aires: Sudamericana, 1990). Mirta Zaida Lobato's research on meatpacking houses has broken new ground by studying workers' individual files in corporate archives. Her analysis, however, does not cover the earliest period of industrialization or the rest of the industrial spectrum. See "Mujeres obreras, protesta y acción gremial en la Argentina: Los casos de la industria frigorífica y textil en Berisso," in Dora Barrancos (ed.), *Historia y género* (Buenos Aires: Centro Editor de América Latina, 1993). For research on women in the putting-out system, see Marcela Nari, *El trabajo a domicilio en la ciudad de Buenos Aires, (1890–1918)*, Informe presentado de las investigaciones realizadas, Universidad de Buenos Aires, 1994. For women and conditions of work, legislation, and unionism, see María Matilde Mercado, *La primera ley de trabajo femenino: "La mujer obrera," (1890–1910)* (Buenos Aires: Centro Editor de América Latina, 1988).

43. Dorfman, *Historia de la industria*, 189; and Ortiz, *Historia económica*, 550 and 657–58. For the 1960s and 1970s, see Ferrer, *La economía*, 190; Jorge, *Industria y concentración económica*; and Oscar Cornblit, "Inmigrantes y empresarios

en la política Argentina," *DE*, January–March 1967, *6*(24), 641–91. For neo-classicism, see Díaz Alejandro, *Essays on the Economic History of the Argentina Republic*. There is no equivalent of agrarian credit analysis for the case of man-ufacturing. See Joseph Tulchin, "El crédito agrario en la Argentina, 1910–1926," *DE*, October–December 1978, *71*, 381–408; and Jeremy Adelman, *Frontier Development: Land, Labor, and Capital on the Wheatlands of Argentina and Canada, 1890–1914* (Oxford: Clarendon Press, 1994), chapter 6.

44. Cortés Conde suggested that part of the industrial sector, for example food processing, did not suffer from capital constraints. Lucio Geller stated that industry was profitable, though his staple-theory framework limited his conclusions to agro-industry. Guy moved the discussion to a fresh area and delved into the legal constraints restricting access to loans, but put too much emphasis on the importance of personal connections in overcoming this challenge. Finally, Paul Lewis highlighted the existence of aggressive entrepre-neurs, in contrast to the passively suffering stereotype, but continued to support the idea of a primitive capital market with personal savings as the main source of financing in an environment of government credit hostility. See Cortés Conde, "Problemas," pp. 66–67; Geller, "El crecimiento industrial," p. 180; Donna Guy, "La industria Argentina, 1870–1940: Legislación comercial, mercado de acciones y capitalización extranjera," *DE*, October–December 1982, *22*(87), 351–74; and Paul Lewis, *The Crisis of Argentine Capitalism*, 65, 67, and 72.

45. See Stephen Haber, *How Latin America Fell Behind: Essays on the Economic History of Brazil and Mexico, 1800–1914* (Stanford, CA: Stanford University Press, 1997). Cliometric studies are also useful for this kind of analysis. See John Coatsworth and Alan Taylor (eds.), *Latin America and the World Economy Since 1800* (Cambridge, MA: Harvard University Press, 1998).

46. Leonard Nakamura and Carlos Zarazaga, "Economic Growth in Ar-gentina in the Period 1900–1930: Some Evidence from Stock Returns," in John Coatsworth and Alan Taylor (eds.), *Latin America and the World Economy Since 1800*; and "Banking and Finance in the Period 1900–35," in Gerardo della Paolera and Alan Taylor (eds.), *The New Economic History of Argentina* (Cambridge, MA: Cambridge University Press, 2003).

47. José Panettieri, *Aranceles y protección industrial, 1862–1930* (Buenos Aires: Centro Editor de América Latina, 1983).

48. For a successful revision of the long-lasting idea of a noninterventionist state, see Topik, *The Political Economy*.

49. See, for instance, Peter Evans, Dietrich Rueschemeyer, and Theda Skopcol (eds.), *Bringing the State Back In* (Cambridge, MA: Cambridge Uni-versity Press, 1985); and Bob Jessop, *State Theory: Putting Capitalist States in Their Place* (University Park, PA: Pennsylvania State University Press, 1990).

50. Jorge Sábato, *La clase dominante en la Argentina moderna: Formación y características* (Buenos Aires: Grupo Editor Latinoamericano, 1988).

51. Colin Lewis, "Industry in Latin America," in Patrick O'Brien (ed.), *Industrialization: Critical Perspectives on the World Economy.*

52. Díaz Alejandro, *Essays on the Economic History of the Argentina Republic,* 277. As Eugene Sharkey put it, "[d]ocumentary evidence of the rationales upon which the import tariff schedules were created before 1906 is largely lacking." See his "Unión Industrial Argentina," 104. To make things worse, Díaz Alejandro's study does not cover material before 1906. See his *Essays on the Economic History of the Argentina Republic,* 277–308.

53. Carl Solberg, "The Tariff and Politics in Argentina 1916–1930," *Hispanic American Historical Review,* May 1973, *53*(2), 260–84.

54. See D.C.M. Platt, *Latin America and British Trade 1806–1914* (London: Adam & Charles Black, 1972), chapter 5; Tim Duncan, "Government by Audacity: Politics and the Argentine Economy, 1885–1892," Ph.D. dissertation, University of Melbourne, 1981; Colin Lewis, "Immigrant Entrepreneurs, Manufacturing and Industrial Policy in the Argentine, 1922–28," *The Journal of Imperial and Commonwealth History,* October 1987, *16*(1), 77–108; Eduardo Zimmermann, *Los liberales reformistas* (Buenos Aires: Sudamericana, 1995); Natalio Botana and Ezequiel Gallo, *De la república posible a la república verdadera (1880–1910)* (Buenos Aires: Ariel, 1997); and Paula Alonso, *Between Revolution and the Ballot Box: The Origins of the Argentine Radical Party* (New York: Cambridge Latin American Studies, Cambridge University Press, 2000). James Scobie suggested the success burlap bag industrialists had in lobbying the government in passive protective tariffs. See his *Revolution in the Pampas: a Social History of Argentine Wheat, 1860–1910* (Austin, TX: Institute of Latin American Studies, 1964). Laura Randall has also mentioned the political pressure by Argentine industrialists on the tariff issue before 1930 in her *An Economic History of Argentina in the Twentieth Century* (New York: Columbia University Press, 1978), chapter 6. José Villarruel has questioned the assumed lack of protectionism in the 1920s in his "Los industrialistas y la tutela del Estado," in Waldo Ansaldi, Alfredo Pucciarelli, and José C. Villarruel (eds.), *Argentina en la paz de dos guerras 1914–1945* (Buenos Aires: Biblos, 1993), 205–209.

55. As Jorge Katz and Bernardo Kosacoff have suggested in their interpretation of Argentina's long-run industrial evolution, scholarly literature on the tariff issue is far from being conclusive and leaves more questions than answers. See Katz and Kosacoff, *El proceso de industrialización,* pp. 22–23.

56. See Jorge Balán, "Una cuestión regional en la Argentina: Burguesías provinciales y el mercado nacional en el desarrollo agroexportador," *DE,* April–June 1978, *18*(69), 49–87; Jorge Balán and Nancy López, "Burguesías y gobiernos provinciales en la Argentina: La política impositiva de Tucumán y Mendoza entre 1874 y 1914," *DE,* October–December 1977, *17*(67),

391–435; Donna Guy, *Argentine Sugar Politics: Tucumán and the Generation of Eighty* (Tempe, AZ: The Center for Latin American Studies, 1980); Noemí Girbal de Blacha, "Azúcar, poder político y propuestas de concertación para el noroeste Argentino en los años '20: Las conferencias de gobernadores de 1926–1927," *DE*, April–June 1994, *34*(133), 107–122; Daniel Campi (ed.), *Estudios sobre la historia de la industria azucarera Argentina* (San Salvador de Jujuy: Universidad Nacional de Tucumán, Serie Ciencia, Colección Jujuy, 1991); and José Antonio Sánchez Román, "La dulce crisis: Finanzas, estado e industria azucarera en Tucumán, Argentina (1853–1914)," Ph.D. dissertation, Universidad Complutense de Madrid, Instituto Universitario 'Ortega y Gasset', Madrid, 2001. For meatpacking houses, see Peter Smith, *Beef and Politics in Argentina: Patterns of Conflict and Change* (New York: Columbia University Press, 1969).

57. The use of the same criteria for all industrial activity, regardless of regional and temporal differences, has been highly criticized both in business and labor history. Alfred Chandler's revisionism from the perspective of "business history" has been especially successful by stressing interindustrial variation in the growth of scale and the application of powered machinery. Bruce Laurie and Mark Schmitz addressed the difficulty of considering firm size as a homogeneous standard in their study of Philadelphia's industry. See their "Manufacture and Productivity: The Making of an Industrial Base, Philadelphia, 1850–1880," in Theodore Herschberg (ed.), *Philadelphia: Work, Space, Family, and Group Experience in the Nineteenth Century: Essays Toward an Interdisciplinary History of the City* (New York and Oxford: Oxford University Press, 1981). The new social history's challenge has grown from the opposition to the romanticised idea of skilled artisans versus unskilled factory workers. See David Montgomery, "Workers' Control of Machine Production in the Nineteenth Century," *Labor History*, Fall 1976, *17*(4), 485–509. In the case of Argentina, Mirta Lobato has applied a new methodology based on the firm perspective to study labor. See her *'El Taylorismo' en la gran industria exportadora Argentina: 1907–1945* (Buenos Aires: Centro Editor de América Latina, 1988); and "Mujeres obreras, protesta y acción gremial en la Argentina: Los casos de la industria frigorífica y textil en Berisso," in Dora Barrancos, *Historia y género* (Buenos Aires: Centro Editor de América Latina, 1993). The extrapolation of the textile industrial paradigm, epitomized by the Lancashire mills, has elicited as many criticisms as the entire English model of industrialization. Some authors have offered an alternative to this paradigm that captures the complexity of any regional or national case. See Raphael Samuel, "The Workshop of the World: Steam-Powered and Hand Technology in Mid-Victorian Britain," *History Workshop Journal*, Spring 1977, *3*, 6–72. A model pointing out the coexistence of overlapping work settings has been drawn by Jeremy Attack in his "Industrial Structure and the Emergence of the Modern Industrial Corporation," *Explorations in Economic History, January 1985, 22*(1), 29–52.

Chapter 1

1. Adrián Patroni, *Los trabajadores en la Argentina* (Buenos Aires: Imprenta Chacabuco, 1897), p. 9.

2. *La Nación*, Buenos Aires, December 17, 1894, p. 5.

3. *The Review of the River Plate*, Buenos Aires, (hereafter cited as *RRP*), June 6, 1896, pp. 5–6; for Buenos Aires in the 1890s, see Francis Korn, *Buenos Aires 1895: Una ciudad moderna* (Buenos Aires: Instituto Torcuato Di Tella, 1981).

4. *RRP*, p. 6. Imitation was possible in a country where trademark laws were not a governmental concern. See United Kingdom, Public Record Office Archives, Foreign Office (hereafter cited as FO), 6/465 "Report on the Law and Regulations Respecting Trade Marks in the Argentine Republic" by F. S. Clarke (Secretary of the Legation), Buenos Aires, May 7, 1900; 6/469, 20 Commercial, Buenos Aires, September 12, 1901, Barrington; and 6/487, 14, Commercial, Buenos Aires, May 10, 1904, Haggard.

5. Ricardo Napp, *La República Argentina* (Buenos Aires: Impreso por la Sociedad Anónima, 1876), 338.

6. Hilda Sabato, *Capitalismo y ganadería en Buenos Aires: La fiebre del lanar 1850–1890* (Buenos Aires: Sudamericana, 1989).

7. Vicente Vázquez Presedo, *Estadísticas históricas Argentinas: Primera parte 1875–1914* (Buenos Aires: Macchi, 1971), 15–16.

8. The 1876 law established tariffs of 40 percent or more upon liqueurs, wines, sugar, beer, other alcohols, shoes, and ready-to-wear clothing; 35 percent on luggage, preserved food, biscuits, pasta, printed matter, furniture, cheese, and hats; and 25 percent on a variety of goods such as textiles and cured hides. See José Carlos Chiaramonte, *Nacionalismo y liberalismo económicos en la Argentina, 1860–1880* (Buenos Aires: Solar-Hachette, 1971); and José Panettieri, *Aranceles y protección industrial, 1862–1930* (Buenos Aires: Centro Editor de América Latina, 1983).

9. Emile Daireaux, *La vie et les moeurs á la Plata*, vol. 2 (Paris: Librairie Hachette, 1884), 124; and Ezequiel N. Paz y Manuel Mendoza, *La Exposición Continental celebrada en el año 1882*, 234, cited in Alfredo Malaurie and Juan Gazzano, *La industria Argentina y la exposición del Paraná* (Buenos Aires: Editada por la Agencia General de Publicidad de Juan M. Gazzano y Cía, 1888), 90. In earlier exhibitions, industrial presence was not so noticeable. In 1880, a joint exhibition was held by the *Club Industrial*, the *Sociedad Rural Argentina*, the *Centro Comercial de Buenos Aires*, and the *Sociedad Científica Argentina*. See *Exposición universal, industrial y agrícola de 1880 en Buenos Aires* (Buenos Aires: Imprenta de la Oficina Técnica, 1878). In 1877 the Club Industrial organized one of its own. See its *Primera Exposición Industrial Argentina celebrada en Buenos Aires en el mes de enero de 1877: Catálogo de los productos naturales e industriales que componen la exposición* (Buenos Aires: Imprenta de Pablo Coni, 1877).

10. Vicente Vázquez Presedo, *Estadísticas históricas Argentinas: Primera parte 1875–1914* (Buenos Aires: Macchi, 1971), 15–16; Roberto Cortés Conde, *La economía Argentina en el largo plazo (Siglos XIX y XX)* (Buenos Aires: Sudamericana/San Andrés, 1997), 230–31 and 236–37; and Irving Stone, "British Direct and Portfolio Investment in Latin America before 1914," *Journal of Economic History*, 1977, (37), 695.

11. Roberto Cortés Conde, "Estimaciones del producto bruto interno de Argentina 1875–1935," working paper, Universidad de San Andrés, Victoria, Buenos Aires, October 1994, 17–20.

12. Workforce is the only indicator I can use as a measure of growth (I could not create a similar table for some other economic indicators such as capital, output, or steam-powered use for lack of data). As Janyce Rye Kinghorn and John Vincent Nye correctly assert in a revisionist comparison of the dimension of industrial firms in the developed world at the turn of the twentieth century, measuring establishment size is problematic. Number of workers, whatever the problems of not accounting for labor productivity changes, continues to be considered a good proxy for size. See "The Scale of Production in Western Economic Development: A Comparison of Official Industry Statistics in the United States, Britain, France, and Germany, 1905–1913," *Journal of Economic History*, March 1996, *56*(1), 95. For other works using this proxy, see David Landes, "French Entrepreneurship and Industrial Growth in the Nineteenth Century," *Journal of Economic History*, 1949, *9*(1), 45–61; François Caron, *An Economic History of Modern France* (New York: Columbia University Press, 1979); and Charles Kindleberger, *Economic Growth in France and Britain 1851–1950* (Cambridge, MA: Harvard University Press, 1961).

13. See H. S. Ferns, *Britain and Argentina in the Nineteenth Century* (Oxford: Clarendon Press, 1960); Alec Ford, *The Gold Standard, 1880–1914: Britain and Argentina* (Oxford: Clarendon Press, 1962); Roberto Cortés Conde, *Dinero, deuda y crisis* (Buenos Aires: Sudamericana, 1989); Gerardo della Paolera and Alan M. Taylor, *Straining the Anchor: The Argentine Currency Board and the Search for Macroeconomic Stability, 1880–1935* (Chicago: University of Chicago Press, 2002); and Pablo Gerchunoff, Fernando Rocchi, and Gastón Rossi, "Un hito en la historia Argentina: La crisis de 1890, sus orígenes y sus efectos," paper presented at the Terceras Jornadas de Historia, Universidad Torcuato Di Tella, September 2003.

14. *Boletín de la Unión Industrial Argentina* (hereafter cited as *BUIA*), March 13, 1890, p. 1.

15. José Panettieri, *Proteccionismo, liberalismo y desarrollo industrial* (Buenos Aires: Centro Editor de América Latina, 1983), 19; and Chiaramonte, *Nacionalismo y liberalismo*.

16. See Victor Bulmer-Thomas, *The Economic History of Latin America Since Independence* (Cambridge, MA: Cambridge University Press, 1994), 41–42;

and Hilda Sabato and Luis Alberto Romero, *Los trabajadores de Buenos Aires: La experiencia del mercado 1850–1880* (Buenos Aires: Sudamericana, 1992), 75.

17. Club Industrial, "Movimiento industrial habido en la República Argentina desde el año 1874 hasta el presente: 15 de Septiembre de 1880," Para nuestro socio honorario Dr. Victorino de la Plaza (For our distinguished and honorary member Dr. Victorino de la Plaza). In Archivo General de la Nación, Buenos Aires, Archivo Victorino de la Plaza (hereafter cited as AGN, AVP) 5-6-12, pp. 1–2.

18. "Estadística industrial de la Capital Federal encomendada a Angel Ramón Cartavio y Enrique Raymond por el Consejo Directivo de la Unión Industrial Argentina para promover la concurrencia de la industria nacional a la Exposición Universal de 1889 en París," *BUIA*, June 8, 1889 (hereafter cited as "Estadística industrial 1889"), p. 3.

19. Félix de Ugarteche, *Las industrias del cuero en la República Argentina* (Buenos Aires: Talleres Gráficos de Roberto Canals), 286.

20. *La Nación*, March 9, 1883, 1.

21. *Censo General de Población, edificación, comercio e industrias de la ciudad de Buenos Aires levantado en los días 17 de agosto, 15 y 30 de septiembre de 1887*, Vol II (Buenos Aires: Companía Sudamericana de Billetes de Banco, 1889), 321.

22. Malaurie and Gazzano, *La industria Argentina*, 136.

23. Daireaux, *La vie et les moeurs*, vol 2, 128.

24. Club Industrial, "Movimiento," 6–7; *Censo General, 1887*; and Sabato and Romero, *Los trabajadores*, 198.

25. Comitato della Camera Italiana di Commercio ed Arti, *Gli italiani nella Repubblica Argentina* (Buenos Aires: Stabilimento Grafico della Compañía General de Fósforos, 1906), Parte Prima, 159.

26. Club Industrial, "Movimiento," 9–10; Manuel Chueco, *Los pioneers de la industria Argentina*, Vols. 1 and 2 (Buenos Aires: Peuser, 1886 and 1896); and *BUIA*, December 15, 1916, 42.

27. P. M. de Corvetto, *Les industries Françaises à Buenos Aires* (Buenos Aires: Librairie Française, 1886), 99.

28. Sabato and Romero, *Los trabajadores*, 72; and Ricardo Yomal, "Humo, un delicioso producto final . . . ," *Todo es historia*, September 1977, (124), 24–30.

29. Corvetto, *Les industries Françaises*, 17–20; Malaurie and Gazzano, *La industria Argentina*, 175–81; and "Estadística industrial 1889," 2.

30. Malaurie and Gazzano, *La industria Argentina*, 142–44.

31. "Estadística industrial 1889," 2; and Corvetto, *Les industries Françaises*, 60–66.

32. "Estadística industrial 1889," 5; Chueco, *Los pioneers*, vol. II, 407; and *BUIA*, January 11, 1888, 1.

33. Corvetto, *Les industries Françaises*, 67–72; Malaurie and Gazzano, *La industria Argentina*, 182–86; *César Ambrosio Tognoni, Fábrica de aceites vegetales*

"La Italia": Pequeña historia de una industria 1876–1951 (Buenos Aires: Kraft, 1951), 11; "Estadística industrial 1889," 2; and Chueco, *Los pioneers*, vol. I, 262–78.

34. "La estadística comercial y la renta," El Nacional, Buenos Aires, September 18, 1878, in D. F. Sarmiento, *Obras completas*, Vol. XLI (Buenos Aires: Editorial Luz del Día, 1951), 67–68.

35. Bagley S.A., *Cien años produciendo calidad* (Buenos Aires: 1964); and *BUIA*, January 15, 1894, 2.

36. Francisco Latzina, *Estadística retrospectiva del Comercio Exterior Argentino, 1875–1904* (Buenos Aires: Cía. Sudamericana de Billetes de Banco, 1905), 86.

37. Club Industrial, "Movimiento," 15; and Corvetto, *Les industries Françaises*, 45.

38. *Censo General, 1887*, 328.

39. Cervecería Bieckert S.A., *Centenario Bieckert, 1860–1960, Historia de una cerveza centenaria* (Buenos Aires, 1960), 6–22; Malaurie and Gazzano, *La industria Argentina*, 86–87; Corvetto, *Les industries Françaises*, 2; and Louis Guilaine, *La Republique Argentine, Physique et Économique* (Paris, Librairie des Imprimeries Réunies, 1889), 161.

40. *BUIA*, February 6, 1889, 3.

41. Quilmes produced three million liters in 1891, four million in 1892, and ten million in 1898. See *Finanzas, comercio e industria en la República Argentina*, Buenos Aires (hereafter cited as *Finanzas*), January 1, 1899, (1), 101–105. The five new breweries that opened in the 1890s started as large factories. See *Exposición Nacional de 1898*, Buenos Aires (hereafter cited as *Exposición*), January 18 and 25, 1899, 439–40; and *BUIA*, April 20, 1899, 32.

42. Dimas Helguera, *La producción Argentina en 1892: Descripción de la industria nacional. Su desarrollo y progreso en toda la República. Ampliación del retrospecto publicado en LA PRENSA* (Buenos Aires: Goyoaga y Cía, 1893), 146; and Leandro Gutiérrez and Juan Carlos Korol, "Historia de empresas y crecimiento industrial en la Argentina: El caso de la Fábrica Argentina de Alpargatas," in *Desarrollo Económico* (hereafter cited as *DE*), October–December 1988, *28*(111), 405–406.

43. Data are from Juan Posse's firm La Popular that already had twelve Bonsack machines in 1898. See *Finanzas*, January 1, 1899, (1), 96; and *La Nación*, February 18, 1893, 6. For quality, see *BUIA*, January 30, 1889, 3; and *La Cámara del Tabaco de la UIA en el primer congreso nacional del tabaco: Comentarios y fragmentos bibliográficos* (Buenos Aires: Talleres Gráficos de la Cía. Fabril Financiera, 1944), 15.

44. See Richard Tennant, *The American Cigarette Industry* (New Haven: Yale University Press, 1950), 18–20; and Alfred Chandler, *Scale and Scope: The Dynamics of Industrial Capitalism* (Cambridge, MA: Cambridge University Press), 63–64.

45. Fabril Financiera S.A., *Historia de un grupo de empresas industriales en la Argentina, 1888–1948* (Buenos Aires: Fabril Financiera, 1948), 4; and *BUIA*, September 12, 1889, 4.

46. *El País*, Buenos Aires, June 28, 1900, 6.

47. Worthington, T. The Special Commissioner Appointed by the Board of Trade to Inquire into and Report Upon the Conditions and Prospects of British Trade in Certain South American Countries. *Commercial Mission to South America, Third Report: The Argentine Republic* (London: Eyre and Spottiswoode, 1898), 23.

48. Dr. Moorne, *Las industrias fabriles en Buenos Aires: Colección de artículos publicados en "El Nacional,"* Vol. I (Buenos Aires: Librairie Française de Joseph Escary, 1893), 86–94.

49. *RRP*, August 5, 1893, 7; and *La Nación*, October 18, 1903, 3.

50. See *BUIA*, January 11, 1888, 1; April 16, 1891, 3; October 15, 1892, 2; and March 1, 1893, 1; Chueco, *Los pioneers*, 407; *César Ambrosio Tognoni*, 11 and 15; *La Prensa*, Buenos Aires, April 8, 1891, 3; and *El País*, June 18, 1900, 6.

51. *La Nación*, April 10, 1885, 10; and *Finanzas*, January 1, 1899, (1), 105. Devoto-Rocha distillery more than doubled its alcohol output between 1891 and 1895. See *BUIA*, December 1, 1896, 21; and Carlos Lix-Klett, *Estudios sobre producción, comercio, finanzas e intereses generales de la República Argentina*, Vol. I (Buenos Aires: Establecimientos tipográficos de Tailhade y Roselli, 1900), 477–78 and 1369.

52. See *Exposición*, November 25, 1897, 70; and December 9, 1897, 83; *Finanzas*, January 1, 1899, (1), 53–5; *El País*, June 13, 1900, 6; Francesco Scardin, *La Argentina y el trabajo* (Buenos Aires: Jacobo Peuser, 1906), 552–53; and Chandler, *Scale and Scope*, 147.

53. Corvetto, *Les industries Françaises*, 78–83; *Finanzas*, January 1, 1900, (2), 93; and T. Worthington, *The Argentine Republic*, 15.

54. Newsprint production started as early as 1864 thanks to legislative support, but it later stagnated. See Antonio Vaquer, *Historia de la ingeniería en la Argentina* (Buenos Aires: Eudeba, 1968), p. 191. La Argentina opened a large establishment located on the Paraná river (in the city of Zárate) in 1888 and, for the first time, one newspaper, *El Diario*, used domestically produced newsprint and started a trend that would later slowly continue. See Club Industrial, "Movimiento," p. 20; Malaurie and Gazzano, *La industria Argentina*, 227–31; Dr. Moorne, *Las industrias fabriles*, vol. I, 23–37; Carlos Lix Klett, *Estudios sobre producción, comercio, finanzas e intereses generales de la República Argentina*. Tomo I (Buenos Aires: Establecimientos Tipográficos de Tailhade y Rosselli, 1900), 469; and *BUIA*, October 3, 1888, 5; and February 13, 1890, 5.

55. Dr. Moorne, *Las industrias fabriles*, vol. I, 38–46; and *BUIA*, December 15, 1893, 1.

56. *BUIA*, January 1, 1893, 1; and Ugarteche, *Las industrias del cuero*, 292. As a result of the new tariffs, shoe imports dramatically dropped. See *Segundo Censo Nacional de la República Argentina*, Mayo 10 de 1895, Vol. III (Buenos Aires: Talleres Tipográficos de la Penitenciaría Nacional, 1898), XCIX.

57. T. Worthington, *The Argentine Republic*, 14; *Segundo Censo Nacional, 1895*, vol. III, XCII; and Dr. Moorne, *Las industrias fabriles*, vol. I, 66–7.

58. Cortés Conde, *La economía Argentina*, 209.

59. Lynden Briscoe, *The Textile and Clothing Industries of the United Kingdom* (Manchester: Manchester University Press, 1971), 2, 3–6, 186, 190, and 192–93.

60. *BUIA*, May 15, 1893, 1. By 1893, eight factories had 7,400 spindles. See *RRP*, November 25, 1893, 17.

61. Corvetto, *Les industries Françaises*, 12.

62. Taken from an interview in *La Prensa*, reproduced in *BUIA*, August 15, 1893, 2.

63. Corvetto, *Les industries Françaises*, 13–14. The second woolen textile factory founded in the country, Fusy, followed the integration strategy of Prat. See *BUIA*, October 3, 1889, 1.

64. D. T. Jenkins and K. G. Ponting, *The British Wool Textile Industry, 1770–1914* (Aldershot, England: Scolar Press, 1987), 175–79; and Gerschenkron, *Economic Backwardness*.

65. *La Nación*, September 10, 1898, 2–3; *El País*, January 1, 1900, 6; and *BUIA*, December 25, 1899, 22. Imports of woolen cloth increased from 294,174 kilos in 1890 to 1,532,868 in 1894, because it was the input for the booming industry of ready-to-wear goods. These imports, however, remained stagnated after then, so that consumption growth beyond that time was supplied by domestic production. See Latzina, *Estadística*, 65–67 and 164.

66. Daireaux, *La vie et les moeurs*, vol. 2, 129; and *La Prensa*, July 27, 1889, 6.

67. Ministero degli Affari Esteri, R. Consolato d'Italia in Rosario al R. Ministro degli Affari Esteri, Serie Politica A, 1888–91, *Pacco* December 12, 1890, (3), 7; Luigi Einaudi, *Un principe mercante: Studio sulla espansione coloniale Italiana* (Torino: Bocca, 1900); and Eugenia Scarzanella, *Italiani d'Argentina: Storie di contadini, industriali e missionari Italiani in Argentina, 1850–1912* (Venice: Marsilio, 1983), 41–42.

68. *Finanzas*, January 1, 1899, (1), 125; and *El País*, August 11, 1901, 3.

69. *Anuario de la Dirección General de Estadística correspondiente a 1898*, Estadística retrospectiva del Comercio Especial Exterior a cargo del Sr. Ricardo Kleine (Buenos Aires: Cía. Sudamericana de Billetes de Banco, 1899), 312–20. Cotton and woolen finished good imports fell from 1,008,800 and 172,217 kilos respectively in 1889 to 421,405 and 86,553 in 1904. See Latzina, *Estadística*, 48–50.

70. T. Worthington, *The Argentine Republic*, 33.

71. *Album ilustrado de la República Argentina*, August 1, 1891, (2), 77. For the consumption of wood in the construction of Buenos Aires, see Francisco Liernur, "La ciudad efímera," in his work with Graciela Silvestri, *El umbral de la metrópolis: Transformaciones técnicas y cultura en la modernización de Buenos Aires (1870–1930)* (Buenos Aires: Sudamericana, 1993).

72. "Estadística industrial 1889," 4. For the increase in production of strongboxes and lockers, see *Finanzas*, January 1, 1900, (2), 123–24; and *El País,* June 24, 1900, 3.

73. *La Nación*, September 26, 1895, 3; and T. Worthington, *The Argentine Republic,* 37.

74. Dr. Moorne, *Las industrias fabriles*, vol. I, 4–5.

75. See *Fray Mocho*, Buenos Aires, May 5, 1916, 46–55; *BUIA*, July 24, 1890, 3; Malaurie and Gazzano, *La industria Argentina*, 268; *Exposición 1898*, November 18, 1897, 64; and *El País*, January 2, 1900, 6.

76. *Finanzas*, January 1, 1900, (2), 63–65; and January 1, 1899, (1), 81–3; Emilio Korkus, *La industria metalúrgica Argentina: Reseña histórica de su desarrollo*, pamphlet, Buenos Aires, December 1922; and Alfred Chandler, *The Visible Hand: The Managerial Revolution in American Business* (Cambridge, MA: The Belknap Press, 1977), 57.

77. In addition, those industries with relative success were producing only the coarsest goods but still relying on imports for the finest items, such as occurred with soap. See "Manufacture and Prices of Soap and Candles in the Argentine Republic" in FO, 6/471, Commercial, no. 71, October 11, 1901, Carnegie Ross, 160; Lix Klett, *Estudios*, 444; Corvetto, *Les industries Françaises*, 36; and Malaurie and Gazzano, *La industria Argentina*, 215–16 and 199–200.

78. Francisco Seguí, "Investigación parlamentaria sobre agricultura, ganadería, industrias derivadas y colonización (provincia de Buenos Aires)," Tenerías, *BUIA*, November 20, 1898, 2–7; *El País*, January 6, 1900, 3; and *BUIA*, November 15, 1902, 9–10.

79. *El País*, January 29, 1900, 5.

80. *RRP*, December 21, 1901, 95; see also G. G. Vivaldi, Regio Vice-Console, "Le industrie Argentine e il loro avvenire," *Rivista Coloniale*, January–June 1907, *3*(3), 176.

81. José Comin, *El tabaco: Contribución al estudio de los tabacos Argentinos* (Buenos Aires: Talleres Poligráficos, 1906), 51; *Monitor de Sociedades Anónimas*, Buenos Aires (hereafter cited as *MSA*), 1916, *XXII*, 73; and Cuadro tipeado en el Ministerio de Agricultura, Dirección General de comercio e Industrias. Sección Industrias, Pesos y Medidas, Warrants, circa 1917.

82. Vivaldi, "Le industrie Argentine," 189–90.

83. FO 368/85, Commercial, 38, Buenos Aires, May 10, 1907, Townley, 1–2; and Adolfo Dorfman, *Historia de la industria Argentina* (Buenos Aires: Losada, 1942), 135–41.

84. Vivaldi, "Le industrie Argentine," 186–87.

85. D.C.M. Platt, *Latin America and British Trade, 1806–1914* (London: Adam & Charles Black, 1972), 90.

86. FO 6/471, 14, Commercial, August 14, 1901, Carnegie Ross, 154–55; and FO 6/478, 1, Commercial, January 8, 1902, Carnegie Ross, 94–5.

87. Latzina, *Estadística*, 18 and 162.

88. Enclosure in FO 368/85, Commercial, 56, June 27, 1907, Towney, 1–2.

89. Diversity of British interests is energetically argued in "Argentine Customs Tariff: Summary of the Representations received from Chambers of Commerce & C, with reference to the effect of the Argentine Customs Tariff of 1906 upon British Trade and Industry," document elaborated by the Board of Trade with suggestions from the Chambers of Commerce. In FO, 368/85, Paper 11321, April 8, 1907.

90. Memorandum made by Baird. Enclosure in FO, 368/85, Commercial, 38, May 10, 1907, W. Towney, 8.

91. Paul B. Goodwin, "Anglo-Argentine Commercial Relations: A Private Sector View, 1922–1943," *Hispanic American Historical Review*, February 1981, *LXI*(1), 29–51.

92. Efforts to grow cotton were as varied as they were unsuccessful. See Donna Guy, "Oro Blanco: Cotton, Technology and Family Labor in Nineteenth Century Argentina," *The Americas*, April 1993, *XLIX*(4), 457–78; and FO, 6/488, August 26, 1904, Commercial, no. 9, 150. For the Brazilian case, see Stanley Stein, *The Brazilian Cotton Industry* (Princeton, NJ: Princeton University Press, 1957), p. 44.

93. *BUIA*, December 1, 1892, 3.

94. *La Prensa*, May 21, 1890, 2.

95. *Censo General, 1887*, vol. II, 339; Lix Klett, *Estudios*, 399–403; and Guilaine, *La Republique Argentine*, 176.

96. Ernesto Tornquist & Co., Limited, *The Economic Development of the Argentine Republic in the Last Fifty Years* (Buenos Aires: 1919), 285–86; and CEPAL, *El desarrollo económico*. For the growth of state capacities before 1880, see Oscar Oszlak, *La formación del estado Argentino* (Buenos Aires: Editorial de Belgrano, 1982), chapter 4.

97. Malaurie and Gazzano, *La industria Argentina*, 100–2; and Ugarteche, *Las industrias del cuero*, 40. Mr. Cirio, who bought Videla's firm later, continued supplying the state with boots; see T. Worthington, *The Argentine Republic*, 36.

98. *BUIA*, January 15, 1894, 2; and *Hombres del Día. 1917* (Buenos Aires: Sociedad Inteligencia Sud Americana, 1918), LXXVI.

99. Daniel Bassi, *Unpublished Memoirs of Don Daniel Bassi*, March 1942, Part II, p. 5 (hereafter cited as Bassi Memoirs). I am grateful to Juan María Veniard for lending me such valuable material.

100. Quoted in Dorfman, *Historia de la industria*, 136.

101. *BUIA*, November 20, 1898, 1.

102. BUIA, November 15, 1893, 1.

103. Robert Barrett, *Paper, Paper Products, and Printing Machinery in Argentina, Uruguay, and Paraguay*, United States, Department of Commerce, Bureau of Foreign and Domestic Commerce (hereafter cited as USD-CBFDC), Special Agents Series, no. 168 (Washington, DC: GPO, 1918), 36; see also USDCBFDC, Special Consular Reports, *Paper and Stationery Trade of the World*, no. 73 (Washington, DC: GPO, 1915), 290.

104. This was the case of Prat, Gratry, Dell'Acqua, Barolo, and Remigio Monteros. See Reginald Lloyd, *Argentina in the Twentieth Century* (London: Lloyd Greater Britain Publishing, 1911), 424; and Scardin, *La Argentina*, 526–27. For the public health efforts, see Hugo Vezzetti, *La locura en la Argentina* (Buenos Aires: Paidós, 1985); and Ricardo González Leandri, *Curar, persuadir, gobernar* (Madrid: CSHIC,1999).

105. Lilia Ana Bertoni, *Patriotas, cosmopolitas y nacionalistas: La construcción de la nacionalidad Argentina a fines del siglo XIX* (Buenos Aires: Fondo de Cultura Económica, 2001), chapters IV and VII.

106. FO 6/460, Buenos Aires, April 11, 1899, Commercial, no. 12, Barrington, fs. 158–59; Dimas Helguera, *La producción*, 69; and Donna Guy, "Carlos Pellegrini and the Politics of Early Industrialization in Argentina, 1876–1906," *Journal of Latin American Studies*, 1979, *11*(1), 123–44.

107. *Exposición*, October 21, 1897, 32; and *RRP*, December 31, 1898. General Viejobueno tried to support this factory no matter at what cost. See his report in *BUIA*, September 25, 1890, 2–3. For President Uriburu's reorganization of the establishment, see *La Nación*, September 17, 1895, 4.

108. *La Nación*, October 25, 1898, 3; and *Almanaque La Razón, 1917*, 47.

109. *El País*, July 26, 1901, 3.

110. *La Nación*, March 26, 1903, 5; *RRP*, October 8, 1901, 207; and *El País*, April 24, 1903, 5.

111. FO, 6/463, Foreign Office to the Law Officers of the Crown, Martin Gosselin, July 4, 1899, 240; and FO, 460, Buenos Aires, October 11, 1899, Commercial, 29, Barrington, 225.

112. See, for example, the noisy protest by the firm E. Dell'Acqua, one of the usual state providers, when the War Intendency threatened to buy fabric elsewhere. See *BUIA*, May 30, 1899, 28–30.

113. Américo Guerrero, *La industria Argentina: Su origen, organización y desarrollo* (Buenos Aires: Establecimientos Plantié S.A., 1944), 29.

114. *BUIA*, April 20, 1899, 32–3. As an example of the industrialist discourse, see the continuing attack on the *Intendente de Guerra* Mr. Seeber in *BUIA*, January 15, 1902, 21–2.

115. *La Nación*, March 29, 1896, 4.

116. FO 368/166, paper no. 27892, October 8, 1908, and paper no. 34207, January 10, 1908, Board of Trade; *La Nación: Edición aniversario de la independencia, 1916* (hereafter cited as *La Nación, 1916*), 60.

117. Bureau of the American Republics, *Handbook of the Argentine Republic*, Bulletin no. 67 (Washington, DC: GPO, 1892), 94.

118. Cortés Conde, *La economía Argentina*, Table A5, 236.

119. *South American Journal and Brazil and River Plate Mail* (hereafter cited as *SAJ*), January 28, 1898, 128.

120. Centro del Comercio, *Informe de la Comisión Especial. Nombrada en Asamblea del Centro del Comercio, el 1 de junio de 1987, para dictaminar sobre las causas de la crisis comercial. Informes parciales de los delegados de los gremios* (Buenos Aires: July 16, 1897).

121. Liga de Defensa Comercial, *Informe leído por el Presidente Sr: Antonio León Lanusse en la Asamblea General Ordinaria del 29 de Diciembre de 1914* (Buenos Aires: Imprenta Enrique L. Frigerio, 1914).

122. U.S. Dept. of State, May 6, 1899, no. 686, vol. 38, roll 33. The variation in exchange rate (or the value of one gold peso in local currency) changed from 3.74 in 1891 to 2.57 in 1898 and continued dropping. By 1902, when the gold standard was finally established, it had reached 2.34. See Juan Alvarez, *Temas de historia económica Argentina* (Buenos Aires: El Ateneo, 1929), 122–23. For industrialists' fears, see Rufino Varela, *Ley de Aduana. Aforos y derechos. Su influencia sobre el comercio y la industria. Reformas convenientes* (n.d.), in Biblioteca Tornquist, Buenos Aires, Comercio 432.

123. Silvio Gesell, *La cuestión monetaria Argentina* (Buenos Aires: Imp. La Buenos Aires, 1898); and *La razón económica del desacuerdo Chileno-Argentino* (Buenos Aires: 1898).

124. *SAJ*, July 30, 1898, 116. See also *The Economist*, May 8, 1897, 672; June 5, 1897, 811; July 17, 1897, 1023; September 18, 1897, 1323; and January 1, 1898, 7.

125. *La Prensa*, July 27, 1899, 5.

126. *La Nación, Revista político-económica*, September 16, 1898, 9.

127. Centro del Comercio, *Informe de la comisión*, 18.

128. *The Economist*, May 20, 1899, 723.

129. *Tarifas de Aduana: Estudios y antecedentes para su discuión legislativa por la Comisión Revisora nombrada por el Poder Ejecutivo* (Buenos Aires: Cía Sudamericana de Billetes de Banco, 1894), 269. See also pages 271 and CXLIII.

130. The consumption of candles was 120,000 per year, while output capacity was 180,000. See *Finanzas*, January 1, 1899, (1), 139. For tin–plate, glass, and hats, see Dr. Moorne, *Las industrias fabriles*, vol. I, 46, 50, and 72–85. For household wares, see *Finanzas*, January 1, 1899, (1), 143. For textiles, see *El País*, June 21, 1900, 2; and BUIA, February 15, 1894, 2. For paper, see *Finanzas*, January 1, 1900, (2), 126. For bags, see Adrián Gustavo Zarrilli, "Estado, semillas y bolsas: Prestaciones extraordinarias para el productor rural

santafesino (1890–1930)," *Res Gesta*, January–December 1992), (31), 297. For chocolate and spirits, see Bureau of the American Republics, *Handbook of the Argentine Republic*, Bulletin no. 67 (Washington, DC: GPO, 1892), 97–98 and 100.

131. Dr. Moorne, *Las industrias fabriles*, vol. I, 13–22. For different goods, see also T. Worthington, *The Argentine Republic*, passim.

132. *BUIA*, February 10, 1897, 25.

133. Manuel Bilbao, *Buenos Aires desde su fundación hasta nuestros días: Especialmente el período comprendido en los siglos XVIII y XIX* (Buenos Aires: Imprenta de Juan A. Alsina, 1902), 605.

134. *Finanzas*, January 1, 1900, (2), 139 and 142; Acta no. 13, August 23, 1894 in *Tarifas de Aduana*, CXI; and *El País*, January 22, 1900, 5.

135. *BUIA*, March 15, 1903, 10.

136. Chueco, *Los pioneers*, 407; *BUIA*, January 11, 1888, 1 and December 25, 1899, 22; *La Nación*, September 10, 1898, 2–3; and *El País*, January 1, 1900, 6.

137. *Diario de Sesiones de la Cámara de Diputados* (hereafter cited as DSCD), October 24, 1894, 318; Fabril Financiera S.A., *Historia de un grupo*; Gutiérrez and Korol, "Historia de empresas"; and Raúl Jacob, *Breve historia de la industria en Uruguay* (Montevideo: Fundación de Cultura Universitaria, 1981). The problems faced by Argentine flour in Brazil were a symbol of the economic relations between the Latin American countries. See Ricardo Pillado, *Estudio sobre el comercio Argentino con las naciones limítrofes* (Buenos Aires: Imprenta de Juan Kidd y Cía, 1910); and *RRP*, August 22, 1896, 10. In spite of delegation visits, Chile was not open to Argentine industrial goods. See "Delegación comercial Argentina en Chile," *BUIA*, December 15, 1910, 1–7.

138. Roberto Cortés Conde, "Some Notes on the Industrial Development of Argentina and Canada in the 1920s," in D. C. Platt and Guido Di Tella (ed.), *Argentina, Canada and Australia: Studies in Development, 1870–1965* (Oxford: MacMillan, 1985).

139. Haber has pointed out a similar case of unsuccessful export attempts for the Mexican manufactures in his *Industry and Underdevelopment: The Industrialization of Mexico, 1890–1940* (Stanford, CA: Stanford University Press, 1989), 30–34.

140. *La Nación*, September 23, 1898, 5.

Chapter 2

1. Martin Tow, *Memorias de un comerciante* (Buenos Aires: Editorial La Facultad, 1934), 69–70.

2. Tow, *Memorias*, 72–79, and 103–104.

3. Roger Burlingame, *Engines of Democracy* (New York: C. Scribner's Sons, 1940), 391.

4. David A. Hounshell, *From the American System to Mass Production, 1800–1932: The Development of Manufacturing Technology in the United States* (Baltimore and London: The Johns Hopkins University Press, 1984).

5. Roberto Cortés Conde, "The Vicissitudes of an Exporting Economy: Argentina (1875–1930)," in Enrique Cárdenas, José Antonio Ocampo, and Rosemary Thorp (eds.), *An Economic History of Twentieth-Century Latin America, Volume 1: The Export Age* (Oxford: Palgrave-St. Antony's College, 2000), 267.

6. Jorge Fodor and Arturo A. O' Connell, "La Argentina y la economía atlántica en la primera mitad del siglo XX," *DE*, April–June 1973, *13*(49), 3–65.

7. For increase in real wages, see Jeffrey Williamson, "Real Wages and Relative Factors Prices in the Third World, 1820–1940: Latin America," discussion paper no. 1853, November 1998, Harvard Institute of Economic Research, Harvard University, Table 2.

8. Angus Maddison, "Explaining the Economic Performance of Nations, 1820–1989," in William J. Baumol, Richard R. Nelson, and Edward N. Wolff, *Convergence of Productivity: Cross-National Studies and Historical Evidence* (Oxford: Oxford University Press, 1994), Tables 2.1 and 2.4, pp. 22 and 27.

9. Charles Sargent, *The Spatial Evolution of Greater Buenos Aires, Argentina, 1870–1930* (Tempe: Arizona State University, 1974), 120; Vicente Vázquez Presedo, *Estadísticas históricas Argentinas: Primera parte 1875–1914* (Buenos Aires: Macchi, 1971); and Primer censo de la República Argentina verificado en los días 15, 16 y 17 de septiembre de 1869 (Buenos Aires: Imprenta del Porvenir, 1872), 92, 115, 241, and 347.

10. Alejandro Bunge, *La Economía Argentina: La conciencia nacional y el problema económico* (Buenos Aires: Agencia de General de Librerías y Publicaciones, 1928), 123–48.

11. Pierre Bourdieu, *La distinción: Criterios y bases sociales del gusto* (Madrid: Taurus, 1988), 227–28.

12. Arjun Appadurai (ed.) *The Social Life of Things: Commodities in Cultural Perspective* (Cambridge, UK: Cambridge University Press, 1986).

13. L. M. de Marancour, *Guide pratique d'Europe au Rio de la Plata* (Paris: n.p., 1883), 64–5; Hilda Sabato and Luis Alberto Romero, *Los trabajadores de Buenos Aires: La experiencia del mercado 1850–1880* (Buenos Aires: Sudamericana, 1992), 72; and Ricardo Yomal, "Humo, un delicioso producto final . . . ," *Todo es historia*, September 1977, (124), 24–30.

14. *Boletín de la Unión Industrial Argentina* (hereafter cited as *BUIA*), Buenos Aires, December 15, 1891, 2. See also *La Cámara del tabaco de la UIA en el primer congreso nacional del tabaco* (Buenos Aires: Cía. Fabril Financiera, 1944), 15–16.

15. Jordan Goodman, *Tobacco in History: The Cultures of Dependence* (London and New York: Routledge, 1993), 90–99.

16. Théodore Child, *Les republiques Hispano-americaines* (Paris: Librairie-illustrée, 1891), 296.

17. For women's smoking habits, see José Antonio Wilde, *Buenos Aires desde setenta años atrás (1810–1880)* (Buenos Aires: Eudeba, 1961 [first published in 1881]), 164; and Victor Gálvez (Seudónimo de Vicente G. Quesada) *Memorias de un viejo, Vol. 1* (Buenos Aires: Peuser, 1888), 125. For the American case, see Stuart Ewen, *Captains of Consciousness: Advertising and the Social Roots of the Consumer Culture* (New York: McGraw-Hill, 1976), 160; and James D. Norris, *Advertising and the Transformation of American Society, 1865–1920* (New York: Greenwood, 1990), chapter 4.

18. *BUIA*, September 10, 1897, 18–9; Administración General de Impuestos Internos, *Memoria correspondiente al ejercicio del año 1913* (Buenos Aires: Cía. Sudamericana de Billetes de Banco, 1914), 42; "Industria tabacalera." Cuadro tipeado en el Ministerio de Agricultura. Dirección General de Comercio e Industrias. Sección Industrias, Pesos y Medidas, Warrants, ca. 1917; and Manufactura Piccardo y Cía, *El 43*. For the American comparison, see Norris, *Advertising and the Transformation*, 125, 136–37.

19. *BUIA*, March 15, 1901, 19–20. For the worldwide transformation of this industry, see Nicoletta Nicolini, *Il pane attossicato: Storia dell'industria dei fiammiferi in Italia 1860–1910* (Bologna: Documentazione Scientifica Editrice, 1995), chapter V.

20. See Archivo de la Cía General de Fósforos, PEHESA-Facultad de Filosofía y Letras-UBA (hereafter cited as CGF), Estadística General. Libro 1, Avellaneda, Paraná, Tucumán y Santa Fé. Resumen de gruesas vendidas, 1–23.

21. CGF, Ventas en $ moneda nacional (sales in domestic currency), 33–34. For rough estimates on inflation, see Rosemary Thorp, *Progress, Poverty and Exclusion: An Economic History of Latin America in the 20th century* (Washington DC: Inter-American Development Bank and Princeton University Press, 1998), Table V.1., 332.

22. *BUIA*, March 15, 1901, 19–20. For the worldwide transformation of this industry, see Nicolini, *Il pane attossicato*, chapter V; and Compañía General de Fósforos S.A. Archives (Biblioteca PEHESA, Facultad de Filosofía y Letras, UBA), *Libros de Actas del Directorio* (minutes of the board of directors meetings, hereafter cited as *CGF, BD*), May 2, 1927.

23. *Revista de impuestos internos, patentes y marcas*, Buenos Aires, no. 177, March 15, 1901.

24. *La Nación: Edición conmemorativa de la revolución del 25 de mayo 1810*. Published in 1910 (hereafter cited as La Nación, 1910), 85.

25. Beer, as a Centennial commemoration pointed out, "was fifty years ago . . . an almost unknown beverage in the Republic." See Carlos Urien and Ezio Colombo, *La República Argentina en 1910*, Vol. I (Buenos Aires: Casa Editora Maucci Hnos., 1910), 541.

26. *BUIA*, October 31, 1888, 2; and Louis Guilaine, *La Republique Argentine, Physique et Économique*, Paris, Librairie des Imprimeries Réunies, 1889, 161.

27. Urien and Colombo, *La República Argentina*, vol. I, 541.

28. República Argentina, *Memoria presentada al Ministro de Hacienda de la Nación por el Administrador General de Impuestos Internos correspondiente al ejercicio del 1 de mayo de 1891 al 31 de mayo de 1892* (Buenos Aires: Imprenta y Papelería "Del Pueblo", 1892), 5; Administración General de Impuestos Internos, *Memoria* . . . (1914), 51; and Javier Padilla, *Datos sobre industria cervecera recopilados por la Sección Industria, Pesas y Medidas, Warrants de la Dirección General de Industria de Javier Padilla, director general a Honorio Pueyerredón, ministro de Agricultura*, April 15, 1917, 5.

29. *Finanzas, comercio e industria en la República Argentina*, Buenos Aires (hereafter cited as *Finanzas*), January 1, 1899, (1), 101; Galileo Massei, *La Repubblica Argentina nel primo centenario della sua independenza* (Milano: Arnaldo De Mohr Editore, 1910), 366; *La Epoca*, Buenos Aires, August 31, 1918, 3; and *La Nación*, November 5, 1894, 6.

30. *La Nación*, February 2, 1893, 3. For socially segmented consumption of beer, see *Diario de Sesiones de la Cámara de Diputados* (hereafter cited as DSCD), October 23, 1894, 305.

31. Ricardo Llanes, *El barrio de Almagro* (Buenos Aires, Municipalidad de la ciudad de Buenos Aires, 1967), 43–4.

32. *BUIA*, December 20, 1898, 21.

33. Aníbal Latino, *Tipos y costumbres bonaerenses* (Buenos Aires: Hyspamérica, 1984 [first published in 1886]), 20.

34. *La Nación: Edición aniversario de la independencia, 1916* (hereafter cited as *La Nación, 1916*), 67.

35. P. M. de Corvetto, *Les industries Françaises à Buenos Aires* (Buenos Aires: Librairie Française, 1886), 2; Massei, *La Repubblica Argentina*, 365–66; and República Argentina. *Impuestos internos. Memoria de 1908* (Buenos Aires: Imprenta de la "Prisión Nacional," 1910), 10. On ice consumption, see Eugenio Garzón, *Amerique Latine: Republique Argentine* (París: Bernard Grasset, 1913), 297; and *The Review of the River Plate*, Buenos Aires, (hereafter cited as *RRP*), August 4, 1900, 9–10 and August 11, 1900, 11.

36. *El País*, February 4, 1900, 5.

37. *Monitor de Sociedades Anónimas*, Buenos Aires (hereafter cited as *MSA*), 1916, *XXII*, 71.

38. *BUIA*, November 15, 1915, 36–38. Consumption of beer, however, was only of ten liters per person, whereas in the United States it was eighty-two liters per year.

39. Wilde, *Buenos Aires*, 186.

40. Santiago de Calzadilla, *Las beldades de mi tiempo* (Buenos Aires: Centro Editor de América Latina, 1982 [first published in 1891]), 26; and Judith Sweeney, *Las costureras de Buenos Aires, 1850–1910*, mimeograph.

41. Octavio Battolla, *La sociedad de antaño* (Buenos Aires: Moloney & De Martino, 1908), 111–12.

42. *BUIA*, June 8, 1889, 3.

43. *BUIA*, December 10, 1897, 1–2. See also *BUIA*, October 1, 1895, 19–20; Dr. Moorne, *Las industrias fabriles en Buenos Aires: Colección de artículos publicados en "El Nacional,"* Vol. *I* (Buenos Aires: Librairie Française de Joseph Escary, 1893), 73; and *El País*, January 25, 1900, 3.

44. *La Nación, 1910*, 294.

45. T. Worthington, *The Argentine Republic*, 562.

46. Lew Clark, *Wearing Apparel in Argentina*, United States, Department of Commerce, Bureau of Foreign and Domestic Commerce, Special Agents Series (hereafter cited as USDCBFDC) Miscellaneous Series, no. 68 (Washington, DC: GPO, 1918), 48 and 53–4.

47. Arthur Burman, *Shoe and Leather Trade*, USDCBFDC, Special Agents Series no. 37, (Washington, DC: GPO, 1910), 13–15.

48. M. A. Phoebus, *Argentine Markets for United States Goods*, USDCBFDC, Special Consular Reports (Washington, DC: GPO, 1926), 11.

49. *El País*, April 11, 1903, 4.

50. Clark, *Wearing Apparel*, 10.

51. Luis Roque Gondra, *Historia económica de la República Argentina* (Buenos Aires: Sudamericana, 1943) 464–65; Clark, *Wearing Apparel*, 38–41; and Roger Gravil "El comercio minorista británico en la Argentina, 1900–1940," in Marcos Giménez Zapiola (ed.), *El régimen oligárquico: Materiales para el estudio de la realidad argentina (hasta 1930)* (Buenos Aires: Amorrortu, 1975), 312–332.

52. *La Nación*, October 2, 1910, 8.

53. Clark, *Wearing Apparel*, 123.

54. *La Nación, 1910*, 74.

55. *La Nación*, October 6, 1910, 28; *Almanaque La Razón, 1917*, 10 and 14.

56. *La Nación, 1916*, 59.

57. Gravil, "El comercio minorista," 320–21.

58. *Bodas de oro de la Casa Escasany, 1892–1942* (Buenos Aires: Talleres Guillermo Kraft, 1942).

59. *BUIA*, March 26, 1891, 2.

60. *El País*, January 30, 1904, 2.

61. Alejandro Galarce, *Bosquejos de Buenos Aires, capital de la nación Argentina* (Buenos Aires: n.p., 1886), 73; and *La Nación, 1910*, 186–87.

62. *BUIA*, November 15, 1909. Quotes from pages 1, 3, 5, and 2 respectively.

63. U.S. Department of State, dispatches, October 7, 1891, vol. 29, no. 156.

64. Middle class is an elusive concept. Eric Hobsbawn has remarked on the difficulty of separating members of the middle class from the upper and lower classes due to their very mobile and internally divided nature. See "La 'classe

media' inglese 1780–1920," in Jürgen Kocka (ed.), *Borghesie europee dell'otto-cento* (Venezia: Marsilio, 1989), 102–106. Kocka addressed these difficulties as well as the national and regional differences in "The Attractiveness of a Concept Rarely Correlates with Its Precision: The Middle Classes in Europe," *The Journal of Modern History*, December 1995, *67*(4), 783–805.

65. This reckoning coincides with Ricardo Ortiz's estimates based on the 1914 census, which considers that the middle-class amounted to 42 percent of the population (the rest divided between 3 percent of upper-class and 55 percent of proletarians). See his *Historia económica Argentina* (Buenos Aires: Raigal, 1955), 191. The cutting bracket in the failed income tax project ($1,500) suggests what might be considered poverty at that time. See Carlos F. Soares, *Economía y finanzas de la Nación Argentina, 1916–1922*, Vol. II (Buenos Aires: Imprenta Rodríguez Giles, 1922), 135–45.

66. Working class consumption during this period has not attracted major attention, an exception being Leandro Gutiérrez's "Condiciones de vida material de los sectores populares en Buenos Aires, 1880–1914," *Revista de Indias*, January–June 1981, *XLI*(163–64), 167–202. The main indication of consumption at that time is still the old study by Alejandro Bunge on working class families, from when he was director of statistics. Bunge calculated that 50 percent of the budget went to food, 20 percent to housing, 15 percent to clothing, and a similar percentage to other items. See his "Costo de vida en la Argentina de 1910 a 1917, números indicadores," *Revista de Economía Argentina, July 1918, I*(1), 39–63.

67. *Mundo Argentino*, Buenos Aires, September 25, 1912, 11. *La Protesta* continuously ran advertisements of cheap suits, pants, and overcoats offered by department stores and furniture produced in Argentine factories. See, for example, March 6, 1908, 3 and October 8, 1908, 3. For the brand, see *BUIA*, May 15, 1902, 31.

68. Susana Saulquin, *La moda en la Argentina* (Buenos Aires: Emecé, 1990), 51–52.

69. Juan Suriano, "Ideas y prácticas 'políticas' del anarquismo Argentino," *Entrepasados*, 1995, *V*(8), 21–48; and *Anarquistas: Cultura y política libertaria en Buenos Aires, 1890–1910* (Buenos Aires: Manantial, 2001); and Ricardo Falcón, "Izquierdas, régimen político, cuestión étnica y cuestión social en Argentina (1890–1912)," *Anuario, Escuela de Historia, Universidad Nacional de Rosario*, 1986/7, (12), 365–89.

70. *BUIA*, March 15, 1905, 25; April 15, 1905, 38–9; and March 15, 1907, 46.

71. Manuel Bilbao, *Buenos Aires* (Buenos Aires: n.p., 1902), 142. See also Francis Korn, "La gente distinguida y la aventura del ascenso," in José Luis and Luis Alberto Romero, *Buenos Aires, historia de cuatro siglos* (Buenos Aires: Abril, 1977).

72. *Finanzas*, January 1899, *1*(1), 138.

73. Clark, *Wearing Apparel*, 44.

74. CGF, BD, November 5, 1924, 21.

75. Alfredo Malaurie and Juan Gazzano, *La industria Argentina y la exposición del Paraná* (Buenos Aires: Editada por la Agencia General de Publicidad de Juan M. Gazzano y Cía, 1888), 215.

76. Pierre Bourdieu challenges the homogeneity of the concepts of consumption and taste since they do not mean the same for individuals of different social classes. For him, taste can be divided into two different categories according to class: freedom and necessity. See his *La distinción*, 177.

77. G. G. Vivaldi, Regio Vice-Console, "Le industrie Argentine e il loro avvenire," *Rivista Coloniale*, January–June 1907, *3*(3), 191; and Eugenia Scarzanella, *Italiani d'Argentina: Storie di contadini, industriali e missionari Italiani in Argentina, 1850–1912* (Venice: Marsilio, 1983), 55. For a discussion on the limits of the ethnic market, see Alejandro Fernández, *Un "mercado étnico" en el Plata: Emigración y exportaciones Españolas a la Argentina, 1880–1935* (Madrid: Consejo Superior de Investigaciones Científicas, 2004).

78. Carole Shammas, *The Preindustrial Consumer in England and America* (Oxford: Clarendon Press, 1990), 78.

79. *El País*, November 1, 1901, 8.

80. Letter to Mariano de Sarratea, Buenos Aires, May 29, 1855, in Domingo F. Sarmiento, *Obras completas*, Vol. XXIV (Buenos Aires: Editorial Luz del Día, 1951), 32. For the evolution of dressing in the pre-1852 period, see Ricardo Salvatore, "Fiestas federales: Representaciones de la República en el Buenos Aires rosista," *Entrepasados*, 1996, *5*(11), 45-68.

81. Ernest White, *Cameos from the Silver Land: or, The Experience of a Young Naturalist in the Argentine Republic*, Vol. I (London: J. Van Voorst, 1881), 165.

82. Federico Rahola, *Sangre nueva: Impresiones de un viaje a la América del Sud* (Barcelona: "La Académica," 1905), 83.

83. *La Nación*, January 7, 1903, 3.

84. Manuel Chueco, *La República Argentina en su primer centenario*, Vol. II (Buenos Aires: Cía. Sudamericana de Billetes de Banco, 1910), 659 and 660–61.

85. Richard Sennett, *Il declino dell' uomo pubblico* (Milano: Bompiani, 1982), 19–20.

86. Calzadilla, *Las beldades*, 121.

87. For Palermo, see Diego Armus, "La idea del verde en Buenos Aires," *Entrepasados*, 1996, *V*(10), 9–22; and Richard Walter, *Politics and Urban Growth in Buenos Aires, 1910–1942* (Cambridge, MA, and New York: Cambridge University Press, 1993).

88. Jules Huret, *Del Plata a la cordillera de los Andes* (París: Fasquelle, 1912), 12–13; and Roberto Gache, *Glosario de la farsa urbana* (Buenos Aires: Centro Editor de América Latina, 1968), 50, quoted in Oscar Troncoso, "Las formas del ocio," in J. L. and L. A. Romero, *Buenos Aires*, 103.

89. Child, *Les republiques Hispano-Americaines*, 16.

90. Quoted from David Viñas, *El ocaso de la ciudad liberal*, in Horacio Salas, *El Centenario: La Argentina en su período más glorioso* (Buenos Aires: Planeta, 1996), 63.

91. Juan Piaggio, *Tipos y costumbres bonaerenses* (Buenos Aires: Félix Lajouane, 1889), 28–29.

92. George J. Stigler and Gary S. Becker, "De Gustibus Non Est Disputandum," *American Economic Review*, March 1977, *67*(2), 76–90.

93. *Caras y Caretas*, February 11, 1899, 8.

94. de Marancour, *Guide pratique*, 71; *Censo General de Población, edificación, comercio e industrias de la ciudad de Buenos Aires levantado en los días 17 de agosto, 15 y 30 de septiembre de 1887*, Vol II (Buenos Aires: Companía Sudamericana de Billetes de Banco, 1889), 335; *Finanzas*, January 1, 1900, (2), 117.

95. Dr. Moorne, *Las industrias fabriles*, 153–54; and *BUIA*, April 15, 1893, 2.

96. For a critical view of this literature, see Fernando Aliata, "Ciudad o Aldea: La construcción de la historia urbana del Buenos Aires anterior a Caseros," *Entrepasados*, 1992, *II*(3), 51–67; and Jackson Lears, *Fables of Abundance: A Cultural History of Advertising in America* (New York: Basic Books, 1994). For a study of the nostalgic traces in the otherwise optimistic Generación del ochenta, see Jeffrey D. Needell, "Optimism and Melancholy: Elite Response to the *fin de siècle bonaerense*," *Journal of Latin American Studies*, 1999, *31*, 551–88. For an example of nostalgic revival, see Gastón Federico Tobal, *De un cercano pasado* (Buenos Aires: L. J. Rosso, 1950).

97. Mariquita Sánchez de Thompson, *Recuerdos del Buenos Ayres Virreynal*, Prólogo y notas por Liniers de Estrada (Buenos Aires, ENE Editorial, 1953), especially chapters "El Virreynato" and "Algunas Costumbres," pp. 23–29 and 53–62.

98. Gálvez, *Memorias*, vol. I, 209 and vol III, 23; Calzadilla, *Las beldades*, 119 and 85; and Wilde, *Buenos Aires*, 185. On the Spanish fashion prevailing in the old times, see the descriptions of C. Skogman, *Viaje en la fragata sueca "Eugenia" (1851–1853): Brasil, Uruguay, Argentina, Chile, Perú* (Buenos Aires: Solar, 1942), 70; and Frederick Gestäcker, *Gestäcker's Travels. Rio de Janeiro, Buenos Aires, Ride Through the Pampas. Winet Journey Across the Cordilleras. Chili-Valparaíso-California and the Gold Fields* (London: T. Nelson and Sons, 1854), 38.

99. Bilbao, *Buenos Aires*, 50; Lucio V. Mansilla, *Mis Memorias* (Buenos Aires: Eudeba, 1966), 37; and Calzadilla, *Las beldades*, 66.

100. Calzadilla, *Las beldades*, 119; and Bilbao, *Buenos Aires*, 145.

101. E. J. Clemens, *La Plata Countries of South America* (Philadelphia: J.B. Lippincott, 1886), 165.

102. See Arsène Isabelle, *Viaje a la Argentina, Uruguay y Brasil, 1830–1834* (Buenos Aires, Emecé, 2001 [first printed in 1835]), chapter X.

103. Sir Horace Rumbold, *The Great Silver River; Notes of a Residence in Buenos Aires in 1880 and 1881* (London: J. Murray, 1890), 265. For similar comments, see also pages 40–41 and 257.

104. Wilde, *Buenos Aires*, 164.

105. *La Nación, 1910,* 170–74.

106. On the simplicity of old commerce, see Wilde, *Buenos Aires,* 173–74; and Víctor Gálvez, *Memorias,* vol. I, 300. On the mid-century store dynamism, see Benjamín Vicuña Mackenna, *Páginas de mi diario durante tres años de viaje, 1853–4–5* (Santiago: Imprenta del Ferrocarril, circa 1855), 367.

107. William Leach, *Land of Desire: Merchants, Power, and the Rise of a New American Culture* (New York: Pantheon, 1993), 41.

108. Clark, *Wearing Apparel,* 40–41.

109. Battolla, *La sociedad,* 87–88.

110. Calzadilla, *Las beldades,* 101.

111. The department store A la ciudad de Londres pioneered fixed-price practices in the 1880s. See Marancour, *Guide pratique,* 67. Fixed price, however, did not generalize until the beginning of the twentieth century. See *La República Argentina pintoresca,* 324; and *La República Argentina 1906–1907,* 78.

112. J. W. Sanger, *Advertising Methods in Argentina, Uruguay, and Brazil,* USDCBFDC, Special Agents Series, no. 190 (Washington, DC: GPO, 1920), 17–18.

113. *Almanaque La Razón 1917,* p. 6.

114. William Beezley, *Judas at the Jockey Club and Other Episodes of Porfirian Mexico* (Lincoln and London: University of Nebraska Press, 1987); Michael Johns, *The City of Mexico in the Age of Díaz* (Austin: University of Texas Press, 1997); Jeffrey Needell, *A Tropical Belle Epoque: Elite Culture and Society in Turn-of-the-Century Rio de Janeiro* (Cambridge: Cambridge University Press, 1987).

115. James R. Scobie, *Secondary Cities of Argentina: The Social History of Corrientes, Salta, and Mendoza, 1850–1910,* compiled and edited by Samuel Baily (Stanford, CA: Stanford University Press, 1988), chapter 7.

116. *La Nación,* May 12, 1895, p. 5. Benito Cabral had an establishment with sixty-eight workers in 1895. See Archivo General de la Nación (Buenos Aires), *Segundo Censo Nacional de la República Argentina,* May 10, 1895, Manuscripts, (hereafter cited as AGN-Manuscripts 1895) Area Capital Federal. Sección Industrias. Legajos 103–108, Section 4, Legajo 104, 308.

117. Wilde, *Buenos Aires,* 57; and Bilbao, *Buenos Aires,* 103.

118. *La Nación,* February 11, 1895, 5 and March 23, 1895, 4; and *BUIA,* June 15, 1904, 21 and February 15, 1905, 28.

119. *La Nación,* May 12, 1895, 5.

120. Cissie Fairchilds, "The Production and Marketing of Populuxe Goods in Eighteenth-Century Paris," in John Brewer and Roy Porter, *Consumption and the World of Goods* (London and New York: Routledge, 1993).

121. *Almanaque La Razón 1917*, p. 124.

122. Bilbao, *Buenos Aires*, 48.

123. Bilbao, *Buenos Aires*, 103–104.

124. Battolla, *La sociedad*, 9.

125. Rumbold, *The Great Silver River*, 44–45 and 313. For old ways of fashion, see Saulquin, *La moda en la Argentina*, 42.

126. Jules Huret, *De Buenos Aires al Gran Chaco* (Buenos Aires: Hyspamérica, 1986 [first published in 1911]), 67–68.

127. Sennett, *Il declino*, 27, and 47–53. In Walter Benjamin's observation, fashion, with its constant variability, reenacted the coexistence of life and death. In Georg Simmel's perception, coquetry is the source of this century's metropolitan hysteria. See Walter Benjamin, *Paris, capitale du XIX siècle* (Paris: Les Editions Du Cerf, 1989), 88–89; and Georg Simmel, "Filosofía de la coquetería," in *Filosofía de la coquetería y otros ensayos* (Madrid: Revista de Occidente, 1924), 12.

128. *Correo del Domingo*, Buenos Aires, December 3, 1885, quoted in Saulquin, *La moda en la Argentina*, 59.

129. Saulquin, *La moda en la Argentina*, 33.

130. L. S. Garry, *Textile Markets of Argentina, Uruguay, and Paraguay*, USD-CBFDSC, Special Agents Series, no. 194 (Washington, DC: GPO, 1920), 14 and 68.

131. Herman Brock, *Boots and Shoes, Leather, and Supplies in Argentina, Uruguay, and Paraguay*, USDCBFDC, Special Agents Series, no. 177 (Washington, DC: GPO, 1919), 31; and U.S. Department of State papers, December 7, 1903, vol. 42, roll 37, no. 312, p. 1.

132. Clark, *Wearing Apparel*, 89 and 101.

133. Brock, *Boots and Shoes*, 67.

134. Georg Simmel,"Filosofía de la moda," in *Filosofía de la coquetería*, 67–68.

135. Fairchilds, "The Production," 2, 7–8, and 27–28; and Philippe Parrot, *Fashioning the Bourgeoisie: A History of Clothing in the Nineteenth Century* (Princeton: Princeton University Press, 1994), 80–86.

136. Rumbold, *The Great Silver River*, 166.

137. *Finanzas*, January 1, 1899, (1), 183.

138. Wolfgang Fritz Haug, *Publicidad y consumo. Crítica de la estética de mercancías* (Mexico City: Fondo de Cultura Económica, 1989), 24–25. The role of advertising in a consumer society has been a highly debated issue. Since Vance Packard's famous book *The Hidden Persuaders* (Montreal: Random House, 1957), economists have usually followed the idea that advertising manipulated and created people's habits and desires. See Ewen, *Captains of Consciousness*, 33 and 45. More recently, scholars have argued that marketers achieved influence by perceiving cultural change as much as by attempting to create it; the long list of advertising failures prove this point. See Susan

Strasser, *Satisfaction Guaranteed: The Making of the American Mass Market* (New York: Pantheon Books, 1989).

139. CGF, BD, October 8, 1924.

140. Rolando Lagomarsino, *Un medio para la consolidación de nuestra prosperidad comercial e industrial* (Buenos Aires: Peuser, 1944), 19–20; and Bagley S.A., *Cien años produciendo calidad* (Buenos Aires: 1964). For the success of Hesperidina, see Clemens, *La Plata Countries*, p. 145; and Tulio Halperin Donghi, *José Hernández y sus mundos* (Buenos Aires: Sudamericana, 1985), 198.

141. Quote from Ezequiel Paz y Manuel Mendoza in Malaurie and Gazzano, *La industria Argentina*, 90.

142. *La Prensa*, November 23, 1911, 2.

143. Quoted in Eduardo Romano, "Fray Mocho: El costumbrismo hacia 1900," *Historia de la literatura Argentina*, Vol. II (Buenos Aires: Centro Editor de América Latina, 1986), 270. Magazines such as *Caras y Caretas, Fray Mocho*, and *PBT* published 112,000; 100,000; and 20,000 to 35,000 issues per week. See USDCBFDC, Miscellaneous Series, *Foreign Publications for Advertising Goods*, no. 10 (Washington, DC: GPO, 1913), 50.

144. Richard Ohmann, *Selling Culture: Magazines, Markets, and Class in the Turn of the Century* (London, New York: Verso, 1996), 107.

145. *La Nación, 1910*, 94.

146. *La Nación, 1910*, 87.

147. *BUIA*, May 15, 1902, 32; July 12, 1902, 32 and 33; August 15, 1902, 28; November 15, 1902, 23; January 15, 1903, 33; March 15, 1903, 33; November 15, 1902, 23; and February 15, 1903, 31.

148. *La Nación, 1916*, p. 71.

149. Brand *43* sales jumped from 316,445 packs in 1900 to 8,548,919 in 1905, 46,012,184 in 1910, and 140,051,357 in 1913. See Manufactura Piccardo y Cía, *El 43*, 29–23 and 63–64.

150. See the report of the American Consul in Buenos Aires, Leo J. Keena, *South American Market for Soap*, USDCBFDC, Special Consular Reports, no. 66 (Washington DC: GPO, 1915), 4–5.

151. *El País*, November 1, 1901, 8 and April 1, 1903, 2.

152. Reginald Lloyd, *Argentina in the Twentieth Century* (London: Lloyd Greater Britain Publishing, 1911), 416. The mentioned announcement can be seen in *Revista Municipal*, November 21, 1910, 10. For the publicity through prices, see Asociación Argentina de Fabricantes de Jabón, *La propaganda comercial a base de premios o regalos adjudicados mediante el azar* (Buenos Aires, 1941), 35–44.

153. Lloyd, *Argentina*, 203.

154. *La Nación, 1910*, 185.

155. Quoted in Salas, *El Centenario*, 210.

156. *Almanaque La Razón 1917*, 176.

157. Sanger, *Advertising Methods*; especially see the illustrations on pp. 16–17, 24–25, and 32–33.

158. Sanger, *Advertising Methods*, 14–16.

159. Eduardo Romero, *Medios más adecuados para fomentar el comercio Hispanoamericano* (Madrid: Imprenta y Litografía de Bernardo Rodríguez, 1905), 20.

160. The Argentine newspaper with the largest circulation, *La Prensa*, charged $US 3.77 per inch while its main Latin American counterparts were behind: the Chilean *El Mercurio* $US 1.20, the Uruguayan *El Día* $US 0.80, the Brazilian *O Estado de Sao Paulo* $US 2, the Mexican *El Imparcial* $US 1.40, and the Bolivian *El Diario* de Bolivia $US 0.08. See USDCBFDC, Miscellaneous Series, *Foreign Publications for Advertising Goods*, no. 10 (Washington, DC: GPO, 1913), 33, 44, 52, 54, 57, and 65.

161. Sanger, *Advertising*, 25–26. For Belgrano and San Martín, see *BUIA*, May 15, 1902, 31; and August 15, 1902, 27. For Sarmiento, see March 10, 1902, 35; and April 15, 1902, 42. There were wine, biscuit, cigarette, perfume, and a wide variety of brands with the name of Mitre. See *La Nación*, August 10, 1908, 8; *Caras y Caretas*, August 30, 1902; *Revista Municipal*, December 12, 1910, 10; and *BUIA*, April 2, 1891, 3.

162. Lloyd, *Argentina*, 424 and 426.

163. See David A. Hounshell, *From the American*, 84.

164. Latino, *Tipos*, 26. Window displays arrived much later to areas outside the downtown. As an example, in the neighborhood of Almagro the practice was not used until the 1920s. See Llanes, *El barrio*, 39.

165. Gálvez, *Memorias*, vol. III, p. 27.

166. Manuel Chueco, *Los pioneers de la industria Argentina*, Vols. 1 and 2 (Buenos Aires: Peuser, 1886 and 1896), 406.

167. Child, *Les republiques Hispano-Americaines* 296; and Lloyd, *Argentina*, 415.

168. *BUIA*, January 15, 1903, 28. For similar comments see *BUIA*, June 15, 1903, 21; Malaurie and Gazzano, *La industria*, 160; *La República Argentina pintoresca*, 279; and *La Nación*, October 5, 1910, 24.

169. *La Nación, 1910*, 186–87.

170. Sanger, *Advertising*, 30–33.

171. United Kingdom, Public Record Office Archives, Foreign Office 368/86, Commercial, 59, Confidential, Buenos Aires, July 18, 1907, Baird, 6.

172. Brock, *Boots and Shoes*, 47–49.

173. Archivo General de la Nación, Tribunal Comercial, Letra "C", 6, 1911–1914, 1912, 7.

Chapter 3

1. *The Review of the River Plate*, Buenos Aires, (hereafter cited as *RRP*), November 17, 1900, 5.

2. Félix de Ugarteche, *Las industrias del cuero en la República Argentina* (Buenos Aires: Talleres Gráficos de Roberto Canals), 322.

3. Emphasis in the original. United States, Department of State papers, Report no. 1, "Upon the Conditions and Opportunities of Commercial and Agricultural Development in the Argentine Republic," December 15, 1904, no. 99, 1.

4. Francesco Scardin, *La Argentina y el trabajo* (Buenos Aires: Jacobo Peuser, 1906)

5. Pablo Gerchunoff, Fernando Rocchi, and Gastón Rossi, "Un hito en la historia Argentina: La crisis de 1890, sus orígenes y sus efectos," paper presented at the Terceras Jornadas de Historia, Universidad Torcuato Di Tella, September 2003.

6. *Boletín de la Unión Industrial Argentina* (hereafter cited as *BUIA*), October 20, 1902, 15; Gerardo della Paolera, "How the Argentine Economy Performed During the International Gold Standard: A Reexamination," Ph.D. dissertation, University of Chicago, 1988; Ezequiel Gallo, "El contexto histórico de la ley de convertibilidad de 1899," in Ana M. Martirena-Mantel, *Aspectos analíticos e históricos de la convertibilidad monetaria* (Buenos Aires: Academia Nacional de Ciencias, 1996); and Lucio Geller, "El modelo de poder de la generación del 80; Política cambiaria Argentina, 1899 y 1914," Buenos Aires, Cuadernos de CICSO, 1982.

7. Francisco Liernur and Graciela Silvestri, "El torbellino de la electricidad," in *El umbral de la metrópolis: Transformaciones técnicas y cultura en la modernización de Buenos Aires (1870–1930)* (Buenos Aires: Sudamericana, 1993).

8. These data are from Angus Maddison, *The World Economy: A Milennial Perspective* (Paris: Organisation for Economic Co-operation and Development, Development Centre Seminars, 2001) Appendix A. For the argument of lack of demand restricting industrial growth, see D.C.M. Platt, *Latin America and British Trade 1806–1914* (London: Adam & Charles Black, 1972), 86.

9. *BUIA*, February 15, 1916, 30. The UIA was especially keen in complaining about lack of industrial school education.

10. Genaro Bevioni, *Argentina 1910: Balance y memoria* (Buenos Aires: Leviatán, 1995), 169.

11. H. O. Chalkley, U.K. Department of Overseas Trade, *Commercial, Economic and Financial Conditions in the Argentine Republic: Buenos Aires, Report of the Year 1919* (London: Published by His Majesty's Stationery Office, 1920), 23; and *Commercial, Economic and Financial Conditions in the Argentine Republic: Buenos Aires, Report of October 1928* (London: Published by His Majesty's Stationery Office, 1928), 6.

12. Vicente Vázquez Presedo, *Estadísticas históricas Argentinas: Primera parte 1875–1914* (Buenos Aires: Macchi, 1971), 16; and Angus Maddison, "Explaining the Economic Performance of Nations, 1820–1989," in William J. Baumol, Richard R. Nelson, and Edward N. Wolff, *Convergence of Productivity:*

Cross-National Studies and Historical Evidence (Oxford: Oxford University Press, 1994), Tables 2.1 and 2.4, pp. 22 and 27.

13. Ernesto Tornquist & Co., Limited, *The Economic Development of the Argentine Republic in the Last Fifty Years* (Buenos Aires: 1919), 285–86.

14. United Kingdom, Public Record Office Archives, Foreign Office (hereafter cited as FO) 368/165, Commercial, no. 17, March 16,1908, Townley, 4; Memorandum on German Activities in South America, FO 368/86, July 22, 1907; FO 371/1573, no. 2, Confidential, Buenos Aires, January 3, 1913, Tower; *RRP*, February 4, 1910, 269; Roger Gravil, *The Anglo-Argentine Connection* (Boulder: Westview Press, 1985); and Platt, *Latin America,* chapter VII.

15. Eduardo Romero, *Medios más adecuados*; *Monitor de Sociedades Anónimas,* Buenos Aires (hereafter cited as *MSA*), 1909, *VIII*, 297; *La Nación,* December 4, 1902, 6.

16. Herman Brock, *Boots and Shoes, Leather, and Supplies in Argentina, Uruguay, and Paraguay*, United States, Department of Commerce, Bureau of Foreign and Domestic Commerce (hereafter cited as USDCBFDC), Special Agents Series, no. 177 (Washington, DC: GPO, 1919), 110.

17. See, as an example, the Memorandum on German Activities in South America, FO 368/86, July 22, 1907. For the perspective sustaining efficient British pressure, see Laura Randall, *An Economic History of Argentina in the Twentieth Century* (New York: Columbia University Press, 1978), chapter 6.

18. Fernando Rocchi, "Britain Versus Newcomers: The Struggle for the Argentine Market, 1900–1914," paper presented at the Second Annual Argentina Conference, "British-Argentine Relations, 1780–1914," The Latin American Centre, University of Oxford, St Antony's College, May, 14–15, 2001. For the British performance, see FO 368/86, no. 62, Commercial, Very confidential, Buenos Aires, Townley, July 20, 1907; and *The Times*, London, South American Supplement, February 28, 1911, 8. This outcome coincides with the reconsideration of the alleged British industrial decline at that time. See Nicholas Crafts, "Foreign Ahead and Falling Behind: The Rise and Relative Decline of the First Industrial Nation," *Journal of Economic Perspectives,* 1998, *12*(2), 133–210.

19. *El País*, April 22, 1900, 5.

20. *BUIA*, March 15, 1904, 19; Informe del inspector Miguel Vidal al Sr. Jefe de Inspección y Vigilancia del Departamento Nacional de Trabajo Dr. Alejandro Unsain, April 25, 1915, in Manuel Vidal, *Algunos de mis trabajos relacionados con las industrias nacionales* (Buenos Aires: Sociedad Gráfica Argentina, 1916), 29–30; and W. D. Boyce, *Illustrated South America* (Chicago and New York: Rand McNally & Co, 1912), 390–91. For the United Shoes's strategy, see Carl Kaysen, *Shoe Machinery Corporation: An Economic Analysis of an Anti-Trust Case* (Cambridge, MA: Harvard University Press, 1956), 9.

21. *La Nación, 1910*, 306.

22. M. A. Phoebus, *Argentine Markets for United States Goods*, USDCBFDC, Special Consular Reports (Washington, DC: GPO, 1926), 11; and Ugarteche, *Las industrias del cuero*, 328 and 397–98.

23. Brock, *Boots and Shoes, 48*–49.

24. *La Nación, 1916*, 214–15; Brock, *Boots and Shoes*, 49 and 63–64.

25. My own elaboration based on Manufactura de tabacos Piccardo y Cía, *El 43* (Buenos Aires, circa 1914), 32.

26. Reginald Lloyd, *Argentina in the Twentieth Century* (London: Lloyd Greater Britain Publishing, 1911), 440; USDCBFDC, SCR, *Tobacco Trade of the World* (Washington, DC: GPO, 1915), no. 38, 41.

27. *Anuarios de la Dirección Estadística de la República Argentina*, 1876–1910. For the business of burlap bagss, see Adrián Gustavo Zarrilli, "Estado, semillas y bolsas: Prestaciones extraordinarias para el productor rural santafesino (1890–1930)," *Res Gesta*, January–December 1992, (31), 281–306.

28. *La Prensa*, September 7, 1891; *BUIA*, January 2, 1890, 2; Scardin, *La Argentina*, 539–40; and Jorge Schvarzer, *Bunge & Born: Crecimiento y diversificación de un grupo económico* (Buenos Aires: CISEA/GEL, 1989), 32.

29. Lloyd, *Argentina*, 423.

30. *La Nación, 1916*, 473.

31. Daniel Bassi, *Unpublished Memoirs of Don Daniel Bassi*, March 1942, Part II, p. 5 (hereafter cited as Bassi Memoirs), 23.

32. Bagley S.A. Archives, *Minutes of the Board of Directors Meetings* (hereafter cited as Bagley, BD), May 5, 1905.

33. FO 368/2, in papers 41619 and 42076, Bristol, December 10 and 19, 1906; and *Album de la República Argentina 1906–1907* (Buenos Aires: Talleres Gráficos de L.J. Rosso, 1907), 160.

34. Galileo Massei, *La Repubblica Argentina nel primo centenario della sua indepedenza* (Milano: Arnaldo De Mohr Editore, 1910), 366.

35. My own elaboration based on Javier Padilla, *Datos sobre industria cervecera*, April 15, 1917, 2–6.

36. *El País*, January 3, 1900, 5; and Scardin, *La Argentina*, 587–89.

37. Reports of the Buenos Aires and Rosario consuls L. J. Keena and William Dawson in USDCBFDC, Special Consular Reports, *Paper and Stationery Trade of the World*, no. 73 (Washington, DC: GPO, 1915), 289–305; and Robert Barrett, *Paper, Paper Products, and Printing Machinery in Argentina, Uruguay, and Paraguay*, USDCBFDC, Special Agents Series, no. 168 (Washington, DC: GPO, 1918), 36–37.

38. *BUIA*, June 15, 1901, 23; Scardin, *La Argentina*, 534–35.

39. Carlos Lix-Klett, *Estudios sobre producción, comercio, finanzas e intereses generales de la República Argentina*, Vol. I (Buenos Aires: Establecimientos tipográficos de Tailhade y Roselli, 1900), 463–65; and Scardin, *La Argentina*, 528–30.

40. *La Nación, 1916*, 201; and Georges Lafond, *L'Argentine au travail* (Paris: Editorial Pierre Roger, 1929), 294–95. Tin-box production also grew to such an extent that Bunge y Born opened a firm in that activity. See *La Argentina monumental en la exposición de París de 1900* (Buenos Aires: Da Costa y Cía, 1900), 27; and Schvarzer, *Bunge y Born*.

41. CEPAL, "Estudio de la industria siderúrgica e informe sobre la reunión de expertos celebrada en Bogotá," E/CN, 12/293, pp. 23 and 30.

42. *La Epoca*, October 10, 1918. On this firm, see *Almanaque La Razón, 1917*, 66; *Fray Mocho*, May 5, 1916, 46–55; and "Una visita a los Talleres Metalúrgicos Pietro Vasena e hijos Ltda," *La Ingeniería*, Buenos Aires, first semester 1921, *XXV*, 104. TAMET switched names a couple of times. First it was called Talleres Metalúrgicos Ex-Rezzónico Ottonello; later it became Talleres Metalúrgicos San Martín and adopted the acronym TAMET. For simplicity, I use this acronym for the company since its inception. For TAMET, see *La Ingeniería*, second semester 1916, *XX*, 93, and first semester 1921, *XXV*, 304.

43. J. A. Massel, *Markets for Machinery and Machine Tools in Argentina*, USDCBFDC, Special Agents Series, no. 116 (Washington, DC: GPO, 1916), 28.

44. Francisco Liernur, "La ciudad efímera," in Liernur and Silvestri, *El umbral de las metrópolis*.

45. *BUIA*, March 15, 1912, 38–39; and G. G. Vivaldi, Regio Vice-Console, "Le industrie Argentine e il loro avvenire," *Rivista Coloniale*, January–June 1907, *3*(3), 171. By 1915 TAMET was producing ninety centrifugal pipes a year. See Enrique Poncini, ingeniero civil, "Caños de fundición centrifugados. Su fabricación en la Argentina," *La Ingeniería*, second semester 1915, XVIII, 757, republished in Buenos Aires, Biblioteca Tornquist, Industrias 400. For the role played by engineers in the diffusion of the bases of the Scientific Labor Organizations in Argentina in the period 1914–1945 through magazine *La Ingeniería*, see Mirta Zaida Lobato, "La Ingeniería: Industria y organización del trabajo en la Argentina de entreguerra," *Revista Estudios del Trabajo*, September 1998, *16*, 47–68.

46. Antonio Vaquer, *Historia de la ingeniería en la Argentina* (Buenos Aires: Eudeba, 1968). By 1920 Vasena had a monthly capacity to produce eight hundred tons of steel and TAMET a capacity of six hundred. See W. S. Ewing, *Construction Materials and Machinery in Argentina and Bolivia*, USDCBFDC, Special Agents Series, no. 188, (Washington, DC: GPO, 1920), 71.

47. Bernardo Duggan, "Iron and Steel Production in Argentina c. 1920–1952: Attempts at Establishing a Strategic Industry", Ph.D. dissertation, London School of Economics and Political Science, 1998, 46–47, 62–65.

48. La Cantábrica S.A., *Memorias y balances (Annual Reports) 1903/4*; and La Cantábrica S.A. *La Cantábrica, sus primeros 50 años 1902–1952* (Buenos Aires: 1952).

49. *RRP*, January 9, 1904, 57; *BUIA*, February 15, 1904, 22; and Vivaldi, "Le industrie argentine", 171 and 174.

50. For Prat, see *RRP*, May 3, 1902, 951; for Dell'Acqua, see Scardin, *La Argentina*, 520–23; for Campomar, see *La Epoca*, October 16, 1918, 4.

51. FO, 6/465, Commercial, no. 22, September 7, 1900, Buenos Aires, Barrington; and Bradford Chamber of Commerce to Marquis of Salisbury, secretary of state for Foreign Affairs, May 21, 1900, enclosed in FO, 6/467, p. 267.

52. *La Nación, 1916*, 208 and 473.

53. *La Nación*, October 2, 1910, 8; *La Nacion, 1910*, 229.

54. Brock, *Boots and Shoes*, 21.

55. See the comments of travelers John Foster Fraser, *The Amazing Argentine: A New Land of Enterprise* (London: Cassell and Co, 1914), 259; W. A. Hirst, *Argentina* (London: T. Fisher Unwin, 1910), 195; Hiram Bingham, *Across South America: An Account of a Travel from Buenos Aires to Lima by Way of Potosí with notes on Brazil, Argentina, Bolivia, Chile, and Perú* (Boston and New York: Houghton Mifflin, 1911), 39; and James Bryce, *South America* (New York: Macmillan, 1912), 336.

56. H. Foster Bain, C. E. Williams, and E. B. Swanson, *Las posibilidades de las manufactura de hierro y acero en la Argentina* (Buenos Aires: Talleres Gráficos del Instituto Geográfico Militar, 1925).

57. For iron, see *The Economist*, May 22, 1920, 1044. For silk, see Sedalana S.A., *Diez años de labor: El fomento de una industria nacional, 1924–1934* (Buenos Aires: Kraft, 1934); and Hugo Miatello, *La industria sericícola: Cultivo de la morera y cría del gusano de seda* (Santa Fé: Nueva Epoca, 1896). For jute, see Dasso y Cía, *La industria textil. Cultivo de las plantas textiles. Explotación manufacturera de sus fibras. Comercio. Necesidad de propender al desarrollo de esta nueva fuente de riqueza. La Nación debe abastecerse a sí misma*, circa 1914, brochure donated to the National Library (Buenos Aires) by Mss. Carballido. Lack of jute prompted failed experiments with other fibers of native species such as chaguar, pita, caraguatá, sbira, and ramio. See *RRP*, September 8, 1900, 10, and July 14, 1900, 7; *La Epoca*, June 22, 25, and 28, 1918, in Biblioteca Tornquist, Industrias, 379; and *Notas de un proyecto para desarrollar la industria textil Argentina: Formación de la Cía Titan Textile Company*, 1919, brochure. For cotton, see Donna Guy, "Oro Blanco: Cotton, Technology and Family Labor in Nineteenth Century Argentina," *The Americas*, April 1993, *XLIX*(4). Colonizers in Santa Fé tried to harvest cotton, but only those in the Chaco experienced successful results. See FO, 368/266, memorandum enclosed in Mr. Russell's Commercial of February 1, 1909, 2; and *RRP*, April 9, 1904, no. 645, 680.

58. Stephen Haber, *Industry and Underdevelopment: The Industrialization of Mexico, 1890–1940* (Stanford, CA: Stanford University Press, 1989); and Stanley Stein, *The Brazilian Cotton Industry* (Princeton, NJ: Princeton University Press, 1957).

59. Federico Cibils, "El algodón," *BUIA*, April 15, 1902, 24.

60. This led the firm Enrico Dell'Acqua to retreat from the idea of founding a spinning mill in Argentina and continue importing yarn from Italy. See Federico Cibils, "El algodón," 25.

61. FO, 3687/2, C.I.B., no. 4, Buenos Aires, January 3, 1906, Ross to the Board of Trade, pp. 1–2. See also *BUIA*, October, November, and December, 1906, pp. 37–38. A new cotton-spinning mill opened in 1907 producing 1,000 kilos a day while the stock company's output was of 4,500 kilos. See *BUIA*, October 15, 1907, 41.

62. The factory had eight thousand spindles and produced five hundred tons of yarn, which equaled 10 percent of imports. See Adolfo Dorfman, *Historia de la industria Argentina* (Buenos Aires: Losada, 1942), 341–42.

63. República Argentina, Secretaría de Industria y Comercio, Dirección del Algodón, *La industrialización de fibra de algodón en la República Argentina* (Buenos Aires: 1947), quoted in Colin Lewis, "Immigrant Entrepreneurs, Manufacturing and Industrial Policy in the Argentine, 1922–28," *The Journal of Imperial and Commonwealth History*, October 1987, *16*(1), 83.

64. Stein, *The Brazilian Cotton*, 101.

65. Dorfman, *Historia de la industria*, 277, and 341–42.

66. Alfred Chandler, *The Visible Hand: The Managerial Revolution in American Business* (Cambridge, MA: The Belknap Press, 1977), 58; and John Brown, "Market Organization, Protection, and Vertical Integration: German Cotton Textiles Before 1914," *Journal of Economic History*, June 1992, *52*(2), 339–51.

67. Barrett, *Paper, Paper Products*, 37. Attempts to obtain wood pulp failed, such as the experimental tests under an Argentine government supervisor to produce it from the native araucarina pine. See Roger E. Simmons, *Markets of the Lumber in the East Coast of South America*, USDCBFDC, Special Agents Series, no. 112 (Washington, DC: GPO, 1916). Similarly, efforts to manufacture cellulose were a failure until 1943. See Américo E. Rava, "Historia y estado actual de la industria del papel en la Argentina," *Los ingenieros Argentinos en la industria nacional* (Buenos Aires, 1914), 123–38; *La Nación*, November 20, 1916, and R. Del Campo, "Industrias nuevas," *Revista de Ciencias Económicas*, 1927, *XXVIII*, 327.

68. USDCBFDC, Special Consular Reports, *Paper and Stationery Trade of the World*, no. 73 (Washington, DC: GPO, 1915), 305.

69. Brock, *Boots and Shoes*, 46.

70. *La Nación, 1916*, 315.

71. Phoebus, *Argentine Markets*, 11.

72. Harold Everley, *Furniture Markets of Argentina, Uruguay, Paraguay, and Brazil*, USDCBFDC, Special Agents Series, no. 183 (Washington, DC: GPO, 1919), 24–26.

73. Rosemary Thorp, in *Progress, Poverty and Exclusion: An Economic History of Latin America in the 20th Century* (Washington DC: Inter-American Development Bank and Princeton University Press, 1998), showed the volatility of the Argentine GDP growth in Table II.3, p. 319.

74. *El País*, February 15, 1900, 5; and *BUIA*, February 20, 1900, 28.

75. Barrett, *Paper, Paper Products*, 39–40.

76. Compañía General de Fósforos S.A. Archives (Biblioteca PEHESA, Facultad de Filosofía y Letras, UBA), *Libros de Actas del Directorio* (minutes of the board of directors meetings, hereafter cited as *CGF, BD*), June 12, and December 31, 1925.

77. Waldo Ansaldi, *Una industrialización fallida: Córdoba, 1880–1914* (Córdoba: Ferreyra Editor, 2000), 145–46.

78. Ewing, *Construction Materials and Machinery*, 59 and 74–75. In 1913, only eight establishments (all in Buenos Aires city) produced cement with a mere total workforce of 121 people. See *Tercer Censo Nacional levantado el 1° de junio de 1914*, Vol. VII (Buenos Aires: Talleres Gráficos de L. J. Rosso y Cía, 1916), 314. For constraints during the war, see FO, 371/2601, 1, Confidential, January 1, 1916, Tower, p. 125 reverse. For construction growth, see Roberto Cortés Conde, "Estimaciones del producto bruto interno de Argentina 1875–1935," working paper, Universidad de San Andrés, Victoria, Buenos Aires, Working Paper 3, October 1994, 17.

79. Waldo Ansaldi, *Una industrialización fallida: Córdoba, 1880–1914*, pp. 129–44.

80. Archivo SIAM Di Tella, Pieza 1.3.16, pamphlet "Calera Argentina S.A."

81. Alfredo Malaurie and Juan Gazzano, *La industria Argentina y la exposición del Paraná* (Buenos Aires: Editada por la Agencia General de Publicidad de Juan M. Gazzano y Cía, 1888), 172–74; *Exposición*, IV, November 4, 1897, 48; Dr. Moorne, *Las industrias fabriles*, vol. I, 130.

82. *El País*, March 27, 1904, 5.

83. The most successful cases were the firms of Nicolás Schneider and Juan Istilart. Shneider's company was based at Esperanza, province of Santa Fé, in the area of farmers' colonies. It turned out one thousand wheel plows and twenty-five-hundred walking plows per year, and prices were 10 percent lower than those of the American counterparts. Istilart was located in Tres Arroyos, province of Buenos Aires, another colonizing area. It produced land rollers, disk-harrows, and stalk cutters. See Sherwood H. Avery, *Markets for Agricultural Implements and Farm Machinery in Argentina and Uruguay*, USDCBFDC, Special Agents Series, (Washington, DC: GPO, 1926), 27–28.

84. Vivaldi, "Le industrie argentine," 174.

85. T. Worthington, *The Argentine Republic*, 564.

298   *Notes to Chapter 3*

86. For the case of the Bianchetti firm, see Lloyd, *Argentina*, 446; and *La Nacion 1916*, 163.

87. Interview with Hugo and Jorge Fontana at Talleres Fontana Hermanos, Buenos Aires, 1998.

88. Thomas C. Cochran and Ruben E. Reina, *Entrepreneurship in Argentine Culture: Torcuato Di Tella and S.I.A.M.* (Philadelphia: University of Pennsylvania Press, 1962), 37–43; and Torcuato S. Di Tella, *Torcuato Di Tella: Industria y política* (Buenos Aires: Tesis, 1993).

89. Interview with Isidoro Lagoisty, quoted in Cochran and Reina, *Entrepreneurship in Argentine Culture*, 52.

90. *The Economist*, June 5, 1897, 811; July 17, 1897, 1023; and September 18, 1897, 1323; and T. Worthington, *The Argentine Republic*, 4.

91. Barrett, *Paper, Paper Products*, 40. Small paper firms produced only wrapping paper. See *BUIA*, March 20, 1899, 27 and October 20, 1899, 28–29.

92. Centro del Comercio, *Informe de la Comisión*, 24–33.

93. The 1887 survey is not complete and did not take into account many small establishments employing one, two, or three people. This fact does not affect the trend expressed in the text.

94. Ideally, a concentration index should relate to the economic theory of market behavior and provide some insight into the degree of "market power." The choice of indexes is difficult and may affect the outcome of the research, since each index has a different meaning. See M. A. Adelman, "The Measurement of Industrial Concentration," *Review of Economics and Statistics*, 1951, *XXXIII*(4), 271.

95. Arturo Goetz, "Concentración y desconcentración en la industria Argentina desde la década de 1930 a la de 1960," *DE*, January–March 1976, *15*(60), 507–548.

96. Yovanna Pineda has used the CR4 and HHI index of industrial concentration for 1895 and, with the exception of blacksmithing, all branches show high levels. See Yovanna Yvonne Pineda, "The Firm in Early Argentine Industrialization, 1890–1930: A Study of Fifty-Five Joint-Stock Companies' Owners, Finance Sources, Productivity, and Profits," Ph.D. dissertation, University of California, Los Angeles, 2002, section 2.5 and Table 2.4.

97. "Establecimientos metalúrgicos en la capital de la República Argentina en 1825 y 1907," in *BUIA*, February 15, 1908, 25.

98. *El País*, January 1, 1900, 6.

99. *BUIA*, October 20, 1902, 1.

100. For hats, see *Finanzas, comercio e industria en la República Argentina*, Buenos Aires (hereafter cited as *Finanzas*),(1), January 1, 1899, 51; *Caras y Caretas*, Buenos Aires March 25, 1899, 4 and 25; *BUIA*, October 20, 1899, 16–17 and December 25, 1899, 22; *El País*, January 1, 1900, 6; and La Nación, September 10, 1898, 2–3. For liqueur, see Vaquer, *Historia de la inge-*

niería, 175–76. For biscuits, see Bagley S.A. Archives, *Memoria y balance anual (Annual Memory and Balance Sheet)*, 1905. For cigarettes, see USDCBFDC, Special Consular Reports, *Tobacco Trade of the World*, 41; and *La Nación, 1916*, 70.

101. Rezzónico, Ottonello y Cía Buenos Aires, *Talleres Metalúrgicos, Fábricas de Bulones, remaches, tornillos, etc. Talleres de construcción, fundición y mecánica*, pamphlet, circa 1903; and *BUIA*, July 12, 1902, 31.

102. Lloyd, *Argentina*, 417. In 1909, TAMET became a joint stock company. At the same time, the Tornquist Group acquired agricultural machinery firms Zimmermann, Noé and Co, and Eugenio Noé and Co. See TAMET, "30 años de presidencia 1914–1944," *Revista TAMET*, Buenos Aires, issue dedicated to the thirtieth anniversary of Carlos Antonio Tornquist's presidency, no. 164, April–May 1944, pp. 4–5.

103. Duggan, "Iron and Steel Production in Argentina c. 1920–1952."

104. S.A. Talleres Metalúrgicos San Martín, brochure, December 26, 1928; and "TAMET S.A, *La Metropole*, Anvers, July 12 and 13, 1947, p. 19. Both are in Biblioteca Tornquist. TAMET also absorbed the metallurgical firm Zublin, de Bary y Cía. See *La Ingeniería*, Buenos Aires, *IX*, April 1905, 365.

105. *Diario de Sesiones de la Cámara de Diputados* (hereafter cited as DSCD), October 22, 1894, 283; and T. Worthington, *The Argentine Republic*, 36. In 1914, paper companies reached an agreement to limit production after the 1913 depression. See Barrett, *Paper, Paper Products*, 40.

106. *BUIA*, February 15, 1894, 1.

107. Brock, *Boots and Shoes*, 61.

108. Kenneth Sokoloff, "Was the Transition from the Artisanal Shop to the Small Factory Associated with Gains in Efficiency?" *Explorations in Economic History*, October 1984, *21*(24), 351–58. For support on the importance of economies of scale, see Jeremy Attack, "Economies of Scale and Efficiency Gains in the Rise of the Factory in America, 1820–1900," in Peter Kilby (ed.), *Quantity and Quiddity: Essays in U.S. Economic History* (Middletown, CT: Wesleylan University Press, 1988). For the opposite view, see John Vincent Nye, "Firm Size and Economic Backwardness: A New Look at the French Industrialization Debate," *Journal of Economic History*, September 1987, *47*(3), 649–69.

109. Chandler, *The Visible Hand* and *Scale and Scope: The Dynamics of Industrial Capitalism* (Cambridge, MA: Cambridge University Press); and Oliver Williamson in his *The Economic Institutions of Capitalism* (New York: Free Press, 1985).

110. William Lazonick, *The Myth of the Market Economy* (Cambridge, MA: Cambridge University Press, 1991); and Patrick O'Brien, "Factory Size, Economies of Scale, and the Great Merger Wave of 1898–1902," *Journal of Economic History*, September 1988, *XLVIII*(3), 639–49.

111. Naomi Lamoreaux, *The Great Merger Movement in American Business,*

1895–1904 (Cambridge, MA: Cambridge University Press, 1985), 30, 46, 86, 116, and 154–55.

112. Yovanna Pineda, "The Firm in Early Argentine Industrialization, 1890–1930," 37–47. In beer, cement, glass, matches, alpargatas, burlap sacks, and textiles there was a decrease from 2.14 to 2.04, 2.45 to 2.11, 2.47 to 1.89, 2.10 to 2.05, 2.22 to 1.91, 2.23 to 2.28, and 2.21 to 1.78 respectively. In iron and steel, small-scale machinery, paper, soap, and tobacco there was an increase of 1.99 to 2.06, 1.86 to 2.04, 2.24 to 2.06, 2.19 to 2.20, 1.86 to 1.91. See Table 2.2.

113. Ezequiel Gallo, *La pampa gringa* (Buenos Aires: Sudamericana, 1983).

114. *BUIA*, October 12, 1897, 1–2. See also *Censo General 1887*, 321; and *BUIA*, October 20, 1899, 17.

115. Dorfman, *Historia de la industria*, 84–85 and 123; and Dr. Moorne, *Las industrias fabriles*, vol. I, 72–85.

116. *El País*, January 1, 1900, 6.

117. Large breweries crushed small ones in the city of Buenos Aires, and virtually none of the latter could survive. By 1895, three small breweries barely continued working, employing from five to thirty-five people. See Archivo General de la Nación (Buenos Aires), *Segundo Censo Nacional de la República Argentina*, May 10, 1895, Manuscripts, Económico Social, Legajo 99, Fábricas de cerveza.

118. See the case of Armengol in Archivo General de la Nación, Tribunal Comercial, Letra A, Año 1910, 7 and 8, 34–38.

119. *El País*, January 29, 1900, 5.

120. Brock, *Boots and Shoes*, 44; *BUIA*, February 15, 1911, 15–16; and Ugarteche, *Las industrias del cuero*, 429.

121. ADOT S.A., Industrial, Comercial y Financiera, *50 Aniversario* (Buenos Aires: Departamento Publicitario Adot, 1942), 4.

122. ADOT S.A., 1942, 4–12.

123. Capitán Nemo (Guillermo Heins), *Ernesto Tornquist: Homenaje* (Buenos Aires: Cía Impresora Argentina, 1936), 34.

124. *Exposición*, LIV and LV, January 18 and 25, 1899, 439; Lix Klett, *Estudios*, vol 1, 473; and Donna Guy, "Refinería Argentina, 1888–1930: Límites de la tecnología azucarera en una economía periférica," *DE*, October–December 1988, *28*(111). For the Tornquist Group, see Donna Guy, "La industria Argentina, 1870–1940," 362–63; Paul Lewis, *The Crisis of Argentine Capitalism* (Chapel Hill and London: The University of North Carolina Press, 1990), 65–66; and Jorge Gilbert, "Un grupo diversificado: Ernesto Tornquist y Compañía," paper presented to the Conference on Empresarios y empresas en la historia Argentina, UADE, Buenos Aires, 2001.

125. *MSA*, 1908, *V*(31), 216–17 and 1910, *IX*, 218; and Cía. Fabril Financiera, *Historia de un grupo de empresas industriales en la Argentina, 1888–1948* (Buenos Aires: Fabril Financiera, 1948). The tannery was Gaggino-Lauret. See

Boletín Oficial de la Bolsa de Comercio (hereafter cited as *BOBC*), July 16, 1906, 49. For a comprehensive study of this group, see María Inés Barbero, "De la Compañía General de Fósforos al Grupo Fabril: Origen y desarrollo de un grupo económico en la Argentina (1889–1965)," in *Universidad Nacional de General Sarmiento: Secretaría de Investigación. Problemas de investigación, ciencia y desarrollo*, November 2001, (2), 327–360.

126. The group was founded by Robert Williams Roberts, who formed a society with Hilary Leng to represent exporters and British investors in Argentina. See Paul Lewis. *The Crisis*, 65. At the same time, its members started to appear in the directorships of corporations in which they operated as brokers. See *MSA*, 1913, *XVI*, 151–53 and 1909, *IX*, 325–27. I am grateful to Alberto López for discussing some issues of this group (Interview with Alberto López, Grupo Roberts, Buenos Aires, 1987).

127. Georges Lafond, *L'Argentine*, 295–96; and Sergio López, "La Empresa en la Historia: El caso de la Cervecería Quilmes (1890–1990)," Master's dissertation, Buenos Aires, Universidad de San Andrés, 2001.

128. Yovanna Pineda, "The Firm in Early Argentine Industrialization, 1890–1930," 70–102.

129. *RRP*, January 25, 1902, 312.

130. Cámara de Diputados de la Nación, Comisión Investigadora de los Trusts, *Informe*. (Buenos Aires: 1919); Aníbal Arcondo, "El conflicto agrario pampeano de 1912. Ensayo de interpretación," *DE*, (October–December 1980, *20*(79), 351–81; and Zarrilli, "Estado, semillas y bolsas," 281–306.

131. For the portrayal of Otto Bemberg, see José Luis Torres, *Los perduelis* (Buenos Aires: Talleres Gráficos Padilla y Contreras, 1943); and Aníbal del Valle, *Juan de Afuera* (Buenos Aires: Porter Hnos, 1941).

132. Letter from Ricardo Pillado to Victorino de la Plaza, June 15, 1902, Archivo General de la Nación, Buenos Aires, Archivo Victorino de la Plaza, 5–2–4.

133. By using census data and information on large firms, Janice Rye Kinghorn and John Vincent Nye arrived at iconoclastic conclusions such as finding that German industry was less concentrated than the French. See their "The Scale of Production in Western Economic Development: A Comparison of Official Industry Statistics in the United States, Britain, France and Germany, 1905–1913," *Journal of Economic History*, March 1996, *56*(1), 90–112. For the comparison, see Table 1, p. 97, and for Argentina, the manuscripts of the 1895 Census (See Appendix 4).

134. Charles Kindleberger, *Economic Growth in France and Britain, 1851–1950* (Cambridge, MA: Harvard University Press, 1961), 122 and 179; and François Caron, *An Economic History of Modern France* (New York: Columbia University Press, 1979), 171.

135. Lamoreaux, *The Great Merger*, 30 and 46.

136. The case of the New Zealand brewing industry is clear. In 1881 there

were 102 independent breweries; in 1971 there were only 2. The process of concentration was due to economies of scale in a market of a very limited size. See S.R.H. Jones and D. R. Paul, "Concentration and Regulation in the New Zealand Brewing Industry," *Australian Economic History Review*, September 1991, *31*(2), 66–94. For Mexico see Haber, *Industry and Underdevelopment*.

137. Chandler, *Scale and Scope*.

138. Integration by itself did not guarantee a deeper industrialization. The existence of vertically integrated firms in Mexico, for instance, did not foster a full-fledged process of industrialization in that country. See Haber, *Industry and Underdevelopment*.

139. Fabril Financiera, *Historia de un grupo*, 4–10.

140. La Cantábrica S.A., *Memorias y balances (Annual Reports) 1913/14*.

141. Roberto Cortés Conde, *La economía Argentina en el largo plazo (Siglos XIX y XX)* (Buenos Aires: Sudamericana/San Andrés, 1997), chapter 1. Due to Argentina's links with Britain rather than the United States, the country did not suffer the 1907 crisis with the intensity felt in Mexico. See FO, 368/86, 3, Commercial, Rosario, April 29, 1907, and 368/165, Commercial, Buenos Aires, March 2, 1908, Townley, p. 1. For a general overview of the interwar period, see Vicente Vázquez-Presedo, *Crisis y retraso: Argentina y la economía internacional entre las dos guerras* (Buenos Aires: Eudeba, 1978).

142. Guido Di Tella and Manuel Zymelman, *Las etapas del crecimiento económico Argentino* (Buenos Aires: Eudeba, 1967).

143. Rory Miller, "Latin American Manufacturing and the First World War: An Explanatory Essay," *World Development, August 1981, 9*(8), 707–716.

144. Bill Albert, *South America and the First World War: The Impact of the War on Brazil, Argentina, Peru, and Chile* (Cambridge, MA, and New York: Cambridge University Press, 1988), 181.

145. Cortés Conde, *La economía Argentina*, Table A.1, pp. 230–31.

146. On the boom in wool washing, see Dorfman, *Historia de la industria*, 340. On the hosiery industry, see *Almanaque La Razón 1917*, p. 47. The collapse in construction left around thirty thousand carpenters unemployed; the cessation of European imports propelled a large number of them to open small companies of five or six men producing for their own accounts or retail and by copying the European models. See Everley, *Furniture Markets*, 24.

147. Shoe production grew from 33.5 to 49.5 million pairs of shoes between 1913 and 1918. See Dorfman, *Historia de la industria*, 328 and 395.

148. Brock, *Boots and Shoes*, 30 and 44.

149. *El Economista Argentino*, Buenos Aires, March 18, 1916, 3, and September 2, 1916, 1. The firm Quilmes started to produce malt in 1918, but hop production only started in 1946. See *Argentina Fabril*, Buenos Aires, July 17, 1986, 8; and Primera Maltería Argentina S.A., *Historia de dos conquistas: La cebada cervecera y el lúpulo* (Buenos Aires: ed. por Primera Maltería Ar-

gentina, 1946). For the general problems of local industry during the war, see Chalkley, *Report of the Year 1919*, 12; and *Commercial, Economic and Financial Conditions in the Argentine Republic: Buenos Aires, Report of September 1921* (London: Published by His Majesty's Stationery Office, 1921), 37.

150. *BUIA*, August 15, 1915, 27, and October 15, 1915, 30; *La Epoca*, October 16, 1918, 4; and Unión Industrial Argentina, *Confederación Argentina de Industrias Textiles* (Buenos Aires: 1934), 8.

151. *La Metropole*, Anvers, July 12 and 13, 1947, p. 20.

152. Javier Villanueva, "El origen de la industrialización Argentina," *DE*, October–December 1972, *12*(47); Cortés Conde, *La economía Argentina*, Table A.1, pp. 230–31; and Randall, *An Economic History*, chapter 6.

153. Francis Korn, *Buenos Aires: Los huéspedes del 20* (Buenos Aires: Grupo Editor Latinoamericano, 1985); and Beatriz Sarlo, *Buenos Aires: Una modernidad periférica: Buenos Aires 1920 y 1930* (Buenos Aires: Nueva Visión, 1988).

154. Di Tella and Zymelman, *Las etapas del crecimiento*.

155. See Alan Taylor, "External Dependence, Demographic Burdens, and the Argentine Economic Decline After the Belle Époque," *Journal of Economic History*, December 1992, *52*(4); and Cortés Conde, *La economía Argentina*.

156. See Carlos Díaz Alejandro, *Essays on the Economic History of the Argentina Republic* (New Haven and London: Yale University Press, 1970); and Leonard Nakamura and Carlos Zarazaga, "Economic Growth in Argentina in the Period 1900–1930: Some Evidence from Stock Returns," in John Coatsworth and Alan Taylor (eds.), *Latin America and the World Economy Since 1800* (Cambridge, MA: Harvard University Press, 1998).

157. Albert Carreras, "An Annual Index of Spanish Industrial Output," in Nicolás Sánchez-Albornoz, *The Economic Modernization of Spain, 1830–1930* (New York and London: New York University Press, 1984), Table 4.4A, p. 84. Data on Argentina are taken from Cortés Conde, "Estimaciones."

158. Villanueva, "El origen de la industrialización argentina"; and Cortés Conde, *La economía Argentina*, Table A.1, pp. 230–31. See also Dudley Maynard Phelps, *Migration of Industry to Latin America: Evolution of International Business, 1800–1945 (The Rise of International Business)* (London, Routledge, 2002).

159. H. O. Chalkley, U.K. Department of Overseas Trade. *Commercial, Economic and Financial Conditions in the Argentine Republic: Buenos Aires, Report of September 1925* (London: Published by His Majesty's Stationery Office, 1925), 58.

160. Fernando Rocchi, "Inventando la soberanía del consumidor: Publicidad, privacidad y revolución del mercado en Argentina, 1860–1940," in Fernando Devoto and Marta Madero, *Historia de la vida privada en la Argentina*, Vol. II (Buenos Aires: Taurus, 1999).

161. Enrique Loncán, *Las charlas de mi amigo (motivos porteños)* (Buenos Aires: Gleizer Editores, 1923), 40–41. The quote is from p. 139.

162. Juan Agustín García, "Los snobs," in *Obras completas*, Vol. II (Buenos Aires: Antonio Zamora, 1955), 1297.

163. Enrique Loncán, "El optimismo de los 'guarangos,'" in *Las charlas de mi amigo* (Buenos Aires: Emecé, 1981 [first published in 1932]), 108–111.

164. *Bandera Proletaria*, Buenos Aires, March 9, 1929, 3; April 28, 1928, 3; and July 3, 1926, 4.

165. Chalkley, *Report of October 1928*, 48.

166. Roberto Cortés Conde, "The Vicissitudes of an Exporting Economy: Argentina (1875–1930)," in Enrique Cárdenas, José Antonio Ocampo, and Rosemary Thorp (eds.), *An Economic History of Twentieth-Century Latin America. Volume 1: The Export Age. The Latin American Economies in the Late Nineteenth and Early Twentieth Centuries* (London and Oxford: Palgrave and St Antony's College, 2000).

167. María Inés Barbero and Mariela Ceva, "El catolicismo social como estrategia empresarial: El caso de Algodonera Flandria," *Anuario IEHS*, 1997, (12); and Colin Lewis, "Immigrant Entrepreneurs, Manufacturing and Industrial Policy in the Argentine, 1922–28."

168. *MSA*, 1925, *XXXIX*, 21–22.

169. Chalkley, *Report of September 1921*, 39.

170. José Villarruel, "Los industrialistas y la tutela del Estado," in Waldo Ansaldi, Alfredo Pucciarelli, and José C. Villarruel (eds.), *Argentina en la paz de dos guerras 1914–1945* (Buenos Aires: Biblos, 1993), 205–207.

171. Chalkley, *Report of September 1925*, 59. For local competition, see pp. 19–20.

172. U.K., Survey of Overseas Market, Committee on Industry and Trade, H.M.S.O., Balfour Report, London, March 12, 1925, p. 10. For a more realistic depiction of the Argentine industrial setting, see Paul Souweine, *L'Argentine au seuil de l'industrie* (Paris: Ecole de Sciences Politiques de Louvaine, 1927).

173. Del Campo, "Industrias nuevas," 327.

174. E. Joint, U.K. Department of Overseas Trade report, Commercial, *Economic*, and Financial *Conditions in the Argentine Republic. Buenos Aires, Report of November 1929* (London: Published by His Majesty's Stationery Office, 1930), 48–49; H. O. Chalkley, U.K. Department of Overseas Trade report, *Commercial, Economic, and Financial Conditions in the Argentine Republic: Buenos Aires, Report of September 1923* (London: Published by His Majesty's Stationery Office, 1924), 24.

175. Barrett, *Paper, paper products*; Cía Fabril Financiera, *Historia de un grupo*, 11, 13, and 14; and *MSA*, 1927, *XLII*, 59–60.

176. Yovanna Pineda, "The Firm in Early Argentine Industrialization, 1890–1930," 100–103.

177. *The Times*, London, December 30, 1922.

178. *MSA*, 1920, *XXIX*, 120–21; 1921, *XXII*, 9; and 1922, *XXXIII*, 158–59.

179. S.A. Talleres Metalúrgicos San Martín, brochure, December 26, 1928; *MSA*, 1929, *XLVII*, 166; and "TAMET S.A", *La Metropole*, Anvers, July 12 and 13, 1947, 19.

180. American Trade Commissioner Charles Ducoté, "The Argentine Iron and Steel Industry and Trade," USDCBFDC, Trade Bulletin no. 776 (Washington, DC: GPO, 1931), 4.

181. *MSA*, 1929, *XLVII*, 166; and 1939, *XLIX*, 175.

182. Duggan, "Iron and Steel Production in Argentina c. 1920–1952," p. 166.

183. Chalkley, *Report of October 1928*, 29.

184. *MSA*, 1926, *XLI*, 149.

185. Barbero, "De la Compañía General de Fósforos al Grupo Fabril."

186. *MSA*, 1925, *XXXIX*, 58.

187. CGF, BD, February 23, 1929; Fabril Financiera, *Historia de un grupo*, 4–10.

188. Barbero, "De la Compañía General de Fósforos al Grupo Fabril."

189. CGF, BD, May 22 and December 2, 1925; February 9, 1927; June 20, 1928; and March 20, 1929. Another exception was the tanning industry, probably the Argentine industrial branch with the most success in integration. The firm La Francia Argentina had a quebracho factory in Chaco, Luppi a sawdust mill, and Casimiro Gomez large extensions of land to raise cattle. See Ugarteche, *Las industria del cuero*, 63–70; Scardin, *La Argentina*, 533–34; and Vidal, *Algunos de mis trabajos*, 10.

190. H. O. Chalkley, U.K. Department of Overseas Trade, *Commercial, Economic and Financial Conditions in the Argentine Republic: Buenos Aires, Report of September 1924* (London: Published by His Majesty's Stationery Office, 1920), 19 and *Commercial, Economic and Financial Conditions in the Argentine Republic: Buenos Aires, Report of September 1927* (London: Published by His Majesty's Stationery Office, 1927), 23.

191. Fábrica Argentina de Alpargatas S.A., minutes of the Board of Directors meetings, March 23, 1923. The company made the decision to begin this production in 1920. See the minutes of April 19, 1920.

192. República Argentina, Secretaría de Industria y Comercio, Dirección del Algodón, *La industrialización de fibra de algodón en la República Argentina* (Buenos Aires: 1947) quoted in Colin Lewis, "Immigrant Entrepreneurs, Manufacturing and Industrial Policy in the Argentine, 1922–28," 83. For industrial evolution in the 1930s, see Barbero and Rocchi, "Industry," and Alberto Petrecolla, "Prices, Import Substitution and Investment in the Argentine Textile Industry (1920–1939)," Buenos Aires, Centro de Investigaciones Económicas, Instituto Torcuato Di Tella, mimeograph, 1968.

193. Howard H. Tewksbury, "The Automotive Market in Argentina,"

USDC, Trade Promotion Series no. 84 (Washington, DC, GPO, 1929), 11–12.

194. Chalkley, *Report of September 1925*, 34; and *Report of October 1928*, 46.

195. Cochran and Reina, *Entrepreneurship in Argentine Culture*, 59–81; Torcuato S. Di Tella, *Torcuato Di Tella*, 46–8.

196. Interview with Antonio Sudeiro, quoted in Cochran and Reina, *Entrepreneurship in Argentine Culture*, 75–76.

197. Cochran and Reina, *Entrepreneurship in Argentine Culture*, chapter III.

198. Capitán Nemo (Guillermo Heins), *Ernesto Tornquist: Homenaje*. Reproducción de la obra América industrial y comercial del Capitán Nemo (Buenos Aires: Cía Impresora Argentina, 1936) 2.

199. Cortés Conde, *La economía Argentina*, 207.

200. As Cortés Conde has signaled, "the industrial development of the 1930s corresponded to a substitution of imported inputs rather than final goods(. . . .) [C]hanges in the 1920s—investment in industrial machinery and cotton—were responsible in one way or another for the expansion of the later period." See his "The Vicissitudes of an Exporting Economy," 269.

201. James R. Scobie, *Secondary Cities of Argentina: The Social History of Corrientes, Salta, and Mendoza, 1850–1910*, compiled and edited by Samuel Baily (Stanford, CA: Stanford University Press, 1988), 224.

Chapter 4

1. *República Argentina*, October 12, 1905, 310–14; *La Nación, 1910*, 104.

2. *La Nación, 1910*, 104; and *La Nación*, Un homenaje al Brasil en la fecha de su primer centenario 1822, September 7, 1922, 4.

3. Alfredo Malaurie and Juan Gazzano, *La industria Argentina y la exposición del Paraná* (Buenos Aires: Editada por la Agencia General de Publicidad de Juan M. Gazzano y Cía, 1888); and Ramón Gutiérrez, "Arquitectura lúdica: Los pabellones del Centenario," in Margarita Gutman (ed.), *Buenos Aires 1910: Memoria del Porvenir* (Buenos Aires: Gobierno de la Ciudad de Buenos Aires-Consejo del Plan Urbano Ambiental, Facultad de Arquitectura y Urbanismo de la Universidad de Buenos Aires, Instituto Internacional de Medio Ambiente y Desarrollo, 1999), 342–57.

4. Juan Alvarez, *Buenos Aires* (Buenos Aires: n.p., 1919). For the modest industrial development of Rosario in the 1880s, see Gabriel Carrasco, *Descripción geográfica y estadística de la provincia de Santa Fé* (Buenos Aires: Imprenta de Stiller & Laas, 1886), 499–506; and *Segundo censo municipal de la ciudad de Rosario de Santa Fe (República Argentina)*, levantado el 19 de octubre de 1906 (Rosario: La Capital, 1908), 309–22.

5. Michael Johns and Fernando Rocchi, "Capital industrial y espacio urbano: Buenos Aires durante el auge del proceso agroexportador," Paper presented at the conference "Buenos Aires moderna: Historia y perspectiva

urbana (1870–1914)," Jornadas del Instituto de Arte Americano e Investigaciones Estéticas Mario J. Buschiazzo, Buenos Aires, 1990.

6. Michael Johns, "The Urbanisation of a Secondary City: The Case of Rosario, Argentina, 1870–1920," *Journal of Latin American Studies*, October 1991, *23*(3), 489–513.

7. José Carlos Chiaramonte, *Ciudades, provincias, estados: Orígenes de la nación Argentina* (Buenos Aires: Ariel, 1997).

8. Miron Burgin, *The Economic Aspects of Argentine Federalism, 1820–1852* (New York: Russel & Russel, 1971), 134–36 and 237–42; D.C.M. Platt, *Latin America and British Trade, 1806–1914* (London: Adam & Charles Black, 1972), 20–21; and Oscar Oszlak, *La formación del estado Argentino* (Buenos Aires: Editorial de Belgrano, 1982), chapters 3 and 4.

9. Vicente Balbín, *Sistema de pesas y medidas de la República Argentina* (Buenos Aires: n.p., 1881); and Juan Alvarez, *Temas de historica económica argentina* (Buenos Aires: El Ateneo, 1929), 155–57.

10. *La Nación*, January 24, 1877, 1.

11. *La Nación*, January 24, 1877, 1.

12. For the case of Córdoba, see Félix Converso, *Un mercado en expansión: Córdoba, 1870–1914* (Córdoba: Centro de Estudios Históricos "Profesor Carlos S. A. Segreti," 2001), 349–50.

13. Eugene Sharkey, "Unión Industrial Argentina, 1887–1920: Problems of Industrial Development," Ph.D. dissertation, Rutgers University, October 1977. See *Diario de Sesiones de la Cámara de Diputados (hereafter referred to as DSCD)*, October 17, 1894, p. 183.

14. Liga de Defensa Comercial, *Informe 1915*, 23 and 70.

15. José S. Acuña, "Las aduanas interiores y el 'dumping' interprovincial ante la Suprema Corte," *Revista de Economía Argentina*, April 1929, *XXII*(39), 301–304.

16. Enclosure in United Kingdom, Public Record Office Archives, Foreign Office (hereafter cited as FO), 6/448, no. 10, Commercial, Buenos Aires, November 24, 1896, Barrington, 332–33.

17. FO, 6/469, no. 18, Commercial, Buenos Aires, June 9, 1901, Barrington, 128–29.

18. *La Nación*, March 15, 1896, 5.

19. *Boletín de la Unión Industrial Argentina* (hereafter cited as *BUIA*), November 15, 1911, 4.

20. FO, 368/86, Commercial 59, Confidential, Buenos Aires, July 18, 1907, Baird, 1.

21. Alejandro Galarce, *Bosquejos de Buenos Aires, capital de la nación Argentina, Vol. I* (Buenos Aires: n.p., 1886), 734 and 742.

22. *La Nación, 1910*, p. 61. *La República Argentina pintoresca, comercial e industrial*, 1906, 45; *La Nación*, October 1, 1910, 24; October 6, 1910, 28; and October 19, 1910, 5; and *Almanaque La Razón 1917*, 128.

23. P. M. de Corvetto, *Les industries Françaises à Buenos Aires* (Buenos Aires: Librairie Française, 1886), 68.

24. *Censo General*, 1887, vol II, 323.

25. Ezequiel Gallo, *La pampa gringa* (Buenos Aires: Sudamericana, 1983).

26. *Exposición 1898*, December 9, 1897, *XI*, 83.

27. Waldo Ansaldi, "Las prácticas sociales de la conmemoración en la Córdoba de la modernización, 1880–1914," *Sociedad*, April 1996, (8), 95–127; "Una modernización provinciana: Córdoba, 1880–1914," *Estudios*, UNC, 1996–1997, (7–8), 51–80; and "Lo sagrado y lo secular-profano en la sociabilidad en la Córdoba de la modernización provinciana, 1880–1914," *Cuadernos de historia*, November 1997, *1*(1), 7–43.

28. For the case of Jujuy, see Gustavo Paz, "Province and Nation in Northern Argentina: Peasants, Elite, and the State, 1780–1880," Ph.D. dissertation, Emory University, 1999.

29. Lorenzo Fazio, *Memoria descriptiva de la provincia de Santiago del Estero*, 1889, quoted in Alberto Tasso, *Aventura, trabajo y poder: Sirios y libaneses en Santiago del Estero, 1880–1980* (Santiago del Estero: Ediciones Indice, 1988), 80 and 82–83.

30. For peculiar standards of consumption in Córdoba, see Fernando J. Remedi, *Entre el gusto y la necesidad: La alimentación en Córdoba a principios del siglo XX* (Córdoba: Centro de Estudios Históricos, 1992) and "El consumo alimentario y sus diferencias en Córdoba, 1915–1930," in Beatriz Moreira et al., *Estado, mercado y sociedad: Córdoba, 1820–1950*, Vol. 1 (Córdoba: Centro de Estudios Históricos "Profesor Carlos S. A. Segreti", 2000).

31. *Censo General de 1887*, vol. II, pp. 335–36; and *DSCD*, October 23, 1894, 306.

32. Malaurie and Gazzano, *La industria Argentina*, 143.

33. *El Progreso*, Córdoba, April 13, 1883, 2.

34. Gath y Chaves opened branches in Rosario, Paraná, Córdoba, Mendoza, Tucumán, Mercedes, and La Plata; the Fábrica Nacional de Calzado in Rosario, La Plata, Córdoba, San Nicolás, Bahía Blanca, Santa Fé, Salta, and Corrientes; Lutz Ferrando in Rosario, Córdoba, Tucumán, and Mar del Plata; Escasany in Tucumán and Mar del Plata. See *Almanaque La Razón 1917*, 92; *La Nación, 1910*, 147; Reginald Lloyd, *Argentina in the Twentieth Century* (London: Lloyd Greater Britain Publishing, 1911), 426; Dr. Moorne, *Las industrias fabriles en Buenos Aires: Colección de artíuclos publicados en "El Nacional,"* Vol. I (Buenos Aires: Librairie Française de Joseph Escary, 1893), 144; and *Bodas de oro de la Casa Escasany, 1892–1942* (Buenos Aires: Talleres Guillermo Kraft, 1942).

35. *La Nación, 1916*, 327. For Grandes Almacenes Zamboni, employing two hundred workers, see *Centenario Argentino*, Vol. II (Buenos Aires: Editorial Cabral, Font y Cía, 1910), 130 and 114; and *La Nación, 1916*, 323.

36. *La Nación, 1916*, 323.

37. *Anuario Comercial y Bancario de la República Argentina.* Director propietario Teodoro Marco (Buenos Aires: Peuser, 1913), 76, 259.

38. Ernst B. Filsinger, *Commercial Travelers' Guide to Latin America,* United States, Department of Commerce, Bureau of Foreign and Domestic Commerce (hereafter cited as USDCBFDC), Miscellaneous Series, no. 89, (Washington, DC: GPO, 1920), 428.

39. Archives de Ministère des Affaires Etrangeres, NS 23, November 1913, no. 114, Jullemiert to Ministry, pp. 104–105. I thank Karen Mead for providing this material.

40. *La Nación, 1916,* 78.

41. *La Nación, 1910,* 100.

42. *Caras y Caretas,* September 23, 1900, 41.

43. *El Independiente,* La Rioja, February 15, 1918, 3.

44. *La Nación, 1916,* 134 and 156; Herman Brock, *Boots and Shoes, Leather, and Supplies in Argentina, Uruguay, and Paraguay,* USDCBFDC, Special Agents Series, no. 177 (Washington, DC: GPO, 1919), 54–58; *La Nación. Un homenaje al Brasil en la fecha de su primer centenario 1822,* September 7, *1922,* 284; and Compañía General de Fósforos S.A. Archives (Biblioteca PEHESA, Facultad de Filosofía y Letras, UBA), *Libros de Actas del Directorio* (minutes of the board of directors meetings, hereafter cited as CGF, BD), July 15, 1925.

45. *El Independiente,* La Rioja, May 8, 1913, 3; and January 5, 1917, 3.

46. *La Nación, 1910,* 187; and *La Nación, 1916,* 59.

47. U.S. Department of State papers, December 25, 1905, vol. 46 and 47, roll 40, no. 281; *Proyecto de creación de una fábrica de carburo de calcio en San Roque* (Provincia de Córdoba). Basada en la concesión Alfredo Molet. Otorgada por el Excmo. Gobierno de la Provincia de Córdoba el 3 de marzo de 1899 (Buenos Aires: Establecimientos tipográficos Revista Técnica, 1899), 3–18; *The Review of the River Plate,* Buenos Aires, (hereafter cited as *RRP*), November 3, 1900, 7–8; and *El País,* April 28, 1900, 6.

48. Waldo Ansaldi, *Una industrialización fallida: Córdoba, 1880–1914* (Córdoba: Ferreyra Editor, 2000); Ofelia Pianetto, "Industria y formación de la clase obrera urbanas en la ciudad de Córdoba, 1880–1906," in A.A.V.V., *Homenaje al Doctor Ceferino Garzón Maceda* (Córdoba: Universidad Nacional de Córdoba, 1973); "Mercado de trabajo y acción sindical: Córdoba, 1880–1930," Córdoba, Consejo Latino Americano de Ciencias Sociales, mimeograph, 1976–77; *El País,* October 14, 1901, 2; and *BUIA,* November 15, 1902; January 15, 1903, 27–28; June 15, 1903, 27; August 15, 1905, 4–5; October 15, 1905, 10–1; and November 15, 1905, 9–15.

49. Waldo Ansaldi, *Una industrialización fallida: Córdoba, 1880–1914,* 145–45.

50. Jorge Schvarzer, *Bunge & Born: Crecimiento y diversificación de un grupo económico* (Buenos Aires: CISEA/GEL, 1989).

51. *Finanzas, comercio e industria en la República Argentina*, Buenos Aires (hereafter cited as *Finanzas*), January 1, 1899, (1), 105; and *BUIA*, August 10, 1898, 19. Among the main customers of the Bank of London and River Plate after it opened a branch in Tucumán were the breweries Bieckert and Quilmes, "all doing large business, friends of ours in Buenos Aires," as the bank managers said in 1909. See José Antonio Sánchez Román, "El Banco de Londres y del Río de la Plata y el negocio azucarero en Tucumán, Argentina (1909–1914)," *Revista de Historia Económica*, Spring–Summer 2001, *XIX*(2), 430. There were large breweries in Azul, Bahía Blanca, Tucumán, Mendoza, and San Juan. See *Argentina fabril*, Buenos Aires, July 17, 1986, 8. Some regional producers, usually colonists of German and Swiss descent in the province of Santa Fé, could keep themselves in the market by maintaining handicraft quality. Cervecería Santa Fé, which employed 180 people, could supply a large portion of the provincial consumption of beer and ice. See *La Nación, 1916*, 196.

52. *RRP*, June 4, 1904, 1091. See also *BUIA*, September 15, 1905, 11–12.

53. *Centenario Argentino*, vol. II, p. 38; and George J. Mills, *Argentina; Physical Features, Natural Resources, Means of Communications, Manufactures and Industrial Development* (New York, South American Handbooks, 1914), 151.

54. *BUIA*, October 15, 1905, 9. See also Pianetto, "Industria y formación."

55. Brock, *Boots and Shoes*, 51 and 86.

56. Brock, *Boots and Shoes*, 51; and Hilda Iparaguirre, "Crecimiento industrial y formación de la burguesía en una subregión argentina: Córdoba a finales del siglo XIX y principios del XX," in Enrique Florescano (ed.), *Orígenes y desarrollo de la burguesía en América Latina* (Mexico City: Editorial Nueva Imagen, 1985), 596–98.

57. This was the case of La Curtidora Cordobesa. See *Monitor de Sociedades Anónimas*, Buenos Aires (hereafter cited as *MSA*), 1910, *IX*, 114–16.

58. Ansaldi, *Una industrialización fallida*.

59. Dimas Helguera, *La producción Argentina en 1892: Descripción de la industria nacional. Su desarrollo y progreso en toda la República. Ampliación del retrospecto publicado en LA PRENSA* (Buenos Aires: Goyoaga y Cía, 1893), 233.

60. *El País*, November 30, 1901, 5.

61. *BUIA*, June 27, 1888, 2–3.

62. *BUIA*, February 10, 1897, 20.

63. Donna Guy, "Oro Blanco: Cotton, Technology and Family Labor in Nineteenth Century Argentina," *The Americas*, April 1993, *XLIX*(4).

64. *BUIA*, January 1, 1895, 21; February 1, 1895, 22; November 1, 1895, 23; April 1, 1896, 23; April 15, 1908, 22–23.

65. *BUIA*, October 11, 1897, 20.

66. *BUIA*, September 15, 1916, 21.

67. As an example of the "hidden" resources of Jujuy, the poorest Argen-

tinian province, see Anales del Ministerio de Agricultura, Sección Agricultura, Botánica y Agronomía, Agronomía, tomo II, no. 6, Informe presentado por Eduardo Alejandro Holmberg (hijo), Investigación agrícola en la provincia de Jujuy (Buenos Aires: Cía. Sudamericana de Billetes de Banco, 1904), 164–67.

68. *BUIA*, June 15, 1916, 36–37.

69. Integration in the national and capitalist market has been seen as beneficial (by modernisation theory) or damaging (by the domestic colonialism school) for the Argentine regional economies. See Ian Rutledge, *Cambio agrario e integración: El desarrollo del capitalismo en Jujuy, 1550–1950* (Tilcara, Jujuy, and Buenos Aires: Centro de Investigaciones Sociales, 1987).

70. Club Industrial, "Movimiento industrial habido en la República Argentina desde el año 1874 hasta el presente: 15 de Septiembre de 1880," Para nuestro socio honorario Dr. Victorino de la Plaza. In Archivo General de la Nación, Buenos Aires, Archivo Victorino de la Plaza (hereafter cited as AGN, AVP) 5-6-12, 39; and *BUIA*, October 20, 1899, p. 30.

71. Helguera, *La producción Argentina*, 120–23.

72. The company is Luppi; see *La Nación, 1910*, 328.

73. The company is Gómez; see *La Nación, 1916*, 106.

74. *BUIA*, January 19, 1893, p. 38.

75. Félix de Ugarteche, *Las industrias del cuero en la República Argentina* (Buenos Aires: Talleres Gráficos de Roberto Canals), 32; see also Segundo Censo 1895, vol. III, 271–301; Tercer Censo Nacional 1914, vol VII, 120–376.

76. *Nueva Epoca*, Salta, February 20, 1913, p. 6.

77. Helguera, *La producción*, 38; *Caras y Caretas*, April 8, 1899, 2; and *La Nación*, September 17, 1898, 10.

78. Bagley S.A. Archives, *Minutes of the Board of Directors Meetings* (hereafter cited as Bagley, BD), February 7, 14, and 28, 1902, and May 6, 1904.

79. Ansaldi, *Una industrialización fallida*, 98–100.

80. Bagley, BD, March 14, 1902; February 28, 1902; October 2, 1902; January 2, 1903; April 3, 1903; May 1, 1903; and February 5, 1904. See also Iparaguirre, "Crecimiento industrial," 585–607.

81. For Córdoba's efforts and successes to establish a commercial network in the interior, see Félix E. Converso, *La lenta formación de capitales: Familias, Comercio y Poder en Córdoba, 1850–1880* (Córdoba: Junta Provincial de Historia de Córdoba, 1993), chapters 2 and 3, 38–156; and *Un mercado en expansión*, chapters II and V.

82. Bagley, BD, August 23, 1912 and May 29, 1909. There was even a small workshop in Córdoba that masterfully imitated Bagley's famous Lola biscuits. See *BUIA*, January 1, 1895, 23.

83. Bagley, BD, May 29, 1909.

84. Bagley, BD, September 29, 1909.

85. Bagley, BD, November 13, 1909. The sum of $40,000 was double that paid to the Córdoba corporation as an annual subsidy.

86. Bagley, BD, July 23, 1910; September 28, 1910; and November 23, 1910.

87. Bagley, BD, August 23, 1912; April 28, 1911; June 28, 1911; February 13, 1912; November 29, 1912; and August 1 and 11, 1913.

88. In the areas of Cremades' direct influence (Tucumán, Santiago, Córdoba, and San Luis), increase was of $0.40 per bundle. In areas of indirect influence (San Juan and Mendoza), it only was $0.10. Bagley, BD, August 23, 1912. On the performance of the Fábrica de Galletitas de Córdoba in 1905, see *BUIA*, October 15, 1905, 5–6.

89. Ansaldi, *Una industrialización fallida*, 103.

90. For the convergence, see Bagley, Surtidos Provincial y Libertad, Libro de Precios 1912. For the Patagonia, see Bagley, BD, September 5 and 20, 1915; and Libro de Precios (Price Book) 1911–1917.

91. Data from Bagley is in Table 1.5. For national and Córdoba data, see Segundo Censo Nacional, 1895, vol. III, 270; and Tercer Censo Nacional 1914, vol. VII, 395.

92. Bagley S.A. Archives, Libro de Inventarios (Inventory Book), 1920–1930.

93. Bagley, Libro de Cuentas Corrientes, Saldos Deudores (Current Accounts Book), 1929–1932.

94. Bagley, BD, December 18, 1909. For the offer, see May 10, 1908. A new offer was rejected on August 31, 1910.

95. Bagley, BD, April 19, 1906; October 1 and 30, 1907; November 30, 1907; October 24, 1908; and November 17, 1908.

96. Bagley, BD, February 7, 1905.

97. Bagley, BD, September 28, 1910; October 19, 1910; and October 23, 1911.

98. Archivo de la Cía General de Fósforos, PEHESA-Facultad de Filosofía y Letras-UBA (hereafter cited as CGF), Estadística General. Libro 1, Avellaneda, Paraná, Tucumán y Santa Fé. Resumen de gruesas vendidas, fs. 1–23.

99. Fabril Financiera S.A., *Historia de un grupo de empresas industriales en la Argentina, 1888–1948* (Buenos Aires: Fabril Financiera, 1948), 4.

100. Fabril Financiera, *Historia de un grupo*, 4–9; and CGF, BD, June 15, 1925.

101. CGF, Fósforos Victoria y Estrella, Libro de estadística por regiones, 1–4.

102. CGF, BD, July 15 and September 2, 1925; and August 1, 1928.

103. CGF, BD, August 20, 1924; October 7, 1925; and June 5, 1926.

104. CGF, BD, January 18, 1928; February 1, 1928; and February 15, 1928.

105. CGF, Estadística General. Libro 1, Avellaneda, Paraná, Tucumán y

Santa Fé. Resumen de gruesas vendidas, 1–23; and CGF, BD, January 18, 1928.

106. CGF, BD October 7, 1925; January 14, 1925; and September 15, 1926. For Bahía Blanca see August 20, 1924.

107. Francisco A. Barroetaveña, *La vitivinicultura en el Litoral: El "viñedo Franklin"* (Buenos Aires: Imprenta de M. Biedma, 1907), 4–5. For wine and sugar in the interior, see Jorge Balán, "Una cuestión regional en la Argentina: Burguesías provinciales y el mercado nacional en el desarrollo agroexportador," *DE*, April–June 1978, *18*(69), 49–87; Jorge Balán and Nancy López, "Burguesías y gobiernos provinciales en la Argentina: La política impositiva de Tucumán y Mendoza entre 1874 y 1914," *DE*, October–December 1977, *17*(67), 391–435; Donna Guy, *Argentine Sugar Politics: Tucumán and the Generation of Eighty* (Tempe, AZ: The Center for Latin American Studies, 1980); Joan Supplee, "Provincial Elites and the Economic Transformation of Mendoza, Argentina, 1880–1914," Ph.D. dissertation, University of Texas, Austin, 1988; and José Antonio Sánchez Román, "La dulce crisis: Finanzas, estado e industria azucarera en Tucumán, Argentina (1853–1914)," Ph.D. dissertation, Universidad Complutense de Madrid, Instituto Universitario 'Ortega y Gasset', Madrid, 2001.

108. In 1895 there were only two small wine factories in the city. See Archivo General de la Nación (Buenos Aires), *Segundo Censo Nacional de la República Argentina*, May 10, 1895, Manuscripts, Legajo 99, Section Fabricación de vinos de pasa de uva. In 1904, the pressure of Cuyo's wine producers had been enough to pass the wine law to end the production of artificial wines. See Balán and López, "Burguesías provinciales." By 1910, the vino de pasa represented only 0.01 percent of the national production. See Carlos Urien and Ezio Colombo, *La República Argentina en 1910*, Vol. I (Buenos Aires: Casa Editora Maucci Hnos., 1910), 540.

109. *Finanzas*, January 1, 1899, (1), 42; and *Centenario Argentino*, vol. I, p. 607.

110. U.S. Department of State, Dispatches from U.S. Ministers to Argentina, Roll 28, vol 33, Buenos Aires, January 2, 1896, no. 185, Buchanan, p. 8; "Nuestra industria molinera en 1907," *BUIA*, August 15, 1908, 15–18; and Shvarzer, *Bunge & Born*. For meatpacking houses, see Peter Smith, *Beef and Politics in Argentina: Patterns of Conflict and Change* (New York: Columbia University Press, 1969); for rice mills, see *Nota elevada a la Honorable Cámara de Diputados por Arrocera y Almidonera Argentina*, October 23, 1912, pamphlet. For yerba mate mills, see *Exposición* 1898, January 1, 1899, *LII*, 421–22.

111. David Harvey, *Consciousness and the Urban Experience: Studies in the History and Theory of Capitalist Urbanization* (Baltimore: Johns Hopkins University, 1985).

112. Eugenio Garzón, *L'Amérique Latine: Republique Argentine* (París: Bernard Grasset, 1913), 299–300; Galileo Massei, *La Repubblica Argentina nel*

primo centenario della sua independenza (Milano: Arnaldo De Mohr Editore, 1910), 369–70; and Horacio Ferrari, *Orígenes y desarrollo de la industria lechera Argentina*, UBA, Facultad de Ciencias Económicas, Instituto de la Producción, Publicación no. 39, 1953. For the butter industry, see *El País*, December 10, 1901, 3; and *BUIA*, May 15, 1903, 5–11.

113. The city of Buenos Aires comprised twenty five per cent of the national investments in dairy and cheese industries, and it produced seventy percent of the country's total butter output. See "Nuestra industria lechera," *BUIA*, August 15, 1908, 18–19; *La Nación, 1916*, 211; and Massei, *La Reppublica*, 371.

114. *Caras y Caretas*, March 18, 1899, p. 6.

115. *Revista Municipal*, September 28, 1908, p. 1. See also FO, 6/482, Commercial no. 21, Buenos Aires, April 20, 1903, Hartford, 116.

116. Lloyd, *Argentina*, 418. See also Massei, *La Reppublica*, 369; and Urien and Colombo, *La República*, vol. I 534–35.

117. Garzón, *L'Amérique Latine*, 299–300; and Massei, *La Repubblica*, 369–70.

118. Lida Knecher and Roberto Gerardo Fuld, "Orígenes, desarrollo y desaparición de una empresa de capital nacional: La historia de Kasdorf S.A.," *CICLOS*, 1998, *VIII*(16), 163–90.

119. Ministerio de Obras Públicas de la Provincia de Buenos Aires, *La industria lechera en la provincia*. Memoria presentada por el Comisionado del Gobierno, Ing. Agrónomo Eduardo T. Larguía (La Plata: Tipografía de la Escuela de Artes y Oficios, 1897); and Knecher and Fuld, "Orígenes, desarrollo y desaparición de una empresa de capital nacional," 163–90.

120. Nicolás Granada, *Al campo! Comedia de costumbres nacionales en tres actos y en prosa* (Buenos Aires: J. Bonmati, 1902); and César Duayen, *Stella* (Buenos Aires: Maucci, 1909). On this image in capitalism, see Raymond Williams, *The Country and the City* (New York: Oxford University Press, 1973).

121. FO, 6/469, no. 18, Commercial, Buenos Aires, September 6, 1901, Barrington, 128–29.

Chapter 5

1. Telmo Manacorda, *La gesta callada: Biografía de una industria* (Buenos Aires: Peuser, 1947), 290–91.

2. The industrialist association was, to some extent, what Roger Chartier has labeled a "political classic" in his "Le monde comme répresentation," *Annales Economies. Sociétés. Civilisations*, November–December 1989, *44*(6), 1505–1519.

3. This view is well represented in Eugene Sharkey, "Unión Industrial Argentina, 1887–1920: Problems of Industrial Development," Ph.D. dissertation, Rutgers University, October 1977; and Schvarzer, *La industria*.

4. Henri Weber, *El partido de los patronos: El CNPF (1946–1986)*, (Madrid, Ministerio de Trabajo y Seguridad Social, 1987).

5. Jorge Katz and Ezequiel Gallo, "The Industrialization of Argentina," in Claudio Veliz (ed.), *Latin America and the Caribbean: A Handbook* (London: Anthony Blond, 1968); Sergio Bagú, *Evolución histórica de la estratificación social en la Argentina* (Caracas: Instituto de Investigaciones Económicas y Sociales de la Universidad Central de Venezuela, 1969); and Oscar Cornblit, "Inmigrantes y empresarios en la política argentina," *DE*, January–March 1967, *6*(24), 641–691.

6. Milcíades Peña, *Industrialización y clases sociales en la Argentina* (Buenos Aires: Hyspamérica, 1986, [first published in 1964]); and Jorge Sábato, *La clase dominante en la formación de la Argentina moderna* (Buenos Aires: CISEA/GEL-Centro de Investigaciones Sociales sobre el Estado y la Administración/Grupo Editor Latinoamericano, 1988). For a discussion of this hypothesis, see Fernando Rocchi, "En busca del empresario perdido: Los industriales argentinos y las tesis de Jorge Federico Sábato," *Entrepasados*, 1996, *V*(10), 67–88.

7. Roy Hora, "Empresarios y política en la Argentina, 1880–1916," in Hilda Sabato and Alberto Lettieri (eds.), *La vida política en la Argentina del siglo XIX: Armas, votos y voces* (Mexico City: Fondo de Cultura Económica, 2003), 293–310.

8. Fernando Rocchi, "La armonía de los opuestos: Industria, importaciones y la construcción urbana de Buenos Aires en el período 1880–1920," *Entrepasados*, 1994, *4*(7), 43–66.

9. For a description and analysis of Once, see Francis Korn, *Buenos Aires: Los huéspedes del 20* (Buenos Aires: Grupo Editor Latinoamericano, 1985).

10. Michael Johns and Fernando Rocchi, "Capital industrial y espacio urbano: Buenos Aires durante el auge del proceso agroexportador," in *Buenos Aires moderna: Historia y perspectiva urbana (1870–1914)*, Jornadas del Instituto de Arte Americano e Investigaciones Estéticas Mario J. Buschiazzo, Buenos Aires, 1990; and Fernando Rocchi, "Industria y metrópolis: El sueño de un gran mercado," in Margarita Gutman and Thomas Reese (eds.), *Buenos Aires 1910: El imaginario para una gran capital* (Buenos Aires: Eudeba, 1999). For activities in the neighbourhood of Once, see Francis Korn, *Los huéspedes del 20*.

11. José Carlos Chiaramonte, *Nacionalismo y liberalismo económicos en la Argentina, 1860–1880* (Buenos Aires: Solar-Hachette, 1971), 207–230; Dardo Cúneo, *Comportamiento y crisis de la clase empresaria* (Buenos Aires: Pleamar, 1967); María Inés Barbero and Susana Felder, "Industriales italianos y asociaciones empresarias en la Argentina: El caso de la Unión Industrial (1887–1930)," *Estudios Migratorios Latinoamericanos*, August–December 1987, (6–7), 155–179; Jorge Schvarzer, *Empresarios del pasado: La Unión Industrial Argentina* (Buenos Aires: Centro de Investigaciones Sociales sobre el Estado y la Administración-Imago Mundi, 1991), chapter 1; and Sharkey, "Unión Industrial Argentina," ch. 2.

316 Notes to Chapter 5

12. *Boletín de la Unión Industrial Argentina* (hereafter cited as *BUIA*), May 22, 1889, 3 and May 29, 1889, 2.

13. *BUIA*, October 20, 1902, 21. For the lack of interest among industrialists, see BUIA, September 12, 1889, 3; October 1, 1891, 1–2; February 15, 1893, 3; October 10, 1897, 19–20; and December 20, 1898, 1.

14. *La Nación*, July 19, 1899, 5; Schvarzer, *Empresarios del pasado*.

15. *BUIA*, January 15, 1893, 1.

16. *El País*, May 8, 1903, 5; May 20, 1903, 5; May 23, 1903, 5; May 24, 1903, 5.

17. *La Vanguardia*, Buenos Aires, July 29, 1899, quoted in Sharkey, "Unión Industrial Argentina," 145–46.

18. *The Review of the River Plate*, Buenos Aires, (hereafter cited as *RRP*), January 9, 1904, 57; and *BUIA*, February 15, 1904, 22 and June 15, 1907, 54.

19. Taken from an interview at *La Prensa* reproduced in *BUIA*, August 15, 1893, 2.

20. *La Nación*, December 17, 1894, 5.

21. *La Prensa*, December 12, 1891, 1.

22. For comparative wages between Argentina and Italy, see Roberto Cortés Conde, *El progreso Argentino, 1880–1914* (Buenos Aires: Sudamericana, 1979), chapter 4.

23. Bagley S.A. Archives, *Memorias y Balances* (Annual Memories and Balance Sheet), 1925; 1930; and 1931.

24. Herman Brock, *Boots and Shoes, Leather, and Supplies in Argentina, Uruguay, and Paraguay*, USDCBFDC, Special Agents Series, no. 177 (Washington, DC: GPO, 1919), 52.

25. Maxine Berg, *The Age of Manufactures, 1700–1820: Industry Innovation and Work in Britain* (London: Routledge, 1994); and Sidney Pollard, *The Genesis of Modern Management* (London: Arnold, 1965), 30–37.

26. Agnete Raaschou-Nielsen, "The Organizational History of the Firm: The Putting-Out System in Denmark Around 1900," *Scandinavian Economic History Review*, 1993, *16*(1), 3–12.

27. Censo Industrial de la República Argentina levantado por la Dirección de Comercio e Industria del Ministerio de Agricultura 1908, in Pablo Storni, "La industria y la situación de las clases obreras en la capital de la República," Informe presentado al ex ministro del interior Dr. Joaquín V. González como antecedente para la preparación del Proyecto de Ley Nacional de Trabajo, *Revista Jurídica y de Ciencias Sociales*, July-September 1908, *25*(3), 239.

28. Juan Suriano, "Niños trabajadores: Una aproximación al trabajo infantil en la industria porteña de comienzos de siglo," in Diego Armus (ed.), *Mundo urbano y cultura popular: Estudios de historia social Argentina* (Buenos Aires: Sudamericana, 1990). For seamstress work and the putting out system, see *La*

Prensa, Oct. 19, 1901, 1; and Judith Sweeney, *Las costureras de Buenos Aires*, (1850–1910), mimeograph.

29. Dr. Moorne, *Las industrias fabriles en Buenos Aires: Colección de artíuclos publicados en "El Nacional," Vol. I* (Buenos Aires: Librairie Française de Joseph Escary, 1893), 118–126.

30. For a contemporary and detailed discussion on the census problems, see Storni, "La industria y la situación de las clases obreras", especially pp. 237–40.

31. Storni, "La industria y la situación de las clases obreras," 314–15.

32. Zulma Recchini de Lattes and Alfredo Lattes (eds.), *La población de la Argentina* (Buenos Aires: INDEC, 1975), 149–167; Zulma Recchini de Lattes and Catalina Wainerman, "Empleo femenino y desarrollo económico: Algunas evidencias," *DE*, July–September 1977, *17*(66), 301–317; Ernesto H. Kritz, "La formación de la fuerza de trabajo en la Argentina: 1869–1914," Buenos Aires, Serie Cuadernos del CENEP (Centro de Estudios de Población), no. 30, 1985; and Marysa Navarro and Catalina Wainerman, "El trabajo de la mujer en la Argentina: Un análisis preliminar de las ideas dominantes en las primeras décadas del siglo XX," Buenos Aires, Serie Cuadernos del CENEP (Centro de Estudios de Población), no. 7, 1979.

33. Donna Guy, "Women, Peonage, and Industrialization: Argentina, 1880–1914," *Latin American Research Review*, 1981, *16*(3), 65–90.

34. In clothing, weaving, alpargatas, jute bags, and hat factories with more than one hundred workers, the percentage of female labor was 95 percent, 83 percent, 82 percent, 77 percent, and 49 percent, respectively. See Archivo General de la Nación (Buenos Aires), *Segundo Censo Nacional de la República Argentina*, May 10, 1895, Manuscripts, (hereafter cited as AGN-Manuscripts 1895).

35. AGN-Manuscripts 1895 (See Appendix 4). For criticism on the use of censuses to study women, see Robert W. Smuts, "The Female Labor Force: A Case Study in the Interpretation of Historical Statistics," *Journal of the American Statistical Association*, March 1960, *55*(289), 71–79; Catalina Wainerman and Zulma Recchini de Lattes, *El trabajo femenino en el banquillo de los acusados: La medición censal en América Latina* (Mexico City: Terranova, 1981); and Edward Higgs, "Women, Occupation and Work in 19th Century Censuses," *History Workshop Journal*, Spring 1987, *23*, 59–80.

36. Mirta Lobato, "Una visión del mundo del trabajo: El caso de los obreros de la industria frigorífica. Berisso, 1900–1930," in Armus, *Mundo urbano*, 322.

37. Marcela Nari, *El trabajo a domicilio en la ciudad de Buenos Aires, (1890–1918)*, Informe presentado de las investigaciones realizadas, Universidad de Buenos Aires, 1994.

38. *La Prensa*, October 19, 1901, 1.

39. Horacio Rivarola, *Las transformaciones de la sociedad Argentina y sus conse-*

cuencias institucionales (1853 a 1910) Ensayo histórico (Buenos Aires: Imprenta de Coni Hnos, 1911), 168–69.

40. Segundo Censo Nacional, 1895, vol. III, p. 275.

41. Mirta Lobato, *La vida en las fábricas: Trabajo, protesta y política en una comunidad obrera: Berisso, 1904–1970* (Buenos Aires: Prometeo libros/Entrepasados, 2001).

42. AGN-Manuscripts 1895 (See Appendix 4). Unfortunately, the manuscripts tabulate either the workers' nationality or their gender, but not both. In other words, we have the number of women and men and the number of foreigners and Argentines but not the number of Argentine women, Argentine men, and so on.

43. *La Nación*, December 31, 1902, 5. Donna Guy has suggested that those arriving in the coastal cities from the North filled the vacuum created by the drastic decline in the number of immigrants in the 1890s. See her "Women, Peonage, and Industrialization," 75–76.

44. *RRP*, April 23, 1904, 785. Single status, however, was an administrative classification that did not contemplate whether those women were mothers and/or heads of household. Looking at other immigrant societies' experiences, one tends to think that many immigrant women worked at home in domestic chores. Indeed, in the United States, southern and eastern European male immigrants took for granted their children's labor, while they preferred to keep wives at home. See Alice Kessler-Harris, *Out to Work: A History of Wage-Earning Women in the United States* (New York: Oxford University Press, 1982), 112; Virginia Yans-McLaughlin, *Family and Community: Italian Immigrants in Buffalo, 1880–1930* (Ithaca: Cornell University Press, 1971); and Judith E. Smith, "Our Own Kind: Family and Community Networks in Providence," *Radical History Review*, Spring 1978, *17*, 99–120.

45. *La Nación*, July 24, 1895, 5. For the general context, see Marcela Nari, "El movimiento obrero y el trabajo femenino: Un análisis de los congresos obreros durante el período 1890–1921," in L. Knecher and M. Panaia (eds.), *La mitad del país: La mujer en la sociedad Argentina* (Buenos Aires: Centro Editor de América Latina, 1993).

46. Adrián Patroni, *Los trabajadores en la Argentina* (Buenos Aires: Imprenta Chacabuco, 1897), 94–95.

47. *El País*, January 22, 1900, 5; Storni, "La industria y la situación de las clases obreras", 239; and *La Nación*, December 17, 1894, 5.

48. Clark Naridnelli, *Child Labor and the Industrial Revolution* (Bloomington and Indianapolis: Indiana University Press, 1990); and U.S. Senate, *Report on Condition of Women and Child Wage-Earners in the United States* (Washington, DC: GPO, 1910), vol. IX, 38, 43, 58–60, and 252–53.

49. Alexander Gerschenkron, *Economic Backwardness in Historical Perspective* (Cambridge, MA: Harvard University Press, 1962), 5–31.

50. See Karen Mead, "Gendering the Obstacles to Progress in Positivist Argentina, 1880–1920," *Hispanic American Historical Review*, November 1997, 77(4), 645–75; Marcela Nari, "De la maldición al derecho: Notas sobre las mujeres en el mercado de trabajo. Buenos Aires, 1890–1940," in Hilda Garrido and María Cecilia Bravo (eds.), *Temas de Mujeres: Perspectivas de Género* (San Miguel de Tucumán: Centro de Estudios Históricos Interdisciplinarios sobre las Mujeres, 1998), 139–155.

51. Quoted in Storni, "La industria y la situación de las clases obreras en la capital de la República," Informe presentado al ex ministro del interior Dr. Joaquín V. González como antecedente para la preparación del Proyecto de Ley Nacional de Trabajo, Buenos Aires, 1909, 111. Even Anarchists shared this point. See Marysa Navarro, "Hidden, Silent, and Anonymous: Women Workers in the Argentine Trade Union Movement," in Norbert Soldon, *The World of Women's Trade Unionism: Comparative Historical Essays* (London: Greenwood Press. 1985).

52. *La Nación*, July 29, 1899, 1.

53. *La Prensa*, August 21, 1901, 1.

54. *El País*, January 22, 1900, 5. See also *BUIA*, December 19, 1899, 5.

55. Alberto Cassagne Serres, "La política comercial Argentina relacionada con las industrias nacionales," Tesis presentada a la Facultad de Ciencias Económicas para optar al grado de Doctor en Ciencias Económicas (Buenos Aires: Cía. Sudamericana de Billetes de Banco, 1916), 73.

56. Richard Sennett, *Authority* (London: Secker & Warburg, 1980), chapter 2.

57. Mary Jackman, *The Velvet Glove: Paternalism and Conflict in Gender, Class, and Race Relations* (Berkeley and Los Angeles: University of California Press, 1994), 11.

58. María Inés Barbero and Mariela Ceva, "El catolicismo social como estrategia empresarial: El caso de Algodonera Flandria," *Anuario IEHS*, 1997, (12), 269–89; María Marta Lupano, "Villa Crespo: Una villa obrera entre el modelo higienista y el paternalismo católico," in *Anales del Instituto de Arte Americano e Investigaciones Estéticas Mario J. Buschiazzo*, 1989–91, (27–28), 127–137; and "Organizaciones religiosas y patrones industriales católicos: Política habitacional con refererencia a la mujer obrera, 1890–1930," in Knecher and Panaia, *La mitad del país*.

59. *BUIA*, April 15, 1907, 1.

60. Sharkey, "Unión Industrial Argentina," p. 183.

61. See the series of articles on "La Cuestión Obrera" in BUIA, January 1, 1893, 2–3; January 15, 1893, 2–3; and February 2, 1893, 3. See also Sharkey, "Unión Industrial Argentina," 181–190.

62. *BUIA*, January 15, 1906, 28–29; and October, November, and December 1906, 2–3. A well-known exception was the Sociedad Tipográfica

Bonaerense, an example of a "good union" with which firms usually negotiated. See Silvia Badoza, "The case of the Sociedad Tipográfica Bonaerense," in Jeremy Adelman (ed.), *Essays in Argentine Labor History 1870–1930* (London: Macmillan, 1992).

63. *BUIA*, November 15, 1904, 29.

64. Daniel Bassi, *Unpublished Memoirs of Don Daniel Bassi*, March 1942, Part II, (hereafter cited as Bassi Memoirs), 26–27.

65. Sharkey, "Unión Industrial Argentina", p. 198.

66. *BUIA*, April 15, 1908, 1. See also May 15, 1906, 11–12; and June 15, 1906, 27 and 31.

67. Bassi Memoirs, Part II, 26.

68. *BUIA*, July 15, 1905, 67.

69. Storni, "La industria y la situación de las clases obreras," 305; Manuel Vidal, *Algunos de mis trabajos relacionados con las industrias nacionales* (Buenos Aires: Sociedad Gráfica Argentina, 1916), 11–13; and *BUIA*, June 15, 1904, 1–6; October 10, 1904, 29–30; and November 15, 1904, 25–26.

70. Juan Suriano, *Anarquistas: Cultura y política libertaria en Buenos Aires 1890–1910* (Buenos Aires: Manantial, 2001); Ricardo Falcón, "Izquierdas, régimen político, cuestión étnica y cuestión social en Argentina (1890–1912)," *Anuario, Escuela de Historia, Universidad Nacional de Rosario*, 1986/7, (12), 365–89; and Eduardo Zimmermann, *Los liberales reformistas* (Buenos Aires: Sudamericana, 1995).

71. *BUIA*, May 15, 1900, 3. For the reformist stand, see Zimmermann, *Los liberales reformistas*.

72. *BUIA*, July 15, 1905, 25 and also 21–28.

73. Sharkey, "Unión Industrial Argentina", 198–210.

74. *El País*, May 2, 1903, 3; May 4, 1903, 1; and March 21, 1904, 4; and Ezequiel Gallo, *Carlos Pellegrini* (Buenos Aires: Fondo de Cultura Económica, 1997).

75. *BUIA*, October 15, 1911 and April 11, 1907, 34–35. See Jeremy Adelman, "The Political Economy of Labor in Argentina, 1870–1930," in Adelman, *Essays in Argentine*. For the private nature with which industrialists perceived their relationship with workers, see Juan Suriano, "El estado Argentino frente a los trabajadores urbanos: Política social y represión, 1880–1916," *Anuario de la Universidad Nacional de Rosario*, Segunda época, Escuela de Historia, Facultad de Humanidades y Artes, 1989–1990, *16*, 109–136.

76. The exchange of letters between the police chief Ramón Falcón and a flattering UIA is quite revealing. See *BUIA*, June 15, 1909, 49–50.

77. David Rock, "Lucha civil en la Argentina: La semana trágica de enero de 1919," *DE*, June 1971–March 1972, *11(42–44)*, 165–215.

78. Graciela Silvestri, "El paisaje industrial del Riachuelo: Historia de una forma territorial," Ph.D. dissertation, University of Buenos Aires, 1996.

79. Emphasis in the original.

80. All direct quotes in this paragraph are from Bagley S.A. Archives, *Minutes of the Board of Directors Meetings* (hereafter cited as Bagley, BD), April 29 and 30, and May 2, 8, and 16, 1919.

81. Quoted in Sharkey, "Unión Industrial Argentina," 229 and in Cúneo, *Comportamiento y crisis*, 211.

82. *BUIA*, January 15, 1922, 19–20. For the editorial "La Paz Industrial," see pp. 3–4.

83. Aníbal Jáuregui, "El despegue de los industriales Argentinos," in Waldo Ansaldi, Alfredo Pucciarelli, and José C. Villarruel (eds.), *Argentina en la paz de dos guerras 1914–1945* (Buenos Aires: Biblos, 1993), 189.

84. *El País*, February 9, 1900, 5.

85. *BUIA*, May 15, 1915, 27.

86. *BUIA*, May 15, 1915, 27.

87. Luis María Caterina, *La liga patriótica Argentina: Un grupo de presión frente a las convulsiones sociales de la década del veinte* (Buenos Aires: Corregidor, 1995); María Ester Rapalo and María Victoria Grillo, "Un caso de solidaridad obrera: El conflicto de 1918 entre Bunge y Born y los obreros de sus empresas molineras," in B. de Groof (ed.), *En los Deltas de la Memoria: Bélgica y Argentina en los siglos XIX y XX* (Leuven: Leuven University Press, 1998); and Cúneo, *Comportamiento y crisis*.

88. W. H. Koebel, *The New Argentina* (London: Adelphi Terrace, 1923), 27–30.

89. Sandra McGee Deutsch, *Counterrevolution in Argentina, 1900–1932: The Argentine Patriotic League* (Lincoln: University of Nebraska Press, 1986).

90. Mirta Lobato, '*El Taylorismo' en la gran industria exportadora Argentina: 1907–1945* (Buenos Aires: Centro Editor de América Latina, 1988).

91. Ingeniero Arturo Hoyo, *La organización científica del trabajo y la producción y el problema obrero: Conferencia dada en el "Instituto Popular de Conferencias" el día 2 de junio de 1922* (Buenos Aires: Imprenta Rinaldi, 1922), 7–9; and interview with Mauricio Morris, manager of Grafa S.A. in the 1930s, Buenos Aires, 1986.

92. Barbero and Ceva, "El catolicismo social."

93. Sharkey, "Unión Industrial Argentina", 183 and 181–190.

94. Jackman, *The Velvet Glove*, and Gerald Zahavi, *Workers, Managers, and Welfare Capitalism: The Shoeworkers and Tanners of Endicot Johnson, 1890–1950* (Urbana and Chicago: University of Illinois Press, 1989).

95. Emir Reitano and Manuel A. Fresco, *Antecedentes del gremialismo Peronista* (Buenos Aires: Centro Editor de América Latina, 1992).

96. Barbero and Felder, "Industriales italianos y asociaciones empresariales en la Argentina."

97. *BUIA*, May 15, 1922, 9–16.

98. Roy Hora, *The Landowners of the Argentine Pampas: A Social and Political History, 1860–1945* (Oxford: Clarendon Press-Oxford Historical Monographs, 2001).

99. Cúneo, *Comportamiento y crisis*, 214–15; Colin Lewis, "Immigrant Entrepreneurs, Manufacturing and Industrial Policy in the Argentine, 1922–28," *The Journal of Imperial and Commonwealth History*, October 1987, *16*(1), 96–99; Jáuregui, "El despegue de los industriales", 161–66 and 186.

100. *La Nación*, February 16 and April 2, 1929, reproduced in BUIA, March 1929, 33–35; and April 1929, 33–38.

101. BUIA, March 1929, 54–57.

102. BUIA, September 1929, 40–44.

Chapter 6

1. *El País*, June 6, 1900, 3.

2. Ricardo Ortiz, *Historia económica Argentina* (Buenos Aires: Raigal, 1955), 326–29 and 657, is a symbol of this position.

3. Michael Collins, *Banks and Industrial Finance in Britain, 1800–1939* (Cambridge, MA: Cambridge University Press, 1995), chapters 1 and 2.

4. On the banking system at that time, see J. A. Fernández, *La Banca Argentina: Su actuación y desarrollo* (Buenos Aires: Editores García & Dasso, 1912); Norberto Piñero, *La moneda: El crédito y los bancos en la Argentina* (Buenos Aires: Jesús Menéndez, 1921); Roberto Cortés Conde, *Dinero, deuda y crisis* (Buenos Aires: Sudamericana, 1989); and "Money and Banking in XIX Century," Buenos Aires, Instituto y Universidad Torcuato Di Tella, Serie Seminarios, Working Paper, number 3, 1995; Gerardo della Paolera, "How the Argentine Economy Performed During the International Gold Standard: A Reexamination," Ph.D. dissertation, University of Chicago, 1988; and, with Javier Ortiz, "Money, Financial Intermediation and the Level of Activity in 110 Years of Argentine Economic History," Universidad Torcuato Di Tella, Working Paper no. 36, December 1995; and Andrés Regalsky, "Banking, Trade, and the Rise of Capitalism in Argentina, 1850–1930," Instituto y Universidad Torcuato Di Tella, 1995, in Alice Teichova, Ginette Kurgan-van Hentenryk, and Dieter Ziegler (eds.), *Banking, Trade and Industry: Europe, America and Asia from the Thirteenth to the Twentieth Century* (Cambridge, UK, and New York: Cambridge University Press, 1997), 359–77. Charles Jones maintains that Argentina possessed "the banking system it deserved," a system dedicated only to financing exports. See his "Commercial Banks and Mortgage Companies," in D.C.M. Platt (ed.), *Business Imperialism, 1840–1930* (Oxford: Oxford at the Clarendon Press, 1977).

5. *Anuario Comercial y Bancario 1913*, 3–4.

6. Edward Hurley, *Banking and Credit in Argentina, Brazil, Chile, and Perú*, United States, Department of Commerce, Bureau of Foreign and Domestic Commerce (hereafter cited as USDCBFDC), Special Agents Series, no. 90, (Washington, DC: GPO, 1914), 31; and William H. Lough, *Banking Opportunities in South America*, USDCBFDC, Special Agents Series, no. 106 (Washington, DC: GPO, 1915), 101–102.

7. Samuel Amaral, "Comercio y crédito en Buenos Aires, 1822–1826," *Siglo XIX*, 1990, 5(9), 105–121; and Horacio Cuccorese, *Historia del Banco de la Provincia de Buenos Aires* (Buenos Aires: Macchi, 1972).

8. *Boletín de la Unión Industrial Argentina* (hereafter cited as *BUIA*), January 9, 1889, p. 2.

9. Archivo del Banco de la Provincia de Buenos Aires (hereafter cited as ABP), Libros de Solicitudes Acordadas y Denegadas at the Banco de la Provincia Archives, February 28, 1887, 71 and March 3, 1887, 85.

10. ABP, Legajo 015-2-F. Letter of November 23, 1889. Also, the firm La Argentina found a constant source of financing in the bank. See ABP, 015-2-L. For paper peso value, see Juan Alvarez, *Temas de historia económica Argentina* (Buenos Aires: El Ateneo, 1929), 122.

11. ABP, *Libro de Actas del Directorio del Banco de la Provincia de Buenos Aires* (Minutes of the Board of Directors' meeting) (hereafter cited as *ABP, BPA*) Libro no. 24, December 21, 1885, 274; and Pamphlet of the Club Industrial, ABP 015-2-F.

12. Letters to the Board of Directors, November 7, 1885 and August 25, 1886. See ABP 015-2-F. The center presented the regulations to the bank in order to inform it of the procedures that would support industrial applicants (and asked the bank to inform the club whether its recommended people paid their debts). See *ABP, BPA*, Libro no. 25, September 10, 1886, 186.

13. Letter to the board of directors, January 31, 1885. See ABP 015-2-F.

14. *ABP, BPA*, Libro no. 24, January 12, 1885, 8.

15. *BUIA*, January 4, 1888, 2.

16. *BUIA*, August 8, 1895, 11.

17. *BUIA*, April 2, 1891, 1.

18. Archivo del Banco de la Nación Argentina (hereafter cited as *ABN*), *Memorias del Banco de la Nación Argentina* (hereafter cited as *ABN-MBN*) 1891–92, 9. See also della Paolera "How the Argentine" and della Paolera and Ortiz "Money, Financial Intermediation."

19. *BUIA*, August 1, 1895, 11.

20. *ABN-MBN*, 1894, 16

21. *ABN-MBN*, 1895, 20–22.

22. *ABN-MBN*, 1899, 3.

23. Andrés Lamas highlighted this concept in his *Estudio histórico y científico del Banco de la Provincia de Buenos Aires* (Buenos Aires: Establecimientos Tipográficos de "El Nacional," 1886), Part I, "El crédito." There were four

main mechanisms, for ninety days with the entire return, and with 50 percent, 40 percent, and 25 percent of trimonthly amortization. In credits to industry, the last type prevailed.

24. This period is covered by the *Libros de Actas del Directorio del Banco de la Nación Argentina* (Minutes of the Board of Directors' meeting) (hereafter cited as *ABN-BNA*) no. 2 to no. 18, March 4, 1892, 4; April 27, 1892, 88; June 22, 1892, 53; April 19, 1893, 136; November 27, 1893, 18; December 15, 1893, 43; and January 3, 1894, 64.

25. *BUIA*, December 15, 1893, 1.

26. *BUIA*, May 30, 1888, 1.

27. Juan S. Jaca, *Hernandarias y Benalcázar, o sea al pasado y presente económico, político y social de la República Argentina*, reprinted in *BUIA*, May 30, 1899.

28. *El País*, April 30, 1900, 4.

29. Centro del Comercio, *Informe de la Comisión Especial*, 27–28, 33–34, and 39–40.

30. Ortiz, *Historia económica*, 655–56; *ABN-BNA*, 1894, 16; 1906, 19; 1910, 22; 1913, 24; and 1916, 25.

31. *Monitor de Sociedades Anónimas*, Buenos Aires (hereafter cited as MSA), "Instituciones nacionales de crédito," 1903, *I*, 1903, 145; and Andrés Regalsky, "La evolución de la banca privada nacional en Argentina (1880–1914): Una introducción a su estudio," in Pedro Tedde and Carlos Marichal (eds.), *La formación de los bancos centrales en España y América Latina (Siglos XIX y XX)* Vol II: Suramérica y el Caribe (Madrid: Banco de España, Servicios de Estudios, Estudios de historia económica, no. 30, 1994).

32. See Regalsky, "La evolución," and *Mercados, inversores y elites: Las inversiones francesas en la Argentina 1880–1914* (Buenos Aires, Editorial de la Universidad Nacional de Tres de Febrero, 2002), chapters 4 and 8.

33. F. Agustín Pinedo, *Crítica a la política bancaria en la República Argentina* (Buenos Aires: Talleres Gráficos Rodríguez Giles, 1917), especially p. 17, and "The Banking Development of the Argentine Republic," pamphlet, January 1917, in Biblioteca Tornquist, Bancos 664, p. 7.

34. Cuccorese, *Historia*, 379–98; and Reginald Lloyd, *Argentina in the Twentieth Century* (London: Lloyd Greater Britain Publishing, 1911), 400.

35. ABP, *Memorias del Banco de la Provincia de Buenos Aires* (hereafter cited as *ABP, MBP*), 1906, 7. The bank could grant loans at very low rates, since it had the advantage of being in custody of fiscal and judicial deposits that it received as a gratuity.

36. ABP, Archivo D'Oliveira, 037-2-1, 24 and 21.

37. In 1910, the bank inaugurated the section of *créditos hipotecarios* (mortgage credits), attempting to favor small business. See *ABP, MBP* 1910, 8. The vast majority of these credits went to farmers. See ABP, 001-2-1-1-2-1 and 001-2-1-1-2-2; and Libros de Créditos Hipotecarios, numbers 1 to 6.

38. For Bagley, see Bagley S.A. Archives, *Minutes of the Board of Directors Meetings* (hereafter cited as Bagley, *BD*), June 15, 1910; July 17, 1910; and May 23, 1910. For Braceras, see *Boletín Oficial de la Bolsa de Comercio* (hereafter cited as *BOBC*), February 16, 1914, 238. The list is composed of middle-size and large firms but does not include small workshops, whose names are almost impossible to find.

39. For the case of the sugar industry, see José Antonio Sánchez Román, "El Banco de Londres y del Río de la Plata y el negocio azucarero en Tucumán, Argentina (1909–1914)," *Revista de Historia Económica*, Spring–Summer 2001, *XIX*(2), 415–447. On the development of private banks, see Andrés Regalsky, "La evolución," and Charles Jones, "British Financial Institutions in Argentina, 1860–1914," Ph.D. thesis, University of Cambridge, 1973. David Joslin has pointed out the conservatism of the Banco de Londres y Río de la Plata in *A Century of Banking in Latin America* (London and New York: Oxford University Press, 1963).

40. Andrés Regalsky, "¿Una experiencia de banca industrial en la Argentina exportadora? El Banco Francés del Río de la Plata, 1905–1914," *Anuario del Centro de Estudios Históricos de Córdoba*, 2001, *I*(1), 219–45.

41. María Inés Barbero, "De la Compañía General de Fósforos al Grupo Fabril: Origen y desarrollo de un grupo económico en la Argentina (1889–1965)," mimeograph, 2001; Regalsky, "La evolución," 59; *Finanzas, comercio e industria en la República Argentina*, Buenos Aires (hereafter cited as *Finanzas*), 1898, (1), 39 and 78; and Banco de Italia y Río de la Plata, *100 Años al Servicio del País, 1872–1972* (Buenos Aires, Frigerio Artes Gráficas S.A.C.I., 1972).

42. The Banco de Italia and Río de la Plata board included important industrialists such as E. Mignaquy (Bagley), Manuel Magdalena, and Antonio Saralegui (both of La Cantábrica). In 1909, Carlos Lockwood (La Primitiva) became director of the bank. See Lloyd, *Argentina*, 402, 415, and 420; and *MSA*, 1903, *I*, 208–209. For the U.S. case, see Naomi Lamoreaux, "Banks, Kinship, and Economic Development: The New England Case," *The Journal of Economic History*, September 1986, *46*(3), 647–67.

43. Stephen Haber, "Industrial Concentration and the Capital Markets: A Comparative Study of Brazil, Mexico, and the United States, 1830–1930," *The Journal of Economic History*, September 1991, *51*(3), 559–80; and "Financial Markets and Industrial Development: A Comparative Study of Governmental Regulation, Financial Innovation, and Industrial Structure in Brazil and Mexico, 1840–1930," in Stephen Haber (ed.), *How Latin America Fell Behind* (Stanford, CA: Stanford University Press, 1997). See also Noel Maureer and Stephen Haber, "Institutional Change and Economic Growth: Banks, Financial Markets, and Mexican Industrialization, 1878–1913," in Jeffrey L. Bortz and Stephen Haber (eds.), *The Mexican Economy, 1870–1930: Essays on the*

Economic History of Institutions, Revolution and Growth (Stanford, CA: Stanford University Press, 2002).

44. Cortés Conde, "Money and Banking."

45. *Finanzas*, 1898, (1), 31.

46. *El País*, October 1, 1901, 5.

47. Cuccorese, *Historia*, 379–98; and Lía Sanucci, *Historia del Banco de la Provincia de Buenos Aires: 1822–1946* (Buenos Aires: Editorial del Banco de la Provincia de Buenos Aires, 1993), 133–34 and 147–156.

48. Guy, "La industria Argentina, 1870–1940,"

49. Guy, "La industria Argentina, 1870–1940"; and Paul Lewis, *The Crisis of Argentine Capitalism* (Chapel Hill and London: The University of North Carolina Press, 1990).

50. Pablo Gerchunoff, Fernando Rocchi, and Gastón Rossi, "Un hito en la historia Argentina: La crisis de 1890, sus orígenes y sus efectos," paper presented at the Terceras Jornadas de Historia, Universidad Torcuato Di Tella, September 2003.

51. *La Bolsa de Buenos Aires en su centenario, 1854–1954* (Buenos Aires: Imprenta López, 1954). Without taking into account sugar and flour firms, fourteen industrial corporations (half of them founded before the crisis) listed their shares in the 1890s. *Anuario Pillado de la deuda pública y sociedades anónimas establecidas en las repúblicas Argentina y del Uruguay*, compilado por Ricardo Pillado (Buenos Aires: Cía Sudamericana de Billetes de Banco, 1900), 334–87.

52. Letter from Alejandro to Ernesto Tornquist, Buenos Aires, June 17, 1903, Biblioteca Tornquist, Miscelánea no. 715, Sobre 1, Items 52–54.

53. The new publication was the *Boletín Oficial de la Bolsa de Comercio*.

54. *El País*, March 5, 1904, 4–5.

55. Alfredo P. Calatayud, "Operaciones de Bolsa," Tesis presentada para optar al grado de Doctor en Jurisprudencia. UBA, Facultad de Derecho y Ciencias Sociales (Buenos Aires: Imprenta La Victoria, 1903), 16–19.

56. *Anuario Comercial y Bancario de la República Argentina* (Buenos Aires: Peuser, 1913), 81.

57. *ABN-MBN*, 1910, 7; and Dionisio Donno, "Bolsas de Comercio," Tesis presentada para optar al grado de doctor en Derecho y Ciencias Sociales (Santa Fé: Imprenta, litografía y encuadernación Sanatín Hnos, 1917).

58. Ernesto Tornquist & Co. Limitada, *Confidential Report of 5 March 1915*, in Archivo General de la Nación, Buenos Aires, Archivo Victorino de la Plaza (hereafter cited as AGN, AVP), legajo 5-7-7, 9.

59. Leonard Nakamura and Carlos Zarazaga, "Economic Growth in Argentina in the Period 1900–1930: Some Evidence from Stock Returns," in John Coatsworth and Alan Taylor (eds.), *Latin America and the World Economy Since 1800* (Cambridge, MA: Harvard University Press, 1998).

60. Ezequiel Leguina, "Bolsa de Comercio," Tesis para optar al grado de doctor en jurisprudencia y al premio "Centro Jurídico," Universidad de

Buenos Aires, Facultad de Derecho y Ciencias Sociales (Buenos Aires: Imprenta Europea de M.A. Rosas, 1903); Bolsa de Comercio de Buenos Aires, *Estatutos y Reglamento General, sancionados el 3 de noviembre de 1904, reformados el 25 de septiembre de 1908 y el 24 de julio de 1914* (Buenos Aires: Talleres Gráficos de Juan Perrotti, 1915); and Hiram G. Calógero and Alberto Arévalo, *Bolsa de Comercio* (Rosario: Talleres Gráficos de Emilio Frenner, 1917).

61. Yovanna Pineda has made other estimates of profitability, such as the return on stockholder's equity and the return on physical capital, and had reached the same conclusion. Indeed, she has dedicated a chapter to explaining the consequences of the double-digit rations of profits in industrial firms. See her "The Firm in Early Argentine Industrialization, 1890–1930: A Study of Fifty-Five Joint-Stock Companies' Owners, Finance Sources, Productivity, and Profits," Ph.D. dissertation, University of California, Los Angeles, 2002, chapter 4.

62. The yield is a widely used rate of capital return that represents the percentage derived from dividing the annual return from any investment by the amount of the investment.

63. *BOBC*, January 1, 1912, 14–16; and January 6, 1919, 16–18.

64. Gastón Lestard, "Aspectos de la economía bancaria Argentina," *La Nación*, February 24, 1928; and S. Rosenthal, *"La Bolsa,"* extractado de la Revista de Economía Argentina, no. 285–6, marzo–abril 1942 (Buenos Aires: Guillermo Kraft, 1942), 3–8.

65. Debt securities carrying a fixed rate of interest, issued by a company and secured on its assets. See David W. Pearce, *The MIT Dictionary of Modern Economics* (Cambridge, MA: MIT University Press, 1992), 96.

66. Haber, "Industrial Concentration and the Capital Markets," 571. For my analysis, I consider outstanding debts as bonds and accounts payable (obligaciones hipotecarias and obligaciones a pagar).

67. Roberto A. Ramm Doman, *Manual de la Bolsa de Comercio de Buenos Aires* (Buenos Aires: n.p., 1912), 261–62, 277–78. La Martona, Alpargatas, Bieckert, and Quilmes also issued bonds in Europe. See Ramm Doman, *Manual*, 265–66; Leandro Gutiérrez and Juan Carlos Korol, "Historia de empresas y crecimiento industrial en la Argentina: El caso de la Fábrica Argentina de Alpargatas," in *Desarrollo Económico* (hereafter cited as *DE*), October–December 1988, *28*(111), 420; and Carlos Lix Klett, *Estudios sobre producción, comercio, finanzas e intereses generales de la República Argentina,* Vol. I (Buenos Aires: Establecimientos tipográficos de Tailhade y Roselli, 1900), 472–73.

68. *MSA*, 1912, *XIII*, 43; and 1914, *XVIII*, 198.

69. See the relationship that Stephen Haber establishes between concentration of capital and financial access problems in his "Institutional Change and Economic Growth."

70. *BUIA*, October 3, 1888, 5; February 13, 1890; May 1, 1890, 3–4; September 12, 1889, 4; February 6, 1890, 1, and November 20, 1899, 11;

Cía. Fabril Financiera S.A., *Historia de un grupo de empresas industriales en la Argentina, 1888–1948* (Buenos Aires: Fabril Financiera, 1948), 4; and *BUIA*, September 12, 1889; Manuel Chueco, *Los pioneers de la industria Argentina*, Vols. 1 and 2 (Buenos Aires: Peuser, 1886 and 1896), 324–39; Gutiérrez and Korol, "Historia," 405–6; and Lloyd, *Argentina*, 423. Quilmes brewery opened as a corporation with legal site in Paris but works in Argentina. See Lix Klett, *Estudios*, vol. 1, 472–73.

    71. *BUIA*, May 30, 1899, 366.

    72. Guy, "La industria Argentina, 1870–1940"; Paul Lewis, *The Crisis*; and Jorge Schvarzer, *La industria que supimos conseguir* (Buenos Aires: Planeta, 1996).

    73. *BUIA*, May 30, 1899, 366.

    74. *La Nación*, 1910, 61. Similar to Bacigalupo were the cases of the Cía. Gral. de Envases, The Standard, Elaboración General de Plomo, Cía. Gral. de Tabacos, Cía. Nacional de Muebles S.A., Cristalerías Papini SA, and Curtiembre La Argentina Grunbaum Soulas SA. See *MSA*, 1903, *I*, 238–39; 1909, *VIII*, 131–32; 1907, *IV*, 91; 1906, *II*, 237; 1907, *III*, 54; 1913, *XV*, 102–103; and 1914, *XVII*, 57–58. Sometimes the formation of a stock company did not modify original property, such as the cases of Luis Magnasco y Cía and Angel Braceras. See *MSA*, 1914, *XVII*, 27–29 and 1911, *XI*, 99–101.

    75. Cases of property diversification were Salinas, La Acero Platense, La Cromo-Hojalatería, La Cantábrica, Fundición y Talleres La Unión, Cervecería San Carlos SA, and Manufactura de Tabaco J. M. Ariza. See *MSA*, 1909, *VII*, 243–45; 1909, *VII*, 243–45; 1903, *I*, 238; 1907, *III*, 207–209; 1911, *XII*, 354; 1912, *XIV*, 258; 1914, *XVIII*, 202; *and 1911*, *XII*, 354–55; *BOBC, I*, 2; and *MSA*, 1911, *XII*, 192; 1906, *II*, 108–112; 1913, *XVI*, 110–11; and 1915, *XIX*, 65–66. Cases of majority control by the Tornquist Group were Ferrum, Conen, and TAMET, and of minority participation were J. Soulas, Thompson, Piccardo, and Rigolleau. See *MSA*, 1911, *XII*, 264; 1903, *I*, 37; 1909, *VII*, 81–82; 1916, *XXI*, 182–84; 1916, *XXII*, 222; 1913, *XVI*, 27–29; and 1913, *XVI*, 63–4; and *BOBC*, December 31, 1908, 473–74.

    76. This was the case of the Cía. Metalúrgica Argentina, Cía. Tabacalera Argentina S.A., Hilanderías Argentinas de Algodón, La Unión, La Vascongada, La Martona, La Galvanizadora S.A., Cía Textil Sud Americana, Cía. Fosforera Argentina, Fábrica Nacional de Cerveza, Cía. Nacional de Pólvora S.A., Gran Destilería de Buenos Aires Cusenier, Cía Nacional de Tabacos, Cía Nacional de Aceites, La Refinadora de Aceites, Cía. Metalúrgica Argentina, and Cía Manufactura del Plata. See *MSA*, 1909, *VIII*, 202; 1913, *XV*, 235–36; and 1908, *VI*(37), 230; Ramm Doman, *Manual*, 266–69; and *MSA*, 1911, *XI*, 28; 1912, *XIII*, 229; 1903, *I*, 252–53; 1907, *III*, 102; 1907, *IV*, 265–66; 1907, *V*, 256; 1912, *XIII*, 77–78; 1909, *VIII*, 35; 1913, *XV*, 224–25; 1908, *VI*(34), 141; 1909, *VII*, 142; 1909, *VIII*, 202; and 1906, *II*, 108.

77. Ramm Doman, *Manual*, 259–60 and 273–74; and *MSA*, 1912, *XIII*, 267; and 1909, *VII*, 8.

78. *MSA*, 1912, *XIV*, 154; and *The Times*, London, December 30, 1922. For the Cía Nacional de Tabacos S.A. (The Argentine Tobacco Co), see *MSA*, 1913, *XV*, 224–25. Irving Stone has considered that British investments in industry grew substantially between 1895 and 1913, albeit by including as "industrial" various service activities. See his "British Direct and Portfolio Investment in Latin America before 1914," *Journal of Economic History*, 1977, (37), 690–722.

79. For the "Argentine circle," see letter of Estanislao Zeballos, April 1, 1908, enclosed in United Kingdom, Public Record Office Archives, Foreign Office (hereafter cited as FO), 368/186, no. 23 Commercial, April 3, Townley, 1908. The main Belgian industrial investments before the 1920s were textile firm Gratry and shoe producer Fábrica Nacional de Calzado. The largest German firm was Sternberg. See Lloyd, *Argentina*, 424; and Francesco Scardin, *La Argentina y el trabajo* (Buenos Aires: Jacobo Peuser, 1906), 534–35. Among the Italian firms, textile Enrico Dell' Acqua highlighted the production of hosiery and fabric. See Luigi Einaudi, *Un principe mercante: Studio sulla espansione coloniale Italiana* (Torino: Bocca, 1900); Scardin, *La Argentina*, 520–23; and *MSA*, 1913, *XV*, 1913, 224–25; and 1911, *XII*, 103.

80. Javier Villanueva, "El origen de la industrialización Argentina," *DE*, October–December 1972, *12*(47), 451–76; and Eduardo Jorge, *Industria y concentración económica: Desde principios del siglo hasta el peronismo* (Buenos Aires: Siglo XXI, 1973).

81. Scardin, *La Argentina*, 498. For similar cases, see Chueco, *Los pioneers de la industria*.

82. *BUIA*, May 30, 1899, 366.

83. *MSA*, 1912, *XIII*, 43; 1907, *IV*, 231–32; 1915, *XX*, 104; 1912, *XIV*, 264; and 1915, *XX*, 136. For the cases of firms with a high level of reserves such as La Argentina, Cristalerías Rigolleau, and Bilz, see *MSA*, 1914, *XVIII*, 224; 1915, *XIX*, 192–93; 1916, *XX*, 59–60; 1910, *IX*, 229; 1915, *XX*, 146; and 1910, *IX*, 229. For the Fábrica Argentina de Alpargatas, see Gutiérrez and Korol, "Historia," 415. For the surprise, see *MSA*, 1912, *XIII*, 267.

84. *MSA*, 1911, *XII*, 113.

85. The metallurgical company TAMET followed a similar strategy. See *MSA*, 1914, *XVIII*, 188; 1915, *XIX*, 125; and 1916, *XXII*, 121.

86. José Moya, *Cousins and Strangers: Spanish Immigrants in Buenos Aires, 1850–1930* (Berkeley and Los Angeles: University of California Press, 1998), 285–87; Regalsky, "La evolución," 59; *Finanzas*, 1898, (1), 39 and 78; Banco de Italia y Río de la Plata, *100 Años al Servicio del País*; and Luigi de Rosa, "Emigrantes Italianos, bancos y remesas: El caso Argentino," in Fernando

Devoto and Gianfausto Rosoli (eds.), *La immigración Italiana en la Argentina* (Buenos Aires: Biblos, 1985).

87. *MSA*, 1927, *XLIII*, 60; and 1928, *XLVI*, 155–56.

88. Fábrica Argentina de Alpargatas S.A. *Memorias y Balances (Annual Reports), 1921–1925*; Cristalerías Rigolleau S.A., *Memorias y Balances (Annual Reports), 1924–1925.*

89. *MSA*, 1924, *XL*, 997–98; and 1925, *XLII*, 577.

90. *MSA*, 1926, *XLII*, 171; 1927, *XLIII*, 55; and 1929, *XLVII*, 166.

91. *MSA*, 1928, *XLVI*, 58.

92. *MSA*, 1925, *XLI*, 157–58.

93. *MSA*, 1929, *XLVII*, 71.

94. Nakamura and Zarazaga, "Economic Growth in Argentina in the Period 1905–1930."

95. Daniel Bassi, *Unpublished Memoirs of Don Daniel Bassi*, March 1942, (hereafter cited as Bassi Memoirs), first part, p. 5.

96. I borrow the concept of "immaterial capital" from Giovanni Levi. Levi depicts the creation of a nontangible through the example of a priest who wants to leave some unofficial inheritance to his unrecognised son by using networks as a capital source. See his *L'eredità immateriale: Carriera di un esorcista nel Piemonte del Seicento* (Torino: Einaudi, 1985).

97. Bassi Memoirs, first part, p. 8 and pp. 11–12. For the working of immigrant networks, see Moya, *Cousins and Strangers*.

98. Bassi Memoirs, second part, p. 3, pp. 5–6, and p. 9.

99. Bassi Memoirs, second part, p. 16 and pp. 20, 21, 22.

100. Bassi Memoirs, second part, pp. 22 and 23. For data of the Bassi firm, see *La Nación, 1910*, p. 12.

101. Interview with engineer Mario Piñeyro, CEO, Alejandro Llauró e Hijos S.A., Buenos Aires, 1986.

102. Arturo Goetz, "Concentración y desconcentración en la industria Argentina desde la década de 1930 a la de 1960," *DE*, January–March 1976, *15*(60), 507–548.

103. Archivo General de la Nación, Tribunal Comercial (hereafter cited as AGN, TC), Letra C, no. 6, 1911–1914, (1913) quiebra, 32 v. For a well-documented case of a larger firm's bankruptcy—La Refinadora de Aceites—see AGN, TC, Letra L, legajo no. 62.

104. AGN, TC, Letra C, no. 8, 1921–1922, quiebra, 39 and 39 v.

105. María Inés Barbero and Fernando Rocchi, "Industry," in Gerardo della Paolera and Alan Taylor (eds.), *The New Economic History of Argentina* (Cambridge, MA: Cambridge University Press, 2003).

Chapter 7

1. N. L. Watson, *The Argentine as a Market* (Manchester: Manchester University Press, 1908), 41–42.

2. *The Review of the River Plate*, Buenos Aires, (hereafter cited as *RRP*), November 29, 1902, 931.

3. Roberto Cortés Conde has reckoned the rate of protection for the period 1910–1930. Starting from 20 percent in 1910, it went down during the war; in 1919 it was as low as 7 percent. The trend reversed during the 1920s, reaching the 1910 levels before the depression. See his "The Vicissitudes of an Exporting Economy: Argentina (1875–1930)," in Enrique Cárdenas, José Antonio Ocampo, and Rosemary Thorp (eds.), *An Economic History of Twentieth-Century Latin America, Volume 1: The Export Age* (Oxford: Palgrave-St. Antony's College, 2000), p. 283.

4. Edward Beatty, "Commercial Policy in Porfirian Mexico: The Structure of Protection," in Jeffrey L. Bortz and Stephen Haber (eds.), *The Mexican Economy, 1870–1930: Essays on the Economic History of Institutions, Revolution and Growth* (Stanford, CA: Stanford University Press, 2002), 205–252.

5. In decreasing percentages, duties were as follows: tobacco, 132 percent; wrapping paper and matches, 112 percent; beer in bulk, 112 percent, and in bottles, 92 percent; hats, 72 percent; starch, 65.3 percent; shoes, ties, and ready-to-wear items, 62 percent; spaghetti, 58.2 percent; socks, 57 percent; cigars, 53.6 percent; collars, fabric (silk with cotton and linseed), and cheese, 52 percent; and blankets and chocolate, 47 percent. Francisco Latzina, *Estadística retrospectiva del comercio exterior Argentino, 1875–1904* (Buenos Aires: Cía. Sudamericana de Billetes de Banco, 1905).

6. The substitution rates were as follows: for the period 1900–1904, 414 percent; for 1905–1909, 40.4 percent; for 1910–14, 42 percent; for 1920–24, 53.7 percent; and for 1925–1930, 50.8 percent. Economic Commission for Latin America (CEPAL), *Análisis y proyecciones del desarrollo económico. Vol V: El desarrollo económico de América Latina* (Mexico City, 1959), 159–60.

7. José María Mariluz Urquijo, *Estado e industria, 1810–1862* (Buenos Aires: Macchi, 1969); Juan Carlos Nicolao, *Industria y aduana, 1835–1854* (Buenos Aires: Devenir, 1975) and *Proteccionismo y librecomercio en Buenos Aires (1810–1850)* (Córdoba: Centro de Estudios Históricos, 1995); D.C.M. Platt, *Latin America and British Trade 1806–1914* (London: Adam & Charles Black, 1972), 76; and María Alejandra Irigoin, "Inconvertible Paper Money, Inflation and Economic Performance in Early Nineteenth Century Argentina," *Journal of Latin American Studies*, May 2000, *32*(2), 333–59.

8. José Carlos Chiaramonte, *Nacionalismo y liberalismo económicos en la Argentina, 1860–1880* (Buenos Aires: Solar-Hachette, 1971). D.C.M. Platt has argued that in Latin America the era of state construction, which he termed the "liberal phase," was followed by a period of increasing state intervention. See his *Latin America*, 81.

9. Natalio Botana and Ezequiel Gallo, *De la república posible a la república verdadera (1880–1910)* (Buenos Aires: Ariel, 1997); and Paula Alonso, "Los

orígenes ideológicos de la Unión Cívica Radical", Universidad Torcuato Di
Tella, working paper no. 12, December 1994.

10. Edward Beatty, "Commercial Policy in Porfirian Mexico," 205–252.

11. Cámara de Comercio, *Petición de la Cámara de Comercio al Honorable
Congreso de La Nación con motivo del proyecto de ley de Aduana para 1884 presentado por el Poder Ejecutivo* (Buenos Aires: Imprenta La Nación, 1883), 8.

12. Francisco Seeber pointed out the first issue when relating the opposition for his project of an *impuesto progresivo limitado* (progressive tax) with the
aim of charging the wealthiest. See his *Apuntes sobre la importancia económica y
financiera de la República Argentina* (Buenos Aires: Imprenta de Pablo Coni e
Hijos, 1888), 163.

13. *Diario de Sesiones de la Cámara de Senadores* (hereafter cited as *DSCS*),
October 2, 1884, 687.

14. Cámara de Comercio, *Petición de la Cámara de Comercio al Honorable
Congreso de la Nación con motivo del proyecto de ley de Aduana para 1884 presentado
por el Poder Ejecutivo*, 12.

15. For the political evolution of this period, see David Rock, *State Building and Political Movements in Argentina, 1860–1916* (Stanford, CA: Stanford
University Press, 2002).

16. *La Prensa*, April 11, 1885, 3.

17. Archive de Ministère des Affaires Etrangeres, 58, DP 19, January 26,
1885, Rouvier to Ministre, 109–114. I thank Karen Mead for providing me
with this material.

18. For Mexico, see Edward Beatty, "Commercial Policy in Porfirian
Mexico."

19. Ezequiel Gallo, "Un quinquenio difícil: Las presidencias de Luis Sáenz
Peña y Carlos Pellegrini," in Ezequiel Gallo and Gustavo Ferrari (eds.), *La
Argentina del ochenta al centenario* (Buenos Aires: Sudamericana, 1980).

20. *El Diario*, October 7 and 8, 1894, 1. and October 13, 1894, 1.

21. *El Argentino*, August 21, 1894, 1.

22. *La Nación*, March 22, 1902, 4. On the "Third Argentina," see September 19, 1899, 3.

23. *DSCS*, November 25, 1893, 737.

24. *El Correo Español*, Buenos Aires, October 10, 1894, 1.

25. Darío Cantón, *El Parlamento Argentino en épocas de cambio: 1890, 1916 y
1946* (Buenos Aires: Editorial del Instituto, 1966), 93–110.

26. For the role of the Argentine Congress, see L. C. Fennell, "Congress
in the Argentine Political System: An Appraisal," in Weston H. Agor (ed.),
Latin American Legislatures: Their Role and Influence. Analyses for the Countries
(New York: Praeger, 1971).

27. *El Argentino*, August 16, 1894, 1. On the efforts of these provinces
to lobby national politics, see Jorge Balán, "Una cuestión regional en la Argentina: Burguesías provinciales y el mercado nacional en el desarrollo agroex-

portador," *DE*, April–June 1978, *18*(69), 49–87; Donna Guy, *Argentine Sugar Politics: Tucumán and the Generation of Eighty* (Tempe, AZ: The Center for Latin American Studies, 1980; Orietta Favaro and Marta B. Molinelli, "La cuestión regional en la política argentina: Conflictos y alianzas (1880–1930)," in Waldo Ansaldi, Alfredo Pucciarelli, and José C. Villarruel (eds.), *Argentina en la paz de dos guerras 1914–1945* (Buenos Aires: Biblos, 1993); and José Antonio Sánchez Román, "La dulce crisis: Finanzas, estado e industria azucarera en Tucumán, Argentina (1853–1914)," Ph.D. dissertation, Universidad Complutense de Madrid, Instituto Universitario 'Ortega y Gasset', Madrid, 2001, chapter 6.

28. *La Nación*, August 31, 1894, 5.

29. *Diario de Sesiones de la Cámara de Diputados* (hereafter cited as *DSCD*), November 9, 1894, 491.

30. *El Diario*, December 1, 1894, 1.

31. DSCD, November 14, 1894, 535–36.

32. *DSCD*, December 31, 1894, 1281; July *20*, 1891, 340–42; and November 13, 1895, 236–37; and DSCS, December 22, 1894, 994. In 1898, a Constitutional reform gave the Littoral much more strength in the House than before. Nevertheless, no changes over the issue of protectionism occurred. The number of representatives rose from 88 to 120, and the regional balance changed (the representation from the Pampas districts of Santa Fe and Buenos Aires went from 21 to 40, and the city of Buenos Aires from 9 to 20).

33. *DSCD*, October 14, 1903, 16 and September 5, 1900, 1130. Catamarca's Senator Del Pino supported the protection of pickle production in Buenos Aires. See *DSCS*, December 22, 1894, 1005.

34. *DSCS*, November 9, 1891, 810. Senator Pérez defended hats and tinplate industries, all in Buenos Aires. See *DSCD*, November 30, 1894, 831; December 1, 1894, 844; December 22, 1894, 1005; December 26, 1894, 1027; and December 27, 1894, 1041.

35. *DSCS*, December 26, 1894, 1027 and December 27, 1894, 104.

36. *DSCD*, November 24, 1894, 727.

37. *DSCS*, December 6, 1892, 436.

38. *DSCS*, January 4, 1896, 1035; and Ezequiel Gallo, *Carlos Pellegrini* (Buenos Aires: Fondo de Cultura Económica, 1997).

39. *La Nación*, January 5, 1896, 4; United Kingdom, Public Record Office Archives, Foreign Office (hereafter cited as FO), 368/1, Commercial, no. 64, Buenos Aires, December 27, 1905, Hartford, p. 1.

40. Natalio Botana, *El orden conservador* (Buenos Aires: Sudamericana, 1977); David Rock, *Politics in Argentina, 1890–1930: The Rise and Fall of Radicalism* (Cambridge, MA: Cambridge University Press, 1975); and Roy Hora, "Autonomistas, radicales y mitristas: El orden oligárquico en la provincia de

Buenos Aires (1880–1912)," *Boletín del Instituto de Historia Argentina y Americana Dr. Emilio Ravignani,* 2003, (23), 39–78.

41. *Boletín de la Unión Industrial Argentina* (hereafter cited as *BUIA*), February 26, 1892, 183.

42. Paula Alonso, "The Origins" and "Los orígenes ideológicos de la Unión Cívica Radical," Universidad Torcuato Di Tella, working paper no. 12, December 1994; and Botana and Gallo, *De la república posible.*

43. *La Nación,* December 27, 1894, 3.

44. *DSCD,* December 22, 1897, 513–18.

45. *El País,* March 6, 1904, 4; January 9, 1904, 4; and January 13, 1904, 4.

46. Carlos Malamud, "El Partido Demócrata Progresista: Un intento fallido de construir un partido nacional liberal–conservador," *DE,* July–September 1995, *35*(138), 289–308. See pp. 307–308 for the electoral platform of the party for the 1916 elections.

47. *La Nación,* March 30, 1895, 4; and October 23, 1901, 6.

48. *La Vanguardia,* October 12, 1901, 1. For Palacios' election see *Album biográfico en homenaje de los nuevos representantes del pueblo de la Capital elevados por la voluntad nacional al Honorable Congreso de la Nación* (Buenos Aires: Imprenta J. Tragant y Cía, 1904).

49. José Bianco, "La cuestión económica: Dos partidos en lucha. Conference given in the Ateneo of Córdoba, 1894," in *Orientaciones* (Buenos Aires: G. Mendesky, 1909), 46–48 and 52–62.

50. Botana and Gallo, *De la república posible,* 671 and 675–76. For a more detailed account of the debate, see Instituto Yrygoyeneano, *Hipólito Yrigoyen: Pueblo y gobierno, selección, anotación y ordenamiento a cargo del Instituto Yrigoyeneano* (Buenos Aires: Raigal, 1956), volume III. On Pedro Molina, see Joaquín de Vedia, *Como los vi yo* (Buenos Aires: M. Gleizer, 1954), 209–217.

51. *DSCD,* November 23, 1894, 691 and 707.

52. Agustín Rivera Astengo, *Miguel Navarro Viola: El opositor victorioso* (Buenos Aires: Guillermo Kraft Ltd., 1947), 196; Néstor Tomás Auza, *Católicos y liberales en la generación del 80* (Buenos Aires, Ediciones Culturales Argentinas, 1975) and Héctor Recalde, *La Iglesia y la Cuestión Social* (Buenos Aires: Centro Editor de América Latina, 1985). For Anadón's political career, see Vicente Cutolo, *Nuevo diccionario biográfico Argentino, 1750–1930* (Buenos Aires: Elche, 1958), 159.

53. Contrary to what was thought for so long, the early Radicals were more a remnant of the old liberal past than a force renewing the political scenario. See Paula Alonso, *Entre la revolución y las urnas: Los orígenes de la Unión Cívica Radical y la política Argentina en los noventa* (Buenos Aires: Sudamericana, 1990), chapter 4; Flavio Fiorani, *La fine del caudillismo: Politica e istituzioni liberali in Argentina (1880–1916)* (Roma: Edizioni Associate, 1990), 43–44; and

Hilda Sabato, "La revolución del 90: Prólogo o epílogo?" *Punto de Vista*, December 1990, *13*(39), 27–31.

54. *DSCS*, December 6, 1892, 438.

55. *DSCD*, September 7, 1905, 698–723.

56. *DSCD*, July 20, 1891, 331.

57. *DSCD*, November 9, 1894, 497.

58. *DSCD*, November 24, 1894, 721 and 727. For Berduc's career, see his obituary cuttings from *El Diario*, Paraná, September 28, 1928; *La Prensa*, September 29, 1928; and *La Nación*, September 28, 1928 in Biblioteca Tornquist, Section *Biografías*, 147.

59. *DSCD*, November 9, 1894, 487–88; November 24, 1894, 719; and November 30, 1894, 834; *La Prensa*, October 5, 1894, 4; and *La Nación*, October 31, 1894, 3. See also Roy Hora, *The Landowners of the Argentine Pampas: A Social and Political History, 1860–1945* (Oxford: Clarendon Press-Oxford Historical Monographs, 2001).

60. *DSCS*, December 26, 1894, 1015.

61. *DSCD*, October 17, 1894, 185.

62. *DSCD*, September 19, 1913, 397.

63. *BUIA*, October 20, 1899, 16.

64. *BUIA*, November 20, 1899, 11; and *DSCS*, November 25, 1893, 737. For similar visits, see *La Nación*, October 16, 1894, 4; and *BUIA*, June 15, 1900, 1.

65. *DSCD*, January 3, 1898, 775.

66. *DSCS*, November 25, 1893, 739.

67. *DSCD*, November 9, 1894, 505; and October 22, 1894, 286.

68. *El País*, May 8, 1903, 4.

69. *DSCD*, November 9, 1894, 505; *El País*, May 16, 1900, 5; and *La Nación*, October 14, 1901, 4. As an antidoctrinarian stand, rational protectionism became successful in the university ambience. See Rodolfo Moreno (h), "Proteccionismo industrial," Tesis presentada a la Facultad de Derecho y Ciencias Sociales para optar al grado de Doctor en Jurisprudencia (Buenos Aires: Facultad de Derecho, UBA, 1900); Daniel Antokoletz, "La política aduanera Argentina en sus relaciones con la economía política nacional y el derecho de gentes," *Revista de Derecho, Historia y Letras*, XXIX (Buenos Aires: January–April 1908), 36; Alberto Cassagne Serres, "La política comercial Argentina relacionada con las industrias nacionales," Tesis presentada a la Facultad de Ciencias Económicas para optar al grado de Doctor en Ciencias Económicas (Buenos Aires: Cía. Sudamericana de Billetes de Banco, 1916); Esteban Tiscornia, "Nuestro fiscalismo y proteccionismo en el régimen aduanero," Tesis presentada a la Facultad de Ciencias Económicas para optar al grado de Doctor en Ciencias Económicas (Buenos Aires: Cía. Sudamericana de Billetes de Banco, 1916); and Alejandro Nimo, "Nuestro sistema fiscal y

proteccionista en el régimen aduanero," Tesis presentada a la Facultad de Ciencias Económicas para optar al grado de Doctor en Ciencias Económicas (Buenos Aires: Cía. Sudamericana de Billetes de Banco, 1916). For later implication of this perspective, see Emilio Pellet Lastra, *Evolución industrial Argentina* (Buenos Aires: Imprenta y Casa Editora Coni, 1940), 16.

70. *La Prensa*, July 27, 1899, 5.

71. Colin Lewis has suggested that policy "pragmatism rather than an intransigent adherence to liberal principles may account for a cautious approach to the tariff." See his "Industry in Latin America," in Patrick O'Brien (ed.), *Industrialization: Critical Perspectives on the World Economy* (London, Routledge, 1998).

72. *La Tribuna*, September 25, 1899, 1.

73. Ezequiel Ramos Mexia, *Mis memorias, 1853–1935* (Buenos Aires: Librería La Facultad, 1936), 184–5. For the context of the convertibility law, see Gerardo della Paolera, "How the Argentine Economy Performed During the International Gold Standard: A Reexamination," Ph.D. dissertation, University of Chicago, 1988.

74. *La Prensa*, August 10, 1899. 3.

75. Tulio Halperin Donghi, *Historia de la Universidad de Buenos Aires* (Buenos Aires: Eudeba, 1962), 104–119.

76. Alejandro Gancedo, ¡*Despierta Argentina! Guerra a la decadencia* (Buenos Aires: Imprenta de la Revista Técnica, 1901). For a similar perspective, see Luis Eduardo Molina, *Estudio sobre la política aduanera más conveniente a la Argentina* (Córdoba: n.p., 1907).

77. Alejandro Gancedo, "Protección y librecambio: Refutación a las ideas económicas oficiales," in Liga de Defensa Comercial, *Sumario de los pormenores y antecedentes que se refieren a la reforma aduanera y a los tratados que la Liga de Defensa Comercial ha presentado al Honorable Congreso de la Nación*. Datos acumulados por José Praprotnik (Buenos Aires, 1903), 58–89.

78. *La Nación*, June 29, 1899, 5; and July 27, 1899, 5.

79. *BUIA*, August 20, 1899, 3.

80. Hora, *The Landowners of the Argentine Pampas*, chapter 3.

81. *El País*, January 1, 1900, 4.

82. The party mainly dealt with the treatment of municipal ordinances that could affect factories. See *El País* January 5, 1900, 6; January 9, 1900, 6; January 13, 1900, 8; March 16, 1900, 6; April 8, 1900, 6; April 18, 1900, 6; and October 28, 1901, 5.

83. *BUIA*, March 15, 1908, 5. For the political atmosphere, see Donald Peck, "Las presidencias de Manuel Quintana y José Figueroa Alcorta," in Gallo and Ferrari, *La Argentina del ochenta*.

84. Hora, *The Landowners of the Argentine Pampas*, chapter 3.

85. Jeremy Adelman, "Socialism and Democracy in Argentina in the Age of the Second International," *Hispanic American Historical Review*, May 1992,

72(2), 211–38; and Richard Walter, *The Socialist Party of Argentina, 1890–1930* (Austin: Institute of Latin American Studies, 1977).

86. *BUIA*, April 15, 1914, 29.

87. Javier Padilla, *Fomento y protección industrial: Un proyecto de ley, estudios y antecedentes por* (Buenos Aires: 1925), 27–28.

88. Ian Rutledge, *Cambio agrario e integración: El desarrollo del capitalismo en Jujuy, 1550–1950* (Tilcara, Jujuy, and Buenos Aires: Centro de Investigaciones Sociales, 1987), 170–74; and Noemí Girbal de Blacha, "Azúcar, poder político y propuestas de concertación para el noroeste Argentino en los años '20: Las conferencias de gobernadores de 1926–1927," *DE*, April–June 1994, *34*(133), 107–122.

89. Colin Lewis, "Immigrant Entrepreneurs, Manufacturing and Industrial Policy in the Argentine, 1922–28," *The Journal of Imperial and Commonwealth History*, October 1987, *16*(1); Laura Randall, *An Economic History of Argentina in the Twentieth Century* (New York: Columbia University Press, 1978), 85 and 235; and Aníbal Jáuregui, "El despegue de los industriales Argentinos," in Waldo Ansaldi, Alfredo Pucciarelli, and José C. Villarruel (eds.), *Argentina en la paz de dos guerras 1914–1945* (Buenos Aires: Biblos, 1993), 175–79.

90. Carl Solberg, "The Tariff and Politics in Argentina 1916–1930," *Hispanic American Historical Review*, May 1973, *53*(2), 263–66; Lewis, "Immigrant Entrepreneurs;" and Randall, *An Economic History*, 122–25. See also Juan Carlos Grosso, "Los problemas económicos y sociales y la respuesta radical en el gobierno (1916–1930)," in Luis Alberto Romero (ed.), *El radicalismo* (Buenos Aires: Colección Los Porqués-C. Pérez, 1968).

91. José Villarruel, "Los industrialistas y la tutela del Estado," in Waldo Ansaldi, Alfredo Pucciarelli, and José C. Villarruel (eds.), *Argentina en la paz de dos guerras 1914–1945* (Buenos Aires: Biblos, 1993), 205–207.

92. *BUIA*, March 15, 1922, 11–21; and August 15, 1923, 3–6.

93. Victor M. Molina, "Discurso ante la constitución de la liga de defensa comercial (versión taquigráfica)," in Carlos M. Bustos, *Discursos y actuación parlamentaria del doctor Victor M. Molina* (Buenos Aires: Talleres Gráficos Araujo Hnos., 1922), 371–87.

94. *BUIA*, December 15, 1923, 9–14.

95. *BUIA*, December 15, 1923, 10.

96. For the failed income tax project, see Carlos Soares, *Economía y finanzas de la Nación Argentina, 1916–1922*, Vol. II (Buenos Aires: Imprenta Rodríguez Giles, 1922), 135–45. The "impuesto a la renta" (income tax) was not issued until 1932.

97. Carlos Guido y Spano, *Autobiografía* (Buenos Aires: Ciordia y Rodríguez, 1948 [first published in 1879]), 162.

98. One case is the formation of a group of "estadísticos," who had the task of measuring the variables of the country. See Hernán Otero, "Estadística

censal y construcción de la nación: El caso Argentino, 1869–1914," *Boletín del Instituto de Historia Argentina y Americana Dr. Emilio Ravignani*, 1997–1998, (16–17), 123–49; and Hernán González Bollo, "Para medir el progreso de la Argentina moderna: Formación y consolidación de una burocracia estadística nacional en el estado conservador," Master's thesis, Universidad Torcuato Di Tella, 2000.

99. *El Economista Argentina*, August 12 and 19, 1916, 1; David Rock, *Politics in Argentina*.

100. *BUIA*, November 20, 1898, 22; and December 20, 1898, 14–15. For the trajectory of García's career, see *BUIA*, April 1, 1895, 23.

101. The proclamation of state independence from particular interests as a step in an increasingly complex and bureaucratized administration is one of the typical features in the Weberian analysis. See Max Weber, *Economy and Society: An Outline of Interpretative Society*, Vol. 2 (Berkeley and Los Angeles: University of California Press, 1978), chapter XI. With a different perspective, the "libertarian" school has stressed ideological changes, rather than economic complexities, as the real cause for the creation of a "Big Government." See Robert Higgs, *Crisis and Leviathan: Critical Essays in the Growth of American Government* (New York and Oxford: Oxford University Press, 1987).

102. FO, 368/85, Commercial, 83, Buenos Aires, October 10, 1907, Townley, 2.

103. Adolfo Dorfman, *Historia de la industria Argentina* (Buenos Aires: Losada, 1942); and Eugene Sharkey, "Unión Industrial Argentina, 1887–1920: Problems of Industrial Development," Ph.D. dissertation, Rutgers University, October 1977.

104. Cámara de Comercio, *Petición de la Cámara de Comercio al Honorable Congreso de la Nación con motivo del proyecto de ley de Aduana para 1884 presentado por el Poder Ejecutivo*, 28–30. Evaluating who was right and whether aforos were lower or higher than market prices for every single good goes beyond the scope of this book. For the complexities of such a study, see Vicente Vázquez Presedo, *El caso Argentino: Migración de factores, comercio exterior y desarrollo, 1875–1914* (Buenos Aires: Eudeba, 1971), 211–12. For studies on quantitative levels of tariffs in Latin America, see Graciela Márquez, "Tariff Protection in Mexico, 1892–1909: Ad Valorem Rates and Sources of Variation," in John Coatsworth and Alan Taylor (eds.), *Latin America and the World Economy Since 1800* (Cambridge, MA: Harvard University Press, 1998); and Beatty, "Commercial Policy in Porfirian Mexico."

105. Eduardo de Ezcurra, *Legislación aduanera: Concordancias, jurisprudencia y comentarios* (Buenos Aires: Casa Editora de Jacobo Peuser, 1896), 22; Argentine Customs Tariff, in FO, 368/85, paper 11321, April 8, 1907, and supplement in FO, 368/85, paper 14905, May 6, 1907. The conclusion was that "items of freight, insurance, etc. hardly suffice to explain the English and Argentine dif-

ferences in valuation. The cause is probably to be found in the fictitious value put upon almost every article of import by the Argentine Customs House." See Commercial Memorandum for August 1908, enclosed in FO, 368/165, Commercial, Buenos Aires, September 3, 1908, Townley.

106. Ezcurra, *Legislación aduanera*, 22.

107. Hilda Sabato, "Citizenship, Political Participation and the Formation of the Public Sphere in Buenos Aires, 1850s–1880s," *Past and Present*, 1992, (136), 139–63.

108. The customs house was composed of seven divisions dependent on the administrator, and each one contained a chain of civil servants that included inspectors, storage chiefs, peons, and a large number of employees. See *Reglamento General de las Aduanas de la República presentado al Excmo Gobierno de La Nación por la Dirección General de Rentas* (Buenos Aires: Cía Sudamericana de Billetes de Banco, 1894), especially article 192. This structure shows an extreme complexity compared to the old one. For the old structure, see *Ordenanzas reformadas para el régimen de las aduanas de la República Argentina para el año 1877: Unica publicación oficial autorizada* (Buenos Aires: Imprenta de La Tribuna, 1877). For the process of reorganization, see *La Prensa*, October 17, 1894, 6.

109. *RRP*, May 21, 1904, 981; *El País*, January 15, 1900, 6; and January 20, 1900, 3.

110. *BUIA*, November 14, 1889, 4; and November 20, 1900, 40.

111. FO, 368/2, Commercial 8, Buenos Aires, December 10, 1896, A Carnegie Ross, 1; FO, 6/482, Memorandum by A. Carnegie Ross, June 3, 1903, enclosed in Mr. Hartford's Commercial 31, June 4, 1903, 162; and *RRP*, February 11, 1899, 8.

112. *RRP*, February 11, 1899, 8.

113. FO, 6/437, no. 15, Commercial BA, May 16, 1894, Packenham, 142–46.

114. Ezcurra, *Legislación*, 56 and 24. For the general context of the discussion, see Javier Villanueva, "Las primeras etapas de la política aduanera Argentina," Buenos Aires, Instituto Torcuato Di Tella, 2001.

115. Américo Guerrero, *La industria Argentina: Su origen, organización y desarrollo* (Buenos Aires: Establecimientos Plantié S.A., 1944), 33–39.

116. Cámara de Comercio, *Petición de la Cámara de Comercio al Honorable Congreso de la Nación con motivo del proyecto de ley de Aduana para 1884 presentado por el Poder Ejecutivo*, 32–38. For merchant predominance, see Chiaramonte, *Nacionalismo y liberalismo económicos*.

117. For a description of this negotiation process, see the reports of Senators Doncel and Igarzábal in *DSCS*, December 28, 1894, 1059 and 1064.

118. Gallo, "Un quinquenio difícil."

119. Nota de Comisión Revisora de Leyes Aduaneras al Sr. Ministro de

Hacienda Dr. José A. Terry, Buenos Aires, 20 de Septiembre de 1894, *Tarifa 1894*, V. The government saw the work of the commission as revolutionary. See *Mensaje del PE elevando el Proyecto de ley de Aduana para 1895* (Buenos Aires: Cía. Sudamericana de Billetes de Banco, 1894).

120. *La Nación*, October 23, 1894, 3. For the same complaints, see FO, 6/437, Commercial, no. 19, September 20, 1894, Pakenham, 168.

121. *DSCD*, November 16, 1894, 559. Duties could be of two different kinds: specific and ad valorem. In the first case, the importer paid a fixed sum on the article bought abroad. In the second case, the duty was subject to the aforo value.

122. The idea of having a commission started with the rise in tariffs in 1890. A Special Commission was appointed in 1891 but never had a meeting. See Informe de la Subcomisión de Mercaderías Generales, Acta no. 2, August 8, 1894, *Tarifa 1894*, 264.

123. Nota de la Comisión Revisora de Leyes Aduaneras al Sr. Ministro de Hacienda Dr. José A. Terry, Buenos Aires, September 20, 1894, *Tarifa 1894*, III.

124. *DSCS*, December 28, 1894, 1065; *La Nación*, December 30, 1894, 4. The commission—composed of four industrialists, three civil servants, three merchants, and two journalists—made the effort to appear neutral. See Nota de Comisión Revisora de Leyes Aduaneras al Sr. Ministro de Hacienda Dr. José A. Terry, Buenos Aires, 20 de Septiembre de 1894, *Tarifa 1894*, IX.

125. *DSCD*, November 9, 1894, 484.

126. Mensaje del PE elevando el Proyecto de ley de Aduana para 1895, in *Tarifa 1894*, IX–X; Informe de la Subcomisión de Mercaderías Generales, Acta no. 2, August 8, 1894, *Tarifa 1894*, 261–76.

127. Informe de la Subcomisión de Mercaderías Generales, Acta no. 2, August 8, 1894, *Tarifa 1894*, 270.

128. FO, 6/437, Commercial, no. 19, Buenos Aires, September 20, 1894, Pakenham, 169 and 171.

129. Acta no. 15, August 27, 1894, Sesiones generales de la Comisión Revisora. Discusión de los despachos presentados a las subcomisiones, *Tarifa 1894*, CXXXII. For the beer lobby, see *DSCD*, October 22, 1894, 284–85.

130. *BUIA*, March 15, 1907, 39.

131. *DSCD*, November 9, 1894, 491; and *La Nación*, November 24, 1894, 3.

132. *RRP*, December 28, 1901, 111. The recently created proindustrialist newspaper *El País* accused the commission of supporting "low and *sentimental* aforos" more proper of an African colony. The Congress, as usual, came to the defense of industrial interests, and "the Senate and the same House, with foresight and elevated economic criteria happily ended a major part of the free-trade plan." See *El País*, March 22, 1900, 5.

133. Unión Industrial Argentina, *Tarifa 1902*, 13–14, 18–19, and 42.

134. *BUIA*, March 15, 1907, 1; and July 15, 1909, 13.

135. *La Nación*, September 29, 1910, 3.

136. *BUIA*, September 15, 1909, 8.

137. Jeremy Adelman, "State and Labor in Argentina: The Portworkers of Buenos Aires, 1910–21," *Journal of Latin American Studies*, February 1993, *25*(1), 73–102; and Noemí Girbal de Blacha and María Silvia Ospital, "Elite, cuestión social y apertura política en la Argentina," *Revista de Indias*, 1986, *XLVI*(178), 609–625.

138. *El Economista Argentino*, June 24, 1916, 1; August 5, 1916, 1; and July 1, 1916, 1.

139. *Revista de la Liga de Defensa Comercial*, Buenos Aires, January 15, 1914, 5–8.

140. *BUIA*, January 15, 1923, 3–8; and August 15, 1923, 4–5.

141. *BUIA*, January 7, 1923, 7.

142. *BUIA*, February 15, 1922, 5–7; and May 13, 1924, 39–43.

143. González Bollo, "Para medir el progreso de la Argentina moderna." Tulio Halperin Donghi has studied the limits of bureaucracy in the Ministry of Agriculture in "Canción de otoño en primavera: Previsiones sobre la crisis de la agricultura cerealera argentina (1894–1930)," *DE*, October–December 1984, *24*(95), 367–86. For the agronomists group, see Eduardo Trigo, Martín Piñeiro, and Jorge Sábato, "La cuestión tecnológica y la organización de la investigación agropecuaria en América Latina," *DE*, April–June 1983, *23*(89), 99–119; and Noemí Girbal-Blacha, "Tradición y modernización en la agricultura cerealera Argentina, 1910–1930: Comportamiento y propuestas de los ingenieros agrónomos," *Jahrbuch für Geschicthe von Staat, Wirtschaft und Gesselschaft Lateinamerikas*, 1992, *29,* 369–95.

144. Stephen Skorownek, *Building a New American State: The Expansion of National Administrative Capacities, 1877–1920* (Cambridge, MA: Cambridge University Press, 1982).

145. *BUIA*, January 15, 1909, 31.

146. Peter Hall, *Governing the Economy: The Politics of State Intervention in Britain and France* (New York: Oxford University Press, 1986); and Steven Steinmo, *Taxation and Democracy: Swedish, British and American Approaches to Financing the Modern State* (New Haven, CT and London: Yale University Press, 1993). For the working of Argentine federalism in this period, see Fiorani, *La fine del caudillismo*, p. 14.

Concluding Remarks

1. Tulio Halperin Donghi, "1880: Un nuevo clima de ideas," in *El espejo de la historia: Problemas Argentinos y perspectivas Latinoamericanas* (Buenos Aires: Sudamericana, 1987), 241–52.

2. José Luis Torres, *Los perduelis* (Buenos Aires: Talleres Gráficos Padilla y Contreras, 1943); and Aníbal Del Valle, *Juan de Afuera* (Buenos Aires: Porter Hnos., 1941).

3. Natalio Botana, *El orden conservador* (Buenos Aires: Sudamericana, 1977).

4. Charles Maier, "Accounting for the Achievements of Capitalism: Alfred Chandler's Business History," *Journal of Modern History*, December 1993, *65*, 775.

Archival Sources

BUENOS AIRES

Archivo General de la Nación

Archivo Victorino de la Plaza.
Club Industrial, "Movimiento industrial habido en la República Argentina desde el año 1874 hasta el presente. 15 de Septiembre de 1880," Para nuestro socio honorario Dr. Victorino de la Plaza.
Letters received by Victorino de la Plaza.
Ernesto Tornquist & Co. Limitada. *Confidential Report of 5 March 1915.*
Tribunal Comercial.
Censo Nacional de 1895. Manuscripts. Sección Industrias.

Archivo del Banco de la Nación Argentina

Libros de Actas del Directorio del Banco de la Nación Argentina (Minutes of the Board of Directors' Meeting).
Memorias del Banco de la Nación Argentina.

Archivo del Banco de la Provincia de Buenos Aires

Libro de Actas del Directorio del Banco de la Provincia de Buenos Aires (Minutes of the Board of Directors' Meeting).
Letters to the board of directors.
Libros de Solicitudes Acordadas y Denegadas.
Memorias del Banco de la Provincia de Buenos Aires.
Pamphlet of the Club Industrial.

COMPANY ARCHIVES, BUENOS AIRES

Bagley S.A.

Memoria y balance annual, 1900–1930.
Minutes of the board of directors' meetings, 1900–1930.
Libro de Precios (Price book), 1911–1917.
Libro de Inventarios (Inventory book), 1920–1930.
Libro de Cuentas Corrientes, Saldos Deudores (Current accounts book), 1929–1932.

Compañía General de Fósforos S.A.

Archivo del Programa de Estudios en Historia Económica y Social Americana, Facultad de Filosofía y Letras, Universidad de Buenos Aires.
Minutes of the board of directors meetings, 1924–1929.
Estadística General. Libro 1, Avellaneda, Paraná, Tucumán y Santa Fé. Resumen de gruesas vendidas.
Fósforos Victoria y Estrella, Libro de estadística por regiones.

Fábrica Argentina de Alpargatas S.A.

Minutes of the board of directors meetings, 1920–1924.
Memorias y Balances (Annual reports), 1921–1925.

La Cantábrica S.A.

Memorias y Balances (Annual reports), 1903–1914.

SIAM Di Tella S.A.

Archivo SIAM, Universidad Torcuato Di Tella.

COMPANY'S UNPUBLISHED PAPERS AND INTERVIEWS, BUENOS AIRES

Unpublished memoirs of Don Daniel Bassi, written in March 1942.
Interview with Hugo and Jorge Fontana at Talleres Fontana Hermanos, Buenos Aires, 1998.
Interview with Mauricio Morris, Grafa S.A., Buenos Aires, 1986.
Interview with Ingeneer Mario Piñeyro, Alejandro Llauró e Hijos, Buenos Aires, 1986.
Interview with Alberto López, Grupo Roberts, Buenos Aires, 1987.

LONDON

Public Record Office, Foreign Office papers.

PARIS

Archive de Ministère des Affaires Etrangeres.

ROME

Archivio del Ministero degli Affari Esteri.

Newspapers and Magazines

ARGENTINA

Buenos Aires

Album ilustrado de la República Argentina.
Almanaque La Razón, 1917.
Argentina fabril.

Bandera Proletaria.

Boletín de la Unión Industrial Argentina.

Boletín Oficial de la Bolsa de Comercio de Buenos Aires.

Caras y Caretas.

El Argentino.

El Correo Español.

El Diario.

El Economista Argentino.

El País.

Exposición Nacional de 1898. Revista oficial semanal ilustrada. Autorizada por la Honorable Comisión Directiva de la Exposición, presidida por S.E. el Ministro del Interior. Empresa editora y concesionaria: Alvarez-Centeno y Corti.

Finanzas, comercio e industria en la República Argentina. Editado por la "Oficina de Informes Comerciales" de Papke & Dankert. Buenos Aires: Imprenta Roma de Juan Carbone, no. 1, 1898, pp. 40–2.

Fray Mocho.

La Epoca.

La Ingeniería.

La Nación.

La Nación: Edición conmemorativa de la revolución del 25 de mayo de 1810, published in 1910.

La Nación: Edición aniversario de la independencia, 1916.

La Prensa.

La Nación: Un homenaje al Brasil en la fecha de su primer centenario 1822, September 7, 1922.

La Razón: Almanaque 1917.

La República Argentina 1906–1907.

La República Argentina pintoresca.

Monitor de Sociedades Anónimas.

Mundo Argentino.

República Argentina, 12 de Octubre de 1905.

Review of the River Plate.

Revista de impuestos internos, patentes y marcas.

Revista de la Liga de Defensa Comercial.

Revista Municipal.

Revista TAMET.

Córdoba

El Progreso.

La Rioja

El Independiente.

Salta

Nueva Epoca.

UNITED KINGDOM

The Economist.
South American Journal and Brazil and River Plate Mail.
The Times.

Government Publications

ARGENTINA

Anuarios

Anuarios de la Dirección General de Estadística de la República Argentina, 1876–
    1930.
Anuarios de la Dirección General de Estadística correspondiente a 1894. Estadística
    retrospectiva del Comercio Especial Exterior a cargo del Sr. Ricardo
    Kleine. Buenos Aires: Cía. Sudamericana de Billetes de Banco, 1895.
Anuario correspondiente a 1898. Buenos Aires: Cía. Sudamericana de Billetes de
    Banco, 1899.

Censuses

Primer censo de la República Argentina verificado en los días 15, 16 y 17 de
    setiembre de 1869. Buenos Aires: Imprenta del Porvenir, 1872.
Censo general de la provincia de Buenos Aires: demográfico, agrícola, indus-
    trial, comercial verificado el 9 de octubre de 1881. Buenos Aires: Im-
    prenta El Diario, 1883.
*Censo General de Población, edificación, comercio e industrias de la ciudad de Buenos
    Aires levantado en los días 17 de agosto, 15 y 30 de septiembre de 1887.*
    Buenos Aires: Compañía Sudamericana de Billetes de Banco, 1889.
Segundo Censo Nacional de la República Argentina, Mayo 10 de 1895. Buenos
    Aires: Talleres Tipográficos de la Penitenciaría Nacional, 1898.
Censo general de población, edificación, comercio e industrias de la ciudad
    de Buenos Aires, levantado en los días 11 y 18 de septiembre de 1904.
    Buenos Aires: Compañía Sud-Americana de Billetes de Banco, 1906.
Segundo censo municipal de la ciudad de Rosario de Santa Fe (República Argentina),
    levantado el 19 de octubre de 1906. Rosario: La Capital, 1908.
Censo Industrial de la República Argentina levantado por la Dirección de
    Comercio e Industria del Ministerio de Agricultura, 1908.
Censo general de población, edificación, comercio e industrias de la ciudad de
    Buenos Aires, levantado en los días 16 al 24 de octubre de 1909. Buenos
    Aires: Compañía Sud-Americana de Billetes de Banco, 1910.
Tercer Censo Nacional levantado el 1° de junio de 1914. Buenos Aires: Talleres
    Gráficos de L. J. Rosso y Cía, 1916.
Pequeño censo de 1927. Buenos Aires: Instituto Torcuato Di Tella, 1971.

Censo Bancario de la República Argentina, 1925. Buenos Aires: G. Kraft, 1926.

Congressional Debates

Diario de Sesiones de la Honorable Cámara de Diputados, 1873–1930.
Diario de Sesiones de la Honorable Cámara de Senadores, 1873–1930.

Ministerial and Special Reports

Cámara de Diputados de la Nación, Comisión Investigadora de los Trusts. *Informe*. Buenos Aires, 1919.
Dirección Nacional de Estadísticas y Censos. *Informe demográfico de la República Argentina*. Buenos Aires, 1944.
Latzina, Francisco. *Estadística retrospectiva del Comercio Exterior Argentino, 1875–1904*. Buenos Aires: Cía. Sudamericana de Billetes de Banco, 1905.
Memoria presentada al Ministro de Hacienda de la Nación por el Administrador General de Impuestos Internos correspondiente al ejercicio del 1 de mayo de 1891 al 31 de mayo de 1892. Buenos Aires: Imprenta y Papelería "Del Pueblo," 1892.
Mensaje del PE elevando el Proyecto de ley de Aduana para 1895, Buenos Aires: Cía Sudamericana de Billetes de Banco, 1894.
Ministerio de Agricultura, Dirección General de comercio e Industrias. Sección Industrias, Pesos y Medidas, Warrants, "Industria tabacalera" Cuadro tipeado en el ca. 1917.
Ministerio de Agricultura, Anales del. Sección Agricultura, Botánica y Agronomía, Agronomía, tomo II, no. 6, Informe presentado por Eduardo Alejandro Holmberg hijo, Investigación agrícola en la provincia de Jujuy. Buenos Aires. Cía. Sudamericana de Billetes de Banco, 1904.
Ministerio de Obras Públicas de la Provincia de Buenos Aires, *La industria lechera en la provincia*. Memoria presentada por el Comisionado del Gobierno, Ing. Agrónomo Eduardo T. Larguía, La Plata, 1897: Tipografía de la Escuela de Artes y Oficios.
Ordenanzas reformadas para el régimen de las aduanas de la República Argentina para el año 1877. Unica publicación oficial autorizada. Buenos Aires: Imprenta de La Tribuna, 1877.
Padilla, Javier. *Datos sobre industria cervecera recopilados por la Sección Industria, Pesas y Medidas, Warrants de la Dirección General de Industria de Javier Padilla, director general a Honorio Pueyerredón, ministro de Agricultura*, April 15, 1917.
———. *Fomento y protección industrial. Un proyecto de ley, estudios y antecedentes*. Buenos Aires, 1925.
Reglamento General de las Aduanas de la República presentado al Excmo Gobierno de la Nación por la Dirección General de Rentas. Buenos Aires: Cía Sudamericana de Billetes de Banco, 1894.

Seguí, Francisco "Investigación parlamentaria sobre agricultura, ganadería,
    industrias derivadas y colonización (provincia de Buenos Aires),"
    Tenerías, in *Boletín de la Unión Industrial Argentina*, November 20,
    1898, 2–7.
Storni, Pablo. "La industria y la situación de las clases obreras en la capital d
    e la República," Informe presentado al ex ministro del interior Dr. Joa-
    quín V. González como antecedente para la preparación del Proyecto
    de Ley Nacional de Trabajo. Buenos Aires, *Revista Jurídica y de Ciencias
    Sociales, 25*(3), July–September 1908, 237–321.
*Tarifas de Aduana. Estudios y antecedentes para su discusión legislativa por la
    Comisión Revisora nombrada por el Poder Ejecutivo.* Buenos Aires: Cía
    Sudamericana de Billetes de Banco, 1894.
Vidal, Miguel. Informe al Sr. Jefe de Inspección y Vigilancia del Departa-
    mento Nacional de Trabajo Dr. Alejandro Unsain, 25 April 1915 in
    Manuel Vidal, *Algunos de mis trabajos relacionados con las industrias na-
    cionales.* Buenos Aires: Sociedad Gráfica Argentina, 1916.

UNITED STATES

U.S. Department of Commerce, Bureau of Foreign and Domestic Commerce.

Special Agents Series

Leather and Shoe Industry by Arthur Butman, no 37. Washington, DC: GPO,
    1910.
*Banking and Credit in Argentina, Brazil, Chile, and Perú by Edward Hurley,
    no. 90.* Washington, DC: GPO, 1914.
Banking Opportunities in South America by William H. Lough, no. 106. Wash-
    ington, DC: GPO, 1915.
*Markets of the Lumber in the East Coast of South America by Roger E. Simmons,
    no. 112.* Washington, DC: GPO, 1916.
Markets for Machinery and Machine Tools in Argentina by J. A. Massel, no. 116.
    Washington, DC: GPO, 1916.
*Paper, Paper Products, and Printing Machinery in Argentina by Robert Barrett,
    no. 168.* Washington, DC: GPO, 1918.
*Boots and Shoes, Leather, and Supplies in Argentina, Uruguay, and Paraguay by
    Herman Brock, no. 177.* Washington, DC: GPO, 1919.
*Furniture Markets of Argentina, Uruguay, Paraguay, and Brazil by Harold Everley,
    no. 183.* Washington, DC: GPO, 1919.
*Construction Materials and Machinery in Argentina and Bolivia by W. S. Ewing,
    no. 188.* Washington, DC: GPO, 1920.
Advertising Methods in Argentina, Uruguay, and Brazil by J. W. Sanger, no. 190.
    Washington, DC: GPO, 1920.
Textile Markets of Argentina, Uruguay, and Paraguay by L.S. Garry, no. 194.
    Washington, DC: GPO, 1920.

Special Consular Reports

South American Market for Soap, no. 66. Washington, DC: GPO, 1915.
Tobacco Trade of the World, no. 68. Washington, DC: GPO, 1915.
Paper and Stationery Trade of the World, no. 73. Washington, DC: GPO, 1915.

Miscellaneous Series

Foreign Publications for Advertising Goods, no. 10. Washington, DC: GPO, 1913.
Wearing Apparel in Argentina by Lew Clark, no. 68. Washington, DC: GPO, 1918.
Commercial Travelers' Guide to Latin America by Ernst B. Filsinger, no. 89. Washington, DC: GPO, 1920.
Monthly Bulletin of the International Bureau of the American Republics.
United States Senate. *Report on Condition of Women and Child Wage-Earners in the United States*. Washington, D.C.: GPO, 1910.

UNITED KINGDOM

Worthington, T. The Special Commissioner Appointed by the Board of Trade to Inquire into and Report upon the Conditions and Prospects of British Trade in Certain South American Countries. Third Report. The Argentine Republic. London: Eyre and Spottiswoode, 1898.
Department of Overseas Trade. Commercial, Economic and Financial Conditions in the Argentine Republic.
H. O. Chalkley, Commercial Secretary, His Majesty's Embassy, 1919–27; Commercial Counsellor, His Majesty's Embassy 1928.
E. J. Joint, Acting Commercial Counsellor, His Majesty's Embassy, 1929.
H. O. Chalkley, Buenos Aires, Report of September 1921. London: Published by His Majesty's Stationery Office, 1921.
H. O. Chalkley, Buenos Aires, Report of September 1923. London: Published by His Majesty's Stationery Office, 1924.
H. O. Chalkley, Buenos Aires, Report of September 1925. London: Published by His Majesty's Stationery Office, 1925.
H. O. Chalkley, Buenos Aires, Report of September 1927. London: Published by His Majesty's Stationery Office, 1928.
H. O. Chalkley, Buenos Aires, Report of October 1928. London: Published by His Majesty's Stationery Office, 1929.
E. J. Joint, Buenos Aires, November 1929. London: Published by His Majesty's Stationery Office, 1930.

ITALY

Rivista coloniale. Organo dell'Istituto Coloniale Italiano, Roma.

UNITED NATIONS

CEPAL, *Análisis y proyecciones del desarrollo económico. Vol V: El desarrollo económico de América Latina*. Mexico, 1959.

Published Documents, Books and Articles

COMPANY AND CORPORATE PUBLISHED PAPERS

ADOT S. A., Industrial, Comercial y Financiera, *50 Aniversario*. Buenos Aires: Departamento Publicitario Adot, 1942.

Arrocera and Almidonera Argentina. *Nota elevada a la Honorable Cámara de Diputados por Arrocera y Almidonera Argentina*. October 23, 1912, pamphlet.

Asociación Argentina de Fabricantes de Jabón. *La propaganda comercial a base de premios o regalos adjudicados mediante el azar*. Buenos Aires, 1941.

Bagley S. A. *Cien años produciendo calidad*. Buenos Aires, 1964.

Bolsa de Comercio de Buenos Aires. *Estatutos y Reglamento General, sancionados el 3 de noviembre de 1904, reformados el 25 de septiembre de 1908 y el 24 de julio de 1914*. Buenos Aires: Talleres Gráficos de Juan Perrotti, 1915.

Braceras, Angel. *Conferencia sobre intercambio Hispano-Americano, dado por el Sr. Angel Braceras en el Ateneo de Madrid el día 26 de noviembre de 1918*. Barcelona: Tipo-litografía M. Ricas, 1918.

Cámara del Tabaco de la UIA en el primer congreso nacional del tabaco, La. Comentarios y fragmentos bibliográficos. Buenos Aires: Talleres Gráficos de la Cía. Fabril Financiera, 1944.

Centro de Importadores. *El Centro de Importadores en su Cincuentenario, 1907– 1957*. Buenos Aires: Imprenta López, 1958.

Cervecería Bieckert S.A. *Centenario Bieckert, 1860–1960, Historia de una cerveza centenaria*. Buenos Aires, 1960.

César Ambrosio Tognoni, Fábrica de aceites vegetales "La Italia." Pequeña historia de una industria 1876–1951. Buenos Aires: Kraft, 1951.

Club Industrial. *Primera Exposición Industrial Argentina celebrada en Buenos Aires en el mes de enero de 1877: Catálogo de los productos naturales e industriales que componen la exposición*. Buenos Aires: Imprenta de Pablo Coni, 1877.

Comercio, Cámara de. *Petición de la Cámara de Comercio al Honorable Congreso de la Nación con motivo del proyecto de ley de Aduana para 1884 presentado por el Poder Ejecutivo*. Buenos Aires: Imprenta La Nación, 1883.

Comercio, Centro del. *Informe de la Comisión Especial. Nombrada en Asamblea del Centro del Comercio, el 1 de junio de 1897, para dictaminar sobre las causas de la crisis comercial. Informes parciales de los delegados de los gremios*. Buenos Aires: 16 de julio de 1897.

Compañía. Fabril Financiera. *Historia de un grupo de empresas industriales en la Argentina, 1888–1948*. Buenos Aires: Fabril Financiera, 1949.

Dasso y Cía. *La industria textil. Cultivo de las plantas textiles. Explotación manufacturera de sus fibras. Comercio. Necesidad de propender al desarrollo de esta nueva fuente de riqueza. La Nación debe abastecerse a sí misma*. Circa 1914 brochure donated to the National Library in Buenos Aires by Mss. Carballido.

Escasany S.A. *Bodas de oro de la Casa Escasany 1892–1942*. Buenos Aires: Talleres Guillermo Kraft, 1942.

Hombres del Día. 1917. Buenos Aires: Sociedad Inteligencia Sud Americana, 1918.

La Bolsa de Buenos Aires en su centenario, 1854–1954. Buenos Aires: Imprenta López, 1954.

La Cantábrica S.A. *Informes anuales*. Annual Reports, 1904–1914.

————. *La Cantábrica, sus primeros 50 años 1902–1952*. Buenos Aires, 1952.

Liga de Defensa Comercial, *Sumario de los pormenores y antecedentes que se refieren a la reforma aduanera y a los tratados que la Liga de Defensa Comercial ha presentado al Honorable Congreso de la Nación*. Datos acumulados por José Praprotnik. Buenos Aires, 1903.

————. *Informe leído por el Presidente Sr. Antonio León Lanusse en la Asamblea General Ordinaria del 29 de Diciembre de 1914*. Buenos Aires: Imprenta Enrique L. Frigerio, 1914.

Manufactura de tabacos Piccardo y Cía, *El 43*. Buenos Aires, circa 1914.

Primera Maltería Argentina S.A. *Historia de dos conquistas: La cebada cervecera y el lúpulo*. Buenos Aires, 1946.

Proyecto de creación de una fábrica de carburo de calcio en San Roque. Provincia de Córdoba. Basada en la concesión Alfredo Molet. Otorgada por el Excmo. Gobierno de la Provincia de Córdoba el 3 de marzo de 1899. Buenos Aires: Establecimientos tipográficos Revista Técnica, 1899.

Rezzónico, Ottonello y Cía Buenos Aires, *Talleres Metalúrgicos, Fábricas de Bulones, remaches, tornillos, etc.: Talleres de construcción, fundición y mecánica*, pamphlet, circa 1903.

Sedalana S.A., *Diez años de labor: El fomento de una industria nacional, 1924–1934*. Buenos Aires: Kraft, 1934.

Síntesis publicitaria 1938. Buenos Aires, 1938.

Titan Textile Co. *Notas de un proyecto para desarrollar la industria textil argentina: Formación de la Cía Titan Textile Company*, brochure, 1919.

Tornquist, Ernesto & Cía. *Antecedentes de Ernesto Tornquist y Compañía y de sus compañías afiliadas*. Buenos Aires, 1932.

————. *1842–1942. TAMET. Reseña gráfica, origen y antecedentes*. Buenos Aires, 1946.

Unión Industrial Argentina. *Guía descriptiva de la UIA*. Buenos Aires, 1895.

————. *Confederación Argentina de Industrias Textiles*. Buenos Aires, 1934.

DATA AND STATISTICAL REPORTS

Anonymous. "The Banking Development of the Argentine Republic." Pamphlet in Biblioteca Tornquist, Bancos 664, January 1917.

Anuario Comercial y Bancario de la República Argentina. Director propietario Teodoro Marco. Buenos Aires: Peuser, 1913.

Instituto de Economía Bancaria. Facultad de Ciencias Económicas. Universidad de Buenos Aires. *Análisis estadístico y económico de algunas series bancarias y afines en el período 1901 a 1927.* Primera parte. Buenos Aires: Imprenta de la Universidad, 1929.

Pillado, Ricardo. *Anuario Pillado de la deuda pública y sociedades anónimas establecidas en las Repúblicas Argentina y del Uruguay.* Buenos Aires: Cía. Sudamericana de Billetes de Banco, 1899 and 1900.

—————. *Estudio sobre el comercio argentino con las naciones limítrofes.* Buenos Aires: Imprenta de Juan Kidd y Cía, 1910.

Tornquist, Ernesto & Cía. *The Economic Development of the Argentine Republic in the Last Fifty Years.* Buenos Aires, 1919.

COMMEMORATIVE PUBLICATIONS

Album biográfico en homenaje de los nuevos representantes del pueblo de la Capital elevados por la voluntad nacional al Honorable Congreso de la Nación. Buenos Aires: Imprenta J. Tragant y Cía, 1904.

Album de la República Argentina, 1906–1907. Buenos Aires: Talleres Gráficos de L.J Rosso, 1907.

Argentina monumental en la exposición de París de 1900, La. Buenos Aires: Da Costa y Cía, 1900.

Camba, Francisco, and Mas y Pi, Juan. *Los españoles en el Centenario.* Buenos Aires: Imprenta Mestres, 1910.

Centenario Argentino. Buenos Aires: Editorial Cabral, Font y Cía, 1910.

Comitato della Camera Italiana di Commercio ed Arti, *Gli italiani nella Republica Argentina.* Buenos Aires: Stabilimento Grafico della Compañía General de Fósforos, 1906.

Exposición universal, industrial y agrícola de 1880 en Buenos Aires. Buenos Aires: Imprenta de la Oficina Técnica, 1878.

Urien, Carlos, and Colombo, Ezio. *La República Argentina en 1910.* Buenos Aires: Casa Editora Maucci Hnos., 1910.

CONTEMPORARY SECONDARY SOURCES, MEMOIRS, AND TRAVELERS ACCOUNTS

Acuña, José S. "Las aduanas interiores y el 'dumping' interprovincial ante la Suprema Corte." *Revista de Economía Argentina*, April 1929, *XXII*(39), 301–4.

Alvarez, Juan. *Buenos Aires.* Buenos Aires: n.p., 1919.

—————. *Temas de historia económica Argentina.* Buenos Aires: El Ateneo, 1929.

Antokoletz, Daniel. "La política aduanera Argentina en sus relaciones con la economía política nacional y el derecho de gentes." *Revista de Derecho, Historia y Letras, XXIX*, January–April 1908.

Bain, H. Foster, Williams, C. E., and Swanson, E. B. *Las posibilidades de las manufactura de hierro y acero en la Argentina.* Buenos Aires: Talleres Gráficos del Instituto Geográfico Militar, 1925.

Balbín, Vicente. *Sistema de pesas y medidas de la República Argentina*. Buenos Aires: n.p., 1881.

Banco de Italia y Río de la Plata, *100 Años al Servicio del País*. 1872–1972. Buenos Aires, Frigerio Artes Gráficas S.A.C.I., 1972.

Barroetaveña, Francisco A. *La vitivinicultura en el Litoral: El "viñedo Franklin."* Buenos Aires: Imprenta de M. Biedma, 1907.

Battolla, Octavio. *La sociedad de antaño*. Buenos Aires: Moloney & De Martino, 1908.

Bevioni, Genaro. *Argentina 1910: Balance y memoria*. Buenos Aires: Leviatán, 1995 (first published as *L'Argentina*).

Bianco, José. *Orientaciones*. Buenos Aires: G. Mendesky, 1909.

Bilbao, Manuel. *Buenos Aires desde su fundación hasta nuestros días; especialmente el período comprendido en los siglos XVIII y XIX*. Buenos Aires: Imprenta de Juan A. Alsina, 1902.

Bingham, Hiram. *Across South America: An Account of a Travel from Buenos Aires to Lima by Way of Potosí with Notes on Brazil, Argentina, Bolivia, Chile, and Perú*. Boston and New York: Houghton Mifflin, 1911.

Boyce, W. D. *Illustrated South America*. Chicago and New York: Rand McNally, 1912.

Bryce, James. *South America*. New York: Macmillan, 1912.

Bunge, Alejandro. "Costo de vida en la Argentina de 1910 a 1917, números indicadores." *Revista de Economía Argentina I*, July 1918.

———. *Los problemas económicos del presente*. Buenos Aires: n.p., 1920.

———. *La Economía Argentina: La conciencia nacional y el problema económico*. Buenos Aires: Agencia de General de Librerías y Publicaciones, 1928.

———. *Una nueva Argentina*. Buenos Aires: Kraft, 1940.

Bustos, Carlos M. *Discursos y actuación parlamentaria del doctor Victor M. Molina*. Buenos Aires: Talleres Gráficos Araujo Hnos., 1922.

Calatayud, Alfredo P. "Operaciones de Bolsa." Tesis presentada para optar al grado de Doctor en Jurisprudencia. UBA, Facultad de Derecho y Ciencias Sociales, Imprenta La Victoria, 1903.

Calógero, Hiram G., and Arévalo, Alberto. *Bolsa de Comercio*. Rosario: Talleres Gráficos de Emilio Frenner, 1917.

Calzadilla, Santiago de. *Las beldades de mi tiempo*. Buenos Aires: CEAL, 1982 (first published in 1891).

Carrasco, Gabriel. *Descripción geográfica y estadística de la provincia de Santa Fé*. Buenos Aires: Imprenta de Stiller & Laas, 1886.

Cassagne Serres, Alberto. "La política comercial argentina relacionada con las industrias nacionales." Tesis presentada a la Facultad de Ciencias Económicas para optar al grado de Doctor en Ciencias Económicas. Buenos Aires: Cía. Sudamericana de Billetes de Banco, 1916.

Child, Théodore. *Les republiques Hispano-Americaines*. Paris: Librairie Illustrée, 1891.

Chueco, Manuel. *Los pioneers de la industria Argentina*. Buenos Aires: Peuser, 1886 (Vol. I) and 1896 (Vol. II).

———. *La República Argentina en su primer centenario*. Buenos Aires: Cía. Sud-americana de Billetes de Banco, 1910.

Clemens, E.J. *La Plata Countries of South America*. Philadelphia: J.B. Lippincott, 1886.

Comin, José. *El tabaco: Contribución al estudio de los tabacos Argentinos*. Buenos Aires: Talleres Poligráficos, 1906.

Corvetto, P. M. De. *Les industries françaises à Buenos Aires*. Buenos Aires: Librairie Française, 1886.

Daireaux, Emile. *La vie et les moeurs á la Plata*. Paris: Librairie Hachette, 1884.

de Ezcurra, Eduardo. *Legislación aduanera: Concordancias, jurisprudencia y comentarios*. Buenos Aires: Casa Editora de Jacobo Peuser, 1896.

de Marancour, L.M. *Guide pratique d'Europe au Rio de la Plata*. Paris: n.p., 1883.

de Ugarteche, Félix. *Las industrias del cuero en la República Argentina*. Buenos Aires: Talleres Gráficos de Roberto Canals, 1927.

Del Campo, R. "Industrias nuevas." *Revista de Ciencias Económicas, XXVIII*, 1927.

Del Valle, Aníbal. *Juan de Afuera*. Buenos Aires: Porter Hnos., 1941.

Donno, Dionisio. "Bolsas de Comercio," Tesis presentada para optar al grado de doctor en Derecho y Ciencias Sociales. Santa Fé: Imprenta, litografía y encuadernación Sanatín Hnos., 1917.

Duayen, César. *Stella*. Buenos Aires: Maucci, 1909.

Einaudi, Luigi. *Un principe mercante: Studio sulla espansione coloniale Italiana*. Torino: Bocca, 1900.

Fernández, J. A. *La Banca Argentina: Su actuación y desarrollo*. Buenos Aires: Editores García & Dasso, 1912.

Fraser, John Foster. *The Amazing Argentine: A New Land of Enterprise*. London: Cassell and Co Ltd, 1914.

Galarce, Alejandro. *Bosquejos de Buenos Aires, capital de la nación Argentina*. Buenos Aires: n.p., 1886.

Gálvez, Víctor. Seudónimo de Vicente G. Quesada. *Memorias de un viejo*. Buenos Aires: Peuser, 1888.

Gancedo, Alejandro. *¡Despierta Argentina! Guerra a la decadencia*. Buenos Aires: Imprenta de la Revista Técnica, 1901.

———. "Protección y librecambio. Refutación a las ideas económicas oficiales." In Liga de Defensa Comercial, *Sumario de los pormenores y antecedentes que se refieren a la reforma aduanera y a los tratados que la Liga de Defensa Comercial ha presentado al Honorable Congreso de la Nación*. Datos acumulados por José Praprotnik. Buenos Aires, 1903, 58–89.

García, Juan Agustín. "Los snobs." In *Obras completas, vol. II*. Buenos Aires: Antonio Zamora, 1955.

García Merou, Martín. *Discurso del Ministro de Agricultura, Comercio e Industria, Sr. Martín García Merou. Presidente Honorario del Congreso Industrial Argentino.* Buenos Aires: Imprenta L. Mortlock, 1900.

Garzón, Eugenio. *Amerique Latine: Republique Argentine.* París: Bernard Grasset, 1913.

Gesell, Silvio. *La cuestión monetaria Argentina.* Buenos Aires: Imp. La Buenos Aires, 1898.

———. *La razón económica del desacuerdo chileno-Argentino.* Buenos Aires: 1898.

Gestäcker, Frederick. *Gestäcker's travels. Rio de Janeiro, Buenos Aires, Ride Through the Pampas. Winet Journey Across the Cordilleras. Chili-Valparaíso-California and the Gold Fields.* London: T. Nelson and Sons, 1854.

Granada, Nicolás. *Al campo! Comedia de costumbres nacionales en tres actos y en prosa.* Buenos Aires: J. Bonmati, 1902.

Guido y Spano, Carlos. *Autobiografía.* Buenos Aires: Ciordia y Rodríguez, 1948 (first published in 1879).

Guilaine, Louis. *La Republique Argentine: Physique et Économique.* Paris, Librairie des Imprimeries Réunies, 1889.

Helguera, Dimas. *La producción Argentina en 1892. Descripción de la industria nacional. Su desarrollo y progreso en toda la República. Ampliación del retrospecto publicado en LA PRENSA.* Buenos Aires: Goyoaga y Cía, 1893.

Hirst, W. A. *Argentina.* London: T. Fisher Unwin, 1910.

Hoyo, Ingeniero Arturo. *La organización científica del trabajo y la producción y el problema obrero: Conferencia dada en el "Instituto Popular de Conferencias" el día 2 de junio de 1922.* Buenos Aires: Imprenta Rinaldi, 1922.

Huret, Jules. *Del Plata a la cordillera de los Andes.* París: Fasquelle, 1912.

———. *De Buenos Aires al Gran Chaco.* Buenos Aires: Hyspamérica, 1986 (first published in 1911).

Instituto Yrygoyeneano. *Hipólito Yrigoyen: Pueblo y gobierno, selección, anotación y ordenamiento a cargo del Instituto Yrigoyeneano.* Buenos Aires: Raigal, 1956.

Isabelle, Arsène. *Viaje a la Argentina, Uruguay y Brasil, 1830–1834.* Buenos Aires: Emecé, 2001 (first published in 1835).

Jaca, Juan S. *Hernandarias y Benalcázar, o sea al pasado y presente económico, político y social de la República Argentina,* reprinted in *Boletín de la Unión Industrial Argentina,* May 30, 1899.

Koebel W. H. *The New Argentina.* London: Adelphi Terrace, 1923.

Korkus, Emilio. *La industria metalúrgica Argentina. Reseña histórica de su desarrollo.* pamphlet. Buenos Aires, December 1922.

Lafond, Georges. *L'Argentine au travail.* Paris: Editorial Pierre Roger, 1929.

Lagomarsino, Rolando. *Un medio para la consolidación de nuestra prosperidad comercial e industrial.* Buenos Aires: Peuser, 1944.

Lamas, Andrés. *Estudio histórico y científico del Banco de la Provincia de Buenos Aires.* Buenos Aires: Establecimientos Tipográficos de "El Nacional," 1886.

Latino, Aníbal. *Tipos y costumbres bonaerenses*. Buenos Aires: Hyspamérica, 1984 (first published in 1886).

Leguina, Ezequiel. "Bolsa de Comercio." Tesis para optar al grado de doctor en jurisprudencia y al premio "Centro Jurídico," Universidad de Buenos Aires, Facultad de Derecho y Ciencias Sociales. Buenos Aires: Imprenta Europea de M.A. Rosas, 1903.

Lestard, Gastón. "Aspectos de la economía bancaria Argentina." *La Nación*, February 24, 1928.

Lix Klett, Carlos. *Estudios sobre producción, comercio, finanzas e intereses generales de la República Argentina*. Tomo I. Buenos Aires: Establecimientos Tipográficos de Tailhade y Rosselli, 1900.

Lloyd, Reginald. *Argentina in the Twentieth Century*. London: Lloyd Greater Britain Publishing, 1911.

Loncán, Enrique. *Las charlas de mi amigo: Motivos porteños*. Buenos Aires: Gleizer editores, 1923.

————. "El optimismo de los 'guarangos.' In *Las charlas de mi amigo*. Buenos Aires: Emecé, 1981 (first published in 1932).

Malaurie, Alfredo, and Gazzano, Juan. *La industria Argentina y la exposición del Paraná*. Buenos Aires: Editada por la Agencia General de Publicidad de Juan M. Gazzano y Cía, 1888.

Manacorda, Telmo. *La gesta callada: Historia de una industria*. Buenos Aires: Peuser, 1947.

Massei, Galileo. *La Repubblica Argentina nel primo centenario della sua indipendenza*. Milano: Arnaldo De Mohr Editore, 1910.

Miatello, Hugo. *La industria sericícola: Cultivo de la morera y cría del gusano de seda*. Santa Fé: Nueva Epoca, 1896.

Mills George J. *Argentina: Physical Features, Natural Resources, Means of Communications, Manufactures and Industrial Development*. New York, South American Handbooks, 1914.

Molina, Luis Eduardo. *Estudio sobre la política aduanera más conveniente a la Argentina*. Córdoba: n.p., 1907.

Moorne, Dr. *Las industrias fabriles en Buenos Aires: Colección de artículos publicados en "El Nacional."* Buenos Aires: Librairie Française de Joseph Escary, 1893.

Moreno, Rodolfo. "Proteccionismo industrial." Tesis presentada a la Facultad de Derecho y Ciencias Sociales para optar al grado de Doctor en Jurisprudencia. Buenos Aires: Facultad de Derecho, UBA, 1900.

Napp, Ricardo. *La República Argentina*. Buenos Aires: Impreso por la Sociedad Anónima, 1876.

Nimo, Alejandro. "Nuestro sistema fiscal y proteccionista en el régimen aduanero." Tesis presentada a la Facultad de Ciencias Económicas para optar al grado de Doctor en Ciencias Económicas. Buenos Aires: Cía. Sudamericana de Billetes de Banco, 1916.

Pascarella, Luis. *La guerra europea y las industria nacionales: Necesidad de bastarse a si mismos.* Buenos Aires: M & B, 1914.

Patroni, Adrián. *Los trabajadores en la Argentina.* Buenos Aires: Imprenta Chacabuco, 1897.

Piaggio, Juan. *Tipos y costumbres bonaerenses.* Buenos Aires: Félix Lajouane, 1889.

Pinedo, F. Agustín. *Crítica a la política bancaria en la República Argentina.* Buenos Aires: Talleres Gráficos Rodríguez Giles, 1917.

Piñero, Norberto. *La moneda: El crédito y los bancos en la Argentina.* Buenos Aires: Jesús Menéndez, 1921.

Rahola, Federico. *Sangre nueva: Impresiones de un viaje a la América del Sud.* Barcelona: "La Académica," 1905.

Ramm Doman, Roberto A. *Manual de la bolsa de comercio de Buenos Aires.* Buenos Aires: n.p., 1912.

Ramos Mexia, Ezequiel. *Mis memorias, 1853–1935.* Buenos Aires: Librería La Facultad, 1936.

Rava, Américo E. "Historia y estado actual de la industria del papel en la Argentina." *Los ingenieros Argentinos en la industria nacional,* 1914, 123–38.

Rivarola, Horacio. *Las transformaciones de la sociedad Argentina y sus consecuencias institucionales: 1853 a 1910: Ensayo histórico.* Buenos Aires: Imprenta de Coni Hnos., 1911.

Rumbold, Sir Horace. *The Great Silver River: Notes of a Residence in Buenos Aires in 1880 and 1881.* London: J. Murray, 1890.

Sarmiento, Domingo F. *Obras completas.* Buenos Aires: Editorial Luz del Día, 1951.

Scardin, Francesco. *La Argentina y el trabajo.* Buenos Aires: Jacobo Peuser, 1906.

Seeber, Francisco. *Apuntes sobre la importancia económica y financiera de la República Argentina.* Buenos Aires: Imprenta de Pablo Coni e Hijos, 1888.

Soares, Carlos F. *Economía y finanzas de la Nación Argentina 1916–1922.* Buenos Aires: Imprenta Rodríguez Giles, 1922.

Souweine, Paul. *L'Argentine au seuil de l'industrie.* Paris: Ecole de Sciences Politiques de Louvaine, 1927.

Tiscornia, Esteban. "Nuestro fiscalismo y proteccionismo en el régimen aduanero." Tesis presentada a la Facultad de Ciencias Económicas para optar al grado de Doctor en Ciencias Económicas. Buenos Aires: Cía. Sudamericana de Billetes de Banco, 1916.

Tobal, Gastón Federico. *De un cercano pasado.* Buenos Aires: L. J. Rosso, 1950.

Torello, Florentino N. "La industria del calzado en la República Argentina." *Revista de Ciencias Económicas, 30,* May 1928.

Tow, Martin. *Memorias de un comerciante.* Buenos Aires: Editorial La Facultad, 1934.

Varela, Rufino. *Ley de Aduana. Aforos y derechos. Su influencia sobre el comercio y la industria. Reformas convenientes.* n.d.

Vicuña Mackenna, Benjamín. *Páginas de mi diario durante tres años de viaje: 1853–4–5.* Santiago: Imprenta del Ferrocarril, circa 1855.

Watson, N. L. *The Argentine as a Market.* Manchester: Manchester University Press, 1908.

White, Ernest. *Cameos from the Silver Land, or, The Experience of a Young Naturalist in the Argentine Republic.* London: J. Van Voorst, 1881.

Wilde, José Antonio. *Buenos Aires desde setenta años atrás, 1810–1880.* Buenos Aires: Eudeba, 1961 (first published in 1881).

SECONDARY SOURCES: BOOKS, ARTICLES, AND WORKING PAPERS

A.A.V.V., Comité Internacional de Ciencias Históricas, Comité Argentino, Historiografía Argentina, 1958–1988. "Historiografía de la historia regional." In *Una evaluación crítica de la producción histórica Argentina,* 87–147. Buenos Aires: Palabra Gráfica y Editorial, 1990.

Adelman, Jeremy (ed.). *Essays in Argentine labor history 1870–1930.* London: Macmillan, 1992.

———. "Socialism and Democracy in Argentina in the Age of the Second International." *Hispanic American Historical Review,* May 1992, 72(2), 211–238.

———. "State and Labor in Argentina: The Portworkers of Buenos Aires, 1910–21." *Journal of Latin American Studies,* February 1993, 25(1), 73–102.

———. *Frontier Development: Land, Labour, and Capital on the Wheatlands of Argentina and Canada, 1890–1914.* Oxford: Clarendon Press, 1994.

Adelman, M. A. "The Measurement of Industrial Concentration." *Review of Economics and Statistics,* November 1951, XXXIII(4), 269–96.

Aglietta, Michel. *A Theory of Capitalist Regulation.* London: New Left Books, 1979.

Albert, Bill. *South America and the First World War: the Impact of the War on Brazil, Argentina, Peru, and Chile.* Cambridge and New York: Cambridge University Press, 1988.

Aliata, Fernando. "Ciudad o Aldea: La construcción de la historia urbana del Buenos Aires anterior a Caseros." *Entrepasados,* 1992, II(3), 51–67.

Alonso, Paula. "Los orígenes ideológicos de la Unión Cívica Radical," Universidad Torcuato Di Tella, Working Paper no. 12, December 1994.

———. *Between Revolution and the Ballot Box: The Origins of the Argentine Radical Party.* Cambridge: Cambridge Latin American Studies, 2000.

Amaral, Samuel. "Comercio y crédito en Buenos Aires, 1822–1826." *Siglo XIX. Revista de Historia,* 1990, 5(9), 105–21.

Ansaldi, Waldo. "Notas sobre la formación de la burguesía Argentina, 1780–
1880." In Enrique Florescano (ed.), *Orígenes y desarrollo de la burguesía en
América Latina.* Mexico: Editorial Nueva Imagen, 1985.
———. "Las prácticas sociales de la conmemoración en la Córdoba de la
modernización, 1880–1914." *Sociedad*, April 1996, (8), 95–127.
———. "Una modernización provinciana: Córdoba, 1880–1914." *Estudios*,
UNC, 1996–1997, (7–8), 51–80.
———. "Lo sagrado y lo secular-profano en la sociabilidad en la Córdoba de
la modernización provinciana, 1880–1914." *Cuadernos de historia*, No-
vember 1997, *1*(1), 7–43.
———. *Una industrialización fallida: Córdoba, 1880–1914.* Córdoba: Ferreyra
Editor, 2000.
Ansaldi, Waldo, Pucciarelli, Alfredo, and Villarruel, José C. (eds.). *Argentina en
la paz de dos guerras 1914–1945.* Buenos Aires: Biblos, 1993.
Arcondo, Aníbal. "El conflicto agrario pampeano de 1912: Ensayo de inter-
pretación." *Desarrollo Económico*, October–December 1980, *20*(79),
351–81.
———. *Historia de la alimentación en la Argentina: Desde los orígenes hasta 1920.*
Córdoba: Ferreyra Editor, 2002.
Armus, Diego (ed.). *Mundo urbano y cultura popular: Estudios de historia social Ar-
gentina.* Buenos Aires: Sudamericana, 1990.
———. "La idea del verde en Buenos Aires." *Entrepasados*, 1996, *V*(10),
9–22.
Attack, Jeremy. "Industrial Structure and the Emergence of the Modern
Industrial Corporation." *Explorations in Economic History*, January 1985,
22, 29–52.
———. "Economies of Scale and Efficiency Gains in the Rise of the Factory
in America, 1820–1900." In Peter Kilby (ed.), *Quantity and Quiddity:
Essays in U.S. Economic History.* Middletown, CT: Wesleyan University
Press, 1988.
Auza, Néstor Tomás. *Católicos y liberales en la generación del 80.* Buenos Aires:
Ediciones Culturales Argentinas, 1975.
Badoza, Silvia. "The Case of the Sociedad Tipográfica Bonaerense." In
Jeremy Adelman (ed.), *Essays in Argentine Labor History 1870–1930.*
London: Macmillan, 1992.
Bagú, Sergio. *Evolución histórica de la estratificación social en la Argentina.* Caracas:
Instituto de Investigaciones Económicas y Sociales de la Universidad
Central de Venezuela, 1969.
Balán, Jorge. "Una cuestión regional en la Argentina: Burguesías provinciales
y el mercado nacional en el desarrollo agroexportador." *Desarrollo
Económico*, April–June 1978, *18*(69), 49–87.
Balán, Jorge, and Nancy López. "Burguesías y gobiernos provinciales en la
Argentina: La política impositiva de Tucumán y Mendoza entre 1874

y 1914." *Desarrollo Económico,* October–December 1977, *17*(67), 391–435.

Bandieri, Susana. "Espacio, economía y sociedad en Neuquén: El auge del ciclo ganadero y la organización social del espacio, 1880–1930." *Entrepasados,* 1991, *1*(1), 35–79.

———. "The Argentina-Chile Frontier as Social Space: A Case Study of the TransAndean Economy of Neuquén." In Paul O. Girot (ed.), *The Americas: World Boundaries.* vol 4. London: Routledge, 1994.

Barbero, María Inés, "De la Compañía General de Fósforos al Grupo Fabril: Origen y desarrollo de un grupo económico en la Argentina, 1889–1965," in *Universidad Nacional de General Sarmiento. Secretaría de Investigación. Problemas de investigación, ciencia y desarrollo,* November 2001, (2), 327–360.

———. "Grupos empresarios, intercambio comercial e inversiones Italianas en la Argentina: El caso de Pirelli, 1910–1920." *Estudios Migratorios Latinoamericanos,* August–December 1990, *5*(15–16), 311–41.

———. "Treinta años de estudios sobre la historia de empresas en la Argentina." *Ciclos,* 1995, *5*(8), 179–200.

Barbero, María Inés, and Felder, Susana. "Industriales Italianos y asociaciones empresarias en la Argentina: El caso de la la Unión Industrial, 1887–1930." *Estudios Migratorios Latinoamericanos,* 1987, (6–7), 155–79.

Barbero, María Inés, and Rocchi, Fernando. "Industry." In Gerardo della Paolera and Alan Taylor, (eds.), *The New Economic History of Argentina.* Cambridge: Cambridge University Press, 2003.

Barbero, María Inés, Felder, Susana, and Ceva, Mariela. "El catolicismo social como estrategia empresarial: El caso de Algodonera Flandria." *Anuario IEHS,* 1997, (12), 269–89.

Bauer, Arnold J. "Industry and the Missing Bourgeoisie: Consumption and Development in Chile, 1850–1950," *Hispanic American Historical Review,* May 1990, *70*(2), 228–53.

———. *Goods, Power and History.* Cambridge: Cambridge University Press, 2001.

Bauer, Arnold J., and Orlove, Benjamin (eds.). *The Allure of the Foreign: Imported Goods in Postcolonial Latin America.* Ann Arbor: The University of Michigan Press, 1997.

Beatty, Edward. "Commercial Policy in Porfirian Mexico: The Structure of Protection." In Jeffrey L. Bortz and Stephen Haber (eds.), *The Mexican Economy, 1870–1930: Essays on the Economic History of Institutions, Revolution and Growth.* Stanford, CA: Stanford University Press, 2002.

Beezley, William. *Judas at the Jockey Club and Other Episodes of Porfirian Mexico.* Lincoln and London: University of Nebraska Press, 1987.

Benjamin, Walter. *Paris, capitale du XIXe siècle.* Paris: Les Editions du Cerf, 1989.

Berg, Maxine. *The Age of Manufactures, 1700–1820: Industry Innovation and Work in Britain.* London: Routledge, 1994.

Bertoni, Lilia Ana. *Patriotas, cosmopolitas y nacionalistas: La construcción de la nacionalidad argentina a fines del siglo XIX.* Buenos Aires: Fondo de Cultura Económica, 2001.

Botana, Natalio. *El orden conservador.* Buenos Aires: Sudamericana, 1977.

Botana, Natalio, and Gallo, Ezequiel. *De la república posible a la república verdadera, 1880–1910.* Buenos Aires: Ariel, 1997.

Bourdieu, Pierre. *La distinción: Criterios y bases sociales del gusto.* Madrid: Taurus, 1988.

Brennan, James, and Pianetto Ofelia. *Region and Nation: Politics, Economy, and Society in Twentieth-Century Argentina.* New York: St. Martin's Press, 2000.

Briscoe, Lynden. *The Textile and Clothing Industries of the United Kingdom.* Manchester: Manchester University Press, 1971.

Brown, John. "Market Organization, Protection, and Vertical Integration: German Cotton Textiles Before 1914." *Journal of Economic History*, June 1992, *52*(2), 339–51.

Bulmer-Thomas, Victor. *The Economic History of Latin America Since Independence.* Cambridge: Cambridge University Press, 1994.

Burgin, Miron. *The Economic Aspects of Argentine Federalism 1820–1852.* New York: Russel & Russel, 1971.

Burlingame, Roger. *Engines of Democracy.* New York: Charles Scribner's Sons, 1940.

Campi, Daniel (ed.). *Estudios sobre la historia de la industria azucarera argentina.* San Salvador de Jujuy: Universidad Nacional de Tucumán, Serie Ciencia, Colección Jujuy, 1991.

Cantón, Darío. *El Parlamento Argentino en épocas de cambio: 1890, 1916 y 1946.* Buenos Aires: Editorial del Instituto, 1966.

Capitán Nemo (Guillermo Heins). *Ernesto Tornquist: Homenaje.* Reproducción de la obra América industrial y comercial del. Buenos Aires: Cía Impresora Argentina, 1936.

Caron, François. *An Economic History of Modern France.* New York: Columbia University Press, 1979.

Carreras, Albert. "An Annual Index of Spanish Industrial Output." In Nicolás Sánchez-Albornoz (ed.), *The Economic Modernization of Spain, 1830–1930.* New York and London: New York University Press, 1987.

Caterina, Luis María. *La liga patriótica Argentina: Un grupo de presión frente a las convulsiones sociales de la década del veinte.* Buenos Aires: Corregidor, 1995.

Chandler, Alfred. *The Visible Hand: The Managerial Revolution in American Business*. Cambridge: The Belknap Press, 1977.

———. *Scale and Scope: The Dynamics of Industrial Capitalism*. Cambridge, MA: Harvard University Press, 1990.

Chartier, Roger. "Le monde comme répresentation." *Annales Economies. Sociétés. Civilisations*, November–December 1989, *44*(6), 1505–19.

Chiaramonte, José Carlos. *Nacionalismo y liberalismo económicos en la Argentina, 1860–1880*. Buenos Aires: Solar-Hachette, 1971.

———. *Ciudades, provincias, estados: Orígenes de la nación Argentina*. Buenos Aires: Ariel, 1997.

Coatsworth, John, and Taylor, Alan (eds.). *Latin America and the World Economy Since 1800*. Harvard: Harvard University Press, 1998.

Cochran, Thomas C., and Reina, Ruben E. *Entrepreneurship in Argentine Culture: Torcuato Di Tella and S.I.A.M.* Philadelphia: University of Pennsylvania Press, 1962.

Collins, Michael. *Banks and Industrial Finance in Britain, 1800–1939*. Cambridge: Cambridge University Press, 1995.

Converso, Félix E. *La lenta formación de capitales: Familias, Comercio y Poder en Córdoba 1850–1880*. Córdoba: Junta Provincial de Historia de Córdoba, 1993.

———. *Un mercado en expansión: Córdoba 1870–1914*. Córdoba: Centro de Estudios Históricos "Profesor Carlos S. A. Segreti," 2001.

Cornblit, Oscar. "Inmigrantes y empresarios en la política Argentina." *Desarrollo Económico*, January–March, *6*(24), 641–91.

Cortés Conde, Roberto. "Problemas del crecimiento industrial Argentino, 1880–1914." In Torcuato Di Tella, Gino Germani, et al., (eds.), *Argentina sociedad de masas*. Buenos Aires, EUDEBA, 1967.

———. *El progreso Argentino*. Buenos Aires: Sudamericana, 1979.

———. "Some Notes on the Industrial Development of Argentina and Canada in the 1920s." In D. C. Platt and Guido Di Tella (eds.), *Argentina, Canada and Australia: Studies in Development, 1870–1965* (Oxford: MacMillan, 1985).

———. *Dinero, deuda y crisis: Evolución fiscal y monetaria en la Argentina*. Buenos Aires: Sudamericana, 1989.

———. "Estimaciones del Producto Bruto Interno de Argentina 1875–1935." Department of Economics, Universidad de San Andrés, Victoria, Working Paper 3, October 1994.

———. "Money and Banking in XIX Century." Buenos Aires, Instituto y Universidad Torcuato Di Tella, Serie Seminarios, Working Paper, number 3, 1995.

———. *La economía Argentina en el largo plazo*. Buenos Aires: Sudamericana, 1997.

————. "The Vicissitudes of an Exporting Economy: Argentina, 1875–1930." In Enrique Cárdenas, José Antonio Ocampo, and Rosemary Thorp (eds.), *An Economic History of Twentieth-Century Latin America, Volume 1: The Export Age*. Oxford: Palgrave-St. Antony's College, 2000.

Crafts, Nicholas. "Foreign Ahead and Falling Behind: The Rise and Relative Decline of the First Industrial Nation." *Journal of Economic Perspectives*, 1998, *12*(2), 133–210.

Cramer, Gisela. "Argentine Riddle: The Pinedo Plan of 1940 and the Political Economy of the Early War Years." *Journal of Latin American Studies*, October 1998, *30*(3), 519–550.

Cuccorese, Horacio. *Historia de los ferrocarriles en la Argentina*. Buenos Aires: Macchi, 1969.

————. *Historia del Banco de la Provincia de Buenos Aires*. Buenos Aires: Macchi, 1972.

Cúneo, Dardo. *Comportamiento y crisis de la clase empresaria*. Buenos Aires: Pleamar, 1967.

Cutolo, Vicente. *Nuevo diccionario biográfico Argentino 1750–1930*. Buenos Aires: Elche, 1958.

de Rosa, Luigi. "Emigrantes Italianos, bancos y remesas: El caso Argentino." In Fernando Devoto and Gianfausto Rosoli, (eds.), *La inmigración Italiana en la Argentina*. Buenos Aires: Biblos, 1985.

de Vries, Jan. "The Industrial and the Industrious Revolution." *Journal of Economic History, June 1994, 54*(2), 249–70.

della Paolera, Gerardo. "How the Argentine Economy Performed During the International Gold Standard: A Reexamination." Ph.D. dissertation, University of Chicago, 1988.

della Paolera, Gerardo, and Ortiz, Javier. "Money, Financial Intermediation and the Level of Activity in 110 years of Argentine Economic History." Universidad Torcuato Di Tella, Working paper no. 36, December 1995.

della Paolera, Gerardo, and Taylor, Alan M. *Straining the Anchor: The Argentine Currency Board and the Search for Macroeconomic Stability, 1880–1935*. Chicago: University of Chicago Press, 2002.

Díaz Alejandro, Carlos. *Essays on the Economic History of the Argentina Republic*. New Haven and London: Yale University Press, 1970.

Di Tella, Guido, and Zymelman, Manuel. *Las etapas del crecimiento económico Argentino*. Buenos Aires: Eudeba, 1967.

————. *Rentas, cuasi-rentas, ganancias normales y crecimiento: Argentina y las áreas de colonización reciente*. Buenos Aires: Instituto Torcuato Di Tella. Centro de Investigaciones Económicas, 1986.

Di Tella, Torcuato S. *Torcuato Di Tella: Industria y política*. Buenos Aires: Tesis, 1993.

Dorfman, Adolfo. *Historia de la industria Argentina*. Buenos Aires: Solar-Hachette, 1942.

Duggan, Bernardo. "Iron and Steel Production in Argentina c. 1920–1952: Attempts at Establishing a Strategic Industry." Ph.D. dissertation, London School of Economics and Political Science, 1998.

Duncan, Tim. "Government by Audacity: Politics and the Argentine Economy, 1885–1892." Ph.D. dissertation, University of Melbourne, 1981.

Evans, Peter, Rueschemeyer, Dietrich, and Skopcol, Theda (eds.). *Bringing the State Back In*. Cambridge: Cambridge University Press, 1985.

Ewen, Stuart. *Captains of Consciousness, Advertising and the Social Roots of the Consumer Culture*. New York: McGraw-Hill, 1976.

Fairchilds, Cissie. "The Production and Marketing of Populuxe Goods in Eighteenth-Century Paris." In John Brewer and Roy Porter, (eds.), *Consumption and the World of Goods*. London and New York: Routledge, 1993.

Falcón, Ricardo. "Izquierdas, régimen político, cuestión étnica y cuestión social en Argentina, 1890–1912." *Anuario, Escuela de Historia, Universidad Nacional de Rosario*, 1986–1987, (12), 365–89.

Favaro, Orietta, and Molinelli, Marta B. "La cuestión regional en la política Argentina: Conflictos y alianzas, 1880–1930." In Waldo Ansaldi, Alfredo Pucciarelli, and José C. Villarruel (eds.), *Argentina en la paz de dos guerras, 1914–1945*. Buenos Aires: Biblos, 1993.

Feijóo, María del Carmen, "Las trabajadoras porteñas a comienzos del siglo." In Diego Armus (ed.), *Mundo urbano y cultura popular: Estudios de historia social Argentina*. Buenos Aires: Sudamericana, 1990.

Fennell, L. C. "Congress in the Argentine Political System: An Appraisal." In Weston H. Agor (ed.), *Latin American Legislatures: Their Role and Influence. Analyses for the Countries*. New York: Praeger, 1971.

Fernández, Alejandro. *Un "mercado étnico" en el Plata: Emigración y exportaciones Españolas a la Argentina, 1880–1935*. Madrid: Consejo Superior de Investigaciones Científicas, 2004.

Ferns, H.S. *Britain and Argentina in the Nineteenth Century*. Oxford: Clarendon Press, 1960.

Ferrari, Horacio. *Orígenes y desarrollo de la industria lechera Argentina*, UBA, Facultad de Ciencias Económicas, Instituto de la Producción, Publicación no. 39, 1953.

Ferrer, Aldo. *La economía Argentina*. Buenos Aires: Fondo de Cultura Económica, 1964.

Fiorani, Flavio. *La fine del caudillismo: Política e istituzioni liberali in Argentina, 1880–1916*. Rome: Edizioni Associate, 1990.

Fleming, William. "Regional Development and Transportation in Argentina: Mendoza and the Gran Oeste Railway, 1885–1914." Ph.D. dissertation, Indiana University, 1976.

————. *Region vs. Nation: Cuyo in the Crosscurrents of Argentine National Development, 1861–1914*. Tempe: Arizona State University, The Center for Latin American Studies, 1988.

Fodor, Jorge, and O'Connell, Arturo A. "La Argentina y la economía atlántica en la primera mitad del siglo XX." *Desarrollo Económico*, April–June 1973, *13*(49), 3–65.

Fogarty, John, Gallo, Ezequiel, and Dieguez, Héctor. *Argentina y Australia*, Serie Jornadas, Instituto Torcuato Di Tella, 1979.

Ford, Alec. *The Gold Standard, 1880–1914: Britain and Argentina*. Oxford: Clarendon Press, 1962.

Fuchs, Jaime. *La penetración de los trusts yanquis en la Argentina*. Buenos Aires: Cartago, 1959.

Gallo, Ezequiel. "Agrarian Expansion and Industrial Development in Argentina, 1880–1930." In Raymond Carr (ed.), *Latin American Affairs St. Antony's Papers* no. 22, Oxford, 1970.

————. *La pampa gringa*. Buenos Aires: Sudamericana, 1983.

————. "Un quinquenio difícil: Las presidencias de Luis Sáenz Peña y Carlos Pellegrini." In Ezequiel Gallo and Gustavo Ferrari (eds.), *La Argentina del ochenta al centenario*. Buenos Aires: Sudamericana, 1980.

————. "El contexto histórico de la ley de convertibilidad de 1899." In Ana M. Martirena-Mantel (ed.), *Aspectos analíticos e históricos de la convertibilidad monetaria*. Buenos Aires: Academia Nacional de Ciencias, 1996.

————. *Carlos Pellegrini*. Buenos Aires: Fondo de Cultura Económica, 1997.

Geller, Lucio. "El crecimiento industrial Argentino hasta 1914 y la teoría del bien primario exportable." In Marcos Giménez Zapiola, (ed.), *El régimen oligárquico: Materiales para el estudio de la realidad Argentina, hasta 1930*. Buenos Aires: Amorrortu, 1975.

————. "El modelo de poder de la generación del 80: Política cambiaria Argentina, 1899 y 1914." Buenos Aires: Cuadernos de CICSO, 1982.

Gerchunoff, Pablo, and Llach, Lucas. *El ciclo de la ilusión y el desencanto*. Buenos Aires: Ariel, 1998.

Gerchunoff, Pablo, Llach, Lucas, and Salazar, Eduardo. *Argentine economic database, 1875–1930*. Mimeograph, Universidad Torcuato Di Tella, 2002.

Gerchunoff, Pablo, Rocchi, Fernando and Rossi, Gastón. "Un hito en la historia Argentina: La crisis de 1890, sus orígenes y sus efectos." Paper presented at the Terceras Jornadas de Historia, Universidad Torcuato Di Tella, September 2003.

Gerschenkron, Alexander. *Economic Backwardness in Historical Perspective*. Cambridge, MA: Harvard University Press, 1962.

Girbal de Blacha Noemí. "Tradición y modernización en la agricultura cerealera Argentina, 1910–1930: Comportamiento y propuestas de los ingenieros agrónomos." *Jahrbuch für Geschicthe von Staat, Wirtschaft und Gesselschaft Lateinamerikas*, 1992, *29*, 369–95.

————. "Azúcar, poder político y propuestas de concertación para el noroeste Argentino en los años '20: Las conferencias de gobernadores de 1926–1927." *DE*, April–June, *34*(133), 107–22.

Girbal de Blacha Noemí, and Ospital, María Silvia. "Elite, cuestión social y apertura política en la Argentina." *Revista de Indias*, 1986, *XLVI*(178), 609–25.

Goetz, Arturo. "Concentración y desconcentración en la industria Argentina desde la década de 1930 a la de 1960." *Desarrollo Económico*, January–March 1976, *15*(60), 507–48.

Gondra, Luis Roque. *Historia económica de la República Argentina*. Buenos Aires: Sudamericana, 1943.

González Bollo, Hernán. "Para medir el progreso de la Argentina moderna: Formación y consolidación de una burocracia estadística nacional en el estado conservador." Master thesis, Department of History, Universidad Torcuato Di Tella, 2000.

González Leandri, Ricardo. *Curar, persuadir, gobernar*. Madrid: Consejo Superior de Investigaciones Científicas, 1999.

Goodman, Jordan. *Tobacco in History: The Cultures of Dependence*. London and New York: Routledge, 1993.

Goodwin, Paul B. "Anglo-Argentine Commercial Relations: A Private Sector View, 1922–1943." *Hispanic American Historical Review*, February 1981, *LXI*(1), 29–51.

Gravil, Roger. *The Anglo-Argentine Connection*. Boulder: Westview Press, 1985.

————. "El comercio minorista británico en la Argentina, 1900–1940." In Giménez Zapiola (ed.), *El régimen oligárquico: Materiales para el estudio de la realidad Argentina, hasta 1930*. Buenos Aires: Amorrortu, 1975.

Grosso, Juan Carlos. "Los problemas económicos y sociales y la respuesta radical en el gobierno, 1916–1930." In Luis Alberto Romero (ed.), *El radicalismo*. Buenos Aires: Colección Los Porqués–C. Pérez, 1968.

Guerrero, Américo. *La industria Argentina: Su origen, organización y desarrollo*. Buenos Aires: Establecimientos Plantié S.A., 1944.

Gutiérrez, Leandro. "Condiciones de vida material de los sectores populares en Buenos Aires, 1880–1914." *Revista de Indias*, January–June 1981, *XLI*(163–4), 167–202.

Gutiérrez, Leandro, and Korol, Juan Carlos. "Historia de empresas y crecimiento industrial en la Argentina: El caso de la Fábrica Argentina de Alpargatas." *Desarrollo Económico*, October–December 1988, *28*(111), 401–24.

Gutiérrez, Ramón, "Arquitectura lúdica: Los pabellones del Centenario." In Margarita Gutman (ed.), *Buenos Aires 1910: Memoria del Porvenir*. Buenos Aires: Gobierno de la Ciudad de Buenos Aires–Consejo del Plan Urbano Ambiental, Facultad de Arquitectura y Urbanismo de la

Universidad de Buenos Aires, Instituto Internacional de Medio Ambiente y Desarrollo, 1999.

Guy, Donna. "Carlos Pellegrini and the Politics of Early Industrialization in Argentina, 1876–1906." *Journal of Latin American Studies*, 1979, *11*(1), 123–44.

———. *Argentine Sugar Politics: Tucumán and the Generation of Eighty*. Tempe: Arizona State University, The Center for Latin American Studies, 1980.

———. "Women, Peonage, and Industrialization: Argentina, 1880–1914." *Latin American Research Review*, 1981, *16*(3), 65–89.

———. "La industria Argentina, 1870–1940: Legislación comercial, mercado de acciones y capitalización extranjera," *Desarrollo Económico,* October–December 1982, *22*(87), 351–74.

———. "Refinería Argentina, 1888–1930: Límites de la tecnología azucarera en una economía periférica." *Desarrollo Económico*, October–December 1988, *28*(111), 353–73.

———. *Sex & Danger in Buenos Aires: Prostitution, Family, and Nation in Argentina*. Lincoln: University of Nebraska Press, 1991.

———. Argentine Sugar Politics. *Tucumán and the Generation of Eighty.* Tempe: Arizona State University, The Center for Latin American Studies, 1991.

———. "Oro Blanco: Cotton, Technology and Family Labor in Nineteenth Century Argentina." *The Americas*, April 1993, *XLIX*(4), 457–78.

Haber, Stephen. *Industry and Underdevelopment: The Industrialization of Mexico, 1890–1940*. Stanford, CA: Stanford University Press, 1989.

———. "Industrial Concentration and the Capital Markets: A Comparative Study of Brazil, Mexico, and the United States, 1830–1930." *The Journal of Economic History*, September 1991, *51*(3), 559–80.

———. "Assessing the Obstacles to Industrialization: The Mexican Economy, 1830–1940." *Journal of Latin American Studies*, February 1992, *24*(1), 1–32.

———. "Financial Markets and Industrial Development: A Comparative Study of Governmental Regulation, Financial Innovation, and Industrial Structure in Brazil and Mexico, 1840–1930." In Stephen Haber (ed.), *How Latin America Fell Behind*. Stanford, CA: Stanford University Press, 1997.

Hall, Peter. *Governing the Economy: The Politics of State Intervention in Britain and France*. New York: Oxford University Press, 1986.

Halperin Donghi, Tulio. *Historia de la Universidad de Buenos Aires*. Buenos Aires: Eudeba, 1962.

———. "Canción de otoño en primavera: Previsiones sobre la crisis de la agricultura cerealera Argentina, 1894–1930." *DE*, October–December 1984, *24*(95), 367–86.

———. *José Hernández y sus mundos*. Buenos Aires: Sudamericana, 1985.

————. "¿Para qué la inmigración? Ideología y política inmigratoria en la Argentina, 1810–1914." In *El espejo de la historia: Problemas Argentinos y perspectivas Latinoamericanas*. Buenos Aires: Sudamericana, 1987.

————. "1880: Un nuevo clima de ideas." In *El espejo de la historia: Problemas Argentinos y perspectivas Latinoamericanas*. Buenos Aires: Sudamericana, 1987.

————. *Proyecto y construcción de una nación, 1846–1880*. Buenos Aires: Ariel, 1995.

Harvey, David. *Consciousness and the Urban Experience: Studies in the History and Theory of Capitalist Urbanization*. Baltimore: Johns Hopkins University, 1985.

Haug, Wolfgang Fritz. *Publicidad y consumo: Crítica de la estética de mercancías*. Mexico City: Fondo de Cultura Económica, 1989.

Higgs, Edward. "Women, Occupation and Work in 19th-Century Censuses." *History Workshop Journal*, Spring 1987, *23*, 59–80.

Higgs, Robert. *Crisis and Leviathan: Critical Essays in the Growth of American Government*. New York and Oxford: Oxford University Press, 1987.

Hobsbawn, Eric. *Industry and Empire*. Harmondsworth: Penguin Books, 1969.

————. "La 'classe media' Inglese, 1780–1920." In Jürgen Kocka (ed.), *Borghesie europee dell'ottocento*. Venezia: Marsilio, 1989.

Hora, Roy. *The Landowners of the Argentine Pampas: A Social and Political History, 1860–1945*. Oxford: Clarendon Press-Oxford Historical Monographs, 2001.

————. "Empresarios y política en la Argentina, 1880–1916." In Hilda Sabato and Alberto Lettieri (eds.), *La vida política en la Argentina del siglo XIX: Armas, votos y voces*. Mexico City: Fondo de Cultura Económica, 2003.

————. "Autonomistas, radicales y mitristas: El orden oligárquico en la provincia de Buenos Aires, 1880–1912." *Boletín del Instituto de Historia Argentina y Americana Dr. Emilio Ravignani*, 2003, (23), 39–78.

Hounshell, David A. *From the American System to Mass Production, 1800–1932: The Development of Manufacturing Technology in the United States*. Baltimore and London: The Johns Hopkins University Press, 1984.

Iparaguirre, Hilda. "Crecimiento industrial y formación de la burguesía en una subregión Argentina: Córdoba a finales del siglo XIX y principios del XX." In Enrique Florescano (ed.), *Orígenes y desarrollo de la burguesía en América Latina*. Mexico City: Ed. Nueva Imagen, 1985.

Irigoin, Alfredo M. "La evolución industrial en la Argentina, 1870–1940." *Libertas*, 1984, (1), 247–88.

Irigoin, María Alejandra. "Inconvertible Paper Money, Inflation and Economic Performance in Early Nineteenth Century Argentina," *Journal of Latin American Studies*, May 2000, *32*(2), 333–59.

Jackman, Mary. *The Velvet Glove: Paternalism and Conflict in Gender, Class, and Race Relations.* Berkeley and Los Angeles: University of California Press, 1994.

Jacob, Raúl. *Breve historia de la industria en Uruguay.* Montevideo: Fundación de Cultura Universitaria, 1981.

Jáuregui, Aníbal. "El despegue de los industriales Argentinos." In Waldo Ansaldi, Alfredo Pucciarelli, and José C. Villarruel (eds.), *Argentina en la paz de dos guerras, 1914–1945.* Buenos Aires: Biblos, 1993.

Jenkins, D.T., and Ponting, K. G. *The British Wool Textile Industry, 1770–1914.* Aldershot, England: Scolar Press, 1987.

Jessop, Bob. *State Theory: Putting Capitalist States in their Place.* University Park, PA: Pennsylvania State University Press, 1990.

Johns, Michael. "The Urbanisation of a Secondary City: The Case of Rosario, Argentina, 1870–1920." *Journal of Latin American Studies,* October 1991, *23*(3), 489–513.

———. *The City of Mexico in the Age of Díaz.* Austin: University of Texas Press, 1997.

Johns, Michael, and Rocchi, Fernando. "Capital industrial y espacio urbano: Buenos Aires durante el auge del proceso agroexportador." Paper presented at the conference "Buenos Aires moderna: Historia y perspectiva urbana, 1870–1914," Jornadas del Instituto de Arte Americano e Investigaciones Estéticas Mario J. Buschiazzo, Buenos Aires, 1990.

Jones, Charles A. "British Financial Institutions in Argentina, 1860–1914." Unpublished Ph.D. thesis, University of Cambridge, 1973.

———. "Commercial Banks and Mortgage Companies." In D.C.M. Platt (ed.), *Business Imperialism, 1840–1930.* Oxford: Oxford at the Clarendon Press, 1977.

Jones, S.R.H., and Paul, D.R. "Concentration and Regulation in the New Zealand Brewing Industry." *Australian Economic History Review,* September 1991, *31*(2), 66–94.

Jorge, Eduardo. *Industria y concentración económica.* Buenos Aires: Siglo XXI, 1973.

Joslin, David. *A Century of Banking in Latin America.* London and New York: Oxford University Press, 1963.

Katz, Jorge, and Gallo, Ezequiel. "The Industrialization of Argentina." In Claudio Veliz (ed.), *Latin America and the Caribbean: A Handbook.* London: Anthony Blond, 1968.

Katz, Jorge, and Kosacoff, Bernardo. *El proceso de industrialización en la Argentina: Evolución, retroceso y prospectiva.* Buenos Aires: CEAL, 1989.

———. "Multinationals from Argentina." In Sanjaya Lall (eds.), *The New Multinationals: The Spread of Third World Enterprises.* New York: John Wiley, 1984.

Kaysen, Carl. *Shoe Machinery Corporation: An Economic Analysis of an Anti-Trust Case*. Cambridge, MA: Harvard University Press, 1956.

Kessler-Harris, Alice. *Out to Work: A History of Wage-Earning Women in the United States*. New York: Oxford University Press, 1982.

Knecher, Lida, and Fuld, Roberto Gerardo. "Orígenes, desarrollo y desaparición de una empresa de capital nacional: La historia de Kasdorf S.A." *CICLOS*, 1998, *VIII*(16), 163–90.

Kindleberger, Charles. *Economic Growth in France and Britain, 1851–1950*. Cambridge, MA: Harvard University Press, 1961.

Kinghorn, Janyce Rye, and Nye, John Vincent. "The Scale of Production in Western Economic Development: A Comparison of Official Industry Statistics in the United States, Britain, France, and Germany, 1905– 1913." *Journal of Economic History*, March 1996, *56*(1), 90–112.

Kocka, Jürgen. "The Middle Classes in Europe." *The Journal of Modern History*, December 1995, *67*, 783–805.

Korn, Francis. "La gente distinguida y la aventura del ascenso." In José Luis and Luis Alberto Romero (eds.), *Buenos Aires, historia de cuatro siglos*. Buenos Aires: April, 1977.

———. *Buenos Aires 1895: Una ciudad moderna*. Buenos Aires: Instituto Torcuato Di Tella, 1981.

———. *Buenos Aires: Los huéspedes del 20*. Buenos Aires: Grupo Editor Latinoamericano, 1985.

Korol, Juan Carlos, and Sabato, Hilda. "Incomplete Industrialization: An Argentine Obsession." *Latin American Research Review*, 1990, *25*(1), 7–30.

Kritz, Ernesto H. "La formación de la fuerza de trabajo en la Argentina: 1869–1914." Serie Cuadernos del CENEP (Centro de Estudios de Población), no. 30, 1985.

Kuntz Ficker, Sandra. *Empresa extranjera y mercado interno: El Ferrocarril Central Mexicano, 1880–1907*. Mexico City: El Colegio de Mexico, 1995.

Lamoreaux, Naomi. *The Great Merger Movement in American Business, 1895– 1904*. Cambridge: Cambridge University Press, 1985.

———. "Banks, Kinship, and Economic Development: The New England Case." *The Journal of Economic History*, September 1986, *46*, 647–67.

Landes, David. "French Entrepreneurship and Industrial Growth in the Nineteenth Century." *Journal of Economic History*, 1949, *9*(1), 45–61.

———. *The Wealth and Poverty of Nations*. New York and London: W.W. Norton, 1998.

Langer, Erick. *Economic Change and Rural Resistance in Southern Bolivia, 1880– 1930*. Stanford, CA: Stanford University Press, 1989.

Langer, Erick, and Conti, Viviana E. "Circuitos comerciales tradicionales y cambio económico en los Andes centromeridionales, 1830–1930." *Desarrollo económico*, April–June 1991, *31*(121), 91–111.

Laurie, Bruce, and Schmitz, Mark. "Manufacture and Productivity: The Making of an Industrial Base, Philadelphia, 1850–1880." In Theodore Herschberg (ed.), *Philadelphia: Work, Space, Family, and Group Experience in the Nineteenth Century: Essays Toward an Interdisciplinary History of the City*. New York and Oxford: Oxford University Press, 1981.

Lazonick, William. *The Myth of the Market Economy*. Cambridge, MA: Cambridge University Press, 1991.

Leach, William. *Land of Desire; Merchants, Power, and the Rise of a New American Culture*. New York: Pantheon, 1993.

Lears, Jackson. *Fables of Abundance: A Cultural History of Advertising in America*. New York: Basic Books, 1994.

Levi, Giovanni. *L'eredità immateriale. Carriera di un esorcista nel Piemonte del Seicento*. Torino: Einaudi, 1985.

Lewis, Colin. *British Railways in Argentina 1857–1914: A Case Study of Foreign Investment*. London: Athlone, 1983.

———. "Industry in Latin America Before 1930." In Leslie Bethell (ed.), *The Cambridge History of Latin America*. Cambridge. MA: Cambridge University Press, 1984.

———. "Railways and Industrialization: Argentina and Brazil, 1870–1929." In C. Abel and C. M. Lewis (eds.), *Latin America, Economic Imperialism and the State*. London: ILAS, 1985.

———. "Immigrant Entrepreneurs, Manufacturing and Industrial Policy in the Argentine, 1922–28." *The Journal of Imperial and Commonwealth History*, October 1987, *16*(1), 77–108.

———. "Industry in Latin America." In Patrick O'Brien (ed.), *Industrialization: Critical Perspectives on the World Economy*. London, Routledge, 1998.

Lewis, Paul. *The Crisis of Argentine Capitalism*. Chapel Hill and London: The University of North Carolina Press, 1990.

Liernur, Francisco, and Silvestri, Graciela. *El umbral de la metrópolis: Transformaciones técnicas y cultura en la modernización de Buenos Aires, 1870–1930*. Buenos Aires: Sudamericana, 1993.

Llach, Juan José. *La Argentina que no fue. Tomo I*. Buenos Aires: Ediciones del IDES, 1985.

Llanes, Ricardo. *El barrio de Almagro*. Buenos Aires, Municipalidad de la Ciudad de Buenos Aires, 1967.

Lobato, Mirta. *'El taylorismo' en la gran industria exportadora Argentina: 1907–1945*. Buenos Aires: Centro Editor de América Latina, 1988.

———. "Una visión del mundo del trabajo: El caso de los obreros de la industria frigorífica. Berisso, 1900–1930." In Diego Armus (ed.), *Mundo urbano y cultura popular: Estudios de historia social Argentina*. Buenos Aires: Sudamericana, 1990.

———. "Mujeres obreras, protesta y acción gremial en la Argentina: Los casos de la industria frigorífica y textil en Berisso." In Dora Barrancos (ed.), *Historia y género*. Buenos Aires: Centro Editor de América Latina, 1993.

——. *La vida en las fábricas: Trabajo, protesta y política en una comunidad obrera. Berisso, 1904–1970*. Buenos Aires: Prometeo libros/Entrepasados, 2001.

——. "La Ingeniería: Industria y organización del trabajo en la Argentina de entreguerra," *Revista Estudios del Trabajo*, September 16, 1998.

Lobato, Mirta, and Suriano, Juan. "Trabajadores y movimiento obrero: Entre la crisis de los paradigmas y la profesionalización del historiador." *Entrepasados*, 1993, *III*(4–5), 41–64.

——. *La protesta social en la Argentina*. Buenos Aires: Fondo de Cultura Económica, 2003.

Lupano, María Marta. "Villa Crespo: Una villa obrera entre el modelo higienista y el paternalismo católico." In *Anales del Instituto de Arte Americano e Investigaciones Estéticas Mario J. Buschiazzo*, no. 27–28, 1989–91, 127–137.

——. "Organizaciones religiosas y patrones industriales católicos: Política habitacional con refererencia a la mujer obrera, 1890–1930." In L. Knecher and M. Panaia (eds.), *La mitad del país: La mujer en la sociedad Argentina*. Buenos Aires: Centro Editor de América Latina, 1993.

Maddison, Angus. "Explaining the Economic Performance of Nations, 1820–1989." In William J. Baumol, Richard R. Nelson, and Edward N. Wolff (eds.), *Convergence of Productivity: Cross-National Studies and Historical Evidence*. Oxford: Oxford University Press, 1994.

——. *The World Economy: A Milennial Perspective*. Paris: Organisation for Economic Co-operation and Development, Development Centre Seminars, 2001.

Maier, Charles. "Accounting for the Achievements of Capitalism: Alfred Chandler's Business History." *Journal of Modern History*, December 1993, *65*, 771–82.

Malamud, Carlos. "El Partido Demócrata Progresista: Un intento fallido de construir un partido nacional liberal-conservador." *DE*, July–September 1995, *35*(138), 289–308.

Mariluz Urquijo, José María. *Estado e industria, 1810–1862*. Buenos Aires: Macchi, 1969.

Márquez, Graciela. "Tariff Protection in Mexico, 1892–1909: Ad Valorem Rates and Sources of Variation." In John Coatsworth and Alan Taylor, (eds.), *Latin America and the World Economy Since 1800*. Cambridge, MA: Harvard University Press, 1998.

Maureer, Noel, and Haber, Stephen. "Institutional Change and Economic Growth: Banks, Financial Markets, and Mexican Industrialization, 1878–1913." In Jeffrey L. Bortz and Stephen Haber (eds.), *The Mexican*

Economy, 1870–1930: Essays on the Economic History of Institutions, Revolution and Growth. Stanford, CA: Stanford University Press, 2002.

Mayo, Carlos. Mirand, Julieta, and Cabrejas, Laura. "Anatomía de la pulpería porteña." In Carlos Mayo (ed.), *Pulperos y pulperías de Buenos Aires 1740–1830.* Mar del Plata: Universidad Nacional de Mar del Plata, 1996.

McGee Deutsch, Sandra. *Counterrevolution in Argentina, 1900–1932: The Argentine Patriotic League.* Lincoln: University of Nebraska Press, 1986.

McKendrick, Neil, Brewer, John, and Plumb, J.H. *The Birth of a Consumer Society: The Commercialization of Eighteenth-Century England.* Bloomington: Indiana University Press, 1982.

Mead, Karen. "Oligarchs, Nuns, and Doctors." Ph.D. dissertation, University of California, Santa Barbara, 1996.

———. "Gendering the Obstacles to Progress in Positivist Argentina, 1880–1920." *Hispanic American Historical Review*, November 1997, 77(4), 645–75.

Mercado, María Matilde. *La primera ley de trabajo femenino: "La mujer obrera", 1890–1910.* Buenos Aires: Centro Editor de América Latina, 1988.

Miller, Daniel (ed.). *Acknowledging Consumption.* London and New York: Routledge, 1994.

Miller, Rory. "Latin American Manufacturing and the First World War: An Explanatory Essay." *World Development*, 1981, 9(8), 707–16.

Montgomery, David. "Workers' Control of Machine Production in the Nineteenth Century." *Labor History*, Fall 1976, 17(4), 485–509.

Moya, José. *Cousins and Strangers: Spanish Immigrants in Buenos Aires, 1850–1930.* Berkeley and Los Angeles: University of California Press, 1998.

Nakamura, Leonard, and Zarazaga, Carlos. "Economic Growth in Argentina in the Period 1900–1930: Some Evidence from Stock Returns." In John Coatsworth and Alan Taylor, (eds.), *Latin America and the World Economy Since 1800.* Cambridge, MA: Harvard University Press, 1998.

———. "Banking and Finance in the Period 1900–35." In Gerardo della Paolera and Alan Taylor (eds.), *The New Economic History of Argentina.* Cambridge, MA: Cambridge University Press, 2003.

Nari, Marcela. "El movimiento obrero y el trabajo femenino: Un análisis de los congresos obreros durante el período 1890–1921." In L. Knecher and M. Panaia (eds.), *La mitad del país: La mujer en la sociedad Argentina.* Buenos Aires: Centro Editora de América Latina, 1993.

———. *El trabajo a domicilio en la ciudad de Buenos Aires. 1890–1918.* Informe presentado de las investigaciones realizadas, Universidad de Buenos Aires, 1994.

———. "De la maldición al derecho: Notas sobre las mujeres en el mercado de trabajo. Buenos Aires, 1890–1940." In Hilda Garrido and María

Cecilia Bravo (eds.), *Temas de Mujeres: Perspectivas de Género*. San Miguel de Tucumán: Centro de Estudios Históricos Interdisciplinarios sobre las Mujeres, 1998, 139–155.

Naridnelli, Clark. *Child Labor and the Industrial Revolution*. Bloomington and Indianapolis: Indiana University Press, 1990.

Navarro, Marysa, and Wainerman, Catalina. *El trabajo de la mujer en la Argentina: Un análisis preliminar de las ideas dominantes en las primeras décadas del siglo XX,*" Buenos Aires, Serie Cuadernos del CENEP (Centro de Estudios de Población), no. 7, 1979.

———. "Hidden, Silent, and Anonymous: Women Workers in the Argentine Trade Union Movement." In Norbert Soldon, *The World of Women's Trade Unionism: Comparative Historical Essays*. London: Greenwood Press, 1985.

Needell, Jeffrey. *A Tropical Belle Epoque: Elite Culture and Society in Turn-of-the-Century Rio de Janeiro*. Cambridge: Cambridge University Press, 1987.

———. "Optimism and Melancholy: Elite Response to the *fin de siècle bonaerense*." *Journal of Latin American Studies*, October 1999, *31*(3), 551–88.

Nicolau, Juan Carlos. *Industria y aduana, 1835–1854*. Buenos Aires: Devenir, 1975.

———. *Proteccionismo y librecomercio en Buenos Aires, 1810–1850*. Córdoba: Centro de Estudios Históricos, 1995.

Nicolini, Nicoletta. *Il pane attossicato: Storia dell'industria dei fiammiferi in Italia 1860–1910*. Bologna: Documentazione Scientifica Editrice, 1995.

Norris, James D. *Advertising and the Transformation of American Society, 1865–1920*. New York: Greenwood, 1990.

Nye, John Vincent. "Firm Size and Economic Backwardness: A New Look at the French Industrialization Debate." *Journal of Economic History*, September 1987, *47*(3), 649–69.

O'Brien, Patrick. "Factory Size, Economies of Scale, and the Great Merger Wave of 1898–1902." *Journal of Economic History*, September 1988, *XLVIII*(3), 639–49.

———. (ed.). *Industrialization: Critical Perspectives on the World Economy*. London: Routledge, 1998.

Ohmann, Richard. *Selling Culture: Magazines, Markets, and Class in the Turn of the Century*. London and New York: Verso, 1996.

Orlove, Benjamin (ed.). *The Allure of the Foreign: Imported Goods in Postcolonial Latin America*. Ann Arbor: The University of Michigan Press, 1997.

Ortiz, Ricardo. *Historia económica de la Argentina*. Buenos Aires: Raigal, 1955.

Oszlak, Oscar. *La formación del estado Argentino*. Buenos Aires: Editorial de Belgrano.

Otero, Hernán. "Estadística censal y construcción de la nación: El caso Argentino, 1869–1914." *Boletín del Instituto de Historia Argentina y Americana Dr. Emilio Ravignani*, 1997–1998, (16–17), 123–49.

Packard, Vance. *The Hidden Persuaders*. Montreal: Random House, 1957.

Panettieri, José. *Aranceles y protección industrial, 1862–1930*. Buenos Aires: Centro Editor de América Latina, 1983.

———. *Proteccionismo, liberalismo y desarrollo industrial*. Buenos Aires: Centro Editor de América Latina, 1983.

Parrot, Philippe. *Fashioning the Bourgeoisie: A History of Clothing in the Nineteenth Century*. Princeton, NJ: Princeton University Press, 1994.

Paz, Gustavo. "Province and Nation in Northern Argentina: Peasants, Elite, and the State 1780–1880." Ph.D. dissertation, Emory University, 1999.

Pearce, David W. *The MIT Dictionary of Modern Economics*. Cambridge, MA: MIT University Press, 1992.

Peck, Donald. "Las presidencias de Manuel Quintana y José Figueroa Alcorta." In Ezequiel Gallo and Gustavo Ferrari (eds.), *La Argentina del ochenta al centenario*. Buenos Aires: Sudamericana, 1980.

Pellet Lastra, Emilio. *Evolución industrial Argentina*. Buenos Aires: Imprenta y Casa Editora Coni, 1940.

Peña, Milcíades. *Industrialización y clases sociales en la Argentina*. Buenos Aires: Hyspamérica, 1986 (first published in 1964).

Peralta Ramos, Mónica. *Etapas de acumulación y alianzas de clase en la Argentina, 1930–1970*. Buenos Aires: Siglo XXI, 1973.

Petrecolla, Alberto. "Prices, Import Substitution and Investment in the Argentine Textile Industry, 1920–1939." Mimeograph. Buenos Aires: Centro de Investigaciones Económicas, Instituto Torcuato Di Tella, 1968.

Phelps, Dudley Maynard. *Migration of Industry to Latin America: Evolution of International Business, 1800–1945: The Rise of International Business*. London: Routledge, 2002.

Pianetto, Ofelia. "Industria y formación de la clase obrera urbanas en la ciudad de Córdoba, 1880–1906." In A.A.V.V., *Homenaje al Doctor Ceferino Garzón Maceda*. Córdoba: Universidad Nacional de Córdoba, 1973.

———. "Mercado de trabajo y acción sindical. Córdoba, 1880–1930." Mimeograph. Córdoba: CLACSO (Consejo Latino Americano de Ciencias Sociales), 1976–77.

Pineda, Yovanna Yvonne. "The Firm in Early Argentine Industrialization, 1890–1930: A Study of Fifty-Five Joint-Stock Companies' Owners, Finance Sources, Productivity, and Profits." Ph.D. dissertation, University of California, Los Angeles, 2002.

Platt, D.C.M. *Latin America and British Trade, 1806–1914*. London: Adam & Charles Black, 1972.

————. *Business Imperialism, 1840–1930.* Oxford: Clarendon Press, 1977.

————. (ed.). *Argentina, Australia and Canada: Studies in Development, 1870–1965.* Oxford: Macmillan, 1985.

Pollard, Sidney. *The Genesis of Modern Management.* London: Arnold, 1965.

Prieto, Adolfo. *El discurso criollista en la Argentina moderna.* Buenos Aires: Sudamericana, 1988.

Punzi, Orlando Mario. *Historia de la conquista del Chaco.* Buenos Aires: Editorial Vinciguerra, 1997.

Raaschou-Nielsen, Agnete. "The Organizational History of the Firm: The Putting-Out System in Denmark Around 1900." *Scandinavian Economic History Review,* 1993, *16*(1), 3–12.

Randall, Laura. *An Economic History of Argentina in the Twentieth Century.* New York: Columbia University Press, 1978.

Rapalo, María Ester, and Grillo, María Victoria. "Un caso de solidaridad obrera: El conflicto de 1918 entre Bunge y Born y los obreros de sus empresas molineras." In B. de Groof (ed.), *En los Deltas de la Memoria: Bélgica y Argentina en los siglos XIX y XX.* Leuven: Leuven University Press, 1998.

Recalde, Héctor. *La Iglesia y la Cuestión Social.* Buenos Aires: Centro Editor de América Latina, 1985.

Recchini de Lattes, Zulma, and Lattes, Alfredo (eds.). *La población de la Argentina.* Buenos Aires: INDEC (Instituto Nacional de Estadísticas y Censos), 1975.

Recchini de Lattes, Zulma, Lattes, Alfredo, and Wainerman, Catalina. "Empleo femenino y desarrollo económico: algunas evidencias." *Desarrollo Económico,* July–September 1977, *17*(66), 301–17.

Regalsky, Andrés. "La evolución de la banca privada nacional en Argentina, 1880–1914: Una introducción a su estudio." In Pedro Tedde and Carlos Marichal (eds.), *La formación de los bancos centrales en España y América Latina: Siglos XIX y XX.* Vol II: Suramérica y el Caribe. Madrid: Banco de España, Servicios de Estudios, Estudios de historia económica, no. 30, 1994.

————. "Banking, Trade, and the Rise of Capitalism in Argentina, 1850–1930." In Alice Teichova, Ginette Kurgan-van Hentenryk, and Dieter Ziegler (eds.), *Banking, Trade and Industry: Europe, America and Asia from the Thirteenth to the Twentieth Century* (Cambridge, UK and New York: Cambridge University Press, 1997), 359–77.

————. "¿Una experiencia de banca industrial en la Argentina exportadora? El Banco Francés del Río de la Plata, 1905–1914." *Anuario del Centro de Estudios Históricos de Córdoba, 2001, I*(1), 219–45.

————. *Mercados, inversores y elites: Las inversiones francesas en la Argentina 1880–1914.* Buenos Aires: Editorial de la Universidad Nacional de Tres de Febrero, 2002.

Remedi, Fernando J. *Entre el gusto y la necesidad: La alimentación en Córdoba a principios del siglo XX.* Córdoba: Centro de Estudios Históricos, 1992.

————. "El consumo alimentario y sus diferencias en Córdoba, 1915–1930." In Beatriz Moreira et al. (eds.), *Estado, mercado y sociedad: Córdoba, 1820–1950.* Vol. 1. Córdoba: Centro de Estudios Históricos "Profesor Carlos S. A. Segreti," 2000.

Rivera Astengo, Agustín. *Miguel Navarro Viola: El opositor victorioso.* Buenos Aires: Guillermo Kraft Ltd., 1947.

Rocchi, Fernando. "La armonía de los opuestos: Industria, importaciones y la construcción urbana de Buenos Aires en el período 1880–1920." *Entrepasados*, 1994, *4*(7), 43–66.

————. "En busca del empresario perdido: Los industriales argentinos y las tesis de Jorge Federico Sábato." *Entrepasados*, 1996, *5*(10), 67–88.

————. "Consumir es un placer: La industria y la expansión de la demanda en Buenos Aires a la vuelta del siglo pasado." *DE*, January–March 1998, *37*(148), 533–58.

————. "Inventando la soberanía del consumidor: Publicidad, privacidad y revolución del mercado en Argentina, 1860–1940." In Fernando Devoto and Marta Madero (eds.), *Historia de la vida privada en la Argentina.* Vol. II. Buenos Aires: Taurus, 1999.

————. "Industria y metrópolis: El sueño de un gran mercado." In Margarita Gutman and Thomas Reese (eds.), *Buenos Aires 1910: El imaginario para una gran capital.* Buenos Aires: Eudeba, 1999.

————. "Britain Versus Newcomers: The Struggle for the Argentine Market, 1900–1914." Paper presented at the Second Annual Argentina Conference, "British-Argentine Relations, 1780–1914." The Latin American Centre, University of Oxford, St Antony's College, May 14–15, 2001.

Rock, David. "Lucha civil en la Argentina: La semana trágica de enero de 1919." *DE*, June 1971–March 1972, *11*(42–44), 165–215.

————. *Politics in Argentina, 1890–1930: The Rise and Fall of Radicalism.* Cambridge: Cambridge University Press, 1975.

————. *Argentina, 1515–1987.* Berkeley and Los Angeles: University of California Press, 1985.

————. *State Building and Political Movements in Argentina, 1860–1916.* Stanford, CA: Stanford University Press, 2002.

Romano, Eduardo. "Fray Mocho: El costumbrismo hacia 1900." *Historia de la literatura Argentina.* Buenos Aires: Centro Editor de América Latina, 1986.

Romero, Eduardo. *Medios más adecuados para fomentar el comercio Hispanoamericano.* Madrid: Imprenta y Litografía de Bernardo Rodríguez, 1905.

Rosenthal, S. "La Bolsa." Extractado de Revista de Economía Argentina, no. 285–6. Buenos Aires: Guillermo Kraft, 1942.

Rougier, Marcelo. "El Banco de Crédito Industrial Argentino y la política económica del peronismo, 1944-1949." Master dissertation, University of Buenos Aires, 1999.

Rutledge, Ian. *Cambio agrario e integración: El desarrollo del capitalismo en Jujuy 1550–1950.* Tilcara, Jujuy, and Buenos Aires: Centro de Investigaciones Sociales, 1987.

Sabato, Hilda. *Capitalismo y ganadería en Buenos Aires: La fiebre del lanar 1850– 1890.* Buenos Aires: Sudamericana, 1989.

———. "La revolución del 90: Prólogo o epílogo?" *Punto de Vista*, December 1990, *13*(39), 27–31.

———. "Citizenship, Political Participation and the Formation of the Public Sphere in Buenos Aires 1850s-1880s." *Past and Present*, 1992, (136), 139–63.

Sabato, Hilda, and Romero, Luis Alberto. *Los trabajadores de Buenos Aires: La experiencia del mercado: 1850–1880.* Buenos Aires: Sudamericana, 1992.

Sábato, Jorge. *La clase dominante en la formación de la Argentina moderna.* Buenos Aires: Centro de Investigaciones Sociales sobre el Estado y la Administración/Grupo Editor Latinoamericano, 1988.

Salas, Horacio. *El Centenario: La Argentina en su período más glorioso.* Buenos Aires: Planeta, 1996.

Salvatore, Ricardo. "Fiestas federales: Representaciones de la República en el Buenos Aires rosista," *Entrepasados*, 1996, *5*(11), 45–68.

———. "Repertoires of Coercion and Market Culture in Nineteenth-Century Buenos Aires Province." *International Review of Social History*, 2000, *45*, 409–48.

Samuel, Raphael. "The Workshop of the World: Steam-Powered and Hand Technology in Mid-Victorian Britain." *History Workshop Journal*, Spring 1977, *3*, 6–72.

Sánchez, Mariquita. *Recuerdos del Buenos Ayres Virreynal*, Prólogo y notas por Liniers de Estrada. Buenos Aires: ENE Editorial, 1953.

Sánchez Román, José Antonio. "La dulce crisis: Finanzas, estado e industria azucarera en Tucumán, Argentina, 1853–1914." Ph.D. dissertation, Universidad Complutense de Madrid, Instituto Universitario 'Ortega y Gasset', Madrid, 2001.

———. "El Banco de Londres y del Río de la Plata y el negocio azucarero en Tucumán, Argentina, 1909–1914." *Revista de Historia Económica*, Spring– Summer 2001, *XIX*(2), 415–47.

Sanucci, Lía. *Historia del Banco de la Provincia de Buenos Aires: 1822–1946.* Buenos Aires: Editorial del Banco de la Provincia de Buenos Aires, 1993.

Sargent, Charles. *The Spatial Evolution of Greater Buenos Aires, Argentina, 1870–1930.* Tempe: Arizona State University Press, 1974.

Sarlo, Beatriz. *Buenos Aires: Una modernidad periférica: Buenos Aires 1920 y 1930*. Buenos Aires: Nueva Visión, 1988.

Saulquin, Susana. *La moda en la Argentina*. Buenos Aires: Emecé, 1990.

Scalabrini Ortiz, Raúl. *Historia de los ferrocarriles Argentinos*. Buenos Aires: Editorial Reconquista, 1940.

Scarzanella, Eugenia. *Italiani d'Argentina: Storie di contadini, industriali e missionari Italiani in Argentina, 1850–1912*. Venice: Marsilio, 1983.

Schvarzer, Jorge. *Bunge & Born: Crecimiento y diversificación de un grupo económico*. Buenos Aires: Centro de Investigaciones Sociales sobre el Estado y la Administración/Grupo Editor Latinoamericano, 1989.

———. *La industria que supimos conseguir*. Buenos Aires: Planeta, 1996.

———. *Empresarios del pasado: La Unión Industrial Argentina*. Buenos Aires: CISEA Centro de Investigaciones Sociales sobre el Estado y la Administración-Imago Mundi, 1991.

Schwartz, Hugh. "The Argentine Experience with Industrial Credit and Protection Industries." Ph.D. dissertation, Yale University, 1967.

Scobie, James R. *Revolution in the Pampas: A Social History of Argentine Wheat, 1860–1910*. Austin, TX: Institute of Latin American Studies, 1964.

———. *Secondary Cities of Argentina: The Social History of Corrientes, Salta, and Mendoza, 1850–1910*. Compiled and edited by Samuel Baily. Stanford, CA: Stanford University Press, 1988.

Sennett, Richard. *Authority*. London: Secker & Warburg, 1980.

———. *Il declino dell' uomo pubblico*. Milan: Bompiani, 1982.

Sereni, Emilio. *Capitalismo e mercato nazionale*. Rome: Editori Riuniti, 1974.

Shammas, Carole. *The Preindustrial Consumer in England and America*. Oxford: Clarendon Press, 1990.

Sharkey, Eugene. "Unión Industrial Argentina 1877–1920: Problems of Industrial Development." Ph.D. dissertation, Rutgers University, 1977.

Silvestri, Graciela. "El paisaje industrial del Riachuelo: Historia de una forma territorial." Ph.D. dissertation, Universidad de Buenos Aires, 1996.

Simmel, Georg. *Filosofía de la coquetería y otros ensayos*. Madrid: Revista de Occidente, 1924.

———. *Filosofía del dinero*. Madrid: Instituto de Estudios Políticos, 1976.

Skogman, C. *Viaje en la fragata sueca "Eugenia," 1851–1853: Brasil, Uruguay, Argentina, Chile, Perú*. Buenos Aires: Solar, 1942.

Skorownek, Stephen. *Building a New American State: The Expansion of National Administrative Capacities, 1877–1920*. Cambridge: Cambridge University Press, 1982.

Smith, Judith E. "Our Own Kind: Family and Community Networks in Providence." *Radical History Review*, Spring 1978, *17*, 99–120.

Smith, Peter. *Beef and Politics in Argentina: Patterns of Conflict and Change*. New York: Columbia University Press, 1969.

Smuts, Robert W. "The Female Labor Force: A Case Study in the Interpretation of Historical Statistics." *Journal of the American Statistical Association*, March 1960, *55*(289), 71–79.

Sokoloff, Kenneth. "Was the Transition from the Artisanal Shop to the Small Factory Associated with Gains in Efficiency?" *Explorations in Economic History*, October 1984, *21*(4), 351–82.

Solberg, Carl. "The Tariff and Politics in Argentina 1916–1930." *Hispanic American Historical Review*, May 1973, *53*(2), 260–84.

Sommi, Luis V. *Los capitales yanquis en la Argentina*. Buenos Aires: Monteagudo, 1949.

Stein, Stanley. *The Brazilian Cotton Industry*. Princeton, NJ: Princeton University Press, 1957.

Steinmo, Steven. *Taxation and Democracy: Swedish, British and American Approaches to Financing the Modern State*. New Haven and London: Yale University Press, 1993.

Stigler, George J., and Becker, Gary S. "De Gustibus Non Est Disputandum." *American Economic Review*, March 1977, *67*(2), 76–90.

Stone, Irving. "British Direct and Portfolio Investment in Latin America Before 1914." *Journal of Economic History*, 1977, (37), 690–722.

Strasser, Susan. *Satisfaction Guaranteed: The Making of the American Mass Market*. New York: Pantheon Books, 1989.

Supplee, Joan. "Provincial Elites and the Economic Transformation of Mendoza, Argentina, 1880–1914." Ph.D. dissertation, University of Texas, Austin, 1988.

Suriano, Juan. "El estado Argentino frente a los trabajadores urbanos: Política social y represión, 1880–1916." *Anuario de la Universidad Nacional de Rosario*, Segunda época, Escuela de Historia, Facultad de Humanidades y Artes, 1989–1990, (16), 109–36.

———. "Niños trabajadores: Una aproximación al trabajo infantil en la industria porteña de comienzos de siglo." In Diego Armus (ed.), *Mundo urbano y cultura popular: Estudios de historia social Argentina*. Buenos Aires: Sudamericana, 1990.

———. "Ideas y prácticas 'políticas' del anarquismo Argentino." *Entrepasados*, 1995, *V*(8), 21–48.

———. *Anarquistas: Cultura y política libertaria en Buenos Aires 1890–1910*. Buenos Aires: Manantial, 2001.

Sweeney, Judith. *Las costureras de Buenos Aires*. Mimeograph. n.d.

Tasso, Alberto. *Aventura, trabajo y poder: Sirios y libaneses en Santiago del Estero, 1880–1980*. Santiago del Estero: Ediciones Indice, 1988.

Taylor, Alan. "External Dependence, Demographic Burdens, and the Argentine Economic Decline After the Belle Epoque." *Journal of Economic History*, December 1992, *52*(4), 907–936.

———. "Argentine Economic Growth in Comparative Perspective." Ph.D. dissertation, Harvard University, 1992.

Tennant, Richard. *The American Cigarette Industry*. New Haven, CT: Yale University Press, 1950.

Thorp, Rosemary. *Progress, Poverty and Exclusion: An Economic History of Latin America in the 20th Century*. New York: Banco Interamericano de Desarrollo, Johns Hopkins University Press, 1998.

Topik, Steven. "The State's Contribution to the Development of Brazil's Internal Economy, 1850–1930." *Hispanic American Historical Review*, 1985, *65*(2), 203–28.

———. "The State's Contribution to the Development of Brazil's Internal Economy, 1850–1930." *Hispanic American Historical Review*, 1985, *65*(2), 203–228.

———. *The Political Economy of the Brazil State, 1889–1930*. Austin: University of Texas Press, 1987.

Torres, José Luis. *Los perduelis*. Buenos Aires: Talleres Gráficos Padilla y Contreras, 1943.

Torres Rivas, Edelberto. "La Nación: Problemas teóricos y políticos." In A.A.V.V., *Estado y política en América Latina*. Mexico City: Siglo XXI, 1983.

Trigo, Eduardo, Piñeiro, Martín, and Sábato, Jorge. "La cuestión tecnológica y la organización de la investigación agropecuaria en América Latina." *Desarrollo Económico*, April–June 1983, *23*(89), 99–119.

Troncoso, Oscar. "Las formas del ocio." In José Luis and Luis Alberto Romero, (eds.), *Buenos Aires, historia de cuatro siglos*. Buenos Aires: April, 1977.

Tulchin, Joseph. "El crédito agrario en la Argentina, 1910–1926." *Desarrollo Económico*, October–December 1978, *18*(71), 381–408.

Vaquer, Antonio. *Historia de la ingeniería en la Argentina*. Buenos Aires: Eudeba, 1968.

Vázquez Presedo, Vicente. "Sobre un período de protección industrial inevitable." Mimeograph, Buenos Aires, 1969.

———. *Estadísticas históricas Argentinas: Primera parte 1875–1914*. Buenos Aires: Macchi, 1971.

———. *El caso Argentino: Migración de factores, comercio exterior y desarrollo, 1875–1914*. Buenos Aires: Eudeba, 1971.

———. *Crisis y retraso: Argentina y la economía internacional entre las dos guerras*. Buenos Aires: Eudeba, 1978.

Veblen, Thornstein. *The Theory of the Leisure Class*. Boston: Houghton Mifflin, 1973.

Vezzetti, Hugo. *La locura en la Argentina*. Buenos Aires: Paidós, 1985.

Villanueva, Javier. "El origen de la industrialización Argentina." *Desarrollo económico*, 1972, *12*(47), 451–76.

————. "Industrial Development in Argentina: The Process up to the 1960s."
     Buenos Aires: Instituto Torcuato Di Tella, 1987.
————. "Las primeras etapas de la política aduanera Argentina." Buenos
     Aires: Instituto Torcuato Di Tella, 2001.
Villarruel, José. "Los industrialistas y la tutela del Estado." In Waldo Ansaldi,
     Alfredo Pucciarelli, and José C. Villarruel (eds.), *Argentina en la paz de
     dos guerras 1914–1945*. Buenos Aires: Biblos, 1993.
Wainerman, Catalina, and Recchini de Lattes, Zulma. *El trabajo femenino en el
     banquillo de los acusados: La medición censal en América Latina*. Mexico
     City: Terranova, 1981.
Waisman Carlos. *Reversal of Development in Argentina*. Princeton, NJ: Princeton
     University Press, 1987.
Walther, Juan Carlos. *La conquista del desierto: Lucha de frontera con el indio*.
     Buenos Aires: Eudeba, 1970.
Walter, Richard. *The Socialist Party of Argentina, 1890–1930*. Austin, TX: In-
     stitute of Latin American Studies, 1977.
————. *Politics and Urban Growth in Buenos Aires, 1910–1942*. Cambridge
     and New York: Cambridge University Press, 1993.
Warwick, Armstrong. "The Social Origins of Industrial Growth: Canada,
     Argentina and Australia, 1870–1930." In D.C.M. Platt and Guido Di
     Tella (eds.), *Argentina, Australia and Canada: Studies in Comparative Devel-
     opment, 1870–1965*. London: MacMillan and Oxford: St. Antony's
     College, 1985.
Weber, Henri. *El partido de los patronos: El CNPF, 1946–1986*. Madrid:
     Ministerio de Trabajo y Seguridad Social, 1987.
Weber, Max. *Economy and Society: An Outline of Interpretative Society*. Berkeley
     and Los Angeles: University of California Press, 1978.
Williams, Raymond. *The Country and the City*. New York: Oxford University
     Press, 1973.
Williamson, Jeffrey. "Real Wages and Relative Factors Prices in the Third
     World 1820–1940: Latin America." Discussion paper no. 1853,
     November 1998, Harvard Institute of Economic Research, Harvard
     University
Williamson, Oliver. *The Economic Institutions of Capitalism*. New York: Free
     Press, 1985.
Wright, Winthrop. *British-Owned Railways in Argentina: Their Effect on
     Economic Nationalism, 1854–1948*. Austin: University of Texas Press,
     1974.
Yans-McLaughlin, Virginia. *Family and Community: Italian Immigrants in Buf-
     falo, 1880–1930*. Ithaca: Cornell University Press, 1971.
Yomal, Ricardo. "Humo, un delicioso producto final." *Todo es historia*, Sep-
     tember 1977, (124), 24–30.

Zahavi, Gerald. *Workers, Managers, and Welfare Capitalism: The Shoeworkers and Tanners of Endicot Johnson, 1890–1950.* Urbana and Chicago: University of Illinois Press, 1989.

Zamagni, Vera. *The Economic History of Italy, 1860–1990.* Oxford: Clarendon Press, 1993.

Zarrilli, Adrián Gustavo. "Estado, semillas y bolsas: Prestaciones extraordinarias para el productor rural santafesino, 1890–1930." *Res Gesta,* Rosario, January–December 1992, (31), 281–306.

Zimmermann, Eduardo. *Los liberales reformistas.* Buenos Aires: Sudamericana, 1995.

DATE DUE